BIBLIOGRAPHY OF THE INDONESIAN REVOLUTION

KONINKLIJK INSTITUUT
VOOR TAAL-, LAND- EN VOLKENKUNDE

Bibliographical Series 21

H.A.J. KLOOSTER

BIBLIOGRAPHY OF
THE INDONESIAN REVOLUTION

Publications from 1942 to 1994

1997
KITLV Press
Leiden

Published by:

KITLV Press
Koninklijk Instituut voor Taal-, Land- en Volkenkunde
(Royal Institute of Linguistics and Anthropology)
P.O. Box 9515
2300 RA Leiden
The Netherlands

ISBN 90 6718 089 0

Printed in the Netherlands

Contents

Preface

The purpose of this bibliography is to make accessible the literature concerning the Indonesian revolution, the West Irian issue and the South Moluccan question, up to and including 1994. Also considered are works on the Japanese occupation, the 'prelude' to the revolution. The titles in this bibliography are categorized by subject, with several indices and an introduction serving as a guide to the voluminous literature on the subjects mentioned. Most of the titles are in Indonesian, Dutch or English; titles in other languages such as German, French, Russian and Japanese are also taken into account. I am aware that the listing of titles in the last two languages (given here in English translation) is not complete.

My experience in compiling this bibliography has shown that many authors are not sufficiently familiar with previously published literature on their subject, especially works written in a foreign language. The 'language barrier' clearly plays a role here. The bibliography presented here is an endeavour to remove the separation between the different bodies of literature.

The introduction gives some of the main lines of development in the historiography of the Indonesian revolution, its prelude and aftermath. 'Historiography' should be interpreted here in a broad sense: works from the revolutionary period itself (1945-1949) are also included. On the other hand, I wish to stress that the introduction is meant merely as an overview, mentioning only a small, representative selection of the works included in the bibliography. For a more complete picture of the existing literature, the user should consult the indices. A full historiography of the Indonesian revolution has yet to be written; it is the compiler's hope that this bibliography will contribute to such an undertaking.

During the last fifty years, much has been written on the Indonesian revolution, an international conflict with numerous aspects. Many new publications are still appearing, particularly in Indonesia, but also in the Netherlands and elsewhere. The body of work is so voluminous that some restrictions on inclusion in this bibliography were inevitable. Articles from the daily and weekly press have been left out, unless separately published. Unpublished items, as a rule, are not included, with the exception of MA theses in the collections of major libraries (particularly KITLV in Leiden) or mentioned in bibliographies and reading lists. Indonesian theses are also included, although they are often only available at the relevant university or IKIP (teachers' training school).

The selection of material was not based on 'scientific' criteria, because I believe not only academic work is of importance, but also material such as pamphlets, works by journalists, memoirs and fiction (*belles-lettres*). Works that do not treat the revolution as the main subject, but still devote attention to it in a substantial way, are also included: surveys of (modern) Indonesian history, works concerning a particular region or town, and biographies.

Each entry in this bibliography is preceded by a number. Titles with no indication of source are in the holdings of the KITLV library. Titles in a library other than KITLV carry an abbreviation of that library in round brackets at the end of the entry. A key to these library codes is on page 93. For items included in this bibliography that I have not actually seen, at the end of the entry in square brackets is the number of the reading list or bibliography in which that title was mentioned; this number can be found elsewhere in the book.

This bibliography was compiled from information available in the Netherlands. Field research in Indonesia undoubtedly would have added more material; however, the KITLV collection in Leiden possesses such a high degree of completeness that it can be safely assumed that most of the important Indonesian literature has been included.

I wish to thank all those who helped, especially Cock van den Aardweg of the acquisition department of KITLV, Marjan Groen of the editorial department, and Dr Harry Poeze who kindly searched his large private book collection for additional titles which would otherwise have been overlooked. Thanks also go to Judith Bellés Knijnenburg, Marianne van der Brugge, Matty Mos and Janet Ranke, who assisted in translating the introduction into English. A special word of gratitude should be addressed to my wife Marlies Klooster-Ranke, who besides filling a full-time job and caring for the children, supported my work for more than ten years.

The user is invited to bring to my attention (by contacting KITLV) any literature unintentionally omitted, so that it can be included in a future supplement.

Throughout the introduction most personal and geographical names are given in the current spelling of Indonesian.

Introduction

Bibliographical notes

In compiling this survey, more than a hundred bibliographies were consulted. Not all of these were of equal interest; some contained many relevant titles, others did not. For this reason I have indicated here which bibliographies were the most useful. It should also be noted that a considerable number of titles was not found in any bibliography, but was taken from the catalogues and accession lists of KITLV (which were thoroughly examined) and from reading lists.

Indonesian bibliographies. For the Japanese occupation, the *Katalog terbitan Indonesia selama pendudukan Jepang* (1983) was used. The most specialized works on the revolutionary period are the *Bibliografi terpilih Perpustakaan 45* (1976-1977) and *Daftar buku-buku Perpustakaan 45*; the latter has appeared in the periodical *Gema Angkatan 45* since 1980. For MA theses, I used the *Bibliografi skripsi*, published by LIPI in cooperation with KITLV. Unfortunately, no new volumes have appeared since 1981.

Dutch bibliographies. The most complete and specialized work on the revolutionary period is H.B. Donkersloot's *Bibliografie van de Nederlandse buitenlandse politiek* (1982). The author delves deeply into Dutch and Western literature, but does not consider Indonesian publications; moreover, the work is poorly indexed and already more than ten years old. Military works are surveyed in the more recent *Herinneringsliteratuur betreffende het Nederlandse militaire optreden te land in Indonesië* (1989) by J.M. Verhoog. Important serial works are the *Repertorium van boeken en tijdschriftartikelen betreffende de geschiedenis van Nederland*, with volumes appearing annually, and *Excerpta Indonesica*, published twice a year by KITLV. MA theses were found in Donkersloot, the *Repertorium* and particularly in *Doctoraalscripties geschiedenis* by H.J. Smit, of which new volumes regularly appear.

Other bibliographies. The *Preliminary checklist of Indonesian imprints during the Japanese period* (1963) and the *Preliminary checklist of Indonesian imprints (1945-1949) with Cornell University holdings* (1965), both compiled by John Echols, are of great interest. For the Japanese period, the *Nishijima Collection* (1973) was very useful. Articles from periodicals are

described in Attar Chand's *Southeast Asia and the Pacific; A select bibliography, 1947-1970* (1979), and in the serial *Bibliography of Asian studies*
(1971-), preceded by the *Cumulative bibliography on Asian studies* (1970-
1972). PhD dissertations are registered in *Doctoral dissertations on Asia*
(1975-). Sardesai and Sardesai also include MA theses in their *Theses and
dissertations on Southeast Asia* (1970).

Japanese period

Indonesian authors. The Indonesian writings published during the Japanese
occupation were, understandably, submitted to Japanese censorship, or du-
plicated the opinion of the occupying force. Important bibliographies
include the *Preliminary checklist of Indonesian imprints during the
Japanese period* (1963) by John Echols and *Katalog terbitan Indonesia selama
pendudukan Jepang* (1983). In the present bibliography, only a few titles
from this period were included.

During the Japanese occupation, it was difficult to write about Indonesia's
aspirations for independence; only in the last year were the rules made
more flexible. A short book by Prijono, *Sedikit tentang sedjarah Asia Timoer
Raja dan sedjarah Tanah Djawa* (1945), still holds to the Japanese war
ideology. In a booklet from 1945, *Perang Asia Timoer Raya*, the importance
of the war in Asia to *Indonesia merdeka* is finally mentioned. Some short
writings were intended to strengthen the spirit of the people, especially its
youth. The youth movement, Seinendan, included paramilitary units: see
the collection of prescriptions, *Atoeran-atoeran tentang Seinendan* (1945).
The Peta (Pembela Tanah Air), an auxiliary corps under the command of
Japanese officers, was influential in the development of the Indonesian
army. There were also militias, such as Hizbullah, established on an Islamic
foundation. Literature on these groups, written during the occupation and
revolutionary years, can be found in contemporary periodicals. After the
occupation, Peta history received attention in many writings, because it was
this corps that rebelled against the Japanese in February 1945.

After the end of the occupation, it became possible for Indonesian authors
to write about recent events unhindered. The number of authors of Chinese
descent who narrated the misbehaviour of the Japanese is striking; included
are Nio Joe Lan, Piso Tjoekoer, Pouw Kioe An and Tjamboek Berdoeri. One
explanation for this could be that the Indonesian Chinese suffered more
than most during the occupation. Tjamboek Berdoeri, a pseudonym
meaning 'thorny whip' behind which an unknown Chinese is hidden,
reports on the misconduct of the Japanese in a touching and sometimes
cynical way in his *Indonesia dalem api dan bara* (1947). He also considers the
first months of the revolution and ponders what improvement the

departure of the Japanese has really brought to the Chinese community. His report centres on the Malang region.

The first general account of the Japanese occupation is G. Pakpahan's *1261 hari dibawah sinar 'Matahari Terbit'* (1947, second printing 1979). The author, a Batak clergyman, pays special attention to the deferral of Christians to Muslims by the occupying force. He describes the mood of the population, which at first was full of expectation, but quickly turned into aversion. The fact that many prominent Indonesians cooperated with the Japanese can be explained by their desire for independence; it did not arise from affinity with Japanese ideology.

During the revolution, several publications appeared on the Joyoboyo-prophecy. Since ancient times, the prediction had been made on Java that small yellow-skinned men would come from the north, and freedom for the Javanese would be achieved thereafter. This prophecy seemed to have been miraculously fulfilled with the arrival of the Japanese (Soekmono 1946, Radèn Tanojo 1946, Tjantrik Mataram 1948, Imam Supardi 1949).

Many Indonesian writings on the Japanese occupation which appeared after 1950 were devoted to insurrections against Japanese authority. A survey of anti-Japanese resistance was made by Prawiroatmodjo (1953). The most celebrated rebellion is undoubtedly by a Peta battalion in Blitar, East Java, in February 1945. In 1977, Nugroho Notosusanto earned his doctoral degree with a study on the Peta and its origins. In this dissertation, *The Peta army during the Japanese occupation of Indonesia*, Nugroho made use of oral history methods, interviewing persons involved in Peta history. He also consulted contemporary periodicals. His conclusion is that the military training received by the Indonesian youth during the occupation was of importance to the independence struggle, because self-confidence had increased. Other Indonesian authors described the rebellions of different Peta units such as those in Gumilir (Legowo 1970) and Bandung. The leader of the great rebellion, Raden Supriyadi, was honoured in several biographies.

'Ordinary' civilians also rose against the Japanese a number of times. The Acehnese, who had resisted the Dutch previously, did not immediately submit to the Japanese and fought two 'wars' with them: Perang Bayu and Perang Pandrah. An Acehnese author who wrote much about the region's history during the Japanese occupation and revolutionary periods, T. Alibasyah Talsya, emphasized that the Acehnese, shortly before the arrival of the Japanese, had already seized power from the Dutch (Talsya 1985), and had successfully seized a large quantity of weapons before their return (Talsya 1982). Another rebellion against the Japanese, which is described in several publications, originated in the *pesantren* (Muslim school) in Singaparna near Tasikmalaya; it was led by K.H. Zainal Mustofa (Hidajat 1961, Danoemihardjo 1972, Marlina 1990).

Many publications give a general description of Japanese rule. Of course, the picture is negative: the population was oppressed and starved, and was submitted to forced labour. Terms like 'fascism' and 'imperialism' are commonly used. More distance was kept by A.A. Zorab in his PhD dissertation at Leiden University, *De Japanse bezetting van Indonesië* (1954). Many writings, including congress papers, are locally specialized: Gandasubrata (1953) on Banyumas, Djamhari (1965, 1970) on Malang, Zuhdi (1979, 1982) on Bogor, Jogaswara (1990) on Bandung and Sinar (1992) on East Sumatra.

The cooperation of prominent nationalist leaders such as Soekarno and Hatta with the Japanese oppressors remains an embarrassing chapter in Indonesian historiography. The explanation is always the same: it was to bring nearer the ultimate goal, *Indonesia merdeka*. The course of history seems to confirm this view. Interesting in this respect are the *Putera reports* of Mohammed Hatta, published in 1971. The Putera (Pusat Tenaga Rakyat) was a Japanese-created mass organization through which nationalist leaders should become subservient to the Japanese war objectives. Hatta did not let things go that far; he thought it intolerable that Indonesians should remain passive under Japanese rule. By means of Putera, it was possible for Hatta to propagate his own ideas on Indonesia's future. In his view, the Japanese occupation was only an interval on the journey to *kemenangan akhir*, the final victory of the Indonesian people.

Fiction (novels and short stories) was also written with the Japanese occupation as a background. H.B. Jassin's 'classic' survey *Kesoesasteraan Indonesia dimasa Djepang* (1948; several reprints) is important in this area. After 1950, many novels and short stories appeared which are situated in the Japanese period. Here we mention two novels on *romusha* (forced labourers) by Sudrajat (1976) and Suparna Sastra Diredja (1987), as well as the award-winning novel *Dan perang pun usai* (1979) by Ismail Marahimin, situated in Sumatra at the end of the occupation, which was translated into English.

Dutch authors. Many Dutch writings on the Japanese occupation concern experiences in internment camps. Although several of these writings cover the first months following the capitulation, the so-called *bersiap* period, they are left out of this bibliography. For this subject, one should consult Arno de Bruin's *Bibliografie van de Nederlands-Indische kampliteratuur van 1946 tot 1987* (1988) and Rolf Utermöhlen's *Japanse vrouwenkampen in Nederlands-Indië 1942-1945* (1993). D. van Velden's PhD dissertation *De Japanse interneringskampen voor burgers gedurende de Tweede Wereldoorlog* (1963, second printing 1977) remains a standard work.

The development of the relations between the Dutch East Indies and Japan prior to 1942 is described by Lieutenant-Governor-General H.J. van

Mook in *The Netherlands Indies and Japan* (1944). The author deals with the negotiations on access to natural resources such as oil and ores, in which he himself was deeply involved; these negotiations resulted in the rejection of many Japanese demands. Other surveys of Dutch-Japanese relations can be found in the collective volume *Van vriend tot vijand* (1945) and in volume 11a of L. de Jong's *Het Koninkrijk der Nederlanden in de Tweede Wereldoorlog* (1984).

Much has been written about the Japanese attack on the East Indies. Deserving of first mention is the detailed survey *Nederlands-Indië contra Japan* (1949-1961), which describes the battles which went on in various places. Since the 1980s the Japanese attack has received renewed attention in a literature 'boom' which has not yet subsided: P.C. Boer (1987, 1990) on the air battles in the Indies, and O.G. Ward (1985) on the KNIL air force; P.M. Bosscher (1986, 1990) on the Royal Navy and the famous battle of the Java Sea; Teitler (1982), Nortier (1988), Groen and Touwen-Bouwsma (1992) and Nortier and others (1994) writing mainly on the land battle. Of course, the standard work of L. de Jong is also of importance in relation to these subjects. Recently much has appeared on guerrilla fighting against the Japanese and the operations of the Dutch-East Indies (allied) secret service: Nortier (1981) and Hegener (1992) on the guerrillas in central Sulawesi; Nortier (1985) and Touwen-Bouwsma (1986) on intelligence operations.

Publications on Japanese rule and policy in the Indies are less numerous. An early account is by K. de Weerd, *The Japanese occupation of the Netherlands East Indies* (1946), compiled for the international tribunal on Japanese war criminals in Tokyo. Better known is *Indië onder Japanschen hiel* (1946) by W.H.J. Elias, reprinted in 1988 under a different title. The documents edited by I.J. Brugmans, *Nederlandsch-Indië onder Japanse bezetting* (1960), from the RIOD collection in Amsterdam are also important. A rich variety of writing is included on Japanese policy, military affairs, the youth movement, the economic situation and resistance against the Japanese.

Two authors who regularly published writings on Japanese occupation policy are Rodney de Bruin and László Sluimers. De Bruin who worked at the RIOD, wrote an interesting MA thesis on the Japanese-trained youth movement, *De Seinendan in Indonesië* (1968), in which the different regions of the archipelago are compared. In his PhD dissertation (1982), De Bruin analysed the Japanese attitude towards the nationalist movement. He also wrote on Japanese policy towards Islam in Indonesia (1982). Sluimers searched the backgrounds of Japanese occupation policy, emphasizing the diverse traditions in Japanese military and political circles (1968). Sluimers sometimes compares Indonesia with other occupied regions such as the Philippines (1972, 1978).

An interesting reading category includes the memoirs of those who remained outside the internment camps. Such memoirs contain vivid descriptions of everyday life. Here we can note the diary of L.F. Jansen, *In deze halve gevangenis* (1988), describing the situation in Batavia. In *Vogelvrij* (1984), Moscou-de Ruyter tells about the circumstances in Malang in East Java. The MA thesis of Paula de Haas (1992) also concerns Malang and is based on personal memoirs and interviews; it also covers the first two years of the revolution.

A special place is occupied by A.J. Piekaar's study *Atjèh en de oorlog met Japan* (1949). It is the only thorough Dutch research on developments in a particular region. Piekaar describes Japanese policy aimed at advancing the status of the *ulama* (religious leaders) at the cost of the *ulèebalang* (local chiefs). Other aspects, such as the socio-economic situation and anti-Japanese resistance, are also discussed.

During the Japanese occupation, several writings appeared outside Indonesia on the political future of the archipelago. Queen Wilhelmina's well-known speech of 7 December 1942 was the first in a long sequence of discussions which continued after the Japanese were defeated. A survey of this literature is made on pages 18-19 and 27-31.

Other Western authors. Part of Western literature on the Japanese period deals with the progress of the war in Southeast Asia. This kind of literature is not fully covered in this bibliography (see the index entry 'Second World War').

An early, little-known dissertation on the Japanese occupation of Indonesia was written by Janus Poppe, *Political development in the Netherlands East Indies during and immediately after the Japanese occupation* (Georgetown University, Washington DC, 1948). The author used documents from the Allied Persecution Section of the War Tribunal in Tokyo. Poppe's thesis is also important for its coverage of the events having to do with the Proclamation. He regrets that the Japanese intermezzo disturbed the relationship between the Dutch and Indonesians; he would have preferred a gradual development towards independence, which would have taken place under Dutch rule in any case. 'Evolution instead of revolution', is Poppe's motto.

The first elaborate study to receive wide attention was Harry Benda's *The crescent and the rising sun* (1958, several reprints). It analyses Japanese policy towards Indonesian Islam and its leaders; moreover, the book can be read as a general survey of the occupation years, including an introductory description of developments since 1900. Benda, too, refers to the Japanese policy of favouring Islam at the expense of the traditional secular leadership which had been subordinate to Dutch rule. The modern nationalist leaders also grew in prestige, but real power was given them only in the last phase, when it became evident that the war was lost. The controversy between Islam and secular nationalism, sharpened by the Japanese, influenced the situation after the Proclamation of August 1945.

Another important, detailed survey of the Japanese occupation is the PhD dissertation by George S. Kanahele (Cornell University, 1967). Here, the emphasis is not placed on Islam but on the secular movement. The author concludes that the self-confidence of the nationalists increased through Japanese intervention. Through his knowledge of the Japanese language, Kanahele had access to primary sources; he also interviewed several of the Japanese involved. Another survey, by L.M. Demin (1963), is written in Russian and therefore is not generally accessible. Benedict Anderson's *Some aspects of Indonesian politics under the Japanese occupation* (1961) discusses only the last year of the occupation and is, in fact, a preliminary study to *The pemuda revolution* (1967).

Many specialized studies have also appeared. Of the regional publications, we mention Reid on North Sumatra and Aceh (1975), Van Langenberg on East Sumatra (1986) and Webb on Flores (1986). Under the editorship of Anton Lucas, a volume appeared on underground (communist) resistance against the Japanese, *Local opposition and underground resistance* (1986), including two contributions by Indonesians (Melati and Soeryana). Legge's monograph on Sjahrir and illegality in Jakarta (1988) considers various aspects of resistance. To suppress all opposition, the Japanese had their own Kenpeitai (secret police), about which Shrimer and Hobbs compiled a volume (1986). A comparison of Japanese policy in Indonesia and other regions of Southeast Asia was made by Elsbree (1953). In *The blue-eyed enemy* (1988), Theodore Friend considers Japanese anti-Western propaganda in Java and the Philippines.

Japanese authors. An important part of the extensive Japanese literature on the occupation of Indonesia is collected in three bibliographies: *The Nishijima Collection* (1973), *Final report of the exhibition of historical materials on the Japanese occupation of Indonesia* (1988), and *Japan and Southeast Asia* (1983) by Ikuo Iwasaki. Of course, most titles are in Japanese and can be consulted only by the specialist. The first-mentioned bibliography was edited by Waseda University in Tokyo, an important research centre in this field. By 1959 a source book had already appeared at Waseda University, which was translated into English in 1963: *Japanese military administration in Indonesia*. This voluminous publication (nearly 700 pages) is still considered important in the study of the Japanese occupation. Professor Kenichi Goto, who works at Waseda University, is considered one of the most prominent authorities on the occupation of Indonesia. In 1989, several of his articles were re-edited into one volume. Professor Goto wrote, *inter alia*, about 'Abdul Rachman' (Ichiki Tatsuo), a Japanese who after the capitulation fought at the side of the Indonesian Republic. In addition, the memoirs of Japanese soldiers are an important source of information; these include Utsumi (1969), Miyamoto (1973), Saito (1977), Yamamoto (1979) and Mizugaki (1984). Because these and other memoirs are written in Japanese, a volume containing fragments translated into English appeared in 1986: *The Japanese experience in Indonesia*, under the editorship of A. Reid and Akira Oki. Various aspects of Japanese rule are considered, as well as the events relating to the Proclamation of the Republic (see the section on the Proclamation, pp. 44-46).

Edited by a renowned expert on Indonesian history, Akira Nagazumi, in 1988 a volume of articles appeared on the insurrections against the Japanese, translated into Indonesian. During the 1980s several thorough, regionally specialized studies were written on the 'ordinary people' of the Japanese period: a favourite subject for the younger generation of Japanese researchers. To begin, we mention the thorough dissertation by Aiko Kurasawa, *Mobilization and control* (Cornell University, 1988), in which the effects of the occupation on Java's rural districts are analysed. Among other aspects, new Japanese institutions on village level, the policy towards Islam, the enlisting of *romusha* (forced labourers), Japanese propaganda and forced rice deliveries, often leading to famine or revolt, are considered. In a congress paper *Social change in rural Java* (1992), Kurasawa concentrates her research on a particular village near Surakarta; this kind of 'social history' is, as far as the revolutionary period is concerned, principally studied by Western authors. Another Japanese study which deserves mention in this respect is *Desa Cimahi* (1988) by Fukuo Ueno, treating the social history of a village in West Java in 1943.

Contemporary writings - Indonesian authors

a. Government publications. Quite soon after the Proclamation of 17 August 1945, the central government of the Republic of Indonesia showed considerable activity in the field of publishing, which continued through the revolutionary period. Many official magazines appeared, which are not considered here (see the bibliography of Thung and Echols 1966, 1973). Also, much non-periodical literature was published, varying from books that number several hundred pages to small brochures and pamphlets (*siaran kilat*). The bulk of government publications was aimed towards the Indonesian reader, yet a considerable number was also intended to be read by the outside world: the Republic's survival was in part dependent on public relations, and a degree of publishing activity could serve as proof of its vitality.

Most publications derive from the Ministry of Information, Kementerian Penerangan. A number of these were meant to clarify the republican standpoint at the negotiation table. One example is a brochure on the draft agreement of Linggajati, *Naskah persetoedjoean boekan à la Vietnam, boekan reëele Unie* (1946). It was intended to anticipate internal criticism on Linggajati by emphasizing the equality of the partners in negotiation, unlike the agreement between France and Vietnam. The Republic of Indonesia, as the future United States of Indonesia, would not be part of the Kingdom of the Netherlands. Moreover, the draft Netherlands-Indonesian Union was not a real union, meaning that the participating states would have their own head of state and would be fully sovereign. Consequently, the United States of Indonesia would conduct an independent foreign policy; at all levels, the population would be able to choose its own administrators.

In 1949, a publication of the Kementerian Penerangan appeared as the voluminous *Perdjuangan di Konperensi Medja Bundar*, which, like the previous brochure, was intended as an explanation of the negotiations and their results. It contains a detailed survey of the issues on which agreement was reached, as well as Dutch and Indonesian press commentary expressing a preponderantly positive tendency.

The Kementerian Penerangan also published booklets with educational purposes, to teach the people about democracy, representative government and political parties. Many of these booklets were included in the PEPORA series on 'political education of the people'. In addition, the department furnished a long series of pamphlets (*siaran kilat*) on pressing issues of the day. One of these issues was the citizenship of the new Republic, about which some minorities had doubts, especially Indo-Europeans and Chinese. The pamphlet *Bagaimana? Apa artinja saja djadi warga negara Indonesia?* (1946), in which the government assures minorities that they will occupy an equal place in the new independent Indonesia, is exemplary. Other issues dealt with in *siaran kilat* are religious freedom, money purification, rice deliveries to India and many more.

In publications with a generally informative purpose, anti-Dutch feelings are not obvious. On the other hand, some writings were intended to keep alive the revolutionary spirit, or were directed at foreign readers, such as the brochure *List of material and personal outrages and injuries* (1946), edited by the Department of Foreign Affairs, in which the misbehaviour of Dutch soldiers in Jakarta is detailed. NICA crimes against the population are summed up in this calendar-style pamphlet. No direct comment on the events is given; the reader is left to draw his own (obvious) conclusions. In describing the period October-December 1945, the pamphlet in fact urges the allied (British) military authorities to prevent the return of Dutch troops.

Evidence of the Republic's publicity activities was also found abroad. In

New York and London, a Republic of Indonesia Office was established from which pamphlets, as well as magazines, were distributed. For instance, in 1949 a *History of Indonesia's national movement* appeared in New York, suggesting that the roots of the Indonesian people's pursuit of freedom extend far back in history. In Melbourne an Indonesian Independence Committee was established to influence Australian public opinion in favour of the Republic during the first years of the revolution. It published a pamphlet on repression under Dutch colonial rule, *inter alia*, illustrated by the imprisonment of nationalists in the isolated camp of Boven-Digul: *Dutch imperialism exposed* (1946).

Most government publications were anonymous, but the speeches of prominent leaders, such as Soekarno, Hatta and Sjahrir, were also issued. Each year on 17 August, Soekarno addressed the people, as well as on other occasions such as the Madiun affair of September 1948. In its entirety, Soekarno's bibliography of the years 1945-1949 numbers many volumes. In 1945 an influential brochure appeared, written by Sjahrir, *Perdjoeangan kita*, which was reprinted several times and also translated. Sjahrir expresses his disapproval of political extremism and emphasizes the merits of diplomacy. During the Japanese occupation, youth was strongly indoctrinated, which resulted in violence against non-Indonesians in revolutionary times; such violence damaged the image of the Republic abroad. Also among the leaders of the Republic were persons who worked with the Japanese, and therefore were not effective in satisfactorily fighting anarchy. Sjahrir found it essential for the Republic to respect civil rights, such as the right to vote and the establishment of political parties. The fate of the Republic was in the hands of the great Western powers such as Britain and the United States, with their 'capitalist-imperialist' systems; it was useless to deny this. The struggle of the Republic would have to be targeted at winning sympathy and support abroad. *Perdjoeangan kita* bears the personal stamp of the author, but was published by the government (Pertjetakan Repoeblik Indonesia); during Sjahrir's premiership, the main points of the pamphlet could be recognized in government policy.

Apart from the publications of the Republic, a number of writings derived from the authorities of the federal states. These writings occupy a special place, because the federal states were a creation of Dutch policy, and at the same time were ruled mainly by Indonesians. Consequently, the attitude towards Dutch authority and Dutch involvement in Indonesian affairs differs from that of the Republic. The most developed, also as regards publishing, was the state of East Indonesia. The Department of Information at Makasar published several booklets with a political-educational character, such as *Pendidikan politik rakjat* (1949), intended to prepare the population for participation in the new representative bodies. A survey of these new institutions is given in *Van onmondige tot burger* (1949). The relations between East Indonesia and the Republic are treated in *Kita sama kita* (1949), a report on two inter-Indonesian conferences. Following the Second Police Action, there was a rapprochement to the side of the Republic, as is evident from the pamphlet *Bendera dan lagu kebangsaan* (1949), stating that East Indonesia had the same red-and-white flag and also the same national anthem, *Indonesia Raya*, as the Republic.

Another federal state that showed activity in publishing was Pasundan in West Java. J. Tuhuteru (1948) wrote about the birth of this *negara*. Further, some guide books appeared on the regional parliament and its members: *Zakboek parlemen Pasoendan* (1948-1949) and *Parlemen Pasundan satu tahun* (1949).

b. Political parties. At the beginning of November 1945 the republican government called for the establishment of political parties; soon after, party activities began to develop. In the same month, the Masyumi (Majelis Syuro Muslimin Indonesia), an organization that had existed during the Japanese occupation, was re-established as a political party. In December, the PSI (Partai Sosialis Indonesia) was founded, followed by the PNI (Partai Nasional Indonesia) in January 1946. The PKI (Partai Komunis Indonesia) gradually gave up its underground existence after the Japanese capitulation. Most parties published magazines, as well as pamphlets.

The booklet *Anggaran dasar roemah tangga* (1946) is an important evaluation of Masyumi's place in the political spectrum. As for internal politics, the party's aim was to penetrate Indonesian society with the principles of Islam. In an economic sense, this meant that capitalism was rejected where it led to egoism. Private enterprise was important, but should not damage the common cause. Foreign policy was aimed at the recognition of the Republic as an equal member of the international community. The principles of Masyumi were explained in detail in a pamphlet by Darwis Thaib, *Toentoetan perdjoeangan* (1946). The author repudiated Western values such as individualism, materialism and capitalism, preferring a society based on social justice. Another aim of Masyumi was the unification of all Indonesian Muslims into one political organization (p. 33).

As for the Partai Sosialis Indonesia, we consider a pamphlet by Abdoelmadjid, *Mentjapai masjarakat sosialis* (1946). The author was Deputy Minister of Social Affairs in a Sjahrir cabinet. The pamphlet presents a Marxist argument, placing the Indonesian revolution within the international struggle of the working classes. However, in Abdoelmadjid's opinion Indonesian society was not yet ripe for socialism; first, a democratic system would have to be developed and the remnants of feudalism and imperialism removed (p. 14).

The Partai Nasional Indonesia paid the least attention to its principles, if we consider the few publications which are at our disposal. It was primarily a leftist, anti colonial party, pursuing *Indonesia merdeka* and offering a political home to secular nationalists of assorted plumage. The pamphlet *Sekitar statements Rum-Van Royen* (1949) scarcely gives any information on the party and its standpoints; it is in fact a collection of press statements. On the other side, there is a booklet concerning the 'struggle' of the PNI in parliament, *Perdjuangan PNI dalam parlemen* (1950; not consulted). The party's mood can further be determined from the writings of prominent members including the journalist-publicist Adi Negoro and the jurist Sunario. Finally, there is Rocamora's study from 1974, entitled – appropriately enough – *Nationalism in search of ideology*.

In contrast with the PNI, the Partai Komunis Indonesia had a firm and well-developed ideology. Some of its principles can be found in *PKI dan KNI Pusat* (1947). It held that economic cooperation was a necessity; an 'economic police' should combat abuse of power (usury). Indonesian enterprise and native industries should be protected against usurpation by foreign capital; foreign trade should, in the vision of the PKI, be placed under strict government control. In matters of war and peace, the party propagated a 'people's army'. The party magazine *Bintang Merah*, published after 1945, is also an important source of information. In the course of 1948, the party's opposition against the government intensified as the result of the new, polarizing course of the international communist movement (*Djalan baroe*, 1948). The return of Muso in August 1948, a PKI leader who had been in Moscow for a long time, further sharpened its oppositionary role, with the Renville Agreement acting as a thorn in its side. In September 1948, this development resulted in the Madiun affair, which was quickly suppressed by the army. As a consequence, the party was again forced into illegality. In the early 1950s, the party once more became manifest under the leadership of Aidit, who explained the Madiun affair as being 'provoked' by the forces of the right to diminish the PKI's influence. During the revolution, PKI leader Alimin (Prawirodirdjo) was most active in the field of publishing. He wrote several pamphlets, for instance on the Linggajati Agreement: *Perdjuangan naskah dan mempertegak de facto* (1947).

Another oppositionary movement was the Persatuan Perdjuangan (PP), in which several political parties cooperated with each other. The PP was led by Tan Malaka, who marked the movement to such an extent that we refer to his writings as the prime source of information (see pp. 15-16). Of the smaller political organizations, we mention here the Protestant and Roman Catholic parties. The Catholic party was led by I.J. Kasimo, who published a political standpoint in 1948, *Dasar perdjuangan*.

c. Islamic and Christian authors. In this bibliography, we are not concerned with strictly religious writings, but only with those which connect religion with the events of 1945-1949. A further distinction can be made between writings treating the relationship of religion, politics and democracy in general terms, and those referring to actual circumstances and events in a more concrete way.

Islamic authors. Several gradations are discernible in the work of Zainal Abidin Ahmad, a leading Muslim publicist who, during the revolution, wrote several books on the 'Islamic state'. In *Mentjari negara sempoerna* (1947), written on the occasion of a Masyumi congress in November 1946, Ahmad provides a historical survey of Islamic political thinkers and their views on the shape of the state; the opinion of Ahmad himself remains in the background. A similar, but more extensive survey is *Konsepsi tata negara Islam* (1949). The author discusses the foundations of the *negara Islam*, namely *keadilan* (justice), *ketuhanan* (belief in God) and *kedaulatan rakyat* (people's sovereignty). He argues that parliamentary democracy and the republican form of government fit in very well with the Islamic concept of the state, leaving room for other (religious) convictions in the representative bodies (p. 113). More directly related to the situation in Indonesia is *Kemerdekaan Indonesia dan Islam* (1946), in which Ahmad views the recently proclaimed independence as compatible with the principles of Islam; the Proclamation is even seen as a consequence of these principles. The pursuit of freedom and resistance against oppression are essential characteristics of the Islamic belief. Moreover, belief in God was recognized by the Republic as one of the principles in the Pancasila. A consequence of the recently acquired independence is that Indonesians became responsible for their own future; Islam summons them to accept that responsibility. In the booklet *Konstitusi negara* (1946), Ahmad explains the republican constitution, showing that it is quite compatible with the beliefs of the religious Muslim, because the state, in recognizing belief in God as one of its principles, is no longer neutral in religious matters. Ahmad defends the constitution as the outcome of debates on the fundamentals of the Indonesian state: creating a state which does not prescribe the *syariah* (Islamic law) to all its citizens, yet is based on belief in God (toward the end of the Japanese occupation, the debate on the fundamentals of an independent Indonesia had become intensive and emotional; see Boland 1982). The last work of Ahmad mentioned here is *Perdjoeangan politik dan sendjata* (1946), a booklet containing a defence of the Republic and an overview of the first year of the independence struggle. A discourse on the position of Islam in the new state is not included.

The best known and most prolific Islamic author is Hamka, pseudonym of Haji Abdul Malik Karim Amrullah. Like Ahmad, he agrees with Pancasila and the constitution; but he is less preoccupied with the Islamic state concept than Ahmad is. Hamka's *Repoloesi agama* (1946) is comparable with Ahmad's *Kemerdekaan Indonesia dan Islam*; the author confirms that Islam calls for liberation. To reach this goal, a social revolution may be inevitable. At the same time, the author states, religion has to renew itself, in order to give the pursuit of liberation a new impulse. Of Hamka's non-religious writings, we refer here to *Merdeka* (1945), disclosing general information on democratic institutions and the rights and duties of civilians; and *Sesudah naskah Renville* (1948), which defends the change in Soekarno's and Hatta's policy from armed struggle to *perjuangan pikiran* (mental struggle). Hamka asserts that the Prophet himself once had to undergo such a mental struggle, more grave and more intense than any other.

Although moderate authors such as Ahmad and Hamka call for social revolution and religious renewal, this remains within the limits of loyalty to the republican government. S.M. Kartosuwirjo is more radical in his pamphlet *Haloean politik Islam* (1946), an address to members of Masyumi and other Islamic organizations in Garut (West Java). Kartosuwirjo, the future leader of the separatist Darul Islam movement, proposes an 'action programme' for the Islamization of Indonesian society. First he states that the political consciousness of the people, underdeveloped in the Dutch and Japanese periods, must overcome its backwardness. Only then would it become possible to build up the revolution with renewed strength, a revolution which shows two aspects: *revolusi nasional*, achieved when Indonesian independence is recognized abroad, and *revolusi sosial*, achieved from within. *Revolusi nasional* must be the first objective, but that does not mean the postponement of *revolusi sosial*. Indonesian society must be changed immediately, at the regional and local levels. The ultimate goal is the establishment of *Darul Islam*, which means that the Republic becomes based on Islam and derives its laws from it. To realize this, it is necessary that Muslims be well represented in regional bodies and in parliament. Religious Muslims were actually under-represented in executive bodies; when opportunities arose, Muslims should occupy seats in order to exert more influence on administration and legislation. Kartosuwirjo advises starting at the local village level, because it is there that the fundamentals of the people's sovereignty are situated.

Christian authors. The only Christian author mentioned here is J. Leimena, leader of the Indonesian Protestants. In 1949, his *Perselisihan Indonesia-Belanda* appeared (also translated into English), presenting a survey of the Indonesian-Dutch conflict. In Leimena's view, the Dutch made the mistake of pressing their concept for an independent Indonesia at any cost, while the Indonesians – though far from having the ideal solution – preferred to follow their own insights. As for the Police Actions, Leimena points out the protests of Dutch Protestant churches. The Indonesian Christians, the majority of them loyal republicans, cannot consent to a violent solution. Moreover, the progress of missionary work will benefit from a quick settlement of the conflict.

d. Three prolific writers. The lawyer-politician-poet Muhammad Yamin, already a prominent nationalist in pre-war times, was a critic of Sjahrir's diplomacy during the revolution. In *Pembelaan Repoeblik Indonesia* (1946), a lyric defence of the revolution, Yamin qualifies the pursuit of freedom as an essential and justified need of all nations; political convictions and creeds are of secondary importance. He holds that every nation has the right to defend its freedom, with arms if necessary. It must be a comprehensive freedom, *kemerdekaan bulat*, leaving no room for compromise. Sjahrir's policy was seen as concessive and weak, also in regard to foreign relations. Yamin felt the Republic must present itself more clearly to the outside world and seek support, as Aceh did half a century before (p. 69). Yamin preferred Tan Malaka as a national leader; in a 1946 pamphlet, he calls Tan Malaka the 'father of the Indonesian Republic'. Yamin's oppositional feelings involved him in the Tiga Juli affair (1946), leading to his imprisonment. When brought to trial, he submitted a defence plea: *Sapta Dharma, patriotisme Indonesia* (1948), in which he presents the 'seven obligations' of patriotism, referring to international literature on law and politics and argues that he himself has always respected these obligations. *Sapta Dharma* also contains many details on the Tiga Juli affair.

Though Tan Malaka was imprisoned during a great deal of the revolutionary period, several titles appeared by his hand, some of which had been written earlier. For example, the pamphlet *Massa actie*, written on the occasion of the disturbances in Java and Sumatra in 1926-1927, was reprinted in 1947. The remarkable, lengthy writing *Madilog* (1946) was conceptualized during the Japanese occupation. In *Madilog*, Tan Malaka's world view is combined with several philosophical and social systems (such as Marxism). The content shows no direct relationship with actual events. This is in contrast to other shorter works such as *PARI* (1946), in which Tan Malaka presents a strategy for the revolution. He stresses the importance of an organized proletarian mass movement, *gerakan murba teratur*, as the only way to drive out Dutch imperialism. The people's unity, eventually in a one-party system, is indispensable for victory. This unity, however, must be based on consensus, *mufakat*, and not on dictatorship. Another condition necessary for success is the fulfilment of the people's basic needs: food, clothing and shelter. Further, foreign capital must not be allowed to dominate the Indonesian economy. These aims can be reached only through an economic development which is strongly guided by the government. In the third part of his autobiography *Dari pendjara ke pendjara* (1948), which remained unpublished, Tan Malaka analyses the policy of the republican government. Negotiations with the British and Dutch are rejected as long as foreign soldiers remain on Indonesian soil. The Linggajati and Renville Agreements are seen as intolerable limitations of the Republic's sovereignty; in fact, such agreements return the Republic to the position of a colony.

A third productive writer of the revolutionary period is the prominent journalist and publicist Adi Negoro, brother of Yamin. His writings often serve didactic purposes and treat general political concepts such as democracy and people's sovereignty. In *Dasar kerakjatan dalam Repoeblik Indonesia* (ca. 1945), Adi Negoro explains the constitution and offers advice to representatives on how to act effectively. A more thorough work on democracy is *Bajangan pergolakan dunia* (1949), stating that the young Republic can only defend itself against the dangers of capitalism and communism by the existence of a well-functioning democracy with a constitution and a parliament. The government must be controlled effectively and the actions of politicians critically observed. These are not principles borrowed from abroad; traditional Indonesian society includes the concept of *adat menyanggah*, resistance against bad rule (p. 102). The author contemplates the American independence war and constitution, using it as an example for his readers. In *Revolusi dan kebudajaan* (1950, written in 1949), Adi Negoro states that Indonesian culture after 1945 should be directed toward the future, and should be based on *kemerdekaan sejati* (real freedom), *kemakmuran* (prosperity) and *demokrasi*. In the past, Indonesian culture had been suppressed; in post-war Indonesia it could develop unhampered.

Not all of Adi Negoro's writings contain general observations. The pamphlet *Apa sebab peroendingan Indonesia dan Nederland mesti gagal?* (1946) deals with a particular stage of the negotiations. The author predicts their failure as long as the Dutch refuse to accept the republican demand of *kemerdekaan seratus persen*; since the Dutch continued to send troops and had set up an economic blockade, Adi Negoro believes their acceptance will not be forthcoming.

e. Other independent authors. In the years 1945-1949, many other writings by independent authors appeared which cannot be adequately described in the scope of this introduction (see nos 2057-2755). Only a few characteristic publications are mentioned here, intended to give an impression of the diversity of pro-republican writing during the revolution.

We first refer to an important short book by the prominent *pemuda* Adam Malik, *Riwajat dan perdjuangan sekitar Proklamasi kemerdekaan Indonesia* (1948). It is the first attempt to describe the events of the Proclamation by one who was closely involved. The author endeavours to correct the picture of the Proclamation which emerges from memorial articles and speeches, especially concerning the role of prominent nationalist leaders (such as Soekarno and Hatta). These persons are usually depicted as self-assured, while in reality they were indecisive. Soekarno and Hatta, and others who derived their leading positions from the Japanese, were inclined to receive independence as a gift from them. For some *pemuda* groups, and for the Indonesian people as a whole, this was unacceptable; independence had to be an Indonesian initiative and not a *kemerdekaan hadiah* (granted freedom). Soekarno, Hatta and others had alienated themselves from the people by their ties with the Japanese, while the *pemuda* had kept in touch with and knew the people's desires. Malik vividly describes the kidnapping of Soekarno and Hatta and the discussions at Rengasdengklok led by *pemuda* Soekarni. After the Proclamation, too, the *pemuda* resisted the influence of the Japanese. Malik also discusses Sjahrir and his following; he admits that Sjahrir had no ties with the Japanese, but did not fully support the *pemuda* initiatives because he failed to appreciate the mood of the population (p. 23).

Another remarkable booklet describing actual events was written by Abdullah Arif, *Disekitar peristiwa penchianat Tjoembok* (1946). It deals with the disturbances in Aceh in December 1945-January 1946 (see also the translation, with an introduction by A. Reid, 1970). The *adat* chiefs in some regions of Aceh (*ulèebalang*) had witnessed a decline in their authority during the Japanese occupation, in favour of the Islamic leaders (*ulama*). After the Japanese surrender they aspired, under the leadership of *ulèebalang* Teuku Mohammad Daud Cumbok, to restore their position with the help of the Dutch. They received military training, oppressed the people and refused to recognize the recently proclaimed Republic. Arif describes how the *ulama*, assisted by republican forces and *pemuda*, drove out the 'traitors' and led the Acehnese back to the bosom of the Republic. Their own position was, of course, strongly enforced.

Finally, we mention a fine short book by Abu Hanifah, *Kita berdjoeang* (1946), which differs completely from the previous titles. It is a lyric description of Indonesian society during the revolution and afterwards. The author repeatedly uses the opening word *saudaraku*, as if speaking to a person. He considers several aspects of Indonesian society, including education, well-being, youth, the position of women and belief in God. In all these fields, according to the author, progress can be achieved through an incessant struggle against imperialism and for freedom, against capitalist oppression and for a decent existence. Considering the future of his country, Abu Hanifah gets more specific: the revolution will succeed because the Netherlands is a small country that can do little without foreign aid. To

prove this, he reminds the reader of the fate of the Dutch during the Second
World War. He believes that the Indonesian revolution must attract the
attention of other countries and win their sympathy. Abu Hanifah himself
attempted to achieve this goal: in 1947, he represented the Republic at the
Inter-Asiatic Conference in New Delhi.

Contemporary writings - Dutch authors

a. Government publications; Plans concerning Dutch-Indonesian relations.
Following the occupation of the Netherlands in May 1940, the government
of the Dutch East Indies was left to take many of its own decisions. The
circumstances led to a more independent course; the Indies stood, more
than before, on their own feet. It was against this background that in
September 1940 the Commission for the Study of Constitutional Reforms
was installed, to register various opinions in the Indies. This 'Visman
Commission' (named after its chairman Frans Visman), which included the
participation of Dutch as well as Indonesians, issued its report on December
1941, shortly before the Japanese invasion. A reprint of this report appeared
in New York in 1944.

The desires of more radical nationalists were also included in the final
report, namely a confederation with a separate head of state for Indonesia,
and a two-chamber representative system copied from the Netherlands.
These desires, however, were 'wrapped' in such a manner that the
Commission's inventory was useful for conservatives, too. In 1946 the
rightist Nationaal Comité Handhaving Rijkseenheid published a synopsis
entitled *Dit vroeg Indië*, selecting those elements which fit into its own
views.

The Visman Commission noted a broad desire for more autonomy, and
for the instalment of a Rijksraad with advisory and even legislative com-
petence. It held that more Indonesians should be appointed to leading
positions. Discrimination on racial grounds in franchise, penal and civil law
should be gradually abolished. The desire for 'East Indies citizenship', however, was not adopted by the Commission.

A Dutch pendant of the Visman Commission was the 'Commission to
Investigate the Opinion in the Netherlands Concerning the Place of the
Overseas Territories in the Kingdom', installed on August 1945 under the
chairmanship of W.H. van Helsdingen. Its voluminous report appeared in
September 1946, presenting a survey of many reform plans. Most of these
recommended new representative bodies such as a Rijksparlement and a
Rijksraad, with decisive powers on matters concerning the Kingdom as a
whole. For the rest, the parts of the Kingdom should look after themselves.
The general opinion was that the 'mother country' interfered too much in

East Indies matters. A Rijksconferentie (conference of the Realm's parts) should be held to settle the new relationship.

The Visman and Van Helsdingen Commissions were primarily intended to assemble various ideas and opinions on constitutional reforms. Their reports contain no government standpoint. The government's view, however, could be distilled from Queen Wilhelmina's radio speech on 7 December 1942, a speech which influenced many of the post-war plans listed in the Van Helsdingen report. The Queen had spoken about a Rijksconferentie 'at a round table', including representatives from the Indies, where discussions on new relations could take place. There should be an 'equal partnership' among the Kingdom's parts, based on the 'voluntary acceptance' of mutual ties. Internal affairs should be handled by the parts themselves; discrimination based on *landaard* (racial grounds) should disappear. This rough scheme could be worked out in several ways. In later government publications, the Queen's speech is often referred to as a starting point, but actual developments such as the Proclamation of the Republic prevented the development of a new relationship between the Netherlands and Indonesia as it was imagined in 1942 (Fasseur 1982).

b. Other government publications. Even before the Japanese capitulation, the population of the East Indies was addressed by the Nederlandsch-Indische Publiciteits Dienst in Melbourne, Australia. This bureau furnished information on the progress of the Pacific War (*Pertempoeran di Pacific*, 1945) and on the return of Dutch authority (*Kepada seloeroeh ra'jat Indonesia*, 1945). After the capitulation, the Regeerings Voorlichtings Dienst (RVD) in Batavia took over. It explained certain aspects of Dutch policy regarding the Indonesian question, such as federalism. It also provided unbiased information on political organizations: *Politieke groeperingen in Indonesië* (1948). Some publications appeared in English and were obviously intended for an international reading public. An example of a propaganda brochure is *Indonesië herleeft!* (1948) which contains positive socio-economic and factual information, and also addresses issues concerning the Indies' future government. It emphasizes the indispensability of Dutch assistance in rebuilding Indonesia. The 'Republic of Yogyakarta', however, was carrying out its own 'irresponsible' economic policy (p. 15). Federal policy was explained by the RVD in two short books by W.A. van Goudoever, *Malino maakt historie* (1946) and *Denpasar bouwt een huis* (1947). The first title contains a synopsis of the Malino conference minutes as well as a defence of the federal ideas intended to lead to the United States of Indonesia, a policy supported by many Indonesians, according to the author.

A survey of the first years of the Dutch-Indonesian conflict can be found in the RVD brochure *Het politieke gebeuren rondom de Repoeblik Indo-*

nesia (1947), published on the occasion of the First Police Action. It describes the Dutch Government's repeated attempts to come to terms with the Republic, a policy that failed due to the numerous violations of the Linggajati Agreement. The Republic had no authority over terrorists who chose as victims so-called disloyal elements such as the Chinese. Many gruesome pictures of massacres by *pelopor* bands are included. The brochure *Het politieke gebeuren*, being a justification of the military operations of July 1947, was also published in English as *The Indonesian problem, facts and factors* (1947). Other English-language RVD publications also show anti-republican sentiments. In *What's it about in Indonesia?* (1947) the pro-Dutch argument from *Indonesië herleeft!* is contrasted with examples of republican mismanagement; a pictorial appendix suggests that the Republic is in reality a Japanese creation and the powerless prey of extremist gangs. The pamphlet *Why political negotiations failed* (1948) is intended as a justification of the Second Police Action.

In New York the Netherlands Information Bureau (NIB) was established, which interpreted Dutch policy in the Indies for an American public. In 1945, *The Netherlands Commonwealth and the future* appeared, containing the speeches of Queen Wilhelmina and positive reactions by the Dutch and American press. As the conflict sharpened, the NIB gave the American public the information it craved on sensitive issues: *Communism in the Republic of Indonesia* (1948). American press articles were repeatedly searched for pro-Dutch statements, which were collected and published; one example is seen in the collection of newspaper and magazine articles on the Second Police Action: *Many American voices that count say that Holland was right...* (1949). One of the last NIB publications, *Towards the United States of Indonesia* (1949), contains Dutch statements made for the UN Security Council, emphasizing the necessity of the second action in the effectuation of the agreement reached with the Republic. Other writings by the Dutch and East Indies governments were also intended to show the outside world that the Republic violated agreements achieved under UN supervision: *Documents submitted to the Committee of Good Offices* (1948), *Documents reveal* (ca. 1948, exposing the opium trade of the Republic; see Maas and Van Oerle 1983), *Three months of truce* (1948), *Miscellaneous documents* (1948) and *Activities of the republican Indonesians* (1948). Apart from these biased writings, 'objective' reproductions of speeches in relation to UN interference also appeared, published by the Department of Foreign Affairs: *Indonesië in de Veiligheidsraad van de Verenigde Naties* (7 vols, 1947-1950). After the Roem-Van Royen Agreement of May 1949, Dutch government publications gave up their anti-republican attitudes. The writings related to the Round Table Conference are generally unbiased and optimistic concerning future cooperation: for example, *Resultaten van de*

Ronde Tafel Conferentie (1950). The Netherlands-Indonesian Union, a cooperative body that would die a premature death, led to the publication of the results of several ministerial conferences in the early 1950s (see Index).

c. Political parties. Dutch political parties published magazines, appearing weekly or less frequently, for instance, *Paraat* from the Partij van de Arbeid and *De Opmars* from the Katholieke Volkspartij. These magazines were not consulted in compiling this bibliography. The parties' standpoints are, of course, clearly visible in these publications. Moreover, political parties published pamphlets which contemplated topical questions. Sometimes proceedings of party congresses appeared. The larger parties had study bureaus which published monthly periodicals: *Socialisme en Democratie* (PvdA), *Katholiek Staatkundig Maandschrift* (KVP). In these periodicals, straightforward party standpoints are not expressed, but the opinions and background stories of authors associated with the party can be discerned. Finally, assorted publications (articles and brochures) by affiliated authors are also treated in this section, although no party standpoint is taken by them.

The social-democratic Partij van de Arbeid (PvdA) was strongly represented in the Dutch government during the whole Indonesian crisis. The party desired liquidation of the colonial relationship and aimed at a constitutional reform of the Kingdom which would lead to voluntary and lasting ties between the Netherlands and Indonesia, coordinated within the Realm ('in gecoördineerd Rijksverband'). To reach this goal, negotiations with the Republic were regarded as the most important tool. This standpoint was expressed in the party brochure *Indonesië* (1947), written by J.H.A. Logemann, former Minister of Overseas Territories. The author assesses the Linggajati Agreement as a guarantee for successful cooperation between the peoples. One year later, W. Schermerhorn, former prime minister and former member of the Commission General, authored an article in *Socialisme en Democratie*, 'Het Nederlands-Indonesisch conflict' (1948). He described the Linggajati Agreement, which he himself had shaped, as an attempt to achieve a Dutch-Indonesian cooperation 'by declaring in advance the Indonesian freedom struggle as won, and accepting the sovereign United States of Indonesia as an equal partner in the Netherlands-Indonesian Union under Her Majesty the Queen' (p. 4). Schermerhorn deplores the so-called 'dressing up' of Linggajati by the Dutch Second Chamber, and the Police Action of July 1947, justified by the party board as 'a limited action to put an end to an emergency situation'. The two Police Actions indeed provoked deep controversy within the party. At the congress on Indonesia in September 1946 (see *Verslag* 1946), sending in troops was already being spoken about with reservation. The First Police Action led to the pamphlet *Linggadjati-militaire actie-wat nu?* (1947) by concerned party members. One of the fiercest opponents of military action was J. de Kadt, who with his article 'Rondom de 20ste Juli 1947', published in *Socialisme en Democratie*, became the spokesman of the dissident wing. In 1949, De Kadt published a monograph with the significant title *De Indonesische tragedie*, in which he argued that not all had been tried to preserve peace during the negotiations with the Republic. The Second Police Action also led to a dissident pamphlet, *Het fiasco van Romme* (1949). The authors, F.W. Michels and Joh.W. Riemens, accused their fellow-party members in government of being too concessionary towards the Katholieke Volkspartij led by Romme, in order to protect the survival of the coalition. Finally, the social democrats of the PvdA were again optimistic about future cooperation with Indonesia, as evident from the pamphlets *Samenwerking na souvereiniteitsoverdracht* (1949) and *Grondslagen van de Nederlands-Indonesische Unie* (1949), both published by the Wiardi Beckman Stichting, the party's study bureau.

Within the Katholieke Volkspartij (KVP) too, the need was felt to change the relationship between the Netherlands and Indonesia. The party's urgency programme wrote about 'the liquidation of the colonial relationship, and the quick realization of constitutional reforms on an equal footing, coordinated within the Realm, 'in gecoördineerd Rijksverband, in accordance with the Royal words of 7 December 1942' (Romme, *Rijkseenheid*, p. 22). This text nearly matches that of the PvdA programme; nevertheless, there were differences between the parties, especially concerning the role played by the Republic and the interpretation of the Linggajati Agreement. According to later authors, the leading KVP politicians in fact aimed at elimination of the Republic (Hendrix 1976:100; Bank 1983:488), which did not fit in with Romme's 'heavy, real Union'. International pressure and protest finally prevented the elimination of the Republic at the Second Police Action. However, KVP circles were not insensitive to Indonesia's national aspirations. The Catholic member of parliament Van Poll had participated in the Commission General which had designed the draft Agreement of Linggajati; during his stay in the Indies, he was impressed by the force of nationalism. In a series of articles in the Catholic periodical *Streven* (1947-1948), Van Poll argued that a quick suppression of the revolution might possibly have been the best solution, but had been impossible under the circumstances. He pleaded for understanding of revolutionary feelings, because the colonialism which existed before the war had failed. Talks with nationalist leaders were seen as 'a political necessity and a moral duty'; the alternative was an endless guerrilla war with no perspective. Van Poll justifies the draft Agreement of Linggajati by emphasizing the equality of the Realm's parts, mentioned in the Queen's speech, which could only be realized if Indonesia's sovereignity became equal to that of the Netherlands; consequently, Indonesia could not be part of the Kingdom. A Netherlands-

Indonesian Union, with its own institutions and headed by the King of the Netherlands, would shape all future cooperation.

The brochure by F. Sybesma, *Linggadjati* (1947), published by the KVP secretariat, generally reflects the same opinion. Having depicted the Republic as a Japanese creation, the author nevertheless shows that he is aware that the revolution is an expression of justified nationalism (p. 42). Before the war 'justified resistance against a spasmodically maintained colonial relationship' was already being exhibited. Through Sjahrir's efforts, the Republic acquired a democratic image and goodwill from abroad. Suppression of the revolution had been impossible from the beginning, primarily due to the attitude of the British.

The leader of the KVP fraction in the Second Chamber, C.P.M. Romme, indicated in his speech to the party council, *Rijkseenheid* (1947), that a reasonable agreement with the Republic was necessary for the creation of a commonwealth of both peoples (p. 5). The draft Agreement of Linggajati was criticized by Romme as being too vague; the clarification given by the Commission General, however, had elucidated much and the Agreement now offered an adequate basis for a lasting association of the Netherlands and Indonesia in a Netherlands-Indonesian Union. Romme stressed the 'weight' of the Union, in an effort to appease rightist opposition under the leadership of the former Minister of Overseas Colonies, Ch.J.I.M. Welter. To oppose Welter's dissent, a pamphlet was issued: *De Katholieke Volkspartij en Indonesië* (1947). The KVP published *Indonesische documentatie* from 1948 to 1950, a factual chronicle without much political colour. A special volume (no. 24) is devoted to Romme's speeches of December 1949. Finally, an important source of information is *Katholiek Staatkundig Maandschrift*, a periodical of the Centrum voor Staatkundige Vorming, the study bureau of the KVP; it contains many contributions concerning the Indonesian question. In 1947 the Centrum published *De economische toekomst van Indonesië*, a report by experts affiliated with the party.

The Protestant Anti-Revolutionaire Partij (ARP) was oppositionary for the duration of the Indonesian conflict. The party held to its opinion that a return to Dutch authority and the end of chaos should come first; it opposed negotiations with the Republic, which it considered a revolutionary movement (Bosscher 1980). The leader of the ARP fraction in the Second Chamber, J. Schouten, rejected the draft Agreement of Linggajati in his speech *Je maintiendrai* (1947). In ARP circles, too, the necessity of a new relationship with the Indies was clear, but there was reluctance to accept the 'equal partnership' of which Queen Wilhelmina had spoken. A.A.L. Rutgers, chairman of the East Indies Commission within the party, wrote several articles on the Indonesian question in *Antirevolutionaire Staatkunde*, the periodical of the Dr Abraham Kuyperstichting, the study bureau of the ARP. As for the new structure of the Kingdom, Rutgers was sympathetic to Van Mook's federal principles. The prominent ARP politician and former prime minister P.S. Gerbrandy reviewed the Indonesian question in *De scheuring van het Rijk* (1951). It presents the main points of the ARP programme: restoration of Dutch authority and termination of the chaos, no talks with revolutionaries and rejection of UN involvement as this would limit Dutch sovereignty.

The Christelijk-Historische Unie (CHU), another, less tightly organized Protestant party, was divided on the Indonesian question (De Jonge 1980). All CHU representatives had voted against Linggajati in the first place. Following the constitutional alterations of 1948, and after the CHU had joined the government, the progressive line of its political leader H.W. Tilanus became more prominent. More of its representatives at last voted in favour of a transfer of sovereignty; in doing so, they showed understanding of the Indonesian call for independence. The conservative line was maintained by C. Gerretson, who in his *Indië onder dictatuur* (1946) stressed the unlawfulness and arbitrariness of the acts of the East Indies government when it started talks with Soekarno. In his pamphlet *Tilanus contra de Christelijk-Historische Unie* (1950), Gerretson opposed the Netherlands-Indonesian Union, and especially the Crown's place in it. Commentaries by prominent CHU members on the Indonesian question were brought together as 'De overzeese gebiedsdelen' in the volume *Wat zeggen ze er van?* (1948), appearing at the party's 40th anniversary.

The liberal Volkspartij voor Vrijheid en Democratie (VVD) originated from a fusion of the Partij van de Vrijheid and a group of former PvdA members, under the leadership of P.J. Oud (Bargeman 1976, Nabbe 1989). Like the CHU, the VVD had joined the government in 1948 after a period of opposition. During the 1948 election campaign, the VVD attacked government policy with the slogan 'The Republic of Indonesia, have you also had enough of it?' In a pamphlet *Het Indische beleid van onze regering* (1948), government policy was fiercely opposed because it was 'disastrous for the Indies and the Netherlands'. Once it joined the government, the VVD pursued a 'heavy Union'; its representatives finally supported the transfer of sovereignty, although in their opinion the Union was not 'heavy' enough. To oppose the results of the Round Table Conference, however, would have made matters still worse. Minister of Foreign Affairs D.U. Stikker, a prominent VVD member, understood the international situation and finally accepted a 'lighter' Union.

Finally, we refer to a party which fully sympathized with the Indonesian revolution and pleaded for full independence: the Communistische Partij van Nederland (CPN). An important source is the party newspaper *De Waarheid*, as well as its periodical *Politiek en Cultuur*, which included many contributions on the Indonesian question. One of the authors was Amir, an Indonesian communist, who wrote a remarkable article 'De contra- revolutie van Hatta' (1948), in which he condemns the suppression of the Madiun rebellion. Party leader Paul de Groot wrote *Het militaire avontuur in Indonesië* (1947), in reaction to the First Police Action. At the same time a party pamphlet appeared, *De wapens neer* (1947), in which the military option is rejected.

d. Christian authors. In general, the Protestant mission took a progressive standpoint on the Dutch-Indonesian conflict. In October 1945, the governing bodies of the Samenwerkende Zendingscoöperaties at Oegstgeest had already stated that a 'complete liquidation of the colonial relationship' was neces- sary and that Indonesia should become an equal partner in a voluntary relationship within the Realm. They plead for a generous honouring of Queen Wilhelmina's 7 December speech (Boland 1946:67; Scharffenorth 1983). This statement was adopted by the Nederlandse Zendingsraad, a cooperative body of the Nederlands Hervormde and the Gereformeerde Kerken. Remarkably an opposing standpoint was taken by Protestant politicians from ARP, CHU and SGP, who in general held conservative views on the Indonesian question (with the exception of the progressive line in the CHU; see the previous paragraph). This discrepancy is even more remarkable if the writings of individual missionaries are taken into account: in these, a clearly progressive standpoint is visible; even the relationship within the Realm (Rijksverband) is abandoned by some authors.

In the Nederlands Hervormde Kerk, the missionary J.A. Verdoorn was the first to write a pamphlet, *De zending en het Indonesisch nationalisme* (1945). He argues that a colonial status would become an obstacle for missionary workers; it had to be abolished as soon as possible. The mission itself, however, should not be identified with the nationalist struggle because it had its own particular tasks and responsibilities (p. 69). A short book by B.J. Boland, *Zending, wat denkt gij van Indië?* (1946) can be con- sidered a popular version of Verdoorn's argument. It contains a historical survey of the nationalist movement; the author points out the nationalists' tendency to identify the mission with colonial policy. Therefore, he states, the mission should distinguish itself more clearly from colonialism. Prominent missionaries like Kruyt, Adriani and Kraemer had already understood the nationalist desires before the War. The autonomy of the Indonesian Protestant churches, initiated by Hendrik Kraemer, combined very well with decolonization. Professor Kraemer, the highest authority among the missionaries of the Nederlands Hervormde Kerk, turned against Dutch policy in an article 'Nederland in de waagschaal' (1947), written on the occasion of the First Police Action. In Kraemer's opinion, military force was incompatible with a policy aimed at forging 'voluntary ties' between peoples. He accused the Dutch government of 'blindness of the fundamental urge towards freedom in Asia' (p. 379). He also disapproved of federal policy as providing 'a support for separatist movements'. Of a different character is *Een waaiende kipas* (1948) by the missionary W.A. Zeydner, narrating the adventures of the mission during the Japanese period and revolutionary years.

In the Gereformeerde Kerken, too, were missionaries who turned against the conservative line of the Protestant political parties, primarily the ARP. In 1946, the missionary H. van den Brink issued *Een eisch van recht*, blaming his fellow-members of the Gereformeerde Kerken for showing 'too little understanding' of the Indonesian pursuit for freedom. Van den Brink's pamphlet broke the unity of opinion concerning East Indies policy in the Gereformeerde Kerken. The author prefers the moderate Sjahrir and shows some reservation towards Soekarno. The pamphlet is introduced by fellow-missionaries, such as the prominent Reverend J. Verkuyl, clergyman at Batavia. In his own brochure *De achtergrond van het Indonesische vraagstuk* (1946), Verkuyl explains and comments on Dutch government policy; he does not deal with questions related to missionary work. He comes close to the government's standpoint when he declines support for an unconditional recognition of the Republic (pp. 54-55); on the other hand, he calls for understanding of the Indonesian desire for freedom. To solve the Indonesian question, Verkuyl recommends negotiations and retainment of the Rijksverband. A conservative standpoint was taken by the missionary S.U. Zuidema in *De Indische kwestie* (1946), a speech made at an ARP meeting. Zuidema turns against the Republic, and calls for a restoration of Dutch authority.

Apart from the writings of individual missionaries, the report of the Protestant missionary conference at Batavia by J.C. Hoekendijk, *Zending in Indonesië* (1946), is of importance in obtaining an impression of the mood in Indonesian Protestant churches on the road to independence. The brochures *Situatie en taak in Indonesië* (1949) and B.J. Boland's *Op weg naar oecumenische samenwerking in Indonesië* (1949) present much information on future prospects for ecumenical cooperation.

As for the Roman Catholic Church, a Vatican decree commanded that its representatives should abstain from politics. Public statements were not made; polemics such as occurred in Protestant circles did not take place. Father L. van Ryckevorsel's pamphlet *Naar Indië?* (1945) is simply a call to resume missionary work. In 1947 the *Indisch Missietijdschrift* included a contribution by the apostolic vicar of Batavia, Mgr P.J. Willekens, entitled 'Toespraak tot katholiek Nederland', in which the neutrality of the Church was emphasized. An article (1949) by Father J.W.M. Bakker in the same periodical, appearing shortly before the transfer of sovereignty, discusses the efforts of the Indonesian nationalists. The author shows some under- standing of 'healthy' nationalism, because 'love of one's mother country is an authentic virtue' (p. 238). He further stresses that the republican leaders had tried to temper the fanatic *pemuda*. Father Bakker's view on the position of the Protestant mission is noteworthy: it was confused by the events, because many Indonesians identified it with colonial rule, unlike the Catholic mission. Consequently, the latter could adapt itself with ease to the new situation. The Roman Catholic Church had no special ties with any country, so that it could be equally subservient to all nations. Represent- atives of the Church were not allowed to participate in politics, but there was no objection against solidarity with the people amongst whom one lived.

Information on the Roman Catholic Church during the Japanese occu- pation and the revolutionary period is given in *Indisch Missietijdschrift* and in several short monographs such as by Boddeke (1950).

e. Three prolific writers. During the revolution, many articles, pamphlets and other writings on the Indonesian question appeared by independent authors. These authors wrote on their own initiative, or were instigated by certain pressure groups such as the conservative Nationaal Comité Hand- having Rijkseenheid or the progressive Vereniging Nederland-Indonesië. Some exhibited a high degree of productivity; they followed the decoloniz- ation process with their comments. It is obvious that such pamphlet writers usually rejected the government's policy; otherwise, there would have been no need to repeatedly state their own opinions.

The most prolific pamphlet writers, Cort van der Linden, Feuilletau de Bruyn and Meijer Ranneft, attacked government policy from the right. R.A.D. Cort van der Linden, a conservative liberal and son of a former prime minister, argued in his pamphlets *De tijger die het Rijk vaneenrijt* (1946) and *Nederlandsch-Indië* (1946) that the Dutch government was too weak in its actions concerning East Indies affairs. The role played by the British brought on the beginning of all misery: they had hindered the timely return of Dutch troops, and at the same time had started talks with representatives of the Republic. As a result, the Dutch could not exercise their authority, while the Republic could develop itself. Van Mook became involved in this policy and threw away the birthright of the Dutch. Cort van der Linden was not in principle against a new relationship with the Indies, because 'the peoples of the Indies are free if they can and want to be' (*De tijger*, p. 9). But first, the people's will had to be expressed in a proper way; the Republic was founded by accomplices of Japan and stood isolated from the masses. In his later pamphlets *De rede van Churchill* (1947) and

Linggadjati (1947), Cort van der Linden rejects the Agreement of November
1946 as not having the support of the people. He suggests that the Indonesians had been better off under the Dutch, whose policy was aimed at
'colonial conciliation'. The sudden retreat of the Dutch was to be avoided, in
view of the experiences in British India, where Hindu and Muslim com-
munities opposed each other.

W.K.H. Feuilletau de Bruyn wrote a still larger number of pamphlets
than Cort van der Linden, and their content is more thoughtful. De Bruyn, a
KNIL officer, had been a member of the Volksraad before the War. In *Indië's
toekomst* (1945), written before Japan's surrender, he stated that the Indies
were not yet ripe for fully-developed democracy. A strong executive must
remain; apart from that, far-reaching social measures were necessary to
persuade more Indonesians to join the civil service and to develop a native
middle class. In this way, the Indies would be able to defend themselves
against a new Japanese attack – expected by De Bruyn. The last pages of
Indië's toekomst briefly refer to the rebellious 'Soekarno movement' which
does not fit into De Bruyn's scheme. In the later brochures *Het politieke en
militaire beleid* (1945) and *Het oude en het nieuwe leger* (1946), De Bruyn
was more concerned about the 'Soekarno movement'. Van Mook and the
Dutch government-in-exile had waited too long to form an army corps to
pacify the Indies after the Japanese capitulation. When it became evident
that the Republic could not be quickly eliminated, De Bruyn launched direct
attacks against it. In the pamphlets *Welk aandeel heeft Dr Van Mook gehad
in de gezagsschemering in Nederlandsch-Indië?* (1946) and *The truth about
the Indonesian Republic* (1946, 'by Dr William F. de Bruyn'), he depicts
Soekarno's 'separatists' as brainwashed by the Japanese, and holds that they
created the Republic to retain their influence in Southeast Asia. In *Naar de
Sovjet-republiek Indonesia* (1947), De Bruyn tries another strategy: he uses
Marxist literature found in republican territory to suggest that the Republic
is becoming increasingly influenced by communism – 'So there is only one
solution: march against Yogya and exterminate this hearth of communism'
(p. 42).

In the pamphlets of J.W. Meijer Ranneft, the same pattern is visible as in
De Bruyn's: first, plans for the Indies after the War; then, disappointment
over government policy towards the Republic, the disturbing factor for all
future schemes. Meijer Ranneft was president of the Volksraad before the
war (on his person: Caminada and Otten 1971, Heijs 1991). In *De weg voor
Indië* (1945), issued at the time of the liberation of the Netherlands, Meijer
Ranneft gives his view on the future of the Indies. He pleads for autonomy
within Rijksverband, as stated in Wilhelmina's speech of 7 December 1942,
and further holds that because of its ethnic diversity, Indonesian society
requires a special constitutional structure to avoid conflict (p. 49). The upper

class should be expanded, so that all races can participate in it. A revolutionary takeover of all leading functions, pursued by the 'nationalists', is rejected. General suffrage should be postponed until society is ripe for it. Executive power is in the hands of a Governor-General, who is responsible only to representatives in the Indies and no longer to the Minister of Colonies. Moreover, this last function should be abolished, to emphasize the autonomy of the Indies. Meijer Ranneft's pamphlets *Rechtvaardigheid voor Indië* (1946) and *Indië in nood* (1946) reveal the author's uneasiness about the Republic and the permissive attitude of the British. He feels that the Republic, set up by the Japanese, will only stir up ethnic controversy instead of aiming at conciliation, which is indispensable for a 'mixed society'. Van Mook lost Meijer Ranneft's confidence when he started talks with the 'enemy'. Three years later, *Het land dat verdween* (1949) appeared, an elegy on the failure of the 'mixed society' in the Indies. The tone is acquiescent, not bitter; future cooperation between the Netherlands and Indonesia is not excluded.

f. Further plans for the future. Before the War, some independent authors had already developed plans for a new relationship between the Netherlands and the Indies in rather extensive writings. During the occupation, these plans were worked out, using Queen Wilhelmina's speech of 7 December 1942 as a directive. In this speech, reference was made to an equal partnership of the Kingdom's regions. Publications in the illegal press (Pluvier 1953-1954) contained many suggestions for a new relationship. In the southern parts of the Netherlands, which were liberated in 1944, such ideas could be issued a bit earlier. In the same year, *En nu... Indië* appeared by A. Voortland and W.G.N. de Keizer. The authors pleaded for a construction which would leave the parts of the Realm 'equal and autonomous' (p. 184) with their own governments and representative bodies, superimposed by a government and a council (or parliament) for the Realm as a whole, to handle matters concerning all parts. The authors emphasize that the Dutch vocation in the East had not yet ended, and that there was still a long way to go before a new constitutional structure was realized. First, the Dutch should promote economic activity in the Indies. A prerequisite was that peace and order be restored by a strong executive. Voortman and De Keizer expected that the Dutch, on their return to the Indies, would meet few problems because of the population's warm acceptance of them (p. 189).

An elaborate study on the future of the Indies was published in 1946 by J.A. Eigeman, a professor of constitutional law. This study, *De bouw van het nieuwe Koninkrijk*, is connected with some of the author's pre-war writings on this subject. Eigeman's argument is that the autonomous parts of the Realm should fall under the Crown (Council of Ministers), to guarantee a

'strong coherence'. The Governor-General should be directly responsible to
the president of the Council, and no longer to the Minister of Colonies. In
this way, subordination of the Indies' interests to the Netherlands is
avoided; at the same time, the relationship between the parts of the Realm
remains close. Eigeman is irritated by the Republic's existence, seeing it as a
Fremdkörper disturbing his schemes. The Netherlands cannot be expected
to tolerate 'any form of government that the parts of the Realm [such as the
Indies] desire for themselves' (p. 205).

Also written from a conservative point of view is E.C. van den Ende's
pamphlet *Hoe verder met Indië?* (1946). The author's plea is more polemic
than Eigeman's, and less based on constitutional knowledge. The Republic
plays a central role in the argument, which is primarily intended as a
commentary on the events following the Japanese capitulation. Van den
Ende's starting point is Wilhelmina's 7 December speech which spoke of
full partnership, to be worked out in a Rijksconferentie. Complete independence as pursued by the republicans would be contradictory to the tenor
of the Queen's speech, notwithstanding its reference to the voluntary
character of the relationship. Van den Ende condemns Van Mook's talks
with the Republic, a Japanese creation that cannot be trusted, and believes
that a recognition of the Republic and its incorporation into an Indonesian
commonwealth will not lead to any lasting results. The fact that Van den
Ende's plea is introduced by Admiral C.E.L. Helfrich reveals affinity with the
Nationaal Comité Handhaving Rijkseenheid.

In the progressive camp there were, of course, also many ideas on the
future of the Indies. In August 1945 Th.A. Fruin, former president of the
Algemeene Volkskredietbank at Batavia, lectured on this subject: *De toekomstige status van Indonesië*. This speech was a powerful defense of the
autonomy of the Indies, whereby the Indonesians themselves should
occupy the leading positions because 'it is abnormal and outdated that a
gifted nation is ruled by strangers' (p. 6). Priority should be given to
'Indianization' by improving education, so that Indonesians themselves
could take over in due course. It was seen as desirable that autonomy be
granted as soon as possible. The ties between the Netherlands and the Indies
should not be too strong; there should be a common diplomatic corps but
separated Ministries of Foreign Affairs (p. 19). During the first years of
autonomy, many Dutchmen would still occupy leading positions; their
number would diminish as more qualified Indonesians became available.
Fruin did not recommend the immediate introduction of full parliamentary
democracy; the vote was to be extended in accordance with the repelling of
illiteracy. Fruin's constitutional ideas were not worked out in his later
publications; some concerned the growth towards economic independence,
while *De worsteling om een nieuwe verhouding tussen Nederland en Indo-*

nesië (1948) held a survey of political events up until the end of 1947, with no reference to the author's earlier ideas expressed in 1945.

A plea for far-reaching autonomy for the Indies was made by the Verbond van Indonesische Burgers in their pamphlet *De plaats van Indonesië in het herbouwde Koninkrijk* (1945). The Verbond tried to maintain the ties between the Netherlands and Indonesia, but without the subordination of the Indies' interests that was the case before the War. There had to be a Rijksregering, to handle the 'imperial' (common) cause; therefore, the ties between the parts of the Realm were more solid than in Fruin's plans. Much attention was given to an Indonesian citizenship that did not discriminate between race or minorities, and that was intended, *inter alia*, to advance the integration of Dutchmen in Indonesian society (p. 17).

A notable pamphlet, *Ons standpunt*, was issued in 1946 by the group known as the Progressieve Groepen at Batavia; some members of this grouping, like the above-mentioned Th.A. Fruin, were connected with the PvdA. The authors of *Ons standpunt*, among whom were D.M.G. Koch, Alb. de la Court and J.H.W. Veenstra, recognized the right to self-determination of the Indonesians and recommended 'acceptance of the Republic of Indonesia' (p. 19). They believed the moment had arrived for a recognition of Indonesian (republican) authority; consequently a treaty could be pursued between Indonesia and the Netherlands as independent states. They found no need for a 'transition period' to politically educate the Indonesians, asserting that their political consciousness was well enough developed, as could be seen from recent events.

To conclude this section on future plans for Indonesia, mention should be made of the reports of the Visman and Van Helsdingen commissions, which contain many schemes and proposals for a new relationship with the 'mother country'. For a brief survey of these reports, see the section on government publications.

g. Reports and commentaries on the events of 1945-1949. The first book deserving mention here, although it did not appear until 1949, was written by H.J. van Mook, the highest Dutch official in the Indies from 1945 to 1948. It was Van Mook who determined to a great extent Dutch policy towards decolonization and the Republic. In his memoirs *Indonesië, Nederland en de wereld*, Van Mook justifies his acts and decisions, and explains the choices made by himself and the Dutch government following the Japanese capitulation. In his view, the Netherlands in August 1945 (and before) faced the task of liberating the Indies from the yoke of the Japanese, with the help of its allies; at the same time, Indonesia had to be preserved for democracy (p. 9). For this purpose, the country had to be transformed into a nation; Western aid was indispensable, as it was for the whole of Southeast Asia. It was a disadvantage that post-war policy initially had to be concerted with the British; in fact the policy was under their determination. Another complication was the proclamation of the Republic, a fact that hampered Dutch-Indonesian rapprochement (p. 81). Van Mook is not impressed by the qualities of the republican leaders, with the exception of Sjahrir, about whom he writes with sympathy. Sjahrir sincerely wished to reach an agreement with the Dutch; his position, however, was continually threatened by radicals.

A return to pre-war conditions was, according to Van Mook, undesirable as well as impossible. Indonesia should become independent, but under Dutch guidance. Van Mook was irritated by the attitude of the Dutch, who did not understand much about the situation in the Indies; the 'dressing up' of the Linggajati Agreement can serve as an example. The First Police Action was inevitable to restore order and safety, and to make room for a constructive policy (p. 184). The occupation of Yogyakarta, 'hearth of agitation and action' (p. 186) where moderate leaders such as Sjahrir had given way to the radicals, should have already taken place during the First Police Action. Van Mook devotes special attention to federalism, in his view the best form of government for an independent Indonesia. He rejects the accusation that federalism was intended to limit the Republic's influence: there were also republicans among the supporters of a federal Indonesia. Van Mook ends with some thoughts on democracy in Southeast Asia; Indonesia (educated by the Dutch) could play a role in its development. This idea was elaborated by Van Mook in *The stakes of democracy in Southeast Asia* (1950).

Of a different character are two books by G.W. Overdijkink, a prominent civil servant at Batavia: *Het Indonesische probleem; De feiten* (1946) and *Het Indonesische probleem; Nieuwe feiten* (1948). The author presents a survey of developments within the Republic, using the Indonesian press and Dutch intelligence as a source. He noted the polemic undertone of many Dutch writings on the Indonesian question, which were not supported by facts. Overdijkink's 'objective' reproduction of facts, however, at times exhibits a pro-Dutch and anti-republican bias. He does not deny the urge for freedom in Indonesia, but stresses the internal quarrels of the republicans and the shortcomings of republican authority. He finds it alarming that more and more concessions were made to the radicals, who rejected any agreement with the Dutch.

Finally, we mention another voluminous work by W.H. van Helsdingen, *Op weg naar een Nederlands-Indonesische Unie* (1947), which, as is also the case with Overdijkink's writings, is principally informative. It contains many official documents concerning a new relationship between the Netherlands and Indonesia, up to the draft Agreement of Linggajati. Most documents are in Dutch, but many republican papers are also included, such as the *Manifes Politik* of November 1945, and radio speeches by prominent leaders such as Soekarno and Sjahrir.

h. Military writings. The attention for the military aspect of Indonesia's decolonization is pronounced. Prior to 1950 many titles had already appeared, especially those which concerned the army. *De Militaire Spectator* was a magazine featuring many contributions on the Dutch military presence in Indonesia, often with a technical aspect; *Ons Leger* was more popular and aimed at a general public. Many army sections had their own periodicals; most of these were not consulted for this bibliography. A survey of this 'small literature' is given by Verhoog (1989) and Draak (1993).

Military writings can be divided into several categories, such as official information, memorial books and personal memoirs. An example of official information is a brochure by the Legervoorlichtingsdienst (LVD) entitled *Indië, waarom wij er heen gaan* (ca. 1946), destined for conscripts of the 7 December Division. The LVD stresses that the mission of Dutch soldiers is not directed against nationalism, but against the Japanese-drilled, fanatic *pemuda* who were terrorizing even their fellow-countrymen: 'It is impossible to reach constructive cooperation until terrorism has come to an end'. It held that Dutch assistance was indispensible to the future development of Indonesia; without it, Indonesia should fall prey to its powerful neighbours. The Malino conference had made obvious that Indonesians wished to cooperate.

In 1947, the first of four volumes of the *Herinneringsalbum* of the 7 December Division appeared, describing operations in West Java. The album was edited by the association Ons Leger. It contains sketches of several Division sections, bringing 'order and peace' by pursuing and arresting *pelopor*. The album is primarily intended for the conscripts' relatives in the Netherlands. Not only in the first volume, but also in the following two, anti-republican sounds are sometimes discernible: 'Yogya continued to instruct gangs which had stayed behind' (vol. III, p. 45). But the real adversaries were these gangs, with their disrespect for any Agreement.

A fine example of a memorial book describing the adventures of a particular battalion is *Bren naar voren partisanen!* (1949). It is a handsome edition, with pictures, drawings, maps and statistics, telling the story of the volunteer battalion 1-12 RI, operative in East Java, around Surabaya and Malang. It gives an impression of the soldiers' daily life, including anecdotes as well as unpleasant events. Here, the adversaries are primarily the 'extremists': the Republic and its army remain in the background. *Bren naar voren partisanen!* was published in the Netherlands (Groningen); memorial books published in the Indies were usually more modest in appearance,

such as *Wij waren in... Jogja!* (1949) concerning the Second Police Action
and the role of the T-Brigade in the occupation (and later evacuation) of the
republican capital. Apart from a description of the military events, the
booklet gives an impression of the local population's feelings: 'But when
they [the Indonesians] had watched the actions of those tall, blond boys, and
found that they had not come to submit and suppress, but only to take their
share in liberation and restoration of justice [...] then Yogya revived in a few
days'. The evacuation of the town did not amuse the soldiers: 'they refused
to believe that all had been in vain'.

There are also personal impressions of soldiers and (military) reporters'
accounts of their stay in the Indies. Here we mention the booklet *Demarcatielijn* (1947) by the journalist Willem Brandt, who served at the Z-Brigade
in Sumatra. In Brandt's view, the Dutch brought freedom and justice to a
chaotic Indonesia: 'we have only one concern: to guard and protect this
people' (p. 125); the soldiers' purpose is protection against the extremists,
who terrorize peaceful villagers. The tragedy of the situation is that the
Dutch soldiers are not allowed to cross the demarcation line into republican
territory, to bring terrorism to an end. Brandt points out the difficult
circumstances in republican territory: 'regularly a stream of ragged, leaned
refugees came across the line to our camp' (p. 14). Moreover, the Republic
does not honour Agreements, such as demilitarization.

Another personal document is *De hitte van de dag* (1947) by reporter J.W.
Hofdijk, who stayed with the Marines in East Java. His story is less literary
than Brandt's, but more idealized: including tales of sturdy men who greatly
suffered to protect the Indonesian people. Hofdijk gives a vivid impression
of military life; yet, political subjects are not touched upon. Sometimes, the
author grumbles at those remaining behind in the Netherlands, who
understand nothing of circumstances in the Indies.

Contemporary writings - other authors

Outside the countries most involved (the Netherlands and Indonesia), the
Indonesian question also drew a lot of attention. The Western countries:
Great Britain, the United States and Australia should be mentioned first. In
(former British) India and Pakistan, too, a number of small monographs
appeared; less attention was received in other Asian countries. After 1947,
the United Nations concerned themselves intensively with the conflict,
which yielded a stream of reports (see Henderson 1954).

A substantial British contribution to contemporary literature is *The birth
of Indonesia* by David Wehl (1948). The author naturally pays much
attention to the British role in the conflict, particularly to the Battle of
Surabaya and its prelude. Because of the violence in Surabaya, Wehl

developed a keen eye for the radical nationalist faction and the excesses it committed. On the other hand he points out that without the impetuousness of the *pemuda*, the majority of the Indonesian people might have meekly let themselves be returned to Dutch authority. In general, the Dutch point of view in the conflict receives more understanding from Wehl than the Indonesian viewpoint. Wehl sees in Soekarno a radical who thwarted the execution of the Linggajati Agreement and who tied the hands of more moderate characters such as Sjahrir. He seems to understand the Dutch decision to carry out the First Police Action; in his view, the majority of the Indonesian population was mainly interested in 'a quiet life and the cultivation of paddy fields' (p. 163).

More critical towards Dutch policy is the American author Charles Wolf Jr., vice consul in Batavia from 1946 until 1947. A great deal of his *Indonesian story* (1948) is based on personal observations. This book is primarily instructive: Wolf's goal is to inform the American public about the political and economic situation in the Republic, and to present the views of its leaders. A short biography is included of the most important republican politicians. Although pro-republican, Wolf occasionally tries to place himself in the position of the Dutch, but his understanding is limited, for example concerning federalism, which he sees as little more than a policy of encirclement. More than Wehl, he is convinced that the Republic is able to stand on its own feet.

A second contemporary American author who deserves our attention is Paul Kattenburg, who in his voluminous dissertation *The Indonesian question in world politics* (1949) elucidates several aspects of the conflict. First, he gives a survey of the policies of the countries most involved: the Netherlands, Great Britain, Australia, a number of Asiatic countries (Arab states, China, India), the United States and the Soviet Union; followed by an explanation of United Nations policy. Kattenburg's main point is that, in the Indonesian question, the various countries involved put their national interests first and foremost – especially the Netherlands. Great Britain and the United States allowed the Dutch room to pursue their own policy, mainly aimed at the continuation of their presence in the region. During the course of the conflict, Kattenburg notes increasing international cooperation embodied in the United Nations, where an 'anti-imperialistic' atmosphere reigned, which ultimately forced the Netherlands to adjust their course. The author distinguishes two trends in the Dutch attitude: one, the 'Indies-Dutch', was expressed by those such as Van Mook and Logemann, who desired an agreement with the Republic and wished to safeguard Dutch interests by means of a 'new deal'. Opposing this viewpoint was a large conservative faction, those who would not hear of leaving the colony, considering it as an important subject of national pride, and who in fact disapproved of the Linggajati Agreement. The conservatives wanted no curtailment of the Netherlands' exclusive right to cope with the Indonesian question as they thought fit. Kattenburg's vision of the United States' policy is also worth mentioning: in spite of their anti-imperialistic tradition, the United States had left the Dutch ample space because they did not want to estrange the West European countries in the growing polarization with the Soviet Union.

That the atmosphere in the United States was indeed 'anti-imperialistic' is apparent from the relatively unknown thesis of the American J.R. Klinkert: *The second Netherlands military action* (1949), in which he compares world press commentary in the period from December 1948 to January 1949. He consulted Dutch, British, French, Swiss, American and Australian daily newspapers, and remarks that most papers had a keen eye for the interests of their own countries in the conflict. Furthermore, he points out the simplification of reality, a phenomenon structurally bound up with newspaper journalism.

Illustrative of the atmosphere in former British India (Pakistan) is I. Chaudhry's *The Indonesian struggle* (1950; preface 1949). The author states that he is presenting 'personal views and observations', but it is clear that he has borrowed much factual material from Wolf's book. The tone is sharply anti-Dutch and often anti-Western as well. He states that in 1945 the Dutch only wanted to recolonize Indonesia for economic reasons, for 'all international conflicts arise fundamentally from the economic issue' (p. 219). The author holds the role played by the United Nations and the Security Council in low esteem, quickly deteriorating into 'nerve centre[s] of power politics and a shelter for aggressors and imperialists' (p. 69). The heroic struggle of the Indonesian people was mainly supported by Asian countries. In 1949, at the Roem-Van Royen Agreement, the most important goal – an independent state – had not yet been reached; the Republic had been reduced to one federal state among many, and the United States of Indonesia was still to be bound to the Netherlands in the fields of foreign policy and economics.

To the United Nations, the Indonesian question was its first test in settling a larger international conflict. UN interference led to a spate of publications in the years 1947-1950. For instance, articles concerning the Indonesian question appeared in the periodicals *United Nations World* and *United Nations Bulletin*. Also of great importance is the series *Official Records of the Security Council*. There were three commissions which, in a large number of accounts, reported to the Security Council: the Consular Commission, the Commission of Good Offices on the Indonesian Question and the United Nations Commission for Indonesia. A survey of the most important reports has been given by Henderson (1954). The Dutch Ministry of Foreign Affairs also published a large number of documents related to the UN, for example, *Indonesië in de Veiligheidsraad van de Verenigde Naties*, which consists of six volumes. Shortly after the Round Table Conference, two concise UN publications appeared in which Indonesia's decolonization was summarized: *The Indonesian question* (1950) and *Peaceful settlement in Indonesia* (ca. 1950).

Later writings

a. Surveys of the revolutionary period 1945-1949

Indonesian authors. Understandably, after 1950 numerous monographs appeared by Indonesian authors, offering a summary of the years of the revolution or a portion of them. These reviews vary from small editions to extensive standard works of several volumes. The author's personal experiences are often incorporated.

During the 1950s, the Indonesian Ministry of Information produced abundant material. In 1950 *Lembaran sedjarah* appeared, a concise calendar, and *Illustrations of the revolution*, an extensive photo book with comments, was produced in 1954; an Indonesian edition, *Lukisan revolusi rakjat Indonesia*, had already appeared in 1949. The same Ministry of Information reprinted the laws, declarations and regulations issued during the revolution: *Dokumentasi Republik Indonesia* (1950); due to the Second Police Action, many republican archives and libraries had been damaged. We found only two small volumes, comprising the years 1945 and 1946. Another attempt to record the period of the revolution is Osman Raliby's *Documenta historica* (1953), mainly consisting of a calendar to which law texts and speeches have been added. Raliby's summary, announced as the first volume of a series which apparently was not continued, stops at 1946. On the tenth anniversary of the revolution, a volume of recollections was edited by Darius Marpaung, *Bingkisan nasional* (1955). Many of the contributions are regionally specialized and refer to the repercussions of the Proclamation in the areas involved. The abundance of the contributions provides full coverage of the whole archipelago. The volume is completed with a chronological review of the revolution.

The 1960s yield few summaries. In these years of guided democracy, Soekarno breathed new life into the term 'revolution', which was also used to indicate the present. At the introduction of this guided democracy, Soekarno had spoken of the 'rediscovery of the revolution'. An example of this kind of literature is *Basic documents of the Indonesian revolution* (1960), published by the Ministry of Information. It contains texts, speeches and declarations from the years 1945-1949, such as the presidential constitution of 1945. For the purposes of guided democracy, this constitution was 'rediscovered', and soon replaced the provisional constitution that gave more influence to the representing bodies. *Basic documents* provides the impression that with the reintroduction of the original constitution, revolutionary spirit would return as well.

A 'proper' summary of the revolutionary period is found in Susanto Tirtoprodjo's *Sedjarah revolusi nasional Indonesia* (1963). It is mainly an enumeration of facts, cabinets and ministers; in his preface the author considers the book fit for use at secondary schools. In 1966, General A.H. Nasution published his *Sedjarah perdjuangan nasional dibidang bersendjata*, stressing the role of the army in the struggle for independence. It is no coincidence that this book appeared shortly after the failed coup of 30 September 1965: it confirms the leading role of the army in Indonesian society. The book also offers a taste of Nasution's magnum opus, which was to appear in the 1970s.

The last title from the 1960s to be mentioned here was not published in Indonesia itself but at Monash University, Australia. It comprises a volume of lectures by Moenander and other authors, *Indonesian nationalism and revolution* (1969), with personal recollections from various parts of the archipelago. The tone is down-to-earth and descriptive, differing from most of the often ideologically-coloured publications which appeared in Indonesia itself.

During the 1970s, the voluminous standard work on the revolution appeared, *Sekitar perang kemerdekaan Indonesia* by General A.H. Nasution (first edition 1973, second edition 1977-1979). Unsurpassed in size even today, this eleven-volume work gives an extensive survey of the revolutionary period, with emphasis on the military aspect: it was published under the auspices of the Dinas Sejarah Angkatan Darat. Yet, Nasution's epic can be considered a general history, because other aspects, such as internal political entanglements and diplomacy, also receive their share of attention. Nasution's personal experiences play an important role: in those days he was commander of the famous Siliwangi Division, active mainly in West Java. In the preface Nasution relates that the material for his book was collected and edited in the years 1952-1955. The author warns that his epic cannot be considered the 'official' history of the revolution; for that it bears too personal a stamp. There are few references to sources or literature; Nasution has tried to fill the gaps in his memory by means of interviews with the main characters. He admits that the result is somewhat unbalanced by the prominence of personal recollection. Indeed, the martial exploits of the Siliwangi Division are described far more extensively than the fighting in remote parts of the archipelago. In fact, the theme of the book is *perjuangan semesta*, the total struggle of the Indonesian people, of which the armed struggle is only one, though important, aspect. In the second volume, attention is also given to the *revolusi sosial* in Aceh and Sumatera Timur, amongst other places. Guerrilla warfare against the Dutch, which takes up the major part of the book, was supported by the whole population. Following two Police Actions, the *perang gerilya semesta* intensified, proving to the Dutch that the population had turned against them and that their position was untenable.

A different and more concise survey is to be found in volume 6 of the *Sejarah Nasional Indonesia*, the standard work on Indonesian history, written by an authors' collective at the instigation of the Indonesian Ministry of Education and Culture. Volume 6 was edited by Nugroho Notosusanto, a well-known military historian. The first edition appeared in 1975, followed by many new editions and reprints; in 1993, a wholly revised version appeared, edited by a team of prominent historians including Anhar Gonggong and R.Z. Leirissa. After the first edition had been released, a great deal of criticism immediately followed, the gist of which was that this standard work, intended to be the basis (*buku induk*) for future history schoolbooks, was not patriotic enough. When one compares the first (1975) and the revised (1993) editions, it can be seen that the compilers have remained true to their work; the most conspicuous difference is a rearrangement of chapters. Volume 6 remains a reservoir of facts without much nationalist exaltation, though the argument is, of course, pro-republican. Contrary to Nasution's epic, *Sejarah Nasional Indonesia* contains many source references, intended to guide the reader through the flood of publications on the revolution. Contemporary sources are also referred to, including Antara press reports and papers such as *Merdeka* and *Siasat*.

At the beginning of the 1980s a series was published by the Ministry of Education and Culture, *Sejarah revolusi kemerdekaan daerah [...]*, an approximately twenty-volume description of the revolutionary period divided per region, following the modern division into provinces. The series was intended to be an inventory of facts and literature, and to fit within the framework of a ministerial project to 'take stock' of the regions historically and culturally. In fact, the series does not yield many new points of view; it only suggests a starting point for further research. The reading list in each volume refers to regional publications and theses. Often, oral history methods are used as well.

In conclusion, M. Idris Adrianatakesuma's dissertation *Suatu studi tentang hubungan Indonesia-Belanda tahun 1945-1950* (Universitas Gadjah Mada, 1980), which reads like a general survey of the revolution, is also worth noting. Not only are Indonesian-Dutch relations dealt with here, but also many internal republican matters. The author interviewed many of the persons involved, although no Dutch, giving the story a republican point of view. To be sure, in his consultation of the source edition *Officiële bescheiden*, the author has given serious consideration to the Dutch viewpoint.

Dutch authors. Shortly after the transfer of sovereignty, a *Parlementaire geschiedenis van het Indonesische vraagstuk* by A. Stempels appeared, based on the *Handelingen* of the States General. It contains summaries of debates, with short outlines of the political situation in the Netherlands and the Republic (the latter are the more concise). The book gives insight into complicated political relations in the Netherlands, which co-decided the course of the Indonesian crisis, and which are often difficult to fathom by foreign authors. Unfortunately, Stempels does not offer a retrospective view; after all, time has still been too short for that. However, he does incorporate biographical sketches of the most important debaters.

If Stempels's reflection is a distant chronicle, *De scheuring van het Rijk* (1951) by former prime minister P.S. Gerbrandy, takes quite a different tone in its complaint about the loss of the Dutch empire. In Gerbrandy's opinion, Van Mook had bartered away the Indies to the republican 'rebels' under pressure from Britain, the United States and the United Nations. This interference by the great powers was seen as an inadmissible meddling in the internal affairs of the Netherlands. Did the countries abroad have so little respect for all the good things the Netherlands had brought to the Indies? To Gerbrandy it was an established fact that the Republic was a Japanese creation, a time bomb ready to explode because the British had remained aloof and had hindered the speedy return of Dutch troops. An English version of Gerbrandy's book had already appeared in 1950.

In 1952 another survey came to light, which was much less personal than Gerbrandy's and fit more into Stempels's style: *De Indonesische quaestie* by C. Smit, a specialist on international law. Smit's survey has become the best known Dutch summary of the revolution: the book has been re-edited several times. It is wholly based on published material: the *Handelingen*, the *Official Records of the Security Council* and other printed sources. In some places the account is somewhat dry and official. The author comprehends the Indonesian aspiration for independence, because the Netherlands had not dealt with nationalism in a constructive manner before the war and had offered no prospects for self-government to the Indonesians. Surprised by the war, the Dutch had no solution for the intensified nationalist feelings aroused by the Japanese occupation. Following Japan's surrender the Republic had the opportunity to consolidate itself, which was of crucial importance to the course of events: the Republic had won a place under the sun and could no longer be eliminated. Van Mook's federal policy could only be explained by the republicans as a policy of encirclement, intended to degrade the Republic to an 'ordinary' federal state. The political constructions and transitional arrangements worked out by the Dutch appeared useless in practice because the great powers, especially the United States, insisted on a speedy decolonization.

Thus, the early 1950s yielded three monographs on the Indonesian question. After that ensued a long silence lasting until the 1970s, when interest in decolonization once again increased. Prior to that period, in 1962, another revised edition of Smit's book appeared, *De liquidatie van een imperium*, for which the author had tapped new sources such as information from persons who had been involved and the exchange of telegrams between The Hague and Batavia. We further refer to a short book by a man of letters and former government official, A. Alberts: *Het einde van een verhouding* (1968), in which the chapter on decolonization is in fact a popularized version of Smit's monograph.

The revival of publicity in the early 1970s was made evident by the official investigation into war crimes committed by Dutch troops in Indonesia (see L. Stam's thesis *De Hueting-affaire*, 1972). The sociologist J.A.A. van Doorn, with W.J. Hendrix, wrote *Ontsporing van geweld* (1970) on the conduct of Dutch soldiers (see further under Military writings). The time was ripe for an extensive edition of source material: *Officiële bescheiden betreffende de Nederlands-Indonesische betrekkingen 1945-1950*, of which the first volume appeared in 1971. Volumes 1-8 were edited by S.L. van der Wal, and later volumes by P.J. Drooglever and M.J.B. Schouten. By 1996, all twenty volumes had appeared. After the completion of the series, a similar source publication on the New Guinea question will follow. The *Officiële bescheiden* are based on the archives of the Dutch ministries involved, collected at the Algemeen Rijksarchief (ARA) in The Hague. This impressive edition has made it possible to follow day-to-day opinion and decision making on the issue from the Dutch viewpoint.

Interest in and investigation of Indonesia's decolonization have noticeably increased since the first edition of *Officiële bescheiden*, considering the large numbers of articles and, particularly, MA theses appearing in the course of the 1970s and 1980s. P.J. Drooglever published many articles as a 'by-product' of his editorship, in which the role of the great powers is frequently illuminated. In the Netherlands, the Indonesian question was again made 'discussable'; this is also evident from the fact that it has been regularly chosen as a topic for final exams in secondary education since 1970 (Pluvier 1970, K. van Dijk 1974, J. Goedhart 1975).

The 1980s yielded a number of concise, popular surveys: Van Esterik and Van Twist (1980), Schumacher (1980), Verhoog (1982) and Bosdriesz and Soeteman (1985). L. de Jong's survey in volume 12 of *Het Koninkrijk der Nederlanden in de Tweede Wereldoorlog* (1988) provides a weightier survey; the chapter concerned is entitled 'De worsteling met de Republiek Indonesië'. Although De Jong's emphasis is on Dutch policy, much attention is also paid to developments within the Republic. Like Smit, De Jong concludes that internal political considerations quite often played a part on the Dutch side, to the irritation of Van Mook, who reproached the politicians in The Hague as having an insufficient understanding of Indonesian relations. Above all, it had been the strength of the Republic (p. 1104) which, in spite of two Police Actions, had turned the ideal of independence into reality. Van Mook's plans for the political structure of Indonesia ultimately did not prove to be viable.

The 1980s also brought the first Dutch dissertations on decolonization (if Doeleman's medical thesis of the mid-1950s is not included). Jan Bank, actually a professor of Dutch history at Leiden University, earned his doctoral degree in 1983 with *Katholieken en de Indonesische revolutie*, in which principally Dutch Catholics and their political party, the KVP, have been investigated. In 1985, G.C. Zijlmans followed with *Eindstrijd en ondergang van de Indische bestuursdienst*, concerning Dutch civil administration in Java in 1945-1949. Both studies can also be read as general reviews of the revolutionary period. This is also true of J.J.P. de Jong's dissertation *Diplomatie of strijd* (1988), in which the Dutch policy leading up to the First Police Action is analysed; at the same time, a careful attempt is made to rehabilitate that policy. Until now, only one dissertation has appeared in the 1990s, *Marsroutes en dwaalsporen* (1991) by P.M.H. Groen, on Dutch military policy in the Indies (see Military writings).

Finally, we refer to two volumes of papers to which non-Dutch authors also contributed. The first is *Decolonization of Indonesia* (1988), edited by C.A. van Minnen, illuminating international aspects. The second is *The Indonesian revolution* (1986), edited by J. van Goor, including papers on various subjects.

Other authors. Kattenburg's dissertation, about which some remarks were made earlier (see Contemporary writings), can be considered a 'borderline case' of a survey of the revolutionary period, in the sense that it was defended during that era, and at the same time offered a retrospective view of the major time period.

The first 'real' retrospective work is the well-known study by George McTurnan Kahin, *Nationalism and revolution in Indonesia* (1952). The author resided in republican territory as a correspondent and researcher and witnessed the revolution. Yet, his book was not written as a personal recollection, but was set up as a scholarly study, the political development in the Republic being the main subject. Kahin's sources are the contemporary republican press, and numerous contacts and interviews with the main personalities. His vision is openly pro-republican, showing a predilection for Sjahrir and his adherents. Dutch policy receives little sympathy. For example, federal policy is seen by Kahin as an attempt to maintain Dutch influence by means of indirect rule. As for the federal state of East Indonesia, he remarks that the traditional élite benefited from the continuation of Dutch presence; consequently, democratic development in the region was delayed. The Republic was seen as a 'proper' democracy on which the free world could pin its hopes. Kahin's exposure of Dutch policy as 'neo-colonial' greatly influenced its image with foreign authors.

In the Asian countries that acquired independence after the Second World War, solidarity was felt with the Indonesian struggle for freedom, not only coming from an anti-colonial mentality as with Kahin, but also inspired by a feeling of solidarity of fate. This is evident in several surveys of the Indonesian revolution which appeared in these countries. As an example, we have already mentioned *The Indonesian struggle* by the Pakistan author I. Chaudhry. In addition, we note *Transfer of power in Indonesia* (1967) by the Indian J.K. Ray, and *L'Indonésie: introduction à une décolonisation* (1965) by the Vietnamese Tran Buu Khanh; the latter work, incidentally, was published in Brussels. An inter-Asian solidarity may also appear in some Japanese surveys (Kinoshita 1958, Koshino 1958; not consulted). Understandably, Japan was uniquely involved in the Indonesian struggle for independence, especially at its onset. Several surveys have also been written by authors from the Soviet Union, from a Marxist perspective, of course: A.I. Ionova (1964), E. Kiamilev (1968) and V.I. Gidaspov (1970).

Returning to Western authors, it is striking that it was not until the early 1960s that other monographs were devoted to the revolution. Kahin's book was a 'forerunner', conceived on the spot and published shortly after the conflict. Only in 1964 did *Bandung in the early revolution* by J.R.W. Smail appear, the first of a complete series of regional studies by Anglo-Saxon authors (see Regional and local aspects). If we limit ourselves to general surveys, then Benedict Anderson's dissertation *The pemuda revolution* (1967) should be considered first. This study, which appeared in 1972 as *Java in a time of revolution*, is restricted to the end of the Japanese era and the first year of the revolution. The original title reveals the prominent role Anderson grants the revolutionary youth, *pemuda*. The Japanese had provided them with military training and taught them an anti-Western attitude. The Proclamation of 17 August had been their initiative, and afterwards they demonstrated truly revolutionary dynamics that greatly influenced republican policy during the first year. According to Anderson, *pemuda* were the driving force behind many revolutionary reforms. In the end, however, they were disappointed by the compromises made by the republican leaders.

The whole period of the revolution is covered by Anthony Reid in his survey *The Indonesian national revolution 1945-1950* (1974), a worthwhile small book suitable for use as a general introduction. Of course, the Republic occupies a central place; less attention is paid to Dutch policy and its framework. The author seems to have taken to heart Kahin's call (in the preface of the 1970 edition of *Nationalism and revolution in Indonesia*) to pay more attention to areas outside Java; he also directs attention to developments in Sumatra, of which a considerable part was under republican administration.

The German specialist on Indonesia Bernhard Dahm, who took his doctoral degree in 1964 with a study on Soekarno, describes in some detail the revolutionary years in *Indonesien; Geschichte eines Entwicklungslandes* (1978). Oey Hong Lee, born in the Dutch East Indies but educated and residing abroad, devotes attention to the interplay of British, American, Dutch and republican policies in his survey *War and diplomacy in Indonesia 1945-1950* (1981). Finally, we turn to the important study by Yong Mun Cheong, *H.J. van Mook and Indonesian independence* (1982), a unique attempt by a non-Dutch author to gain insight into Dutch policy on the Indonesian revolution. Yong's book describes the years 1945-1948 and can also be read as a survey of that period. Oey Hong Lee's and Yong Mun Cheong's studies differ from earlier surveys in not taking the Republic and its policy as a starting point.

b. The Proclamation

The independence Proclamation of the Indonesian people by Soekarno and Hatta on 17 August 1945 is the most radical event in the period described here, especially when long-term effects are considered. For Indonesians the Proclamation heralded the freedom of the nation; in the writing of national history it is, understandably, a much greater moment than the transfer of sovereignty (*penyerahan/pengakuan kedaulatan*) by the Netherlands on 27 December 1949. The Proclamation is pivotal in every review of modern Indonesian history. It took place during the final phase of the Japanese occupation, and is often given consideration by many Indonesian authors who have written primarily about the Japanese era. Furthermore, the Proclamation is of interest from a historiographical point of view, because the authors (including Indonesian authors) offer divergent views on the developments of the time.

Indonesian authors. As mentioned earlier, in 1948 Adam Malik published his *Riwajat dan perdjuangan sekitar Proklamasi kemerdekaan Indonesia*, in which the part of the *pemuda* was seen as crucial. Soekarno and Hatta are said to have hesitated to make a proclamation, and it was feared that independence would be received as a gift from the Japanese. The kidnapping at Rengasdengklok was necessary in order to persuade Soekarno and Hatta to make their proclamation. Malik's booklet was reprinted several times (a sixth edition was published in 1975). In 1951, Hatta defended himself against Malik's version in an article in *Mimbar Indonesia*; a Dutch translation 'Legende en realiteit rondom de Proclamatie van 17 Augustus' was included in Hatta's *Verspreide geschriften* (1952). Hatta argues that he and Soekarno had planned to proclaim independence as soon as possible, after it had become obvious that Japan had lost the war. But it had to be an 'organized revolution' and not a putsch in which power was grasped from the hands of the Japanese by the Peta, *pemuda* and the people. The kidnapping at Rengasdengklok had been intended to provoke such a putsch in Jakarta, in the absence of the two leaders who were against it. Because it was badly organized the plan failed, and after 24 hours the *pemuda* had no choice but to return Soekarno and Hatta to the capital, where independence was proclaimed the same day. It was obvious that nobody could attempt anything without them. This version of events, playing down the role of *pemuda* and depicting them as thoughtless hotheads, was reintroduced by Hatta in *Sekitar Proklamasi 17 Agustus 1945* (1969), in which he also responds to other publications, such as those of Achmad Subardjo Djojo-adisurjo.

Achmad Subardjo, a jurist and prominent nationalist, had been Hatta's assistant when he advised the Japanese military government on socio-economic issues; later on during the occupation Subardjo himself acted as advisor to the Japanese navy. His experiences concerning the Proclamation were published in *Lahirnja Republik Indonesia* (1972). During the 1960s, Subardjo already published material on the Proclamation in the periodical *Penelitian Sedjarah*. His account is not complimentary to the pemuda, although he admires their enthusiasm. Soekarno and Hatta wanted to wait for official news on the Japanese surrender before taking action; Admiral Maeda, who was in favour of the nationalists, had promised to inform them. But the *pemuda* were impatient; there were plans for a large Peta demonstration in Jakarta, to accelerate the transfer of power to the Indonesian people. The kidnapping was intended to bring Soekarno and Hatta into safety in case riots broke out. Subardjo warned the *pemuda* not to irritate the Japanese, as they would remain responsible for preserving the status quo after the surrender. The young Republic would soon be suppressed if action was taken without the Japanese being informed, especially the well-meaning Maeda. By promising that the Proclamation would follow soon, Subardjo was able to succeed in releasing Soekarno and Hatta from Rengasdengklok. Talks followed with Maeda, who agreed to take responsibility with the Allies. The Proclamation was made the morning after the Committee for the Preparation of Independence had met. In this way, the Indonesian initiative followed Maeda's approval. Whatever the differences concerning the role of the *pemuda*, Indonesian authors agree that the Proclamation was indeed an Indonesian initiative (an exception to this is found in the pamphlets written by the pro-Dutch Mas Slamet (1946), which appeared shortly after the Proclamation).

Other authors. In the work of non-Indonesian authors, a more prominent role is sometimes assigned to the Japanese, mainly by conservative Dutch authors who wanted the world to believe that the Republic was of Japanese design and was not supported by the Indonesian people. In 1959, H.J. de Graaf published the article 'The Indonesian declaration of independence', for which he consulted printed sources as well as unpublished Indonesian and Japanese documents. At first glance, De Graaf's reconstruction does not essentially differ from Achmad Subardjo's account; however, the author repeatedly suggests that Maeda's involvement was larger than usually assumed. He states (p. 323) that Maeda prepared the Proclamation together with the Indonesian leaders, and that the Japanese admiral in fact founded the Republic by his firm conduct (a rather far-reaching assumption), where-as the Indonesian leaders were unable to take decisions and the *pemuda* were unequipped to take over command (p. 326).

Several Japanese authors have also written on the events surrounding the Proclamation. Most of their accounts are in Japanese and therefore not widely accessible. An exception are the memoirs of the interpreter Nishiji-ma Shigetada, of which English and Indonesian translations appeared in 1986 and 1987. In 'The independence Proclamation in Jakarta', Nishijima describes Indonesian plans for the Proclamation and Maeda's cooperation (thus, Nishijima's version includes an Indonesian initiative, too). Soekarno and Hatta courteously awaited official confirmation of Japan's surrender, whereas the *pemuda*, impatient as they were, wished to avoid any semb-lance of Japanese interference in the Proclamation. Nishijima concludes that the *pemuda* actions were favourable for the image of the Proclamation; if everything had worked out as Soekarno and Hatta had in mind, it would have been an unromantic event arousing little excitement.

c. Military writings

Indonesian authors. There are numerous Indonesian writings on the armed struggle in the years 1945-1949. Physical resistance against the colonial authority trying to re-establish itself in the archipelago after the Japanese surrender seems to be more appealing than the diplomatic side, considering the number of publications devoted to these subjects. This is not surprising, because the resistance concerns manifest acts which speak of courage and heroism. The revolutionary period is also the era in which the Indonesian armed forces took shape and started to take on an increasingly important role in Indonesian society, far more prominent than in most Western countries. This also explains the large amount of contemporary military publications.

The armed resistance against Dutch colonialism throughout history and against Japanese rule has been compiled in the multipartite series *Sejarah perlawanan terhadap kolonialisme dan imperialisme* (ca. 1981-1984). The revolution itself has been described in a similar series *Sejarah revolusi kemerdekaan daerah [...]* (ca. 1980). Both series were edited under the auspices of the Indonesian Ministry of Education and Culture. In them, the military aspect is not stressed continually. It is more important in General Nasution's eleven-volume standard work *Sekitar perang kemerdekaan Indonesia* (second edition 1977-1979), which has been previously discussed. Finally, the military dominates all other aspects in the publications by the Ministry of Defence (Departemen HANKAM) and by the historical bureaus of the three main divisions of the armed forces: Pusat Sejarah Militer Angkatan Darat (PUSSEMAD) for the army, Dinas Sejarah TNI-Angkatan Udara for the air force and Dinas Sejarah TNI-Angkatan Laut for the navy (the names of these bureaus are subject to change).

As the republican air force and navy were small in revolutionary times, most relevant publications concern the army. Some incomplete bibliographies on army history exist, for example, *Bibliografi sedjarah HANKAM/ABRI* (second edition, 1971). An important periodical containing many relevant contributions is *Madjalah Sedjarah Militer Angkatan Darat*, renamed *Vidya Yudha* in the early 1970s.

Apart from overviews of the armed struggle there are also many studies dedicated to large (Sumatra) or smaller (Bali) islands, to regions or provinces (Riau, Sulawesi Utara, Maluku, etc.) and to cities and other places. Of course, much literature is dedicated to the scenes of high points in the war for freedom, such as Bandung ('Bandung lautan api'), Semarang ('Lima hari di Semarang'), Surabaya (the 'Battle of Surabaya') and Yogyakarta ('Serangan umum'). As an example we mention a book on the last event, which took place on 1 March 1949, when several districts of Yogyakarta that had been occupied by Dutch troops during the Second Police Action were reconquered by republican forces. This particular book, *Serangan umum 1 Maret 1949 di Yogyakarta*, was published in 1989 under the auspices of the Sekolah Staf dan Komando Angkatan Darat (SESKOAD); the second edition, which is referred to here, appeared in 1990. As is customary, the book opens with several prefaces by high officers, recommending the book to the reader. President Soeharto also wrote a *sambutan* (recommendation), in which he stresses the importance of the *serangan umum* (general attack) to the self-respect of the Indonesian people, inspiring them to stand up against oppression and to take on a respected and equal place amongst nations.

Soeharto himself participated in the struggle (see his 'Pendjelasan tentang serangan umum', 1968, as well as his autobiography). The book goes on to give an extensive overview of the first four years of the revolution, in which the genesis of the Indonesian army occupies a central place. Then a description of the 'general attack' is related, in such detail that the action can be followed from hour to hour. It is repeatedly stressed that the people of Yogyakarta and its surroundings supported the guerrilla fighters in various ways, for instance, *pelajar* (secondary school children) carried messages for them. The book is richly illustrated with pictures from the republican photographic service IPPHOS, and with maps. Appendices provide the texts of important agreements between the Republic and the Netherlands, as well as a list of participants in a 1988 seminar dedicated exclusively to the *serangan umum*, which led to the publication of the standard work.

Another topic of military history is the genesis of the armed forces, in particular the army. The tradition of armed resistance against the colonial oppressors is often referred to in relation to this subject, for instance, in the Java and Aceh Wars. During the Japanese occupation, the first Indonesian army corps was formed. The Peta (Pembela Tanah Air), one unit of which rebelled against the Japanese in February 1945 at Blitar (see Japanese period), is the best known of these corps. Other militias were affiliated with the youth movement, Seinendan, or were based on the principles of Islam, such as Hizbullah. During the revolution, the regular army (TRI, later TNI) tried to get control of the 'wild', unofficial armed groups (*laskar, lasykar*), to which many youths had turned. These *laskar* are often depicted in literature as carriers of the true revolutionary spirit. An important *pelajar* corps was the TRIP (Tentara Republik Indonesia Pelajar), mainly active in East Java. Outside Java, there were many *laskar* in South Sulawesi; the booklet *Badan-badan perjuangan* (1983), published by the Ministry of Defence, contains an overview of armed groups in the whole archipelago.

Not only the *laskar*, but also the regular army avoided open confrontations with the Dutch troops. There was an extensive guerrilla force that could not be fought sufficiently by the Dutch; after the Second Police Action, guerrilla activity even intensified. General Nasution wrote a famous manual on the organization of guerrilla warfare, *Pokok-pokok gerilja* (1953, fourth edition 1980), which was translated into English and German. Nasution describes the regional set-up of the guerrilla troops, based on *Wehr-kreise*, explaining it as the only way for a people that is militarily weaker than its adversary to continue armed resistance. Furthermore, it is necessary that soldiers are able to receive supplies and can be hidden by the local population. Nasution's book contains many reflections on guerrilla theory. An account taken solely from practice is *Laporan dari Banaran* (1960) by General T.B. Simatupang, which, just as Nasution's book, also became well-known outside Indonesia. Simatupang vividly describes the last year of the independence struggle, based on field notes he recorded from the fall of Yogyakarta (December 1948) until the transfer of sovereignty. The renowned general Soedirman was also present in the Yogya region, and understandably plays an important part in Simatupang's notes.

As early as 1954, Simatupang wrote a book on the position of the army in Indonesian society: *Pelopor dalam perang, pelopor dalam damai*. It discusses the Japanese era as well as the revolution, with the interweaving of the army and population as its theme. This bond was brought into existence through guerrilla warfare and continued to exist in peacetime. After the failed coup in 1965, the position of the army in society and politics became pronounced and many works on the subject have since appeared; Simatupang's book was actually a predecessor of this kind of reading. Attention for the revolutionary period, when the ties between the people and the army were forged, is understandably large. As an example we refer to the voluminous *Kemanunggalan ABRI dengan rakyat* (1985).

The most impressive history of the army's genesis is Nasution's epic *Sekitar perang kemerdekaan Indonesia* (1977-1979). Several other reviews are restricted to the revolutionary period; still others confine themselves to the history of regional military commands, Komando Daerah Militer (KODAM), also dealing with recent years. We mention here *Dua windhu KODAM I/Iskandar Muda* (1972) concerning North Sumatra (Aceh). In this account, the number of prefaces by military officers is so large that they take up the first 65 pages of the book. Following is an overview of the revolution with lists of units and their officers. It is a genuine military history without much attention to political developments, providing the impression that in 1945 a vast, well-organized army stood ready to give the Dutch a warm welcome in Indonesia. A description of how weapons were captured from the Japanese and used in the struggle for independence is given. However, the book is not a vivid, readable account as are the notes of Simatupang, but a dry enumeration of persons and facts. In addition, the greater part of the book is dedicated to the years after 1950; the regional command in question, KODAM I, was not founded until 1956. In total, sixteen regional commands exist, each with a historiography of its own.

Another method used to record the Indonesian army's birth and development is the military biography. In Indonesia, the biography is a cultivated genre (see Biographies); it is therefore understandable that in a country where the armed forces play a prominent part, many officers have been honoured with a biography, or even with several biographies, as is the case with the generals Oerip Soemohardjo, I Gusti Ngurah Rai and Soeharto (who held the rank of lieutenant colonel during the revolution). Some wrote autobiographies, such as A.H. Nasution, with his voluminous *Meme-*

nuhi panggilan tugas (1982-1987), in which he describes the revolution in minute detail. The memoirs by A.E. Kawilarang, translated into Dutch under the title *Officier in dienst van de Republiek Indonesië* (1990), also offer a good insight into the early years of the army. However, the military officer who has inspired the most biographies is Soedirman, Panglima Besar (commander-in-chief) of the republican army during the revolution. This outstanding figure clearly appeals to the imagination. His health was poor; during the guerrilla struggle he was transported in a sedan chair, and his death came shortly after the end of the independence struggle in January 1950. The place and date of his birth are somewhat unclear. His father worked at a sugar mill near Rembang in Central Java. Soedirman himself was trained as a schoolteacher; during the Japanese occupation he became a Peta officer, and after gaining honours in the fight for Ambarawa, was appointed commander-in-chief of the republican army in November 1945. Soedirman did not consider himself subordinate to political leadership and was inclined to set his own course, a trait receiving little attention in his biographies. The *route gerilya* between Yogyakarta and Kediri, followed by Soedirman after the occupation of the republican capital in December 1948, has become renowned. Shortly after his death, the Panglima Besar was venerated; by 1950 biographies full of praise were being published, such as *Djendral Soedirman pahlawan sedjati* by the Ministry of Information, which attempts to shed light on his youth and also stresses the romantic aspects of his stature: the depiction of his transformation from a simple *desa* boy to commander-in-chief, weak in body but strong in mind, and so on. The legend around his person particularly focuses on the *route gerilya*, as is evident in the book by N.S.S. Tarjo, *Dari atas tandu* (1984). There were strong protests when S.I. Poeradisastra suggested in the article 'Hubungan Panglima Besar Soedirman dengan Persatuan Perjuangan' (1983) that the commander-in-chief had been sympathetic to the conspirators in the Tiga Juli affair, who wanted to push Sjahrir aside in 1946 because of his inclination to compromise with the Dutch. A more detached approach to Soedirman's image can be found in the remarkable American dissertation by Salim Said, *Genesis of power* (1985).

Most Indonesian military writings on the period 1945-1949 concern the army; the republican air force and navy were much smaller and played a less important role. However, there is still much reading available on these branches of the armed forces. Concerning the air force, a memorial book, *Sewindu Angkatan Udara RI* was published in 1954, mainly dealing with the revolution. A more recent memorial book is *Catur windu TNI-AU* (1977). Further we mention the concise survey *Sedjarah AURI* (1970) and a more detailed work by S. Trihadi, *Sedjarah perkembangan Angkatan Udara* (1971). *Sejarah operasi penerbangan Indonesia periode 1945-1950* (1980) is a work which focuses on the revolution. Specialized studies include *Sejarah perhubungan/komunikasi TNI-AU* (1978) on air connections, and *Sejarah pendidikan perwira penerbang* (1979) on the training of air force officers during the revolution. Biographies appeared on Agustinus Adisucipto, Halim Perdana Kusuma, Iswahyudi and Abdulrachman Saleh. This last-mentioned officer, who was also a medical doctor and radio pioneer, fell near Yogyakarta in 1947 when his aircraft was shot down by the Dutch. Moving on to the navy, we mention first a general survey by Sudono Jusuf (1971). The book *Sejarah TNI-Angkatan Laut* (1973) and the photo book by Muchri and Sugeng Sudarto focus on the revolution. Regionally specialized works include Zamzulis Ismail's publications on the expeditions to Kalimantan (1980) and on the navy in Aceh (1980). Biographies of the naval officers R.E. Martadinata and Yos Sudarso also appeared.

Dutch authors. Most Dutch writings on the military conflict with Indonesia were collected in J.M. Verhoog's bibliography *Herinneringsliteratuur betreffende het Nederlandse militaire optreden te land in Indonesië* (1989). As is evident from the title, air force and navy operations are not included. Otherwise, Verhoog shows a high measure of completeness; not only the general military periodicals *De Militaire Spectator* and *Ons Leger* were consulted, but also smaller, specialized magazines such as *Oud-Wapenbroeders* (Nederlands Veteranenlegioen), *De Groene Baret* (Commandovereniging) and *Stabelan* (Oud-KNIL-militairen). These and other smaller magazines have not been included in our bibliography; they are catalogued most completely by Sjak Draak (1993). Prior to Verhoog's publication, the reading list in *Het woordenboek van Jan Soldaat in Indonesië* (1980) by H. Salleveldt was the most comprehensive for memorial books, whereas De Ruyter's bibliography (second edition 1976) was useful in tracing articles in military magazines.

As already stated, Dutch military literature can be divided into several categories. There are publications with a military-technical aspect, as *De Militaire Spectator*, which might, for instance, detail the construction of a bridge in West Java. There are also memorial books, describing the exploits of a particular battalion. This kind of reading not only contains much factual information, but also reveals the personal and emotional involvement of the compilers, whereby their own achievements are stressed. Doubts about the Dutch military presence in the Indies are seldom expressed.

Memorial books are an important source because they offer insight into the day-to-day life of the soldiers. Their number is large, although they are sometimes difficult to find in libraries: often these publications only received distribution among the soldiers themselves. The Sectie Militaire Geschiedenis in The Hague has the largest collection of these publications, and the KITLV in Leiden is now also well provided. A small wave of memorial books appeared in the early 1950s; since that time they have continued to appear regularly, for instance on the occasion of reunions. Another category is formed by personal documents, such as memoirs, diaries and short stories. Much of this reading first appeared in the 1950s; after a slack period in the 1960s and 1970s, these personal documents are now again being published in abundance, largely because their authors have reached retirement and now have the time to write their memoirs or edit their diaries. Furthermore, on the approach of the fiftieth anniversary of the birth of the 'Indonesian question', the behaviour of Dutch soldiers in the Indies has again become subject to public discussion. A last category of writing consists of a few scientific studies on the Dutch military presence and policy, reluctantly begun in the early 1970s and only further developed in the 1980s and 1990s, with the Sectie Militaire Geschiedenis as an important centre.

The memorial books from the early 1950s vary in content. For instance, *Het fiere eendje* (1950) on the achievements of 4-1 RI in South Sumatra is mainly a photo book with captions. *Awas, Pijp-Pijp datang!* (1950), about 5-5 RI in Central Java, contains many photographs as well as text which consists of short sketches by soldiers and their officers. The last pages list men killed in action or through mishap. An example of a recent memorial book is *Noorderlicht op Midden-Java* (1992) on the 403rd Infantry Battalion, published on the occasion of its reunion.

Among the personal documents, we mention *Front op Java* (ca. 1952) by G. van Heek, a well-written account of the author's service with 4-9 RI. The author is convinced of the usefulness of Dutch military presence: providing protection of the civilians against the terror of the *peloppers* and the establishment of law and order. At the end of his story, the author ponders the future of Indonesia after the Dutch have had to withdraw. A more critical account is given by Jan Schilt in his *Soldaatje spelen onder de smaragden gordel* (1969). A recently edited diary is *Dagboek van een oorlogsvrijwilliger* (1994) by G. Deters, who served with the Stoottroepen in South Sumatra and Java. The author gives an impression of the soldier's daily life with its moments of action and weariness. In his preface, the author relates that he was finally moved to edit his diary out of anger over the present discussion on the behaviour of Dutch soldiers in the Indies, which was compared by some (for instance the author Graa Boomsma) with 'Nazi methods'.

As already stated, scientific literature started to be produced in the early 1970s, following the debate on the excesses of Dutch soldiers. In 1969, the psychologist J.E. Hueting gave stimulus to this debate in a television interview (see the thesis by L. Stam, *De Hueting-affaire*, 1972), leading to the official *Nota betreffende het archievenonderzoek naar gegevens omtrent excessen in Indonesië begaan door Nederlandse militairen* (1969; reprinted

1995). Soon following was the important study by J.A.A. van Doorn and W.J. Hendrix, *Ontsporing van geweld* (1970). The authors, both Indies veterans, chose as a theme 'social intercourse with violence', whereby the actions of Dutch soldiers in the Indies served as practical examples. They concluded that a society is inclined to conceal violence by leaving it to the armed forces and the police. These institutions tend to secrecy and allow only limited public scrutiny. As a result, it was possible to keep Indonesian excesses silent for years, except for a few acknowledged cases such as the Bondowoso affair and Westerling's behaviour in South Sulawesi.

Following the debate on excesses, a number of years passed until the number of relevant scientific publications increased. In 1983 H.L. Zwitzer, associated with the Sectie Militaire Geschiedenis, edited *Documenten betreffende de eerste politionele actie*, intended as a military-technical supplement to the source publication *Officiële bescheiden*. Nonetheless, an in-depth study exploring the military-technical side of Dutch involvement has yet to appear. Two younger associates of the Sectie Militaire Geschiedenis, J. Hoffenaar and P.M.H. Groen, are now active in this field. Hoffenaar is specialized in military publicity and the Dutch retreat from Indonesia. After producing a large number of preliminary publications, Groen took her doctoral degree in 1991 with *Marsroutes en dwaalsporen*, concerning the Dutch military-strategic policy in Indonesia in the years 1945-1950. She states that Van Mook soon abandoned the plan for a speedy reoccupation of Java: such a move would be too strong an effort for the Netherlands. Van Mook instead decided to decolonize and launched his federal plans (which were in fact older) for an independent Indonesia; it was intended that the Republic be incorporated into these plans. When the Republic obstructed this decolonization scheme, the plan had to be altered, using military force. The First Police Action was intended to reduce the size of the Republic, even though Van Mook and Commander Spoor initially had wanted to occupy the capital Yogyakarta and install a more cooperative government. Because of international pressure, however, the action was limited. Furthermore, the goal to reduce the Republic's size was only partially achieved. During the Second Police Action, Yogya was occupied and the Republic temporarily neutralized as a political factor, but international protest was so strong that the republican leaders were soon released. The military situation was also becoming more difficult, caused by a revival of the guerrilla struggle. Overcoming these forces was a task beyond Dutch power. General Spoor's conviction, that the revolution would die out if radical elements were eliminated, turned out to be false.

Apart from the Sectie Militaire Geschiedenis, other authors also dealt with militaria. W. IJzereef wrote on Westerling's actions in *De Zuid-Celebesaffaire* (1984). J.A. de Moor, associated with Leiden University, published work concerning the Korps Speciale Troepen and is currently working on a biography of Westerling. Nevertheless, military biographies are scarce; only two short books have appeared on the engrossing figure of Spoor, which contain memoirs (Schilling 1953, Smulders 1988); a 'real' biography of this outstanding personality has yet to be written. Two very different personality types have written their memoirs: General H.J. Kruls (1975) and Captain R. Westerling (1952), the latter trying to justify and downplay his disputed actions in South Sulawesi. His memoirs have been translated into English, German and French. Finally, mention is made of several volumes with articles on the Police Actions: *De politionele acties* (1987), edited by G. Teitler and P.M.H. Groen, and *De politionele acties; Afwikkeling en verwerking* (1990), edited by G. Teitler and J. Hoffenaar. Articles on the navy are also included in these volumes.

Concerning the air force, of primary importance is *De militaire luchtvaart van het KNIL in de naoorlogse jaren 1945-1950* (1980) by O.G. Ward and others, which can be considered the standard work on the revolutionary period. Hugo Hooftman gives an overview of the period 1940-1949 in the second volume of his *Militaire luchtvaart in Nederlandsch-Indië* (1981). For literature on the Luchtvaarttroepen (airborne troops) and the Marine Lucht-vaart Dienst, see the index. Here we will only make reference to W.J.A.M. de Kock's *Commando Luchtvaarttroepen; Nederlands-Indië 1947-1950* (1990). Finally we mention the informative memoirs of Dick Asjes, *Startklaar* (1985). Asjes was the first Dutch aviator to set foot on Indonesian soil after the Japanese surrender; he was charged with the organization of RAPWI. Concerning the Dutch navy (Koninklijke Marine) and its presence in the East Indies waters, much has been written by G. Teitler, associated with the Koninklijk Instituut voor de Marine in Den Helder. In 1990, Teitler publish-ed *Vlootvoogd in de knel*, on Vice-Admiral A.S. Pinke and an analysis of his policy towards the revolution. Various books have also appeared on the Korps Mariniers, active in East Java. In 1955, C.J.O. Dorren wrote *Onze mariniersbrigade*; in addition the daily life of marines was described as early as 1950 by W. Dussel. Another popular author is Wim Hornman, who wrote several voluminous books on the marines in the Indies; the most recent is *De laatste man; Mariniers in de gordel van smaragd* (1992). From an academic point of view, the study by D.C.L. Schoonoord, *De mariniers-brigade 1943-1949; Wording en inzet in Indonesië* (1988), is of great value.

Other authors. The other authors who have dealt with the military aspects of the revolution can be divided into two groups: those who wrote about the presence of British (British-Indian) and Australian troops in Indonesia, and those who investigated the genesis and development of the Indonesian armed forces and their place in society.

A well-known book on the British-Indian troops in Indonesia (and Southeast Asia) is *The Fighting Cock* (1951) by A.J.F. Doulton, which describes the exploits of the 23rd Indian Division. Naturally, much attention is given to the heavy fighting in Surabaya in November 1945, where a high officer, Brigadier A.W.S. Mallaby, was killed. Another event which is dealt with is the occupation of Bandung in March 1946, when retreating republican troops set part of the city on fire, an event known as *Bandung lautan api* in Indonesian historiography. A later study on British-Indian troops is J.G.A. Parrott's thesis (1977), which concerns the prelude to the Battle of Surabaya. Also of importance are the writings and biographies of Lord Mountbatten, commander of the Allied Forces on Java and Sumatra in 1945 and 1946.

The place of the armed forces, and the role of the revolution, in Indonesian society has been the subject of study by several Anglo-Saxon authors. Harold Crouch briefly describes the revolution in *The army and politics in Indonesia* (1978). Ulf Sundhaussen's treatment of the revolution in *The road to power* (1982) is more extensive. David C. Anderson wholly dedicated a SOAS thesis to the years 1945-1949: *Military politics in East Java* (1976), a regionally focused study which investigated the social backgrounds of army officers. These officers reluctantly conformed to the guidelines of republican military leadership, which strove for centralism, and exhibited an attitude towards central leadership during the Madiun crisis that can be described as 'decidedly ambiguous'.

d. Regional and local aspects

Indonesian authors. Shortly after the *revolusi physik*, a considerable amount of regionally and locally specialized writings appeared, steadily increasing up until the present. Most of these writings are not specifically focused on the revolution; rather they review the entire history of a particular region or place, in which the revolutionary period is just another chapter. These books are sometimes published on the occasion of a special event, such as *Kota Jogjakarta 200 tahun* (1956).

The first inventory of regional history is the series *Republik Indonesia, propinsi[...]* published by the Ministry of Information in 1953. In this work, the revolution receives much attention. The province (*daerah*) is also the basis for two later series on anti-colonial resistance and the revolution, respectively, *Sejarah perlawanan terhadap imperialisme dan kolonialisme di [...]* (ca. 1982) and *Sejarah revolusi kemerdekaan (1945-1949) daerah [...]* (1979-). These series, published by the Ministry of Education and Culture, are a new attempt to map out the regional differentiation of the whole archipelago. Each volume is compiled by a collection of authors, chosen for their regional specialization.

Apart from these all-encompassing series, many regional and local initiatives have been carried out on the history of the revolution, sometimes set within a larger period of time (for instance, that including the Japanese period). These writings concern a whole island or parts of it, for example, South Sulawesi, a region to which a conference was devoted in 1982, yielding a large amount of papers. Much literature is available on cities such as Jakarta, Bandung, Semarang, Surakarta, Yogyakarta, Surabaya, Medan, Padang and Makasar (Ujung Pandang). The revolution in numerous smaller places and islands has also been described. Sometimes local administrations made the first move for publication, while on other occasions this came from private initiative.

Since the 1970s, there has been interest in the theory and methods of regional and local history. The prominent historian Taufik Abdullah has published writings on the subject and in 1982 a seminar was dedicated to it. Oral history, recorded by means of interviews, has been very important in reconstructing the revolution in a certain region or place. A large amount of theses on local history exist, although these are poorly distributed and often can only be consulted at the university or IKIP concerned. Nevertheless, these titles are included in our bibliography as completely as was possible.

Regional and local literature is indexed by geographical name and easy to trace. The entries 'Oral History/Interviews' and 'Regional/Local Aspects' should also be consulted.

Dutch authors. Unlike the abundant Indonesian regional literature, the Dutch production of these publications was quite limited. Interestingly, many military memorial books give information on local circumstances. An in-depth study was written by W. IJzereef on the Zuid-Celebesaffaire (1984). Non-military aspects are dealt with in *Bersiap in Bandoeng* (1989) by Mary C. van Delden, concerning the initial phase of the revolution. C.H.M. de Bruin wrote a thesis on Mojokerto (1981), and Tattersall on Bali (1990). Other theses deal with the federal states East Indonesia (Groen 1979, Bunnik 1981), Pasundan (De Boer-van Meurs 1984), East Sumatra (G.C.M. de Bruin 1985) and Madura (Keyzer-Grooten 1984).

Other authors. It was mainly Anglo-Saxon authors who, since the 1960s, researched the impact of the revolution in specific regions (see A. Reid, 'The revolution in regional perspective', 1986). The first such study was *Bandung in the early revolution* (1964) by J.R.W. Smail; in this, the author pays much attention to the role of the *pemuda* and their militias during the first six months of the revolution. Their endeavours to influence or even take over the local republican administration led to intervention by the Japanese and, when almost total anarchy ensued, by the British. In March 1946 the city had to be evacuated, an event known as *Bandung lautan api*. Smail describes the competition and power struggle between the various social groups: republican politicians, the army, traditional administrators (*pamong praja*), Islamic leaders and *pemuda*. The shifting between these groups, known as 'social revolution', is also a theme in other regional studies. A second study was not published until 1976, *National revolution in North Sumatra*, by Michael van Langenberg as a doctoral dissertation at Sydney University. The author describes the establishment of the Republic in East Sumatra (capital: Medan) and Tapanuli. At first the native élite, which had cooperated with the Dutch colonial administration, was set aside under pressure from the *pemuda*; this development was reversed when the Dutch again took control over the area and created the federal state of East Sumatra in 1947. Van Langenberg's account ends in 1950, when the federal states merged into the Indonesian unitary state. *Indonesian urban society in transition* (1978) by William H. Frederick, a dissertation at the University of Hawaii, is focused on Surabaya in the years 1926-1946. The author probes the background of the Battle of Surabaya in November 1945, by exploring local late-colonial society, the Japanese intermezzo and the first months of the revolution. He reveals special characteristics of the *arek Surabaya*, the common citizens, who in the 1930s already had demonstrated the self-awareness which was expressed in an extreme form in the outburst of November 1945. The Japanese occupation caused little change, contrary to the idea given by most literature. The *pemuda* of Surabaya were not opposed to the nationalist élite, as was the case elsewhere. This viewpoint is disclosed in Ben Anderson's well-known study *The pemuda revolution* (1967). Frederick emphasizes the longer lines of development which do not fit into the radical change associated with the word 'revolution'. In 1989 his study was published as *Visions and heat; The making of the Indonesian revolution*.

Another important regional study is by A.J.S. Reid, *The blood of the people* (1979), dealing with Aceh and East Sumatra during the revolution. The late colonial days and the Japanese occupation are also treated. Reid describes the 'social revolution' in which the traditional native élite (*ulèebalang*) was pushed aside in favour of the religious leaders (*ulama*). In 1979, Audrey R. Kahin took her doctoral degree at Cornell University with *Struggle for independence; West Sumatra in the Indonesian national revolution*. This detailed study describes the establishment of republican authority in the area and also deals with military aspects. The theme 'social revolution' is again important in an ANU dissertation by Anton E. Lucas, *The bamboo spear pierces the payung* (1981). This study concerns the Tiga Daerah, three *kabupaten* in the Pekalongan residence on the north coast of Central Java: Brebes, Tegal and Pemalang. Here, a classic 'social revolution' took place, with a clearly economic background. In colonial times there was

a gap between the native élite (*pangreh praja*) and the common people. This
gap further widened when the Japanese ordered the élite to supervise hard
labour and forced deliveries of rice. After the outbreak of the revolution, the
native élite was expelled; for six weeks local revolutionaries took charge,
until the republican army put an end to their rule. Lucas's dissertation was
later published as *One soul, one struggle* in 1991.

In 1984, another regional dissertation was defended, this time by Robert B.
Cribb at the SOAS. His study *Jakarta in the Indonesian revolution* describes
the unique 'double government' consisting of both the Dutch and the
republicans, which existed in the city for some time. Special attention is
given to the poorer levels of society in Jakarta and surroundings, where
gang leaders and their followers roamed. Due to the revolutionary situation,
their status was 'politicized'. In an adaptation, *Gangsters and revolutionaries* (1991), this aspect of Jakarta's recent history is given a central place. In
addition, Cribb wrote numerous papers on revolutionary Jakarta, also
dealing with other aspects as diplomacy.

A final regional study worth noting is by Geoffrey B. Robinson, *The
politics of violence in modern Bali, 1882-1966*, a PhD thesis defended at
Cornell University in 1992. Robinson was interested in the large number of
victims in Bali in the aftermath of the failed 1965 coup. He has endeavoured
to correct the image of Bali as a peaceful island where people live harmoni-
ously, by writing a political history with an emphasis on disharmony and
conflict. The revolution plays an important part in Robinson's study. When
Bali was reoccupied by the Dutch in 1946, the population turned out to be
'politicized' beyond all expectation; the Dutch were quickly confronted with
a stubborn guerrilla force. The causes of this political consciousness, such as
the traces left by the Japanese occupation, are extensively analysed.

In 1985 a volume was edited by Audrey Kahin, *Regional dynamics of the
Indonesian revolution*, with summaries of the studies mentioned above;
other authors who are not discussed here also made contributions: Michael
Williams on Banten, Eric Morris on Aceh, Barbara Harvey on South
Sulawesi and Richard Chauvel on Ambon. This last author will be dealt
with in the section on the South Moluccan question.

e. Dutch-Indonesian negotiations

The literature on talks and negotiations between the Dutch and Indonesians
can be divided into two categories: talks with representatives of the Republic, and talks with the 'federalists'. Concerning the Republic, the following
events were significant: the Hoge Veluwe talks (April 1946), the Linggajati
Agreement (November 1946), the Renville Agreement (January 1948), the
Roem-Van Royen Agreement (May 1949) and the Round Table Conference
(August-November 1949). Talks with the federalists took place in Malino

(July 1946), Denpasar (December 1946) and Bandung (1948-1949); the 'minority conference' at Pangkalpinang (1946) should also be mentioned.

Indonesian authors. After 1950, few publications were specifically dedicated to negotiations. When compared with writings on the armed struggle (*diplomasi* versus *perjuangan*), their number is quite humble. Most of these essays are included in general surveys on the revolution, memoirs, biographies and autobiographies of prominent politicians such as Soekarno, Hatta, Sjahrir, M. Roem and H. Agus Salim.

In 1958 *The beginnings of the Indonesian-Dutch negotiations and the Hoge Veluwe talks*, by Idrus Nasir Djajadiningrat, appeared at Cornell University, the only monograph written on this conference. Some theses and articles cover the Linggajati Agreement, for example by Rosad Amidjaja (1970), who considers the Agreement incompatible with the tone of the Proclamation and the 1945 constitution. The volume *Menelusuri jalur Linggarjati* is especially noteworthy as a collection of papers on an Indonesian-Dutch scholarly conference in November 1991, with Linggajati as a special subject. A few years earlier, K.M.L. Tobing published a trilogy on the political struggle of the Indonesian people, *Perjuangan politik bangsa Indonesia* (1986-1987). The three volumes are dedicated respectively to Linggajati, Renville and the Round Table Conference; together they form an overview of the diplomatic side of the revolution, in which the role of the United Nations is also considered.

Finally, we mention the dissertation (University of Utrecht) by the 'federalist' Ide Anak Agung Gde Agung, former prime minister of the federal state of East Indonesia. This dissertation, *Renville als keerpunt in de Nederlands-Indonesische onderhandelingen* (1980), deals with the period lasting from the Renville Agreement until the transfer of sovereignty. Anak Agung takes Renville as a turning point because the execution of the Agreement encountered such difficulties that the Dutch deemed it necessary to initiate a second military action. This action again led to international isolation, forcing the Dutch to transfer sovereignty before the end of 1949. The author is one of the few Indonesian researchers who has tried to gain a deeper insight into the background of Dutch policy and has consulted Dutch archives for his research. He emphasizes the fact that the federalists, united in the BFO, distanced themselves from the Second Police Action and refused to participate in the Round Table Conference until the Republic was represented.

Dutch authors. Most considerations on Dutch-Indonesian negotiations by Dutch authors are to be found in general surveys, for instance Jan Bank's *Katholieken en de Indonesische revolutie* (1983), J.J.P. de Jong's *Diplomatie of strijd* (1988) and L. de Jong's *Het Koninkrijk der Nederlanden in de Tweede Wereldoorlog* (1988). Memoirs and diaries of prominent politicians and administrators are also significant. Concerning the latter category, we mention *Het dagboek van Schermerhorn* (1970), edited by C. Smit. As chairman of the Commission General for the East Indies, Schermerhorn was closely involved in the realization of the Linggajati Agreement. His diary covers the period from September 1946 until October 1947. Smit had previously edited fragments of his diary as *Het accoord van Linggadjati* (1959).

Another diary that sheds light on these negotiations is by H.N. Boon, a high official who worked closely with Van Mook. In 1986 his *Indonesische dagboeknotities* were published by C. Wiebes and B. Zeeman. Several autobiographies are also of significance, for instance that of W. Drees (1962), prime minister at the time of the revolution, J.A. Jonkman (1977), Minister of Overseas Territories, and D.U. Stikker (1966), Minister of Foreign Affairs in the closing stage of the conflict.

Finally, numerous papers by P.J. Drooglever, editor of the source publication *Officiële bescheiden*, should be noted. These have appeared since the early 1980s and illustrate various aspects of Dutch-Indonesian negotiations.

Other authors. Only a few publications are specifically dedicated to negotiations, although reflections by 'other authors' can also be found in general surveys. The important study by A.A. Schiller *The formation of federal Indonesia* (1955) is worth mentioning, in which attention is directed principally on the negotiations with the 'federalists'. In Yong Mun Cheong's *H.J. van Mook and Indonesian independence* (1982), talks with the republicans and others are a main issue. Finally, a number of authors have studied the role of the United Nations in bringing the Dutch and Indonesians back to the conference table (see International aspects).

f. Federal policy

Indonesian authors. At the transfer of sovereignty in December 1949, the United States of Indonesia were established, a federative structure with several states having their own government. As early as 1950, federalism was abolished and replaced by a unitary state. The literature on federalism consists mostly of contemporary writings stemming from the federal states themselves. In later writings, federalism is usually considered as a system forced on the Indonesians by the Dutch, having its roots in a divide-and-rule policy and intended to encircle and isolate the Republic. A more nuanced approach is found in the writings of Anak Agung Gde Agung, former prime minister of the federal state of East Indonesia and also a respected republican. According to Anak Agung, federalism initially was a sensible form of government, respecting the cultural and ethnic variety of the archipelago. Later on it was carried too far by Van Mook, with the establishment of small, unviable states degrading the whole system.

The end of federalism was accompanied by publications from the republican Ministry of Information, such as *Madura kembali ke asalnja* (1950): independent Indonesia had begun as a unitary state, and the federal states then returned to their source. Elsewhere it is stressed that the Republic had never acknowledged the federal states as equal: an example is *Republik Indonesia ta' pernah mengakui negara-negaraan* (1950). The republican point of view can also be found in books on the structure of the Indonesian state, such as Soenarko's manual (1951-1955). In addition, there are studies such as The Liang Gie's (1950) on the development of regional government in Indonesia, and A. Muslimin's (1960) on regional autonomy during the period 1903-1958.

The American dissertation by M.A. Nawawi, *Regionalism and regional conflicts in Indonesia* (1968), largely deals with the revolution and federalism, although the secession of the Republik Maluku Selatan (RMS) is also discussed. The South Moluccan question is considered by some authors (for example Manuputty 1970) to be a result of the discord caused by federalism.

A number of writings on the federal states were produced, especially on East Indonesia and Pasundan. The most developed of these were on East Indonesia; the writings of Anak Agung deal with its internal politics and relations with the Netherlands and with the Republic. In their conference papers, G.R. Pantouw (1982) and R.A. Daud (1982) give attention to the resistance of the people of South Sulawesi against the *negara* East Indonesia. Theses on Pasundan were written by Tanu Suherly (1968; adapted into an extensive conference paper, 1970) and by Lindayanti (1984).

Dutch authors. The writings on this subject by the great promoter of federalism, H.J. van Mook (1949, 1950) should receive first mention. In 1952 an article by Jaquet appeared on the elimination of the federal states. J.J.P. de Jong extensively discusses the federal concept in his dissertation *Diplomatie of strijd* (1988). A number of theses are devoted to individual federal states: Groen (1979) and Bunnik (1981) on East Indonesia, De Boer-van Meurs (1984) on Pasundan, G.C.M. de Bruin (1985) on East Sumatra and Keyzer-Grooten (1984) on Madura.

Other authors. The standard work on Indonesian federalism was written by the American professor A. Arthur Schiller: *The formation of federal Indonesia, 1945-1949* (1955). He was impressed by the dedication of both Dutch and Indonesians in building up a federal structure. He does not comment on the early death of federalism but is pleased to note that the unitary state recognized the advantages of a decentralized government in the first years of its existence.

In his remarkable study, *H.J. van Mook and Indonesian independence* (1982), Yong Mun Cheong, associated with the National University of Singapore, devoted ample attention to federalism. While Schiller observed matters from the angle of public administration, Yong stresses the political aspects. According to his interpretation, Van Mook's paternalism forced federalism upon the Indonesians; therefore, it was not surprising that soon after the transfer of sovereignty the whole system was scrapped and replaced by unitarism.

g. Political parties

Indonesian political parties - Indonesian authors. Since Indonesian political parties played an important role during the revolution, they are mentioned in many kinds of publications. The subject remains difficult to define. Nevertheless, it is useful here to mention some party histories, including literature on the theme 'party and parliament'. In order to get a more complete picture, biographies of prominent party members should be consulted. Histories of political parties were mostly written by adherents; thus, a biased point of view can be expected.

Partai Nasional Indonesia (PNI). Many details on the PNI can be found in biographies, autobiographies and other writings of prominent members, such as Roeslan Abdulgani and Sunario. An official history is *Empat windu Partai Nasional Indonesia* (1950), which describes the ups and downs of the party since its establishment in 1927. A more recent survey of the party's history can be found in Sunario's *Banteng segitiga* (second edition 1988).

Partai Komunis Indonesia (PKI). The events of 1965 were pivotal for the PKI and its historiography. Before the coup, the PKI had published some brief reviews, such as *Lahirnja PKI dan perkembangannja* (1955), and an address by chairman D.N. Aidit, in which he also deals with the role the party played during the revolution. In other publications, Aidit describes the Madiun affair, attempting to whitewash the party's role. After 1965, the PKI is depicted in a sinister manner and characterized as an association of traitors, for instance by Sutomo (1965) who places the Madiun affair and the Gestapu on the same level. The same is done in a photo book published by the Indonesian army, *Lukisan pemberontakan PKI* (1979). Another angle comes from Hartono's (American) thesis *The Indonesian communist movement* (1959), which also deals with the party's relationship with the Soviet Union.

The publicity concerning the Marxist-inspired *Partai Murba* of Tan Malaka had its own development. Tan Malaka's disappearance (or probable death) in 1949 caused a decline in printed matter on the subject, although the stream did not dry up entirely. Regular publications on Tan Malaka and his doctrine and role during the revolution have appeared up until the present, for instance, those by the 'Murbaist' Djamaluddin Tamim (1965) and M. Kaisiepo (1982).

A third Marxist party was the *Partai Sosialis Indonesia* (PSI) of Sjahrir and Sjarifuddin. Very little has been published in Indonesia on this party. Most literature concerns the two politicians mentioned above. Similarly, little information is to be found on the small Christian parties; these are best described in foreign studies. The important Islamic parties *Masyumi* and *Nahdatul Ulama* (NU) are, understandably, better documented. Deliar Noer is specialized in their history and in 1960 wrote an extensive study on Masyumi at Cornell University. His *Partai Islam di pentas nasional* (1987) concerns both Masyumi and NU, but mainly focuses on the first party. A history of NU since 1926 was written by H. Abdul Basit Adnan (1982). For parties not mentioned here, consult the index.

Indonesian political parties - other authors. This survey is restricted to a few important studies. The PNI was described by Rocamora (1974), and the PSI by Myers (1959) and Kiessling (1983). Much has been written on the PKI and on the unfortunate history of Indonesian communism, mainly by American authors, in part related to the containment of communism in Southeast Asia. Most PKI studies concern the party's history since 1950, under Aidit's chairmanship; however, there are also some excursions into pre-war and revolutionary times. Worth mentioning are the overviews by Brackman (1963), McVey (1965) and Mintz (1965). Concerning the revolution, the Madiun affair attracts most attention; a recent study has been written by Ann Swift, *The road to Madiun* (1989). Islamic parties are treated by Boland (1982) and by literature concerning Darul Islam: Jackson (1971), C. van Dijk (1981) and Dengel (1986). Finally, Christian parties are described by Webb (1978).

Dutch political parties. The historiography of Dutch political parties seems to be the exclusive domain of Dutch authors, especially in relation to the 'Indonesian question'. The viewpoints of the various parties in this matter are a favourite subject for Dutch theses; a number of articles and monographs are also devoted to it. In addition, biographies and memoirs by politicians are useful in gaining insight into the rather complicated political spectrum of the Netherlands.

Political relations in the Netherlands are detailed by Duynstee (1966), on the formation of cabinets in 1946-1965, and by Duynstee and Bosmans (1977), on the first post-war cabinet Schermerhorn-Drees. Van Oerle (1989) wrote about the political structure in 1948, using the diaries of leading politicians: Beel, Drees, Van der Goes van Naters and Romme. Stempels's overview *De parlementaire geschiedenis van het Indonesische vraagstuk* (1950) is also quite informative regarding the Dutch political scene and its main characters.

Partij van de Arbeid (PvdA). Van Baardewijk (1975) was the first to write a thesis on the PvdA and the Indonesian question; later on (in 1980) he summarized its contents in a magazine article. Additionally, there are articles by Bank, Poeze and Van 't Veer. Former prime minister Drees reviewed government policy towards the Indies in two articles (1961, 1972). Also of interest are writings by and about prominent social-democrats such as Drees, Schermerhorn, Van der Goes van Naters, Palar and Goedhart.

Katholieke Volkspartij (KVP). Since the appearance of Bank's voluminous dissertation *Katholieken en de Indonesische revolutie* (1983), the KVP has been the most thoroughly studied of all parties concerning the Indonesian question. The author describes how the party with the least outspoken colonial tradition came to decide decolonization policy in the last phase of the conflict. Under Romme's leadership the KVP favoured Indonesian independence permeated by Dutch conditions and by continued ties with the motherland in a Dutch-Indonesian Union. The Catholics who opposed decolonization united in the Voorlopig Katholiek Comité van Actie, led by the former Minister of Colonies Welter. Bank's study not only concerns party-political aspects, but also the attitude of the Roman Catholic Church and its leaders in the Netherlands and Indonesia. Apart from Bank's dissertation, there are several theses on the KVP (for example, H.L. Hendrix 1976). Furthermore, the role of a number of prominent Catholic politicians was studied, including Maas (1982) on Sassen and Gase (1986) on Beel. Bosmans (1991-) is currently at work on Romme's biography, and Giebels' Beel biography was published in 1995.

Anti-Revolutionaire Partij (ARP). The orthodox Protestant ARP did not participate in government in the years 1945-1949 and resisted decolonization. In *Om de erfenis van Colijn* (1980), D. Bosscher describes post-war party history under Schouten's leadership, giving much attention to the Indonesian issue. The author wrote his thesis on this subject (1974). Books by the former prime minister Gerbrandy (1950, 1951), imbued with a conservative spirit, were already discussed earlier.

Christelijk-Historische Unie (CHU). The Protestant CHU, too, was oppositional (until 1948) but exhibited a less-closed front than the ARP. Part of the party in the Second Chamber, including the political leader Tilanus, voted for the transfer of sovereignty. The conservative Gerretson opposed it for constitutional reasons. The controversy within the party, known as 'Tilanus contra Gerretson', is discussed in two theses written on the CHU and the Indonesian question, by H. Verheijen (1976) and by A.B.L. de Jonge (1980).

Volkspartij voor Vrijheid en Democratie (VVD). Initially, the liberals of the VVD opposed 'East Indies policy', but beginning in 1948 the party supported the government's position. Theses on the VVD and other Dutch liberals in connection with the Indonesian question were written by Ria Bargeman (1976), C. van Geel (1989) and A. Nabbe (1989). A prominent liberal politician, Minister of Foreign Affairs D.U. Stikker, wrote an autobiography (1966) and further was the subject of a number of publications, of which the dissertation by M.F. Westers (1988) is most detailed.

In conclusion, two small parties will be mentioned which, although from totally different backgrounds, both rejected the policy of the government. The *Communistische Partij van Nederland* (CPN) had a strong anti-colonial tradition and wanted Indonesia to become independent as soon as possible. The viewpoint of the party has never been thoroughly researched because the archives were sealed until recently; a biased book was written by J. Morriën, *Indonesië los van Holland* (1982). The orthodox Protestant *Staatkundig Gereformeerde Partij* (SGP) wished to hold the Indies at any cost, in order that the Netherlands could continue its historic and God-given task of ruling and civilizing overseas possessions. M.N. de Visser (1987) wrote an interesting and informative thesis on the conservative viewpoints of the SGP and its adherents.

h. International aspects

Foreign policy of the Republik Indonesia - Indonesian authors. The first extensive publication on foreign affairs is by Mohammad Moein, *Sistem penjelenggaraan perdjoangan diplomasi dan politik luar negeri* (1951); the revolution, however, is dealt with only marginally. Mohammad Bondan's *Genderang Proklamasi di luar negeri* (1971), on republicans abroad during the revolution, makes a more significant contribution. Anak Agung Gde Agung, former prime minister of the federal state of East Indonesia, and later a prominent diplomat of the Republik Indonesia, is the author of an overview work, *Twenty years of Indonesian foreign policy, 1945-1965* (1973). A unique aspect of foreign relations is treated by M. Zein Hassan in *Diplomasi revolusi di luar negeri* (1980), which concerns the role of republican students in the Middle East. The first history of the republican Ministry of Foreign Affairs was written by M. Wongsodirdjo (1955).

Several publications by Hatta and Roeslan Abdulgani devote attention to foreign policy in the period 1945-1949. The establishment of relations with foreign countries was of great importance to the young Republic in its striving for acknowledgement. In 1954 a selection was published of the work of H. Agus Salim, Minister of Foreign Affairs during the revolution. In addition, a number of biographies have been dedicated to him.

Foreign policy of the Republik Indonesia - other authors. Non-Indonesian authors have also devoted a fair amount of attention to republican foreign policy. Much is also found in general overviews on this aspect of the independence struggle, which became a hot issue in negotiations with the Dutch. In his thesis (1981), J. van der Werff describes the tension between the two countries on this particular point, which was one reason for the First Police Action. In 1948, new problems arose when the Republic established consular relations with the Soviet Union, an incident known as the 'Suripno affair' (see B. van de Sande 1984).

Regarding work from Anglo-Saxon authors, we first mention Robert W. Harper, who in his dissertation (American University, Washington DC, 1957) gives lavish attention to republican foreign policy during the revolution. Reinhardt (1971) and Leifer (1983) devote a chapter to this subject as well. Several studies on Indonesian foreign relations also stem from the former socialist countries: the Soviet author V.I. Gidaspov (1970) wrote exclusively on the revolution (unfortunately his study is not available; see Gidaspov's article on the historiography of Indonesian foreign policy, 1974). The Czech author M. Jankovec (1966) deals with the period 1945-1955; the revolution receives special consideration, and a chapter on the West Irian issue is also included. A study by the Indian author Nagarajan (1973) discusses the period 1956-1962, which mainly addresses the West Irian question.

Great Britain. In 1945 and 1946, the British had considerable involvement in Indonesia, especially since British (British-Indian) soldiers took over command from the Japanese in Sumatra and Java. As a consequence, much literature concerns military affairs; Commander-in-chief Mountbatten also receives much consideration. Writings also treat other aspects of British involvement, for instance their mediatory role between the Dutch and the Republic. Here we mention three important dissertations: S.M. Smith (1978) on British and Dutch foreign policy in the period 1945-1963; S.H. Drummond (1979) on British involvement in Indonesia during the same era; and C.W. Squire (1979) on Britain and Indonesia during the first year of the revolution. Other great powers are also treated in Oey Hong Lee's study (1981) on the intricacies of diplomacy concerning the Indonesian question. J.J.P. de Jong pays much attention to British policy in his dissertation *Diplomatie of strijd* (1988). The Siauw Giap wrote a thesis on the response of the British press to the Indonesian question (1955) as a sequel to Boas's booklet (1946).

Australia. Even before 1945, there was already much sympathy with the Indonesian nationalists' strive for freedom in Australia. Beverley Male's thesis (1965) and an article by Rupert Lockwood (1970) concern Indonesian nationalists in Australia during the Second World War and thereafter.

Further, in general writings on Australia's role during the War, chapters are found on the situation in Indonesia, especially concerning the eastern parts which were liberated by Australian troops (Wigmore 1957; Long 1963, 1973). The Australian military presence in South Sulawesi in 1945 is treated by A. Reid (1986). The most important study to correlate Australian policy and the Indonesian revolution is by Margaret George (1973, 1980), which was also translated into Indonesian. In *Black Armada* (1982), Rupert Lockwood treats the Australian trade unions' support of the Indonesian independence struggle, particularly as concerns the 'wharfies'.

The Indonesian (and West Irian) question is also dealt with in works that treat Australian foreign policy in a wider context (Casey 1954, A. Watt 1967). Recently, a source publication concerning Australia and the Indonesian revolution appeared, edited by Philip Dorling (1994); two more volumes will follow. In this publication, the communications of the Australian mediator Richard Kirby assume an important place. Kirby's biography was written by Blanche d'Alpuget (1977). Finally, we note two studies dealing with Australian-Indonesian relations by Indonesians: M. Asal Siman-djuntak (1963), who discusses the years 1947-1949 in his University of Chicago thesis, and Hilman Adil (1973), who deals with the years 1945-1962 in his Leiden dissertation.

United States of America. Historically, the United States were considered an anti-imperialistic power, aiming at the elimination of the European colonial empires, especially after the Second World War. Initially the United States kept neutral in the Indonesian question, but after the Madiun affair (September 1948) it became clear that the republican government was able to suppress the communist threat under its own force. After that time the United States pressed the Netherlands for a speedy decolonization. Several studies were made on US policy before and during the war concerning the future of the East Indies: Buisman (1967), Wolthuis (1968), Sullivan (1969) and Zonderwijk (1982). Those works specifically concerned with the revolution are the dissertations by Nolton (1972), Leupold (1976) and McMahon (1977, 1982). Gerlof Homan wrote a number of articles on divergent aspects of US involvement, including military and economic. Other studies concern Southeast Asia as a whole, such as those of Ohn (1967) and Hess (1987); American interest in the region can also be seen as an effort to 'contain' communism. American-Indonesian relations were also dealt with outside of the United States; these works include the German dissertation of Steltzer (1965) treating the years 1940-1949 and a study of the Czech Rudolf Mràzek (1978) on American 'intervention' in the Indonesian military. There are also some shorter writings by Dutch and other authors: Droog-lever (1981), Zwitzer (1982) and Van der Eng (1988); this last writer deals

with the American threat to stop Marshall aid if the Netherlands did not
speedily decolonize. Schiethart wrote his thesis (1985) on American-Dutch
relations in the years 1947-1949. Only one Indonesian writer is known to
have discussed more fully the relations of the United States and Indonesia
after 1945: Tribuana Said (1983). Ultimately, the United States played such a
prominent part in the Indonesian question that it receives attention in
almost every general survey. Thus, this kind of literature can also be
consulted.

Soviet Union. Concerning Soviet writings on the Indonesian revolution,
the Soviet author Sholmov (1966, not consulted), who describes Soviet-
Indonesian relations in the period 1945-1963, deserves first mention. The
same subject is dealt with by Aleshin (1963). A number of studies con-
centrate on the efforts of Soviet republics (Russia and the Ukraine) to win
United Nations' recognition for the young Indonesian republic, such as the
works by Voina (1949) and Aleshin (1978, Indonesian translation).
Vaschinskii (1965) deals with relations between Indonesia and the socialist
countries of Eastern Europe.

   As for non-Soviet authors, Ruth McVey wrote an important essay on the
Soviet view of the Indonesian revolution (1957); its bibliography also
contains many contemporary titles on the subject. Earlier, in 1954, McVey
had written about the ties between the PKI and the Communist Party of the
Soviet Union. In his dissertation (1966), R.M. Rodes analyses Soviet policy
regarding independence movements in South and Southeast Asia in the
years 1945-1952; Sylvia W. Fain (1971) also handles the same subject. One
Indonesian author should also be mentioned here: J. Soedjati, who in his
London dissertation (1983) dealt with Soviet-Indonesian relations, giving
some attention to the revolution, but concentrating principally on the West
Irian issue.

India/Pakistan. The independence of British India in 1947 was important to
the morale of the Indonesian freedom fighters; conversely, (British) Indians
showed solidarity with the Republic. Several Indian authors wrote about
Indian-Indonesian relations in the years 1945-1949 in shorter writings:
B. Prasad (1977), V. Suryanarayan (1981) and S. Gupta (1984). Others concerned themselves with broader subjects, of which the Indonesian revolution formed a part, such as the recognition policy of independent India
towards other Asian countries: Satya Swarup (1956) and B.N. Mehrish
(1964). Of the non-Indian authors, we mention here Constance Freydig who
wrote a thesis (1954) on India and Indonesian foreign policy, and Angelika
Weber (1988). G.M. van Beek's thesis (1988) is also of note; it deals with
relations between India and the Netherlands in the years 1946-1960, with a

complete treatment of the Indonesian revolution. A distinctive place is held by writings related to the British-Indian soldiers who took over from the Japanese in the western parts of the archipelago. See the index entry 'British Forces/Troops'.

Other countries. For entries on other countries which had some degree of involvement with the Indonesian question, such as Belgium or the Arab states, see the index of geographical names.

United Nations. The United Nations had intervened in the Dutch-Indonesian conflict since the time of the First Police Action (July 1947). The UN played a mediating role and pressed the parties to resume negotiations. A Committee of Good Offices was installed to bring the parties closer; the Indonesian question was on the Security Council's agenda repeatedly. Furthermore, 'Indonesia' was the first case in which the young organization could prove itself. Publications of the UN on the Indonesian question are chiefly contemporary; in the early 1950s a few more appeared, such as on the Round Table Conference. The first independent analysis of the UN's role is to be found in Kattenburg's dissertation (1949) which was reviewed earlier. This was soon followed by J. Foster Collins (1950) and Henderson (1954); Henderson's review also contains a bibliography of relevant UN publications. The standard work on UN involvement remains A.M. Taylor (1960). Other important monographs are by T.L. Wilborn (1965), concerning the period 1945-1961, and by D.W. Wainhouse (1966), on UN peace observation, with a great deal of attention to the Indonesian issue. George A. Tune (1977) examined the role of the United Nations in the decolonization process in South and Southeast Asia.

There are several writings on the positions of individual countries in UN discussions concerning the Indonesian issue: Jessup (1974) and Karns (1975) on the United States; Hudson (1970) on Australia; Voina (1949) and Aleshin (1978) on the Soviet Union. The writings of Indonesian authors on this matter are mainly theses; an exception is Adrianatakesuma's congress paper (1970). Hoenderkamp (1973) compiled a modest bibliography on UN involvement.

i. Biographies

Indonesian authors. In Indonesia, the biography is a well-developed genre and numerous titles have appeared on persons who played an important role in the revolution. Autobiographies and memoirs are also abundant. A popular genre is the collective biography, containing short descriptions of several persons in one volume. Official, government-edited series also exist, such as the *Seri pahlawan nasional* from the Ministry of Education and

Culture. Indonesian national historiography retains a prominent place for individuals who are considered model patriots. The most illustrious characters are honoured after their death with the title *pahlawan* (hero), bestowed on them by presidential decree for extraordinary merits (regarding this phenomenon, see Schreiner-Brauch 1993).

There are many biographies of the 'Father of the Fatherland' Soekarno, who was, however, not recognized as a *pahlawan* until 1990. Following the failed coup of 1965, his person was shrouded in biographical silence, until he was 'rediscovered' in the 1980s. Recently, several biographies have been published, including careful treatment of the last years of his presidency, characterized by *konfrontasi* policy and increasing influence of the PKI. Soekarno's role in the 'physical revolution' is praised: while cabinets came and went, his authority guaranteed the continuity of the Republic.

Many other prominent politicians have also been honoured with biographies: Hatta, Sjahrir, Yamin, Roem, Sunario, H. Agus Salim, Sartono, R.W. Mongisidi, Adam Malik, and others. Persons with a pronounced religious background include Hamka (Muslim), Mgr Sugyopranoto (Roman Catholic) and Leimena (Protestant). In the cultural sphere, prominent figures are Ki Hajar Dewantara, the first republican Minister of Education, and St. Takdir Alisjahbana, cultural philosopher and propagator of the national language, Bahasa Indonesia. From the world of science come Professor Supomo, a jurist and expert on Indonesian constitutional law, but also a minister of justice, and Professor Yohannes, a physician and politician.

The lives of persons who, at one time or another, resisted republican authority are also described: Sjafruddin Prawiranegara, who played an important role during the revolution and was a leader of the PRRI-Permesta rebellion in the 1950s; Daud Beureueh, an Acehnese who wanted to break away from Jakarta; and Darul Islam leaders Kartosuwirjo and Kahar Muzakkar. Publications are still regularly appearing on the remarkable figure of Tan Malaka. This abundance of literature is not the case, however, concerning the former PKI leadership. No biography of Muso is found (although his role in the Madiun rebellion is referred to in many publications), nor of D.N. Aidit, PKI foreman in the 1950s and 1960s. Evidently, this matter is still too sensitive. A separate category is formed by the biographies of military men; these are treated elsewhere (see Military writings).

Indonesian authors themselves paid little attention to the biographies of non-Indonesians, although one exception is Westerling, who serves as an example of the cruelty of Dutch colonialism.

Autobiographies and memoirs. This category is difficult to define, because much autobiographical material is concealed in general surveys, military writings and *belles-lettres*. In the 1940s, memoirs appeared by Chinese authors concerning the Japanese occupation. Adam Malik published his memoirs on the events around the Proclamation. Later, this subject returned in several autobiographies (A. Subardjo Djojoadirsurjo, M. Hatta and others). Other important events, such as the Battle of Surabaya, also serve as a framework for personal memoirs (an example is Roeslan Abdulgani). In addition, some memoirs encompass an entire lifetime. Almost every leading politician has left behind autobiographical notes: Soekarno, Soeharto, Hatta, Roem, Natsir, Ali Sastroamidjojo, Adam Malik and Abu Hanifah (but not Sjahrir). Many military men also wrote their memoirs, as well as persons with religious and cultural backgrounds.

Though memoirs were already appearing in the 1940s, a peak occurred in the 1970s and 1980s. This is partly a consequence of the growth of Indonesian publishing in general, but is also related to the fact that many who witnessed the revolution had reached an age which invites contemplation. Further, institutions played a stimulating role, as in the case of the autobiographical project of the Ministry of Social Affairs (ca. 1986), led by Soekandarno and others. This project, however, especially concerned the pre-war nationalist movement.

Dutch and other authors. In the Netherlands, biographies are scarcer than in Indonesia. This is also evident from the relatively modest number of biographies concerning persons who were involved in the decolonization of Indonesia. Most titles are about politicians such as Schermerhorn, Drees, Stikker and Romme, whose careers as a whole are described, within which the Indonesian question forms just one aspect. Writings specifically addressing the Indonesian aspect were mostly magazine articles. Only one Dutch monograph has appeared concerning the crucial figure Van Mook, *De laatste landvoogd* (1982) by J.C. Bijkerk, a journalistic work.

Published Dutch writings on Indonesian major characters were also modest and consisted mainly of magazine articles; one concise monograph appeared on Soekarno (Van 't Veer 1964). A number of theses were devoted to Indonesians: Van Tuijl (1985) on Palar and Dingemans (1989) on Sultan Hamid II. Further, H.G. Schulte Nordholt (1959) wrote an extensive article on Hatta. Poeze's biography of Tan Malaka (1976) goes no further than 1945.

Other Western authors concerned themselves almost exclusively with Indonesian characters. An exception is Yong Mun Cheong's monograph (1982) on Van Mook and his policy. Several studies have appeared on Soekarno (Adams, Dahm, Legge, Palmier, Penders, Tarling), and around the 1980s, two monographs were devoted to Hatta (Rose, Siebeck). Recently, a biography of Sjahrir also appeared (Mrázek 1994).

Autobiographies and memoirs. Several prominent Dutch politicians wrote their memoirs: Schermerhorn, Drees, Van der Goes van Naters,

Jonkman, Van Kleffens, Stikker and others. High civil servants also wrote about their experiences during the time of the Indonesian question: Jaquet, Van Baal, Visser. The volume *Besturen overzee* (1977), edited by Van der Wal, contains memoirs of civil servants. Numerous military men also described their involvement in the Indies: high officers such as Kruls and Helfrich, but conscripts too, told about their tropical experiences, sometimes in a romanticized form. There are also journalistic accounts: Fabricius and Ritman. It can generally be said that autobiographies and memoirs provide a richer source of information than 'genuine' biographies.

Of the Anglo-Saxon authors, three are mentioned: John Coast, a British who fought at the Republic's side; K'tut Tantri (Sue Manx) who assisted Sutomo, 'Bung Tomo', with his revolutionary radio broadcasts in Surabaya; and Tim Carew, a British soldier who witnessed the early revolution.

There are also numerous memoirs of Japanese soldiers on the occupation and the revolutionary period. Most of these writings are in Japanese and therefore of limited access. The memoirs of Shigetada Nishijima on the Proclamation, and of Fusayama Takao on North Sumatra in the early revolution were translated into English.

j. Religious aspects

Islam - Indonesian authors. From the survey of contemporary writings it became clear that a considerable amount had an Islamic background. 'Islam and revolution' remained an important subject, even after 1950. First, there are writings on the general or twentieth-century history of Islam in Indonesia (T. Ismail Ja'kub 1956, Chaidir Anwar 1972). In addition, a number of writings are devoted to the revolution itself, often regionally specialized, such as those concerning Aceh, where Islam played an important role in resisting the return to colonial authority (Nazaruddin Sjamsuddin 1974, M. Isa Sulaiman 1985).

The debate on the fundamentals of the Indonesian state and on the Jakarta Charter, Piagam Jakarta, an addition to the Constitution prescribing Muslims to obey Islamic law, was a 'hot issue'. Several studies were made on the genesis of Piagam Jakarta; the most detailed is by H. Endang Anshari (1981). Other writings were dedicated to Darul Islam and its leaders S.M. Kartosuwirjo and Kahar Muzakkar. The DI/TII rebellion had started in the 1940s in West Java and lasted until the 1960s, when it was definitively suppressed.

Many monographs were written on the Islamic political parties Masyumi and Nahdatul Ulama (for instance that by Deliar Noer 1987), and Islamic militias such as Hizbullah. Prominent Muslims Hamka, H. Agus Salim, M. Natsir, M. Roem and others were honoured with biographies.

Islam - other authors. First to be mentioned here is Harry Benda's well-known study *The crescent and the rising sun* (1958) on Indonesian Islam during the Japanese occupation (see on this subject also Rodney de Bruin 1982). Concerning Islam under the Republic, studies were made by Alers (1956), Boland (1971), Ionova (1972) and Samson (1972). Dutch Islam policy after 1945, which until recently had only received attention in a few articles by Van Nieuwenhuyze, has now been thoroughly analysed in the SOAS dissertation by Ismail Göksoy (1991). Darul Islam was studied in three extensive monographs: Jackson (1971), C. van Dijk (1982) and Dengel (1986); the last study chiefly concerns Kartosuwirjo's leadership.

Christianity - Indonesian authors. In general works such as *Sejarah Gereja Katolik Indonesia* (1973-), much attention is paid to the revolutionary period. The contribution of Simatupang and others to the volume *Partisipasi Kristen dalam nation building di Indonesia* (1968) specifically concerns the revolution, emphasizing the Christians' role in contrast to that of Muslims and seculars in the freedom struggle. The volume referred to, edited by W.B. Sidjabat, makes obvious that the discussion on the fundamentals of the Indonesian state was of concern to Christians too. The editor Sidjabat took his doctoral degree in 1960 at Princeton University with a dissertation on religious tolerance related to the Indonesian Constitution. Further, biographies of prominent Christians are of significance, such as of Mgr Sugiyopranoto (proclaimed a *pahlawan*), the Catholic politician Kasimo and Leimena, who all chose the republican side.

Christianity - other authors. The attitude of Roman Catholics in the Netherlands and Indonesia was given attention in Bank's dissertation (1983). The Protestant churches in the Netherlands as well as their missions were examined in several monographs, including Tiat Han Tan (1967) and Scharffenorth (1984). The viewpoint of Indonesian Christians was studied by Webb (1978), who was primarily concerned with their political parties, and Haire (1981), who focused on the church of Halmahera. Biographies were written by Van Leeuwen (1959) on Kraemer and by Verkuyl (1977) on Leimena. Kraemer as well as Verkuyl were prominent Protestant missionaries who took a progressive standpoint on the Indonesian question. Finally, we mention the study by M.P.M. Muskens (Pipitseputra) on the Catholic contribution to Indonesian national identity (1969), which considers the revolutionary period as well.

k. Socio-economic aspects

Indonesian authors. Publications which detail the economic aspects of the revolution are rather scarce. Most information is to be found in general works such as *Sejarah Nasional Indonesia*. Sonda (1963) describes the development of Indonesian economy in the period 1800-1950, although the revolution is only covered in the closing phase. Sutjiatiningsih (1979, not consulted) goes into more detail in her notes on the economy of the revolution. Commemorative writings of the Bank Nasional Indonesia and other banks contain passages on the years 1945-1949. Margono Djojohadikusumo (1978) wrote a small article on the role of foreign banks during the revolution. Republican currency was considered by Natasuwarna (1979) and in the illustrated jubilee volume *Rupiah di tengah rentang sejarah* (1991), an edition of the Ministry of Finance. Halilintars wrote the biography of businessman B.R. Motik (1986), and H.M. Sulchan, a successful entrepreneur, tells his story 'from newsboy to millionaire' in an autobiography (1979) devoting much attention to the revolution.

The term 'social revolution' (*revolusi sosial*) is also used by Indonesian authors, but few writings are specifically dedicated to it; two instances are works by M. Said (1973) and Hersry (1983) on East Sumatra. The aspect 'social revolution' implicitly arises from numerous publications on the *pemuda*, who launched attacks on the establishment in several places. Most volumes of the series *Sejarah sosial [...]* (1983-), edited by the Ministry of Social Affairs, also discuss the revolution. Finally, a significant paper was written by Jang Aisjah Muttalib and Sudjarwo (1982) on the homeless and vagabonds in Yogyakarta during the revolution, a first attempt to reveal the fringe elements of society.

Other authors. The second volume of D.H. Burger's survey of the socio-economic history of Indonesia (1975) deals with the revolution. The detailed study by J.O. Sutter (1959) on the 'Indonesianizaton' of politics and economy in the period 1940-1955 is also significant. Webb (1986) describes the socio-economic history of Nusatenggara (the Southeastern islands) over the years 1930-1975. A relatively large amount of attention is spent on the rubber and tobacco estates of East Sumatra: in Pelzer (1978, 1982) and Stoler (1985); Dutch authors who wrote on this subject were Dootjes (1952), Biemans and Kleingeld (1985, 1986) and Van Doorn and Hendrix (1987). H. Baudet wrote several articles, sometimes in cooperation with others, on the economic relations between the Netherlands and Indonesia before, during and after decolonization. In 1983, he and M. Fennema edited the volume *Het Neder-lands belang bij Indië*. An Anglo-Saxon author who dealt with the economic aspect of the revolution in several papers is Robert Cribb, who in 1984 took his doctoral degree on revolutionary Jakarta. Cribb wrote on the currency (1981) and on the opium trade (1988) of the Republic; at present, he is studying the financial aspects of the revolution. The Republic earned its foreign currency not only with the opium trade, but also through rice export, as detailed by Anderson (1966). Banking in Indonesia since World War II was described in the Tilburg dissertation of Scheffer (1951). As for 'social revolution', there are several important, regionally-specialized studies by Anglo-Saxon authors which were reviewed previously (see Regional and local aspects).

The West Irian question

At the Round Table Conference it was agreed that a Dutch-Indonesian commission would present proposals for the future status of West Irian (West New Guinea) within a year. However, the commission could not reach agreement and it was not until 1963 that West Irian, following a year of UN interim government, was transferred to Indonesia. The conflict escalated to such a degree that diplomatic relations between the Netherlands and Indonesia were broken off for some time.

Indonesian authors. Strong ideological tensions are apparent in Indonesian publications on the West Irian dispute, which appeal some times to history and at other times to international law. In *Perdjoangkan Irian Barat* (1955), E. Katoppo established that politically Irian had already belonged to the Indonesian archipelago for centuries. The Sultan of Tidore claimed the north coast of the island, a claim that was later taken over by the Dutch. Consequently, the Dutch effort to give Irian a different political future than the rest of the archipelago was inappropriate. In 1956, Muhammad Yamin published *Pembebasan Irian Barat atas dasar Proklamasi*, in which he, like Katoppo, notes the historical arguments for Irian's joining the Republic. However, he also stresses the meaning of the Proclamation in this respect, as this great event had given new life to the sovereignty of the peoples of the archipelago, so long oppressed by the Dutch. Yamin also makes a number of recommendations in an address to the Indonesian government concerning Irian's liberation. He ends with a verbose reflection on the Irian resolutions taken by the Kongres Rakyat Indonesia in 1955.

The Irian dispute was actuated by numerous speeches, partly within the framework of the United Nations. Included in these is a long oration by Minister of Foreign Affairs Soebandrio, *West Irian* (1961), and a volume of speeches by Soekarno, *Pembebasan Irian Barat* (1962), made in Indonesia and abroad (Tokyo, Belgrade), which often bear a political-ideological tendency.

As for the military aspect, M. Cholil offers a useful factual survey in *Sedjarah operasi pembebasan Irian Barat* (1971). The endeavour to liberate Irian from the Dutch, if necessary by military means, arose from Soekarno's 1961 triple command to the Indonesian people, Tri Komando Rakyat (TRIKORA). It consisted of a. rejection of the 'puppet government' which the Dutch wanted to plant in West Irian, ostensibly for the benefit of the Papuans; b. bringing West Irian under Indonesian authority; c. preparation of a general mobilization to fight for freedom and unity (pp. 29-30). In connection with the third point of TRIKORA volunteers were recruited, and a Komando Mandala was established with Makasar as headquarters. All branches of the armed forces participated in this Komando Mandala, which stood under Soeharto's command and which participated in raids on the Irian coast in 1962. A devoted volunteer for Irian's liberation was J. Herlina, who was already active before the Komando came into being. Herlina has written extensively on her experiences in *Pending emas* (1985), a romanticized narration of the guerrilla movement. At present, she is revered as the most prominent fighter for Irian's freedom.

Following Irian's transfer to Indonesia, many writings were dedicated to the development of this remote territory, such as *Buatlah Irian Barat satu zamrud jang indah* (1964), edited by the Ministry of Information. Besides a number of speeches, the volume contains schemes for the administration of the region and plans for the founding of Cenderawasih University at Kotabaru (formerly Hollandia).

Of the later writings on the West Irian issue, we mention the extensive survey *Api perjuangan pembebasan Irian Barat* (1986) dealing with all aspects, from military operations to development plans.

Dutch authors. In his dissertation on the West Irian issue (1984), P.B.R. de Geus mentions three considerations of the Dutch for desiring to keep this remote part of the archipelago under Dutch rule for the time: a. the region's importance as a colonization territory, especially for Indo-Europeans; b. the realization of political self-determination of the Papuans, following their reaching a sufficient level of development; c. the region's usefulness as a barrier against communism, in connection with the Cold War. According to De Geus, at the Round Table Conference certain 'uncomfortable feelings' felt by the Dutch at the conclusion of colonial rule in the East played a role. The colonization argument was hardly used at the time. Yet, this 'New Guinea longing' (Tutupoly 1981) of the Indo-Europeans was the oldest consideration to treat the region differently. The idea of colonization had come into existence in the 1920s; attempts to accomplish this, however, had failed. After 1945 the idea gained new life, caused by the difficult position of the Indo-Europeans. A fervent plea for colonization was made in 1950 by K. Snijtsheuvel in his brochure *De Indische Nederlanders staan voor een gigantische taak.* A colonization in which pioneers from the Netherlands would also be involved was considered in plans for the economic development of the region. In 1947, the Department of Social Affairs at Batavia published a *Nota inzake Nieuw-Guinea* concerning the 'opening up' of the area. Studies on the possibilities for economic development were especially numerous after 1950, when it became evident that West Irian would remain under Dutch rule for the time being. Several dissertations were dedicated to this subject: Stratenus (1952), Leslie-Miller (1952) and Cannegieter (1959). In the years 1953-1954, an extensive collective work on West Irian was published under the editorship of W.C. Klein. Most attention is directed at the economic aspect, but history, ethnology and politics are also considered. Klein's standard work was published by the Staatsuitgeverij, proof that the Dutch government took an interest in the area's development. Another confirmation of government concern was the Pieters Commission, in which officials of several departments participated; its report, called *Toekomstige ontwikkeling van Nieuw-Guinea* was published in 1953. Various periodicals were dedicated to the development of the area: *Nederlands Nieuw-Guinea*, *Nieuw-Guinea Studiën* and *Mededelingen van het Nieuw-Guinea Instituut*. The contents of these periodicals have not been included in this bibliography.

Apart from the purely economic aspect, the development of the Papua population received ample attention in the writings of J.P.K. van Eechoud, Resident of New Guinea from 1944 to 1950. In *Vergeten aarde* (1951), Van Eechoud states that 'the education of the Papuan must extend itself to all fields of life' (p. 208). The spread of education, with the help of Catholic and Protestant missions, must have been an important objective of the Dutch government. In 1961, the education of the political conscience of the Papuans led to elections and to the establishment of the New Guinea Council, a representative body which, as a consequence of the end of Dutch rule, existed for only a short period (Wolters 1986). At the occasion of the Council's instalment, Dutch authorities published brochures with cheerful titles such as *Papoea's bouwen aan hun toekomst*. There was also an awareness that the international community was watching; therefore a number of brochures were published in English, for example, *The New Guinea Council opened* (1961).

As the conflict between the Netherlands and Indonesia over West Irian's future escalated, international concern grew accordingly. Discussions within the framework of the Netherlands-Indonesian Union had reached a deadlock in the 1950s. The United Nation's attention was drawn to the territory as Indonesia repeatedly put the conflict on the agenda of the General Assembly. Every year the Dutch gave an account of their rule of West Irian to the United Nations: *Rapport inzake Nederlands Nieuw-Guinea* (1951-1962), and *Report on Netherlands New Guinea* (1951-1962). In addition, the volumes *Statements met betrekking tot Nederlands Nieuw-Guinea* (1959) and *Regeringsuitspraken* (1961) appeared, giving a survey of the Dutch government's viewpoints.

In addition to the government, many other authors wrote about the conflict; a few outstanding authors are mentioned here. One significant work is F.J.F.M. Duynstee's *Nieuw-Guinea als schakel tussen Nederland en Indonesië* (1961). Duynstee, a prominent member of the Katholieke Volkspartij (KVP; also the party of the Dutch Minister of Foreign Affairs), pleads for a transfer to Indonesia, because he fears the last 'link' connecting the Netherlands and Indonesia will break in an armed conflict, and that cooperation to develop the Papuans will no longer be possible. A diversion of the threat of war and a restoration of diplomatic relations were conditional for the preservation of Dutch influence in the East. Besides, the danger existed that Indonesia would be driven into the arms of communism in case of an armed conflict. This last argument arose from reasoning contrary to that of conservative circles, namely that New Guinea must be kept for the Netherlands as a stronghold against communism, which was progressing both within and outside Indonesia. This reasoning can be found, for instance, in a brochure by G. Goossens, *Nieuw-Guinea, de Koude Oorlog en de Anti-Revolutionaire Partij* (1962). The author was concerned about the alteration in the standpoint of the ARP, which formerly had resisted the transfer to Indonesia (Berghuis 1962, Kaan 1983).

As far back as the 1950s, voices arose to the left of the Dutch political spectrum supporting the dissociation of New Guinea from the Netherlands. Here we point out the (still very cautious) report by the Wiardi Beckman Stichting, the research bureau of the social-democratic Partij van de Arbeid (PvdA), *Het vraagstuk Nieuw-Guinea* (1958). The report objects to the government's standpoint, and insists on a policy resulting in the resolution of the New Guinea question 'as a Dutch problem'. Transfer to Indonesia is not excluded in principle, but is considered undesirable 'as long as no lasting changes have occurred in Indonesia's political stature and its economic and political capacities' (p. 16). Guarantees for the development of the Papuan population were necessary; for the time being, development should take place under the aegis of the South Pacific Commission. In this sense, the PvdA commission was pleading for an international solution. The administration of the area by the United Nations, also an international solution, was advocated by J. de Kadt in *De huidige stand van het Nieuw-Guinea vraagstuk* (1960), published by the PvdA. The Dutch communist party (CPN) pleaded for an unconditional transfer, although its affection for Soekarno and Hatta had waned since the 1948 Madiun rebellion. In any case, Dutch colonialism in the East should end as soon as possible; see the articles by H. de Vries (pseudonym of J. Morriën) in *Politiek en Cultuur* (1953, 1956, 1958). The CPN also resisted sending troops when the conflict sharpened: see *Geen oorlog om Nieuw-Guinea* (1962).

The standpoint of the General Synod of the Nederlands Hervormde Kerk is of interest: as early as 1956, the Synod urged the government to change its New Guinea policy. This *Oproep van de Generale Synode* led to agitation in Protestant circles; a Landelijk Comité was established, which bundled its objections against the Synod's call in a brochure, *Kerk en Nieuw-Guinea* (1956). A. Teeuw, a professor of Indonesian languages at Leiden University, pleaded in his brochure *Het conflict met Indonesië als spiegel voor Neder-land* (1956) for a speedy transfer to Indonesia, because this country had 'very evident and strong rights' (p. 12). He considers the argument of 'historical continuity' the only one relevant: the Dutch East Indies had been ruled as a single state; therefore, why amputate a part when it came to transferring sovereignty? Teeuw also participated in a study commission reporting in 1961 under the title *De kwestie Nieuw-Guinea*, in which a plea is made for conveyance to Indonesia. A volume of essays, *Terdege ter discussie*, had appeared in 1958, in which the contributors (among whom was Reverend J. Verkuyl) urged for a change in government policy. In spite of these and other 'dissident' voices, the Dutch government held on to West Irian until the early 1960s. In 1962 the Netherlands, under strong pressure from the United States, yielded administration to the United Nations; a year later, the area was annexed to Indonesia.

When in 1960 diplomatic relations were broken off between the Nether-lands and Indonesia, war threatened for a short time. Several writings had previously been dedicated to the military aspect of the Dutch presence in West Irian. The Dutch navy (Koninklijke Marine) and its marine corps (Korps Mariniers) were principally involved in New Guinea's defence; when the conflict escalated, action was taken against Indonesian infiltrators. J. Hokke's article on the Dutch navy in New Guinea, published in *Marine-blad* (1950) is quite extensive. Later, a series of articles by J.J.M. Antonietti appeared in *De Militaire Spectator*, concerning New Guinea's defence, for instance, on the formation of a Papua corps (1959). Because of growing tension, less was published on military affairs; after the end of the conflict, the number of publications again rose.

Later Dutch writings. After West Irian's transfer to the United Nations, two more studies on Dutch development work appeared: Lagerberg (1962) and Bakker (1965). In his *Jaren van reconstructie*, Kees Lagerberg states that it would take at least one more generation of development workers to set up the projects needed. However, it all turned out differently; the ambitious work of the Dutch remained unfinished. Lagerberg's irritation with the way Jakarta promoted Papuan interests is evident in his *West Irian and Jakarta imperialism* (1981). J.C.M. Bakker's *Strategie van het ontwikkelingswerk* (1965) pays no attention to the political aspect; it is intended to analyse Dutch development policy 'from a greater mental distance' (p. 7) than had been possible previously.

It was not until 1977 that J.G. de Beus illuminated the diplomatic aspects of the conflict. His account is in fact a defence of Dutch policy; he finds it humiliating that the Netherlands had to transfer sovereignty to a dictator (Soekarno) without the population having had the opportunity to express itself concerning its political future. More critical towards Dutch policy is P.B.R. de Geus in his dissertation *De Nieuw-Guinea kwestie* (1984), stating that the Dutch held 'legalistic-moralistic' views, without much under-standing of real power politics. He discerns in Dutch foreign policy the same irrational factors as the 'Dutch American' A. Lijphart had already noted in 1966 (see p. 81). A look behind the scenes of Dutch diplomacy is offered by J.L.R. Huydecoper van Nigtevecht in his *Nieuw-Guinea, het einde van een koloniaal beleid* (1990). At the time, the author was closely involved in the negotiations which ultimately led to the conveyance of West Irian to Indonesia. In the 1950s, Huydecoper was ambassador to Jakarta, thus prov-iding a first-hand account of the development of the Indonesian standpoint.

Several other memoirs of Dutch politicians offer information on Dutch New Guinea policy, such as those by Foreign Minister Luns (Van der Plas 1971). The memoirs by J.V. de Bruyn (1978) and J. van Baal (1986-1989) lay a stronger accent on administration and ethnography. J. Derix's biography of Resident Van Eechoud (1987) and a recent dissertation by S.R. Jaarsma (1990) give information on Dutch development policy. A number of specialized studies were made of the viewpoints of Dutch political parties: see Koole (1979) on the KVP and Coerts (1983) on the ARP. The latter party made, under its leader Bruins Slot, a remarkable turnabout in its policy in favour of a transfer to Indonesia (Kaan 1983).

After the end of the conflict, the military aspect received ample attention in the six-volume series *De Nederlandse strijdkrachten in Nieuw-Guinea* (1964-1989). The series had a limited distribution and included some confi-dential sections. It was edited by the Afdeling Maritieme Historie of the Dutch navy, in cooperation with the historical bureaus of the army and air force. Other militaria deserving mention are *Nieuw-Guinea: de mariniers-kant van het verhaal* (1979) by G.K.R. de Roos and, destined for a wider reading public, *Patrouilleren voor de Papoea's* (1989-1990) by R.E. van Holst Pellekaan and others, describing the exploits of the Dutch navy. Not much was published concerning the Dutch army (Koninklijke Landmacht) in New Guinea, which played a more modest role (see Nortier 1978).

Regarding Dutch New Guinea, memoirs also took the form of novels and short stories. Here we refer to *De balenkraai* (1967) by Aad Nuis, a critical account of a conscript who is convinced of the senselessness of the Dutch presence in this outlying corner of the world; the subtle stories by the diplomat F. Springer, *Bericht uit Hollandia* (1962) and *Zaken overzee* (1978); and a collection of stories by Joop van den Berg, *Een mors huis* (1991).

Other authors. The West Irian question also received attention from Anglo-Saxon authors. Their contemporary writings were principally magazine articles; an exception is the report by Robert C. Bone, *The dynamics of the Western New Guinea problem* (1957, reprinted in 1962). Bone's study was the first in which the Indonesian and Dutch points of view are discussed in depth. Sources were consulted in both the Indonesian and Dutch language, which increases the quality of the investigation, and the author has tried to render the standpoints of both parties objectively.

Shortly after the conflict, the 'Dutch American' sociologist Arend Lijphart earned his doctoral degree at Yale University with *The West New Guinea problem in Dutch domestic politics* (1963); a few years later the study was published as *The trauma of decolonization; The Dutch and West New Guinea* (1966). Lijphart analyses in depth the Dutch arguments for holding onto New Guinea and comes to the surprising conclusion that these were all irrational in character. Lijphart contends that no 'objective' interests, political or economical, were involved. The Dutch concern with the destiny of the Papuans was not sincere; soon after the territory's transfer to the United Nations, interest in the population disappeared. Lijphart's dissection of Dutch society as expressed by political parties, the parliament and many types of pressure groups is very thorough. Understandably, there was much Dutch criticism of Lijphart's pronounced conclusions.

A few other specialized studies on the West Irian question concern the mediatory role of the United States: see Hermanson (n.d.), Bunnell (1969) and McMullen (1981). Australian involvement, too, received ample attention: see Warmenhoven (1965, 1971) and Haupt (1970). Finally, several studies were devoted to the role of the United Nations: see Brown (1975) and Tunnicliff (1984).

The South Moluccan question

On 25 April 1950, the Republic of the South Moluccas (Republik Maluku Selatan, RMS) was proclaimed in Ambon. That same day the parliament of the federal state East Indonesia had dismissed a pro-federal cabinet; it was replaced by a cabinet which intended to merge East Indonesia into a unitary Indonesian state. Part of the population of Ambon and other South Moluccan islands, mostly KNIL soldiers of Moluccan descent, feared that in a unitary state the right to self-determination would fall into the background. The Moluccan KNIL soldiers, who had faithfully served the Dutch colonial authorities, were to be absorbed into the armed forces of the RIS.

Moluccan soldiers who were in Java at the time were prevented by the Indonesian government from returning to Ambon as long as the rebellion lasted. In December 1950, the Court of Justice in The Hague ruled that Moluccan KNIL soldiers on Java could not be carried off to Ambon or any other area reigned by the Republik Indonesia against their will. Consequently, some thousands of Moluccan ex-KNIL soldiers and their families were transported to the Netherlands in the first months of 1951. Thus, the South Moluccan question acquired two aspects: on one side was the rebellion in Ambon itself and the rightfulness of the RMS proclamation, on the other the South Moluccan community in the Netherlands and its problems.

Indonesian authors. Understandably, all Indonesian (republican) authors condemned the revolt in Ambon and rejected the RMS proclamation. In April 1950, a few days after the proclamation, a peace mission was sent to Ambon under J. Leimena, a prominent Protestant leader. In a brochure *The Ambon question* (1950), Leimena states that the RMS proclamation was not based on the will of the South Moluccan population, but was forced upon them under armed pressure by the KNIL troops present in Amboina (p. 38). This view is also found in other Indonesian writings; the most extensive is by Jusuf A. Puar in his *Peristiwa Republik Maluku Selatan* (1956). Apart from a survey of the events in Ambon and an account of the revolt's suppression, the book also contains excerpts from documents of the court-martial against RMS leaders. The second president of the RMS, Dr Soumokil, was involved in resistance in Seram until December 1963. Soumokil's role in the proclamation and the guerrilla movement is described in Agoes Anwar's booklet *Soumokil dan hantjurnja 'RMS'* (1964), published in connection with his death sentence on 25 April 1964. Two other studies place the RMS revolt in an historical perspective: I.O. Nanulaitta's *Timbulnja militarisme Ambon* (1966) is almost entirely dedicated to the earlier history of the Moluccas, while R.Z. Leirissa in his *Maluku dalam perjuangan nasional Indonesia* (1975) devotes ample attention to the revolt. Also of significance are the biographies of Ignatius Slamet Rijadi (1971, 1976), an Indonesian officer who fell in November 1950 in the struggle against the RMS.

RMS authors. The South Moluccans who came to the Netherlands consisted mostly of RMS partisans and their families. In exile, the ideal of a free Ambon was continually propagated. Their best-known leader was undoubtedly J.A. Manusama, president-in-exile of the RMS until 1992. In 1953, Manusama published *Om recht en vrijheid*, in which an account is given of the RMS proclamation and of administration and army organization in

Ambon and other South Moluccan islands. The book also contains the text of the provisional RMS constitution. The author states that the RMS had developed into a democratic state, supported by the majority of the population. In The Hague, the Bureau Zuid-Molukken was established, which edited and distributed several brochures, including *Ambon's strijd tegen de leugens van Djocja* (ca. 1951) by P.W. Lokollo, 'head of the Department of Food Supply of the RMS'. The brochure concerns the legality of the RMS proclamation and the right to self-determination of the South Moluccan people. Another bureau which published brochures and pamphlets was the 'Department of Public Information' of the RMS in Rotterdam. Most publications from this bureau were in English, to draw the attention of the international community to the South Moluccan struggle. An example is by J.P. Nikijuluw, *The forgotten war; An appeal from the RMS* (1950).

In the 1970s armed actions such as train hijackings were carried out by young South Moluccans in the Netherlands. In *Minne strijd voor de RMS* (ca. 1980), Abé Sahetapy gives a touching account of his involvement in a train hijacking in December 1975. He also writes about his youth and education in the Netherlands and about the frustrations which led to his desperate action.

Dutch authors. Most Dutch who sympathized with the South Moluccan case rallied around the Stichting Door de Eeuwen Trouw, which tried to influence Dutch and international public opinion with numerous brochures, pamphlets and the magazine *De Stem van Ambon*. A nearly complete inventory of publications by the Stichting is given in Donkersloot's bibliography (1982). For information on the Stichting itself, consult Waaldijk (1982) and Bosscher and Waaldijk (1985). The ideologies of many (but not all) donors of the Stichting leaned to the right of the Dutch political spectrum and fit into orthodox Protestant circles. An example of a brochure by the Stichting is *Ambon; Mena Moeria; Om de vrijheid van de Zuid-Molukken* (ca. 1951), which emphasized that centuries of Ambonese loyalty to Dutch colonial authority led to the Netherlands' moral obligation to support the South Moluccan freedom struggle. Moreover, the right to self-determination had been stipulated by the Netherlands in negotiations with the Republik Indonesia, such as in the Renville Agreement.

In 1960, a volume of articles on the South Moluccan case was edited by J.C. Bouman. Although this volume, called *The South Moluccas; Rebellious province or occupied state*, was not published by the Stichting Door de Eeuwen Trouw, the contributors upheld the RMS, this time in a more sophisticated way. Much attention was paid to the status of the RMS in international law (see the contribution by Gesina van der Molen); the strategic significance of the RMS against advancing world communism (contributions by General Kruls and Admiral Helfrich) is also in evidence. A well-known sympathizer of the RMS, Gerhard Knot, under the pseudonym Bung Penonton ('the Observer'), wrote a survey of the South Moluccan struggle called *De Zuid-Molukse Republiek* (1970, fourth enlarged edition 1977). In addition to an account of the physical struggle in Ambon and other islands, the book contains much information on the South Moluccan community in the Netherlands and on the Vrije Zuidmolukse Jongeren, who were radicalized and carried out several violent actions. Bung Penonton pleads for understanding, not for their actions but for the frustrations behind them, which had accumulated over twenty years.

Of the Dutch publications which do not adopt the RMS standpoint, the first deserving mention is the government statement, *De problematiek van de Molukse minderheid in Nederland* (1978). It asserts that the Dutch government did everything possible to secure the right to self-determination of the federal states, and that ultimately the Netherlands could not interfere in what had become an Indonesian domestic concern. No promise on the self-determination of the South Moluccas had been made. Also of interest is the study by Bosscher and Waaldijk, *Ambon; Eer en schuld* (1985) in which the role of the South Moluccan question in Dutch domestic politics is analysed. A thesis by M.H. Mariën (1968) is concerned with the South Moluccan community in the Netherlands and its numerous organizations, and the more recent study by Dieter Bartels, *Moluccans in exile* (1989) is most detailed on this subject.

Other authors. Of the remaining writings on the South Moluccan question, we first refer to *Republik Maluku Selatan; Die Republik der Süd-Molukken* (1957) by Günter Decker, which devotes much attention to international law. An extensive study by Richard Chauvel, *Nationalists, soldiers and separatists* has recently appeared (1990), which narrates the history of twentieth-century Ambon; the South Moluccan community in the Netherlands is not considered. Chauvel's study was originally defended at the University of Sydney (1984). The author concludes that adherents of the RMS were primarily found among the former 'pillars' of Dutch colonial authority, those who thought they had something to fear from Indonesian nationalism.

Abbreviations

AAT	Aan- en Afvoertroepen
ABK	Anak Buah Kapal
ABRI	Angkatan Bersenjata Republik Indonesia
AD	Angkatan Darat
AK	Angkatan Kepolisian
AKRI	Angkatan Kepolisian Republik Indonesia
AL	Angkatan Laut
ALRI	Angkatan Laut Republik Indonesia
AMKRI	Angkatan Muda Katolik Republik Indonesia
ANJV	Algemeen Nederlands Jeugd Verbond
ANU	Australian National University
API	Angkatan Pemuda Indonesia
APRA	Angkatan Perang Ratu Adil
APRI	Angkatan Perang Republik Indonesia
APWI	Allied Prisoners of War and Internees
ARJOS	Anti-Revolutionaire Jongeren Sociëteit
ARP	Anti-Revolutionaire Partij
AS	Amerika Serikat
ASAA	Asian Studies Association of Australia
AU	Angkatan Udara
AURI	Angkatan Udara Republik Indonesia
AVRO	Algemene Vereniging Radio Omroep
BA	Bachelor of Arts
BAPERKI	Badan Permusyawaratan Kewarganegaraan Indonesia
BB	Binnenlands Bestuur
BBC	British Broadcasting Corporation
BE	Brigade
BFI	Berita Film Indonesia
BFO	Bijeenkomst voor Federaal Overleg
BI	Bataljon Infanterie
BIO	Bewind (Bestuursregeling) Indonesië in Overgangstijd
BKR	Badan Keamanan Rakyat
BN	Batalyon
BNI	Bank Negara Indonesia
BPI	Badan Perguruan Indonesia
BPKI	Badan Penyelidik Kemerdekaan Indonesia
BPKKP	Badan Penolong Keluarga Korban Perjuangan
BPKNP	Badan Pekerja Komite Nasional Pusat

BPNK	Badan Pengawas Negeri dan Kota
BPRI	Badan Perjuangan Republik Indonesia
BPSKNP	Badan Pembaharuan Susunan Komite Nasional Pusat
BPUPKI	Badan Penyelidik Usaha-Usaha Persiapan Kemerdekaan Indonesia
CASA	Centre for Asian Studies Amsterdam
CBS	Centraal Bureau voor de Statistiek
CCPKI	Centraal Comité Partai Komunis Indonesia
CDA	Christen-Democratisch Appèl
CEP	Christelijk Ethische Partij
CHU	Christelijk-Historische Unie
CIA	Central Intelligence Agency
CIE	Compagnie
CM	Corps Mahasiswa
CORHAS	Corps Hasanuddin
CPN	Communistische Partij van Nederland
CRM	Cultuur, Recreatie en Maatschappelijk Werk
CSP	Christelijk Staatkundige Partij
D'66	Democraten '66
DAM	Daerah Militer
DAMRI	Jawatan (Djawatan) Angkutan Motor Republik Indonesia
DC	District of Columbia
DCI	Daerah Chusus Ibukota
Dep.	Departemen
DI	Daerah Istimewa
DI/TII	Darul Islam/Tentara Islam Indonesia
DISJARAH	Dinas Sejarah
DIY	Daerah Istimewa Yogyakarta
DKI	Daerah Khusus Ibukota
DMI	Daerah Militer Istimewa
DPA	Dewan Pertimbangan Agung
DPR	Dewan Perwakilan Rakyat
DPR-GR	Dewan Perwakilan Rakyat-Gotong Royong
EEG	Europese Economische Gemeenschap
FDR	Front Demokrasi Rakyat
FKPS	Fakultas Keguruan Pengetahuan Sosial
FKUI	Fakultas Kedokteran Universitas Indonesia
G30S	Gerakan Tiga Puluh September
GAPIS	Gabungan Pemuda Indonesia Soppeng
GAPRI	Gabungan Pemberontak Rakyat Indonesia
GASBIINDO	Gabungan Serikat-Serikat Buruh Islam Indonesia
GBI	Gezags Bataljons Indië
GERPOLEK	Gerilya-Politik-Ekonomi
GESTAPU	Gerakan September Tiga Puluh
GESURI	Genta Suara Revolusi
GID	Gevechts Inlichtingen Dienst
GKBI	Gabungan Koperasi Batik Indonesia
GKMI	Gereja Kristen Muria Indonesia

GM	Gadjah Mada
GM	Gubernur Militer
GMU	Gadjah Mada University
GOM	Gerakan Operasi Militer
GPII	Gerakan Pemuda Islam Indonesia
GRI	Gerakan Rakyat Indonesia
HAMKA	Haji Abdul Malik Karim Amrullah
HAMOT	Hare Majesteits Ongeregelde Troepen
HANKAM	Pertahanan Keamanan
HKAG	Hoofdkwartier van de Adjudant-Generaal
HUT	Hari Ulang Tahun
IAHA	International Association of Historians of Asia
IAIN	Institut Agama Islam Negeri
ICODO	Informatie- en Coördinatie-orgaan Dienstverlening Oorlogs-getroffenen
IID	Indische Inlichtingen Dienst
IKADA	Ikatan Atletik Jakarta (Jakarta)
IKAPI	Ikatan Penerbit Indonesia
IKIP	Institut Keguruan dan Ilmu Pendidikan
IKON	Inter-Kerkelijke Omroep Nederland
IMAM	Indonesia Merdeka Atau Mati
IPI	Ikatan Pelajar Indonesia
IPK	Ilmu Pengetahuan Kemasyarakatan
IPPHOS	Indonesia(n) Press and Photo Service
IPPI	Ikatan Pemuda Pelajar Indonesia
IPSO	Instituut voor Politiek en Sociaal Onderzoek
ISOR	Interdisciplinair Sociaal-Wetenschappelijk Onderzoeksinstituut Rijksuniversiteit Utrecht
ITB	Institut Teknologi Bandung
IVIO	Instituut voor Individueel Onderwijs
JABAR	Jawa Barat
JARAHDAM	Jawatan Sejarah Daerah Militer
JATIM	Jawa Timur
Kab.	Kabupaten
KALSEL	Kalimantan Selatan
KALTIM	Kalimantan Timur
KANWIL	Kantor Wilayah
Kem.	Kementerian
KEMPEN	Kementerian Penerangan
KGSS	Kesatuan Gerilya Sulawesi Selatan
KIM	Koninklijk Instituut voor de Marine
KIT	Koninklijk Instituut voor de Tropen
KITLV	Koninklijk Instituut voor Taal-, Land- en Volkenkunde
KKM	Komite Ketatanegaraan Minahasa
KKO	Korps Komando
KL	Koninklijke Landmacht
KLu	Koninklijke Luchtmacht
KM	Koninklijke Marine

KMA	Koninklijke Militaire Academie
KMB	Konferensi Meja Bundar
KNIL	Koninklijk Nederlands-Indisch (Indonesisch) Leger
KNIP	Komite Nasional Indonesia Pusat
KNP	Komite Nasional Pusat
KODAK	Komando Daerah Kepolisian
KODAM	Komando Daerah Militer
KODM	Komando Onder Distrik Militer
KOLA	Komando Mandala
KOWANI	Kongres Wanita Indonesia
KPM	Koninklijke Paketvaart Maatschappij
KRI	Keputerian Republik Indonesia
KRIM	Kebaktian Rakyat Indonesia Maluku
KRIS	Kebaktian Rakyat Indonesia Sulawesi
KRU	Kesatuan Reserve Umum
KSAU	Komandan Sumatera Angkatan Udara
KUDP	Kantor Urusan Demobilisan Pelajar
KVP	Katholieke Volkspartij
LAKSDA	Laksamana Muda
LAM	Lambung Mangkurat
LAPRIS	Laskar Pemberontak Republik Indonesia Sulawesi
LASWI	Laskar Wanita
LB	Labuhan Balik
LEKNAS	Lembaga Ekonomi Kemasyarakatan Nasional
LIB	Lichte Infanterie Bataljons
LIDESCO	Leiden Institute of Development Studies and Consultancy Services
LIPI	Lembaga Ilmu Pengetahuan Indonesia
LP3ES	Lembaga Penelitian, Pendidikan dan Penerangan Ekonomi dan Sosial
LPI	Laskar Putri Indonesia
LRKN	Lembaga Research Kebudayaan Nasional
LuA	Luchtdoelartillerie
LVRI	Legiun Veteran Republik Indonesia
LVT	Luchtvaarttroepen
MA	Master of Arts
MADILOG	Materialisme-Dialektika-Logika
MASYUMI	Majelis Syuro Muslimin Indonesia
MBKD	Markas Besar Komando Jawa (Djawa)
MBKS	Markas Besar Komando Sumatera
MBO	Markas Besar Umum (Oemoem)
MDPP	Markas Daerah Perjuangan Pertahanan Priangan
MIPI	Majelis Ilmu Pengetahuan Indonesia
MLD	Marine Luchtvaart Dienst
MMC	Merapi-Merbabu Complex
MOTIK	Majukan Olehmu Tanah Air Indonesia Kita
MPPP	Majelis Persatuan Perjuangan Priangan
MPR	Majelis Permusyawaratan Rakyat
Mubes	Musyawarah Besar

MZS	Middelbare Zeevaart School
NASSI	Nationale Actie Steunt Spijtoptanten Indonesië
NEFIS	Netherlands (Eastern) Forces Intelligence Service
NEI	Netherlands East Indies
NHK	Nederlands Hervormde Kerk
NIAS	Netherlands Institute for Advanced Studies
NIB	Netherlands Information Bureau
NICA	Netherlands Indies Civil Administration
NIT	Negara Indonesia Timur
NIU	Nederlands-Indonesische Unie
NIWIN	Nationale Inspanning Welzijnsverzorging Indonesië
NRC	Nieuwe Rotterdamsche Courant
NRI	Negara Republik Indonesia
NSB	Nationaal-Socialistische Beweging
NST	Negara Sumatera Timur
NU	Nahdatul Ulama
NV	Naamloze Vennootschap
OVW	Oorlogsvrijwilligers
P dan K	Pendidikan dan Kebudayaan
PANGSAR	Panglima Besar
PARI	Partai Republik Indonesia
PATI	Perwira Tinggi
PAW	Pantserwagens
PBB	Perserikatan Bangsa-Bangsa
PDRI	Pemerintah Darurat Republik Indonesia
PEMA	Penyelidik Masyarakat
PEMDA	Pemerintah Daerah
PEPERA	Penentuan Pendapat Rakyat
PEPORA	Pendidikan Politik Rakyat
PERMOERI	Persatuan Masyarakat Usaha-Usaha (Oesaha-Oesaha) Rakyat Indonesia
PERSADJA	Persatuan Jaksa-Jaksa (Djaksa-Djaksa) Seluruh Indonesia
PERTIP	Persatuan Tionghoa Peranakan
PESINDO	Pemuda Sosialis Indonesia
PETA	Pembela Tanah Air
PGP	Peraturan Gaji Pegawai
PhD	Doctor of Philosophy
PII	Pelajar Islam Indonesia
PJM	Paduka Yang (Jang) Mulia
PKI	Partai Komunis Indonesia
PKRI	Partai Katolik Republik Indonesia
PKRI	Perjuangan Kemerdekaan Republik Indonesia
PMT	Pasukan Mobil Teras
PNI	Partai Nasional Indonesia
POD	Peraturan Urusan (Oeroesan) Dalam
POLRI	Polisi Republik Indonesia
POPDA	Panitya Urusan (Oeroesan) Pengangkutan Jepang (Djepang) dan APWI

PP	Persatuan Perjuangan
PP	Pimpinan Pusat
PPB	Pendaftaran Pelabuhan
PPF	Pertemuan Permusyawaratan Federal
PPI	Pemuda Puteri Indonesia
PPKI	Panitya Persiapan Kemerdekaan Indonesia
PRIMA	Pejuang Republik Indonesia Medan Area
PRIW	Penegak Republik Indonesia Wajo
PROP	Propinsi
PRRI-PERMESTA	Pemerintah Revolusioner Republik Indonesia - Perjuangan Semesta
PRSI	Partai Rakyat Sarekat Indonesia
PS	Partai Sosialis
PSI	Partai Sosialis Indonesia
PT	Perseroan Terbatas
PTPI	Pusat Tenaga Pelukis Indonesia
PTT	Post-Telegraaf-Telefoon
PUSHUMAS	Pusat Hubungan Masyarakat
PUSSEM	Pusat Sejarah Militer
PUSSEMAD	Pusat Sejarah Militer Angkatan Darat
PUTERA	Pusat Tenaga Rakyat
PvdA	Partij van de Arbeid
PvdV	Partij van de Vrijheid
PWI	Persatuan Wartawan Indonesia
RAHTIHKU	Merah Putih Jiwaku, Merah Putih Semangatku
RAPWI	Rehabilitation (Recovery) of Allied Prisoners of War and Internees
RI	Regiment Infanterie
RI	Republik Indonesia
RIOD	Rijksinstituut voor Oorlogsdocumentatie
RIS	Republik Indonesia Serikat
RMS	Republik Maluku Selatan
RRI	Radio Republik Indonesia
RS	Regiment Stoottroepen
RTC	Ronde Tafel Conferentie
RTP	Resimen Team Pertempuran
RVA	Regiment Veld Artillerie
RVD	Regerings Voorlichtings Dienst
SAB	Staf Angkatan Bersenjata
SARBUPRI	Sarekat Buruh Perkebunan Republik Indonesia
SBG	Serikat Buruh Gula
SBPI	Serikat Buruh Percetakan Indonesia
SDAP	Sociaal-Democratische Arbeiders Partij
SEMDAM	Sejarah Militer Daerah Militer
SESKOAD	Sekolah Staf dan Komando Angkatan Darat
SGP	Staatkundig Gereformeerde Partij
SH	Sarjana Hukum
SKI	Serikat Kerakyatan Indonesia
SNI	Sejarah Nasional Indonesia
SO	Serangan Umum (Oemoem)

SOAS	School of Oriental and African Studies
SOB	Staat van Oorlog en Beleg
SOBSI	Sentral Organisasi Buruh Seluruh Indonesia
SSN	Seminar Sejarah Nasional
SU	Serangan Umum
SULSEL	Sulawesi Selatan
SULUT	Sulawesi Utara
SUM	Sumatera
SUMBAGSEL	Sumatera Bagian Selatan
SUMBAR	Sumatera Barat
SUMUT	Sumatera Utara
SUN	Socialistiese Uitgeverij Nijmegen
SWIDOC	Sociaal-Wetenschappelijk Informatie- en Documentatiecentrum
SWK	Sub Wehr Kreise
SWT	Subhanahu Wa Ta'ala
TGP	Tentara Genie Pelajar
TKR	Tentara Keamanan Rakyat
TNI	Tentara Nasional Indonesia
TNI-AD	Tentara Nasional Indonesia-Angkatan Darat
TNI-AL	Tentara Nasional Indonesia-Angkatan Laut
TNI-AU	Tentara Nasional Indonesia-Angkatan Udara
TP	Tentara Pelajar
TRI	Tentara Republik Indonesia
TRIKORA	Tri Komando Rakyat
TRIP	Tentara Republik Indonesia Pelajar
TRM	Tentara Rakyat Mataram
TS	Taman Siswa
UGM	Universitas Gadjah Mada
UI	Universitas Indonesia
UN	United Nations
UNPAD	Universitas Padjadjaran
UNTEA	United Nations Temporary Executive Administration
US	United States
USA	United States of America
USSR	Union of Socialist Soviet Republics
UUD	Undang-Undang Dasar
VARA	Vereniging van Arbeiders Radio Amateurs
VBM	Vereniging Belangenbehartiging Militairen
VEW	Vechtwagens
VKNG	Vereniging tot Kolonisatie van Nieuw-Guinea
VNI	Vereniging Nederland-Indonesië
VOC	Verenigde Oostindische Compagnie
VPRO	Vrijzinnig Protestantse Radio Omroep
VS	Verenigde Staten
VSI	Verenigde Staten van Indonesië
VU	Vrije Universiteit
VVD	Volkspartij voor Vrijheid en Democratie
WAMPA	Wakil Menteri Pertama

WEL	Wiweko Experimental Light Plane
WK	Wakil
YAPERNA	Yayasan Perpustakaan Nasional
YAVITRA	Yayasan Historia Vitae Magistra

Library codes

The absense of a code or reference means that the title is available at KITLV.

amh	Afdeling Maritieme Historie, The Hague
ara	library Algemeen Rijksarchief, The Hague
eur	library Erasmus Universiteit, Rotterdam
kb	Koninklijke Bibliotheek, The Hague
kit	Koninklijk Instituut voor de Tropen, Amsterdam
kitlv	Koninklijk Instituut voor Taal-, Land- en Volkenkunde, Leiden
kitlv-m	available at KITLV, in *Indonesian monographs on microfiche* [57]
kitlv-smg	a copy from the SMG collection was placed at KITLV
lmd	Legermuseum, Delft
lijst Leiden	list of MA theses kept at the Faculty of Arts, Rijksuniversiteit Leiden
mhm	Moluks Historisch Museum, Utrecht
riod	Rijksinstituut voor Oorlogsdocumentatie, Amsterdam
smg	Sectie Militaire Geschiedenis, The Hague
uba	library Universiteit van Amsterdam
ubl	library Rijksuniversiteit Leiden
ubn	library Katholieke Universiteit Nijmegen
ubt	library Katholieke Universiteit Brabant, Tilburg
ubu	library Universiteit Utrecht
vp	Vredespaleis, The Hague

List of periodicals

Acta Historiae Neerlandicae. 's-Gravenhage.
Acta Politica. Meppel.
Administrative Science Quarterly. Ithaca.
Aliran Islam. Bandung.
Amerasia; Review of America and Asia. New York.
American Historical Review. New York.
American Journal of Sociology. Chicago.
American Perspective. Washington.
American Sociological Review. Albany.
Annals of the American Academy of Political and Social Science. Philadelphia.
Antirevolutionaire Staatkunde. 's-Gravenhage.
Archipel; Etudes Interdisciplinaires sur le Monde Insulindien. Paris.
Archiv des Völkerrechts. Tübingen.
Armamentaria. Leiden.
Asia. New York.
Asia and the Americas. New York.
Asia Quarterly. Brussels.
Asian Affairs. New York.
Asian Horizon. London.
Asian Profile. Hong Kong.
Asian Studies. Quezon City.
Asian Studies Review. Nathan.
Asian Survey. Berkeley.
Asiatic Review. London.
Asien, Afrika, Lateinamerika. Berlin.
Austral-Asiatic Bulletin. Melbourne.
Australian Army Journal. Canberra.
Australian Journal of Politics and History. St Lucia.
Australian Outlook. Melbourne.
Australian Quarterly. Sydney.
Basis. Yogyakarta.
Berita Buana. Jakarta.
Bestuursvraagstukken/Soal-Soal Pemerintahan. Batavia/Djakarta.
Blackwood's Magazine. Edinburgh.
British Survey. London.
De Brug/Djambatan. Amsterdam.
Budaya Jaya. Jakarta.
Bulletin of Concerned Asian Scholars. San Francisco.

Bulletin of Indonesian Economic Studies. Canberra.
Bulletin van de Nederlandse Arbeidersbeweging. Groningen.
Bulletin Yaperna. Jakarta.
Bijdragen en Mededelingen betreffende de Geschiedenis der Nederlanden. 's-Graven-
    hage.
Bijdragen tot de Taal-, Land- en Volkenkunde. 's-Gravenhage, Leiden.
Cahiers du Monde Nouveau. Paris.
Christelijk-Historisch Tijdschrift. 's-Gravenhage.
Christen-Democratische Verkenningen. 's-Gravenhage.
Civis Mundi. 's-Gravenhage.
Columbia Law Review. New York.
Common Cause. Chicago.
Communist Review. London.
Contemporary Review. London.
Crisis. New York.
Cultures et Développement. Louvain.
Current Economic Comment. Urbana (Ill.).
Current History; The Monthly Magazine of World Affairs. Philadelphia.
The Developing Economies. Tokyo.
Documentatieblad Lutherse Kerkgeschiedenis. Haarlem.
Economic Review of Indonesia. Batavia.
De Economist. Amsterdam.
Europa Archiv. Frankfurt.
Excerpta Indonesica. Leiden.
Far Eastern Economic Review. Hong Kong.
Far Eastern Quarterly. New York.
Far Eastern Survey. New York.
Fibula, Orgaan van de Nederlandse Jeugdbond ter Bestudering van de Geschiedenis.
    Heemstede.
Foreign Affairs. New York.
Foreign Policy Reports. New York.
Fortnightly. London.
Fortune. Chicago.
Gema Angkatan 45. Jakarta.
Het Gemeenebest. Haarlem.
Genie; Maandblad van de Vereniging van Officieren der Genie. Utrecht.
De Gids; Algemeen Cultureel Maandblad. Amsterdam.
Great Britain and the East. London.
Groniek; Onafhankelijk Gronings Historisch Studentenblad. Groningen.
Harper's Magazine. New York.
Hemisphere. Canberra.
Histori. Jakarta.
The Historian. Albuquerque.
Hollands Maandblad; Tijdschrift voor Literatuur en Politiek. 's-Gravenhage.
l'Homme et l'Humanité. N.p.
ICODO-Info. Utrecht.
India Quarterly. New Delhi.
Indisch Missietijdschrift. 's-Gravenhage.

Indisch Tijdschrift van het Recht. Batavia/Djakarta.
Indische Letteren. Alphen aan den Rijn.
Indonesia. Ithaca.
Indonesia. Jakarta.
Indonesia Circle. London.
Indonesia-Holland Line. Wychen.
Indonesia Magazine. Jakarta.
Indonesian Quarterly. Jakarta.
Indonesian Review. Jakarta.
Indonesian Review of International Affairs. Jakarta.
Indonesië; Tweemaandelijks Tijdschrift gewijd aan het Indonesisch Cultuurgebied.
    's-Gravenhage.
International Affairs. London.
International Conciliation. New York.
International Journal. Toronto.
International Organization. Boston.
International Relations. London.
International Review of Missions. Geneva.
International Studies. Delhi.
Internationale Spectator. 's-Gravenhage.
Internationale Studiën/Etudes Internationales. Haarlem.
Internationales Recht und Diplomatie. Hamburg.
Intisari. Jakarta.
The Islamic Review. Woking.
Itinerario. Leiden.
Jaarboek voor het Democratisch Socialisme. Amsterdam.
Jaarboek Documentatiecentrum Nederlandse Politieke Partijen. Groningen.
Jaarboek voor de Geschiedenis van Socialisme en Arbeidersbeweging in Nederland.
    Nijmegen.
Jaarboek Katholiek Documentatie Centrum. Nijmegen.
Jaarboek Mediageschiedenis. Amsterdam.
Jambatan; Tijdschrift voor de Geschiedenis van Indonesië. Amsterdam.
Janus. Utrecht.
Journal of Asian Studies. Ann Arbor.
Journal of the Australian War Memorial. Canberra.
Journal of Contemporary Asia. London.
Journal of Contemporary History. London.
Journal of East Asiatic Studies. Manila.
Journal of the Historical Society of the University of Malaya. Kuala Lumpur.
Journal of Indian History. Allahabad.
Journal of the Indian Institute of International Affairs. New Delhi.
Journal of Politics. Gainsville.
The Journal of the Royal Artillery. London.
Journal of Southeast Asian History. Singapore.
Journal of Southeast Asian Studies. Singapore.
Kabar; Magazine of the Australian-Indonesian Association. N.p.
Kabar Seberang Sulating Maphilindo. Townsville.
Katholiek Cultureel Tijdschrift Streven. Amsterdam.

Katholiek Staatkundig Maandschrift. 's-Gravenhage.
KIM-Spiegel. Den Helder.
Kleio. 's-Gravenhage.
Leidschrift. Leiden.
Lembaran Berita Sejarah Lisan. Jakarta.
Liberaal Reveil. Amsterdam.
Libertas; Maandschrift voor het Koninkrijk der Nederlanden. 's-Gravenhage.
Libertinage. Amsterdam.
Loekisan Soeasana. Jakarta.
Maandschrift van het CBS. 's-Gravenhage.
Maatschappij en Krijgsmacht. 's-Gravenhage.
Maatstaf; Maandblad voor Letteren. 's-Gravenhage.
Madjalah Ilmu-Ilmu Sastra Indonesia. Jakarta.
Madjalah Sedjarah Militer Angkatan Darat. Bandung.
Majalah Canang. Pekanbaru.
Majalah Ketahanan Nasional. Jakarta.
Marineblad. Den Helder.
Mars et Historia. Leidschendam.
Masyarakat Indonesia. Jakarta.
Mededelingen Sectie Militaire Geschiedenis Landmachtstaf. 's-Gravenhage.
The Middle East Journal. Washington.
Militair Rechtelijk Tijdschrift. 's-Gravenhage.
De Militaire Spectator. 's-Gravenhage.
Mimbar Ulama. Jakarta.
Modern Asian Studies. London.
Moesson; Onafhankelijk Indisch Tijdschrift. 's-Gravenhage.
The Moslem World. Hartford.
The Nation. New York.
Nederlands Juristenblad. Zwolle.
De Nieuwe Stem; Maandblad voor Cultuur en Politiek. Arnhem.
Nineteenth Century. London.
Notes et Etudes Documentaires. Paris.
Ons Erfdeel. Rekkem.
Ons Leger. 's-Gravenhage.
Oost-West. Scheveningen.
Opstand; Tijdschrift van de Beweging 'Christenen voor het Socialisme'. Zeist.
Orbis. Philadelphia.
Oriëntatie; Cultureel Maandblad. Batavia/Djakarta.
Orion. 's-Gravenhage.
Pacific Affairs. Honolulu.
Pacific Historical Review. Berkeley.
Pakistan Horizon. Karachi.
Panji Masyarakat. Jakarta.
Pembaroean. Djakarta.
Penelitian Sedjarah. Djakarta.
Peninjau. Jakarta.
Pers Indonesia. Jakarta.
Persepsi. Jakarta.

Philippine Quarterly of Culture and Society. Cebu City.
Podium; Tweemaandelijks Literair Tijdschrift. Leeuwarden.
Political Affairs; Journal of Marxist Thought and Analysis. New York.
Political Quarterly. London.
Political Science Quarterly. Boston.
Politiek en Cultuur. Amsterdam.
Politieke Kroniek. Utrecht.
Politieke Opstellen. Nijmegen.
Politique Etrangère. Paris.
Prisma; Indonesian Journal of Social and Economic Affairs. Jakarta.
Prisma; Informasi dan Forum Pembahasan Masalah [...] Jakarta.
Pudjangga Baru. Batavia/Djakarta: Pustaka Rakjat.
Quality and Quantity; European-American Journal of Methodology. Padova.
Quarterly Review of Historical Studies. Calcutta.
Race and Class. London.
Rechtsgeleerd Magazijn Themis. Zwolle.
Rekenschap. Utrecht.
Review of Indonesian and Malayan/Malaysian Affairs. Sydney.
Revue Française de Science Politique. Paris.
Revue de l'Histoire de la Deuxième Guerre Mondiale. Paris.
Round Table; The Commonwealth Journal of International Affairs. London.
Sinar Darussalam. Banda Aceh.
Skript. Amsterdam.
Social Forces. Chapel Hill.
Socialisme en Democratie. Amsterdam.
Sociologia Neerlandica. Assen.
Sociologische Gids; Tijdschrift voor Sociologie en Sociologisch Onderzoek. Meppel.
South East Asian Review. Gaya (India).
South East Asian Spectrum. Bangkok.
Soviet Press Translations. Washington.
Spiegel Historiael; Maandblad voor Geschiedenis en Archeologie. Bussum.
Statistische en Economische Onderzoekingen. Utrecht.
Sumatra Research Bulletin. Hull.
Synthèses; Revue Internationale Mensuelle. Brussels.
Tanah Air. Jakarta.
Tempo; Majalah Berita Mingguan. Jakarta.
Tirade. Amsterdam.
Tong Tong. 's-Gravenhage.
Tijdschrift voor Diplomatie. Brussels.
Tijdschrift voor Geschiedenis. Groningen.
Tijdschrift voor Parapsychologie. Amsterdam.
United Asia; International Magazine of Afro-Asian Affairs. Bombay.
United Nations Bulletin. Lake Success.
United Nations World. New York.
Vidya Yudha. Bandung.
Vierteljahrshefte für Zeitgeschichte. Stuttgart.
VU-Magazine. Amsterdam.
War and Society; Yearbook of Military History. London.

Warta Pendidikan dan Kebudayaan. N.p.
Wending; Maandblad voor Evangelie en Cultuur. 's-Gravenhage.
World Affairs. London.
World Justice. Louvain.
World Politics. Princeton.
The World Today. London.
Yale Review. New Haven.
The Yearbook of World Affairs. London.
ZWO-Jaarboek. 's-Gravenhage.

Bibliographies

0001 *Abstraksi skripsi sarjana Fakultas Sastra Universitas Padjadjaran.* Bandung: Universitas Padjadjaran, 1974, 155 pp.

0002 Anderson, Benedict R.O'G.
Bibliography of Indonesian publications; Newspapers, non-government periodicals and bulletins 1945-1958 at Cornell University. Ithaca: Cornell University, 1959, 69 pp.

0003 Baal, J. van; K.W. Galis and R.M. Koentjaraningrat
West Irian; A bibliography. Dordrecht/Cinnaminson: Foris, 1984, 307 pp.

0004 *Berita bibliografi.* Djakarta: Gunung Agung, 1956-61. Many vols.

0005 Berton, Peter and Alvin Z. Rubinstein
Soviet works on Southeast Asia; A bibliography of non-periodical literature, 1946-1965. Los Angeles: University of South California Press, 1967, 201 pp.

0006 *Bibliografi Nasional Indonesia/Indonesian National Bibliography.* Djakarta: Kem. P dan K/Perpustakaan Nasional Indonesia, 1963-. Many vols.

0007 *Bibliografi perpustakaan.* Jakarta: Dewan Harian Nasional Badan Penggerak Pembina Potensi Angkatan 45, 1981, 15+155 pp.

0008 *Bibliografi sedjarah HANKAM/ABRI dan masalah-masalah HANKAM.* Djakarta: Dep. HANKAM, 1969, 34 pp. [Second edition, 1971, 97 pp.]

0009 *Bibliografi skripsi beranotasi.* Jakarta: Kem. P dan K, 1973, 622 pp.

0010 *Bibliografi skripsi IKIP Bandung, 1960-1976.* Jakarta: LIPI/KITLV, 1977, 186 pp.

0011 *Bibliografi skripsi IKIP Jakarta, 1961-1976.* Jakarta: LIPI/KITLV, 1977, 119 pp.

0012 *Bibliografi skripsi IKIP Malang, 1958-1975.* Jakarta: LIPI/KITLV, 1977, 65 pp.

0013 *Bibliografi skripsi IKIP Medan, 1962-1975.* Jakarta: LIPI/KITLV, 1977, 56 pp.

0014 *Bibliografi skripsi IKIP Padang, 1965-1976.* Jakarta: LIPI/KITLV, 1977, 14 pp.

0015 *Bibliografi skripsi IKIP Semarang, 1968-1976.* Jakarta: LIPI/KITLV, 1977, 31 pp.

0016 *Bibliografi skripsi IKIP Surabaya, 1969-1975.* Jakarta: LIPI/KITLV, 1977, 15 pp.

0017 *Bibliografi skripsi IKIP Yogyakarta, 1960-1976.* Jakarta: LIPI/KITLV, 1977, 239 pp.

0018 *Bibliografi skripsi Universitas Indonesia, 1952-1970.* Jakarta: LIPI/KITLV, 1979, 169 pp.

0019 *Bibliografi skripsi Universitas Indonesia, 1971-1978.* Jakarta: LIPI/KITLV, 1981, 278 pp.

0020 *Bibliografi skripsi Universitas Padjadjaran, 1957-1980.* Jakarta: LIPI/KITLV, 1981, 406 pp.

0021 *Bibliografi tentang bibliografi Indonesia.* Jakarta: Balai Pustaka/Kem. P dan K, 1977, 139 pp.

0022 *Bibliografi terpilih Perpustakaan 45.* Jakarta: Dewan Harian Nasional Angkatan 45, 1976, 1977, 129 pp. 2 vols.

0023 *Bibliografi tesis dan disertasi.* Ujung Pandang: IKIP Ujung Pandang, 1983, 40 pp.

0024 *Bibliografie overzeese gebiedsdelen.* 's-Gravenhage: Regerings Voorlichtings Dienst, 1950, 49 pp.

0025 *Bibliography of Asian studies.* Ann Arbor: Association for Asian Studies, 1971-. Many vols.

0026 *A bibliography on Indonesian material for the humanities and social sciences 1960-1970.* Djakarta: LIPI, 1972, 19+147 pp.

0027 Bloomfield, B.C.
Theses on Asia accepted by universities in the United Kingdom and Ireland, 1877-1964. London: Cass, 1967, 127 pp.

0028 *Brinkman's (cumulatieve) catalogus van boeken en tijdschriften, die [...] in Nederland uitgegeven of herdrukt zijn.* Alphen aan den Rijn: Samsom/Stafleu, 1931-. Many vols.

0029 Bruin, Arno de
Bibliografie van de Nederlands-Indische kampliteratuur van 1946 tot 1987. 1988. [MA thesis Rijksuniversiteit Leiden.] [unpaged]

0030 Buck, H. de
Bibliografie der geschiedenis van Nederland. Leiden: Brill, 1968, 712 pp. (ubl)

0031 *Bung Karno; Sebuah bibliografi memuat daftar karya oleh dan tentang Bung Karno.* Second edition. Jakarta: Idayu, 1981, 128 pp. [First edition 1979.]

0032 Buur, Dorothée
Persoonlijke documenten Nederlands-Indië/Indonesië; Keuze-bibliografie. Leiden: KITLV, 1973, 241 pp.

0033 *Centrale militaire catalogus.* 's-Gravenhage: Ministerie van Defensie, 1947-. Many vols. (kb)

0034 Chand, Attar
Southeast Asia and the Pacific; A select bibliography, 1947-1970. New Delhi: Sterling Publishers, 1979, 378 pp.

0035 Coolhaas, W.Ph.
A critical survey of studies on Dutch colonial history. The Hague: Nijhoff, 1960, 8+154 pp. [Second edition, revised by G.J. Schutte, 1980, 8+264 pp.]

0036 *Cumulative bibliography on Asian studies 1941-1965.* Boston: Association of Asian Studies, 1970, 749+752+725+734 pp. 4 vols.

0037 *Cumulative bibliography on Asian studies 1966-1970.* Boston: Association of Asian Studies, 1972, 797+750+738 pp. 3 vols.

0038 *Current annotated bibliography of Dutch expansion studies.* Leiden: Centre for the History of European Expansion, 1976-. Many vols.

0039 *Daftar buku 20 th. penerbitan Indonesia, 1945-1965.* Djakarta: IKAPI, 1965, 416 pp.

0040 'Daftar buku-buku Perpustakaan 45', *Gema Angkatan 45,* 1980-.

0041 Damian, Eddy and Robert N. Hornick
Bibliografi hukum Indonesia. Bandung: Lembaga Penelitian Hukum dan Kriminologi (UNPAD), 1971, 28+352 pp. [Third edition, Bandung: Universitas Padjadjaran, 1984, 20+845 pp.]

0042 Dengel, Holk H.
Annotated bibliography of new Indonesian literature on the history of Indonesia. Stuttgart: Steiner, 1987, 114 pp.

0043 *Doctoraalscripties geschiedenis.* Samengesteld door H.J. Smit. Amsterdam: SWIDOC/Universiteit van Amsterdam, 1980-92, 26+97+66+96 pp. 4 vols. (ubl)

0044 *Doctoral dissertations on Asia.* Ann Arbor: Association for Asian Studies, 1975-. Many vols.

0045 Donkersloot, H.B.
Bibliografie van de Nederlandse buitenlandse politiek; Nederland-Indonesië 1942-1980; Geannoteerde systematische bibliografie. Amsterdam: Universiteit van Amsterdam, 1982, 100 pp.

0046 Draak, J.G.F. (Sjak)
Bibliografie van Indië-tijdschriften. Delft: Legermuseum, 1993, 43 pp.

0047 Duin, Kees van
Bibliografie Zuidmolukkers. Hoevelaken: Christelijk Pedagogisch Studiecentrum, 1982, 81 pp.

0048 Echols, John M.
Preliminary checklist of Indonesian imprints during the Japanese period (March 1942-August 1945). Ithaca: Cornell University, 1963, 56 pp.

0049 Echols, John M.
Preliminary checklist of Indonesian imprints (1945-1949) with Cornell University holdings. Ithaca: Cornell University, 1965, 186 pp.

0050 *Excerpta Indonesica.* Leiden: KITLV, 1970-. Many vols.

0051 *Final report of the exhibition of historical materials on the Japanese occupation of Indonesia 1942-1945.* Tokyo: Forum for Research Materials on the Japanese Occupation of Indonesia, 1988, 55 pp.

0052 Galis, K.W.
Bibliographie van Nederlands Nieuw-Guinea. Hollandia: n.n., 1951, 61 pp. [Second edition, 1955, 165 pp.; Third edition, 's-Gravenhage: Ministerie van Binnenlandse Zaken, 1962, 275 pp.]

0053 Hoenderkamp, Mariëtte
De Verenigde Naties en de Indonesische kwestie 1947-1963. Amsterdam: Koninklijk Instituut voor de Tropen, 1973, 8 pp.

0054 *Indeks artikel-artikel tentang negara-negara Asia Tenggara dalam bidang sedjarah, politik dan sosial/Index of articles on Southeast Asia in the field of political and social history.* Djakarta: Kem. P dan K, 1969, 42 pp. [Second edition, 1971, 92 pp.]

0055 *Index of Indonesian learned periodicals/Indeks madjalah ilmiah.* Djakarta: MIPI, 1961-. Many vols.

0056 *Indonesia microfiche editions.* Zug: Inter Documentation Company, ca. 1975, 87 pp.

0057 *Indonesian monographs on microfiche 1945-1968.* Zug: Inter Documentation Company, 1975, 154 pp.

0058 'Inventarisatie doctoraalscripties', *Jambatan; Tijdschrift voor de geschiedenis van Indonesië,* 1981-.

0059 Iwasaki, Ikuo
Japan and Southeast Asia; A bibliography of historical, economic and political relations. Tokyo: Institute of Developing Economies, 1983, 176 pp.

0060 Johnson, D.C.
Index to Southeast Asian journals, 1960-1974; A guide to articles, book reviews, and composite works. Boston: Hall, 1977, 23+811 pp.

0061 *Katalog majalah terbitan Indonesia 1942-1979; Koleksi Perpustakaan Museum Nasional.* Jakarta: Perpustakaan Museum Nasional, 1980, 150 pp.

0062 *Katalog sejarah Indonesia; Koleksi Perpustakaan Museum Nasional.* Jakarta: Museum Nasional, 1980, 236 pp.

0063 *Katalog sejarah Indonesia koleksi Perpustakaan Nasional Republik Indonesia/ Indonesian history catalog of the National Library of Indonesia collections.* Jakarta: Perpustakaan Nasional RI, 1992, 204 pp.

0064 *Katalog terbitan Indonesia selama pendudukan Jepang 1942-1945.* Jakarta: Kem. P dan K, 1983, 101 pp.

0065 *Katalog terbitan pemerintah.* Jakarta: Kem. P dan K, 1982, 500 pp.

0066 *Katalogus penerbitan Departemen Penerangan semendjak tahun 1950-1961.* Djakarta: Dep. Penerangan, 1961, 28 pp. (kitlv-m)

0067 Kemp, Herman C.
Annotated bibliography of bibliographies on Indonesia. Leiden: KITLV Press, 1990, 433 pp.

0068 Kozicki, Richard J. and Peter Ananda
South and Southeast Asia; Doctoral dissertations and master's theses completed at the University of California at Berkeley, 1906-1968. Berkeley: University of California at Berkeley, 1969, 8+49 pp.

0069 Kratz, Ernst Ulrich
A bibliography of Indonesian literature in journals; Drama, prose, poetry/Bibliografi karya sastra Indonesia dalam majalah; Drama, prosa, puisi. Yogyakarta: Gadjah Mada University Press, London: School of Oriental and African Studies, 1988, 901 pp.

0070 Lev, Daniel S.
A bibliography of Indonesian government documents and selected Indonesian writings on government in the Cornell University library. Ithaca: Cornell University, 1958, 58 pp.

0071 *Library of Congress catalog; A cumulative list of works represented by Library of Congress printed cards.* Ann Arbor: Edwards. Many vols. (ubl)

0072 *Literatuurlijst betreffende het conflict tussen Nederland en Indonesië, 1945-1951.* N.p.: n.n., 1969, 17 pp.

0073 Looyenga, A.J.
Overzicht van Nederlandse studies over de geschiedenis der Europese expansie, verschenen sinds 1945/A survey of Dutch studies on the history of European expansion, published since 1945. Leiden: Werkgroep Geschiedenis der Europese Expansie, 1977, 33 pp.

0074 McVey, Ruth T.
Bibliography of Soviet publications on Southeast Asia. Ithaca: Cornell University, 1959, 109 pp.

0075 Martodiredjo, Soedarminto
Bibliography on the struggle for the Indonesian independence. Amsterdam: Koninklijk Instituut voor de Tropen, 1972, 8 pp.

0076 *Molukkers in Nederland; Een keuze uit de literatuur.* Rijswijk: Ministerie van Cultuur, Recreatie en Maatschappelijk Werk, 1980, 72 pp.

0077 Müller, Werner
Bibliographie deutschsprachiger Literatur über Indonesien. Hamburg: Institut für Asienkunde, 1974, 96 pp. [Second edition, 1979, 201 pp.; Third edition, 1983, 228 pp.]

0078 Nagelkerke, Gerard A.
The Chinese in Indonesia; A bibliography, 18th century-1981. Leiden: KITLV, 1982, 21+238 pp.

0079 Nakamura, Mitsuo
Checklist of microfilm holdings on the Japanese occupation of Indonesia in the Cornell University Library (Wason Collection). Ithaca: Cornell University, 1970, 86 pp.

0080 Nash, Vivien
Monash University theses on Southeast Asia 1961-1987. Clayton: Monash University, 1988, 45 pp.

0081 *The Nishijima Collection; Materials on the Japanese military administration in Indonesia.* Tokyo: Waseda University, 1973, 97 pp.

0082 Ockeloen, G.
Catalogus dari buku-buku jang diterbitkan di Indonesia. Bandung: Kolff, 1950-55.
Djilid 1, 1945-1949, 140 pp.

0083 Ockeloen, G.
Catalogus dari buku-buku jang diterbitkan di Indonesia. Bandung: Kolff, 1950-55.
Djilid 2, 1950-1951, 312 pp.

0084 Ockeloen, G.
Catalogus dari buku-buku jang diterbitkan di Indonesia. Bandung: Kolff, 1950-55.
Djilid 3, published by Gedung Buku Nasional, 1952-1953, 276 pp.

0085 Ockeloen, G.
Catalogus dari buku-buku jang diterbitkan di Indonesia. Bandung: Kolff, 1950-55.
Djilid 4, published by Gedung Buku Nasional, 1953-1954, 220 pp.

0086 Oki, Akira
Japanese studies on contemporary Southeast Asia, 1973-1983. Tokyo, 1985, 15 pp.

0087 *Overzicht van de literatuur betreffende Nieuw-Guinea, aanwezig in de bibliotheek van het Ministerie voor Uniezaken en Overzeese Rijksdelen.* 's-Gravenhage: Ministerie voor Uniezaken en Overzeese Rijksdelen, 1952, 1953, 84+60 pp. 2 vols.

0088 *Perslijst Indonesië/Daftar persuratkabaran/Daptar poestakamangsa/Pratélan kalawarti/ List of publications; Een nominatieve opgave van in Indonesië verschijnende periodieken (dag-, week-, maandbladen enz.) [...].* Batavia: Landsdrukkerij, 1948, 40 pp. (kitlv-m) [Second edition, Batavia: Regerings Voorlichtings Dienst, 1949, 58 pp.]

0089 Postma, Nel; Zeina Hadad and Hernando
Bibliografi wanita Indonesia/Bibliography of women in Indonesia. Jakarta: LIPI, 1980-85, 162+120+77 pp. 3 vols.

0090 Pringgoadisurjo, Luwarsih
Badan-badan pemerintah Indonesia 1950-1969; Bibliografi penerbitan. Djakarta: LIPI, 1971, 412 pp.

0091 Purawidjaja, Sukarsih
Bibliografi tentang pergerakan wanita Indonesia sesudah tahun 1945. Amsterdam: KIT, 1972, 33 pp.

0092 Reid, A.; Annemarie Jubb and J. Jahmin
Indonesian serials 1942-1950 in Yogyakarta libraries with a list of government publications in the Perpustakaan Negara, Yogyakarta. Canberra: Australian National University, 1974, 133 pp.

0093 *Repertorium van boeken en tijdschriftartikelen betreffende de geschiedenis van Nederland.* 's-Gravenhage: Nijhoff/Instituut voor Nederlandse Geschiedenis, 1943-. Many vols.

0094 *Ringkasan tesis IKIP Malang.* Malang: IKIP, 1981, 265 pp.

0095 *Ringkasan tesis IKIP Padang.* Padang: IKIP, 1977, 233 pp.

0096 Ruyter, M.J.L. de
De Nederlandse militaire tijdschriften; Een bibliografie. Breda: KMA, 1964, 76 pp.
(kb) [Second edition, 1976, 107 pp.]

0097 Sardesai, D.R. and Bhanu D. Sardesai
Theses and dissertations on Southeast Asia; An international bibliography in social sciences, education and fine arts. Zug: Inter Documentation Company, 1970, 176 pp.

0098 Schutte, G.J.
Beknopt overzicht van de geschriften over de Molukse geschiedenis en cultuur. Rijswijk: Ministerie van Welzijn, Volksgezondheid en Cultuur, 1983, 63 pp.

0099 *Sejarawan Indonesia dan karya tulisnya.* Disusun oleh Masyarakat Sejarawan Indonesia. Jakarta: Lembaga Ilmu Pengetahuan Indonesia, 1978, 13+89 pp.

0100 Seleky, W.A.
Bibliografi tentang penduduk dan kebudajaannja dari kepulauan Maluku, 1934-1964. Amsterdam: Koninklijk Instituut voor de Tropen, 1972, 13 pp.

0101 Stephens, Helen L.
Theses on South-East Asia 1965-1985, accepted by universities in the United Kingdom and Ireland. Hull: University of Hull, 1986, 74 pp.

0102 Stucki, Curtis W.
American doctoral dissertations on Asia, 1933-June 1966, incl. appendix on Master's theses at Cornell University, 1933-June 1968. Ithaca: Cornell University, 1968, 304 pp.

0103 Suhardi, P. Alfons S.
Bibliografi Islam Indonesia. Bandung: Universitas Katolik Parahyangan, 1985, 164 pp.

0104 *Sukarno; A select bibliography of works by and about President Sukarno in the National Library of Australia.* Canberra: National Library of Australia, 1981, 21 pp.

0105 Sumantri, Bambang
Bibliografi hubungan Indonesia-Belanda 1945-1950. Amsterdam: Koninklijk Instituut voor de Tropen, 1972, 9 pp.

0106 The, Lian and Paul W. Van der Veur
Treasures and trivia; Doctoral dissertations on Southeast Asia accepted by universities in the United States. Athens: Ohio State University, 1968, 141 pp.

0107 *Les thèses françaises sur l'Asie du Sud-Est depuis 1980.* Paris: Association Française pour la Recherche sur l'Asie du Sud-Est (AFRASE), 1986, 50 pp.

0108 *Thesis abstract Institut Keguruan dan Ilmu Pendidikan Bandung, 1960-1968.* Bandung: IKIP, 1969, 145 pp.

0109 Thung, Y. and John M. Echols
A guide to Indonesian serials (1945-1965) in the Cornell University Library. Ithaca: Cornell University, 1966, 151 pp.

0110   Thung, Y. and John M. Echols
       Checklist of Indonesian serials in the Cornell University Library (1945-1970). Ithaca:
       Cornell University, 1973, 225 pp.

0111   *Universitas Hasanuddin; Skripsi-tesis sampai dengan Agustus 1972*. Ujung
       Pandang: Universitas Hasanuddin, ca. 1972, 66 pp.

0112   Utermöhlen, Rolf
       De Japanse vrouwenkampen in Nederlands-Indië 1942-1945; Een bibliografie. Am-
       sterdam: Rijksinstituut voor Oorlogsdocumentatie, 1993, 60 pp.

0113   Van der Veur, P.W.
       The Eurasians of Indonesia; A political-historical bibliography. Ithaca: Cornell
       University, 1971, 115 pp.

0114   Verhoog, J.M.
       *Herinneringsliteratuur betreffende het Nederlandse militaire optreden te land in
       Indonesië 1945-1950*. 's-Gravenhage: Sectie Militaire Geschiedenis Landmacht-
       staf, 1989, 13+100 pp.

General works
Indonesian authors

0115 *17 tahun yang lalu Bung Karno wafat, 21 Juni 1970.* Jakarta: Yayasan Marinda, 1987, 58 pp.

0116 *20 tahun ABRI; 5 Oktober 1965.* Djakarta: Pusat Penerangan AD-AL-AU-AK, 1965, 92 pp.

0117 *20 tahun Indonesia merdeka.* Djakarta: Dep. Penerangan, 1965, 1098+962+963 pp. 3 vols.

0118 *20 tahun perkembangan Angkatan Kepolisian Republik Indonesia (AKRI).* Djakarta: Inkoprak, 1967, 362 pp.

0119 *21 tahun ABRI; 5 Oktober 1966.* Djakarta: Pusat Penerangan AD-AL-AU-AK, 1966, 110 pp.

0120 *30 tahun Angkatan Bersenjata Republik Indonesia.* Jakarta: Departemen HANKAM, Pusat Sejarah ABRI, 1976, 502 pp.

0121 *30 tahun Indonesia merdeka 1945-1975.* Jakarta: Sekretariat Negara Republik Indonesia, 1977, 1030 pp. [Second edition, 1978, 1039 pp. 3 vols. (Part I: 1945-1949); Third edition, Jakarta: Tira Pustaka, 1980, 1030 pp.]

0122 *30 tahun perkembangan peradilan militer di negara Republik Indonesia.* Disusun oleh Soegiri dan kawan-kawan. Jakarta: Indra Djaja, 1976, 569 pp.

0123 *35 tahun Bank Negara Indonesia 1946 (5 Juli 1946-1981).* Jakarta: BNI, 1981, 148 pp.

0124 *35 tahun Siliwangi, 20 Mei 1946-20 Mei 1981.* Bandung: KODAM VI/Siliwangi, 1981, 254 pp.

0125 *39 tahun Radio Republik, 11 September 1945-1984.* Jakarta: RRI, 1984, 41+14 pp.

0126 *40 tahun Angkatan Bersenjata Republik Indonesia. Jilid 1, Masa perang kemerdekaan, konsolidasi awal dan masa integrasi (1945-1965).* Jakarta: Markas Besar Angkatan Bersenjata Republik Indonesia, Pusat Sejarah dan Tradisi ABRI, 1985, 298 pp.

0127 *40 tahun Bank Negara Indonesia; 5 Juli 1946-1986.* Jakarta: BNI, 1986, 112 pp.

0128 *40 tahun peranan pertambangan dan energi Indonesia, 1945-1985.* Jakarta: Dep. Pertambangan dan Energi, 1985, 473 pp.

0129 *40 tahun PKI 1920-1960.* Djakarta: Lembaga Sedjarah PKI, 1960, 87 pp.

0130   *40 tahun perjalanan pengabdian TNI-ABRI*. Jakarta: Pusat Penerangan ABRI, 1985, 160 pp.

0131   *41 tahun PKI*. Djakarta: Pembaruan, 1961, 47 pp.

0132   *45 tahun Sumpah Pemuda*. Jakarta: Yayasan Gedung-Gedung Bersejarah Jakarta, 1974, 372 pp.

0133   *45 tahun Zeni TNI-AD*. Jakarta: Direktorat Zeni TNI-AD, 1991, 43+168 pp.

0134   *50 tahun kebangkitan nasional; 20 Mei 1908-20 Mei 1958*. Djakarta: UPENI, 1958, 100 pp. (kitlv-m)

0135   Abdulgani, H. Roeslan
        Pantjasila the prime mover of the Indonesian revolution. Djakarta: Prapantja, ca. 1965, 374 pp.

0136   Abdulgani, Roeslan
        Nationalism, revolution and guided democracy in Indonesia; Four lectures. Clayton: Monash University, 1973, 63 pp.

0137   Abdullah, Makmun; Nangsari Ahmad; F.A. Sutjipto and Mardanas Safwan
        Kota Palembang sebagai kota dagang dan industri. Jakarta: Kem. P dan K, 1985, 138 pp.

0138   Abdullah, Taufik
        'The hero in historical perspective', *Prisma* no. 4 (November 1976):27-32.

0139   Abdullah, Taufik
        'Manusia dalam sejarah; Sebuah pengantar', in: Abdullah, Taufik; Aswab Mahasin and Daniel Dhakidae (eds), *Manusia dalam kemelut sejarah*, pp. 1-19. Jakarta: LP3ES, 1978.

0140   Abdullah, Taufik; Aswab Mahasin and Daniel Dhakidae (eds)
        Manusia dalam kemelut sejarah. Jakarta: Lembaga Penelitian, Pendidikan dan Penerangan Ekonomi dan Sosial, 1978, 287 pp.

0141   Abdulmuchni, Gatot Achmad
        Kepanduan Indonesia dari masa ke masa. Djakarta: Balai Pustaka, 1951, 57 pp.

0142   Abdurachman
        Sedjarah Madura selajang pandang. Sumenep: The Sun, 1971, 78 pp.

0143   Aboebakar, H. (ed.)
        Sedjarah hidup K.H.A. Wahid Hasjim dan karangan tersiar. Djakarta: Panitia Buku Peringatan K.H.A. Wahid Hasjim, 1957, 24+975 pp.

0144   Abu, Rifai and Abdullah Suhadi
        Chatib Suleman. Jakarta: Kem. P dan K, 1976, 44 pp.

0145   Adang S.
        Umar Wirahadikusumah; Anak desa Situraja. Jakarta: Rosda Jayaputra, 1984, 84 pp.

0146   Adil, Hilman
        Australia's relations with Indonesia 1945-1962. N.p.: n.n., 1973, 200 pp. [PhD thesis Rijksuniversiteit Leiden.]

0147 Adil, Hilman
The significance of the defense-security dimension in Australian-Indonesian relations, 1945-1962. Paper Sixth International Conference on Asian History, Yogyakarta, 1974, 17 pp.

0148 Adil, Hilman
Hubungan Australia dengan Indonesia 1945-1962. Jakarta: Djambatan, 1993, 17+258 pp.

0149 Adinegoro, Djamaludin
Eropah sumber perang dunia. Djakarta: Bulan Bintang, 1952, 192 pp.

0150 Adnan, H. Abdul Basit
Kemelut di NU; Antara kyai dan politisi. Solo: Mayasari, 1982, 108 pp.

0151 Aidit, D.N.
Lahirnja PKI dan perkembangannja (1920-1955). Djakarta: Pembaruan, 1955, 52 pp.

0152 Aidit, D.N.
Pilihan tulisan. Djakarta: Pembaruan, 1959, 537 pp. [Second edition, 1965, 511+352 pp. 2 vols.]

0153 Aidit, D.N.
Peladjaran dari sedjarah PKI. Djakarta: Pembaruan, 1960, 31 pp. (kitlv-m)

0154 Aidit, D.N.
Problems of the Indonesian revolution. N.p.: Demos, 1963, 612 pp.

0155 Aidit, D.N.
Revolusi Indonesia; Latarbelakang sedjarah dan haridepannja. Djakarta: Pembaruan, 1964, 88 pp.

0156 Alamsjah, St. Rais
10 orang Indonesia terbesar sekarang. Bukittinggi/Djakarta/Padang: Mutiara, 1952, 184 pp.

0157 *Album 86 pahlawan nasional dan sejarah perjuangannya.* Jakarta: Bahtera Jaya, 1985, 96 pp.

0158 *Album kenangan perjuangan Siliwangi.* Jakarta: Badan Pembina Corps Siliwangi, 1991, 800 pp.

0159 *Album mini; Mengenal Presiden dan Wakil Presiden RI serta pahlawan-pahlawan nasional.* Jakarta: Simplex, 1984, 86 pp.

0160 *Album pahlawan bangsa.* Jakarta: Mutiara, 1977, 85 pp. [Third edition, 1979, 93 pp.; Eighth printing, Jakarta: Mutiara Sumber Widya, 1986, 96 pp.]

0161 *Album perjuangan PATI ABRI asal SULUT.* Jakarta, ca. 1977, 180 pp.

0162 Alfian
'Tan Malaka; Pejuang revolusioner yang kesepian', *Prisma* 6-8 (August 1977):57-76.

0163 Alfian
'Tan Malaka; The lonely revolutionary', *Prisma* no. 8 (December 1977):16-36.

0164 Alfian
'Tan Malaka; Pejuang revolusioner yang kesepian', in: Abdullah, Taufik; Aswab Mahasin and Daniel Dhakidae (eds), *Manusia dalam kemelut sejarah*, pp. 132-173. Jakarta: LP3ES, 1978.

0165 Alfian
Kasimo sebagai politikus. Jakarta: n.n., 1980, 14 pp.

0166 Algadri, Hamid
Sukaduka dan latar belakang seorang perintis kemerdekaan. Jakarta: Dep. Sosial, 1980, 40+28 pp.

0167 Ali, Fachry
'Hamka dan masyarakat Islam Indonesia; Catatan pendahuluan riwayat dan perjuangannya', *Prisma* 12-2 (February 1983):48-60.

0168 Ali, Fachry
'Mohammad Roem, diplomat pejuang', *Prisma* 13-6 (June 1984):76-86.

0169 Ali, R. Moh. and F. Bodmer
Djakarta Djaja sepandjang masa. Djakarta: Pemerintah DCI, 1969, 158 pp.

0170 Ali, R. Moh. and F. Bodmer
Djakarta through the ages. Djakarta: Government of the Capital City of Djakarta, 1969, 154 pp.

0171 Alisjahbana, St. Takdir
Indonesia; Social and cultural revolution. Kuala Lumpur: Oxford University Press, 1966, 206 pp.

0172 Alisjahbana, St. Takdir
Revolusi masharakat dan kebudayaan di Indonesia. Kuala Lumpur: Oxford University Press, 1966, 236 pp.

0173 *Almanak seperempat abad kepolisian RI; 17 Agustus 1945-17 Agustus 1970.* Djakarta: Markas Besar Kepolisian RI, 1970, 1179 pp.

0174 *Almanak TNI-AD 1945-1963.* Bandung: Dinas Sejarah TNI-AD, 1977, 1614 pp. 3 vols.

0175 Aly, Bachtiar
Geschichte und Gegenwart der Kommunikationssysteme in Indonesien. Frankfurt a. Main: Lang, 1984, 687 pp.

0176 Amier, Andi Baso
Gema revolusi. Makasar: Pustaka Amanna Gappa, 1957, 128 pp.

0177 Amin, S.M.
Disekitar peristiwa berdarah di Atjeh. Djakarta: Soeroengan, 1956, 305 pp.

0178 Amin, S.M.
Kenang-kenangan dari masa lampau. Jakarta: Pradnya Paramita, 1978, 210 pp.

0179 Amin, S.M. (Krueng Raba Nasution)
Perjalanan hidupku selama sepuluh windu. Jakarta: Bulan Bintang, 1987, 416 pp.

0180   Anam, Choirul
       Pertumbuhan dan perkembangan Nahdlatul Ulama. Solo: Jatayu, 1985, 319 pp.

0181   Ananda, Endang Basri (ed.)
       70 tahun Prof. Dr. H.M. Rasjidi. Jakarta: Pelita, 1985, 340 pp.

0182   Anis, M. Junus
       Riwajat hidup K.H.A. Badawi; Djabatan terachir penasehat PP Muhammadijah dan anggota Pertimbangan Agung. Djakarta: GKBI, 1971, 48 pp.

0183   Anshari, H. Endang Saifuddin and M. Amien Rais (eds)
       Pak Natsir 80 tahun; 1. Pandangan dan penilaian generasi muda; 2. Penghargaan dan penghormatan generasi muda. Jakarta: Media Da'wah, 1988, 12+198, 21+231 pp. 2 vols.

0184   Antemas, Anggraini
       Orang-orang terkemuka dalam sedjarah Kalimantan; Dari Mulawarman sampai H. Hasbullah Jasin. Bandjarmasin: Anggraini Features, 1971, 95 pp.

0185   Anwar, Chaidir
       Sedjarah pergerakan ummat Islam di Indonesia. Bandung: IKIP, 1972, 100 pp.

0186   Anwar, Dewi Fortuna
       'Militer dan politik di Indonesia; Sebuah tinjauan', *Masyarakat Indonesia* 10-1 (1983):157-168.

0187   Anwar, Rosihan
       Perdjalanan terachir pahlawan nasional Sutan Sjahrir. Djakarta: Pembangunan, 1966, 76 pp.

0188   Anwar, Rosihan (ed.)
       Mengenang Sjahrir. Jakarta: Gramedia, 1980, 36+343 pp.

0189   Anwar, Rosihan
       Menulis dalam air; Di sini sekarang esok hilang; Sebuah otobiografi. Jakarta: Sinar Harapan, 1983, 376 pp.

0190   Anwar, Rosihan (ed.)
       Musim berganti; Sekilas sejarah Indonesia 1925-1950. Jakarta: Grafiti, 1985, 200 pp.

0191   Any, Andjar
       Bung Karno; Siapa yang punya. Solo: Sasongko, 1978, 252 pp.

0192   Any, Andjar
       Menyingkap tabir Bung Karno. Semarang: Aneka, 1978, 168 pp.

0193   Any, Andjar
       Rahasia ramalan Jayabaya, Ranggawarsita dan Sabdapalon. Semarang: Aneka, 1979, 123 pp.

0194   *Api nan tak kunjung padam; Gelora perjuangan Nusantara sebelum Proklamasi kemerdekaan 17 Agustus 1945.* Jakarta: Badan Penerbit Almanak R.I./Alda, 1983, 11+112 pp.

0195 Arfah, Muhammad; St. Nuraeda; Delila Supeno and Muhammad Amir
Lanto Daeng Pasewang sebagai seorang nasionalis dan patriotik; Biografi pahlawan.
Ujung Pandang: Dep. P dan K, 1994/1995, 14+192 pp.

0196 Ariwiadi
Gerakan Operasi Militer VII; Penjelesaian peristiwa Atjeh. Djakarta: Mega Book-
store/Pusat Sedjarah ABRI, ca. 1967, 12 pp.

0197 Ariwiadi
Ichtisar sedjarah nasional Indonesia (awal-sekarang). Djakarta: Departemen Perta-
hanan Keamanan, Pusat Sedjarah ABRI, 1971, 170 pp. [Second edition,
Jakarta: Departemen Pertahanan-Keamanan, 1979, 10+196 pp.]

0198 Arnowo, H. Doel
H. Doel Arnowo; Seorang pejuang berkerakyatan. Surabaya: Surya Agung, 1984,
23 pp.

0199 Ars, Mohammad Nur; Yunus Rasyid and Hasyim Achmad
Sejarah kota Samarinda. Jakarta: Kem. P dan K, 1986, 91 pp.

0200 Arsyad, A. Syatiri
Majlis Syuro Muslimin Indonesia; Studi tentang pemikiran dan perjuangannya.
1983, 156 pp. [Thesis IAIN Sunan Kalijaga, Yogyakarta.]

0201 Artha, Artum
Sedjarah kota Bandjarmasin. Bandjarmasin: Pemerintah Daerah Prop. KalSel,
1970, 32 pp.

0202 Artha, Artum
Wartawan-wartawan di Kalimantan Raya; Lintas sejarah pers di Kalimantan.
Surabaya: Bina Ilmu Offset, 1981, 144 pp.

0203 Arybowo, Sutamat; Nurinwa Ki S. Hendrowinoto and Mien A. Rifai
Mohammad Noer gubernur pangan. Surabaya: n.n., 1986, 490 pp.

0204 Askandar, L.; Masfar R. Hakim; Zamzulis Ismail and Burhanuddin Sanna
Mengenal Jos Sudarso. Jakarta: Dinas Sejarah TNI-AL, 1976, 210 pp.

0205 Assegaff, Dja'afar
Bunga rampai sejarah media massa. Jakarta: Mecon Press, 1978, 359 pp.

0206 Atmakusumah (ed.)
Tahta untuk rakyat; Celah-celah kehidupan Sultan Hamengku Buwono IX.
Dihimpun oleh: Mohamad Roem, Mochtar Lubis, Kustiniyati Mochtar dan
S. Maimoen. Jakarta: Gramedia, 1982, 24+384 pp.

0207 Atmakusumah (ed.)
Mochtar Lubis, wartawan jihad. Jakarta: Kompas, 1992, 16+527 pp.

0208 Atmodjo, Soebronto K.
Api kemerdekaan Indonesia; Kumpulan pertama. Djakarta: Lembaga Kebudajaan
Rakjat, 1962. [unpaged] (kitlv-m)

0209 Bachtiar, Harsja W.
The formation of the Indonesian nation. 1972. [PhD thesis Harvard University.]
[99]

0210 Bachtiar, Harsja W.
Siapa dia? Perwira tinggi Tentara Nasional Indonesia Angkatan Darat (TNI-AD).
Jakarta: Djambatan, 1988, 16+482 pp.

0211 *Bahaya laten komunisme di Indonesia. Jilid I: Perkembangan gerakan dan peng-
khianatan komunisme di Indonesia (1913-1948).* Jakarta: Markas Besar Angkatan
Bersenjata Republik Indonesia, Pusat Sejarah dan Tradisi ABRI, 1991, 136 pp.

0212 Bakry, Oemar
Bung Hatta selamat jalan; Cita-citamu kami teruskan. Jakarta: Mutiara, 1980, 197
pp.

0213 Bandjaransari, Soedomo
Sedjarah pemerintahan kota Jogjakarta. Jogjakarta: Djawatan Penerangan Kotapradja, ca. 1960, 39 pp.

0214 Bandjaransari, Soedomo and Tjeng Tik Kie
Peringatan 200 tahun kota Jogjakarta, 1756-1956; Buku kenang-kenangan. Jogjakarta: n.n., 1956, 206 pp. (kitlv-m)

0215 Bangun, Payung (ed.)
Melanchton Siregar; Pendidik dan pejuang. Jakarta: Gunung Mulia, 1987,
15+360 pp.

0216 Bangun, Tridah
Dr. T.D. Pardede; Wajah seorang pejuang wiraswasta. Jakarta: Gunung Agung,
1981, 212+51 pp. [Second edition, 1983, 280 pp.]

0217 Bangun, Tridah and Hendri Chairudin
*Kilap sumagan; Biografi Selamat Ginting; Salah seorang penggerak revolusi
kemerdekaan di Sumatera Utara.* Jakarta: Haji Masagung, 1994, 16+463 pp.

0218 *Bank Negara Indonesia 1946 25 tahun.* Djakarta: Panitya Peringatan Hari Ulang
Tahun ke-25 BNI-1946, 1971, 133 pp.

0219 *Banknotes and coins from Indonesia 1945-1990.* Jakarta: Yayasan Serangan Umum
1 Maret 1949/Perum Peruri, ca. 1991, 303 pp.

0220 Bauty, Yusuf
Genderang kemerdekaan dari penjara Hogepad; Otobiografi. Jakarta: Banteng
Sukarna, 1980, 271 pp.

0221 Bhakti, Indra Mulya
Pemikiran politik Tan Malaka; Suatu tinjauan cita-cita Tan Malaka tentang
nasionalisme. 1989, 217 pp. [MA thesis Universitas Nasional, Jakarta.]

0222 *Biografi 9 pahlawan revolusi Indonesia.* Bandung: Dinas Sejarah TNI-AD, 1982,
119 pp.

0223 *Biografi pahlawan nasional dari lingkungan ABRI.* Jakarta: Pusat Sejarah ABRI,
1979, 205 pp. [Second edition, Jakarta: Markas Besar Angkatan Bersenjata
Republik Indonesia, Pusat Sejarah dan Tradisi ABRI, 1988, 175 pp.]

0224 Boentarman
Djakarta kota lambang kemerdekaan. Bandung: Ganaco, 1956, 67 pp. (kitlv-m)

0225 Bondan, Molly
Spanning a revolution; The story of Mohamad Bondan and the Indonesian nationalist movement. Jakarta: Sinar Harapan, 1992, 318 pp.

0226 Bradjanegara, Sutedjo
Sedjarah pendidikan Indonesia. Jogjakarta, 1956, 208 pp. (kitlv-m)

0227 Brotosewojo
Perkembangan politik luar negeri Indonesia. 1970, 89 pp. [MA thesis Universitas Djajabaja, Djakarta.] [9]

0228 Budhiman, Arif
'In memoriam Djenderal anumerta Basuki Rachmat', *Vidya Yudha* no. 6 (1969):53-55.

0229 *Buku kenang-kenangan 39 tahun RRI Stasiun Regional I Bandung.* Bandung: RRI-SR I Bandung, 1984, 50 pp.

0230 *Buku kenang-kenangan sejarah biografi pahlawan negara RI.* Yogyakarta: Yayasan Keluarga Pahlawan Negara, 1973, 119 pp.

0231 *Buku pantja windhu kebangkitan perdjuangan pemuda Indonesia.* Djakarta: Jajasan Kesedjahteraan Keluarga Pemuda 66, 1970, 67+131 pp.

0232 *Buku peringatan 20 tahun 4 Oktober 1945-1965 PT Bank Dagang Nasional Indonesia.* Medan: Bank Dagang Nasional Indonesia, 1965, 72 pp.

0233 *Buku peringatan 30 tahun kesatuan pergerakan wanita Indonesia, 22 Desember 1928-22 Desember 1958.* Djakarta: Kem. Penerangan, 1958, 397 pp.

0234 *Buku peringatan limapuluh tahun Kota-Pradja Palembang.* Palembang: Rhama Publishing House, 1956, 194 pp.

0235 *Buku peringatan Taman Siswa 30 tahun, 1922-1952.* Third edition. Yogyakarta: Majelis Luhur Persatuan TS, 1981, 376 pp. [First edition 1952.]

0236 *Buku sejarah biografi pahlawan kemerdekaan dan revolusi.* Yogyakarta: Dewan Harian Daerah Angkatan 45 DI Yogyakarta, 1973, 149 pp.

0237 *Bung Hatta kita dalam pandangan masyarakat; Mengenang 40 hari wafatnya Bung Hatta.* Jakarta: Yayasan Idayu, 1980, 291 pp.

0238 *Bung Hatta mengabdi pada tjita-tjita perdjuangan bangsa; Beberapa lukisan pribadi dan perdjoangan pada peringatan ulang tahunnja ke-70.* Djakarta: Panitya Peringatan Ulang Tahun Bung Hatta ke-70, 1972, 16+538 pp.

0239 *Bung Karno tentang Partai Murba, Tan Malaka dan perdjuangannja; Pidato amanat Presiden Sukarno kepada resepsi pembukaan Kongres ke V Partai Murba di Bandung 15-17 Desember 1960.* Djakarta: Biro Agitprop D.P. Partai Murba, 1961, 14 pp.

0240 *Bunga rampai nilai-nilai perjuangan perintis kemerdekaan di DKI Jakarta; Seri II.* Jakarta: Dinas Sosial DKI Jakarta, 1986, 160 pp.

0241 *Bunga rampai Soempah Pemoeda.* Jakarta: Balai Pustaka, 1978, 544 pp. [Second edition, 1986, 507 pp.]

0242 Burhanuddin
Autobiografi Burhanuddin selaku perintis kemerdekaan. Jakarta: Dep. Sosial, 1986, 56 pp.

0243 Busyairi, Badruzzaman
Pesan dan kesan; pertemuan silaturrahmi Mohammad Natsir dan Mohamad Roem 70 tahun. Jakarta: Fajar Shadiq, 1978, 93 pp.

0244 Busyairi, Badruzzaman
R.H.O. Djoenaidi; Pejuang, pengusaha, dan perintis pers. Bandung: Yayasan R.H.O. Djoenaidi Manonjaya, 1982, 574 pp.

0245 Busyairi, Badruzzaman
Catatan perjuangan H.M. Yunan Nasution. Jakarta: Panjimas, 1985, 407 pp.

0246 *Butir-butir pejuang kesuma bangsa Indonesia di Minangkabau menuju kemerdekaan.* Jakarta: Panitia Besar Perlawanan Rakyat Minangkabau Menentang Penjajah, 1980, 1981, 22+54 pp. 2 vols.

0247 Buya, R.M.
Dr. Gerungan Saul Jacob Ratulangi (Dr. Sam Ratulangi). Jakarta: Plumpang Raya, 1986, 42 pp.

0248 Buya, R.M.
R.M.T.A. Suryo. Bandung: Sarana Panca Karya, 1987, 38 pp.

0249 *Catur windu TNI-AU 1945-1977; Sejarah bergambar.* Jakarta: Dinas Sejarah TNI-AU, 1977, 338 pp.

0250 Chaniago, J.R.; Kasijanto; Erwiza Erman and M. Hisyam
Ditugaskan sejarah; Perjuangan 'Merdeka' 1945-1985. Jakarta: Pustaka Merdeka, 1987, 13+146 pp.

0251 *A chronology of Indonesian history.* Djakarta: Department of Information, 1960, 83 pp.

0252 *Citra dan perjuangan perintis kemerdekaan; Seri perjuangan ex-Digul.* Jakarta: Direktorat Jenderal Bantuan Sosial, Departemen Sosial, 1977, 9+174 pp.

0253 *D.D.; Riwajat penghidupan dan perdjuangannja.* Jogjakarta: Kem. Penerangan, 1950, 76 pp.

0254 Dahlan, Hanafi
Beberapa tjatatan tentang Muhammad Yamin dan penulisan sedjarah nasional Indonesia. 1967, 99 pp. [MA thesis IKIP Padang.] [14]

0255 Darmaputera, Eka
Pancasila and the search for identity and modernity in Indonesian society; A cultural and ethical analysis. 1982, 466 pp. [PhD thesis University of Michigan, Ann Arbor.]

0256 Darmaputera, Eka
Pancasila and the search for identity and modernity in Indonesian society; A cultural and ethical analysis. Leiden: Brill, 1988, 254 pp.

0257 Daruch, Agus
De nationalistische beweging onder de Indo-Europeanen. Djakarta: Ministerie van Voorlichting, 1955, 110 pp. [Second printing 1957.]

0258 Darwis, Alwir and Ishaq Thaher
Anthology sejarah Indonesia babakan abad Proklamasi. Padang: Jurusan Sejarah FKPS IKIP Padang, 1978, 109 pp.

0259 Dasuki, H.A.; J.P. Sardjono; Sumardjo and Djamara
Sejarah Indramayu. Indramayu: Pemerintah Kab. Daerah Tingkat II Indramayu, 1977, 375 pp.

0260 *Dewan Perwakilan Rakjat Atjeh dalam sedjarah pembentukan dan perkembangan pemerintahan di Atjeh sedjak Proklamasi 1945 sampai awal tahun 1968 dan produk-produk legislatif.* Banda Atjeh: Sekretariat DPR-GR Prop. DI Atjeh, 1968, 274 pp.

0261 Dewantara, Bambang Sokawati
Ki Hadjar Dewantara ayahku. Jakarta: Sinar Harapan, 1989, 172 pp.

0262 Dewantara, Ki Hadjar
Dari kebangunan nasional sampai Proklamasi kemerdekaan; Kenang-kenangan. Djakarta: Endang, 1952, 270 pp.

0263 Dewantara, Ki Hadjar
Karja Ki Hadjar Dewantara. Jogjakarta: Taman Siswa, 1962, 1967, 557+317 pp. 2 vols.

0264 Dhaniswara
Dokumentasi sewindu; Berisi peristiwa-peristiwa jang penting dan bersedjarah di sekitar tanah air Indonesia. Second edition. Djakarta: Jajasan Pendidikan Kedjuruan-Djakarta, 1954, 152 pp. [First edition 1953.]

0265 Diah, B.M.
Meluruskan sejarah; Kumpulan karangan. Pengantar Dr. Alfian. Jakarta: Pustaka Merdeka, 1987, 27+268 pp.

0266 Dimyati, Muhammad
Sedjarah perdjuangan Indonesia. Djakarta: Widjaja, 1951, 222 pp.

0267 Djaja, Tamar
Sedjarah perang Indonesia. Djakarta: Energie, 1951, 45 pp.

0268 Djaja, Tamar
Orang-orang besar Indonesia. Jakarta: Pustaka Antara, 1974, 91+91+96+106 pp. 4 vols. [Second printing 1975.]

0269 Djaja, Tamar
Pahlawan-pahlawan Indonesia. Jakarta: Pustaka Antara, 1979, 160+138+150+163 pp. 4 vols.

0270 Djaja, Tamar
Soekarno-Hatta; Persamaan dan perbedaannya. Jakarta: Sastra Hudaya, 1981, 294 pp.

0271 Djalal, Zaidir
A.F. Lasut. Jakarta: Mutiara, 1978, 50 pp.

0272 Djalal, Zaidir
Dr. F.L. Tobing. Jakarta: Mutiara, 1978, 66 pp.

0273 Djalal, Zaidir
Dr. Sahardjo. Jakarta: Mutiara, 1978, 51 pp.

0274 Djamhari, Saleh As'ad
Ichtisar sedjarah perdjuangan ABRI (1945-sekarang). Djakarta: Pusat Sedjarah ABRI, 1971, 176 pp. [Second edition, *Ikhtisar sejarah perjuangan ABRI,* Jakarta: Departemen Pertahanan-Keamanan, Pusat Sejarah ABRI, 1979, 10+166 pp.]

0275 Djamily, Bachtiar
Hidup dan perjuangan Adam Malik. Cetakan kedua, diperbaiki dan dilengkapkan oleh: A. Hamid Lubis, Fauzi Amrullah, Sjamsudin Lubis. Kuala Lumpur: Pustaka Melayu Baru, 1978, 172 pp. [Second edition, Jakarta: Selecta Group, 1980, 317 pp.]

0276 Djamily, Bachtiar
Harmoko menteri penerangan Republik Indonesia; Anak rakyat insan yang arif. Kuala Lumpur: Pustaka Budiman, 1985, 269 pp.

0277 Djamily, Bachtiar
Ibrahim Yaacob pahlawan Nusantara. Kuala Lumpur: Pustaka Budiman, 1985, 240 pp.

0278 Djarwadi, Radik
Kisah Kahar Muzakar. Surabaja: Grip, 1962, 32 pp. [Second printing 1963.]

0279 Djauharuddin A.R.; H.M. Salim Umar and Ishak Solih
Peranan ummat Islam dalam proses pembentukan dan pembangunan negara Republik Indonesia yang berdasarkan Pancasila dan UUD 1945. Bandung: Angkasa, 1985, 60 pp.

0280 Djazh, Dahlan
Indonesia raya, merdeka, merdeka; Sejarah lagu kebangsaan Republik Indonesia. Jakarta: Bahtera Jaya, 1985, 87 pp.

0281 Djohan, Bahder
Bahder Djohan; Pengabdi kemanusiaan. Jakarta: Gunung Agung, 1980, 418 pp.

0282 Djojohadikusumo, Margono
Herinneringen uit drie tijdperken; Een geschreven familie-overlevering. Djakarta: Indira, 1969, 211 pp. [Second edition, Amsterdam: Nabrink, 1970, 13+191 pp.]

0283 Djojohadikusumo, Margono
Kenang-kenangan dari tiga zaman; Satu kisah kekeluargaan tertulis. Djakarta: Indira, 1971, 176 pp. (ubl)

0284 Djojohadikusumo, Margono
Reminiscences from three historical periods; A family tradition put in writing. Jakarta: Indira, 1973, 200 pp.

0285   Djojohadikusumo, Margono
       Catatan-catatan dari lembaran kertas yang kumal Dr. E.F.E. Douwes Dekker (Dr.
       Danoedirdjo Setia Budi); Seorang yang tak gentar menjunjung tinggi suatu cita-cita
       hidup: kemerdekaan politik Indonesia. Jakarta: Bulan Bintang, 1975, 92 pp.

0286   Djojoprajitno, Sudyono
       P.K.I.-Sibar contra Tan Malaka; Pemberontakan 1926 dan 'kambing hitam' Tan
       Malaka. Djakarta: Jajasan Massa, 1962, 236 pp.

0287   Djojoprajitno, Sudyono
       Dialektika sedjarah menjapubersih segala fitnah terhadap Tan Malaka; Memperingati
       ulang tahun ke-XIV hilangnja Tan Malaka. Djakarta: Jajasan Massa, 1963, 40 pp.

0288   Djojosoebroto, Soetoko
       Sedjarah penderitaan bangsa Indonesia; Tiga setengah abad didjadjah oleh sikulit
       putih, tiga setengah tahun didjadjah oleh sikulit kuning. Djakarta: Harapan Masa,
       1953, 59 pp. (kitlv-m)

0289   *Dua puluh lima tahun Departemen Luar Negeri, 1945-1970.* Djakarta: Panitya
       Penulisan Sedjarah Departemen Luar Negeri, 1971, 15+364 pp.

0290   *Dua puluh tiga tahun Indonesia merdeka.* Bukittinggi: Djawatan Penerangan
       Kotamadya Bukittinggi, 1968, 23 pp.

0291   *Dua windhu KODAM I/Iskandar Muda.* Kutaradja: Sedjarah Militer KODAM I,
       1972, 419 pp.

0292   *Dwi dasa warsa BNI; 5 Djuli 1946-1966.* Djakarta: BNI, 1966, 68 pp.

0293   Dwipayana, G. and Nazaruddin Sjamsuddin
       Diantara para sahabat; Pak Harto 70 tahun. Jakarta: Citra Lamtoro Gung
       Persada, 1991, 15+980 pp.

0294   Dyoyoadisuryo, Achmad Subardjo
       Kesadaran nasional; Otobiografi. Jakarta: Gunung Agung, 1978, 586 pp.

0295   Effendie, S. Anwar (ed.)
       Seminggu berkabung... melepas Bung Hatta. Bandung: Harapan Bandung, 1980,
       192 pp.

0296   Ekadjati, Edi S. a.o.
       Sejarah kota Bandung 1945-1979. Jakarta: Kem. P dan K, 1985, 244 pp.

0297   *Empat windu Partai Nasional Indonesia; 4 Djuli 1927-4 Djuli 1959.* Semarang:
       Dewan Daerah PNI Djawa Tengah, 1959, 310 pp. (kitlv-m)

0298   Erka (ed.)
       Bung Karno; Kepada bangsaku. Semarang: Aneka, 1978, 202 pp.

0299   Erka (ed.)
       Bung Karno...; Perginya seorang kekasih, suami dan kebanggaanku. Semarang:
       Aneka, 1978, 216 pp.

0300   G-Martha, Ahmaddani; Christianto Wibisono and Yozar Anwar (eds)
       Pemuda Indonesia dalam dimensi sejarah perjuangan bangsa. Jakarta: Yayasan
       Sumpah Pemuda, 1984, 443+49 pp. [Second edition, Jakarta: Indo-Media
       Communication, 1992, 205 pp.]

0301 Gafur, Abdul
Siti Hartinah Soeharto; Ibu utama Indonesia. Jakarta: Citra Lamtoro Gung Persada, 1992, 572 pp.

0302 Gandasubrata, S.M.
Kenang-kenangan 1933-1950. Purwokerto: n.n., 1952, 58+56 pp. 2 vols. (kitlv-m)

0303 Gani, M.
Surat kabar Indonesia dalam tiga zaman. Jakarta: Dep. Penerangan, 1978, 151 pp.

0304 *Garis besar perkembangan pers Indonesia.* Djakarta: Serikat Penerbit Suratkabar (SPS), 1971, 264 pp.

0305 Gayatri, Sri Indra
Prof. Dr. M. Soetopo; Hasil karya dan pengabdiannya. Jakarta: Kem. P dan K, 1983, 58 pp.

0306 Ghazaly, A.
Biografi Prof. Teungku Haji Ali Hasjmy. Jakarta: Socialia, 1978, 123 pp.

0307 Gonggong, Anhar
Mgr. Albertus Sugyopranoto S.Y. Jakarta: Kem. P dan K, 1976, 92 pp. [Second edition, 1981, 119 pp.]

0308 Gonggong, Anhar
Abdul Qahhar Mudzakkar dan gerakan DI/TII di Sulawesi Selatan 1950-1965. 1990, 14+461 pp. [PhD thesis Universitas Indonesia, Jakarta.]

0309 Gonggong, Anhar
Abdul Kahar Mudzakkar; Dari patriot hingga pemberontak. Jakarta: Grasindo, 1992, 11+239 pp.

0310 Gonggong, Anhar and Masjkuri
Dr. Johannes Verkuyl berkarya untuk Indonesia. Jakarta: Kem. P dan K, 1977, 15 pp.

0311 Hadhariyah M. and Mukeri
Autobiografi Hadhariyah M. dan Mukeri selaku perintis kemerdekaan. Jakarta: Dep. Sosial, 1986-87, 51 pp.

0312 Hadhi, Kartono
Sedjarah pemimpin Indonesia. Djakarta: Pustaka Dewata, 1961, 94 pp.

0313 Hadi, Syamsu (ed.)
Bung Karno dalam pergulatan pemikiran. Jakarta: Yayasan Pendidikan Soekarno/ Pustaka Simponi, 1991, 11+229 pp.

0314 Hadikusuma, H. Djarnawi
Derita seorang pemimpin; Riwayat hidup, perjoangan dan buah pikiran Ki Bagus Hadikusuma. Second edition. Yogyakarta: Persatuan, 1979, 72 pp. [First edition 1971.]

0315 Hadisutjipto, S.Z.
Sekitar 200 tahun sejarah Jakarta (1750-1945). Jakarta: Dinas Museum dan Sejarah Pemerintah DKI Jakarta, 1979, 143 pp.

0316   Hadiz, Vedi R.
       Politik, budaya dan perubahan sosial; Ben Anderson dalam studi politik Indonesia.
       Jakarta: Gramedia Pustaka Utama/Yayasan Society for Political and Economic
       Studies, 1992, 26+191 pp.

0317   Hakim, Masfar R. and Zamzulis Ismail
       Laksamana R.E. Martadinata. Jakarta: Kem. P dan K, 1980, 141 pp.

0318   Halilintars, Imam
       *B.R. MOTIK: Majukan Olehmu Tanah Air Indonesia Kita; Tokoh perintis ekonomi
       nasional.* Jakarta: Gunung Agung, 1986, 238 pp.

0319   Hamka (ps. H.A.M.K. Amrullah)
       Kenang-kenangan hidup. Kuala Lumpur: Antara, 1966 (edisi baru), 465 pp.
       [First edition, Djakarta: Gapura, 1951.]

0320   Hanafi, A.M.
       'In memoriam: Adam Malik', *Indonesia* no. 39 (1985):149-157.

0321   Hanafiah gelar Sutan Maharaja, Moh. Ali
       77 tahun riwayat hidup. Jakarta: n.n., 1977, 154 pp.

0322   Hanafiah, M.A.; Bahder Djohan and Surono (eds)
       125 tahun pendidikan dokter di Indonesia, 1851-1976. Jakarta: Panitya Peringatan
       125 Tahun Pendidikan Dokter di Indonesia, 1976, 363 pp.

0323   Hanifah, Abu
       *Renungan perjuangan bangsa dulu dan sekarang; Ceramah pada tanggal 6 Nopember
       1977 di Jakarta.* Jakarta: Yayasan Idayu, 1978, 80 pp.

0324   Hardi, Lasmidjah (ed.)
       Sumbangsihku bagi ibu pertiwi; Kumpulan pengalaman dan pemikiran. Jakarta:
       Yayasan Wanita Pejoang, 1981-85, 311+226+170+184+237 pp. 5 vols.

0325   Hardjito
       Risalah gerakan pemuda. Djakarta: Pustaka Antara, 1952, 446 pp.

0326   Hardjono, A.M.
       Dokumentasi perdjuangan pemuda Indonesia, 1915-1950. Medan: Toko Buku
       Islamiyah, 1950, 106 pp.

0327   Hardjosoediro, Soejitno
       Kronologi pergerakan kemerdekaan Indonesia. Jakarta: Pradnya Paramita, 1979,
       77 pp.

0328   Harjoto, R.M.
       'Sepuluh tahun orang penerangan', in: Darius Marpaung (ed.), *Bingkisan
       nasional; Kenangan 10 tahun revolusi Indonesia,* pp. 235-237, 242. Djakarta:
       Usaha Pegawai Nasional Indonesia, 1955.

0329   Harsono, Ganis
       Recollections of an Indonesian diplomat in the Sukarno era. Edited by C.L.M.
       Penders and B.B. Hering. St Lucia: University of Queensland Press, 1977,
       14+324 pp.

0330 Harsono, Ganis
Cakrawala politik era Sukarno. Jakarta: Inti Idayu Press, 1985, 216 pp.

0331 Hasjmy, A.
Peranan agama Islam dalam perang Aceh dan perjuangan kemerdekaan Indonesia. Medan: Panitya Seminar Perjuangan Aceh Sejak 1873 Sampai Kemerdekaan Indonesia, 1976, 116 pp.

0332 Hasjmy, A.
Tanah Merah; Digul bumi pahlawan kemerdekaan Indonesia. Jakarta: Bulan Bintang, 1976, 176 pp.

0333 Hasjmy, A.
Semangat merdeka; 70 tahun menempuh jalan pergolakan dan perjuangan kemerdekaan. Jakarta: Bulan Bintang, 1985, 772 pp.

0334 Hatta, Mohammad
Kumpulan karangan. Djakarta/Amsterdam/Surabaja: Balai Buku Indonesia, 1952-54, 276+156+272+290 pp. 4 vols. [Second printing 1976.]

0335 Hatta, Mohammad
Verspreide geschriften. Djakarta/Amsterdam/Surabaja: Van der Peet, 1952, 585 pp.

0336 Hatta, Mohammad
Demokrasi kita. Djakarta: Pandji Masjarakat, 1960, 36 pp. (kitlv-m) [Second edition, Djakarta: Pustaka Antara, 1966, 36 pp.]

0337 Hatta, Mohammad
Sesudah 25 tahun; Pidato. Djakarta: Djambatan, 1970, 29 pp.

0338 Hatta, Mohammad
Portrait of a patriot; Selected writings by Mohammad Hatta. The Hague/Paris: Mouton, 1972, 604 pp.

0339 Hatta, Mohammad
Bung Hatta menjawab; Wawancara Dr. Mohammad Hatta dengan Dr. Z. Yasni. Jakarta: Gunung Agung, 1978, 8+215 pp.

0340 Hatta, Mohammad
Bung Hatta antwoordt; Een vraaggesprek met Dr. Z. Yasni opgenomen in 1978 ten huize van Dr. Moh. Hatta. Hengelo: Smit, Jakarta: Gunung Agung, 1979, 228 pp.

0341 Hatta, Mohammad
Bung Hatta berpidato; Bung Hatta menulis. Jakarta: Mutiara, 1979, 103 pp.

0342 Hatta, Mohammad
Memoir. Jakarta: Tintamas, 1979, 21+597 pp.

0343 Hatta, Mohammad
Our democracy. Nathan: Griffith University, 1979, 27 pp.

0344 Hatta, Mohammad
Bung Hatta answers; Interviews (of) Dr. Mohammad Hatta with Dr. Z. Yasni. Singapore: Gunung Agung, 1981, 195 pp. [25]

0345   Hatta, Mohammad
       Memoirs. Edited by C.L.M. Penders. Singapore: Gunung Agung, 1981, 13+
       319 pp.

0346   Hatta, Mohammad
       Demokrasi kita, bebas aktif dan ekonomi masa depan. Edited by Sri-Edi Swasono
       and Fauzie Ridjal. Jakarta: Penerbit Universitas Indonesia (UI-Press), 1990,
       22+245 pp.

0347   Hellypradibyo and Herman Pratikno (eds)
       *Memperingati hari ulang tahun ke-62/63 P.J.M. Presiden Republik Indonesia
       Pemimpin Besar Revolusi Bung Karno.* Djakarta: Fadjar Bhakti, 1964, 316 pp.

0348   Hendrowinoto, Nurinwa Ki S.
       A. Aziz, wartawan kita. Jakarta: Yayasan Biografi Indonesia, 1985, 22+620 pp.

0349   Hersri, S.
       'Cornel Simandjuntak; Cahaya, datanglah!', *Prisma* 11-2 (February 1982):73-87.

0350   Hersri, S. and Joebar Ajoeb
       'S.M. Kartosuwirjo; Orang seiring bertukar jalan', *Prisma* 11-5 (May 1982):79-
       96.

0351   Hidayat, R.A.; H. Ikin A. Gani; Abu Chanief; Abdul Kadir and M. Rauf
       Umar Wirahadikusumah; Dari peristiwa ke peristiwa. Jakarta: Yayasan Kesejah-
       teraan Jayakarta, 1983, 311 pp.

0352   *Himpunan peraturan tata tertib Dewan Perwakilan Rakjat Republik Indonesia, 1945-
       1971.* Djakarta: Sekretariat DPR-GR, 1971, 376 pp.

0353   Hitipeuw, Frans
       Karel Sadsuitubun. Jakarta: Dep. P dan K, 1981, 115 pp. [Second edition, 1985,
       124 pp.]

0354   Hitipeuw, Frans
       Ir. Gunung Iskandar; Hasil karya dan pengabdiannya. Jakarta: Kem. P dan K,
       1982, 126 pp.

0355   Hitipeuw, Frans
       Dr. Johannes Leimena; Karya dan pengabdiannya. Jakarta: Kem. P dan K, 1986,
       222 pp.

0356   Husny, T.H.M. Lah
       Biografi-sejarah pujangga dan pahlawan nasional Amir Hamzah. Jakarta: P dan K,
       1978, 105 pp.

0357   Hutagalung, Mangaraja Haolonan
       Perjalanan hidupku; Sebuah buku memoar. Jakarta: Arion, 1983, 121 pp.

0358   Hutagalung, Sutan M.
       The problem of religious freedom in Indonesia, 1800 to the present. 1958. [PhD
       thesis Yale University, New Haven.] [106]

0359   Hutagaol, Said
       The development of higher education in Indonesia, 1920-1979. 1985, 313 pp. [PhD
       thesis University of Pittsburgh.]

0360 Hutauruk, M.
Gelora nasionalisme Indonesia. Jakarta: Erlangga, 1984, 20+79 pp.

0361 Hutauruk, M.
Sejarah ringkas Tapanuli suku Batak. Jakarta: Erlangga, 1987, 13+54 pp.

0362 Ibrahim, Muchtaruddin
Dr. Sukiman Wirjosandjojo; Hasil karya dan pengabdiannya. Jakarta: Kem. P dan K, 1982/83, 125 pp.

0363 Ibrahim, Muchtaruddin
Prof. Dr. Sulaiman Kusumah Atmaja. Jakarta: Kem. P dan K, 1983, 52 pp.

0364 Ibrahim, Muchtaruddin
Prof. Dr. Drs. Notonagoro SH; Hasil karya dan pengabdiannya. Jakarta: Kem. P dan K, 1983/84, 84 pp.

0365 Ibrahim, Thalib
Karya dan tjita-tjita Sutan Sjahrir. Djakarta: Photin, 1966, 25 pp.

0366 Ibrahim, Thalib
Jiwa joang bangsa Indonesia. Jakarta: Mahabudi, 1975, 84 pp.

0367 Ibrahimy, M. Nur el
Kisah kembalinya Tgk. Muh. Daud Beurcueh ke pangkuan Republik Indonesia. Jakarta: M. Nur el Ibrahimy, 1980, 341 pp.

0368 Ibrahimy, M. Nur el
Teungku Muhammad Daud Beureueh; Peranannya dalam pergolakan di Aceh. Second edition. Jakarta: Gunung Agung, 1982, 327 pp. [Third edition, 1986, 344 pp.]

0369 Idris, Rabihatun; Hajrah and Intan Densi Kamar
Peranan wanita di Sulawesi Selatan menentang penjajahan asing. Paper Seminar Sejarah Perjuangan Rakyat Sulawesi Selatan Menentang Penjajahan Asing, Ujung Pandang, 1982, 16 pp.

0370 Imawan, Riswandha
The evolution of political party systems in Indonesia, 1900 to 1987. 1989, 312 pp. [PhD thesis Northern Illinois University, DeKalb.]

0371 Imran, Amrin
Mohammad Hatta; Pejuang, proklamator, pemimpin, manusia biasa. Jakarta: Mutiara, 1981, 156 pp.

0372 Imran, Amrin (ed.)
Pendidikan opsir Divisi IX Banteng Sumatera Tengah, Bukittinggi; Peringatan hari jadi ke-40, 17 Pebruari 1946-17 Pebruari 1986. Jakarta: Yayasan Bukit Apit, 1986, 98 pp.

0373 *Indonesia 17 août 1945-1950.* Paris: Ambassade d'Indonésie, 1950, 38 pp. (ubl)

0374 *Indonesia; 20 years nationhood, 17-8-1945/17-8-1965.* Canberra: Kantor Penerangan RI, 1965, 61 pp. (kitlv-m)

0375 *Indonesia Raya; Brosur lagu kebangsaan Indonesia Raya.* Djakarta: Kem. P dan K, 1972, 139 pp.

0376   The Indonesian revolution; Basic documents and the idea of guided democracy.
       Djakarta: Dept. of Information, 1960, 122 pp.

0377   Iskandar, A. St. and Syarbaini
       Sembilan wanita perkasa. Jakarta: Gama Cipta, 1984, 108 pp.

0378   Iskandar, Nj. K.
       Menudju persatuan dan kedjajaan nusa dan bangsa. Pamekasan: Sunar, 1950,
       10 pp.

0379   Ismail B.D.
       Seorang peradjurit meninggalkan kita; Biografi singkat Djenderal anumerta Ahmad
       Yani. Djakarta: Sasmita Loka, 1967, 39 pp.

0380   Ismail, Zamzulis and B. Sanna
       Siapa Laksamana R.E. Martadinata? Jakarta: TNI-AL, 1976, 202 pp.

0381   Jajak MD
       Biografi presiden dan wakil presiden Republik Indonesia 1945-sekarang. Jakarta: Asri
       Media Pustaka, 1990, 182 pp.

0382   Ja'kub, T. Ismail
       Sedjarah Islam di Indonesia. Djakarta: Widjaya, 1956, 79 pp.

0383   Jarmanto
       Pancasila; Suatu tinjauan aspek historis dan sosio-politis. Yogyakarta: Liberty,
       1982, 154 pp.

0384   Jassin, H.B.
       Chairil Anwar pelopor Angkatan 45; Satu pembitjaraan; Disertai kumpulan hasil-
       hasil tulisannja. Djakarta: Gunung Agung, 1956, 157 pp. [Eighth printing,
       Jakarta: Haji Masagung, 1992, 184 pp.]

0385   Jassin, H.B.
       Surat-surat 1943-1983. Diedit dan diberi pengantar oleh Pamusuk Eneste.
       Jakarta: Gramedia, 1984, 386 pp.

0386   Joeniarto
       Sedjarah ketatanegaraan RI. Jogjakarta: Jajasan Penerbit GM, 1966, 164 pp.
       [Third edition, Jakarta: Bina Aksara, 1984, 176 pp.]

0387   Judono, H.M.
       Kenang-kenangan tiga zaman. Jakarta: Yayasan Penerbitan Ikatan Dokter
       Indonesia, 1990, 262 pp.

0388   Jumenengan Sri Sultan Hamengku Buwono IX; Peringatan 40 tahun 18 Maret
       1940-18 Maret 1980. Jakarta: Gunung Agung/Yayasan Idayu/Panitia
       Peringatan 40 Tahun Jumenengan Sri Sultan Hamengku Buwono IX, 1980, 39
       pp.

0389   Jusuf, Sudono
       Sedjarah perkembangan Angkatan Laut. Djakarta: Departemen Pertahanan-
       Keamanan, Pusat Sedjarah ABRI, 1971, 9+258 pp.

0390   Kabinet-kabinet Republik Indonesia. Djakarta: Kem. Penerangan, 1955, 51 pp.

0391 *Kabinet-kabinet RI; Susunan dan programnja sedjak 1945.* Djakarta: Biro Research Dep. Luar Negeri, 1961, 40 pp.

0392 Kaisiepo, Manuel
'Setengah abad di panggung politik; Perjuangan Bung Adam', *Prisma* 13-11 (November 1984):77-88.

0393 *Kami perkenalkan..!* Djakarta: Kementerian Penerangan R.I., 1950, 108 pp. [Second edition, 1954, 158 pp.]

0394 'Kantor Pusat Sedjarah Militer Angkatan Darat (Pussem)', *Madjalah Sedjarah Militer Angkatan Darat* no. 7 (1960):85-91.

0395 Karim, H. Abdul (ps. Oey Tjeng Hien)
Mengabdi agama, nusa dan bangsa; Sahabat karib Bung Karno. Jakarta: Gunung Agung, 1982, 263 pp.

0396 Karim, M. Rusli
Perjalanan partai politik di Indonesia; Sebuah potret pasang-surut. Jakarta: Rajawali, 1983, 17+304 pp.

0397 Kartadarmadja, Soenjata
Riwayat hidup dan perjuangan Sultan Sarief Kasim II. Jakarta: Kem. P dan K, 1977, 34 pp.

0398 Kartadarmadja. Soenjata
Yos Sudarso. Jakarta: Widjaya, 1978, 48 pp.

0399 Kartadarmadja, Soenjata
Adisucipto; Bapak penerbang Indonesia. Jakarta: Widjaya, 1981, 59 pp.

0400 Kartadarmadja, Soenjata
I Gusti Ngurah Rai. Jakarta: Widjaya, 1982, 55 pp.

0401 Kartadarmadja, Soenjata
Prof. Dr. Wilhelmus Zakharias Yohannes. Jakarta: Kem. P dan K, 1982, 106 pp. [Second edition, 1985, 112 pp.]

0402 Kartodirdjo, Sartono
Modern Indonesia; Transformation and tradition; A socio-historical perspective. Yogyakarta: Gadjah Mada University Press, 1984, 299 pp.

0403 Kartodirdjo, Sartono
'Peasant mobilization and political development in Indonesia', in: Sartono Kartodirdjo, *Modern Indonesia; Transformation and tradition; A socio-historical perspective,* pp. 30-54. Yogyakarta: Gadjah Mada University Press, 1984.

0404 Kartohadikusumo, Setiadi
Soetardjo; Pembuat 'Petisi Soetardjo' dan perjuangannya. Jakarta: Sinar Harapan, 1990, 247 pp.

0405 Kartonagoro, Suwidji
Belajar, membaca sejarah nasional Indonesia. Surakarta: Yayasan Pendidikan Surakarta Hadiningrat, 1980, 711 pp.

0406   Kartosoepadmo, Soegir
       Riwayat hidup dan kenang-kenangan Soegir Kartosoepadmo, 20-8-1900 s/d 11-12-
       1980. Malang: n.n., 1980, 305 pp.

0407   Kartowijono, Sujatin
       Perkembangan pergerakan wanita Indonesia; Ceramah. Second edition. Jakarta:
       Yayasan Idayu, 1977, 32 pp. [First edition 1975.]

0408   *Karya Jaya; Kenang-kenangan lima Kepala Daerah Jakarta, 1945-1966.* Jakarta:
       Pemerintah DKI, 1977, 268 pp.

0409   Kasansengari, Oerip
       Sedjarah lagu kebangsaan Indonesia Raya dan W.R. Soepratman pentjiptanja.
       Surabaja: Kasansengari, 1967, 178 pp.

0410   *I.J. Kasimo; Hidup dan perjuangannya.* Oleh tim wartawan Kompas dan redaksi
       Penerbit Gramedia. Jakarta: Gramedia/Yayasan Kasimo, 1980, 197 pp.

0411   Katoppo, Aristides (ed.)
       80 tahun Bung Karno. Jakarta: Sinar Harapan, 1981, 342 pp.

0412   Kelana, Pandir (ps. R.M. Slamet Danusudirdjo)
       Merah Putih golek kencana; Katharina Khoo Giok Nio menggugat. Jakarta: Sinar
       Harapan, 1982, 199 pp. [Second edition, Jakarta: Gramedia, 1992, 247 pp.]

0413   Kelana, Pandir (ps.)
       Ibu Sinder. Jakarta: Sinar Harapan, 1983, 182 pp. [Second edition, Jakarta:
       Gramedia, 1991, 242 pp.]

0414   *Kemanunggalan ABRI dengan rakyat; Sekelumit catatan sejarah.* Jakarta: Triosa
       Dharma, 1985, 530 pp.

0415   *Kementerian Agama 10 tahun; 3 Djanuari 1946-3 Djanuari 1956.* Djakarta: Kem.
       Agama, 1956, 94 pp. (kitlv-m)

0416   *Kenang-kenangan lima windu Radio Republik Indonesia.* Jember: RRI-Stasiun
       Regional 2, 1985, 51 pp.

0417   *Kenangan tiga puluh tahun Komando Daerah Militer IV/Sriwijaya.* Palembang:
       Dinas Sejarah Militer KODAM IV/Sriwijaya, 1975, 44+211 pp.

0418   *Kepartaian di Indonesia.* Jogjakarta: Kem. Penerangan Republik Indonesia, 1950,
       1951, 203+431 pp. 2 vols. (kitlv-m)

0419   *Kepartaian di Indonesia.* Djakarta: Kem. Penerangan, 1954, 578 pp.

0420   *Kewarganegaraan yang bertanggungjawab; Mengenang Dr. J. Leimena.* Jakarta:
       Gunung Mulia, 1980, 14+408 pp.

0421   *Kisah singkat pendaratan RTP 2/Brawidjaja di SUM Barat; Diselenggarakan sebagai*
       peringatan hari ulang tahun ke-10 Brawidjaja, 17 Desember 1958. Bukittinggi:
       Divisi Brawidjaja, 1958, 92 pp.

0422   Kleden, Ignas
       'The changing political leadership of Java; The significance of Sultan Hamengku
       Buwono IX', *Prisma* no. 46 (1989):21-31.

0423 Koesmen, S.
Kenalilah pahlawan kemerdekaan; Dari Sultan Hasanuddin sampai Djendral Sudirman. Surabaja: Grip, 1962, 56 pp.

0424 Kole, E.Y.
Dr. Sam Ratulangi; Riwayat hidup dan perjuangannya. Menado: Wenang Lima, 1981, 50 pp.

0425 *Komunisme dan kegiatannya di Indonesia*. Bandung: Dinas Sejarah TNI Angkatan Darat, 1972, 311 pp. [Second edition, 1982, 396 pp.]

0426 *Korps Komando AL dari tahun ketahun*. Djakarta: Bagian Sedjarah KKO-AL, 1971, 600 pp.

0427 Kosim, E.; Y. Yogaswara and Rachmat Susatio
Biografi dan perjuangan Dewi Sartika. Bandung: Universitas Padjadjaran, 1980, 91 pp.

0428 *Kota Jogjakarta 200 tahun, 7 Oktober 1756-7 Oktober 1956*. Jogjakarta: Panitya Peringatan Kota Jogjakarta 200 Tahun, 1956, 168 pp.

0429 *Kotapradja Malang 50 tahun, 1-4-1964*. Malang: Seksi Penerbitan 50 Tahun Kotapradja Malang, 1964, 152 pp.

0430 *Kronologi sedjarah TNI-1945*. Bandung: PUSSEMAD, 1963, 132 pp. (kitlv-m)

0431 Kurniadi, H. Eddy
Peranan pemuda dalam pembangunan politik di Indonesia (analistis studi berdasarkan pendekatan sejarah dan sosio kultural). Bandung: Angkasa, 1987, 263 pp.

0432 Kutoyo, Sutrisno
Pahlawan Prof. Mohamad Yamin SH. Jakarta: Kem. P dan K, 1975, 131 pp.

0433 Kutoyo, Sutrisno and Mardanas Safwan
Dr. G.S.S.J. Ratulangi; Riwayat hidup dan perjuangannya. Jakarta: Mutiara, 1972, 71 pp.

0434 Kutoyo, Sutrisno and Mardanas Safwan
Riwayat hidup dan perjuangan H. Agus Salim. Bandung: Angkasa, 1974, 73 pp.

0435 Kutoyo, Sutrisno and Mardanas Safwan
Riwayat hidup dan perjuangan Oto Iskandar Dinata. Jakarta: Mutiara, 1974, 43 pp.

0436 Kutoyo, Sutrisno and Mardanas Safwan
Wage Rudolf Supratman. Jakarta: Mutiara, 1976, 80 pp. [Second printing 1978.]

0437 *Labour legislation Republic of Indonesia (1945-1972)*. Jakarta: Erlangga, 1972, 196 pp.

0438 *Lahir dan perkembangan S.B.G*. Surabaja, 79 pp.

0439 *Lahir-berdjoang-berkembang di alam Indonesia merdeka; 15 tahun Bank Nasional Indonesia, 5 Djuli 1946-5 Djuli 1961*. Djakarta: BNI, 1961, 12 pp.

0440 Lain, Husni (ed.)
Mengenang proklamator RI Soekarno-Hatta. Jakarta: Kreasi Jaya Utama, 1980, 151 pp.

0441 Lapian, A.B. and T.B. Simatupang
'Pemberontakan di Indonesia; Mengapa dan untuk apa?', *Prisma* 7-7 (August 1978):9-13.

0442 Latief, Hasnah
Mengenal pahlawan nasional Dr. G.S.S.J. Ratulangi. Manado: IKIP, 1986, 31 pp.

0443 Latuihamallo, P.D.; V. Matondang; H. Rosihan Anwar; P.K. Ojong and M. Hoetaoeroek (eds)
Kejakinan dan perdjuangan; Buku kenangan untuk Letnan Djenderal Dr. T.B. Simatupang. Djakarta: Gunung Mulia, 1972, 452 pp.

0444 Lee Kam Hing
Schooling in Indonesia; Trends in development and issues of controversy, 1945-1965. 1974, 769 pp. [PhD thesis Monash University, Clayton.]

0445 Lee Kam Hing
'The Taman Siswa in post-war Indonesia', *Indonesia* no. 25 (1978):41-59.

0446 Leirissa, R.Z.
'Biografi Dr. J. Leimena', in: *Kewarganegaraan yang bertanggungjawab*, pp. 1-103. Jakarta: Gunung Mulia, 1980.

0447 Leirissa, R.Z.
Ir. Martinus Putuhena; Karya dan pengabdiannya. Jakarta: Kem. P dan K, 1985, 121 pp.

0448 Leirissa, R.Z.
Terwujudnya suatu gagasan; Sejarah masyarakat Indonesia 1900-1950. Jakarta: Akademik Pressindo, 1985, 108 pp.

0449 Lim Ek Cheang
Light on Indonesia. Djakarta: Suropati, 1950, 110 pp.

0450 Lontaan, Ju. and Gm. Sanusi
Mengenal kabupaten Kotawaringin Barat. Kotawaringin Barat: Pemdati, 1977, 180 pp.

0451 Lubis, Mochtar
Het land onder de regenboog; De geschiedenis van Indonesië. Alphen aan den Rijn: Sijthoff, 1979, 207 pp.

0452 Lubis, Mochtar
Indonesia; Land under the rainbow. Singapore: Oxford University Press, 1990, 218 pp.

0453 Lubis, Mochtar; Suardi Tasrif and Mohammad Said
Visi wartawan 45. Jakarta: Media Sejahtera, 1992, 109 pp.

0454 *Lukisan pemberontakan PKI di Indonesia dan penumpasannya*. Bandung: Dinas Sejarah TNI-AD, 1979, 280 pp.

0455   Lutfi, Muchtar; Suwardi; Anwar Syair and Umar Amin
       Sejarah Riau. Pekanbaru: Universitas Riau, 1977, 38+931 pp.

0456   Maarif, Ahmad Syafii
       Islam as the basis for the state; A study of the Islamic political ideas as reflected in the Constituent Assembly debates in Indonesia. 1983, 338 pp. [PhD thesis University of Chicago.]

0457   Maarif, Ahmad Syafii
       Islam dan masalah kenegaraan; Studi tentang percaturan dalam Konstituante. Jakarta: Lembaga Penelitian, Pendidikan dan Penerangan Ekonomi dan Sosial, 1985, 225 pp.

0458   Machudum Dt.M., St.
       Riwajat perdjuangan bangsa Indonesia dalam masa 150 tahun. Bandung: Nix, 1952, 100 pp.

0459   Madewa, Lukman (ed.)
       Esa hilang dua terbilang; Album kenangan KODAM VI/Siliwangi 1946-1977. Bandung: Jarahdam VI/Siliwangi, 1977, 149 pp.

0460   Mahmud, Syamsuddin
       Monetary developments and policy in the Republic of Indonesia after World War II. 1974, 17+123 pp. [PhD thesis University of Ghent.]

0461   Malaka, Tan
       From jail to jail. Translated, edited, and introduced by Helen Jarvis. Athens: Ohio University Center for International Studies, 1991, 146+303, 8+306, 8+454 pp. 3 vols.

0462   Malik, Adam
       Mengabdi Republik. I. *Adam dari Andalas;* II. *Angkatan 45;* III. *Angkatan pembangunan.* Jakarta: Gunung Agung, 1978-79, 224+258+235 pp. 3 vols.

0463   Malik, Adam
       In the service of the Republic. Singapore: Gunung Agung, 1980, 13+326 pp.

0464   Mangandaralam, Sjahbuddin
       In memoriam St. Sjahrir; Perdjuangan dan penderitaannja. Bandung: Pantjasakti, 1966, 51 pp.

0465   Mangandaralam, Syahbuddin
       Apa dan siapa Bung Hatta? Jakarta: Rosda Jayaputra, 1986, 89 pp.

0466   Mangandaralam, Syahbuddin
       Apa dan siapa Bung Karno? Bandung: Rosda Jayaputra, 1986, 97 pp.

0467   Mangandaralam, Syahbuddin
       Apa dan siapa Sutan Syahrir? Jakarta: Rosda Jayaputra, 1986, 63 pp.

0468   Mangkualam, H. Asnawi
       Padama terletak qadar; Sebuah autobiografi. Jakarta: Haji Masagung, 1989, 10+ 373 pp.

0469 Mangunwidodo, Soebaryo
Dr. K.R.T. Radjiman Wediodiningrat; Perjalanan seorang putra bangsa. Jakarta: Yayasan Dr. K.R.T. Radjiman Wediodiningrat, 1994, 10+255 pp.

0470 Manilet-Ohorella, G.A.
Wim J. Latumeten; Hasil karya dan pengabdiannya. Jakarta: Kem. P dan K, 1983, 64 pp.

0471 Mansoer, M.D.; Amrin Imran; Mardanas Safwan; Asmaniar Z. Idris and Sidi I. Buchari
Sedjarah Minangkabau. Djakarta: Bhratara, 1970, 19+286 pp.

0472 Margono
Ichtisar sedjarah pergerakan nasional (1908-1945). Djakarta: Pusat Sedjarah ABRI, 1971, 222 pp.

0473 Martamin, Maryadi a.o.
Sejarah daerah Sumatera Barat. Padang: Proyek Penelitian dan Pencatatan Kebudayaan Daerah, 1976, 205 pp.

0474 Martha, Fajar
Prof. Dr. Mr. Supomo (sarjana ahli hukum). Jakarta: Karya Unipress, 1984, 63 pp.

0475 Masykuri
Dr. G.S.S.J. Ratulangi. Jakarta: Kem. P dan K, 1975, 118 pp. [Fourth edition 1985.]

0476 Masykuri
Drs. Susanto Tirtoprodjo SH; Hasil karya dan pengabdiannya. Jakarta: Kem. P dan K, 1982/83, 74 pp.

0477 Materu, Mohamad Sidky Daeng
Sejarah pergerakan nasional bangsa Indonesia. Third edition. Jakarta: Gunung Agung, 1985, 8+134 pp. [First edition 1967.]

0478 Matondang, H.M. Victor
Percakapan dengan Dr. T.B. Simatupang. Jakarta: Gunung Mulia, 1986, 87 pp.

0479 Mattalioe, Bahar
Kahar Muzakkar dengan petualangannja. Djakarta: Delegasi, 1965, 168 pp.

0480 Mattulada
'Kahar Muzakkar; Profil patriot pemberontak', in: Abdullah, Taufik; Aswab Mahasin and Daniel Dhakidae (eds), *Manusia dalam kemelut sejarah*, pp. 174-188. Jakarta: Lembaga Penelitian, Pendidikan dan Penerangan Ekonomi dan Sosial, 1978.

0481 Mawi, Bung
Bung Karno milik rakyat Indonesia. Jakarta: Rose Group, 1978, 52 pp.

0482 Melik, Sajoeti
Demokrasi Pantjasila dan perdjoangan ideologi didalamnja. Djakarta: Pesat, 1953, 205 pp. [22, 40, 1348]

0483 *Memperingati tudjuh tahun perdjuangan PII, 1947-1954.* Semarang: Peladjar Islam Indonesia, 1954, 54 pp. (kitlv-m)

0484 *Mengenal dari dekat Komando Daerah Militer XV/Pattimura.* Ambon: KODAM XV/Pattimura, 1974, 216 pp.

0485 Mertokusumo, Sudikno
Sedjarah peradilan dan perundang-undangannja di Indonesia sedjak 1942. 1971, 198 pp. [PhD thesis Universitas Gadjah Mada, Jogjakarta.]

0486 Mertolojo, Soemartono
Hamengku Buwono IX penyelamat RI. Yogyakarta: n.n., 1989, 1991, 20+510, 28+ 685 pp. 2 vols.

0487 Meuraxa, Dada
Lintasan sedjarah perdjuangan rakjat di Atjeh; Atjeh daerah modal Republik Indonesia. Medan: National Book Store, 1952, 80 pp. (kitlv-m)

0488 Meuraxa, Dada
Atjeh 1000 tahun dan peristiwa Teungku Daud Beureueh c.s. Medan: Pustaka Hasmar, 1954, 166 pp.

0489 Meuraxa, Dada
Peristiwa berdarah di Atjeh. Medan: Sedar, 1956, 70 pp.

0490 Moedjanto, G.
Indonesia abad ke-20. Yogyakarta: Kanisius, 1988, 201+181 pp. 2 vols.

0491 Moehkardi
Mohammad Said Reksohadiprodjo; Hasil karya dan pengabdiannya. Jakarta: Kem. P dan K, 1982, 133 pp.

0492 Moein, Mohammad
Sistem penjelenggaraan perdjoangan diplomasi dan politik luar negeri. Djakarta: Pustaka Dewata, 1951, 84 pp.

0493 Moeryantini, M. Henricia
Mgr. Albertus Soegijapranata S.J. Ende: Nusa Indah, 1975, 140 pp.

0494 Mokoginta, A.J.
Sedjarah singkat perdjuangan bersendjata bangsa Indonesia. Djakarta: SAB, 1964, 170 pp.

0495 *Monografi daerah.* Jakarta: Kem. P dan K, ca. 1976. Many vols.

0496 Muhaimin, Jahja
Perkembangan militer dalam politik di Indonesia 1945-1966. Jogjakarta: Lukman, 1971, 210 pp. [Second edition, Yogyakarta: Gadjah Mada University Press, 1982, 245 pp.]

0497 Mukayat
Haji Agus Salim; The grand old man of Indonesia. Jakarta: Kem. P dan K, 1981, 90 pp.

0498 Mukayat
Haji Agus Salim; Karya dan pengabdiannya. Jakarta: Kem. P dan K, 1985, 93 pp.

0499 Mukmin, Hidayat
Beberapa aspek perjuangan wanita di Indonesia; Suatu pendekatan deskriptif-komparatif. Bandung: Binacipta, 1980, 183 pp.

0500 Mulyono
Dr. Muwardi. Jakarta: Kem. P dan K, 1981, 76 pp.

0501 Mulyono and Sutrisno Kutoyo
Haji Samanhudi. Jakarta: Kem. P dan K, 1980, 126 pp.

0502 *Museum dan sejarah.* Jakarta: Dep. P. dan K, Proyek Pembinaan Permuseuman Jakarta, 1993/1994, 142 pp.

0503 Muslimin, Amrah
Ichtisar perkembangan otonomi daerah, 1903-1958. Djakarta: Djambatan, 1960, 157 pp. (kitlv-m)

0504 Mustoffa, Sumono (ed.)
Sukarni dalam kenangan teman-temannya. Jakarta: Sinar Harapan, 1986, 323 pp.

0505 Nalenan, Ruben
Biografi Prof. Dr. W.Z. Johannes. Jakarta: Bhratara Karya Aksara, 1979, 54 pp.

0506 Nalenan, R.
Arnold Mononutu; Portret seorang patriot. Jakarta: Gunung Agung, 1981, 12+ 283 pp.

0507 Nalenan, Ruben
Iskaq Tjokrohadisurjo; Alumni desa bersemangat banteng. Jakarta: Gunung Agung, 1982, 13+207 pp.

0508 Nalenan, Ruben
'Ali Sastroamidjojo; Merombak pola kekuatan dunia', *Prisma* 12-4 (April 1984):77-91.

0509 Nalenan, Ruben and H. Iskandar Gani
Dr. A.K. Gani; Pejuang berwawasan sipil dan militer. Jakarta: Yayasan Indonesianologi, 1990, 22+347 pp.

0510 Nanulaitta, I.O.
Biografi pahlawan kemerdekaan nasional Ir. Haji Juanda. Jakarta: Kem. P dan K, 1979, 243 pp.

0511 Nanulaitta, I.O.
Ir. Haji Juanda Kartawijaya. Jakarta: Kem. P dan K, 1980, 203 pp.

0512 Nanulaitta, I.O.
Mr. Johannes Latuharhary; Hasil karya dan pengabdiannya. Jakarta: Kem. P dan K, 1982, 251 pp.

0513 *Naskah penelitian sedjarah pertumbuhan AURI.* Djakarta: Pushumas AURI, 1968. [4835]

0514 *Naskah ringkas chronologis sedjarah Divisi Siliwangi.* Bandung: KODAM VI/Siliwangi, 1961. [1540]

0515   Nasution, A.H. (Abdul Haris)
       Tjatatan-tjatatan sekitar politik militer Indonesia. Djakarta: Pembimbing, 1955,
       388 pp.

0516   Nasution, A.H.
       General Abdul Haris Nasution; Biographical note. London: Indonesian Embassy,
       1961, 15 pp. (kitlv-m)

0517   Nasution, A.H.
       'Biografi Djenderal A.H. Nasution', *Madjalah Sedjarah Militer Angkatan Darat*
       no. 9 (1962):4-7.

0518   Nasution, A.H.
       Tentara Nasional Indonesia. Bandung/Djakarta: Jajasan Pustaka Militer (vol. 1);
       Djakarta: Seruling Masa (vols 2, 3), 1962, 1968, 1971, 254+274+203 pp. 3 vols.
       [Vol. 1, third edition, Djakarta: Seruling Masa, 1970, 364 pp.]

0519   Nasution, A.H.
       Biographical notes on General Dr. A.H. Nasution. Djakarta: Biro Hubungan
       Masjarakat, 1971, 12 pp. [22]

0520   Nasution, A.H.
       Kekarjaan ABRI. Djakarta: Seruling Masa, 1971, 420 pp.

0521   Nasution, A.H.
       Memenuhi panggilan tugas. Vol. 1, *Kenangan masa muda*, Jakarta: Gunung Agung,
       1982, 12+276 pp.; Vol. 2, *Kenangan masa gerilya*, 1983, 12+374 pp.; Vol. 3,
       Masa pancaroba pertama, 1983, 14+490 pp.; Vol. 4, *Masa pancaroba kedua*, 1984,
       13+518 pp.; Vol. 5, *Kenangan masa Orde Lama*, 1985, 14+501 pp.; Vol. 6, *Masa
       kebangkitan Orde Baru*, 1987, 14+486 pp.; Vol. 7, *Masa konsolidasi Orde Baru*,
       Jakarta: Haji Masagung, 1988, 10+347 pp.; Vol. 8, *Masa pemancangan Orde
       Pembangunan*, 1988, 9+475 pp.; Vol. 8a, *Kenangan masa gerilya*, 1989, 12+359
       pp.; Vol. 9, *Bagi pejuang tiada tugas akhir dan tiada akhir tugas*, 1993, 9+515 pp.
       [Second edition, Jakarta: Haji Masagung, 1989-90.]

0522   Nasution, Adnan Buyung
       *The aspiration for constitutional government in Indonesia; A socio-legal study of the
       Indonesian Konstituante 1956-1959*. 1992, 12+570 pp. [PhD thesis Vrije
       Universiteit, Amsterdam.]

0523   Nasution, Amir Hamzah
       Sedjarah kebangsaan untuk kursus pengetahuan umum. Djakarta: Pustaka Aida,
       1951, 128 pp.

0524   Nasution, Harun
       The Islamic state in Indonesia; The rise of the ideology, the movement for its
       creation and the theory of the Masjumi. 1965, 190 pp. [MA thesis McGill
       University, Montreal.]

0525   Natsir, M.
       Capita selecta II. Djakarta: Pustaka Pendis, 1957, 337 pp. (kitlv-m)

0526   Nawawi, H. Ramli; Tamny Ruslan and Yustan Aziddin
       Sejarah kota Banjarmasin. Jakarta: Kem. P dan K, 1986, 183 pp.

0527 Nawawi, Mohd. A.
Regionalism and regional conflicts in Indonesia. 1968, 368 pp. [PhD thesis Princeton University, Princeton, N.J.]

0528 Nawawi, M.A.
'Punitive colonialism; The Dutch and the Indonesian national integration', *Journal of Southeast Asian Studies* 2-2 (September 1971):159-168.

0529 Ning, Hasjim
Pasang surut pengusaha pejuang; Otobiografi Hasjim Ning. Seperti dituturkan kepada A.A. Navis. Jakarta: Grafitipers, 1986, 11+392 pp.

0530 Noer, Deliar
Masjumi; Its organization, ideology, and political role in Indonesia. 1960, 412 pp. [MA thesis Cornell University, Ithaca.]

0531 Noer, Deliar
The development of our democracy. Nathan: Griffith University, 1978, 27 pp.

0532 Noer, Deliar
'Islam as a political force in Indonesia', in: J.A.C. Mackie (ed.), *Indonesia; The making of a nation*, pp. 633-644. Canberra: Research School of Pacific Studies, Australian National University, 1980.

0533 Noer, Deliar
Partai Islam di pentas nasional 1945-1965. Jakarta: Grafitipers, 1987, 493 pp.

0534 Noer, Deliar
Mohammad Hatta; Biografi politik. Jakarta: Lembaga Penelitian, Pendidikan dan Penerangan Ekonomi dan Sosial, 1990, 14+778 pp.

0535 Notosoetardjo, H.A.
Menggali api revolusi; Dari 11 amanat Bung Karno. Djakarta: Endang, 1962, 252 pp. (kitlv-m) [Second edition, Djakarta: Lembaga Penggali dan Penghimpun Sedjarah Revolusi Indonesia, 1964, 294 pp.]

0536 Notosoetardjo, H.A.
Peranan agama Islam dalam revolusi Indonesia. Djakarta: Endang, 1963, 67 pp. [Second edition, 1964, 68 pp.]

0537 Notosoetardjo, H.A.
Dokumenta Pantja Sila berdasarkan adjaran Bung Karno. Djakarta: Endang, 1965, 306 pp.

0538 Notosusanto, Nugroho
Sedjarah dan HANKAM. Djakarta: Lembaga Sedjarah HANKAM, 1968, 152 pp.

0539 Notosusanto, Nugroho
Ichtisar sedjarah R.I. (1945-sekarang). Djakarta: Departemen Pertahanan-Keamanan, Pusat Sedjarah ABRI, 1971, 10+150 pp.

0540 Notosusanto, Nugroho
Norma-norma dasar penelitian dan penulisan sedjarah; Penerbitan sementara. Djakarta: Dep. HANKAM, 1971, 163 pp.

0541 Notosusanto, Nugroho
Armed forces and society in Indonesia; Past, present and future. Jakarta: Department of Defense and Security, 1974, 34 pp.

0542 Notosusanto, Nugroho
Generations in Indonesia. Jakarta: Dept. of Defense and Security, 1974, 18 pp.

0543 Notosusanto, Nugroho
The national struggle and the armed forces in Indonesia. Jakarta: Department of Defense and Security, Centre for Armed Forces History, 1975, 165 pp. [Second edition, Jakarta: Pusat Sejarah ABRI, 1980, 184 pp.]

0544 Notosusanto, Nugroho
Masalah penelitian sejarah kontemporer (suatu pengalaman). Jakarta: Idayu, 1978, 48 pp.

0545 Nugroho, Tjahyadi
Soeharto bapak pembangunan Indonesia. Semarang: Yayasan Telapak, 1984, 636 pp.

0546 Nurliana S., Nana
Pahlawan nasional Ferdinand Lumban Tobing. Jakarta: Kem. P dan K, 1977, 88 pp.

0547 Nurliana S., Nana
Dr. Ferdinand Lumban Tobing. Jakarta: Kem. P dan K, 1981, 112 pp. [Second edition 1983.]

0548 Oemar, Mohammad
Jenderal Gatot Subroto; Pahlawan nasional. Jakarta: Kem. P dan K, 1975, 114 pp.

0549 Oemar, Moh.
Laksda TNI anumerta Yosaphat Sudarso. Jakarta: Kem. P dan K, 1976, 84 pp. [Second edition, 1984, 111 pp.]

0550 Oesoep (ed.)
Kabinet dan program RI 1945-1956. Semarang: Penerbit Djaja, 1956, 40 pp. (kitlv-m)

0551 Ohorella, G.A.
Prof. Dr. Abu Hanifah Dt. M.E.; Karya dan pengabdiannya. Jakarta: Kem. P dan K, 1985, 116 pp.

0552 Onghokham
'Sukarno; Mitos dan realitas', in: Abdullah, Taufik; Aswab Mahasin and Daniel Dhakidae (eds), *Manusia dalam kemelut sejarah,* pp. 20-46. Jakarta: Lembaga Penelitian, Pendidikan dan Penerangan Ekonomi dan Sosial, 1978.

0553 Onghokham
Rakyat dan negara. Jakarta: Sinar Harapan, 1983, 180 pp.

0554 'Organisasi dan tugas Kantor Pusat Sedjarah Militer Angkatan Darat (PUSSEM)', *Madjalah Sedjarah Militer Angkatan Darat* no. 7 (1960):92-102.

0555 *Padang kota tercinta.* Padang: Genta Silanggang Press, 1983, 100 pp.

0556   Padi, Butir-Butir
       B.M. Diah; Tokoh sejarah yang menghayati zaman. Jakarta: Pustaka Merdeka,
       1992, 553 pp.

0557   *Pahlawan kemerdekaan.* Second edition. Djakarta: Dep. Penerangan, 1960, 36
       pp. [First edition 1953.]

0558   *Pahlawan kemerdekaan nasional.* Djilid 1. Djakarta: Dep. Penerangan, 1967,
       91 pp.

0559   *Pahlawan pembela kemerdekaan.* Djakarta: Dep. Sosial, 1971, 89 pp. [Second
       edition, 1972, 104 pp.]

0560   Pandoyo, S. Toto
       *Ulasan terhadap beberapa ketentuan Undang-Undang Dasar 1945; Proklamasi dan
       kekuasaan MPR.* Yogyakarta: Liberty, 1981, 175 pp.

0561   Panggabean, M.
       Berjuang dan mengabdi. Jakarta: Sinar Harapan, 1993, 496 pp.

0562   *Pantjasila sepandjang zaman.* Djakarta: Panitya Peringatan 'Lahirnja Pantjasila',
       1964, 69 pp.

0563   Panyarikan, Ktut Sudiri
       Dr. Sahardjo SH. Jakarta: Kem. P dan K, 1980, 85 pp. [Second printing 1983.]

0564   Panyarikan, Ktut Sudiri
       Sukarjo Wirjopranoto. Jakarta: Dep. P dan K, Direktorat Sejarah dan Nilai
       Tradisional, Proyek Inventarisasi dan Dokumentasi Sejarah Nasional, 1981,
       140 pp.

0565   Parengkuan, F.E.W.
       A.A. Maramis SH. Jakarta: Kem. P dan K, 1982, 128 pp. [Second edition, 1984,
       127 pp.]

0566   Parengkuan, F.E.W.; L.Th. Manus; Rino S. Nihe and Djoko Suryo
       Sejarah kota Manado. Jakarta: Kem. P dan K, 1986, 113 pp.

0567   Parera, Frans M. (ed.)
       Bung Tomo dari 10 Nopember 1945 ke Orde Baru; Kumpulan karangan. Kata
       pengantar oleh Taufik Abdullah. Jakarta: Gramedia, 1982, 20+448 pp.

0568   Partokoesoemo, Alimoerni
       Riwajat singkat gerakan nasional di Indonesia, 1905-1950. Jogjakarta: Kangguru,
       1950, 21 pp. (kitlv-m)

0569   Patunru, Abd. Razak Daeng
       Sedjarah Wadjo. Makassar: Jajasan Kebudajaan Sulawesi Selatan dan Tenggara,
       1964, 98 pp. [Second edition, Ujung Pandang: Yayasan Kebudayaan Sulawesi
       Selatan dan Tenggara, 1983, 86 pp.]

0570   Patunru, Abd. Razak Daeng
       Sedjarah Gowa. Makassar: Jajasan Kebudajaan Sulawesi Selatan dan Tenggara,
       1969, 164 pp. [Second edition, Ujung Pandang: Yayasan Kebudayaan Sulawesi
       Selatan dan Tenggara, 1983, 159 pp.]

0571 Paulus, B.P.
Kewarganegaraan RI ditinjau dari UUD 1945, khususnya kewarganegaraan pera-nakan Tionghoa; Tinjauan filosofis, historis, yuridis konstitusional. Jakarta: Pradnya Paramita, 1983, 547 pp. [PhD thesis Universitas Gadjah Mada, Yogyakarta.]

0572 *Pemberontakan DI/TII Jawa Tengah dan penumpasannya.* Second edition. Bandung: Disjarah TNI-AD, 1982, 204 pp. [First edition 1974.]

0573 *Pemuda Indonesia dalam dimensi sejarah perjuangan bangsa.* Jakarta: Yayasan Sumpah Pemuda, 1984, 443 pp. [Second edition, Jakarta: Kurnia Esa, 1985, 507 pp.]

0574 *Pendidikan di Indonesia dari jaman ke jaman.* Jakarta: Kem. P dan K/Balai Pustaka, 1979, 246 pp. [Second edition, 1985, 339 pp.]

0575 *Penumpasan pemberontakan DI-TII/S.M. Kartosuwiryo di Jawa Barat.* Bandung: Dinas Sejarah TNI-AD, 1974, 155 pp.

0576 *Peranan dan dharma bhakti KODAM IV/Sriwidjaja.* Palembang: KODAM IV/Sriwidjaja, 1969. [4873]

0577 *Pergerakan pemuda di Indonesia.* Jogjakarta: Kem. Penerangan, 1950, 98 pp. [21, 39]

0578 *Peringatan 38 tahun hilangnya Tan Malaka, 19 Pebruari 1949-19 Pebruari 1987.* Jakarta: Yayasan Massa, 1987, 5+162 pp.

0579 *Peringatan sewindu hilangnja Tan Malaka, bapak Murba dan Republik Indonesia, 19 Pebruari 1949-1957.* Djakarta: Bulletin Murba, 1957, 107 pp.

0580 *Perintis kemerdekaan Indonesia; Riwayat perjuangan/autobiografi perintis kemer-dekaan Sumatera Selatan.* Palembang: Kantor Wilayah, 1980-81, 107+146+120+158 pp. 4 vols.

0581 *Perjalanan TNI-Angkatan Udara dan perkembangannya pada awal dasa warsa 80-an.* Jakarta: Dinas Penerangan Markas Besar TNI-AU, 1982, 142 pp.

0582 *Perjuangan rakyat di daerah Gorontalo menentang kolonialisme dan mempertahankan negara Proklamasi; Latar belakang sejarah gerakan patriotik 23 Januari 1942 dan kaitannya dalam mencapai/mempertahankan Proklamasi kemerdekaan R.I.* N.p.: Yayasan 23 Januari 1942, 1982, 84 pp.

0583 Pinardi
Sekarmadji Maridjan Kartosuwirjo. Djakarta: Aryaguna, 1964, 252 pp.

0584 Poerbakawatja, Soegarda
Pendidikan dalam alam Indonesia merdeka. Djakarta: Gunung Agung, 1970, 520 pp.

0585 Poliman
Prof. Dr. R. Soeharso. Jakarta: Kem. P dan K, 1980, 152 pp. [Second edition, 1983, 176 pp.]

0586 Poliman
Prof. R. Satochid Kartanegara SH; Hasil karya dan pengabdiannya. Jakarta: Kem. P dan K, 1981, 43 pp.

0587 Pondaag, W.S.T.
Pahlawan kemerdekaan nasional mahaputera Dr. G.S.S.J. Ratu Langie. Surabaja: Jajasan Penerbitan Dr. G.S.S.J. Ratu Langie, 1966, 215 pp.

0588 Pradopo, Sri Widati a.o.
Struktur cerita rekaan Jawa modern berlatar perang. Jakarta: Kem. P dan K, 1988, 166 pp.

0589 Pramono a.o. (ed.)
Biografi pahlawan nasional dari lingkungan ABRI. Jakarta: Dep. HANKAM, 1979, 205 pp. [Second edition, Jakarta: Markas Besar Angkatan Bersenjata Republik Indonesia, Pusat Sejarah dan Tradisi ABRI, 1988, 175 pp.]

0590 Pranarka, A.M.W.
Sejarah perkembangan pemikiran tentang Pancasila sebagai ideologi, dasar negara dan sumber hukum (suatu studi explorasi). 1983, 645 pp. [PhD thesis Universitas Katolik Parahyangan, Bandung.]

0591 Pranarka, A.M.W.
Sejarah pemikiran tentang Pancasila. Jakarta: Yayasan Proklamasi, 1985, 509 pp.

0592 Pranata Ssp
Ki Hadjar Dewantara; Perintis perdjuangan kemerdekaan Indonesia. Djakarta: Balai Pustaka, 1959, 116 pp.

0593 Pratignyo, Imam
Ungkapan sejarah lahirnya Golongan Karya; Perjoangan menegakkan kembali negara Proklamasi 17-8-1945. Jakarta: Yayasan Bhakti, 1982, 111 pp.

0594 Prawiranegara, Sjafruddin
Sjafruddin Prawiranegara 75 tahun dalam pandangan tokoh-tokoh, 28 Februari 1911-1986. Jakarta: Panitya Buku 75 Tahun Sjafruddin Prawiranegara, 1986, 68 pp.

0595 Prawirowidjojo, Djoko Said
Bupati Djoko Said; Profil amtenar pejuang (risalah pengalaman tiga zaman). Bandung: Keluarga Besar Djoko Said Prawirowidjojo, 1986, 127 pp.

0596 Pringgodigdo, A.G.
Perubahan kabinet presidensiil mendjadi kabinet parlementer. Jogjakarta: Jajasan Fonds Universitas Negeri Gadjah Mada, ca. 1955, 79 pp. (ubl)

0597 Pringgodigdo, A.K.
Tiga undang-undang dasar. Third edition. Djakarta: Pembangunan, 1966, 115 pp. [First edition 1954.]

0598 Pringgodigdo, A.K.
Kedudukan presiden menurut tiga undang-undang dalam teori dan praktek. Djakarta: Pembangunan, 1956, 66 pp. (kitlv-m)

0599 Pringgodigdo, A.K.
The office of president in Indonesia as defined in the three constitutions in theory and practice. Ithaca: Cornell University, 1957, 59 pp.

0600 Priyadi, Arief
Wawancara dengan Sayuti Melik. Jakarta: Centre for Strategic and International Studies/Yayasan Proklamasi, 1986, 382 pp.

0601 Prodjodikoro, Wirjono
Kenang-kenangan sebagai hakim selama 40 tahun mengalami tiga zaman. Jakarta: Ichtiar Baru, 1974, 50 pp.

0602 Puar, Yusuf Abdullah (ed.)
Muhammad Natsir 70 tahun; Kenang-kenangan kehidupan dan perjuangan. Jakarta: Pustaka Antara, 1978, 613+413 pp. 2 vols.

0603 Puar, Yusuf A. and Matu Mona
Wage Rudolf Supratman; Pencipta lagu kebangsaan kita. Jakarta: Indrajaya, 1976, 72 pp. [Second printing 1977; Third printing 1978; Fourth printing 1979.]

0604 Pulinggomang, Edward
'Beberapa catatan tentang historiografi Sulawesi Selatan', in: *Seminar Sejarah Nasional IV, Sub tema historiografi,* pp. 74-89. Jakarta: Kem. P dan K, 1985.

0605 *Puputan sebagai ungkapan kepahlawanan.* N.p.: n.n., ca. 1965, 17 pp.

0606 Putuwati
Ir. Martinus Putuhena; Menteri Pekerjaan Umum di masa revolusi. Jakarta: Sinar Harapan, 1985, 105 pp.

0607 Rahim, S. Saiful
Perjalanan hidup Kusni Kasdut; Dari pejoang sampai penjahat yang dihukum mati. Jakarta: Pustaka Antar Kota, 1980, 222 pp.

0608 Rahman, Darsjaf
Antara imajinasi dan hukum; Sebuah roman biografi H.B. Jassin. Jakarta: Gunung Agung, 1986, 486 pp.

0609 Rais, Moch. Lukman Fatahullah; Mohammad Syah Agusdin and Nasmay Lofita Anas
Mohammad Natsir pemandu ummat; Pesan dan kesan tasyakkur 80 tahun Mohammad Natsir 17 Juli 1988. Jakarta: Bulan Bintang, 1989, 18+134 pp.

0610 Ramadhan KH
Kuantar ke gerbang; Kisah cinta Ibu Inggit dengan Bung Karno. Jakarta: Sinar Harapan, 1981, 480 pp. [Second printing, 1981, 468 pp.]

0611 *Rangkaian peristiwa pemberontakan komunis di Indonesia.* Oleh Lembaga Studi Ilmu-ilmu Kemasyarakatan. Jakarta: Yudha Gama, 1983, 127 pp. [Second edition, *Rangkaian peristiwa pemberontakan komunis di Indonesia, 1926-1948-1965,* Jakarta: Lembaga Studi Ilmu-Ilmu Kemasyarakatan, 1988, 127 pp.]

0612 Rasid, Gadis
Maria Ullfah Subadio; Pembela kaumnya. Jakarta: Bulan Bintang, 1982, 184 pp.

0613 Rasjid, Sutan Muhamad
Rasjid-70. Jakarta: Panitia Peringatan Ulang Tahun Mr. Rasjid ke-70, 1981, 330 pp.

0614 Rasjidi, H.M.
Documents pour servir à l'histoire de l'Islam à Java. Paris: Ecole Française de l'Extrème Orient, 1977, 282 pp.

0615 Rasjidi, H.M.
70 tahun Prof. Dr. H.M. Rasjidi. Jakarta: Pelita, 1985, 12+340 pp.

0616 Rasjied, Zainal
Riwajat orang-orang politik. Medan: Bakti, 1951, 1952, 32+36 pp. 2 vols.

0617 Rasyad, Aminuddin
'Rahmah El Yunusiyyah; Kartini perguruan Islam', in: Abdullah, Taufik; Aswab Mahasin and Daniel Dhakidae (eds), *Manusia dalam kemelut sejarah*, pp. 219-243. Jakarta: Lembaga Penelitian, Pendidikan dan Penerangan Ekonomi dan Sosial, 1978.

0618 Rasyid, H. St. Mohamad
Autobiografi Mr. Haji Sutan Mohamad Rasyid selaku perintis kemerdekaan. Jakarta: Dep. Sosial, 1985/86, 72 pp.

0619 Razak, Ischaq A.
Prahara Kahar Muzakkar; Bias sebuah kekecewaan. N.p.: n.n., 1985, 188 pp.

0620 Reksowihardjo, Sarjono
Perindustrian Angkatan Darat di Bandung; Satu tinjauan historis tentang perkembangan perindustrian Angkatan Darat di Bandung dari tahun 1945-1971. 1973, 124 pp. [MA thesis IKIP Bandung.] [10]

0621 *Republic of Indonesia; The country, the people, the history.* Washington, D.C.: Republic of Indonesia Embassy, 1951, 80 pp.

0622 *Republik Indonesia; DI Jogjakarta.* Djakarta: Kem. Penerangan, 1953, 887 pp.

0623 *Republik Indonesia; Kotapradja Djakarta Raja.* Djakarta: Kem. Penerangan, 1953, 568 pp.

0624 *Republik Indonesia; Propinsi Djawa Barat.* Djakarta: Kem. Penerangan, 1953, 603 pp.

0625 *Republik Indonesia; Propinsi Djawa Tengah.* Djakarta: Kem. Penerangan, 1953, 455 pp.

0626 *Republik Indonesia; Propinsi Djawa Timur.* Djakarta: Kem. Penerangan, 1953, 954 pp.

0627 *Republik Indonesia; Propinsi Kalimantan.* Djakarta: Kem. Penerangan, 1953, 445 pp.

0628 *Republik Indonesia; Propinsi Sulawesi.* Djakarta: Kem. Penerangan, 1953, 644 pp.

0629 *Republik Indonesia; Propinsi Sumatera Selatan.* Djakarta: Kem. Penerangan, 1953, 827 pp.

0630 *Republik Indonesia; Propinsi Sumatera Tengah.* Djakarta: Kem. Penerangan, 1953, 1198 pp.

0631 *Republik Indonesia; Propinsi Sumatera Utara.* Djakarta: Kem. Penerangan, 1953, 759 pp.

0632 *Republik Indonesia; Propinsi Sunda Ketjil.* Djakarta: Kem. Penerangan, 1953, 245 pp.

0633 Rifai, Bachrudin
Kesatria Kuda Putih. Bandung: Tarate, 1976, 52 pp.

0634 *Risalah pemuda.* Semarang: Masman en Stroink, 1950, 43 pp. (kitlv-m)

0635 *Riwayat hidup dan buku-buku karangan Dr. Moh. Hatta.* Jakarta: Universitas Indonesia, 1975, 6 pp.

0636 *Riwayat hidup dan perjuangan 20 ulama besar Sumatera Barat.* Padang: Islamic Centre Sumatera Barat, 1981, 279 pp.

0637 *Riwayat hidup dan riwayat perjoangan Presiden Soeharto dan Ibu Tien Soeharto dan wakil Presiden Sultan Hamengku Buwono IX.* Surabaya: Grip, 1973, 123 pp.

0638 *Riwayat hidup singkat dan perjuangan Sri Sultan Hamengkubuwono IX.* Jakarta: Dep. Sosial, 1990, 26 pp.

0639 *Riwayat ringkas perjuangan almarhum Haji Andi Mappanyukki, Sultan Ibrahim, Raja Bone ke 31.* Ujung Pandang: Badan Pembina Pahlawan Daerah, 1975, 16 pp.

0640 Riwut, Tjilik
Kalimantan memanggil. Djakarta: Endang, 1958, 404 pp.

0641 Riwut, Tjilik
Kalimantan membangun. Jakarta: Agung Offset, 1979, 421 pp.

0642 Roem, Mohamad
Karena benar dan adil. Djakarta: Hudaya, 1969, 66 pp.

0643 Roem, Mohamad
Bunga rampai dari sejarah. Jakarta: Bulan Bintang, 1972, 1977, 1983, 226+ 303+ 324 pp. 3 vols. [Vol. 3 with subtitle: *Wajah-wajah pemimpin dan orang terkemuka Indonesia.*]

0644 Roem, Mohamad
'Memimpin adalah menderita; Kesaksian Haji Agus Salim', in: Abdullah, Taufik; Aswab Mahasin and Daniel Dhakidae (eds), *Manusia dalam kemelut sejarah*, pp. 103-131. Jakarta: Lembaga Penelitian, Pendidikan dan Penerangan Ekonomi dan Sosial, 1978.

0645 Roem, Mohamad
Mohamad Roem 70 tahun; Pejuang-perunding. Jakarta: Bulan Bintang, 1978, 12+416 pp.

0646 Roem, Mohamad
Diplomasi: Ujung tombak perjuangan RI; Kumpulan karangan. Jakarta: Gramedia, 1989, 18+414 pp.

0647 Roem, Mohamad; Mochtar Lubis and Kustiniati Mochtar
Tahta untuk rakyat; Celah-celah kehidupan Sultan Hamengku Buwono IX. Jakarta: Gramedia, 1982, 24+384 pp.

0648 Rondonuwu, Ch.A.
Profil anak tani; Potret diri H.V. Worang. Manado: Yayasan Manguni Rondor, 1977, 8+317 pp. (ubl)

0649 Rosamona
Matinja Aidit; Marsekal Lubang Buaja. Djakarta: Inkoprak-Hazera, 1967, 116 pp.

0650 Rosidi, Ajip
Sjafruddin Prawiranegara lebih takut kepada Allah SWT; Sebuah biografi. Jakarta: Inti Idayu Press, 1986, 12+316 pp.

0651 Rosidi, Ajip
M. Natsir; Sebuah biografi. Jilid 1. Jakarta: Girimukti Pasaka, 1990, 319 pp. [All published.]

0652 *Rupiah di tengah rentang sejarah; 45 tahun uang Republik Indonesia 1946-1991.* Jakarta: Dep. Keuangan, 1991, 225 pp.

0653 Rustandie, A.M.
Mohammad Roem. Jakarta: Plumpang Raya, 1985, 38 pp.

0654 Sabir, M.
Politik bebas aktif; Tantangan dan kesempatan. Jakarta: Haji Masagung, 1987, 259 pp.

0655 Safwan, Mardanas
Mayor Jenderal anumerta D.I. Panjaitan. Jakarta: Kem. P dan K, 1981, 90 pp.

0656 Safwan, Mardanas
Prof. Mr. Iwa Kusuma Sumantri SH; Hasil karya dan pengabdiannya. Jakarta: Dep. P dan K, Direktorat Sejarah dan Nilai Tradisional, Projek Inventarisasi dan Dokumentasi Sejarah Nasional, 1983, 71 pp.

0657 Safwan, Mardanas
Prof. Dr. Bahder Djohan; Karya dan pengabdiannya. Jakarta: Kem. P dan K, 1985, 110 pp.

0658 Safwan, Mardanas
Pahlawan nasional Teuku Nyak Arif. Jakarta: Balai Pustaka, 1992, 280 pp.

0659 Sagimun M.D.
Ki Hajar Dewantara. Jakarta: Bhratara, 1974, 59 pp.

0660 Sagimun M.D.
Andi Pangerang Daeng Rani; Hasil karya dan pengabdiannya. Jakarta: Kem. P dan K, 1982/83, 108 pp.

0661 Sagimun M.D.
Jakarta dari tepian air ke kota Proklamasi. Jakarta: Pemerintahan Daerah Khusus Ibukota Jakarta, Dinas Museum dan Sejarah, 1988, 18+523 pp.

0662 Sagimun M.D.
Peranan pemuda dari Sumpah Pemuda sampai Proklamasi. Jakarta: Bina Aksara, 1989, 14+388 pp.

0663 Sagimun M.D.
90 tahun Prof. Mr. Sunario; Manusia langka Indonesia. Jakarta: Rosda Jayaputra, 1992, 15+148 pp.

0664 Sagimun M.D.; A. Hamzah; Ribut Subardjo and Roosmalawati
Haji Andi Mappanyukki; Raja Bone ke-XXXII. Jakarta: Kem. P dan K, 1976, 51 pp.

0665 Said, Salim
'Tentara Nasional Indonesia dalam politik; Dulu, sekarang dan pada masa datang', *Prisma* 16-6 (June 1987):80-96.

0666 Said, Syamsuar and Sumar
Patriot dari lembah sungai Serayu. Semarang: Mandira Jaya Abadi, 1984, 62 pp.

0667 Said, Syamsuar and Supriyo Priyanto
GOM VI (Gerakan Operasi Militer VI) di Jawa Tengah. Second edition. Semarang: Mandira Jaya Abadi, 1985, 54 pp.

0668 Said, Tribuana
Indonesia dalam politik global Amerika; Tinjauan atas kebijakan dan strategi pembendungan AS dari Truman hingga Nixon. Medan: Waspada, 1983, 12+187 pp.

0669 Said, Tribuana
Sejarah pers nasional dan pembangunan pers Pancasila. Jakarta: Departemen Penerangan RI, 1987, 246 pp. [Second edition, Jakarta: Haji Masagung, 1988, 11+267 pp.]

0670 Said, Tribuana (ed.)
H. Rosihan Anwar; Wartawan dengan aneka citra. Pengantar Jakob Oetama. Jakarta: Kompas, 1992, 17+298 pp.

0671 Saidi, Ridwan
'Peranan pemuda Islam menghadapi PKI; Catatan sejarah 1945-1966', *Persepsi* 2-1 (1980):52-70.

0672 Saidi, H. Ridwan
Pemuda Islam dalam dinamika politik bangsa 1925-1984. Jakarta: Rajawali, 1984, 18+170 pp.

0673 Sajidiman, Soekamto
The tender power; An autobiography. Fifth edition. Jakarta: n.n., 1977, 214 pp. [First edition 1971.]

0674 Salam, Solichin
Hadji Agus Salim; Hidup dan perdjuangannja. Djakarta: Djajamurni, 1961, 200 pp.

0675 Salam, Solichin
Sedjarah perdjoangan GASBIINDO. Djakarta: GASBIINDO, 1964, 167 pp.

0676 Salam, Solichin
Hadji Agus Salim; Pahlawan nasional. Djakarta: Djajamurni, 1965, 261 pp.

0677 Salam, Solichin
Bung Karno putera fadjar. Djakarta: Gunung Agung, 1966, 301 pp. [Second edition, 1981, 317 pp.]

0678 Salam, Solichin
Adam Malik; Profil seorang pejuang. Jakarta: Gunung Jati, 1978, 10+126 pp.

0679 Salam, Solichin (ed.)
Bung Karno di mata bangsa Indonesia. Jakarta: Dela-Rohita, 1980, 9+116 pp.

0680 Salam, Solichin (ed.)
Bung Karno dalam kenangan. Jakarta: Pusaka, 1981, 374 pp.

0681 Salam, Solichin
Bung Hatta; Profil seorang demokrat. Jakarta: Gunung Muria, 1982, 77 pp.

0682 Salam, Solichin
A.H. Nasution; Prajurit, pejuang dan pemikir. Jakarta: Kuning Mas, 1990, 318 pp.

0683 Salam, Solichin
Sjahrir; Wajah seorang diplomat. Jakarta: Centre for Islamic Studies and Research/Pusat Studi dan Penelitian Islam, 1990, 87 pp.

0684 Salam, Solichin
Wajah-wajah nasional. Jakarta: Centre for Islamic Studies and Research/Pusat Studi dan Penelitian Islam, 1990, 627 pp.

0685 Salam, Solichin (ed.)
90 tahun Bung Karno dalam kenangan. Jakarta: Yayasan Pendidikan Soekarno/Centre for Islamic Studies and Research, 1991, 230+12 pp.

0686 Salam, Solichin
Soekarno-Hatta. Jakarta: Centre for Islamic Studies and Research/Pusat Studi dan Penelitian Islam, 1991, 134 pp.

0687 Salam, Solichin (ed.)
Bung Hatta; Pejuang dan pemikir bangsa. Jakarta: Centre for Islamic Studies and Research/Pusat Studi dan Penelitian Islam, 1992, 85 pp.

0688 Salam, Solichin
Suwirjo; Walikota Jakarta Raya pertama. Jakarta: Yayasan Ananda, 1992, 94 pp.

0689 Salam, Solichin
GPH Djatikusumo; Prajurit-pejuang dari kraton Surakarta. Jakarta: Gema Salam, 1993, 282 pp.

0690 Salam, Solichin
Umar Wirahadikusumah; Pengabdian seorang prajurit. Jakarta: Gema Salam, 1994, 15+220 pp.

0691 Saleh, M. Idwar
Banjarmasih; Sejarah singkat mengenai bangkit dan perkembangannya kota Banjarmasin serta wilayah sekitarnya sampai dengan tahun 1950. Banjarmasin: Pemerintah Daerah, 1975, 153 pp. [Second edition, 1984, 151 pp.]

0692 Salim, H. Agus
Djedjak langkah Hadji Agus Salim; Pilihan karangan, utjapan dan pendapat beliau dari dulu sampai sekarang. Djakarta: Tintamas, 1954, 18+386 pp.

0693 Salim, I.F.M.
Vijftien jaar Boven-Digoel; Concentratiekamp in Nieuw-Guinea; Bakermat van de Indonesische onafhankelijkheid. Amsterdam: Contact, 1973, 436 pp. [Second edition, Hengelo: Smit, 1980, 432 pp.]

0694 Salim, I.F.M.
Lima belas tahun Digul; Kamp konsentrasi di Nieuw Guinea; Tempat persemaian kemerdekaan Indonesia. Jakarta: Bulan Bintang, 1977, 536 pp. (kb)

0695 Salim, Leon
Bung Sjahrir; Pahlawan nasional. Medan: Masadepan, 1966, 78 pp.

0696 *Sam karya bhirawa anoraga; Sedjarah militer KODAM VIII/Brawidjaja.* Malang: Sedjarah Militer KODAM VIII/Brawidjaja, 1968, 349 pp.

0697 Samawi
25 tahun merdeka. Jogja: Kedaulatan Rakjat, 1970, 159 pp.

0698 Sandra
Sedjarah pergerakan buruh Indonesia. Djakarta: Pustaka Rakjat, 1961, 216 pp.

0699 Sangti, Batara
Sejarah Batak. Balige: Karl Sianipar Company, 1977, 520 pp.

0700 Sanna, Burhanuddin
Pahlawan samudera Kapten Samadikun. Jakarta: Dinas Sejarah TNI-AL, 1976, 46 pp.

0701 Sanre, Roel
'Iwa Kusumasumantri; Upaya menertibkan tentara', *Prisma* 13-5 (May 1984): 60-79.

0702 *Santiaji Pancasila; Suatu tinjauan filosofis, historis dan yuridis konstitusionil.* Fifth edition. Malang: Laboratorium Pancasila, 1977, 240 pp. [First edition 1972.]

0703 Santoso, Slamet Iman
Pendidikan di Indonesia dari masa ke masa. Jakarta: Haji Masagung, 1987, 286 pp.

0704 Sanusi, Achmad
Perkembangan sistem pemerintahan Negara Republik Indonesia, 1945-1958. Bandung: Penerbitan Universitas, 1958, 80 pp.

0705 Sanusi, Buntaran a.o.
K.H.A. Wahid Hasjim; Mengapa memilih NU? Jakarta: Inti Sarana Aksara, 1985, 13+164 pp. [42]

0706 Sarli
Autobiografi Sarli selaku perintis kemerdekaan. Jakarta: Dep. Sosial, 1985/86, 47 pp.

0707 Sartono
Sepuluh tahun kemerdekaan Indonesia; Pidato. Djakarta: Sekretariat DPR, 1955, 16 pp. (kitlv-m)

0708 Sastroamidjojo, Ali
Tonggak-tonggak di perjalananku. Jakarta: Kinta, 1974, 596 pp.

0709 Sastroamidjojo, Ali
Milestones on my journey; The memoirs of A.S., Indonesian patriot and political leader. Edited by C.L.M. Penders. St Lucia: Queensland University Press, 1979, 405 pp.

0710 Sastroamidjoyo, Usman
The Indonesian point of view. Buenos Aires: Impresiones el Sol, 1958, 156 pp.

0711 Sastrosatomo, Soebadio
'Perjuangan demokrasi dan demokrasi perjuangan', *Sejarah* 4 (1993):56-60.

0712 Satrio
Perjuangan dan pengabdian; Mosaik kenangan Prof. Dr. Satrio, 1916-1986. Jakarta: Arsip Nasional Republik Indonesia, 1986, 13+362 pp.

0713 *Sedjarah AURI*. Djakarta: AURI, 1970, 23 pp.

0714 'Sedjarah Divisi Brawidjaja', *Madjalah Sedjarah Militer Angkatan Darat* no. 13 (1963):5-9. [55]

0715 *Sedjarah Geredja Katolik di Indonesia*. Djakarta: n.n., 1971, 152 pp.

0716 *Sedjarah perdjuangan pemuda Indonesia*. Disusun oleh Panitia Penjusun Biro Pemuda Departemen P.P. dan K. Djakarta: Balai Pustaka, 1965, 314 pp.

0717 *Sedjarah pergerakan nasional (1908-1964)*. Djakarta: Pengurus Besar Front Nasional, 1964, 111 pp.

0718 *Sedjarah perkembangan pembangunan daerah Djawa Barat tahun 1945-1965*. Bandung: Badan Koordinasi Pembangunan Daerah Tingkat I Djawa Barat, 1965, 364 pp.

0719 *Sedjarah radio di Indonesia*. Djakarta: Dep. Penerangan, 1953, 270 pp. (kitlv-m)

0720 *Sedjarah seperempat abad Korps Komando Angkatan Laut*. Djakarta: Biro Sedjarah KKO, 1970, 269+83 pp.

0721 *Sedjarah TNI-Angkatan Darat, 1945-1965*. Second edition. Bandung: Pusat Sedjarah Militer Angkatan Darat, 1966, 324 pp. [26]

0722 *Segala sesuatu tentang kewarganegaraan Republik Indonesia*. Djakarta: BAPERKI, 1960, 229 pp.

0723 *Sejarah Bekasi*. Jakarta: Pemerintah Daerah Tingkat II Bekasi/Yavitra, 1992, 155 pp.

0724 *Sejarah daerah...* Jakarta: Kem. P dan K, 1977-. Many vols.

0725 *Sejarah DKI Jakarta*. Jakarta: Kem. P dan K, 1978, 166 pp.

0726 *Sejarah Departemen Penerangan RI*. Jakarta: Dep. Penerangan, 1986, 207 pp.

0727 *Sejarah Gereja Katolik Indonesia*. Vols 3a, 3b, 4. Ende: Arnoldus, 1973-74, 714+874+615 pp.

0728 *Sejarah Jambi dari masa ke masa*. Jambi: Badan Pelaksana Pendirian Museum Propinsi Jambi, 1976, 67 pp.

0729   *Sejarah kabupaten Madiun.* Madiun: Pemerintah Kabupaten Daerah Tingkat 2 Madiun, 1980, 23+491 pp.

0730   *Sejarah kabupaten Magetan.* Magetan: Pemerintah Kabupaten Daerah Tingkat 2 Magetan, 1976, 116 pp.

0731   *Sejarah kampung Marunda.* Jakarta: Pemerintah DKI Jakarta, 1985, 46 pp.

0732   *Sejarah kepartaian di Indonesia.* Jakarta: Kem. P dan K, 1985, 194 pp.

0733   *Sejarah kesehatan nasional Indonesia.* Jilid 1. Jakarta: Dep. Kesehatan, 1978, 232 pp.

0734   *Sejarah kesehatan TNI-Angkatan Laut.* Jakarta: TNI-AL, 1975, 284 pp.

0735   *Sejarah kota Denpasar 1945-1979.* Jakarta: Kem. P dan K, 1986, 144 pp.

0736   *Sejarah nasional Indonesia. Jilid 6, Republik Indonesia dari Proklamasi sampai demokrasi terpimpin.* Edisi yang direvisi. Jakarta: Kem. P dan K, 1993, 27+ 392 pp. [First edition 1975.]

0737   *Sejarah organisasi pembinaan dan kegiatan olah raga Indonesia.* Jakarta: Kem. P dan K, 1972, 197 pp.

0738   *Sejarah pendidikan daerah...* Jakarta: Kem. P dan K, 1980-81. Many vols.

0739   *Sejarah pendidikan swasta di Indonesia.* Jakarta: Majelis Pusat Pendidikan Kristen, 1976, 93 pp.

0740   *Sejarah pengabdian Corps Polisi Militer-Angkatan Darat 1945-1978.* Jakarta: Yayasan Gajah Mada, 1981, 442 pp.

0741   *Sejarah perjuangan Komando Daerah Militer II/Bukit Barisan.* Medan: Dinas Sejarah KODAM II/Bukit Barisan, 1977, 49+752 pp.

0742   *Sejarah perjuangan TNI-AD KODAM XIII/Merdeka 1945-1977.* Manado: KODAM XIII/Merdeka, 1978. [4871]

0743   *Sejarah dan perkembangan Bumiputera 1912, 1912-1982; Tujuh puluh tahun menyertai perjuangan bangsa Indonesia.* Jakarta: Yayasan Dharma Bumiputera, 1982, 17+532 pp.

0744   *Sejarah perlawanan terhadap imperialisme dan kolonialisme di...* Jakarta: Kem. P dan K, ca. 1982. Many vols.

0745   *Sejarah pers di Indonesia; Sumber dan hasil penelitian awal.* Jakarta: LEKNAS-LIPI, 1977, 365 pp.

0746   *Sejarah pertumbuhan dan perkembangan KODAM V/Jaya; Pengawal-penyelamat ibukota Republik Indonesia.* Jakarta: KODAM V/Jaya, 1974, 24+722 pp.

0747   *Sejarah rumpun Diponegoro dan pengabdiannya.* Disusun oleh Dinas Sejarah Militer KODAM VII/Diponegoro. Semarang: Dinas Sejarah Militer KODAM VII/Diponegoro/Borobudur Megah, 1977, 36+703 pp.

0748   *Sejarah setengah abad pergerakan wanita Indonesia.* Jakarta: Balai Pustaka, 1978, 32+531 pp. [Second edition, 1986, 523 pp.]

0749   'Sejarah singkat Dinas Sejarah Militer TNI-AD', *Vidya Yudha* no. 18 (1974):66-71.

0750   *Sejarah Skadron I/Pembom TNI-AU.* Jakarta: TNI-AU, 1986, 197+23 pp.

0751   *Sejarah sosial daerah...* Jakarta: Kem. P dan K, 1983-85. Many vols.

0752   *Sejarah Sumatera Barat.* Jakarta: Kem. P dan K, 1978, 202 pp.

0753   *Sejarah ummat Islam Indonesia.* Jakarta: Majelis Ulama Indonesia, 1991, 485 pp.

0754   *Sekilas lintas 25 tahun perkereta-apian, 1945-1970.* Bandung: Perusahaan Negara Kereta Api, 1970, 231 pp.

0755   *Sekilas lintas kepolisian Republik Indonesia.* Jakarta: Dinas Penerangan Polisi, 1976, 99 pp.

0756   *Selamat jalan Bung Tomo.* Jakarta: Aksara Agung, 1981, 127 pp.

0757   Selosoemardjan
       Social changes in Jogjakarta. Ithaca: Cornell University Press, 1962, 27+440 pp.

0758   Selosoemardjan
       'Penggunaan kekerasan secara massal', *Prisma* 7-7 (August 1978):14-25.

0759   Selosoemardjan
       Perubahan sosial di Yogyakarta. Yogyakarta: Gadjah Mada University Press, 1981, 337 pp.

0760   Selosoemardjan
       'In memoriam: Hamengkubuwono IX, Sultan of Yogyakarta, 1912-1988', *Indonesia* no. 47 (1989):115-117.

0761   Semaun
       Skets sedjarah Pak Matosin. Surabaja: Matang, 1962, 131 pp.

0762   *Seminar Sejarah Regional Indonesia Timur; Masalah sejarah perjuangan rakyat Sulawesi Selatan.* Ujung Pandang: Dep. P dan K, Balai Kajian Sejarah dan Nilai Tradisional, 1993, 81 pp.

0763   *Seperempat abad Legiun Veteran Republik Indonesia.* Second edition. Jakarta: Panitya Pusat Peringatan HUT XXV LVRI, 1982, 44+512 pp.

0764   *Seperempat abad Pusjarah ABRI, 1964-1989.* Jakarta: Markas Besar Angkatan Bersenjata Republik Indonesia, Pusat Sejarah dan Tradisi ABRI, 1989, 189 pp.

0765   *Seperempat abad Zeni TNI-AD, 1945-1970.* Second edition. Jakarta: Pusat Zeni AD, 1973, 32+391 pp. [First edition 1971.]

0766   *Sepuluh tahun Pusat Sejarah ABRI.* Jakarta: Dep. HANKAM, 1974, 74 pp.

0767   *Seratus tahun Haji Agus Salim.* Disusun oleh Panitia Buku Peringatan. Jakarta: Sinar Harapan, 1984, 484 pp.

0768   Sewaka
       Tjorat-tjoret dari djaman ke djaman. Bandung: Visser, 1955, 320 pp.

0769   *Si Bung telah pergi; 22 Juli 1917-5 September 1984.* Jakarta: Yayasan Idayu, 1984, 16 pp.

0770 Siahaan, E.K.
K.H. Zainul Arifin. Jakarta: Kem. P dan K, 1982, 82 pp. [Second edition, 1984, 80 pp.]

0771 *Siaran Angkatan Bersendjata Republik Indonesia 17 Maret 1946-17 Maret 1968; Dwi dasa dwi warsa (22 tahun).* Djakarta: Dep. HANKAM, 1968, 74 pp.

0772 Siauw Giok Tjhan
Lima jaman perwujudan integrasi wajar. Jakarta/Amsterdam: Yayasan Teratai, 1981, 11+443 pp.

0773 *Siauw Giok Tjhan remembers; A Chinese peranakan in independent Indonesia.* Vol. 2. Edited by Peter Burns. Townsville: James Cook University of North Queensland, 1984, 83 pp.

0774 *Siauw Giok Tjhan remembers; A peranakan Chinese and the quest for Indonesian nation-hood.* Vol. 1. Edited by Bob Hering. Townsville: James Cook University of North Queensland, 1982, 84 pp.

0775 Siauw Tiong Djin
'Siauw Giok Tjhan; The making of a peranakan leader', in: Angus McIntyre (ed.), *Indonesian political biography; In search of cross-cultural understanding,* pp. 123-159. Clayton: Monash University, 1993.

0776 Sidjabat, Gr.K.
Mamolus galumbang ni lima zaman. Tomok, 1977, 113 pp.

0777 Sidjabat, W.B. (ed.)
Partisipasi Kristen dalam nation building di Indonesia. Djakarta: Badan Penerbit Kristen, 1968, 224 pp.

0778 Sidjabat, Walter Bonar
Religious tolerance and the Christian faith; A study concerning the concept of divine omnipotence in Indonesian constitution in the light of Islam and Christianity. Jakarta: Gunung Mulia, 1982, 284 pp. [PhD thesis Princeton University, 1960.]

0779 *Siliwangi dari masa ke masa.* Oleh Sedjarah Militer Kodam VI/Siliwangi. Djakarta: Fakta Mahjuma, 1968, 714 pp. [Second editon, disusun oleh Disjarahdam VI/Siliwangi, Bandung: Angkasa, 1979, 91+779 pp.]

0780 Simatupang, T.B.
Pelopor dalam perang; Pelopor dalam damai. Djakarta: Jajasan Pustaka Militer, 1954, 234 pp. [Second edition, Jakarta: Sinar Harapan, 1981, 344 pp.]

0781 Simatupang, T.B.
Soal-soal politik militer Indonesia. Djakarta: Gaya Raya, 1956, 136 pp.

0782 Simatupang, T.B.
'Menelaah kembali peranan TNI; Refleksi kesejarahan dan perspective masa depan', *Prisma* 9-12 (December 1980):12-26.

0783 Simatupang, T.B.
'Re-examining the role of the Indonesian army; Historical reflections and future perspectives', *Prisma* 20 (March 1981):13-25.

0784   Simatupang, T.B.
       Kehadiran Kristen dalam perang, revolusi dan pembangunan; Berjuang mengamalkan
       Pancasila dalam terang iman. Jakarta: Gunung Mulia, 1986, 285 pp.

0785   Simbolon, Juster Tumanggor
       Analisa tentang hubungan Republik Indonesia dengan Perserikatan Bangsa-
       Bangsa. 1970, 202 pp. [MA thesis IKIP Medan.] [13]

0786   Simorangkir, J.C.T.
       Tentang dan sekitar Undang-Undang Dasar 1945. Eighth edition. Jakarta:
       Djambatan, 1975, 131 pp. [Second edition, J.C.T. Simorangkir and B. Mang
       Reng Say (eds), 1959.]

0787   Simorangkir, J.C.T. (ed.)
       Sejarah Departemen Kehakiman Republik Indonesia, 1945-1985. Jakarta: Dep.
       Kehakiman, 1985, 659 pp.

0788   Singodimedjo, Kasman
       Hidup itu berjuang; Kasman Singodimedjo 75 tahun. Oleh Panitia Peringatan 75
       Tahun Kasman. Jakarta: Bulan Bintang, 1982, 18+594 pp.

0789   *Sirnaning jakso katon gapuraning ratu; Sedjarah TNI-AD KODAM VII/Diponegoro.*
       Semarang: KODAM VII/Diponegoro, 1968, 1972, 324+255 pp. 2 vols.

0790   Sitohang, J.S. Giovani and Jr. Chaniago
       Suka dan duka seorang pejuang kemerdekaan angkatan 1928-1945; Prof. Mr. Sunario
       delapan puluh tahun (28 Agustus 1902-28 Agustus 1982) dalam napas perjuangan.
       Jakarta: Mars-26, 1982, 8+110 pp.

0791   Sitompul, Agussalim (ed.)
       Sejarah perjuangan Himpunan Mahasiswa Islam, tahun 1947-1975. Surabaya: Bina
       Ilmu, 1976, 189 pp.

0792   Sitompul, Binsar
       Cornel Simandjuntak; Kumpulan lagu-lagu. Jakarta: Gunung Mulia, 1986, 69 pp.

0793   Sitompul, Binsar
       Cornel Simandjuntak; Komponis, penyanyi, pejuang. Jakarta: Pustaka Jaya, 1987,
       58 pp.

0794   Sitompul, Einar M.
       Nahdlatul Ulama dan Pancasila; Sejarah dan peranan NU dalam perjuangan umat
       Islam di Indonesia dalam rangka penerimaan Pancasila sebagai satu-satunya asas.
       Jakarta: Sinar Harapan, 1989, 271 pp.

0795   Sitorus, L.M.
       Sejarah pergerakan dan kemerdekaan Indonesia. Jakarta: Dian Rakyat, 1988,
       123 pp.

0796   Situmorang, Sitor
       Sitor Situmorang seorang sastrawan 45; Penyair Danau Toba. Jakarta: Sinar
       Harapan, 1981, 224 pp.

0797   Siwabessy, G.A.
       Upuleru; Memoar Dr. G.A. Siwabessy. Jakarta: Gunung Agung, 1979, 174 pp.

0798   Sjah, Rochman Djuhajat
       Dari timbul sampai tenggelamnja Masjumi sebagai partai politik Islam di Indonesia (tahun 1945-1960). 1970, 70 pp. [MA thesis IKIP Bandung.] [10]

0799   Sjahrir, Sutan
       Renungan dan perjuangan. Pengantar oleh Charles Wolf Jr; Catatan akhir oleh Soedjatmoko; Penerjemah H.B. Jassin. Jakarta: Djambatan/Dian Rakyat, 1990, 24+295 pp.

0800   Sjamsuddin, Nazaruddin
       The republican revolt; A study of the Acehnese rebellion. Singapore: Institute of Southeast Asian Studies, 1985, 359 pp.

0801   Sjamsuddin, Nazaruddin (ed.)
       Soekarno; Pemikiran politik dan kenyataan praktek. Jakarta: Rajawali, 1988, 17+247 pp.

0802   Sjamsuddin, Nazaruddin
       Pemberontakan kaum Republik; Kasus Darul Islam Aceh. Jakarta: Grafiti, 1990, 377 pp.

0803   Sjamsuri, M.I.
       Sedjarah singkat KODAM X/LAM. Bandjarmasin: KODAM X/LAM, 1970, 52 pp.

0804   Sjariffudin, Amak
       Kisah Kartosuwirjo dan menjerahnja. Third edition. Surabaja: Grip, 1963, 36 pp. (kitlv-m) [First edition 1962.]

0805   Sjureich, M.; Tribuana Said and A.K. Jacobi
       Sejarah pers sepintas. Jakarta: Dep. Penerangan, 1980, 144 pp.

0806   Slametmuljana
       Nasionalisme sebagai modal perdjuangan bangsa Indonesia. Djakarta: Balai Pustaka, 1968, 1969, 238+312 pp. 2 vols.

0807   Soebagijo I.N.
       Bung Karno. Surabaja: Panjebar Semangat, 1952, 32 pp. (kitlv-m)

0808   Soebagijo I.N.
       Sebelas perintis pers Indonesia. Jakarta: Djambatan, 1976, 8+78 pp.

0809   Soebagijo I.N.
       Sejarah pers Indonesia. Jakarta: Dewan Pers, 1977, 199 pp.

0810   Soebagijo I.N.
       Lima windu 'Antara' (sejarah dan perjuangannya). Jakarta: Lembaga Kantor Berita Nasional 'Antara', 1978, 20+235 pp.

0811   Soebagijo I.N.
       'Riwayat hidup Wilopo', in: *Wilopo 70 tahun*, pp. 1-209. Jakarta: Gunung Agung, 1979.

0812   Soebagijo I.N.
       Jusuf Wibisono; Karang ditengah gelombang. Jakarta: Gunung Agung, 1980, 8+429 pp.

0813 Soebagijo I.N.
Sumanang; Sebuah biografi. Jakarta: Gunung Agung, 1980, 8+227 pp.

0814 Soebagijo I.N.
Jagat wartawan Indonesia. Jakarta: Gunung Agung, 1981, 16+635 pp.

0815 Soebagijo I.N.
Sudiro; Pejuang tanpa henti. Jakarta: Gunung Agung, 1981, 8+343 pp.

0816 Soebagijo I.N.
K.H. Mas Mansur; Pembaharu Islam di Indonesia. Jakarta: Gunung Agung, 1982, 8+175 pp.

0817 Soebagijo I.N.
K.H. Masjkur; Sebuah biografi. Jakarta: Gunung Agung, 1982, 251 pp.

0818 Soebagijo I.N.
S.K. Trimurti; Wanita pengabdi bangsa. Jakarta: Gunung Agung, 1982, 7+247 pp.

0819 Soebagijo I.N.
'Wilopo negarawan yang jatmika dan bersahaja', *Prisma* 11-4 (April 1982):72-88.

0820 Soebagijo I.N.
'Biografi Prof.Dr. H.M. Rasjidi', in: Rasjidi, H.M., *70 tahun Prof. Dr. H.M. Rasjidi,* pp. 3-92. Jakarta: Pelita, 1985.

0821 Soebagijo I.N.
Harsono Tjokroaminoto; Mengikuti jejak perjuangan sang ayah. Jakarta: Gunung Agung, 1985, 9+291 pp.

0822 Soebagijo I.N.
Riwayat hidup dan perjuangan H. Zainal Abidin Ahmad. Jakarta: Pustaka Antara, 1985, 218 pp.

0823 Soebagijo I.N.
Tragedi kehidupan seorang komponis; Biografi Wage Rudolf Supratman. Jakarta: Inti Idayu Press, 1985, 87 pp.

0824 Soebagijo I.N.
Tuan Kijang (kisah kepahlawanan Douwes Dekker Setiabudhi). Jakarta: Inti Idayu Press, 1985, 103 pp.

0825 Soebagijo I.N.
Adinegoro; Pelopor jurnalistik Indonesia. Jakarta: Haji Masagung, 1987, 231 pp.

0826 Soebagijo I.N.; Abdurrachman Surjomihardjo and P. Swantoro
Lintasan sejarah P.W.I. Jakarta: P.W.I. Pusat/Departemen Penerangan, 1977, 150 pp.

0827 Soebantardjo
Pahlawan nasional Jenderal anumerta Basuki Rachmat. Jakarta: Kem. P dan K, 1975, 96 pp.

0828 Soebantardjo
Letjen M.T. Haryono. Jakarta: Kem. P dan K, 1981, 43 pp. [Second edition, 1984, 71 pp.]

0829 Soebardi, Soebakin
'Kartosuwirjo and the Darul Islam rebellion in Indonesia', *Journal of Southeast Asian Studies* 14-1 (1983):109-133.

0830 Soedewo, Mang Eri
A freedom fighter; My life with ERI-san. Surabaya: Airlangga University Press, 1994, 16+607 pp.

0831 Soedjati, J.
An analysis of the use and role of a third party in the settlement of international disputes; With special reference to Indonesian-Soviet relations. 1983, 304 pp. [PhD thesis London School of Economics.]

0832 Soegih Arto
Sanul daca; Pengalaman pribadi Letjen (Pur) Soegih Arto. Jakarta: Merdeka Sarana Usaha, 1989, 364 pp.

0833 Soegih Arto
Indonesia & I; An insider's account of 30 years of Indonesian history like it's never been told before... Singapore/Kuala Lumpur: Times Books International, 1994, 247 pp.

0834 Soegito, A.T.
Prof. Mr. Dr. R. Supomo. Jakarta: Kem. P dan K, 1980, 111 pp.

0835 Soegito, A.T.
Dr. K.R.T. Rajiman Wedyodiningrat; Hasil karya dan pengabdiannya. Jakarta: Kem. P dan K, 1982, 110 pp. [Second edition 1985.]

0836 Soeharto
Pikiran, ucapan dan tindakan saya; Otobiografi. Seperti dipaparkan kepada G. Dwipayana dan Ramadhan KH. Jakarta: Citra Lamtoro Gung Persada, 1989, 14+599 pp.

0837 Soeharto
Mijn gedachten, woorden en daden. Co-auteurs: Ramadhan KH. en G. Dwipayana. Franeker: Van Wijnen, 1991, 392 pp.

0838 Soeharto, R.
Saksi sejarah; Mengikuti perjuangan dwitunggal. Jakarta: Gunung Agung, 1982, 10+244 pp.

0839 Soehino
Perkembangan pemerintahan di daerah. Yogyakarta: Liberty, 1980, 185 pp.

0840 Soejito, Irawan
Sejarah pemerintahan daerah di Indonesia. Jilid 1. Jakarta: Pradnya Paramita, 1982, 165 pp.

0841 Soekadri, Heru
Hasil wawancara dengan Doel Arnowo. Malang, 1974. [842]

0842 Soekadri, Heru
Percikan peristiwa-peristiwa sejarah Surabaya. Surabaya: n.n., 1977, 101 pp.

0843 Soekadri, Heru
Kiai Haji Hasyim Asy'ari; Riwayat hidup dan perjuangannya. Jakarta: Kem. P dan K, 1982, 137 pp. [Second edition, 1985, 141 pp.]

0844 Soekardi (ed.)
Tiga puluh tahun Angkatan Bersenjata RI. Jakarta: Dep. HANKAM, 1976, 502 pp.

0845 Soekarjo
Sedikit tentang pemberontakan Dar ul-Islam di Djawa. 1965, 33 pp. [Thesis Universitas Gadjah Mada, Jogjakarta.]

0846 Soekarno
Kepada bangsaku; Karya-karya Bung Karno pada tahun-tahun 1926-1930-1933-1941-1945-1947 dan 1957. Djakarta: Prapantja, 1957, 449 pp.

0847 Soekarno
Dari Proklamasi sampai GESURI; Kumpulan pidato-pidato Presiden Soekarno pada tiap tanggal 17 Agustus. Djakarta: Prapantja, 1963, 597 pp. (kitlv-m)

0848 Soekarno
Dibawah bendera revolusi. Second edition. Djakarta: Panitya Penerbit Dibawah Bendera Revolusi, 1963, 1964, 627+598 pp. 2 vols.

0849 Soekarno
Amanat Proklamasi; Pidato pada ulang tahun Proklamasi kemerdekaan Indonesia. Second edition. Jakarta: Inti Idayu Press/Yayasan Pendidikan Soekarno, 1985-86, 110+116+178+226 pp. 4 vols. [First edition 1966.]

0850 Soekirman, Djoko; Ryadi Gunawan; Sutrisno and A. Adaby Darban
Sejarah kota Yogyakarta. Jakarta: Kem. P dan K, 1986, 139 pp.

0851 Soekirno (ed.)
Semarang. Semarang: Djawatan Penerangan Kota Besar Semarang, 1956, 384 pp.

0852 Soemantoro
Kemerdekaan pikiran dan pers. Djakarta: Pena, 1950, 63 pp.

0853 Soemargono, Farida
Le 'groupe de Yogya', 1945-1960; Les voies javanaises d'une littérature indonésienne. Paris: Archipel, 1979, 282 pp.

0854 Soemohardjo-Soebroto, Rohmah
Oerip Soemohardjo; Luitenant-Generaal T.N.I. (22-2-1893/17-11-1948). Den Haag: Moesson/Tong Tong, 1972, 98 pp.

0855 Soemohardjo-Soebroto, Rohmah
Oerip Soemohardjo; Letnan Jenderal TNI (22 Pebruari 1893-17 Nopember 1948). Jakarta: Gunung Agung, 1973, 136 pp. [22]

0856 Soenario
Banteng segitiga. Jakarta: Yayasan Marinda, 1988, 10+376 pp.

0857 Soenarko
Susunan negara kita. Djakarta/Amsterdam: Djambatan, 1950, 1951, 111+166 pp. 2 vols; I: *Sedjak penjerahan kedaulatan*; II: *Sedjak proklamasi negara kesatuan*.

0858 Soenarman, Stj.
Sedjarah KODAM III/17 Agustus; Sedjarah sedjak perdjuangan/perlawanan rakjat semasa pendjadjahan - sampai perkembangan dan peranan TNI semendjak tahun 1945 hingga masa Orde Baru dan Orde Pembangunan. Padang: KODAM III/17 Agustus, 1970, 470 pp.

0859 Soeratman, Darsiti
Ki Hajar Dewantara. Jakarta: Kem. P dan K, 1981, 170 pp. [Third edition, 1989, 169 pp.]

0860 Soerojo, Soegiarso
Siapa menabur angin akan menuai badai (G30S/PKI dan peran Bung Karno). Jakarta: Soegiarso Soerojo, 1988, 26+578 pp.

0861 Soesatyo
'Pengantar kata tentang perkembangan serta peranan sedjarah militer', *Vidya Yudha* no. 4 (1968):4-15; no. 5 (1968):11-21.

0862 Soetanto, Soetopo
Prof. Dr. Husein Jayadiningrat; Hasil karya dan pengabdiannya. Jakarta: Kem. P dan K, 1982, 82 pp.

0863 Soetarno and Si Uma
Pak Harto; Risalah singkat mengenai riwajat hidup Djenderal Soeharto, Pd. Presiden Republik Indonesia. Surabaja: Usaha Modern, 1967, 53 pp.

0864 Soewarto, W.
Kejayaan dan saat-saat akhir Bung Karno. Jakarta: Gunung Jati, 1978, 248 pp.

0865 Soewidji
Kisah nyata di pinggir jalan Slamet Riyadi di Surakarta; Dalam bentuk ceritera-ceritera, pengalaman-pengalaman dan roman-roman historis sejak tahun 1848-1948. Semarang: Percetakan Universitas Satya Wacana, 1973, 74 pp.

0866 DS. Soewito M.
Cintaku negeriku; Kumpulan lagu-lagu wajib dan perjuangan. Jakarta: Titik Terang, ca. 1994, 125 pp.

0867 Soimun Hp.
HAA. Hamidhan; Pejuang dan perintis pers di Kalimantan. Jakarta: Kem. P dan K, 1986, 79 pp.

0868 Sonda, Amir
Perekonomian Indonesia didalam masa 150 tahun, 1800-1950. Makasar: Jajasan Penerbit Udjungpandang, 1960, 108 pp.

0869 Sonda, Amir
The economy of Indonesia within the last 150 years, 1800-1950/Wirtschaft Indonesiens in den letzten 150 Jahren. Djakarta: Pergrafi, 1963, 49 pp. (kitlv-m)

0870 Sophiaan, Manai
Apa yang masih teringat. Jakarta: Yayasan Mencerdaskan Kehidupan Bangsa, 1991, 16+471 pp.

0871 Sosroatmodjo, Ny. Armistiani Soemarno
Bukit kenangan. Jakarta: n.n., 1986, 242 pp.

0872 Sosroatmodjo, Soemarno
Dari rimba raya ke Jakarta Raya; Sebuah otobiografi. Jakarta: Gunung Agung, 1981, 10+462 pp.

0873 *Sri Sultan; Hari-hari Hamengku Buwono IX; Sebuah presentasi majalah 'Tempo'.* Jakarta: Grafiti, 1988, 188 pp.

0874 Subagyo, Wisnu
Dr. R. Kodiyat; Hasil karya dan pengabdiannya. Jakarta: Departemen Pendidikan dan Kebudayaan, Direktorat Sejarah dan Nilai Tradisional, Proyek Inventarisasi dan Dokumentasi Sejarah Nasional, 1981, 102 pp. [Second edition, 1983, 93 pp.]

0875 Subagyo, Wisnu
Dr. Mohammad Amir; Karya dan pengabdiannya. Jakarta: Kem. P dan K, 1986, 90 pp.

0876 Subandrio
Indonesia on the march; A collection of addresses by Dr. Subandrio, Foreign Minister of the Republic of Indonesia. Djakarta: Department of Foreign Affairs, 1959, 146+357 pp. 2 vols.

0877 Subekti
K.H. Dewantara. Surakarta: Suharir, 1952, 54 pp.

0878 Subhan, O.
Sedjarah pertumbuhan Nahdatul Ulama (1926-1959). 1972, 61 pp. [MA thesis IKIP Bandung.] [10]

0879 *Subversive activities in Indonesia; The Jungschlager and Schmidt affair.* Djakarta: Ministry of Foreign Affairs, 1957, 96 pp.

0880 Sudarmanto, Y.B.
Jejak-jejak pahlawan; Dari Sultan Agung hingga Hamengku Buwono IX. Jakarta: Grasindo, 1992, 162 pp.

0881 Sudarwo, I.M.
Kegagalan pemberontakan Darul Islam S.M. Kartosuwirjo. 1964, 170 pp. [MA thesis IKIP Djakarta.] [11]

0882 Sudirjo, Radik Utoyo
Umar Wirahadikusumah; Wakil presiden RI terpilih. Jakarta: Alda, 1983, 168 pp.

0883 Sudiro
Autobiografi Sudiro selaku perintis kemerdekaan. Jakarta: Dep. Sosial, 1984, 41 pp.

0884 Sudiyarto Ds, Sides
Pahlawan Indonesia dalam puisi. Bandung: Aqua Press, 1979, 124 pp.

0885 Suhadi (ed.)
Kenangan kepada jasa-jasa perjoangan kemerdekaan Brigadir Jenderal TNI anumerta Ignatius Slamet Riyadi. Jakarta: Inaltu, 1976, 124 pp.

0886 Suhandi, Andy
Jakarta dari masa ke masa. Jakarta: Baru, 1987, 128 pp.

0887 Suhardiman (ed.)
Kesetiaan pahlawan revolusi Yani kepada revolusi, pemimpin besar revolusi dan adjaran-adjaran Bung Karno. Djakarta: Matoa, 1966, 32 pp.

0888 Suhatno
Prof. Dr. R. Sutedjo; Hasil karya dan pengabdiannya. Jakarta: Kem. P dan K, 1983, 145 pp.

0889 Suhatno
Dr. H. Affandi; Karya dan pengabdiannya. Jakarta: Kem. P dan K, 1985, 132 pp.

0890 Suhatno
Jenderal Mayor RH Abdul Kadir; Karya dan pengabdiannya. Jakarta: Kem. P dan K, 1986, 100 pp.

0891 Sujudi, Agus
Pers nasional; Lustrum PWI jang pertama. Jogjakarta: PWI, 1951, 50 pp.

0892 *Sukarno, president of Indonesia.* Djakarta: Min. of Information, 1956, 30 pp.

0893 Sukarno, Fatmawati
Fatmawati; Catatan kecil bersama Bung Karno. Jakarta: Dela-Rohita, 1978, 280 pp. [Third edition, *Jilid 1*, Jakarta: Sinar Harapan, 1985, 238 pp.]

0894 Sukawati, Tjokorda Gde Agung
Reminiscences of a Balinese prince, Tjokorda Gde Agung Sukawati, as dictated to Rosemary Hilbery. Honolulu: University of Hawaii, 1979, 93 pp.

0895 Sukisman, W.D.
Masalah Cina di Indonesia. Jakarta: Yayasan Penelitian Masalah Asia, 1975, 116 pp.

0896 Sularto, B.
Wage Rudolf Supratman. Jakarta: Kem. P dan K, 1980, 252 pp. [Second edition, 1985, 256 pp.]

0897 Sularto, B.
Sejarah lagu kebangsaan Indonesia Raya. Jakarta: Balai Pustaka, 1982, 58 pp.

0898 Sularto, B. and M.P. Siagian
Riwayat Pak Harto; Bacaan anak-anak dan remaja. Yogyakarta: Penyebar Musik Indonesia, 1984, 74 pp.

0899 Sulchan, H.M.
Kejutan seorang kacung; Otobiografi. Jakarta: Gunung Agung, 1979, 150 pp.

0900 Sumadi, Umi Prahastuti
Laksamana Muda Udara Prof. Dr. Abdulrachman Saleh; Pelopor kedokteran, radio dan penerbangan. Djakarta: Kem. HANKAM, 1967, 16 pp.

0901 Sumantri, Iwa Kusuma
Riwajat hidup seorang perintis kemerdekaan; Prof. Hadji Iwa Kusuma Sumantri S.H., 1899-1971. Djakarta: n.n., ca. 1972, 304 pp.

0902 Sumardjo, Jakob
Sinopsis roman Indonesia. Bandung: Citra Aditya Bakti, 1990, 342 pp.

0903 Sumarno, Kohar Hari
Manusia Indonesia, manusia Pancasila; Pembahasan mengenai Pancasila, Piagam Jakarta dan Pancasila sebagai satu-satunya asas. Jakarta: Ghalia Indonesia, 1984, 142 pp.

0904 Sumarsono, Tatang
Didi Kartasasmita; Pengabdian bagi kemerdekaan. Jakarta: Dunia Pustaka Jaya, 1993, 13+325 pp.

0905 Sumartana, Anton de
Perintis pesawat terbang Indonesia. Bandung: Pelita Masa, 1985, 100 pp.

0906 *Sumber laporan sejarah radio Indonesia.* Jakarta: Dep. Penerangan, Bandung: UNPAD, 1978, 144 pp.

0907 Sunario
PNI dan perdjuangannja. Djakarta: Partai Nasional Indonesia, 1972, 87 pp.

0908 Sunoto
Filsafat Pancasila. Jilid 2, Pendekatan melalui sejarah dan pelaksanaannya. Second edition. Yogyakarta: Universitas Islam Indonesia, 1984, 151 pp. [First edition 1982.]

0909 Suny, Ismail
Mencari keadilan; Sebuah otobiografi. Jakarta: Ghalia, 1982, 544 pp.

0910 Supomo, R.
The provisional constitution of the Republic of Indonesia. Ithaca: Cornell University, 1964, 98 pp.

0911 Suprapto, Bibit
Perkembangan kabinet dan pemerintahan di Indonesia. Jakarta: Ghalia Indonesia, 1985, 398 pp.

0912 Supriatna, A.
Bung Karno milik kita yang abadi. Jakarta: Lancar Indah, 1987, 105 pp.

0913 Suprijatna, F.A.
Bung Karno milik rakyat semua. N.p.: n.n., ca. 1979, 112 pp.

0914 Suputro
Tegal dari masa ke masa. Djakarta: Kem. P dan K, 1959, 78 pp.

0915 Suratmin
Prof. Ir. Raden Mas Panji Surakhman Cokrodisuryo; Hasil karya dan pengabdiannya. Jakarta: Kem. P dan K, 1981, 66 pp.

0916 Suratmin
Mr. Mohamad Roem; Karya dan pengabdiannya. Jakarta: Kem. P dan K, 1986, 202 pp.

0917 Suratmin and Poliman
Mengenal beberapa tokoh perintis kemerdekaan di Daerah Istimewa Yogyakarta.
Yogyakarta: Kem. P dan K, 1983, 150 pp.

0918 Surianingrat, Bayu
Sejarah pemerintahan di Indonesia; Babak Hindia Belanda dan Jepang. Jakarta:
Dewaruci Press, 1981, 84 pp.

0919 Suripto
*Menudju masjarakat adil dan makmur dengan pembangunan; Kenang-kenangan 25
tahun merdeka.* Surabaja: Kota Madya Surabaja, 1970, 22 pp.

0920 Suripto
'Ir. Soekarno', in: Suripto (ed.), *Dari Napoleon sampai Bung Karno dan Pak Harto
tentang negara dan masyarakat*, pp. 171-197. Second edition. Surabaya: Grip,
1978. [First edition 1966.]

0921 Surjohadiprodjo, Sajidiman
Langkah-langkah perdjoangan kita. Djakarta: Pusat Sedjarah ABRI, 1971,
202 pp. [Second edition, Djakarta: Balai Pustaka, 1972, 202 pp.; Third edition,
1986, 220 pp.]

0922 Surjomihardjo, Abdurrachman
Ki Hadjar Dewantara dan Taman Siswa dalam sejarah Indonesia modern. Jakarta:
Sinar Harapan, 1986, 254 pp.

0923 Suryochondro, Sukanti
Potret pergerakan wanita di Indonesia. Jakarta: Rajawali, 1984, 279 pp.

0924 Suryountoro, S. (ed.)
Sukarno-Hatta-Suharto menggembleng bangsanya. Surabaya: Bina Ilmu, 1980,
139 pp.

0925 *Susunan dan program kabinet Republik Indonesia selama 25 tahun, 1945-1970.*
Djakarta: Pradnja Paramita, 1970, 45 pp.

0926 Sutjiatiningsih, Sri
Gubernur Suryo. Jakarta: Kem. P dan K, 1975, 89 pp. [Second edition, 1982,
179 pp.]

0927 Sutjiatiningsih, Sri
Tokoh nasional Chairil Anwar. Jakarta: Kem. P dan K, 1979, 85 pp.

0928 Sutjiatiningsih, Sri
R. Otto Iskandardinata. Jakarta: Kem. P dan K, 1980, 101 pp. [Second edition,
1983, 108 pp.]

0929 Sutjiatiningsih, Sri
K.H.A. Wahid Hasyim; Riwayat hidup dan perjuangannya. Jakarta: Kem. P dan K,
1984, 8+122 pp.

0930 Sutrisno
Letnan Jenderal anumerta Siswondo Parman. Jakarta: Kem. P dan K, 1980, 197
pp. [Second edition, 1984, 196 pp.]

0931 Sutrisno
Marsekal TNI Suryadi Suryadarma. Jakarta: Kem. P dan K, 1985, 165 pp.

0932 Suwardjo, Suwardi; H. Slamet Sudjono and Edisaputra
Mohamad Rivai; Tanpa pamrih kupertahankan Proklamasi kemerdekaan Indonesia 17 Agustus 1945. Jakarta: Intermasa, 1983, 58+720 pp.

0933 Suwardy
'Prof. Dr. Moestopo; Pejuang kemerdekaan dan pejuang pembangunan', *Gema Angkatan 45* nr. 32 (September 1978):15-19.

0934 Suwarno, P.J.
Hamengku Buwono IX dan sistem birokrasi pemerintahan Yogyakarta 1942-1974; Sebuah tinjauan historis. Yogyakarta: Kanisius, 1994, 472 pp.

0935 Suwarto, Wasid
Tuntunan dan tuntutan perdjuangan rakjat Indonesia. Surabaja: Perintis, 1951, 52 pp. (kitlv-m)

0936 Suwarto, W. (ed.)
Pokok-pokok adjaran Tan Malaka. Djakarta: Biro Pendidikan Kader D.P. Partai Murba, 1960, 66 pp. [22] [Second edition, Jakarta: Yayasan Massa, 1987, 86 pp.]

0937 Suwondo
Sedjarah pergerakan nasional. Djakarta: Universitas Trisakti, 1970, 48 pp.

0938 Swasono, Meutia Farida (ed.)
Bung Hatta; Pribadinya dalam kenangan; 80 artikel mengenai Bung Hatta. Jakarta: Sinar Harapan/Penerbit Universitas Indonesia, 1980, 13+714 pp. [Second edition, 1982, 730 pp.]

0939 Syahadat
Perjuangan rakyat Aceh Tenggara sejak tahun 1873 s/d kemerdekaan RI. Medan: Panitia Seminar Perjuangan Aceh, 1976. [4854]

0940 Syahwil
Si Bung dari Siantar (Adam Malik). Jakarta: Aries Lima, 1978, 88 pp.

0941 Talsya, T. Alibasyah
Sedjarah dan dokumen-dokumen pemberontakan di Atjeh. Djakarta: Kesuma, ca. 1970. [4854, 6286]

0942 Tamim, Djamaluddin
Sedjarah PKI. Djakarta: n.n., 1957, 105 pp.

0943 Tamim, Djamaluddin
Kematian Tan Malaka (19 Februari 1949-19 Februari 1965). Djakarta: n.n., 1965, 63 pp.

0944 Tamim, Djamaluddin
Sambutan pada peringatan 19 tahun hilangnja Tan Malaka. Djakarta, 1968, 19 pp.

0945 Tanumidjaja, Memet
Sedjarah perkembangan Angkatan Kepolisian. Djakarta: Departemen Pertahanan-Keamanan, Pusat Sedjarah ABRI, 1971, 10+218 pp.

0946 Tashadi
Dr. D.D. Setiabudhi. Jakarta: Kem. P dan K, 1981, 96 pp. [Second edition, 1984, 97 pp.]

0947 Tashadi
Prof. K.H. Abdul Kahar Mudzakkir; Riwayat hidup dan perjuangannya. Jakarta: Kem. P dan K, 1986, 89 pp.

0948 Tauchid, Mochammad
Perdjuangan dan adjaran hidup Ki Hadjar Dewantara. Jogjakarta: Taman Siswa, 1963, 68 pp.

0949 Tauchid, Mochammad
Mengenang pahlawan Sjahrir. Jogjakarta: Jajasan Sjahrir, 1966. [26]

0950 Tauchid, Mochammad
Ki Hadjar Dewantara; Pahlawan dan pelopor pendidikan nasional. Jogjakarta: Taman Siswa, 1968, 109 pp.

0951 Taufik, I.
Sejarah dan perkembangan pers di Indonesia. Jakarta: Triyinco, 1977, 87 pp.

0952 Taulu, H.M.
Pahlawan nasional Dr. G.S.S.J. Ratu Langie. Manado: Panitia Peringatan ke-18 Wafatnja Pahlawan Nasional Dr. G.S.S.J. Ratu Langie, 1967, 42 pp.

0953 Taulu, H.M.
Sejarah Sulawesi; Perjuangan-perjuangan rakyat Indonesia/Sulawesi menentang penguasaan bangsa-bangsa Sepanyol, Belanda, Jepang dan NICA (1643-1950). Manado: Kem. P dan K, 1978, 58 pp.

0954 Taulu, H.M. and A.U. Sepang
Sedjarah Bolaang Mongondow. Manado: Rame, 1961, 59 pp.

0955 Team Fact Finding
Haji Rangkayo Rasuna Said. Jakarta: Badan Pembina Pahlawan Pusat, 1974, 15 pp.

0956 Team Fact Finding
I Gusti Ngurah Rai. Jakarta: Badan Pembina Pahlawan Pusat, 1974, 54 pp.

0957 Team Fact Finding
Supriyadi. Jakarta: Badan Pembina Pahlawan Pusat, 1974, 14 pp.

0958 Tedja, Frans
Sedjarah pergerakan nasional Indonesia. Djakarta: Dep. HANKAM, ca. 1970, 48 pp.

0959 Tedjasukmana, Iskandar
The political character of the Indonesian trade union movement. Ithaca: Cornell University, 1959, 10+130 pp.

0960 Tedjasukmana, Iskandar
The development of labor policy and legislation in the Republic of Indonesia. 1961, 566 pp. [PhD thesis Cornell University, Ithaca.]

0961   Thaib, Roestam; Mansyur Yunus and Zainal Arifin Nasution
        50 tahun kotapradja Medan. Medan: Djawatan Penerangan Kotapradja 1
        Medan, 1959, 815 pp.

0962   The, Anne Marie
        Darah tersimbah di Djawa Barat; Gerakan Operasi Militer V. Djakarta: Mega
        Bookstore, 1965, 12 pp. [Second edition, Djakarta: Lembaga Sedjarah
        HANKAM, 1968, 16 pp.]

0963   The, Anne Marie
        Komodor Udara Agustinus Adisutjipto; Bapak penerbang Indonesia. Djakarta:
        Lembaga Sedjarah HANKAM, 1967, 16 pp.

0964   The Liang Gie
        Pemerintahan daerah di Indonesia. Djakarta: Djambatan, 1958, 275 pp. (kitlv-m)

0965   The Liang Gie (ed.)
        Sedjarah pemerintahan kota Djakarta. Djakarta: Kota Pradja Djakarta Raya,
        1958, 194 pp.

0966   Tiardjono B.D.
        *Kisah pemberontakan di Indonesia; Dihimpunkan dan disusun sedjak petjahnja
        revolusi nasional 1945 sampai dengan peristiwa pemberontakan PRRI-Permesta
        tahun 1958.* Surabaja: n.n., 1959, 154 pp.

0967   Tiardjono B.D.
        *Landjutan kisah pemberontakan di Indonesia; Disusun sedjak timbulnja peristiwa
        PRRI-Permesta hingga kini, berdasarkan berita-berita surat kabar, siaran-siaran
        pemerintah, brosur-brosur jang berwadjib berikut pula gambar-gambarnja.* Surabaja:
        Dewi, 1959, 65 pp.

0968   *Tien jaar Republik Indonesia.* 's-Gravenhage: Hoge Commissariaat van de
        Republik Indonesia, 1955, 207 pp.

0969   *Tiga puluh tahun Bank Negara Indonesia (BNI) 1946.* Jakarta: BNI, 1976, 84 pp.

0970   *Tiga puluh tahun pengabdian BPI, 1948-1978.* Bandung: Tarate, 1978, 128 pp.

0971   Tirtoprodjo, Susanto
        Sedjarah pergerakan nasional Indonesia. Third edition. Djakarta: Pembangunan,
        1968, 68 pp. [First edition 1961; Fourth edition, 1970, 72 pp.; Sixth edition,
        1980, 72 pp.]

0972   Tista, Paul (ed.)
        Supeni; Wanita utusan negara. Jakarta: Pembimbing Masa, 1989, 19+258 pp.

0973   Tjiptoning (ps. M. Wonohito)
        Apa dan siapa. Jogja: Kedaulatan Rakjat, 1951, 173 pp.

0974   Tjokroaminoto, Harsono
        Menelusuri jejak ayahku. Jakarta: Arsip Nasional Republik Indonesia, 1983,
        18+247 pp.

0975   Tjokroaminoto, Harsono
        Autobiografi Harsono Tjokroaminoto selaku perintis kemerdekaan. Jakarta: Dep.
        Sosial, 1984, 57 pp.

0976 Tjokrosisworo, R.M. Sudarjo (ed.)
Sekilas perdjuangan sebangsa; Kenangan sedjarah pers sebangsa. Djakarta: Serikat Perusahaan Suratkabar SPS, 1958, 349 pp.

0977 Tjondronegoro, Purnawan
Memburu pasukan merah; Peristiwa Madiun 1948-peristiwa G-30-S/PKI 1965. Jakarta: Nugraha, 1982, 104 pp.

0978 Toer, Pramoedya Ananta
Hoa Kiau di Indonesia. Djakarta: Bintang Press, 1960, 200 pp.

0979 *Tokoh cendekiawan dan kebudayaan.* Jakarta: Kem. P dan K, ca. 1975. Many vols.

0980 *Tokoh-tokoh sejarah perjuangan dan pembangunan pos dan telekomunikasi di Indonesia.* Jakarta: Dep. Pariwisata, Pos dan Telekomunikasi, 1985, 896 pp.

0981 Tomasoa, Peter
Sedjarah pergerakan pemuda Indonesia. Djakarta: n.n., 1972, 346 pp.

0982 Trihadi, S.
Sedjarah perkembangan Angkatan Udara. Djakarta: Departemen Pertahanan-Keamanan, Pusat Sedjarah ABRI, 1971, 9+94 pp.

0983 Trihadi, S.
Riwayat-hidup Halim Perdanakusuma; Laksamana Muda Udara (anumerta). Jakarta: Angkatan Udara, 1974, 10 pp.

0984 Trihadi, S.
Riwayat-hidup Iswahyudi; Komodor Udara anumerta. Jakarta: Angkatan Udara, 1974, 9 pp.

0985 Trimurti, S.K.
'Hidupku sebagai wartawan pejuang', in: *Wartawan wanita berkisah*, pp. 1-38. Jakarta: Indonesia Raya, ca. 1975.

0986 Trimurti, S.K.
Hubungan pergerakan buruh Indonesia dengan pergerakan kemerdekaan nasional. Jakarta: Yayasan Idayu, 1975, 32 pp.

0987 Trimurti, Surastri Karma
'Sukarno si priya', in: Colin Wild and Peter Carey (eds), *Gelora api revolusi*, pp. 115-120. Jakarta: Gramedia, 1986.

0988 Trimurti, S.K.
'Sukarno the man; An interview with Surastri Karma Trimurti', in: C. Wild and P. Carey (eds), *Born in fire; The Indonesian struggle for independence; An anthology*, pp. 103-107. Athens: Ohio University Press, 1986.

0989 Tugiyono Ks
Pahlawan nasional Prof. Dr. Suleiman Kusuma Atmaja SH. Jakarta: Kem. P dan K, 1978/79, 170 pp.

0990 Tugiyono Ks; Sutrisno Kutoyo and Alex Pelatta
Atlas dan lukisan sejarah nasional Indonesia. Vol. 2. Jakarta: Baru, 1985, 219 pp.

0991 Ubani, Bahruddin A.
Sedikit kontribusi politik dan diplomatik untuk nusa dan bangsa. Jakarta: Pustaka Antara, 1992, 106 pp.

0992 Uhuk, H. Abdulmanap and George Obus
Autobiografi H. Abdulmanap Uhuk dan George Obus selaku perintis kemerdekaan. Jakarta: Dep. Sosial, 1986/87, 42 pp.

0993 *Ulasan sedjarah 20 tahun 1945-1965 bidang pemerintahan Perhubungan Laut.* Djakarta: Departemen Perhubungan Laut, 1970, 85 pp.

0994 Umar, Rika
Laksamana Mochamad Nazir; Karya dan pengabdiannya. Jakarta: Kem. P dan K, 1985, 47 pp.

0995 Untung S.
Mengikuti jejak H. Agus Salim dalam tiga zaman. Jakarta: Rosda Jaya Putra, 1987, 104 pp.

0996 Usman, K.
Komponis Indonesia yang kita kenal. Jakarta: Aries Lima, 1979, 122 pp.

0997 Utomo, Djoko
Inventaris van de papieren van Dr. P.J. Koets (geb. 1901) over de jaren 1920-1978. 's-Gravenhage: Algemeen Rijksarchief, 1979, 105 pp.

0998 Utoyo (Sudirjo), Radik
Di ambang fajar Indonesia merdeka; Bacaan sejarah untuk para tunas bangsa Indonesia. Jakarta: Alda, 1976, 94 pp.

0999 *Wadja sampai keputing; Sedjarah singkat KODAM X/Lambung Mangkurat.* Bandjermasin: SEMDAM X/LAM, 1970, 26 pp.

1000 Wahidin, Samsul
MPR-RI dari masa ke masa. Jakarta: Bina Aksara, 1986, 153 pp.

1001 *Wajah dan sejarah perjuangan pahlawan nasional.* Jakarta: Dep. Sosial, 1981/82, 1982/83, 428+462 pp. 2 vols.

1002 Wali A.T., Nyak
Mr. Sartono; Karya dan pengabdiannya. Jakarta: Kem. P dan K, 1985, 121 pp.

1003 Wardhana, Goenawan Ardi
The effects of politics on educational development in Indonesia from the colonial period to the present (1511-1971). 1973, 278 pp. [PhD thesis University of California at Berkeley.]

1004 Watuseke, F.S.
Sedjarah Minahasa. Manado: Pertjetakan Negara, 1962, 72 pp. [Second edition, 1968, 85 pp.]

1005 Wellem, Frederiek Djara
Mr. Amir Syarifuddin; Tempatnya dalam kekristenan dan dalam perjuangan kemerdekaan Indonesia. 1982, 349 pp. [MA thesis Sekolah Tinggi Theologia, Jakarta.]

1006 Widjaja, I Wangsa
      Mengenang Bung Hatta. Jakarta: Haji Masagung, 1988, 11+292 pp.

1007 Widjaja, I Wangsa
      Bung Hatta. Jakarta: Marinda, 1990, 66 pp.

1008 Widjayakusuma, A.L.
      Sedjarah pemuda dan sosialisme Indonesia. Surabaja: Grip, 1961, 74 pp. (kitlv-m)

1009 Wiedjannah, Tuti Nurijah
      Peranan Muhammad Yamin dalam perdjuangan rakjat Indonesia mewudjudkan
      persatuan bangsa. 1970, 57 pp. [MA thesis IKIP Bandung.] [10]

1010 Wignjosoehardjo, Achmad
      *Peneropongan kemerdekaan Indonesia dan pandangan baru terhadap maksudnja
      perimbon-perimbon*. Jogjakarta: Soemodidjojo Maha-Dewa, 1950, 104 pp.

1011 Wilopo
      Zaman pemerintahan partai-partai dan kelemahan-kelemahannya. Jakarta: Yayasan
      Idayu, 1976, 72 pp.

1012 *Wilopo 70 tahun*. Jakarta: Gunung Agung, 1979, 8+556 pp.

1013 Wiriaatmadja, Rochiati
      Dewi Sartika. Jakarta: Kem. P dan K, 1985, 128 pp.

1014 Wiryosukarto, Amir Hamzah (ed.)
      *Wawasan politik seorang muslim patriot; Dr. Soekiman Wirjosandjojo, 1898-1974
      (kumpulan karangan)*. Surabaya: Yayasan Pusat Pengkajian, Latihan dan
      Pengembangan Masyarakat, 1984, 16+358 pp.

1015 Yani, Amelia
      Profil seorang prajurit TNI. Jakarta: Sinar Harapan, 1988, 239 pp.

1016 Yani, Ibu A.
      Ahmad Yani; Sebuah kenang-kenangan. Jakarta: n.n., 1981, 333 pp.

1017 Yap Tjwan Bing
      Meretas jalan kemerdekaan; Otobiografi seorang pejuang kemerdekaan. Kata
      pengantar Abdurrachman Surjomihardjo. Jakarta: Gramedia, 1988, 16+127 pp.

1018 Yatim, Badri
      Soekarno, Islam dan nasionalisme; Rekonstruksi pemikiran Islam-nasionalis. Jakarta:
      Inti Sarana Aksara, 1985, 16+201 pp.

1019 Yoe-Sioe Liem
      Die ethnische Minderheit der Überseechinesen im Entwicklungsprozess Indonesiens.
      Saarbrücken/Fort Lauderdale: Breitenbach, 1980, 626 pp.

1020 Yusra, Abrar and Ramadhan KH
      Hoegeng; Polisi idaman dan kenyataan (sebuah autobiografi). Jakarta: Sinar
      Harapan, 1993, 374 pp.

1021 Zainal, Zuraida (ed.)
      Serumpun melati di bumi pertiwi; Kisah perjuangan Srikandi Sumatera. Jakarta:
      Keluarga Besar Wirawati Catur Panca, 1985, 9+105 pp.

1022 Zamzami, Amran
Belajar dan berjuang. Sebagaimana diceritakan oleh Amran Zamzami kepada penulis Sugiono M.P. Jakarta: Bulan Bintang, 1985, 176+18 pp.

1023 Zed, Mestika
Kepialangan, politik dan revolusi; Palembang 1900-1950. 1991, 6+481 pp. [PhD thesis Vrije Universiteit, Amsterdam.]

1024 *Zeven jaar Republik Indonesia.* The Hague: Information Service Indonesia, 1952, 188 pp.

General works
Dutch authors

1025   *50 jaar Marine Luchtvaartdienst, 1917-1967.* 's-Gravenhage: MLD, 1967, 141 pp.

1026   Alberts, A.
Een kolonie is ook maar een mens. Amsterdam: Van Oorschot, 1989, 129 pp.

1027   Algra, A.
De Gereformeerde Kerken in Nederlands-Indië/Indonesië (1877-1961). Franeker:
Wever, ca. 1965, 360 pp.

1028   Amersfoort, J.M.M. van
*Immigratie en minderheidsvorming; Een analyse van de Nederlandse situatie, 1945-
1973.* Alphen aan den Rijn: Samsom, 1974, 242 pp. [Also PhD thesis Universiteit van Amsterdam.]

1029   Amersfoort, J.M.M. (Hans) van
*Immigration and the formation of minority groups; The Dutch experience 1945-
1975.* Cambridge: Cambridge University Press, 1982, 234 pp.

1030   Ark, Jodien van
'Kerken over Indonesië; Onderzoek naar het kerkelijk spreken in Nederland ten
aanzien van Indonesië na de tweede wereldoorlog', *Opstand* 5-2 (1978):44-58.
(ubl)

1031   Asjes, Dick
Startklaar; Verhalen en anecdotes uit een ruim 50-jarig actief vliegersleven. Amster-
dam/Dieren: De Bataafsche Leeuw, 1985, 142 pp.

1032   Backer Dirks, F.C.
*De Gouvernementsmarine in het voormalige Nederlands-Indië in haar verschillende
tijdsperioden geschetst, 1861-1949 III.* Houten: De Boer Maritiem, 1986, 330 pp.

1033   Bank, Jan; Martin Ros and Bart Tromp
'Gesprek met Jacques de Kadt', in: *Eerste Jaarboek voor het Democratisch Socialisme*, pp. 283-338. Amsterdam: Arbeiderspers, 1979.

1034   Bartels, J.A.C.
Vier eeuwen Nederlandse cavalerie. Deel II. Amsterdam: De Bataafsche Leeuw,
1987, 261 pp.

1035   Bastiaans, W.Ch.J.
Herinneringen III uit het voormalige Ned. Indië en Nederland; Tijdvak 1941-1968.
Groningen: Bastiaans, 1968, 300 pp.

1036 Baudet, H. and C. Fasseur
'Koloniale bedrijvigheid', in: J.H. van Stuijvenberg (ed.), *De economische geschiedenis van Nederland*, pp. 309-350. Groningen: Wolters-Noordhoff, 1977.

1037 Beetsma, J. a.o.
De afbraak van het Britse en Franse wereldrijk; 1918-1949 Nederland en Nederlands-Indië. Groningen: Wolters-Noordhoff, 1987, 71+72 pp. 2 vols.

1038 Berg, Joop van den (ed.)
Zo was Indië 1850-1950; Herinneringen aan een eeuw Nederlands-Indië. Laren: Luitingh, 1976, 160 pp.

1039 Blaas, Piet
Betrokkenheid en distantie; Bernard Vlekke (1899-1970) en de studie van de internationale betrekkingen. Hilversum: Verloren, 1991, 123 pp.

1040 Bogaarts, M.D.
De periode van het kabinet-Beel, 3 juli 1946-7 augustus 1948. 's-Gravenhage: SDU Uitgeverij, 1989-. 4 vols.

1041 Boland, B.J.
The struggle of Islam in modern Indonesia. The Hague: Nijhoff, 1971, 283 pp. [Second edition, 1982, 8+283 pp.]

1042 Boon, Siem and Eva van Geleuken
Ik wilde eigenlijk niet gaan; De repatriëring van Indische Nederlanders 1946-1964. 's-Gravenhage: Stichting Tong Tong, 1993, 120 pp.

1043 Bootsma, N.
'Indonesië, Suriname en de Antillen', in: P. Luykx and N. Bootsma (eds), *De laatste tijd; Geschiedschrijving over Nederland in de 20e eeuw*, pp. 299-345. Utrecht: Het Spectrum, 1987.

1044 Bos, J.
'Soetan Sjahrir; Socialist, nationalist, internationalist', in: *Tiende Jaarboek voor het Democratisch Socialisme*, pp. 153-182. Amsterdam: Arbeiderspers, 1989. (ubl)

1045 Bosch, Rob; Wout Oprel and Gerard Pichèl
Indonesië tot 1950. 's-Gravenhage: Arjos, 1978, 32 pp.

1046 Bosscher, D.F.J.
Om de erfenis van Colijn; De ARP op de grens van twee werelden (1939-1952). Alphen aan den Rijn: Sijthoff, 1982, 480 pp.

1047 Bosscher, Ph.M.
De Nederlandse mariniers. Bussum: Van Dishoeck, 1966, 120 pp.

1048 Broeshart, A.C.; J.R. van Diessen; R.G. Gill and J.P. Zeydner
Soerabaja; Beeld van een stad. Purmerend: Asia Maior, 1994, 160 pp.

1049 Bruin, R. de
'Prediker van de democratie; Hadji Agus Salim (1884-1954), Indonesisch politicus', in: *Onze jaren 45-70*, p. 1119. Amsterdam, 1972.

1050 Bruins Slot, J.A.H.J.S.
...en ik was gelukkig; Herinneringen. Baarn: Bosch en Keuning, 1972, 216 pp.

1051 Bruyn, J. de
'Gerbrandy als Kamerlid', in: C. Bremmer, D.Th. Kuiper and A. Postma (eds), *Pieter Sjoerds Gerbrandy; Herdenkingsbundel*, pp. 125-167. Franeker: Wever, 1985.

1052 Buiter, Hans
Nederlands-Indië (1830-1949); Een kolonie in ontwikkeling. Utrecht/Antwerpen: Kosmos/Z & K, 1993, 160 pp.

1053 Burger, D.H.
Sociologisch-economische geschiedenis van Indonesia; Deel II, Indonesia in de 20e eeuw. Wageningen: Landbouwhogeschool, Afdeling Agrarische Geschiedenis, Amsterdam: Koninklijk Instituut voor de Tropen, Leiden: Koninklijk Instituut voor Taal-, Land- en Volkenkunde, 1975, 16+276 pp.

1054 *Bij het scheiden van de markt; Bloemlezing uit de Indische letterkunde van 1935 tot heden.* Verzameld en ingeleid door R. Nieuwenhuys. Amsterdam: Querido, 1960, 205 pp. [Second edition, 1965, 208 pp.]

1055 Caminada, I.W.L.A. and F.J.M. Otten
Inventaris van de papieren van Dr. J.W. Meyer Ranneft. 's-Gravenhage: Algemeen Rijksarchief, 1971, 128 pp.

1056 Campen, S.I.P. van
The quest for security; Some aspects of Netherlands foreign policy, 1945-50. The Hague: Nijhoff, 1958, 308 pp. (ubl)

1057 Casius, Gerard and Thijs Postma
40 jaar luchtvaart in Indië. Alkmaar: De Alk, 1986, 152 pp.

1058 Cleintuar, G.L.
Indische Nederlanders; Een ontheemde bevolkingsgroep zonder toekomstbeeld. 's-Gravenhage: Moesson/Tong Tong, 1971, 56 pp.

1059 Cottaar, Annemarie and Wim Willems
Indische Nederlanders; Een onderzoek naar beeldvorming. Den Haag: Moesson, 1984, 191 pp.

1060 Dake, A.C.A.
In the spirit of the Red Banteng; Indonesian communists between Moscow and Peking 1959-1965. The Hague/Paris: Mouton, 1973, 16+479 pp.

1061 Dames, G.W.T.
Oom Ambon van het KNIL. 's-Gravenhage: Moesson, 1954, 156 pp.

1062 Djatipit (ps. F.J. Appelman)
Memoires van een houtvester. Amsterdam: De Bezige Bij, 1951, 192 pp.

1063 Dolk, Liesbeth
Twee zielen, twee gedachten; Tijdschriften en intellectuelen op Java (1900-1957). Leiden: KITLV Uitgeverij, 1993, 7+217 pp. [Also PhD thesis Rijksuniversiteit Leiden.]

1064 Dongen, S. van
'De CPN en de Indonesische vrijheidsstrijd', *Politiek en Cultuur* 29-2 (February 1969):49-59.

1065 Doorn, J.A.A. van
De laatste eeuw van Indië; Ontwikkeling en ondergang van een koloniaal project.
Amsterdam: Bakker, 1994, 363 pp.

1066 Dorleijn, Adriaan; Herman Hazelhoff and Jan Scheffers
Welter en de KVP. 1974, 74 pp. [MA thesis Rijksuniversiteit Groningen.]

1067 Drees, W.
Zestig jaar levenservaring. Amsterdam: Arbeiderspers, 1962, 345 pp.

1068 Drees, W.
Herinneringen en opvattingen. Naarden: Strengholt, 1983, 142 pp.

1069 Drooglever, P.J.
'Was er een Nederlandse koloniale ideologie in de twintigste eeuw?', *Kleio* 18
(1977):813-817. (ubl)

1070 Drooglever, P.J.
The Netherlands' colonial empire; Historical outline and some legal aspects. Alphen
aan den Rijn: Sijthoff en Noordhoff, 1978, 63 pp.

1071 Drooglever, P.J. (ed.)
Indisch intermezzo; Geschiedenis van de Nederlanders in Indonesië. Amsterdam: De
Bataafsche Leeuw, 1991, 135 pp. [Second printing 1994.]

1072 Dutilh, M.
Inventaris van de papieren van Dr. H.J. van Mook. 's-Gravenhage: Algemeen
Rijksarchief, 1975, 101 pp.

1073 Duynstee, F.J.F.M.
De kabinetsformaties 1946-1965. Deventer: Kluwer, 1966, 45+462 pp. (ubl)

1074 Duynstee, F.J.F.M. and J. Bosmans
Het kabinet Schermerhorn-Drees, 24 juni 1945-3 juli 1946. Assen/Amsterdam:
Van Gorcum, 1977, 756 pp.

1075 Dijk, C. van
'De strijd om erkenning; Het bestuur na 1942', in: R.N.J. Kamerling (ed.),
Indonesië toen en nu, pp. 109-125. Amsterdam: Intermediair, 1980.

1076 Dijk, C. van
Rebellion under the banner of Islam; The Darul Islam in Indonesia. The Hague:
Nijhoff, 1981, 10+474 pp. [Also PhD thesis Rijksuniversiteit Leiden.]

1077 Dijk, C. van
Darul Islam; Sebuah pemberontakan. Jakarta: Grafiti, 1983, 25+409 pp. [Second
printing 1987.]

1078 *Elk Moment.* Ca. 1958, 45 pp. (kitlv-smg)

1079 Ellemers, J.E. and R.E.F. Vaillant
Indische Nederlanders en gerepatrieerden. Muiderberg: Coutinho, 1985, 159 pp.

1080 Ellemers, J.E. and R.E.F. Vaillant
'Indische Nederlanders en gerepatrieerden; De grootste categorie naoorlogse
immigranten', *Tijdschrift voor Geschiedenis* 100 (1987):412-431.

1081 End, Th. van den (ed.)
De Nederlandse Zendingsvereniging in West-Java, 1858-1963; Een bronnen-publikatie. Alphen aan den Rijn: Raad voor de Zending der Nederlands Hervormde Kerk, 1991, 736 pp.

1082 Eijgelshoven, H.J.
De CEP/CSP; Een christelijke Indische partij toont haar politieke ziel. 1985, 137 pp. [MA thesis Rijksuniversiteit Utrecht.]

1083 Fabricius, Johan
Een wereld in beroering; Verdere mémoires (1936-1946). 's-Gravenhage: Leopold, 1952, 234 pp. [Second printing 1960.]

1084 Fasseur, C.
De indologen; Ambtenaren voor de Oost, 1825-1950. Amsterdam: Bakker, 1993, 552 pp. [Second printing 1994.]

1085 Fèbre, W. le
Taman Siswa. Djakarta/Surabaja: Penerbitan dan Balai Buku Indonesia, 1952, 70 pp.

1086 Ferguson, Margaretha
Brief aan niemand; Dagboekfragmenten 1948-1984. 's-Gravenhage: Nijgh en Van Ditmar, 1985, 437 pp.

1087 *Gedenkboek Ons Aller Belang 1902-1952*. N.p.: n.n., 1952, 205 pp.

1088 *Gedenkboek, uitgegeven ter gelegenheid van het vijf en twintig jarig bestaan van het rechtswetenschappelijk hoger onderwijs in Indonesië, 28 October 1949*. Groningen: Wolters, 1949, 336 pp.

1089 *Gedenkschrift Koninklijk Nederlands-Indisch Leger (1830-1950)*. Dordrecht: Stichting Herdenking KNIL, 1990, 97 pp.

1090 Geel, C.W.J. van
Oud, Stikker en de achterban van de VVD. 1989, 93 pp. [MA thesis Katholieke Universiteit Nijmegen.]

1091 Geldhof, N.
70 jaar Marine Luchtvaartdienst. Leeuwarden: Eisma, 1987, 217 pp.

1092 George, Leonore (ps. L.G. Hoffmeister)
Herrijzenis niet gewenst. 's-Gravenhage: Kleywegt, ca. 1974, 340 pp.

1093 George, M.J.F. (of Podebrad)
Verloren strijd met een verdwijnende achtergrond. N.p.: n.n., ca. 1989, 324 pp.

1094 Gerretson, C.
Verzamelde werken. Bijeengebracht door G. Puchinger. Baarn: Bosch en Keuning, 1974-87; Vols 4-7, 457+408+495+323 pp.

1095 *De geschiedenis van het Korps Mariniers, 10 december 1667-1965*. 's-Gravenhage: n.n., 1965, 64 pp.

1096 Gielen, Corine J.H. and Maureen E. Hommerson
De boot afgehouden? Het Nederlandse beleid ten aanzien van de repatriëring van Indische Nederlanders op Rijksvoorschotbasis, 1949-1959. 1987, 234 pp. [MA thesis Katholieke Universiteit Nijmegen.]

1097 Glissenaar, Frans
Voorheen Nederlands-Indië; Een reis door de geschiedenis. Amsterdam: Contact, 1994, 246 pp.

1098 Go Gien Tjwan
'The role of the overseas Chinese in the South-East Asian revolutions and their adjustment to new states', in: Michael Leifer (ed.), *Nationalism, revolution and evolution in South-East Asia*, pp. 59-73. Zug: Inter Documentation Company, 1970.

1099 Goedhart, F.J.
Een revolutie op drift; Indonesisch reisjournaal. Amsterdam: Van Oorschot, 1953, 220 pp.

1100 Goedhart, J. and J. Algera
Histo-speciaal; Nederland en Nederlands-Indië 1918-1949. Zutphen: Thieme, 1987, 47 pp. (kb)

1101 Goes van Naters, M. van der
Met en tegen de tijd; Een tocht door de twintigste eeuw. Amsterdam: Arbeiders-pers, 1980, 324 pp.

1102 Goor, J. van
Indië/Indonesië; Van kolonie tot natie. Utrecht: HES, 1987, 130 pp.

1103 Goor, J. van
De Nederlandse koloniën; Geschiedenis van de Nederlandse expansie, 1600-1975. 's-Gravenhage: SDU, 1993, 400 pp.

1104 Graaf, H.J. de
Geschiedenis van Indonesië. 's-Gravenhage/Bandung: Van Hoeve, 1949, 513 pp.

1105 Graaf, H.J. de
'Geschichte Indonesiens in der Zeit der Verbreitung des Islam und während der europäischen Vorherrschaft', in: *Handbuch der Orientalistik*, 3. Abteilung, 1. Band, Lieferung 2, pp. 1-118. Leiden/Köln: Brill, 1977.

1106 Groeneboer, Kees
Weg tot het Westen; Het Nederlands voor Indië 1600-1950. Leiden: KITLV Uitgeverij, 1993, 12+580 pp. [Also PhD thesis Rijksuniversiteit Leiden.]

1107 Haas-Engel, Renata Henriëtte de
Het Indonesische nationaliteitsrecht. Deventer: Kluwer, 1993, 449 pp. [Also PhD thesis Rijksuniversiteit Limburg, Maastricht.]

1108 *Handelingen der Staten-Generaal.* 's-Gravenhage: Staatsuitgeverij, 1945-. Many vols.

1109   Heekeren, C. van
       Trekkers en blijvers; Kroniek van een Haags-Indische familie. Franeker: Wever, 1980,
       189 pp.

1110   Heldring, Ernst
       Herinneringen en dagboek van Ernst Heldring, 1871-1954. Uitgegeven door Joh. de
       Vries. Groningen: Wolters-Noordhoff, 1970, 1880 pp. 3 vols. (ubl)

1111   Helfrich, C.E.L.
       Memoires. Amsterdam/Brussel: Elsevier, 1950, 480+411 pp. 2 vols.

1112   Henssen, Emile
       Gerretson en Indië. Groningen: Wolters-Noordhoff/Bouma's Boekhuis, 1983, 231
       pp. [Also PhD thesis Rijksuniversiteit Groningen.]

1113   Heshusius, C.A.
       *KNIL-cavalerie 1814-1950; Geschiedenis van de Cavalerie en Pantsertroepen van het
       Koninklijk Nederlandsch-Indische Leger.* 's-Gravenhage: Sectie Krijgsgeschiedenis
       der Koninklijke Landmacht, 1978, 100 pp.

1114   Heshusius, C.A.
       *Soldaten van de Kompenie; KNIL 1830-1950; Een fotodocumentaire over het
       dagelijks leven van het koloniale leger in Nederlands-Indië.* Houten: De Haan, 1986,
       192 pp.

1115   Heshusius, C.A.
       Het KNIL van tempo doeloe. Amsterdam: De Bataafsche Leeuw, 1988, 144 pp.

1116   Hiltermann, G.B.J.
       De zaak Joseph Luns en andere sterke verhalen. Amsterdam: Europese Publici-
       teitsmaatschappij, 1974, 92 pp.

1117   Hobma-Glastra, T.Y.
       Bandjir; Een Indische kroniek 1935-1950. Naarden: Lunet, 1988, 141 pp.

1118   Hövell tot Westerflier, J.R.C.O. van
       K.R.M.T. Wuryaningrat (1881-1967); Tussen aristocraat en nationalist. 1985,
       125 pp. [MA thesis Universiteit van Amsterdam.]

1119   Hoffenaar, J. and B. Schoenmaker
       Met de blik naar het Oosten; De Koninklijke Landmacht 1945-1990. 's-Gravenhage:
       SDU Uitgeverij Koninginnegracht, 1994, 535 pp.

1120   Hokke, C.
       Opkomst en ondergang van onze Gouvernements Marine 'Setengah Kompenie'.
       Leiden: Leidsche Uitgeversmaatschappij, 1950, 168 pp.

1121   Holtrop, P.N.
       *Selaku perintis jalan keesaan gerejani di Indonesia; Sejarah Majelis Keristen Indonesia
       bahagian Timur, 1947-1956.* Ujung Pandang: ISGIT, 1982, 223 pp.

1122   Honselaar, L.
       Vleugels van de vloot; De geschiedenis van de Marine-Luchtvaartdienst. Rotterdam:
       Wyt, 1950, 336 pp.

1123　Hoogenband, C. van den
'In memoriam het KNIL', *De Militaire Spectator* 119 (1950):461-483.

1124　Hoogstraten, M.G.
*Nederlanders in Nederlands-Indië; Een schets van de Nederlandse koloniale aan-
wezigheid in Zuidoost-Azië tussen 1596 en 1950.* Zutphen: Thieme, 1986, 119 pp.

1125　Houten, Joop van
Nederland bevrijd! Een muzikale terugblik op de meidagen van '45. Zwolle: Rebo,
1994, 64 pp. (kb)

1126　Houwaart, Dick and Corrie Berghuis
*De mannenbroeders door de bocht; Herinneringen aan en van Dr. W.P. Berghuis, van
1956 tot 1968 voorzitter van de Anti-Revolutionaire Partij.* Kampen: Kok, 1988,
131 pp. (ubl)

1127　Huis, Frits and René Steenhorst
Bij monde van Willem Drees; Levensschets van een groot Nederlander. Utrecht/
Antwerpen: Het Spectrum, 1985, 168 pp.

1128　Hulst, J.W. van
Gerretson dichterbij. Amsterdam: Buijten en Schipperheijn, 1985, 175 pp.

1129　Hulzen, Joh. van
Verlaten; Om het recht der Nederlands-Indische staatsburgers. N.p.: Stichting Pro
Patria, ca. 1951, 12 pp.

1130　Ittersum, W. van
Gedenkboek Grenadiers en Jagers, 1939-1954. 's-Gravenhage: Fonds tot Handhaving van de Traditiën der Grenadiers en Jagers, 1954, 220 pp.

1131　Jacobs, Hans and Jan Roelands
*Indisch ABC; Een documentaire over historie en samenleving van Nederland-Indië-
Indonesië.* Amsterdam: Arbeiderspers, 1970, 256 pp.

1132　Jagt, M.B. van der
Memoires van M.B. van der Jagt, oud-gouverneur van Soerakarta. Den Haag:
Leopold, 1955, 383 pp.

1133　Jansen van Galen, John and Herman Vuijsje
Drees; Wethouder van Nederland. Alphen aan den Rijn: Sijthoff, 1980, 188 pp.
[Second edition, Houten: De Haan, 1986, 219 pp.]

1134　Janzen, J.P.
'Willem Schermerhorn en zijn politieke denkbeelden', *Socialisme en Democratie* 22
(1972):537-554. (ubl)

1135　Jaquet, L.G.M.
'Tan Malakka's nationaal communisme', *Internationale Spectator* 5-5 (1951):7-11.

1136　*Jhr. Mr. Dr. A.W.L. Tjarda van Starkenborgh Stachouwer; Bijdragen tot een
kenschets.* Rotterdam: Donker, 1978, 84 pp.

1137　Joël, H.F.
Honderd jaar Java Bode; De geschiedenis van een Nederlands dagblad in Indonesië.
Djakarta: De Unie, 1952, 124 pp.

1138 Jong, A.P. de (ed.)
KLu 75; Vlucht door de tijd; Uitgegeven ter gelegenheid van het vijfenzeventigjarig bestaan van de Koninklijke Luchtmacht, 1 juli 1988. Houten: Van Holkema en Warendorf, 1988, 440 pp.

1139 Jonge, B.C. de
Belevenissen en beschouwingen 1940-1950. N.p.: n.n., 1968. [Various pagings.]

1140 Jonge, J.F. de
Nagelaten nalatenschap; Koloniale handel in koffie – Koopvaardij – Pardon ik schiet. Amsterdam: Centraal Venster, 1989, 224 pp.

1141 Kaam, B. van
'Bij de gratie van welke macht was Indonesië Nederlands kolonie?', *Wending* 39 (1984):426-430.

1142 Kadt, J. de
'Sjahrir; Poging tot plaatsbepaling, benevens een paar persoonlijke herinneringen', *Tirade* 10 (1966):460-478.

1143 Kamerling, R.N.J. (ed.)
Indonesië toen en nu. Amsterdam: Intermediair, 1980, 304 pp.

1144 Kant, Gert
Raddraaiers zijn het! Nederlandsch-Indië 1900-1970 Indonesië. Alkmaar: Centrum voor Internationale Vorming-CEVNO, 1983, 132 pp.

1145 Kikkert, J.G.
De wereld volgens Luns. Utrecht: Het Spectrum, 1992, 279 pp.

1146 Klaauw, Bart van der and Bart M. Rijnhout
De militaire luchtvaart in Nederlands-Indië 1914-1949. Amsterdam: De Bataafsche Leeuw, 1987, 96 pp.

1147 Kleffens, E.N. van
Belevenissen. Deel II, 1940-1958. Alphen aan den Rijn: Sijthoff, 1983, 229 pp.

1148 Klooster, H.A.J.
Indonesiërs schrijven hun geschiedenis; De ontwikkeling van de Indonesische geschiedbeoefening in theorie en praktijk, 1900-1980. Dordrecht/Cinnaminson: Foris, 1985, 10+264 pp. [Also PhD thesis Rijksuniversiteit Leiden.]

1149 Klooster, H.A.J.
'Penelitian Sedjarah; Een Indonesisch geschiedenistijdschrift', *Tijdschrift voor Geschiedenis* 99 (1986):507-516.

1150 Koch, D.M.G.
Verantwoording; Een halve eeuw in Indonesië. 's-Gravenhage/Bandung: Van Hoeve, 1956, 287 pp.

1151 Koch, D.M.G.
Batig slot; Figuren uit het oude Indië. Amsterdam: De Brug/Djambatan, 1960, 8+212 pp.

1152 Koerts, H.J.
Eens vrienden, altijd vrienden ('Sekali sahabat, tetap sahabat'); Herontmoeting met Zuid-Celebes. Garrelsweer: Servo, 1989, 269 pp.

1153 Kort, Th. de
Van Brigade en Garderegiment 'Prinses Irene'; Bijdragen tot de geschiedenis van de Koninklijke Nederlandse Brigade 'Prinses Irene' en haar opvolgers. Rotterdam: Donker, 1983, 128 pp.

1154 Kossmann, E.H.
De Lage Landen 1780-1980; Twee eeuwen Nederland en België. Deel II, 1914-1980. Amsterdam/Brussel: Elsevier, 1986, 446 pp. (ubl)

1155 Kraak, J.M. (ed.)
De repatriëring uit Indonesië; Een onderzoek naar de integratie van de gerepatrieerden uit Indonesië in de Nederlandse samenleving. Amsterdam: Instituut voor Sociaal Onderzoek van het Nederlandse Volk, Utrecht: Sociologisch Instituut van de Nederlandse Hervormde Kerk, 's-Gravenhage: Katholiek Sociaal-Kerkelijk Instituut, 1958, 461 pp.

1156 Krol d'Yovre, L.
Soekarno. Den Haag: Provisor, 1962, 104 pp.

1157 Kruls, H.J.
Generaal in Nederland; Memoires. Bussum: Fibula-Van Dishoeck, 1975, 271 pp.

1158 Kuijk, Otto and Bart van Veen
Soekarno tabeh; Een documentaire in samenwerking met De Telegraaf en De Courant Nieuws van de Dag. Amsterdam: Becht, Bussum: Van Dishoeck/Van Holkema en Warendorf, 1967, 190 pp.

1159 Laanen, J.T.M. van
'De Indonesische economie sedert 1945', *Spiegel Historiael* 21 (1986):128-134.

1160 Last, Jef
Bali in de kentering. Amsterdam: De Bezige Bij, 1955, 208 pp.

1161 Last, Jef
Zo zag ik Indonesië. 's-Gravenhage/Bandung: Van Hoeve, 1956, 319 pp.

1162 Leeuwen, A.Th. van
Hendrik Kraemer; Dienaar der wereldkerk. Amsterdam: Ten Have, 1959, 172 pp.

1163 Leeuwen, G.I. van
De intendance in het voormalige KNIL. Culemborg: Verschoor, ca. 1980, 60 pp.

1164 Leeuwendal, Th.C.
Indonesië als symptoom; De Aziatische bedreiging van het Westen. 's-Gravenhage: Stichting Rijksbehoud, 1954, 30 pp.

1165 Logemann, J.H.A.
Het staatsrecht van Indonesië; Het formele systeem. 's-Gravenhage/Bandung: Van Hoeve, 1954, 214 pp. [Third edition, 1955, 216 pp.]

1166   Lont, Carla M.
       Inventaris van de papieren van Prof. Dr. J.H.A. Logemann (1892-1969). 's-Graven-
       hage: Algemeen Rijksarchief, 1975, 31 pp.

1167   Luitwieler, W.A.
       Bestuursambtenaar van Nederlands-Indië tot Indonesië. Leiderdorp: n.n., 1978,
       60 pp.

1168   Maalderink, P.G.H.; C.M. Schulten and B.J. Kasperink-Taekema (eds)
       Korps Commandotroepen 1942-1982. Roosendaal: De Commando Stichting,
       1982, 176 pp. (smg)

1169   Maas, P.F.
       Het kabinet Drees-Van Schaik (1948-1951). Nijmegen: Gerard Noodt Instituut,
       1991, 27+871 pp.

1170   Maclaine Pont, H.
       Kolonialisme en vrijheid op Java. Den Haag: Maclaine Pont, 1958, 15 pp.

1171   Meel, P. van
       *Tanda mata KNIL; Foto's en verhalen als herinnering aan het Koninklijk Nederlands-
       Indische Leger*. Dordrecht: Stabelan, 1983, 182 pp.

1172   Meel, P. van
       *Getekend als koloniaal; Een relaas over het leven van gewone mensen in het
       vooroorlogse Indië en tijdens de bewogen laatste jaren van het Koninklijk Nederlands-
       Indische Leger*. Dordrecht: Stabelan, 1988, 128 pp.

1173   Mens, Lucie van
       De statusscheppers; Sociale mobiliteit in Wajo, 1905-1950. Amsterdam: CASA,
       1989, 136 pp.

1174   Mevius, Johan
       *Catalogue of paper money of the V.O.C., Netherlands East Indies and Indonesia, from
       1782-1981*. Vriezenveen: Mevius Numisbooks, 1981, 104 pp.

1175   Möller, A.J.M.
       Batavia, a swinging town! Dansorkesten en jazzbands in Batavia, 1922-1949.
       's-Gravenhage: Moesson, 1987, 95 pp.

1176   Mooij, W.
       *Het Indisch avontuur tegemoet; Als officier van gezondheid naar voormalig
       Nederlands-Indië*. 's-Gravenhage: Moesson/Tjalie Robinson, 1978, 71 pp.

1177   Mulder, Gerard and Paul Koedijk
       H.M. van Randwijk; Een biografie. Amsterdam: Nijgh en Van Ditmar, 1988,
       16+809 pp. (ubl)

1178   Muskens, M.P.M.
       Indonesië; Een strijd om nationale identiteit; Nationalisten, islamieten, katholieken.
       Bussum: Paul Brand, 1969, 597 pp. [Second printing 1970; Also PhD thesis
       Katholieke Universiteit Nijmegen.]

1179 Muskens, M.P.M.
      Partner in nation building; The Catholic Church in Indonesia. Aachen: Missio
      Aktuell Verlag, 1979, 339 pp.

1180 Nicolas, C.B. (ed.)
      De Mariniersbrigade te kiek. Amsterdam: Omega Boek, 1986, 100 pp.

1181 Nieuwenhuys, Rob
      *Oost-Indische spiegel; Wat Nederlandse schrijvers en dichters over Indonesië hebben
      geschreven, vanaf de eerste jaren der Compagnie tot op heden.* Amsterdam: Querido,
      1972, 645 pp. [Third edition, 1978, 669 pp.]

1182 Nieuwenhuyze, C.A.O. van
      Aspects of Islam in post-colonial Indonesia; Five essays. 's-Gravenhage/Bandung:
      Van Hoeve, 1958, 248 pp.

1183 *De nood der spijtoptanten in Indonesië; Een gewetenszaak voor onze natie.* 's-Graven-
      hage: NASSI, 1960, 38 pp.

1184 Oerle, J.E.C.M. van (ed.)
      *Kabinetsformatie onder hoogspanning; 1948; De formatiedagboeken van Beel, Drees,
      Van der Goes van Naters en Romme.* Amsterdam: Van Soeren, 1989, 134 pp.

1185 *Officiersopleidingen van het Koninklijk Nederlands-Indisch Leger in Nederlands-Indië,
      1936-1950.* Aerdenhout: Vereniging Officieren Ex-K.M.A. Bandoeng, Ex-K.I.M.
      Soerabaja en Ex-Res. Officieren Bandoeng, 1990, 186 pp.

1186 Oltmans, Willem
      De verraders. Utrecht: Van Amelrooij, 1968, 229 pp.

1187 Oltmans, Willem L.
      Den vaderland getrouwe; Uit het dagboek van een journalist. Utrecht/Antwerpen:
      Bruna, 1973, 680 pp.

1188 Oltmans, Willem
      Memoires. Vol. 1, *1925-1953,* 1985, 280 pp.; Vol. 2, *1953-1957,* 1986, 351 pp.;
      Vol. 3, *1957-1959,* 1987, 338 pp.; Vol. 4, *1959-1961,* 1988, 340 pp.; Vol. 5,
      1961, 1989, 320 pp. Baarn: In den Toren.

1189 Oudenhoven, E.A.J. and H. Ulrich
      'Nederland en Nederlands-Indië 1918-1949', in: *Nederland en Nederlands-Indië
      1918-1949/China 1925-1986; HV-editie,* pp. 2-34. Den Bosch: Malmberg, 1988.

1190 Oudenhoven, E.A.J. and H. Ulrich
      'Nederland en Nederlands-Indië 1918-1949', in: *Nederland en Nederlands-Indië
      1918-1949/China 1925-1986; M-editie,* pp. 2-32. Den Bosch: Malmberg, 1988.

1191 Pipitseputra (ps. M.P.M. Muskens)
      Beberapa aspek dari sejarah Indonesia; Aliran nasionalis, Islam, Katolik. Ende:
      Arnoldus, 1973, 615 pp.

1192 Plas, Michel van der (ps. B.G.F. Brinkel)
      Mooie vrede; Een documentaire over Nederland in de jaren 1945-1950. Utrecht:
      Ambo, 1966, 399 pp.

1193 Plas, Michel van der (ps.)
Luns: 'ik herinner mij...' Vrijmoedige herinneringen van Mr. J.M.A.H. Luns zoals verteld aan Michel van der Plas. Leiden: Sijthoff, 1971, 269 pp.

1194 Pluvier, J.M.
Confrontations; A study in Indonesian politics. Kuala Lumpur: Oxford University Press, 1965, 8+86 pp.

1195 Pluvier, J.M.
'Recent Dutch contributions to modern Indonesian history', *Journal of Southeast Asian History* 8 (1967):201-225.

1196 Pluvier, Jan
South-East Asia from colonialism to independence. Kuala Lumpur: Oxford University Press, 1974, 22+571 pp.

1197 Pluvier, Jan
Indonesië; Kolonialisme, onafhankelijkheid, neo-kolonialisme; Een politieke geschiedenis van 1940 tot heden. Nijmegen: SUN, 1978, 391 pp.

1198 Pluvier, J.
'De politieke ontwikkeling van Indonesië, 1942 tot heden', *Opstand* 5-2 (1978):1-13. (ubl)

1199 Poeze, Harry A.
Tan Malaka; Strijder voor Indonesië's vrijheid; Levensloop van 1897 tot 1945. 's-Gravenhage: Nijhoff, 1976, 7+605 pp. [Also PhD thesis Universiteit van Amsterdam.]

1200 Poeze, Harry A.
Tan Malaka; Pergulatan menuju Republik I. Jakarta: Grafiti, 1988, 32+413 pp.

1201 Polak, Bob en Bart Molenkamp
Indonesië gezien door Jordaan, Opland en Doeve; Een inhoudsanalyse van 259 politieke caricaturen verschenen in de Groene Amsterdammer en Elsevier's Weekblad tussen 1945 en 1970. 1977, 132 pp. [MA thesis Universiteit van Amsterdam.]

1202 Puchinger, G.; W. Drees and A.J. van der Weele
Professor Dr. Ir. W. Schermerhorn; Minister-president van herrijzend Nederland. Naarden: Strengholt, 1977, 285 pp.

1203 Quik, H.G.
Thuisgekomen in Nederland; Indische Nederlanders en gerepatrieerden in de wetten voor oorlogsgetroffenen. Leiden: LIDESCO, Voorburg: Pelita, 1988, 43 pp.

1204 Raatgever, J.G.
Koninklijke Nederlandse Brigade 'Prinses Irene' Garderegiment. 's-Gravenhage: Legervoorlichtingsdienst, 1950, 16 pp. (kitlv-smg)

1205 Raatgever, J.G. (ed.)
Geschiedenis van de garderegimenten Grenadiers en Jagers. 's-Gravenhage: Fonds tot Handhaving van de Traditiën der Grenadiers en Jagers, 1961, 51 pp. (smg)

1206   Randwijk, H.M. van
       Heet van de naald; Keuze uit het werk van een man in verzet. 's-Gravenhage:
       Daamen, 1968, 240 pp.

1207   Ringeling, A.B.
       *Beleidsvrijheid van ambtenaren; Het spijtoptantenprobleem als illustratie van de
       activiteiten van ambtenaren bij de uitvoering van beleid*. Alphen aan den Rijn:
       Samsom, 1978, 273 pp.

1208   Ritman, J.H.
       Journalistieke herinneringen. Den Haag: Moesson, 1980, 176 pp.

1209   Roethof, H.
       Dwars over het Binnenhof; Herinneringen van een liberale socialist. Utrecht etc.:
       Veen, 1990, 287 pp. (kb)

1210   Romein, J.M.
       The Asian century; A history of modern nationalism in Asia. Berkeley: University of
       California Press, 1965, 448 pp. (kb)

1211   Romein, J.M. and J.E. Romein
       *De eeuw van Azië; Opkomst, ontwikkeling en overwinning van het modern Aziatisch
       nationalisme*. Leiden: Brill, 1954, 395 pp.

1212   Rüter, C.F.
       *Enkele aspecten van de strafrechtelijke reactie op oorlogsmisdrijven en misdrijven tegen
       de menselijkheid*. Amsterdam: Amsterdam University Press, 1973, 244 pp. [Also
       PhD thesis Universiteit van Amsterdam.]

1213   Rutgers, S.J.
       Sedjarah pergerakan nasional Indonesia. Second edition. Surabaja: Hajam Wuruk,
       1956, 94 pp.

1214   Rijkens, Paul
       Handel en wandel; Nagelaten gedenkschriften, 1888-1965. Rotterdam: Donker,
       1965, 185 pp.

1215   Rijnhout, Bart M.
       De geschiedenis van Squadron 321. Amsterdam/Dieren: De Bataafsche Leeuw,
       1984, 79 pp.

1216   Salleveldt, H. (ps. L. Verhoeff)
       Het woordenboek van Jan Soldaat in Indonesië. Alphen aan den Rijn: Sijthoff,
       1980, 223 pp.

1217   Schenkhuizen, Marguérite
       Memoirs of an Indo woman; Twentieth-century life in the East Indies and abroad.
       Edited and translated by Lizelot Stout van Balgooy. Athens: Ohio University
       Center for International Studies, 1993, 286 pp.

1218   Schmidt, H.
       In de greep van Soekarno; Achtergronden van een proces tegen een Nederlander.
       Leiden: Sijthoff, 1961, 255 pp.

1219 Schöffer, I.
'Recente Nederlandse memoires', *Tijdschrift voor Geschiedenis* 83 (1970):262-283.

1220 Schoonhoven, J. and K.C. Snijtsheuvel
De Indo-Nederlandse volksgroep in de branding; Een nationaal probleem. 's-Gravenhage: Van Stockum, 1951, 31 pp.

1221 Schulte Nordholt, H.G.
'Mohammed Hatta', in: H. Bergema (ed.), *Pioniers van het nieuwe Azië*, pp. 341-465. Franeker: Wever, 1959.

1222 Schulten, C.M. and F.J.H.Th. Smits
Grenadiers en Jagers in Nederland. 's-Gravenhage: Staatsuitgeverij, 1980, 160 pp.

1223 Schutte, G.J.
'De koloniale geschiedschrijving', in: W.W. Mijnhardt (ed.), *Kantelend geschiedbeeld; Nederlandse historiografie sinds 1945*, pp. 289-310. Utrecht/Antwerpen: Het Spectrum, 1983.

1224 Snijtsheuvel, Karel C.
Onthullingen van achter het bamboegordijn. Breda/Utrecht/Maastricht: Neerlandia, ca. 1958, 160 pp.

1225 Spaans-van der Bijl, T.
Tot betere tijden? Het levensverhaal van Willem van Pelt (1920-1959), rubberplanter op Sumatra. Amsterdam/Antwerpen: Veen, 1991, 167 pp.

1226 *Het spijtoptantenprobleem.* 's-Gravenhage: NASSI, 1961, 22 pp. [45]

1227 Stevens, R.J.J.; L.J. Giebels and P.F. Maas (eds)
De formatiedagboeken van Beel, 1945-1973; Handboek voor formateurs. 's-Gravenhage: SDU Uitgeverij Koninginnegracht, 1994, 20+282 pp.

1228 Stikker, Dirk U.
Bausteine für eine neue Welt; Gedanken und Erinnerungen an schicksalhafte Nachkriegsjahre. Wien/Düsseldorf: Econ, 1966, 494 pp.

1229 Stikker, D.U.
Memoires; Herinneringen uit de lange jaren waarin ik betrokken was bij de voortdurende wereldcrisis. Rotterdam/'s-Gravenhage: Nijgh en Van Ditmar, 1966, 360 pp.

1230 Stikker, D.U.
Men of responsibility; A memoir. London: John Murray, 1966, 418 pp. (kb)

1231 Tadema Sporry, Bob
Geschiedenis van Indonesië. Weesp: Fibula-Van Dishoeck, 1984, 168 pp.

1232 Tas, Sal
Wat mij betreft. Baarn: Ten Have, 1970, 232 pp.

1233 Tas, S.
De onderontwikkelde vrijheid; Indonesia toen en nu. Baarn: Ten Have, 1973, 355 pp.

1234 Tas, S.
Indonesia; The underdeveloped freedom. Indianapolis: Pegasus, 1974, 12+388 pp. (ubu)

1235 Teeuw, A.
Modern Indonesian literature. The Hague: Nijhoff, 1967, 15+308 pp. [Second edition, 1979, 10+232, 10+292 pp. 2 vols.]

1236 Teeuw, A.
Pramoedya Ananta Toer; De verbeelding van Indonesië. Breda: De Geus, 1993, 395 pp.

1237 Teitler, G.
'De staf der zeemacht; Ervaringen in de Oost, 1902-1949', in: L. Brouwer (ed.), *Tussen vloot en politiek; Een eeuw marinestaf 1886-1986*, pp. 51-87. Amsterdam/Dieren: De Bataafsche Leeuw, 1986.

1238 Teitler, G. and C. Homan (eds)
Het Korps Mariniers, 1942-heden. Amsterdam: De Bataafsche Leeuw, 1985, 83 pp.

1239 Thielsch, F. (ed.)
Gedenkboek M.Z.S. Makassar 1947-1977. Alkmaar: Thielsch, 1978, 312 pp.

1240 Tichelman, F.
'De Nederlandse koloniale politiek 1919-1969; Een oriënterende schets', *De Gids* 133 (1970):254-262.

1241 Tichelman, G.L.
Indische Nederlanders. Amsterdam: Stichting IVIO, ca. 1975, 16 pp.

1242 Troevers, Herman (ps. H.J. van der Meer)
Op de waterscheiding; Schetsen van een theeplanter in de 'kentering der tijden', 1906-1956. 's-Gravenhage: Van der Meer, 1992, 245 pp. [Second edition, 1993, 304 pp.]

1243 Tuijl, Peter van
'Mijn positie is helaas niet erg benijdenswaardig'; Nico Palar en de koloniale politiek van de Nederlandse sociaal-democratie, 1930-1947. 1985, 150 pp. [MA thesis Universiteit van Amsterdam.]

1244 Utrecht, Ernst
Soekarno-Soeharto; Indonesië's dekolonisatie dreigt te mislukken. Odijk: Sjaloom, ca. 1969, 52 pp.

1245 Utrecht, E.
The Indonesian army; A socio-political study of an armed, privileged group in the developing countries. Vol. I. Townsville: James Cook University of North Queensland, 1979, 233 pp. [All published.]

1246 Veer, Paul van 't
Soekarno. 's-Gravenhage: Kruseman, 1964, 95 pp.

1247 Veer, Paul van 't (ed.)
Drees; Neerslag van een werkzaam leven; Een keuze uit geschriften, redevoeringen, interviews en brieven uit de jaren 1902-1972. Assen: Van Gorcum, 1972, 283 pp. (ubl)

1248 Veer, Paul van 't
'Vogelvlucht door de geschiedenis van Indonesië (1800-1979)', in: R.N.J. Kamerling (ed.), *Indonesië toen en nu*, pp. 9-33. Amsterdam: Intermediair, 1980.

1249 Velde, J.J. van de
Brieven uit Sumatra, 1928-1949. Franeker: Wever, 1982, 224 pp.

1250 Verheem, Rudy
Bevrijding zonder bevrijders; De 'sinjo' tussen Indië en Nederland. Baarn: Hollandia, 1979, 112 pp.

1251 Verhoeff, L.
Soldatenfolklore; Een inventarisatie van de informele tradities in de Nederlandse militaire samenleving in de jaren rond de Tweede Wereldoorlog. Voorwoord van C.M. Schulten. 's-Gravenhage: Koninklijke Landmacht, 1977, 282 pp.

1252 Verkuyl, J.
'Kort levensbericht van Dr. Johannes Leimena; Medebouwer van de staat en de oecumene in Indonesia', *Wereld en Zending* 6 (1977):329-335.

1253 Verkuyl, J.
Gedenken en verwachten; Memoires. Kampen: Kok, 1983, 348 pp.

1254 Verkuylen, C.
'Het Indo-Europees Verbond als vertegenwoordiger van de Indo-Europese gemeenschap in Nederlands-Indië, 1919-1949', in: P. Luykx and A.F. Manning (eds), *Nederland in de wereld 1870-1950; Opstellen over buitenlandse en koloniale politiek, aangeboden aan Dr. N. Bootsma*, pp. 141-163. Nijmegen: Vakgroep Geschiedenis der Katholieke Universiteit, 1988. (ubl)

1255 Vervloet, L.Th. and Mohamad Jusuf
Pelanggaran ekonomi di Indonesia/Economische delicten in Indonesië. Bandung: Vorkink, 's-Gravenhage: Van Hoeve, 1954, 255 pp.

1256 Vinken, Fred
De dubbele aar; H.J. Friedericy, schrijver en ambtenaar, 1900-1962. 1987, 122 pp. [MA thesis Rijksuniversiteit Utrecht.]

1257 Visser, A.
Een merkwaardige loopbaan; Herinneringen van een bestuursambtenaar in Nederlandsch-Indië/Indonesië (1932-1950). Franeker: Wever, 1982, 192 pp.

1258 Vlekke, B.H.M.
Geschiedenis van den Indischen archipel van het begin der beschaving tot het doorbreken der nationale revolutie. Roermond/Maaseik: Romen, 1947, 526 pp.

1259 Vlekke, Bernard H.M.
Nusantara; A history of Indonesia. Sixth edition. The Hague: Van Hoeve, 1965, 479 pp. [First edition 1943.]

1260 Vlugt, E. van der
Azië in vlammen; Het communisme in het Oosten. 's-Gravenhage: Van Stockum, 1951, 28+299 pp.

1261 Vlugt, Ebed van der
Asia aflame; Communism in the East. New York: Devin-Adair, 1953, 16+294 pp.

1262 *Het vraagstuk der Indische Nederlanders.* 's-Gravenhage: Centrum voor Staatkundige Vorming, 1953, 15 pp.

1263 Vredenburch, H.F.L.K. van
Den Haag antwoordt niet; Herinneringen van Jhr. Mr. H.F.L.K. van Vredenburch. Leiden: Nijhoff, 1985, 14+618 pp.

1264 Vries, D. de (ed.)
D.M.G. Koch; Levensschets en bibliografie ter gelegenheid van zijn 70ste verjaardag. Djakarta: Jajasan Pembangunan, 1951, 40 pp.

1265 Wal, S.L. van der (ed.)
Besturen overzee; Herinneringen van oud-ambtenaren bij het Binnenlands Bestuur in Nederlandsch-Indië. Franeker: Wever, 1977, 331 pp.

1266 Wassenaar-Jellesma, H.C.
Van Oost naar West; Relaas van de repatriëring van 1945 tot en met 1966. 's-Gravenhage: Staatsdrukkerij, 1969, 11+63 pp.

1267 Wentholt, G.J.M.
De aalmoezeniers in de Nederlandse krijgsmacht. Amsterdam: Van Soeren, 1993, 216 pp.

1268 Wentholt, W.
Amerika, Indonesië en wij. Amsterdam: Buijten en Schipperheijn, 1951, 159 pp.

1269 Wertheim, W.F.
Effects of Western civilization on Indonesian society. New York: Institute of Pacific Relations, 1950, 83 pp.

1270 Wertheim, W.F.
Indonesië van vorstenrijk tot neo-kolonie. Meppel: Boom, 1978, 276 pp. [Second printing 1992.]

1271 Wertheim, Wim and Hetty Wertheim-Gijse Weenink
Vier wendingen in ons bestaan; Indië verloren, Indonesië geboren. Breda: De Geus, 1991, 367 pp.

1272 Wesseling, H.L.
'Nederland zonder Indië', *Hollands Maandblad* no. 379/380 (1979):3-14. (ubl)

1273 Wesseling, H.L.
'Post-imperial Holland', *Journal of Contemporary History* 15 (1980):125-142. (ubl)

1274 Wesseling, Henri L.
'Les Pays-Bas et la décolonisation; Politique extérieure et forces profondes', in: *Opinion politique et politique extérieure III, 1945-1981,* pp. 219-239. Rome/Milan, 1985.

1275 Wesseling, H.L.
'Naar een geschiedenis van de dekolonisatie', *Spiegel Historiael* 21 (1986):108-115.

1276 Wesseling, H.L.
Indië verloren, rampspoed geboren en andere opstellen over de geschiedenis van de Europese expansie. Amsterdam: Bakker, 1988, 358 pp.

1277 Westers, M.F.
De kabinetscrisis van 1951; De samenwerking Stikker-Oud. 1984, 231 pp. [MA thesis Rijksuniversiteit Utrecht.] [58]

1278 Westers, M.F.
Mr. D.U. Stikker en de na-oorlogse reconstructie van het liberalisme in Nederland; Een zakenman in de politieke arena. Amsterdam: De Bataafsche Leeuw, 1988, 312 pp. [Also PhD thesis Rijksuniversiteit Utrecht.]

1279 Willems, Wim and Leo Lucassen (eds)
Het onbekende vaderland; De repatriëring van Indische Nederlanders (1946-1964). 's-Gravenhage: SDU Uitgeverij Koninginnegracht, 1994, 183 pp.

1280 Wit, Dick de
De verhouding tussen christendom en islam op Zuid-Celebes voor en na de politieke onafhankelijkheid van Indonesië, 1930-1965. 1988, 116 pp. [MA thesis Rijksuniversiteit Utrecht.]

1281 Witkamp, F. a.o. (ed.)
Gedenkboek van het KNIL 1911-1961. Amersfoort: Van Amerongen, 1961, 334 pp.

1282 Wittert van Hoogland, R.W.C.G.A. (ed.)
Een halve eeuw militaire luchtvaart, 1913-1 juli-1963. 's-Gravenhage: Staatsdrukkerij, 1963, 543 pp.

1283 Wolff, Joop
Uit het rijk der 1000 eilanden; Indonesië zoals het is; Het verhaal van een reis door Indonesië. Amsterdam: Pegasus, 1954, 157 pp.

1284 Woltjer, J.J.
Recent verleden; De geschiedenis van Nederland in de twintigste eeuw. Amsterdam: Balans, 1992, 568 pp. [Second edition, Amsterdam: Muntinga, 1994, 849 pp.]

1285 *'Wij gedenken...' Gedenkboek van de Vereniging van Ambtenaren bij het Binnenlands Bestuur in Nederlandsch-Indië.* Utrecht: Oosthoek, 1956, 11+362 pp.

1286 IJzereef, W.Th.
De wind en de bladeren; Hiërarchie en autonomie in Bone en Polombangkeng (Zuid-Sulawesi), 1850-1950. 1994, 11+278 pp. [PhD thesis Rijksuniversiteit Groningen.]

1287 Zwaag, Jaap van der
Verloren tropische zaken; De opkomst en ondergang van de Nederlandse handel- en cultuurmaatschappijen in het voormalige Nederlands-Indië. Meppel: Feniks, 1991, 319 pp.

1288 Zwitzer, H.L.
'The Netherlands as a colonial power and the United States', *De Militaire Spectator* 151 (1982):193-201. (ubl)

1289 Zwitzer, H.L. and C.A. Heshusius
Het Koninklijk Nederlands-Indisch Leger 1830-1950; Een terugblik. 's-Gravenhage: Staatsuitgeverij, 1977, 175 pp.

General works
Other authors

1290 Abeyasekere, Susan
Jakarta; A history. Singapore: Oxford University Press, 1987, 280 pp.

1291 Adams, Cindy
Sukarno; An autobiography as told to Cindy Adams. Indianapolis/Kansas City/New York: The Bobbs-Merrill Company, 1965, 324 pp.

1292 Adams, Cindy
Bung Karno penjambung lidah rakjat Indonesia. Djakarta: Gunung Agung, 1966, 23+470 pp. [Third printing 1984.]

1293 Adams, Cindy
Sukarno; Een autobiografie uit de mond van de president opgetekend door Cindy Adams. 's-Gravenhage: Van Hoeve, 1967, 358 pp.

1294 Aden, Jean Bush
Oil and politics in Indonesia, 1945-1980. 1988, 545 pp. [PhD thesis Cornell University, Ithaca.]

1295 Albertini, R. von
Dekolonisation; Die Diskussion über Verwaltung und Zukunft der Kolonien, 1919-1960. Köln/Opladen: Westdeutscher Verlag, 1966, 607 pp.

1296 Aleshin, Iurii
Soviet-Indonesian relations during the 1945-1962 period. Moscow: Institute of International Relations, 1963, 176 pp. [In Russian.]

1297 d'Alpuget, Blanche
Mediator; A biography of Sir Richard Kirby. Carlton: Melbourne University Press, 1977, 277 pp.

1298 'Amir Sjarifuddin', in: *Lives given to freedom*, pp. 245-262. Moscow: Progress, 1966.

1299 Amstutz, James B.
The Indonesian youth movement, 1908-1955. 1958, 391 pp. [PhD thesis Fletcher School of Law and Diplomacy, Tufts University, Medford.] (uba)

1300 Andaya, Leonard
'Arung Palakka and Kahar Muzakkar; A study of the hero figure in Bugis-Makassar society', in: *People and society in Indonesia; A biographical approach*, pp. 1-11. Clayton: Monash University, 1977.

1301   Andaya, L.Y.; Charles Coppel and Yuji Suzuki (eds)
        People and society in Indonesia; A biographical approach. Clayton: Monash
        University, 1977, 50 pp.

1302   Andreev, G.A.
        The Indonesian state; Problems of unity and autonomy (1945-1965). Moscow:
        Nauka, 1974, 149 pp. [In Russian.]

1303   Anthonio, Winniefred
        Tjalie Robinson; 'Reflections in a brown eye'. 1990, 418 pp. [PhD thesis University
        of Michigan, Ann Arbor.]

1304   Baker, Elisabeth A. and G. Derwood Baker
        The story of Indonesia. Wichita, 1965, 156 pp. [37]

1305   Baliga, Bantval Mohandas
        *The American approach to imperialism in Southeast Asia; The attitude of the United
        States government in the Philippines, Indo-China and Indonesia, 1945-1958.* 1961,
        245 pp. [PhD thesis Southern Illinois University, Carbondale.]

1306   Ball, W. MacMahon
        Nationalism and communism in East Asia. Melbourne: Melbourne University
        Press, 1952, 210 pp.

1307   Barclay, C.N.
        *The Regimental history of the 3rd Queen Alexandra's Own Gurkha Rifles. Vol. II,
        1927-1947.* London, 1953. [45, 6345]

1308   Bastin, J. and H.J. Benda
        A history of modern Southeast Asia; Colonialism, nationalism and decolonization.
        Englewood Cliffs: Prentice-Hall, 1968, 214 pp. [Second edition, Sydney:
        Prentice-Hall of Australia, 1977, 190 pp.]

1309   Bey, Mohammad Ali
        The Indonesian struggle for independence 1914-1950. 1958, 449 pp. [PhD thesis
        Muslim University, Aligarh.] [97]

1310   Bhattacharjee, G.P.
        Southeast Asian politics; Malaysia and Indonesia. Calcutta: Minerva, 1976, 7+
        264 pp.

1311   Bigalke, Terance William
        A social history of 'Tana Toraja' 1870-1965. 1981, 524 pp. [PhD thesis
        University of Wisconsin, Madison.]

1312   Bonneff, Marcel; Françoise Cayrac-Blanchard; Pierre Labrousse; Jacques
        Leclerc; Denys Lombard and Monique Zaini-Lajoubert
        Pantjasila; Trente années de débats politiques en Indonésie. Paris: Editions de la
        Maison des Sciences de l'Homme, 1980, 427 pp.

1313   Bowen, John R.
        Sumatran politics and poetics; Gayo history, 1900-1989. New Haven/London:
        Yale University Press, 1991, 298 pp.

1314 Brackenridge, Lindy C.
      The Darul Islam movement in West Java; A study of religion and its
      relationship to insurgency. 1975. [MA thesis Australian National University,
      Canberra.] [1348]

1315 Brackman, Arnold C.
      Indonesian communism; A history. New York: Praeger, 1963, 16+336 pp.

1316 Brimmell, J.H.
      Communism in South East Asia; A political analysis. London: Oxford University
      Press, 1959, 10+415 pp.

1317 Britton, Peter A.
      Military professionalism in Indonesia; Javanese and Western military traditions
      in army ideology to the 1970s. 1983, 352 pp. [MA thesis Monash University,
      Clayton.]

1318 Bro, Margueritte Harmon
      Indonesia; Land of challenge. New York: Harper, 1954, 13+263 pp.

1319 Bruhat, Jean
      Histoire de l'Indonésie. Paris: Presses Universitaires de France, 1958, 127 pp.

1320 Buhite, Russell
      'The United States and Indonesia', in: A.M. Schlesinger (ed.), *The dynamics of
      world power; A documentary history of United States Foreign Policy 1945-1973.
      Vol. IV, The Far East*, pp. 677-701. New York: Chelsea House, 1973. (ubl)

1321 Burns, Peter
      Revelation and revolution; Natsir and the Panca Sila. Townsville: James Cook
      University of North Queensland, 1981, 139 pp.

1322 Cady, John F.
      America's post-war role in Southeast Asia. Paper International Conference on
      Asian History, Kuala Lumpur, 1968, 33 pp.

1323 Cady, John F.
      The history of post-war Southeast Asia; Independence problems. Athens: Ohio
      University Press, 1974, 720 pp.

1324 Caldwell, Malcolm
      Indonesia. London: Oxford University Press, 1968, 128 pp.

1325 Caldwell, Malcolm
      Indonesië. Nijkerk: Callenbach, 1969, 102 pp.

1326 Caldwell, Malcolm and Ernst Utrecht
      Indonesia; An alternative history. Sydney: Alternative Publishing Co-operative,
      1979, 208 pp.

1327 Casey, R.G.
      Friends and neighbours; Australia and the world. Melbourne: Cheshire, 1954,
      166 pp.

1328 Cayrac-Blanchard, Françoise
      Le parti communiste indonésien. Paris: Colin, 1973, 217 pp.

1329 Cayrac-Blanchard, Françoise
L'armée et le pouvoir politique en Indonésie; De la révolution au développement.
Paris: l'Harmattan, 1991, 214 pp.

1330 Chang Chiao Xian
Politics and economics of post-war Indonesia. Moscow: Foreign Languages Press,
1958, 439 pp. [In Russian; Translated from the Chinese.]

1331 Colbert, Evelyn
Southeast Asia in international politics, 1941-1956. Ithaca: Cornell University
Press, 1977, 372 pp.

1332 Cooley, Frank L.
'In memoriam: T.B. Simatupang, 1920-1990', *Indonesia* no. 49 (1990):145-152.

1333 Coppel, Charles A.
'The national status of the Chinese in Indonesia', *Papers on Far Eastern History*
no. 1 (March 1970):115-139. (ubl)

1334 Coppel, Charles A.
'Patterns of Chinese political activity in Indonesia', in: J.A.C. Mackie (ed.), *The
Chinese in Indonesia; Five essays*, pp. 19-76. Melbourne: Nelson, 1976.

1335 Coppel, Ch.A.
Indonesian Chinese in crisis. Kuala Lumpur: Oxford University Press, 1983,
236 pp.

1336 Corsino, MacArthur F.
*A communist revolutionary movement as an international state-actor; The case of the
PKI-Aidit.* Singapore: Institute of Southeast Asian Studies, 1982, 8+229 pp.

1337 Cribb, Robert
'The Indonesian Marxist tradition', in: Colin Mackerras and Nick Knight (eds),
Marxism in Asia, pp. 251-272. London/Sydney: Croom Helm, 1985.

1338 Crouch, Harold
Army and politics in Indonesia. Ithaca: Cornell University Press, 1978, 377 pp.
[Second edition, 1988, 384 pp.]

1339 Crouch, Harold
'The trend to authoritarianism; The post-1945 period', in: Harry Aveling (ed.),
The development of Indonesian society, pp. 166-204. St Lucia: University of
Queensland Press, 1979.

1340 Crouch, Harold
Militer dan politik di Indonesia. Jakarta: Sinar Harapan, 1986, 419 pp.

1341 Dahm, Bernhard
Soekarno en de strijd om Indonesië's onafhankelijkheid. Meppel: Boom, 1964, 399
pp.

1342 Dahm, Bernhard
*Sukarnos Kampf um Indonesiens Unabhängigkeit; Werdegang und politische Ideen bis
zu seiner Wahl zum ersten Präsidenten der Republik Indonesien im August 1945.*
1964, 407 pp. [PhD thesis Universität Kiel.]

1343   Dahm, Bernhard
       Sukarno and the struggle for Indonesian independence. Ithaca/London: Cornell
       University Press, 1969, 374 pp.

1344   Dahm, Bernhard
       History of Indonesia in the twentieth century. London: Pall Mall, 1971, 321 pp.

1345   Dahm, Bernhard
       Indonesien; Geschichte eines Entwicklungslandes (1945-1971). Leiden/Köln: Brill,
       1978, 200 pp.

1346   Dahm, Bernhard
       Sukarno dan perjuangan kemerdekaan. Jakarta: Lembaga Penelitian, Pendidikan
       dan Penerangan Ekonomi dan Sosial, 1987, 450 pp.

1347   *A decade of American foreign policy; Basic documents, 1941-49.* Washington:
       Government Printing Office, 1950, 1381 pp.

1348   Dengel, Holk H.
       Darul-Islam; Kartosuwirjos Kampf um einen islamitischen Staat Indonesien. Stutt-
       gart: Steiner, 1986, 255 pp. [Also PhD thesis Universität Heidelberg.]

1349   Dengel, Holk H.
       *Neuere Darstellung der Geschichte Indonesiens in Bahasa Indonesia; Entwicklung und
       Tendenzen der indonesischen Historiographie.* Stuttgart: Steiner, 1994, 269 pp.

1350   Dobbin, Christine
       'The search for women in Indonesian history', in: *Kartini centenary; Indonesian
       women then and now,* pp. 56-68. Clayton: Monash University, 1980.

1351   Doran, Christine
       'Women and Indonesian nationalism', *Kabar Seberang* 17 (June 1986):20-30.

1352   Edman, Peter
       *'Communism à la Aidit'; The Indonesian communist party under D.N. Aidit, 1950-
       1965.* Townsville: James Cook University of North Queensland, 1987,
       7+146 pp.

1353   Emerson, Rupert
       Representative government in Southeast Asia. Cambridge: Harvard University
       Press, 1955, 197 pp.

1354   Entessar, Tahmineh
       Revolution and leadership; A study of four countries. 1983, 312 pp. [PhD thesis St
       Louis University, St Louis.]

1355   Fain, Sylvia Woodby
       *The evolution of Soviet approaches to colonial nationalism; South and Southeast Asia,
       1946-1953.* 1971, 411 pp. [PhD thesis Columbia University, New York.]

1356   Federspiel, Howard M.
       Persatuan Islam; Islamic reform in twentieth century Indonesia. Ithaca: Cornell
       University, 1970, 7+247 pp.

1357   Feith, Herbert
       The decline of constitutional democracy in Indonesia. Ithaca: Cornell University
       Press, 1962, 20+618 pp.

1358   Feith, Herbert
       'Indonesia', in: George McTurnan Kahin (ed.), *Governments and politics of
       Southeast Asia*, pp. 183-278. Second edition. Ithaca: Cornell University Press,
       1964. [First edition, 1959, pp. 153-238.]

1359   Feith, H. and L. Castles (eds)
       Indonesian political thinking, 1945-1965. Ithaca: Cornell University Press, 1970,
       505 pp.

1360   Feith, H. and L. Castles (eds)
       Pemikiran politik Indonesia 1945-1965. Jakarta: Lembaga Penelitian, Pendidikan
       dan Penerangan Ekonomi dan Sosial, 1988, 67+267 pp.

1361   Fel'chukov, Iu.V.
       *The agrarian question in the policies of the government of independent Indonesia,
       1945-1962.* PhD thesis Lomonosov State University, Moscow, 1962, 306 pp.
       [In Russian.] [97]

1362   Fifield, Russell H.
       The diplomacy of Southeast Asia, 1945-1958. New York: Harper, 1958, 15+584
       pp.

1363   Finch, Susan and Daniel S. Lev
       Republic of Indonesia cabinets, 1945-1965. Ithaca: Cornell University Press, 1965,
       66 pp.

1364   Finkelstein, Lawrence S.
       American policy in Southeast Asia. New York: American Institute of Pacific
       Relations, 1950, 66 pp.

1365   Fischer, Louis
       The story of Indonesia. New York: Harper, London: Hamish Hamilton, 1959,
       10+341 pp.

1366   Fitzgerald, C.P.
       China and Southeast Asia since 1945. London: Longman, 1973, 110 pp.

1367   *Foreign relations of the United States.* Washington: U.S. Government Printing
       Office. Many vols. (kb)

1368   Frederick, W.H.
       The man who knew too much; Ch.O. van der Plas and the future of Indonesia,
       1927-1950. Paper Ohio State University, Athens, 1993, 50 pp.

1369   Frederick, William H. and Soeri Soeroto (eds)
       Pemahaman sejarah Indonesia sebelum dan sesuai revolusi. Jakarta: Lembaga
       Penelitian, Pendidikan dan Penerangan Ekonomi dan Sosial, 1982, 486 pp.

1370   Fryer, Donald W. and James C. Jackson
       Indonesia. London: Ernest Benn, Boulder: Westview Press, 1977, 313 pp.

1371 Goetze, Dieter
      Castro-Nkrumah-Sukarno; Eine vergleichende soziologische Untersuchung zur Struk-turanalyse charismatischer politischer Führung. Berlin: Reimer, 1976, 29+323 pp.

1372 Gould, James W.
      Americans in Sumatra. The Hague: Nijhoff, 1961, 185 pp.

1373 Grant, Bruce
      Indonesia. Parkville etc.: Melbourne University Press, 1964, 190 pp. [Second edition, Carlton: Melbourne University Press, 1966, 204 pp.]

1374 Grant, Bruce
      Indonesië. Hilversum: De Haan, Antwerpen: Standaard, 1965, 221 pp.

1375 Greenwood, Gordon
      Approaches to Asia; Australian postwar policies and attitudes. Sydney: McGraw-Hill, 1974, 612 pp. (kb)

1376 Grimal, Henri
      La décolonisation, 1919-1963. Paris: Colin, 1965, 408 pp. (kb)

1377 Grimal, H.
      Decolonization; The British, French, Dutch and Belgian empires 1919-1963. London: Routledge and Kegan Paul, 1978, 443 pp.

1378 Guber, A.A.; A.B. Belenky and O.I. Zabozlaeva (eds)
      The Republic of Indonesia 1945-1960. Moscow: Eastern Languages Press, 1961, 384 pp. [In Russian.]

1379 Habibuddin, S.M.
      'Nationalism in India and Indonesia; A comparative and interpretative appraisal', *Quarterly Review of Historical Studies* 15 (1975-76):31-43. (ubl)

1380 Haire, James
      The character and theological struggle of the church of Halmaheira, Indonesia, 1941-1979. Frankfurt am Main: Lang, 1981, 381 pp.

1381 Hall, D.G.E.
      A history of South-East Asia. London: MacMillan, New York: St Martin's Press, 1955, 807 pp. [Third edition, 1968, 1019 pp.]

1382 Hanna, W.A.
      'Nationalist revolution and revolutionary nationalism; Indonesia', in: K.H. Silvert (ed.), *Expectant peoples; Nationalism and development*, pp. 129-177. New York: Random House, 1963.

1383 Hanna, W.A.
      Eight nation makers; Southeast Asia's charismatic statesmen. New York: St Martin's Press, 1964, 307 pp.

1384 Hanna, Willard A.
      'From jail to jail; The saga of Tan Malaka; An analysis of the qualities necessary for Indonesian political leadership; A report', *American Universities Field Staff, Southeast Asia Series* 7-2 (64-1959):1-22.

1385   Hanna, Willard A.
       Bali profile; People, events, circumstances (1001-1976). New York: American
       Universities Field Staff, 1976, 140 pp.

1386   Hanna, Willard A.
       Indonesian Banda; Colonialism and its aftermath in the nutmeg islands.
       Philadelphia: Institute for the Study of Human Issues, 1978, 164 pp.

1387   Hanna, Willard A.
       Hikayat Jakarta. Jakarta: Yayasan Obor Indonesia, 1988, 15+267 pp.

1388   Harper, Robert W.
       An analysis of the development of the international relations of Indonesia. 1957,
       248 pp. [PhD thesis American University, Washington.]

1389   Harrison, Brian
       A short history of South East Asia. New York: St Martin's Press, 1954, 268 pp.

1390   Harrison, Brian
       Zuidoost-Azië; Een beknopte geschiedenis. Amsterdam: De Spieghel, 1954, 285 pp.

1391   Harvey, Barbara S.
       Tradition, Islam and rebellion; South Sulawesi, 1905-1965. 1974, 513 pp. [PhD
       thesis Cornell University, Ithaca.]

1392   Harvey, Barbara S.
       Pemberontakan Kahar Muzakkar; Dari tradisi ke DI/TII. Jakarta: Grafiti, 1989,
       9+415 pp.

1393   Heinschke, Martina
       *Angkatan 45; Literaturkonzeptionen im gesellschaftspolitischen Kontext; Zur
       Funktionsbestimmung von Literatur im postkolonialen Indonesien.* Hamburg/Berlin:
       Reimer, 1993, 365 pp.

1394   Henderson, William (ed.)
       Southeast Asia; Problems of United States policy. Cambridge, Mass.: The M.I.T.
       Press, 1963, 14+273 pp.

1395   Hess, Gary R.
       The United States' emergence as a Southeast Asian power, 1940-1950. New York:
       Columbia University Press, 1987, 448 pp.

1396   Higgins, Rosalyn (ed.)
       United Nations peacekeeping, 1946-1967; Documents and commentary; Vol II: Asia.
       London: Oxford University Press, 1970, 486 pp.

1397   Hilsman, Roger
       *To move a nation; The politics of foreign policy in the administration of John F.
       Kennedy.* New York: Doubleday, 1967, 583 pp. (ubl)

1398   Hindley, Donald
       The Communist Party of Indonesia 1951-1963. Berkeley/Los Angeles: University
       of California Press, 1964, 17+380 pp. [Second printing 1966.]

1399   *History of the 5th Royal Gurkha Rifles (Frontier Force); Vol. II, 1929-1947.*
       Aldershot, 1956. [45, 6345]

1400 Holland, R.F.
European decolonization 1918-1981; An introductory survey. Houndsmills: MacMillan, 1985, 321 pp.

1401 Horikoshi, Hiroko
'The Dar-ul-Islam movement in West Java (1948-62); An experience in the historical process', *Indonesia* no. 20 (1975):58-86.

1402 Hudson, W.J.
Australia and the colonial question at the United Nations. Sydney: Sydney University Press, 1970, 214 pp. [PhD thesis Australian National University, Canberra, 1967.]

1403 Hussein-Jouffroy, Anne-Marie
'Les mots merdeka et revolusi chez Sukarno; Etude de vocabulaire politique Indonésien', *Archipel* 12 (1976):47-76.

1404 Hyma, A.
A history of the Dutch in the Far East. Second edition. Ann Arbor: Wahr, 1953, 295 pp. [First edition 1942.]

1405 Ingleson, John
'Mohammad Hatta; Cendekiawan, aktivis dan politikus', *Prisma* 11-1 (January 1982):61-74.

1406 Ionova, Alla Ivanovna
The Indonesian bourgeoisie and working class, 1945-1960. Moscow: Nauka, 1966, 138 pp. [In Russian.] (kitlv-m)

1407 Ionova, Alla Ivanovna
Muslim nationalism in modern Indonesia, 1945-1965. Moscow: Nauka, 1972, 283 pp. [In Russian.]

1408 Jackson, Karl D.
Traditional authority, Islam and rebellion; A study of Indonesian political behavior. Berkeley/Los Angeles/London: University of California Press, 1980, 375 pp. [PhD thesis Massachusetts Institute of Technology, Cambridge.]

1409 Jackson, Karl D.
Kewibawaan tradisional, Islam dan pemberontakan; Kasus Darul Islam Jawa Barat. Jakarta: Grafiti, 1990, 393 pp.

1410 Jarvis, Helen
'Tan Malaka; Revolutionary or renegade?', *Bulletin of Concerned Asian Scholars* 19-1 (January-March 1987):41-54.

1411 Jessup, Philip C.
The birth of nations. New York/London: Columbia University Press, 1974, 361 pp.

1412 Jhaveri, Satyavati S.
The presidency in Indonesia; Dilemmas of democracy. Bombay: Popular Prakashan, 1975, 319 pp.

1413   Jones, Garth N.
       A comparison of Indonesia's three constitutions. Jogjakarta: Gadjah Mada University, 1960, 18+120 pp.

1414   Jones, Howard Palfrey
       Indonesia; The possible dream. New York: Harcourt, Brace and Jovanovich, 1971, 19+473 pp. [Second printing, Singapore: Mas Aju, 1973.]

1415   Junge, Gerhard
       The universities of Indonesia; History and structure. Bremen: Bremen Economic Research Society, 1973, 223 pp.

1416   Kahin, George Mc.T.
       'In memoriam: Mohammed Hatta (1902-1980)', *Indonesia* no. 30 (1980):113-119.

1417   Kahin, George McT.
       'In memoriam: L.N. Palar', *Indonesia* no. 32 (1981):169-170.

1418   Kahin, George McT.
       'In memoriam: Sjafruddin Prawiranegara (1911-1989)', *Indonesia* no. 48 (1989):97-100.

1419   Kahin, George McTurnan
       'Molly Bondan: 1912-1990', *Indonesia* no. 50 (1990):158-161.

1420   Kapica, M.S. and N.P. Maletin
       Sukarno; A political biography. Moscow: Mysl, 1980, 331 pp. [In Russian.]

1421   Karns, Margaret Padelford
       The United States, the United Nations and decolonization. 1975, 344 pp. [PhD thesis University of Michigan, Ann Arbor.] [44]

1422   Kemp, Peter
       Alms for oblivion. London: Cassell, 1961, 189 pp.

1423   Kennedy, Malcolm
       A history of communism in East Asia. New York: Praeger, 1957, 9+556 pp.

1424   Khoo, Gilbert
       A history of South-East Asia since 1500. Fifth edition. Singapore: Oxford University Press, 1980, 200 pp.

1425   Khoo, Gilbert and Dorothy Lo
       Asian transformation; A history of South-East, South and East Asia. Kuala Lumpur: Heinemann, 1977, 1164 pp.

1426   Kiessling, Hein Günter
       Partai Sosialis/Partai Sosialis Indonesia 1945-1960; Der demokratische Sozialismus in der Republik Indonesien unter besonderer Berücksichtigung seiner Rolle im Freiheitskampf. 1983, 265 pp. [PhD thesis Ludwig-Maximilians-Universität, München.]

1427   King, Dwight Y.
       Interest groups and political linkage in Indonesia, 1800-1965. DeKalb: Northern Illinois University, 1982, 192 pp.

1428 Kosut, Hal (ed.)
Indonesia; The Sukarno years. New York: Facts on File, 1967, 140 pp.

1429 Krishnamurthy, S.
Central-local relations in Indonesia, 1947-59. 1961. [PhD thesis University of Delhi.] [1412]

1430 Kubitscheck, Hans-Dieter and Ingrid Wessel
Geschichte Indonesiens vom Altertum bis zur Gegenwart. Berlin: Akademie-Verlag, 1981, 13+290 pp.

1431 Labrousse, Pierre
'La deuxième vie de Bung Karno; Analyse du mythe (1978-1981)', *Archipel* 25 (1983):187-214.

1432 Latourette, Kenneth Scott
The American record in the Far East 1945-1951. New York: Macmillan, 1952, 208 pp.

1433 Leclerc, Jacques
'La condition du parti; Révolutionnaires indonésiens à la recherche d'une identité (1928-1948)', *Cultures et Développement* 10-1 (1978):3-70.

1434 Leclerc, J.
'Amir Sjarifuddin 75 tahun', *Prisma* 11-12 (December 1982):53-76.

1435 Leclerc, Jacques
'Amir Sjarifuddin; Between the state and the revolution', in: Angus McIntyre (ed.), *Indonesian political biography; In search of cross-cultural understanding*, pp. 1-41. Clayton: Monash University, 1993.

1436 Legge, J.D.
Indonesia. Englewood Cliffs: Prentice-Hall, 1964, 184 pp.

1437 Legge, J.D.
Sukarno; A political biography. Harmondsworth: Penguin Books, 1972, 431 pp. [Second edition, Sydney: Allen and Unwin, 1984.]

1438 Legge, J.D.
'Sukarno; Traditional or modern leader?', in: Wang Gungwu (ed.), *Self and biography; Essays on the individual and society in Asia*, pp. 171-184. Sydney: Sydney University Press, 1975.

1439 Legge, John
'Sukarno si tokoh politik', in: Colin Wild and Peter Carey (eds), *Gelora api revolusi*, pp. 109-115. Jakarta: Gramedia, 1986.

1440 Leifer, Michael
Indonesia's foreign policy. London: Allen and Unwin, 1983, 198 pp.

1441 Lev, Daniel S.
'In memoriam: R.M. Sartono', *Indonesia* no. 7 (1969):191-193.

1442 Lev, Daniel S.
'In memoriam: Besar Martokoesoemo SH (1894-1980)', *Indonesia* no. 30 (1980):121-123.

1443   McIntyre, Angus (ed.)
        Indonesian political biography; In search of cross-cultural understanding. Clayton:
        Monash University, 1993, 327 pp.

1444   McKemmish, Susan Marilyn
        A political biography of General A.H. Nasution. 1976, 328 pp. [MA thesis
        Monash University, Clayton.]

1445   McLane, Charles B.
        *Soviet strategies in Southeast Asia; An exploration of eastern policy under Lenin and
        Stalin*. Princeton, N.J.: Princeton University Press, 1966, 17+563 pp.

1446   McVey, Ruth T.
        *The development of the Indonesian communist party and its relations with the Soviet
        Union; Summary*. Cambridge (Mass.): Center for International Studies,
        Massachusetts Institute of Technology, 1954, 10 pp. (ubl)

1447   McVey, Ruth T.
        'The post-revolutionary transformation of the Indonesian army', *Indonesia* no. 11
        (1971):131-176.

1448   McVey, Ruth T.
        'In memoriam: Adam Malik (1917-1984)', *Indonesia* no. 39 (1985):144-148.

1449   'Manovar Musso', in: *Lives given to freedom*, pp. 221-242. Moscow: Progress,
        1966.

1450   Mansur, Fatma
        Onafhankelijkheid als proces. Voorwoord Dr. H.J. van Mook. Amsterdam:
        Arbeiderspers, 1965, 224 pp.

1451   Maruyama, Katsuhiko
        A chronology of Japanese-Indonesian relations. Tokyo: Meiji Tosho Shuppan, 1979,
        144 pp. [In Japanese.] [51]

1452   Maryanov, G.S.
        Decentralization in Indonesia as a political problem. Ithaca: Cornell University
        Press, 1958, 118 pp.

1453   Maryanov, Gerald Seymour
        The establishment of regional government in the Republic of Indonesia. 1959, 384 pp.
        [PhD thesis Indiana University, Bloomington.]

1454   Masuda, Ato
        A history of modern Indonesia. Tokyo: Chuo-Koron-sha, 1971, 438 pp. [In
        Japanese.] [81]

1455   Mehrish, B.N.
        India's recognition policy towards the new nations. Delhi: Oriental Publishers,
        1972, 228 pp. (ubl)

1456   Merle, Marcel (ed.)
        Les églises chrétiennes et la décolonisation. Paris: Colin, 1967, 519 pp.

1457 Mestenhauser, Josef A.
Ideologies in conflict in Indonesia, 1945-1955. 1960, 386 pp. [PhD thesis University of Minnesota, Minneapolis.]

1458 Meyvis, L.
De gordel van smaragd; Indonesië van 1799 tot heden. Leuven: Peeters, 1984, 11+189 pp.

1459 Mintz, Jeanne S.
'Marxism in Indonesia', in: Frank N. Trager (ed.), *Marxism in Southeast Asia; A study of four countries*, pp. 171-239. Stanford: Stanford University Press, 1959.

1460 Mintz, Jeanne S.
Mohammed, Marx and Marhaen; The roots of Indonesian socialism. London: Pall Mall, 1965, 8+246 pp.

1461 Morris, Eric Eugene
Islam and politics in Aceh; A study of center-periphery relations in Indonesia. 1983, 325 pp. [PhD thesis Cornell University, Ithaca.]

1462 Morton, Shirley M.
Leadership; Indonesia 1945-67; China 1921-49. London: Whitcoulls, 1978, 87 pp.

1463 Moussay, Gérard
'Un grand figure de l'Islam indonésien: Buya Hamka', *Archipel* 32 (1986):87-111.

1464 Mrázek, R.
'Tan Malaka; A political personality's structure of experience', *Indonesia* no. 14 (1972):1-48.

1465 Mrázek, Rudolf
The United States and the Indonesian military 1945-1965; A study of an intervention. Prague: Czechoslovak Academy of Sciences, 1978, 229+279 pp. 2 vols.

1466 Mrázek, Rudolf
Semesta Tan Malaka. Yogyakarta: Bayu Indra Grafika (Bigraf), 1994, 15+106 pp.

1467 Mrázek, Rudolf
Sjahrir; Politics and exile in Indonesia. Ithaca: Cornell University, 1994, 10+526 pp.

1468 Müller-Krüger, Th.
Sedjarah geredja di Indonesia. Djakarta: Badan Penerbit Kristen, 1959, 249 pp. (kitlv-m) [Second edition, 1966, 291 pp. (kitlv-m)]

1469 Müller-Krüger, Th.
Der Protestantismus in Indonesien; Geschichte und Gestalt. Stuttgart: Evangelisches Verlagswerk, 1968, 388 pp.

1470 Myers, Robert John
The development of the Indonesian socialist party. 1959, 256 pp. [PhD thesis University of Chicago.]

1471   Nakamura, Mitsuo
       The crescent arises over the banyan tree; A study of the Muhammadiyah movement in
       a central Javanese town. 1976, 345 pp. [PhD thesis Cornell University, Ithaca.]

1472   Nakamura, Mitsuo
       Bulan sabit muncul dari balik pohon beringin; Studi tentang pergerakan Muham-
       madiyah di Kotagede, Yogyakarta. Yogyakarta: Gadjah Mada University Press,
       1983, 19+263 pp.

1473   Neill, Wilfred T.
       Twentieth-century Indonesia. New York/London: Columbia University Press,
       1973, 413 pp.

1474   Nöbel, H.W.
       Heer und Politik in Indonesien; Zielsetzung und Zielverwirklichung einer
       militärischen Organisation, 1945-1967. Boppard: Boldt, 1975, 236 pp.

1475   Nyhus, Edward O.V.
       An Indonesian church in the midst of social change; The Batak Protestant Christian
       Church, 1942-1957. 1987, 578 pp. [PhD thesis University of Wisconsin,
       Madison.]

1476   Oey Hong Lee
       Power struggle in South-East Asia. Zug: Inter Documentation Company, 1976,
       614 pp.

1477   Oey Hong Lee
       The Sukarno controversies of 1980/81. Hull: Centre of Southeast Asian Studies,
       1982, 42 pp.

1478   Ohn, Byunghoon
       The United States and Southeast Asia, 1945-1954; The evolution of American policy
       in Southeast Asia. 1967, 378 pp. [PhD thesis University of Kentucky,
       Lexington.]

1479   Oki, Akira
       Social change in the West Sumatran village, 1908-1945. 1977, 291 pp. [PhD thesis
       Australian National University, Canberra.]

1480   Osborne, Milton
       Southeast Asia; An introductory history. Sydney/London: Allen and Unwin,
       1979, 205 pp. [Second edition, 1983, 208 pp.]

1481   Palmier, Leslie H.
       'Soekarno the nationalist', *Pacific Affairs* 30 (June 1957):101-119.

1482   Palmier, L.H.
       'Indonesian-Dutch relations', *Journal of Southeast Asian History* 2-2 (July
       1961):24-34.

1483   Palmier, Leslie H.
       Indonesia and the Dutch. London: Oxford University Press, 1962, 15+194 pp.
       [Second printing 1965.]

1484 Palmier, L.H.
Indonesia. London: Thames and Hudson, 1965, 240 pp.

1485 Palmier, Leslie
Communists in Indonesia; Power pursued in vain. New York: Anchor Press/ Doubleday, 1973, 13+302 pp. [British edition, *Communists in Indonesia*, London: Weidenfeld and Nicolson.]

1486 Pauker, G.J.
'The role of the military in Indonesia', in: John J. Johnson (ed.), *The role of the military in underdeveloped countries*, pp. 185-230. Princeton, N.J.: Princeton University Press, 1962.

1487 Pauker, Guy J.
The rise and fall of the Communist Party of Indonesia. Santa Monica: Rand Corporation, 1969, 63 pp.

1488 Pelzer, Karl J.
Planter and peasant; Colonial policy and the agrarian struggle in East Sumatra, 1863-1947. 's-Gravenhage: Nijhoff, 1978, 11+184 pp.

1489 Pelzer, Karl J.
Planters against peasants; The agrarian struggle in East Sumatra, 1947-1958. 's-Gravenhage: Nijhoff, 1982, 18+186 pp.

1490 Pelzer, K.J.
Toean keboen dan petani; Politik kolonial dan perjuangan agraria di Sumatera Timur, 1863-1947. Jakarta: Sinar Harapan, 1985, 230 pp.

1491 Penders, C.L.M.
The life and times of Sukarno. London: Sidgwick and Jackson, 1974, 11+224 pp.

1492 Penders, C.L.M. and Ulf Sundhaussen
Abdul Haris Nasution; A political biography. St Lucia: University of Queensland Press, 1985, 295 pp.

1493 Plekhanov, Iu.A.
Socio-political reform in Indonesia, 1945-1975. Moscow: Nauka, 1980, 156 pp. [In Russian.]

1494 Purdy, Susan Selden
Legitimation of power and authority in a pluralistic state; Pancasila and civil religion in Indonesia. 1984, 451 pp. [PhD thesis Columbia University, New York.]

1495 Quinn, George
The novel in Javanese; Aspects of its social and literary character. Leiden: KITLV Press, 1992, 330 pp.

1496 Rae, Lindsay
'Sutan Sjahrir and the failure of Indonesian socialism', in: Angus McIntyre (ed.), *Indonesian political biography; In search of cross-cultural understanding*, pp. 43-121. Clayton: Monash University, 1993.

1497 Reinhardt, Jon M.
       Foreign policy and national integration; The case of Indonesia. New Haven: Yale
       University, 1971, 6+230 pp.

1498 Richer, Philippe
       L'Asie du Sud-Est; Indépendances et communismes. Paris: Imprimerie Nationale,
       1981, 430 pp.

1499 Ricklefs, M.C.
       A history of modern Indonesia, c.1300 to the present. London: Macmillan, 1981,
       335 pp. [Second edition, 1993, 378 pp.]

1500 Robertson, J.B. and J. Spruyt
       A history of Indonesia. Melbourne: Macmillan, 1967, 258 pp.

1501 Rocamora, Jose Eliseo
       Nationalism in search of ideology; The Indonesian Nationalist Party 1946-1965.
       1974, 616 pp. [PhD thesis Cornell University, Ithaca.]

1502 Rodes, Robert Michael
       *Soviet attitudes toward the independence movements in South and Southeast Asia,
       1945-1952.* 1966, 318 pp. [PhD thesis Columbia University, New York.]

1503 Roeder, O.G.
       The smiling general; President Soeharto of Indonesia. Djakarta: Gunung Agung,
       1969, 280 pp. [Second edition, 1970, 290 pp.]

1504 Roeder, O.G.
       Soeharto dari pradjurit sampai presiden. Djakarta: Gunung Agung, 1969, 330 pp.

1505 Roeder, O.G. (ed.)
       *Who's who in Indonesia; Biographies of prominent Indonesian personalities in all
       fields.* Djakarta: Gunung Agung, 1971, 32+544 pp. [Second edition by O.G.
       Roeder and Mahiddin Mahmud (eds), Singapore: Gunung Agung, 1980, 6+
       428 pp.]

1506 Roeder, O.G.
       Anak desa; Biografi Presiden Soeharto. Jakarta: Gunung Agung, 1976, 416 pp.

1507 Rose, L.A.
       Roots of tragedy; The United States and the struggle for Asia, 1945-1953.
       Westport, Conn.: Greenwood Press, 1976, 262 pp.

1508 Rose, Mavis
       Indonesia free; A political biography of Mohammad Hatta. Ithaca: Cornell
       University, 1987, 8+237 pp.

1509 Rose, Mavis
       Indonesia merdeka; Biografi politik Mohammed Hatta. Jakarta: Gramedia, 1991,
       24+396 pp.

1510 Rotter, Andrew Jon
       The big canvas; The United States, Southeast Asia and the world, 1948-1950. 1981,
       492 pp. [PhD thesis Stanford University, Stanford.]

1511 Samson, Allan Arnold
Islam and politics in Indonesia. 1972, 411 pp. [PhD thesis University of California at Berkeley.]

1512 Samuel, Christopher D.
Ideological and political aspects of the Indonesian constitutional debates of 1945 and 1956-59. 1971, 13+344 pp. [MA thesis Monash University, Clayton.]

1513 Sardesai, D.R.
Southeast Asia; Past and present. New Delhi: Vikas Publishing House, 1981, 485 pp.

1514 Sarkisyanz, Emanuel
Südostasien seit 1945. München: Oldenbourg, 1961, 180 pp.

1515 Sato, Tasuku and P. Mark Tennien
I remember Flores. New York: Farrar, Straus and Cudahy, 1957, 25+129 pp. (kb)

1516 Sato, Tasuku and P. Mark Tennien
Aku terkenang Flores. Ende: Arnoldus, 1976, 137 pp.

1517 Schaarschmidt-Kohl, Eva-Maria
Die politische Geschichte der indonesischen Gewerkschaftsbewegung bis zur Unabhängigkeit. Köln: Pahl-Rugenstein, 1987, 10+143 pp. [PhD thesis Universität Heidelberg.]

1518 Schlereth, Einar
Indonesien; Die Menschen, das Land, die Kultur und was die holländischen Räuber daraus gemacht haben. Berlin: Wagenbach, 1975, 125 pp.

1519 Schreiner-Brauch, Klaus H.
Nationalismus und Personenkult im indonesischen Geschichtsverständnis. 1993, 293 pp. [PhD thesis Universität Hamburg.]

1520 Sevortyan, R.Z.
The political role of the army in Indonesia, 1945-1957. 1966, 297 pp. [PhD thesis Institute of Asian Peoples of the Academy of Sciences, Moscow.] [In Russian.] [90]

1521 Shin, A.S.
The policy of the United States towards Indonesia after the Second World War, 1945-1960. 1962, 321 pp. [PhD thesis Lomonosov State University, Moscow.] [In Russian.] [97]

1522 Shin, A.S.
American imperialism in Indonesia (1945-1962). Moscow: Eastern Languages Press, 1963, 132 pp. [In Russian.]

1523 Sholmov, Iu.A.
Soviet-Indonesian relations between 1945-1963. 1966, 292 pp. [PhD thesis Institute of Asian Peoples of the Academy of Sciences, Moscow.] [In Russian.] [97]

1524 Sholmov, Iu.A.
Soviet Union-Indonesia 1945-1954. Moscow: Nauka, 1976, 165 pp. [In Russian.]

1525 Siebeck, Christian Albrecht
Mohammed Hatta und der indonesische Sozialismus; Staatsdenken eines indonesischen Nationalisten. 1979, 248 pp. [PhD thesis Universität Heidelberg.]

1526 Silverman, Jerry M.
Indonesianizing Marxism-Leninism; The development and consequences of communist polycentrism (1919-1966). 1967, 309 pp. [PhD thesis Claremont Graduate School, Claremont, Calif.]

1527 Singh, Bilveer
Bear and garuda; Soviet-Indonesian relations from Lenin to Gorbachev. Yogyakarta: Gadjah Mada University Press, 1994, 14+361 pp.

1528 Singh, Vishal
The Indonesian political parties. 1961. [PhD thesis University of Delhi.] [1412]

1529 Smith, Steven Murray
Foreign policy adaptation; Aspects of British and Dutch foreign policies, 1945-63. 1978, 484 pp. [PhD thesis University of Southampton.]

1530 Smith, Tony (ed.)
The end of European empire; Decolonization after World War II. Lexington: Heath, 1975, 23+262 pp. (ubl)

1531 Somers, Mary Frances Ann
Peranakan Chinese politics in Indonesia. 1965, 302 pp. [PhD thesis Cornell University, Ithaca.]

1532 Soriano, Francisco S.
Philippine diplomatic relations with Southeast Asia (1946-1957). 1959, 118 pp. [MA thesis American University, Washington.]

1533 Spruyt, J.
Indonesia; An alternative history of the timeless isles. Third edition. Melbourne: The MacMillan Company of Australia, 1979, 214 pp. [First edition 1967.]

1534 Steinberg, David Joel (ed.)
In search of Southeast Asia; A modern history. Honolulu: University of Hawaii Press, 1987, 590 pp.

1535 Stoler, Ann Laura
In the Company's shadow; Labor control and confrontation in Sumatra's plantation history, 1870-1979. 1983, 387 pp. [PhD thesis Columbia University, New York.]

1536 Stoler, A.L.
Capitalism and confrontation in Sumatra's plantation belt, 1870-1979. New Haven: Yale University Press, 1985, 12+244 pp.

1537 Sundhaussen, Ulf
'The fashioning of unity in the Indonesian army', *Asia Quarterly* 2 (1971):181-202.

1538 Sundhaussen, Ulf
The political orientations and political involvement of the Indonesian officers corps 1945-66; The Siliwangi Division and the Army Headquarters. 1971, 731 pp. [PhD thesis Monash University, Clayton.]

1539 Sundhaussen, Ulf
Social policy aspects in defence and security planning in Indonesia, 1947-1977. Townsville: James Cook University of North Queensland, 1980, 54 pp.

1540 Sundhaussen, Ulf
The road to power; Indonesian military politics 1945-1967. Kuala Lumpur: Oxford University Press, 1982, 304 pp.

1541 Sundhaussen, Ulf
Politik militer Indonesia 1945-1967; Menuju dwi fungsi ABRI. Jakarta: Lembaga Penelitian, Pendidikan dan Penerangan Ekonomi dan Sosial, 1986, 15+503 pp.

1542 Suryadinata, Leo
Indigenous Indonesians, the Chinese minority and China; A study of perceptions and policies. 1975, 302 pp. [PhD thesis American University, Washington.]

1543 Suryadinata, Leo
Eminent Indonesian Chinese; Biographical sketches. Singapore: Institute of Southeast Asian Studies, 1978, 10+230 pp.

1544 Suryadinata, Leo
Pribumi Indonesians, the Chinese minority and China; A study of perceptions and policies. Kuala Lumpur: Heinemann, 1978, 11+227 pp.

1545 Suryadinata, Leo (ed.)
Political thinking of the Indonesian Chinese, 1900-1977; A sourcebook. Singapore: Singapore University Press, 1979, 19+251 pp.

1546 Suryadinata, Leo
Dilema minoritas Tionghoa. Jakarta: Grafiti Pers, 1984, 258 pp.

1547 Suzuki, Yuji
'Tan Malaka; Perantauan and the power of ideas', in: *People and society in Indonesia; A biographical approach*, pp. 31-50. Clayton: Monash University, 1977.

1548 Swarup, Satya
Indian relations and attitudes in regard to Southeast Asia (1947-1952). 1956, 193 pp. [PhD thesis Fletcher School of Law and Diplomacy, Tufts University, Medford.] [97]

1549 Tanner, Rolf
'A strong showing'; Britain's struggle for power and influence in South-East Asia 1942-1950. Stuttgart: Steiner, 1994, 299 pp.

1550 Tarling, Nicholas
A concise history of Southeast Asia. New York: Praeger, 1966, 334 pp.

1551 Tarling, Nicholas
Southeast Asia; Past and present. Melbourne: Cheshire, 1966, 334 pp.

1552   Tarling, Nicholas
       Sukarno and Indonesian unity; Leadership Indonesia 1945-1967. Auckland:
       Heinemann, 1977, 45 pp.

1553   Thayer, Philip W. (ed.)
       Nationalism and progress in free Asia. Baltimore: Johns Hopkins Press, 1956,
       394 pp.

1554   Ton That Thien
       *India and South East Asia, 1947-1960; A study of India's policy towards the South
       East Asian countries in the period 1947-1960.* Genève: Droz, 1963, 384 pp.

1555   Tsuchiya, Kenji
       'Yogyakarta in a time of transition', in: Kenji Tsuchiya (ed.), *States in Southeast
       Asia; From transition to modernity,* pp. 209-256. Kyoto: Center for Southeast
       Asian Studies, Kyoto University, 1984.

1556   Tune, George Albert
       South and Southeast Asia, the U.N., and colonialism. 1977, 381 pp. [PhD thesis
       University of Michigan, Ann Arbor.]

1557   Tziganov, V.A.
       History of Indonesia; Volume 2. Moscow: Moscow University Press, 1993,
       272 pp. [In Russian.]

1558   Van der Kroef, J.M.
       'The Arabs in Indonesia', *The Middle East Journal* 7 (1953):300-323. (kb)

1559   Van der Kroef, J.M.
       'The Eurasian minority in Indonesia', *American Sociological Review* 18 (1953):484-
       493. (ubl)

1560   Van der Kroef, J.M.
       Indonesian social evolution. Amsterdam: Van der Peet, 1958, 189 pp.

1561   Van der Kroef, J.M.
       The communist party of Indonesia; Its history, program and tactics. Vancouver:
       University of British Columbia, 1965, 347 pp.

1562   Van der Veur, P.W.
       'The Eurasians of Indonesia; Castaways of colonialism', *Pacific Affairs* 27-2 (June
       1954):124-137.

1563   Van der Veur, Paul Willem Johan
       Introduction to a socio-political study of the Eurasians of Indonesia. 1955, 8+595 pp.
       [PhD thesis Cornell University, Ithaca.]

1564   Van der Veur, P.W.
       'E.F.E. Douwes Dekker; Evangelist for Indonesian political nationalism', *Journal
       of Asian Studies* 17-4 (August 1958):551-566.

1565   Van der Veur, P.W.
       'Eurasian dilemma in Indonesia', *Journal of Asian Studies* 20-1 (1960):45-60.

1566 Van der Veur, P.W.
'De Indo-Europeaan; Probleem en uitdaging', in: H. Baudet and I.J. Brugmans (eds), *Balans van beleid; Terugblik op de laatste halve eeuw van Nederlandsch-Indië*, pp. 81-101. Assen: Van Gorcum, 1961. [Second printing 1984.]

1567 Vandenbosch, A. and M.B. Vandenbosch
Australia faces Southeast Asia; The emergence of a foreign policy. Lexington: University of Kentucky Press, 1967, 175 pp.

1568 Vaschinskii, L.
Relations between the socialist nations of Eastern Europe and the Republic of Indonesia. 1965, 388 pp. [PhD thesis Lomonosov State University, Moscow.] [In Russian.] [97]

1569 Vickers, Adrian
Bali; A paradise created. Ringwood: Penguin Books, 1989, 240 pp.

1570 Von der Mehden, Fred R.
South-East Asia 1930-1970; The legacy of colonialism and nationalism. London: Thames and Hudson, 1974, 144 pp.

1571 Von der Mehden, Fred R.
Zuidoost-Azië 1930-1970; De erfenis van het kolonialisme en het nationalisme. Leiden: Sijthoff, 1977, 111 pp.

1572 Vos, Luc De
De koude vrede; Koude oorlog en dekolonisatie 1945-1963. Tielt: Lannoo, 1988, 391 pp.

1573 Wainhouse, D.W.
International peace observation; A history and forecast. Baltimore: Johns Hopkins University, 1966, 663 pp. (ubl)

1574 Walker, Millidge P.
Indonesian election and party development 1945-1955. 1957, 118 pp. [MA thesis University of California, Berkeley.]

1575 Watt, Alan
The evolution of Australian foreign policy, 1938-1965. Cambridge: Cambridge University Press, 1967, 387 pp.

1576 Watt, D.C.
'American anti-colonialist policies and the end of the European colonial empires 1941-1962', in: A.N.J. den Hollander (ed.), *Contagious conflict; The impact of American dissent on European life*, pp. 93-125. Leiden: Brill, 1973. (ubl)

1577 Wawer, Wendelin
Muslime und Christen in der Republik Indonesia. Wiesbaden: Steiner, 1974, 326 pp.

1578 Weatherbee, Donald E.
Ideology in Indonesia; Sukarno's Indonesian revolution. New Haven: Yale University, Southeast Asia Studies, 1966, 10+135 pp.

1579 Webb, R.A.F.
Indonesian Christians and their political parties 1923-1966; The role of Partai Kristen Indonesia and Partai Katolik. Townsville: James Cook University of North Queensland, 1978, 8+114 pp.

1580 Webb, R.A.F.
Palms and the Cross; Socio-economic development in Nusatenggara, 1930-1975. Townsville: James Cook University of North Queensland, 1986, 14+284 pp.

1581 Weidemann, Diethelm
Die Entstehung unabhängiger Staaten in Süd- und Südostasien. Berlin: Deutscher Verlag der Wissenschaften, 1969, 416 pp.

1582 Williams, Lea E.
Southeast Asia; A history. New York: Oxford University Press, 1976, 13+299 pp.

1583 Williams, Maslyn
The story of Indonesia. London: Angus and Robertson, 1976, 64 pp.

1584 Willison, M.R.
Leaders of revolution; The social origins of the Republican cabinet members in Indonesia, 1945-55. Ithaca: Cornell University, 1958. [1525]

1585 Willmott, D.E.
The Chinese of Semarang; A changing minority community in Indonesia. Ithaca: Cornell University, 1960, 374 pp.

1586 Willmott, D.E.
The national status of the Chinese in Indonesia, 1900-1958. Ithaca: Cornell University, 1961, 139 pp.

1587 Wilson, Greta O. (ed.)
Regents, reformers and revolutionaries; Indonesian voices of colonial days; Selected historical readings 1899-1949. Honolulu: University Press of Hawaii, 1978, 20+201 pp.

1588 Woodman, Dorothy
The Republic of Indonesia. London: Cresset, 1955, 444 pp.

1589 Wyatt, Woodrow
Southwards from China; A survey of Southeast Asia since 1945. London: Hodder and Stoughton, 1952, 200 pp.

1590 Yefimov, D.
World War Two and Asia's struggle for independence. Delhi: Sterling Publishers, 1975, 124 pp. [Russian edition, Moscow: Novosty Press Agency, 1975.]

1591 Yoder, Lawrence M.
The Church of the Muria; A history of the Muria Christian Church of Indonesia - GKMI. 1981, 634 pp. [PhD thesis Fuller Theological Seminary, School of World Mission, Pasadena.]

1592 Yoder, L.M.
Tunas kecil; Sejarah kelahiran dan perkembangan Gereja Kristen Muria Indonesia. Semarang: Komisi Literatur Sinode GKMI, 1985, 410 pp.

1593 Zainu'ddin, Ailsa
      A short history of Indonesia. Melbourne: Cassell Australia, 1968, 299 pp.

1594 Zainu'ddin, Ailsa
      Indonesia. Hawthorn: Longman, 1975, 155 pp.

1595 Ziegler, Philip
      Mountbatten; The official biography. London: Collins, 1985, 786 pp. (ubl)

Japanese period
Indonesian authors

1596   Abas, Mursjid
        Perdjuangan pemuda 1942-1945. Jogjakarta, 1966, 29 pp. [59]

1597   Abdullah, H.M. Syafei
        Korban pembangunan jalan kereta api maut Muaro Sijunjung-Pekanbaru tahun 1943-1945. Pekanbaru: Yapsim, 1987, 146 pp.

1598   Abdulmuthalib, Muhammad
        Riwajat prang Pandrah dikala pendudukan Djepang 1945. Kutaradja: Maktabah Atjeh Raja, 1960, 39+51 pp. [In Acehnese.] (kitlv-m)

1599   Abdurachman
        Pandangan rakyat terhadap cita-cita prajurit PETA; Ditinjau dari segi pengamatan sejarah kontemporer. Jakarta: Yayasan PETA, 1984, 26 pp.

1600   Achmad, Ja'
        Kalimantan Barat dibawah pendudukan tentara Jepang. Pontianak: Dep. P dan K, 1981, 50 pp.

1601   Adiyati, Siti
        Seni lukis Indonesia masa Jepang. Paper Symposium on Modern Indonesian History, Jakarta, 1992, 9 pp.

1602   Adrianatakesuma, Moh. Idris
        Pemberontakan PETA di Blitar. Yogyakarta: Universitas Gadjah Mada, 1973, 84 pp.

1603   Ali, R. Moh.
        'Ketika Kudus menjadi kota yang tidak ber-tuan (1 Maret 1942-k.l. 15 Maret 1942)', *Vidya Yudha* no. 18 (1974):86-93.

1604   Alisjahbana, St. Takdir
        Kalah dan menang; Fajar menyingsing dibawah mega mendung; Patahnya pedang samurai. Jakarta: Dian Rakyat, 1978, 486 pp.

1605   Anhar, Ratnawati
        Pahlawan nasional Supriyadi. Jakarta: Kem. P dan K, 1977, 117 pp. [Third edition, 1985, 112 pp.]

1606   Anhar, Ny. Ratnawati
        Pahlawan nasional Supriyadi. Jakarta: Balai Pustaka, 1992, 100 pp.

1607 Anwar, Rosihan
Cultural activities under the Japanese occupation. Paper Symposium on Modern Indonesian History, Jakarta, 1992, 7 pp.

1608 Aruan, Musa
Sedjarah Indonesia dalam pendudukan Djepang. 1969, 101 pp. [MA thesis IKIP Medan.] [13]

1609 Atjil, Asmawi Anang
Indonesia menghadapi penjajahan Jepang. 1973, 172 pp. [MA thesis IKIP Malang.] [12]

1610 *Atoeran-atoeran tentang Seinendan.* Djakarta: Gunseikanbu, 2605 (1945), 70 pp.

1611 Auwjong P.K.
Perang Pasifik 1941-1945. Sixth edition. Djakarta: Kinta, 1962, 247 pp. (kitlv-m) [First edition 1958.]

1612 Bagin and Idris Mt. Hutapea
Topan menjelang fajar. Jakarta: Balai Pustaka, 1983, 175 pp.

1613 Bakri, Ahmad
Rangkaian peristiwa zaman Jepang. Jakarta: Pustaka Jaya, 1986, 122 pp.

1614 Bhuwana, Eka Putra
Djawa Sinbun Kai; Situasi persuratkabaran di Jawa pada masa pendudukan Jepang 1942-1945. Paper SSN-V, Semarang, 1990, 28 pp.

1615 *Boekoe pengoempoelan oendang-oendang.* Djakarta: Kokumin Tosyokyoku (Balai Poestaka), 2604 (1944), 422 pp.

1616 Boender, R. Soedirmo
Terhempas prahara ke Pasifik; Kenangan seorang prajurit bekas anggota The Rainbow Division, sebuah divisi yang terkenal selama Perang Pasifik. Jakarta: Sinar Harapan, 1982, 242 pp.

1617 *Buku kumpulan kenang-kenangan Heiho Indonesia 1942-1945.* Jakarta: Yayasan Kesejahteraan Persatuan Keluarga Besar Bekas Heiho Indonesia, 1980, 93 pp.

1618 Chaniago, Jr.
'Memperkenalkan "The Nishijima Collection"' , *Gema Angkatan 45* nr. 15 (March 1977):10-12.

1619 *Citra dan perjuangan perintis kemerdekaan; Seri pemberontakan PETA Blitar.* Jakarta: Direktorat Jenderal Bantuan Sosial Dep. Sosial R.I., 1978, 92 pp.

1620 Danoemihardjo, Sjarief Hidajat
Riwajat perdjuangan K.H. Zainal Mustofa; Pemimpin dan penggerak pemberontakan Singaparna, 25 September 1944. Ca. 1972. [736]

1621 Darmosugito, Pitoyo (ed.)
Menjelang Indonesia merdeka; Kumpulan tulisan tentang bentuk dan isi negara yang akan lahir. Jakarta: Gunung Agung, 1982, 293 pp.

1622 Dasuki, A.
Indonesia dalam Perang Pasifik. Bandung: Sanggabuwana, 1975, 44 pp.

1623 Delly, S.M.
      Suatu tinjauan sejarah mengenai perjuangan Sumatera dalam merealisasikan
      cita-cita pergerakan kemerdekaan Indonesia antara tahun 1942-1945 di
      Sumatera Barat. 1973. [MA thesis IKIP Padang.] [4872]

1624 *Detik-detik peristiwa perdjuangan Gorontalo merdeka, 23 Djanuari-16 Djuni 1942.*
      Makasar: Badan Penerbit Propinsi Sulawesi Tengah, 1957, 113 pp.

1625 *Di bawah pendudukan Jepang; Kenangan empat puluh dua orang yang mengala-
      minya.* Jakarta: Arsip Nasional Republik Indonesia, 1988, 142 pp.

1626 Dini, Nh.
      Padang ilalang di belakang rumah; Cerita kenangan. Jakarta: Pustaka Jaya, 1979,
      155 pp. [Second edition, Jakarta: Gramedia, 1987, 99 pp.; Third printing 1989;
      Fourth printing 1991.]

1627 Diredja, Suparna Sastra
      Romusa; Novel sejarah di jaman pendudukan Jepang di Indonesia, 1942-1945.
      Amsterdam: Khattulistiwa, 1987, 79 pp.

1628 Djajoesman, R.
      'Sedjarah perang Djepang melawan Hindia Belanda', *Madjalah Sedjarah Militer
      Angkatan Darat* nos 7-19 (1960-1965).

1629 Djajusman
      'Pertempuran di Djawa (Maret 1942)', *Vidya Yudha* no. 8 (1969):93-107.

1630 Djajusman
      Hancurnya angkatan perang Hindia Belanda. Bandung: Angkasa, 1978, 226 pp.

1631 Djamhari, Saleh As'ad
      Pendudukan Djepang di Malang. 1965. [MA thesis Universitas Indonesia,
      Djakarta.] [18]

1632 Djamhari, Saleh A.
      Pendudukan Djepang di Malang Sju (Djawa Timur 1942-1945). Paper SSN-II,
      Jogjakarta, 1970, 39 pp.

1633 Djamil, M. Joenoes
      Riwayat Barisan 'F' (Fujiwara Kikan) di Aceh. Banda Aceh: Pusat Latihan
      Penelitian Ilmu-Ilmu Sosial Aceh, 1975. [1461, 4854]

1634 Djanari
      Raden Soeprijadi; Hidup dan peranannya. 1974, 155 pp. [MA thesis IKIP
      Malang.] [12]

1635 Djojoadikusumo, N.C. Tuty Hartati
      Invasi tentara Djepang dalam Perang Dunia II, 1939-1942. 1970. [MA thesis
      Universitas Padjadjaran, Bandung.] [1]

1636 Djuir, Mohammad
      Giyugun; Lasykar rakyat di Sumatera Barat 1943-1945. 1988, 71+10 pp. [MA
      thesis Universitas Andalas, Padang.] [58]

1637   Gandasubrata, S.M.
An account of the Japanese occupation of Banjumas residency, March 1942 to August 1945. Ithaca: Cornell University, 1953, 21 pp.

1638   Gunawan, I Gde Putu
Usaha petani dalam mempertahankan hidup; Kisah pendudukan Jepang di Madiun. Paper SSN-III, Jakarta, 1981, 16 pp.

1639   Gunawan, I Gde Putu
Usaha petani dalam mempertahankan hidup; Kisah pendudukan Jepang di Madiun', in: *Seksi Sejarah Mutakhir (1); Seminar Sejarah Nasional III*, pp. 42-51. Jakarta: Dep. P dan K, Direktorat Sejarah dan Nilai Tradisional, Proyek Inventarisasi dan Dokumentasi Sejarah Nasional, 1982.

1640   Hanafiah, M.A.
Drama kedokteran terbesar. Jakarta: Yayasan Gedung-Gedung Bersejarah, 1976, 65 pp.

1641   Harahap, Parada
Nippon di masa perang! Kesan ringkas jang didapat selama toeroet dalam sekawan oetoesan Djawa melawat ke Nippon (2603). Semarang: Harahap, 2604 (1944), 131 pp.

1642   Hariyono
Kepeloporan pemuda dalam perjuangan pada masa pendudukan Jepang. Paper Musyawarah Kerja Nasional Sejarah, Bandung, 1990, 22 pp.

1643   Hasbi, Mochtar J. and Fauzi Hasbi
Perang Bayu. Medan: Panitya Seminar Perjuangan Aceh, 1976. [4854]

1644   Hassan, Chandra
Sejarah pertumbuhan dan perkembangan prajurit sukarela Pembela Tanah Air (PETA). Jakarta: Yayasan PETA, 1982, 17 pp.

1645   Hatta, Mohammad
The Putera reports; Problems in Indonesian-Japanese wartime cooperation. Ithaca: Cornell University, 1971, 114 pp.

1646   Herawati
Kebiadaban Djepang di Indonesia. Bandjarmasin: Semangat, 1946, 68 pp.

1647   Herkusumo, Arniati Prasedyawati
Chuo Sangi-In; Dewan Pertimbangan Pusat pada masa pendudukan Jepang. Jakarta: Rosda Jayaputra, 1982, 13+138 pp.

1648   Heroesoekarto
Soeprijadi; Pahlawan pemberontakan PETA Blitar. Kediri: Pustaka Rakjat, 1949, 32 pp. [49]

1649   Hidajat, Sjarief
Riwajat singkat perdjuangan K.H. Zainal Mustofa. Tasikmalaja: Soetraco, 1961, 67 pp. (kitlv-m)

1650   Hussain, Abdullah
Terjebak. Kuala Lumpur: Pustaka Antara, 1965, 380 pp.

1651   Hussain, Abdullah
       Fujiwara Kikan; Kolonne kelima melakukan penaklukan tanpa pertempuran
       fisik. Paper Symposium on Modern Indonesian History, Jakarta, 1992, 39 pp.

1652   Ibrahim, Muhammad
       'Gerakan protes masyarakat pedesaan di Aceh terhadap militarisme Jepang;
       Kasus Bayu dan Pandaan', in: *Seminar Sejarah Lokal; Dinamika masyarakat
       pedesaan*, pp. 77-89. Jakarta: Kem. P dan K, 1983.

1653   Imran, Amrin
       Blitar bergolak. Semarang: Mandira Jaya Abadi, 1984, 102 pp.

1654   Iskandar, N.St.
       Tjinta tanah air. Djakarta: Balai Poestaka, 2605 (1945), 148 pp. (ubl) [Third
       edition, 1953, 152 pp.; Fourth edition, 1963, 208 pp.]

1655   Jassin, H.B.
       Kesoesasteraan Indonesia dimasa Djepang. Djakarta: Balai Pustaka, 1948, 189 pp.
       [Second edition, 1954, 184 pp.; Third edition, 1969, 184 pp.; Fourth edition,
       1975, 184 pp.; Fifth edition, 1985, 182 pp.]

1656   Jogaswara, H.J.
       Situasi politik dan militer di kota Bandung pada masa pendudukan Jepang
       (1942-1945). Paper Musyawarah Kerja Nasional Sejarah, Bandung, 1990,
       14 pp.

1657   Kadir, Amir
       Latar belakang historis perlawanan rakyat Unra kabupaten Bone pada masa
       pemerintahan Jepang tahun 1943. 1978. [MA thesis IKIP Ujung Pandang.]
       [1711]

1658   'Kadisjarahad'
       'Pemberontakan PETA di Gumilir', *Gema Angkatan 45* no. 20 (August 1977):18-
       20, 41.

1659   Kartodirdjo, R. Oerip
       'De rechtspraak op Java en Madoera tijdens de Japansche bezetting, 1942-45',
       Indisch Tijdschrift van het Recht 160-1 (1947):8-21.

1660   Kelana, Pandir (ps. R.M. Slamet Danusudirdjo)
       Bara bola api. Jakarta: Gramedia, 1992, 149 pp.

1661   Koesdianawati, Nendah
       Hubungan tentara PETA Daidan Jakarta dengan tokoh pergerakan nasional
       dan pemuda menjelang Proklamasi kemerdekaan. 1987, 152 pp. [MA thesis
       Universitas Indonesia, Jakarta.] [Histori]

1662   Lapian, A.B.
       Pengalaman bersekolah di masa perang. Paper Symposium on Modern
       Indonesian History, Jakarta, 1992, 20 pp.

1663   Latief, A.
       Pers di Indonesia di zaman pendudukan Jepang. Surabaya: Karya Anda, 1980,
       132 pp.

1664 Latif, Nasaruddin
Apa sebab Djepang kalah? Dipandang dari sudut politik, sedjarah, agama. Djakarta: Tandjoeng, 1948, 86 pp.

1665 Legowo, S.D.
'Pemberontakan PETA di Gumilir', *Vidya Yudha* no. 10 (1970):85-90.

1666 Lienau, Sri Setyaningsih
Yogyakarta pada masa pendudukan Jepang, 1942-1945. 1976, 289 pp. [MA thesis Universitas Indonesia, Jakarta.] [19, 1986]

1667 Mangkupradja, R. Gatot
'The PETA and my relations with the Japanese; A correction of Sukarno's autobiography', *Indonesia* no. 5 (1968):105-134.

1668 Mansur, Ahmad
'Sejarah pendudukan dan politik Jepang di Indonesia', *Panji Masyarakat* 16-145 (15 February 1974):11-13; 16-146 (1 March 1974):28-30.

1669 Marahimin, Ismail
Dan perang pun usai. Jakarta: Pustaka Jaya, 1979, 244 pp.

1670 Marahimin, Ismail
And the war is over. Baton Rouge/London: Louisiana State University Press, 1986, 173 pp.

1671 Marboen, Moela
Seinendan, PETA, BKR. 1964. [MA thesis Universitas Indonesia, Djakarta.] [18]

1672 Marboen, Moela
Djaman Djepang pemuda Indonesia mendapat pendidikan latihan militer setjara luas. Paper SSN-II, Jogjakarta, 1970, 30 pp.

1673 Marlina, Iece
K.H.Z. Mustofa dalam perlawanan santri terhadap Jepang tahun 1944; Studi di pesantren Sukamanah, Singaparna, kabupaten Tasikmalaya. Paper SSN-V, Semarang, 1990, 30 pp.

1674 Marunduh, S.U.
Pendaratan Jepang di Minahasa. 1978, 94 pp. [MA thesis Universitas Sam Ratulangi, Manado.]

1675 Mawuntu, Grietje
Awal masa pendudukan Jepang di Bolaang Mongondow. 1979. [BA thesis Universitas Sam Ratulangi, Manado.] [4871]

1676 Melati, Sintha
'In the service of the underground; The struggle against the Japanese in Java', in: Anton Lucas (ed.), *Local opposition and underground resistance to the Japanese in Java 1942-1945*, pp. 121-262. Clayton: Monash University, 1986.

1677 Moejali
Sidang pengadilan mahkamah militer pemerintah Jepang dan keputusan hukuman. 1978. [1619]

1678	Momon
	Pemberontakan pesantren Sukamanah terhadap imperialisme Djepang di pulau
	Djawa. 1968, 97 pp. [MA thesis IKIP Bandung.] [10, 108]

1679	Moo, Ina
	*Sejarah 23 Januari 1942 di Gorontalo; Suatu coup d'état yang berhasil
	menggulingkan pemerintahan Belanda.* Jakarta: Yayasan 23 Januari 1942, 1977,
	136 pp.

1680	Muchtar, Ery
	Cirebon Syu pada masa pendudukan Jepang, 1942-1945. 1979. [MA thesis
	Universitas Indonesia, Jakarta.] [1986]

1681	Mudaryanti, H. Tri Wahyuning
	Priangan Shu pada masa pendudukan Jepang, 1942-1945. 1979, 204 pp. [MA
	thesis Universitas Indonesia, Jakarta.] [1986]

1682	Muis, Abdul
	Hantjurnja tentara Belanda di Indonesia. Surabaja: Grip, 1960. [26]

1683	Mutalib, Abdul
	'Pemberontakan rakjat Pontianak dimasa pendudukan Djepang', *Madjalah
	Sedjarah Militer Angkatan Darat* no. 8 (1961):25-34. [55]

1684	Nio Joe Lan
	*Dalem tawanan Djepang (Boekit-Doeri, Serang, Tjimahi); Penoetoeran pengidoepan
	interneeran pada djeman pendoedoekan Djepang.* Djakarta: Lotus, 1946, 158 pp.

1685	Notosusanto, Nugroho
	'Instansi jang melaksanakan pembentukan tentara PETA', *Madjalah Ilmu-Ilmu
	Sastra Indonesia* 2-8 (June 1964):285-290.

1686	Notosusanto, Nugroho
	Pemberontakan tentara PETA Blitar terhadap kekuasaan fasis Djepang. Djakarta:
	Mega Bookstore/Pusat Sedjarah ABRI, ca. 1965, 17 pp.

1687	Notosusanto, Nugroho
	Pemberontakan tentara PETA Blitar melawan Djepang (14 Pebruari 1945).
	Djakarta: Dep. Pertahanan-Keamanan, 1968, 68 pp.

1688	Notosusanto, Nugroho
	'The revolt of a PETA batallion in Blitar, February 14, 1945', *Asian Studies* 7-1
	(April 1969):111-123.

1689	Notosusanto, Nugroho
	'Kesatuan-kesatuan Djepang di Indonesia', *Intisari* 6-70 (May 1969):17-22.

1690	Notosusanto, Nugroho
	'Djepang kontra Belanda di Djawa Barat dalam Perang Dunia II', *Intisari* 7-78
	(January 1970):87-94.

1691	Notosusanto, Nugroho
	Latar belakang pembentukan tentara PETA. Paper SSN-II, Jogjakarta, 1970,
	12 pp.

1692 Notosusanto, Nugroho
'Versi Djepang mengenai pendudukan Djepang di Indonesia dan perumusan Proklamasi', *Intisari* 7-81 (April 1970). (kitlv-m)

1693 Notosusanto, Nugroho
The PETA-army in Indonesia 1943-1945. Djakarta: Department of Defence and Security, Centre for Armed Forces History, 1971, 23 pp.

1694 Notosusanto, Nugroho
'L'armée PETA en Indonésie (1943-1945)', *Revue de l'Histoire de la Deuxième Guerre Mondiale* 22-86 (April 1972):33-43.

1695 Notosusanto, Nugroho
The revolt against the Japanese of a PETA-batallion in Blitar, February 14, 1945. Jakarta: Department of Defence and Security, Centre for Armed Forces History, 1974, 30 pp.

1696 Notosusanto, Nugroho
The Japanese occupation and Indonesian independence. Jakarta: Department of Defence and Security, Centre for Armed Forces History, 1975, 39 pp.

1697 Notosusanto, Nugroho
'Jakarta dan tentara PETA', *Budaya Jaya* 10-109 (1977):373-379.

1698 Notosusanto, Nugroho
The PETA army during the Japanese occupation of Indonesia (Tentara PETA pada jaman pendudukan Jepang di Indonesia). 1977, 282 pp. [PhD thesis Universitas Indonesia, Jakarta.]

1699 Notosusanto, Nugroho
Tentara PETA pada jaman pendudukan Jepang di Indonesia. Jakarta: Gramedia, 1979, 11+194 pp.

1700 Notosusanto, Nugroho
'The PETA army in Indonesia 1943-1945', in: William H. Newell (ed.), *Japan in Asia 1942-1945*, pp. 32-45. Singapore: Singapore University Press, 1981.

1701 Nurhadi
Poetera (Poesat Tenaga Rakjat) Maret 1943-Maret 1944. 1968. [MA thesis Universitas Indonesia, Djakarta.] [18]

1702 *Oendang-oendang Balatentara Dai Nippon.* Soerabaja: Moelja, ca. 2604 (1944), 138 pp.

1703 Onghokham
Runtuhnja Hindia Belanda (Indonesia dari 1940-Maret 1942). 1968. [MA thesis Universitas Indonesia, Djakarta.] [18]

1704 Onghokham
Runtuhnya Hindia Belanda. Jakarta: Gramedia, 1987, 8+287 pp. [Second printing 1989.]

1705 *Orang Indonesia yang terkemuka di Jawa.* Fourth edition. Yogyakarta: Gadjah Mada University Press, 1986, 12+556 pp. [First edition 2604 (1944).]

1706 Pakpahan, G.
      1261 hari dibawah sinar Matahari Terbit, 6 Maret 2602-17 Agustus 2605. Dja-
      karta: n.n., 1948, 160 pp. [Second edition, Jakarta: Marintan Djaya, 1979,
      200 pp.]

1707 Pamoerahardjo (ed.)
      PETA Rengasdengklok. Jakarta: Yayasan Pembela Tanah Air, 1984. [4765]

1708 Pangemanan, Johannes J.
      Liku cinta Tarakan-Brisbane. Jakarta: Yayasan Pendidikan Gunung Temboan,
      1992, 166 pp.

1709 Parikesit
      Sekitar pembentukan dan perkembangan pasukan PETA di daerah Surakarta
      dan Jogjakarta. 1970. [MA thesis Universitas Gadjah Mada, Jogjakarta.]
      [Histori]

1710 Pattikayhatu, J.A.
      'Kerjasama pasukan Australis-KNIL dan rakyat Ambon menghadap
      penyerbuan tentara Jepang di Pulau Ambon pada Perang Dunia Kedua',
      Indonesian Studies 10 no. 1-2 (1993):18-31.

1711 Pawiloy, Sarita
      Perlawanan rakyat Sulawesi Selatan menentang kekuasaan Jepang. Paper
      Seminar Sejarah Perjuangan Rakyat Sulawesi Selatan Menentang Penjajahan
      Asing, Ujung Pandang, 1982, 16 pp.

1712 *Perang Asia Timoer Raya; Seloek-beloek toedjoean Perang Asia Timoer Raya dengan
      dasar tjita-tjita Indonesia merdeka*. Medan: Pertjetakan KSS, 2605 (1945), 32 pp.
      (kitlv-m)

1713 *Perdjalanan kearah Indonesia merdeka*. Djakarta: Dokuritsu Zyunbi Tyoosakai
      Zinukyoku, 2605 (1945), 145 pp.

1714 'PETA Bandung juga berontak?', *Gema Angkatan 45* no. 15 (March 1977):8-10.

1715 Piso Tjoekoer (ps. Khoe Wie Hin)
      Warisan Djepang. Batavia: Eng Hoat, ca. 1946, 59 pp.

1716 Polontalo, I.
      Sejarah peristiwa 23 Januari 1942. Gorontalo, 1978. [4871]

1717 *Pontianak-affaire; Lembaran hitam sedjarah di Kalimantan*. Jogjakarta: Ikatan
      Perdjuangan Kalimantan, ca. 1947, 14 pp. (kitlv-m)

1718 Pouw Kioe An
      198 hari dalem koengkoengan Kenpeitai. Malang: Perfectas, 1947, 183 pp. (kitlv-
      m)

1719 Prawiroatmodjo, Soehoed
      Perlawanan bersendjata terhadap fasisme Djepang. Djakarta: Merdeka Press, 1953,
      195 pp.

1720 Prijono
      Sedikit tentang sedjarah Asia Timoer Raja dan sedjarah tanah Djawa. Djakarta:
      Gunseikanbu Kokumin Tosyokyoku (Balai Poestaka), 2605 (1945), 40 pp.

1721 Pringgodigdo, A.G.
Tatanegara di Djawa pada waktu pendudukan Djepang; Dari bulan Maret sampai bulan Desember 1942. Jogjakarta: Universitas Gadjah Mada, 1952, 35 pp.

1722 Priyantono, Yuwono Dwi
Jaman Jepang di Jakarta. Paper SSN-V, Semarang, 1990, 25 pp.

1723 Rachmat-Ishaya, F.A.
Indonesian women's organizations during the Japanese occupation, 1942-1945. 1990, 93 pp. [MA thesis Universiteit van Amsterdam.]

1724 Rahardja, Sutia
Islam dan fasisme Djepang di Indonesia. 1971, 85 pp. [MA thesis IKIP Djakarta.] [11]

1725 Rasyidi, Khalid
Pengalaman perjuangan jaman Jepang sampai Proklamasi. Jakarta: Yayasan Idayu, 1979, 35 pp.

1726 Renbarinst
Pahlawan Noesantara. Bandjarmasin: Semangat, 1946, 60 pp.

1727 *Risalah sidang Badan Penyelidik Usaha-Usaha Persiapan Kemerdekaan Indonesia (BPUPKI), Panitya Persiapan Kemerdekaan Indonesia (PPKI), 29 Mei 1945-19 Agustus 1945.* Second edition. Jakarta: Sekretariat Negara RI, 1992, 378+98 pp. [First edition 1980.]

1728 Rivai, Mawardi
Kissah kepahlawanan Pang Suma. Djakarta: Pustaka Antara, ca. 1971, 67 pp.

1729 Rosady, M.
'Riwajat pemberontakan PETA-Blitar', *Madjalah Sedjarah Militer Angkatan Darat* no. 15 (1964):11-20.

1730 Rosidi (Rossidhy), Ajip
'Seorang Djepang', in: Ajip Rossidhy, *Ditengah keluarga,* pp. 85-94. Djakarta: Balai Pustaka, 1956. [Third printing, 1967, pp. 69-79.]

1731 Rosidi, Ajip
'A Japanese', *Indonesia* no. 6 (1968):82-87.

1732 Sagimun M.D.
Perlawanan rakyat Indonesia terhadap fasisme Jepang. Jakarta: Inti Idayu Press, 1985, 10+113 pp.

1733 Salim, Makmun
Ichtisar sedjarah Perang Dunia II. Djakarta: Dep. Pertahanan-Keamanan, 1971, 164 pp.

1734 Santosa, Rochmani
Djakarta Raya pada djaman Djepang. 1969. [MA thesis Universitas Indonesia, Djakarta.] [18]

1735 Santosa, Rochmani
Djakarta Raya pada djaman Djepang. Paper SSN-II, Jogjakarta, 1970, 46 pp.

1736   Saptoto
       Seni lukis dan wartawan dari tahun 1942-1945. Paper Seminar Sejarah Peranan
       Generasi Muda dalam Perjuangan Bangsa 1942-1950, Yogyakarta, 1989, 14 pp.

1737   Sastrosatomo, Soedarpo
       Situasi pergerakan pemuda pada akhir penjajahan Belanda hingga akhir
       pendudukan Jepang. Paper Seminar Lahirnya Suatu Bangsa, Jakarta, 1990,
       17+5 pp.

1738   Senen, Radjab
       Sejarah runtuhnya kekuatan kolonial Belanda di Indonesia. 1973, 180 pp. [MA
       thesis IKIP Semarang.] [15]

1739   Sihombing, Ismail
       Tindjauan tentang situasi politik di Indonesia pada waktu Perang Pasifik
       hingga Proklamasi kemerdekaan. 1972, 133 pp. [MA thesis IKIP Medan.] [13]

1740   Sihombing, O.D.P.
       Pemuda Indonesia menantang fasisme Djepang. Djakarta: Sinar Djaya, 1962,
       220 pp.

1741   Simanungkalit, Coster
       Suatu analisa tentang sebab berachirnja kolonialisme Belanda di Indonesia, 9
       Maret 1942. 1971, 116 pp. [MA thesis IKIP Medan.] [13]

1742   Sinar, Tengku Luckman
       'The East Coast of Sumatra under the Japanese heel', *Sumatra Research Bulletin*
       1-2 (May 1972):29-43.

1743   Sinar, Tengku Luckman
       Perobahan sosial pada masa pendudukan Jepang di Sumatera Timur. Paper
       Symposium on Modern Indonesian History, Jakarta, 1992, 16 pp.

1744   Siregar, Risnauli
       Pers Indonesia di masa pendudukan Jepang. 1978, 158 pp. [MA thesis
       Universitas Indonesia, Jakarta.] [19]

1745   Soebagijo I.N.
       Mr. Sudjono mendarat dengan pasukan Jepang di Banten 1942. Jakarta: Gunung
       Agung, 1983, 8+344 pp.

1746   Soebardjo
       'Mentjari djedjak tokoh pemberontakan PETA Blitar', *Vidya Yudha* no. 12
       (1971):50-56.

1747   Soedarno, Noerhadi
       *Poetera (Poesat Tenaga Rakjat); Wadah perjuangan Soekarno-Hatta beserta para
       perintis kemerdekaan lainnya dalam zaman Jepang.* Jakarta: Tintamas, 1982, 81
       pp.

1748   Soedjanadi
       'Pengalaman dalam pendidikan Seinendan', *Madjalah Sedjarah Militer Angkatan
       Darat* no. 21 (1964):29-32. [6127]

1749   Soeherna, A. Toto
       Masa imperialisme Djepang di pulau Djawa (1942-1945). 1968, 74 pp. [MA
       thesis IKIP Bandung.] [10, 108]

1750   Soeryana
       'Blitar; The changing of the guard', in: Anton Lucas (ed.), *Local opposition and*
       underground resistance to the Japanese in Java 1942-1945, pp. 263-321. Clayton:
       Monash University, 1986.

1751   Soetanto, Soetopo
       Sistem propaganda Jepang melalui penerbitan. Paper Symposium on Modern
       Indonesian History, Jakarta, 1992, 20 pp.

1752   Sompie, K.H.E.
       Sekelumit riwayat perjuangan kemerdekaan Indonesia 1942-1945 di karesidenan
       Manado. Manado, 1979. [4871]

1753   Srijati, C.
       Barisan pemuda di Djawa pada masa pendudukan Djepang (Djawa Seinen-
       dan). 1965, 27 pp. [MA thesis Universitas Gadjah Mada, Jogjakarta.]

1754   Sudrajat, Agrar
       Romusa; Novel di zaman pendudukan Jepang di Indonesia 1942-1945. N.p.: n.n.,
       1976, 518 pp.

1755   Suganda, Her
       'Pemberontakan Peta di Rengasdengklok', in: *Cahaya dari medan laga; Hasil*
       sayembara mengarang dalam rangka peringatan hari ulang tahun kemerdekaan RI
       yang ke 30, pp. 153-170. Jakarta: Dewan Harian Nasional Angkatan 45/Aries
       Lima, 1976.

1756   Suganda, Her
       'Pemberontakan PETA di Rengasdengklok', *Gema Angkatan 45* no. 31 (July-
       August 1978):31-35.

1757   *Suka duka pelajar Indonesia di Jepang sekitar Perang Pasifik 1942-1945.* Jakarta:
       Antarkarya, 1990, 535 pp.

1758   Sukarti
       Perlawanan bangsa Indonesia terhadap Jepang. 1973, 64 pp. [MA thesis IKIP
       Yogyakarta.] [17]

1759   Supartono
       Politik Japanifikasi dan pemuda Indonesia. 1968, 174 pp. [MA thesis IKIP
       Djakarta.] [11]

1760   Surjo, Radjiman
       Romusha (korban politik dan pemerasan fasisme Djepang) di Djawa. 1965,
       30 pp. [MA thesis Universitas Gadjah Mada, Jogjakarta.]

1761   Surjomihardjo, A.
       'Wawancara dengan Tadashi Maeda', *Lembaran Berita Sejarah Lisan* 2 (January
       1974):6-11.

1762 Surjomihardjo, Abdurrachman
Penulis-penulis Indonesia tentang zaman pendudukan Jepang; Sebuah tinjauan ulang. Paper Symposium on Modern Indonesian History, Jakarta, 1992, 9 pp.

1763 Suryanegara, A. Mansur
'Peranan ulama dalam tentara Pembela Tanah Air', *Mimbar Ulama* 2-18 (February-March 1978):49-56.

1764 Suwanto
Gerakan Aron di Pancur Batu; Suatu gerakan perlawanan terhadap Jepang. Paper Seminar Mahasiswa Sejarah se-Indonesia, Jakarta, 1986, 10 pp.

1765 Suwardy
'Kalau mati ingin dikuburkan di Indonesia; In memoriam Tadashi Maeda', *Gema Angkatan 45* no. 24 (December 1977):10-12, 15.

1766 Suwarno, P.J.
'Pedjuang-pedjuang serta gerakan Indonesia pada saat-saat terachir pendudukan Djepang', *Basis* 18-11 (August 1969):368-376.

1767 Suwarno, P.J.
Peranan Djepang pada pendidikan militer di Indonesia. 1971, 92 pp. [MA thesis IKIP Djakarta.] [11]

1768 Suwondo, Purbo S.
Beberapa catatan tentang sejarah tentara PETA dan kaitannya dengan perjuangan kemerdekaan Indonesia dari 1944-1950. Jakarta: Yayasan PETA, 1984, 23 pp.

1769 Talsya, T.A.
'Merebut kekuasaan sebelum Jepang mendarat di Aceh', *Gema Angkatan 45* no. 88/89 (1985):79-80, 103.

1770 Talsya, T.A.
'Pemberontakan melawan Jepang di Aceh', *Gema Angkatan 45* no. 86/87 (September-October 1985):117-121.

1771 Talsya, T.A.
'Sebelum pendaratan tentara Jepang kekuasaan sudah direbut rakyat di Aceh', *Gema Angkatan 45* no. 90/91 (1986):55-57, 63-64.

1772 Tampubolon, R.
Usaha militer Djepang merebut pulau Djawa 1941-1942. 1972, 69 pp. [MA thesis IKIP Bandung.] [10]

1773 Tedja
Rajoean Djepang. Boekit Tinggi: Penjiaran Ilmoe, 1946, 32 pp. (kitlv-m)

1774 Tjamboek Berdoeri (ps.)
Indonesia dalem api dan bara; Ditoelis sebagi peringetan oentoek anak-tjoetjoe saja. Malang: Drukkerij Perfectas, 1947, 222 pp.

1775 *Tokoh-tokoh Badan Penyelidik Usaha-Usaha Persiapan Kemerdekaan Indonesia.* Jakarta: Kem. P dan K, 1993, 162+184 pp. 2 vols.

1776 Wartabone, Nani
Sedjarah singkat perebutan kekuasaan terhadap pemerintah kolonial Belanda 23 Djanuari 1942. Gorontalo, 1968. [4871]

1777 Widijati, Endang
Tentera Pembela Tanah Air di Djawa. 1965, 18 pp. [BA thesis Universitas Gadjah Mada, Jogjakarta.]

1778 Widodo, Sutedjo Kuwat
Peranan pemuda pada masa pendudukan Jepang 1942-1945. Paper Musyawarah Kerja Nasional Sejarah X, Bandung 1990, 12 pp.

1779 Yanis, M.
Kapal terbang sembilan; Kisah pendudukan Jepang di Kalimantan Barat. Pontianak: Yayasan Perguruan Panca Bhakti, 1983, 228 pp.

1780 Zainu'ddin
'The Japanese occupation', in: *Indonesian nationalism and revolution; Six first-hand accounts,* pp. 12-17. Clayton: Monash University, 1969.

1781 Zorab, A.A.
De Japanse bezetting van Indonesië en haar volkenrechtelijke zijde. Leiden: Universitaire Pers Leiden, 1954, 173 pp. [PhD thesis Rijksuniversiteit Leiden.]

1782 Zuhdi, Susanto
Bogor Shu pada masa pendudukan Jepang, 1942-1945. 1979, 8+274 pp. [MA thesis Universitas Indonesia, Jakarta.]

1783 Zuhdi, Susanto
Bogor Shu pada masa pendudukan Jepang (1942-1945). Paper SSN-III, Jakarta, 1982, 15 pp.

Japanese period
Dutch authors

1784   *1940-1945; Indonesische strijd tegen de Duitse bezetters; Het verzet tegen de Japanners; Koloniaal fascisme; Het Indonesische nationalisme.* Amsterdam: Indonesië-Commissie CPN, 1985, 26 pp.

1785   Aalderen, G.R. van
Steunverlening aan Nederlanders gedurende de Japanse bezetting in Nederlands-Indië. 1971, 159 pp. [MA thesis Katholieke Universiteit Nijmegen.]

1786   Alberts, A.
'Verdeelde eenheid; De verwarring in het nationalistische kamp', in: *Bericht van de Tweede Wereldoorlog*, pp. 2653-2656. Amsterdam, 1971.

1787   Alt, M.A.
Ons kampleven gedurende de Japansche en republikeinsche bezetting. Soerabaja: Van Ingen, 1948, 40 pp. (kitlv-m)

1788   Beets, N.
De verre oorlog; Lot en levensloop van krijgsgevangenen onder de Japanner. Meppel: Boom, 1981, 476 pp.

1789   Berg, Irma van den
Van gele terreur tot zwarte moesson; De visie van Willem Brandt op de gebeurtenissen tijdens de Japanse bezetting en de Indonesische revolutie. 1987. [Various pagings.] [MA thesis Rijksuniversiteit Leiden.]

1790   Blom, N.S.
'De verhouding tusschen de gebiedsdelen van het Koninkrijk', in: A.A. van Rhijn (ed.), *Nieuw Nederland; Bijdragen van buiten bezet gebied in verband met den wederopbouw van ons land*, pp. 57-91. New York: Querido, ca. 1945. [Second printing, Amsterdam: Querido, 1946.]

1791   Boer, P.C.
De luchtstrijd rond Borneo; Operaties van de Militaire Luchtvaart KNIL in de periode december 1941 tot februari 1942. Houten: Van Holkema en Warendorf, 1987, 299 pp.

1792   Boer, P.C.; P.A.C. Benjamins and M.T.A. Schep
De luchtstrijd om Indië; Operaties van de Militaire Luchtvaart KNIL in de periode december 1941 tot februari 1942. Houten: Van Holkema en Warendorf, 1990, 9+348 pp.

1793 Boisot (ps. J.G. de Beus)
De wedergeboorte van het Koninkrijk. Fourth edition. Tilburg: Bergmans, 1945, 139 pp. [First edition 1943.] (ubl)

1794 Boissevain, Gon and Lennie van Empel
Vrouwenkamp op Java; Een dagboek. Amsterdam: De Boekerij, 1981, 284 pp. [Second edition, Amsterdam: De Bataafsche Leeuw, 1991, 359 pp.]

1795 Bosscher, Ph.M.
'Opmars in de Oost; De Geallieerde penetratie in de Indische archipel', in: *Bericht van de Tweede Wereldoorlog,* pp. 2634-2638. Amsterdam, 1971.

1796 Bosscher, Ph.M.
De Koninklijke Marine in de tweede wereldoorlog. Vols 2+3. Franeker: Wever/Van Wijnen, 1986, 1990, 675+490 pp.

1797 Bouwer, Jan
Het vermoorde land. Franeker: Van Wijnen, 1988, 405 pp.

1798 Broek, J.O.M.
Indonesia and the Netherlands. New York: Netherlands Information Bureau, 1943, 18 pp.

1799 Broek, J.O.M.
'Indonesia and the Netherlands', *Pacific Affairs* 16 (September 1943):329-338.

1800 Brugmans, I.J.; H.J. de Graaf; A.H. Joustra and A.G. Vromans (eds)
Nederlandsch-Indië onder Japanse bezetting; Gegevens en documenten over de jaren 1942-1945. Franeker: Wever, 1960, 12+664 pp. [Second edition, 1960, 11+661 pp.]

1801 Bruin, R. de
Sense and non-sense in the 3A movement. Paper 27th International Congress of Orientalists, Ann Arbor, 1967, 28 pp.

1802 Bruin, R. de
De Seinendan in Indonesië, 1942-1945. 1968, 98 pp. [MA thesis Universiteit van Amsterdam.]

1803 Bruin, R. de
'Indonesia tidak merdeka; De betekenis van de Koiso-verklaring', in: *Bericht van de Tweede Wereldoorlog,* pp. 2643-2646. Amsterdam, 1971.

1804 Bruin, R. de
'Peta maakt amok; Ontevredenheid en verzet in Indonesië', in: *Bericht van de Tweede Wereldoorlog,* pp. 2650-2652. Amsterdam, 1971.

1805 Bruin, R. de
'Vreemdeling in eigen land; De positie van de Indo-europeanen', in: *Bericht van de Tweede Wereldoorlog,* pp. 2639-2642. Amsterdam, 1971.

1806 Bruin, R. de
'Vrijheid op de valreep; Het voorspel tot de Indonesische onafhankelijkheid', in: *Bericht van de Tweede Wereldoorlog,* pp. 2657-2660. Amsterdam, 1971.

1807   Bruin, Rodney de
       Indonesië; De laatste etappe naar de vrijheid, 1942-1945. 1982, 224+11 pp. [PhD thesis Universiteit van Amsterdam.]

1808   Bruin, R. de
       Islam en nationalisme in door Japan bezet Indonesië, 1942-1945. 's-Gravenhage: Staatsuitgeverij, 1982, 104 pp.

1809   Bruin, Rodney de
       'De Japanse bezetting en de gevolgen ervan voor de verschillende bevolkings-groepen in Nederlands-Indië', in: *Syllabus Nederland en Nederlands-Indië*, pp. 14-52. Ridderkerk: n.n., 1987.

1810   Bruin, Th. de
       Gevolgen der internering van Nederlanders voor de economie van Nederlands-Indië tijdens de Japanse bezetting (maart 1942-augustus 1945). 1962, 36 pp. [MA thesis Nederlandse Economische Hogeschool, Rotterdam.]

1811   Bruynesteyn, W. (ed.)
       Catalogus van de postzegels, uitgegeven in Nederlands-Indië onder Japanse bezetting, 1942-1945. Hilversum: Dai Nippon, 1975, 173 pp.

1812   Bijkerk, J.C.
       Vaarwel, tot betere tijden! Documentaire over de ondergang van Nederlands-Indië. Franeker: Wever, 1974, 283 pp. [Second printing 1974.]

1813   Captain, Esther
       Herinneringen uit gescheiden werelden; Kampliteratuur van vrouwen en mannen uit Nederlands-Indië ten tijde van de Japanse bezetting. 1993, 142 pp. [MA thesis Universiteit Utrecht.]

1814   Chattel, C.J.H. du
       Storm over Java. Assen: Born, 1946, 144 pp.

1815   Dankers, J. and J. Verheul
       Bezet gebied dag in dag uit; Nederland en Nederlands-Indië in de tweede wereld-oorlog; Een chronologisch overzicht. Utrecht/Antwerpen: Het Spectrum, 1985, 190 pp.

1816   *A decade of Japanese underground activities in the Netherlands East Indies.* London: His Majesty's Stationary Office, 1942, 40 pp. (smg)

1817   Drijvers, J.
       Beschouwingen over de Indonesische problemen na een jaar Japansche bezetting. Bussum: Kroonder, 1946, 60 pp.

1818   'De economische toestand van Nederlandsch-Indië tijdens de Japansche bezetting, 1942-1945', *Statistische en Economische Onderzoekingen, Nieuwe Reeks* 2-4 (December 1947):118-127.

1819   *Eenige hoofdpunten van het regeeringsbeleid in Londen gedurende de oorlogsjaren 1940-1945.* 's-Gravenhage: Rijksuitgeverij, 1946, 251 pp.

1820   Elias, W.H.J.
       Indië onder Japanschen hiel. Deventer: Van Hoeve, 1946, 244 pp. [Third printing 1947.]

1821   Elias, W.H.J.
       De Japanse bezetting van Nederlands-Indië; Een ooggetuige-verslag. Amsterdam: Teleboek, 1988, 244 pp. [Reprint of 1820.]

1822   Engers, J.F.
       Indië in de branding; De geallieerde wereld over de toekomst van Nederlandsch Indië van Pearl Harbor tot Hollandia. New York: Querido, 1945, 136 pp.

1823   Fasseur, C.
       'Een wissel op de toekomst; De rede van Koningin Wilhelmina van 6/7 december 1942', in: *Between people and statistics; Essays on modern Indonesian history presented to P. Creutzberg,* pp. 267-281. The Hague: Nijhoff, 1979.

1824   Fasseur, C.
       'A cheque drawn on a failing bank; The address delivered by Queen Wilhelmina on 6th/7th December 1942', *Acta Historiae Neerlandicae* 15 (1982):102-116. (ubl)

1825   Gelder, Ed van
       De Japansche regeering; Haar papieren betaalmiddelen uitgegeven in Nederlandsch-Indië 1942-1945. Heerlen: n.n., 1986, 56 pp.

1826   Gerner, Angelique van
       Wat was cultuur, wat criminaliteit? De Kenpeitai op Java. Paper Universiteit Utrecht, 1990, 24 pp.

1827   Giebel, C.
       Morotai; De bevrijding van de Grote Oost en Borneo (april 1944-april 1946). Franeker: Wever, 1976, 253 pp.

1828   Go Gien Tjwan
       'Wat betekende de Japanse bezetting voor de Chinese bevolkingsgroep?', in: J. Zwaan a.o., *Djojobojo, oorlog en bezetting in Nederlands-Indië 1940-1946,* pp. 23-27. 1986.

1829   Graaf, H.J. de
       'De PETA-opstand te Blitar, 14 febr. 1945', *Moesson* 31-18 (1986-87):11, 14; 31-19 (1986-87):8-9.

1830   Groen, Petra and Elly Touwen-Bouwsma (eds)
       Nederlands-Indië 1942; Illusie en ontgoocheling. 's-Gravenhage: SDU Uitgeverij Koninginnegracht, 1992, 160 pp.

1831   Haas, Paula de
       Indo-Europeanen in Malang buiten de Japanse kampen (9 maart 1942-31 juli 1947). 1992, 65 pp. + appendices. [MA thesis Rijksuniversiteit Leiden.]

1832   Hamel, J.C.
       Soldatendominee. 's-Gravenhage: Van Hoeve, 1948, 248 pp. [Second edition, *Soldatendominee; Ervaringen van een legerpredikant in Japanse krijgsgevangenschap,* Franeker: Wever, 1975, 222 pp.; Third edition 1980.]

1833   Hart, G.H.C.
       Towards economic democracy in the Netherlands Indies. New York: Netherlands
       Information Bureau, 1942, 123 pp. [Second edition, Melbourne: Netherlands
       Indies Government Information Service, 1943, 109 pp.; Third printing 1945.]

1834   Hegener, M.M.
       'De guerrilla op Midden-Celebes in 1942', *Mededelingen Sectie Militaire Geschie-
       denis Landmachtstaf* 12 (1989):51-67.

1835   Hegener, M.M.
       *Guerrilla in Mori; Het verzet tegen de Japanners op Midden-Celebes in de tweede
       wereldoorlog.* Amsterdam: Contact, 1990, 272 pp.

1836   Heshusius, C.A.
       *Bevrijding? Vergeet het maar! Onze kwart miljoen landgenoten in bezet Nederlands-
       Indië gedurende de 2e Wereldoorlog in de Pacific.* Den Haag: Comité Nationale
       Viering Bevrijding, 1985, 8 pp.

1837   Immerzeel, B.
       *Moluks verzet WO II; De rol van Molukkers in het verzet in de Tweede Wereldoorlog/
       Perlawanan orang-orang Maluku dalam Perang Dunia II; Peranan orang-orang
       Maluku dalam perlawanan.* Utrecht: Moluks Historisch Museum, 1992, 128 pp.

1838   Immerzeel, B.R. and F. van Esch (eds)
       Verzet in Nederlands-Indië tegen de Japanse bezetting 1942-1945. Den Haag: SDU
       Uitgeverij Koninginnegracht, 1993, 242 pp.

1839   Jalhay, S.M.
       Jalhay's kleine oorlog. 's-Gravenhage: Thomas en Eras, 1981, 367 pp.

1840   Jansen, L.F.
       *In deze halve gevangenis; Dagboek van Mr Dr L.F. Jansen, Batavia/Djakarta 1942-
       1945.* Bezorgd en geannoteerd door G.J. Knaap. Franeker: Van Wijnen, 1988,
       54+447 pp.

1841   Jappe Alberts, W. and R. de Bruin
       'Rijst op rantsoen; De hongerjaren 1944-1945 in Nederlands-Indië', in: *Bericht
       van de Tweede Wereldoorlog*, pp. 2647-2649. Amsterdam, 1971.

1842   Jong, L. de
       Het Koninkrijk der Nederlanden in de tweede wereldoorlog; Nederlands-Indië. Vols.
       11a-11b-11c. Leiden: Nijhoff, 1984-86, 1199+1116+751 pp. [Popular edition,
       's-Gravenhage: Staatsuitgeverij, 1984-86, 1120+1041+697 pp.]

1843   Kersten, A.E.
       'The Dutch and the American anti-colonialist tide 1942-1945', in: R. Jeffreys-
       Jones (ed.), *Eagle against empire; American opposition to European imperialism,
       1941-1982*, pp. 91-116. Aix-en-Provence: Université de Provence, 1983.

1844   Kleffens, E.N. van
       'The democratic future of the Netherlands Indies', *Foreign Affairs* 20 (October
       1942):87-102. (ubl)

1845 Knaap, Saskia van der
Anak Belanda; Indische jeugdliteratuur over Japanse interneringskampen en de
bersiap. 1994, 186 pp. [MA thesis Rijksuniversiteit Leiden.]

1846 Koch, D.M.G.
'De Japanse bezetting van Indonesië', in: *Onderdrukking en verzet; Nederland in
oorlogstijd; Vol. 4*, pp. 535-587. Arnhem: Van Loghum Slaterus, Amsterdam:
Meulenhoff, 1953.

1847 Kock, P.P. de
De ongelijke strijd in de Vogelkop. Franeker: Wever, 1981, 173 pp.

1848 Kretz, J.Th.W.
In de klauwen van den Jap en den extremist. Dordrecht: Stolk, 1946, 62 pp.

1849 Kriek, David W.N.
Speciale missie nr. 43 in Bantam (Java). Amsterdam: n.n., 1985, 170 pp.

1850 Küpfer, C.C.
*Onze vliegers in Indië; De geschiedenis der Indische militaire luchtvaart van haar
aanvang tot de capitulatie van Bandoeng in 1942.* Haarlem: Boom-Ruygrok, 1947,
358 pp.

1851 Landheer, B.
The Netherlands East Indies comes of age. New York: Netherlands Information
Bureau, 1942, 16 pp.

1852 Liempt, Luc M.D. van
Gelukkig hebben wij het nooit beseft; De ontwikkeling in visie van H.J. van
Mook aangaande de staatkundige toekomst van Nederlands-Indië van 8 maart
1942 tot 2 oktober 1945. 1987, 76 pp. [MA thesis Katholieke Universiteit
Nijmegen.]

1853 Linde, J. de
Anonè... De Europese gemeenschap gedurende de Japanse bezetting. Rotterdam/Ant-
werpen: Donker, 1946, 93 pp.

1854 Luxinger, J.
*Drie Nederlanders bestrijden Japan; Een verhaal van ondergronds gewapend verzet
tegen de Japanners in Indonesië 1942-1943.* Leiden: Brill, 1949, 148 pp.

1855 Man, J.Th.A. de
Opdracht Sumatra; Het Korps Insulinde 1942-1946. Houten: De Haan, 1987,
176 pp.

1856 Manning, A.F.
'De katholieke missie in Nederlands-Indië en de Japanse bezetting; Een verken-
ning', *Jaarboek Katholiek Documentatie Centrum* 17 (1987):112-137. (ubl)

1857 Meel, P. van
*Tanda kehormatan KNIL; Verzet, guerrilla- en bevrijdingsstrijd geleverd door het
Koninklijk Nederlandsch-Indisch Leger, 8 maart 1942-15 augustus 1945.* Dordrecht:
Stabelan, ca. 1985, 45 pp.

1858 Mook, H.J. van
'The position of Europe in Asia', *Asiatic Review* 38 (July 1942):298-302.

1859 Mook, H.J. van
'Japan in Java', *Asiatic Review* 39 (January 1943):82-85.

1860 Mook, H.J. van
Nederlandsch-Indië onder Japansche bezetting; Zeven toespraken gehouden over Radio Oranje in den zomer van 1944; Met een naschrift over de beteekenis van Nederlandsch-Indië door Ch.O. van der Plas. London: The Netherland Publishing Company, 1944, 28 pp.

1861 Mook, H.J. van
The Netherlands Indies and Japan; Battle on paper, 1940-1941. New York: Norton, 1944, 138 pp.

1862 Mook, H.J. van
The Netherlands Indies and Japan; Their relations 1940-1941. London: Allen and Unwin, 1944, 114 pp.

1863 Mook, H.J. van
Nederlandsch-Indië en Japan; Hun betrekkingen in 1940-1941. London: The Netherland Publishing Company, 1945, 140 pp.

1864 Mook, H.J. van
Past and future in the Netherlands Indies. New York: Netherlands Information Bureau, 1945, 16 pp.

1865 Moscou-de Ruyter, M.
Vogelvrij; Het leven buiten de kampen op Java 1942-1945. Weesp: Fibula-Van Dishoeck, 1984, 224 pp.

1866 *Nederlands-Indië contra Japan; Stafwerk in opdracht van wijlen Z.E. Generaal S.H. Spoor, commandant van het leger in Indonesië.* 7 vols. Deel 1: *Voorspel; Invloed van de oorlog 1914-1918.* Door A.J.Th. Boester. 's-Gravenhage: Staatsuitgeverij, Bandoeng: Van Dorp, 1949, 318 pp.; Deel 2: *Nederlands-Indië na de overweldiging van Nederland tot het uitbreken van de oorlog met Japan.* Door A. Treffers. 's-Gravenhage: Staatsuitgeverij, Bandung: Van Dorp, 1950, 292 pp.; Deel 3: *Overzicht van de na het uitbreken van de oorlog met Japan in de Z.W. Pacific gevoerde strijd.* Door C. van den Hoogenband. 's-Gravenhage: Staatsuitgeverij, 1954, 196 pp.; Deel 4: *De verrichtingen van de militaire luchtvaart bij de strijd tegen de Japanners.* Bewerkt door L. Schotborgh. 's-Gravenhage: Staatsuitgeverij, 1956, 211 pp.; Deel 5: *De strijd op Borneo en op Celebes.* Bewerkt door C. van den Hoogenband en L. Schotborgh. 's-Gravenhage: Staatsuitgeverij, 1957, 130 pp.; Deel 6: *De strijd op Ambon, Timor en Sumatra.* Bewerkt door C. van den Hoogenband en L. Schotborgh. 's-Gravenhage: Staatsuitgeverij, 1959, 173 pp.; Deel 7: *De strijd op Java.* Bewerkt door C. van den Hoogenband en L. Schotborgh. 's-Gravenhage: Staatsuitgeverij, 1961, 178 pp.

1867 *Nederlands-Indië in de Tweede Wereldoorlog, 10 mei 1940-15 augustus 1945.* 's-Gravenhage: Stichting Herdenking 15 Augustus 1945, 1980, 71 pp.

1868 Neuman, H.J.
Impasse te Londen; Nederlands veiligheidsbeleid 1940/1945. Utrecht/Antwerpen: Veen, 1990, 302 pp.

1869 Nieuwenhuys, R.
Een beetje oorlog; Java 8 december 1941-15 november 1945. Amsterdam: Querido, 1979, 149 pp.

1870 Nieuwenhuyze, C.A.O. van
What the Japanese did to Islam in Java. Batavia: n.n., 1947, 38 pp. (kitlv-m)

1871 Nortier, J.J.
'De guerilla op Timor (maart 1942 tot februari 1943)', *Mededelingen Sectie Krijgsgeschiedenis* 1-1 (1978):24-74.

1872 Nortier, J.J.
'De herovering van Balikpapan in juli 1945; Veldtocht met een lange politieke voorgeschiedenis', *Ons Leger* 62-12 (1978):54-69. (ubl)

1873 Nortier, J.J.
'De guerilla in Midden-Celebes, april 1942 tot augustus 1942', *Mars et Historia* 15-5 (September-October 1981):127-140. (kb)

1874 Nortier, J.J.
Acties in de archipel; De intelligence-operaties van NEFIS-III in de Pacific-oorlog. Franeker: Wever, 1985, 334 pp.

1875 Nortier, J.J.
De Japanse aanval op Nederlands-Indië. Rotterdam: Donker, 1988, 215 pp.

1876 Nortier, J.J.
De Japanse aanval op Nederlands-Indië; Deel 2: Borneo. Rotterdam: Donker, 1992, 204 pp.

1877 Nortier, J.J.; P. Kuijt and P.M.H. Groen
De Japanse aanval op Java. Amsterdam: De Bataafsche Leeuw, 1994, 326 pp.

1878 *Ons aandeel in den strijd tegen Japan.* Melbourne: Nederlandsch Indische Regeerings Publiciteits Dienst, 1945, 27 pp.

1879 *Pertempoeran di Pacific.* Melbourne: Nederlandsch Indische Regeerings Publiciteits Dienst, 1945, 32 pp.

1880 Piekaar, A.J.
Atjèh en de oorlog met Japan. 's-Gravenhage/Bandung: Van Hoeve, 1949, 15+398 pp.

1881 Piekaar, A.J.
Aceh dan peperangan dengan Jepang. Banda Aceh: Pusat Dokumentasi dan Informasi Aceh, 1977, 1981, 56+255 pp. 2 vols.

1882 Plas, C.O. van der
Recent developments in the Netherlands East Indies. New York: n.n., 1942, 16 pp. (ubn)

1883 Pluvier, J.M.
'Beschouwingen over de toekomst van Indonesië in de ondergrondse pers 1940-1945', *Indonesië* 7 (1953-54):353-374.

1884 Poelgeest, L. van
Nederland en het Tribunaal van Tokio; Volkenrechtelijke polemiek en internationale politiek rond de berechting en gratiëring van de Japanse oorlogsmisdadigers. Arnhem: Gouda Quint, 1989, 169 pp.

1885 Poeze, Harry A.
'1940-1945; Isolement en solidariteit', in: Harry A. Poeze (ed.), *In het land van de overheerser; Indonesiërs in Nederland 1600-1950*, pp. 297-330. Dordrecht/Cinnaminson: Foris, 1986. [Second printing 1986.]

1886 Poeze, Harry A.
'De weg naar de hel; De aanleg van een spoorlijn op West-Java tijdens de Japanse bezetting', in: *Tweede Jaarboek van het Rijksinstituut voor Oorlogsdocumentatie*, pp. 9-47. Zutphen: Walburg Pers, 1990.

1887 Preger, W.
Dutch administration in the Netherlands Indies. Melbourne: Cheshire, 1944, 119 pp.

1888 Quispel, H.V.
Nederlandsch-Indië in den Tweeden Wereldoorlog. London: Netherland Publishing Company, 1945, 247 pp.

1889 Roemit, Ernst
Soeta Winata. Amsterdam: Luitingh, 1962, 232 pp.

1890 Scholte, J.A.
'Imperial allies? Relations between British and Dutch armed forces in Asia 1941-1946', in: M.R.D. Foot (ed.), *Holland at war against Hitler; Anglo-Dutch relations 1940-1945*, pp. 54-67. London: Cass, 1990. (kb)

1891 Schoorel, A.F. (ed.)
Mensen onder druk; Ervaringen van Nederlanders in Zuid-Oost Azië beleefd tijdens de oorlog met Japan, tijdens de Japanse bezetting en tijdens de jaren van confrontatie met de Indonesische nationalisten. Franeker: Wever, 1986, 101 pp.

1892 Sinnighe Damsté, J.S.
Advocaat, soldaat; Oorlogsherinneringen. Den Haag: n.n., 1986, 405 pp.

1893 Sluimers, L.
'Nieuwe orde op Java; De Japanse bezettingspolitiek en de Indonesische elites, 1942-1943', *Bijdragen tot de Taal-, Land- en Volkenkunde* 124 (1968):336-367.

1894 Sluimers, L.E.L.
'Enige theoretische beschouwingen over de Japanse bezettingsperiode op Java', in: *Buiten de grenzen; Sociologische opstellen aangeboden aan Prof. Dr. W.F. Wertheim, 25 jaar Amsterdams hoogleraar 1946-1971*, pp. 240-266. Meppel: Boom, 1971.

1895 Sluimers, L.E.L.
Samurai, Pemuda und Sakdalista; Die Japaner und der Radikalismus in Indonesien und den Philippinen, 1941-1945. Amsterdam: Universiteit van Amsterdam, Antropologisch-Sociologisch Centrum, 1972, 88 pp.

1896 Sluimers, László
A method in the madness? Aanzetten tot een vergelijkende politicologische studie van de Japanse periode in Zuidoost-Azië, 1942-1945. Amsterdam: Universiteit van Amsterdam, Antropologisch-Sociologisch Centrum, 1978, 280 pp.

1897 Sluimers, L.
'Japanese influences upon the genesis of the Indonesian Republic', in: *Modern relations between Japan and the Netherlands*, pp. 18-31. Leiden: The Netherlands Association for Japanese Studies, 1981. (ubl)

1898 Sluimers, L.
The rice situation in Java during the Japanese era, 1942-1945. Amsterdam: Universiteit van Amsterdam, Antropologisch-Sociologisch Centrum, 1983, 20 pp.

1899 Sterenborg, Edward and Joost van der Weiden (eds)
Oorlog en bezetting in Nederlands Indië. Overloon: Nationaal Oorlogs- en Verzetsmuseum, 1986, 133 pp.

1900 Teitler, G. (ed.)
De val van Nederlands-Indië. Dieren: De Bataafsche Leeuw, 1982, 128 pp.

1901 Teitler, G.
De weg terug naar Indië, 1942-1945; Strategieën, conflicten, frustraties. N.p.: n.n., n.y., 143 pp.

1902 *Ten years of Japanese burrowing in the Netherlands East Indies; Official report of the Netherlands East Indies Government on Japanese subversive activities during the last decade.* New York: Netherlands Information Bureau, 1941, 132 pp. [Second edition, 1944, 132 pp. (ubl)]

1903 Termorshuizen, Gerard
'Altijd weer aan denken; De Japanse tijd in Nederlandse bellettrie en ego-documenten', in: D.H. Schram and C. Geljon (eds), *Overal sporen; De verwerking van de tweede wereldoorlog in literatuur en kunst*, pp. 161-188. Amsterdam: VU Uitgeverij, 1990.

1904 *Tien jaar Japansch gewroet in Nederlandsch-Indië.* Batavia: Landsdrukkerij, 1942, 204 pp.

1905 Touwen-Bouwsma, Elly
Verzets- en guerilla-activiteiten in de buitengewesten van Nederlands-Indië tijdens de Japanse bezetting. N.p.: n.n., 1986, 45 pp.

1906 Touwen-Bouwsma, Elly
'De Indische collectie van het Rijksinstituut voor Oorlogsdocumentatie', in: Wim Willems (ed.), *Bronnen van kennis over Indische Nederlanders*; Bundel artikelen naar aanleiding van de 2e Studiedag Indische Nederlanders, pp. 219-233. Leiden: Centrum voor Onderzoek van Maatschappelijke Tegenstellingen, Faculteit der Sociale Wetenschappen der Rijksuniversiteit, 1991.

1907 Touwen-Bouwsma, Elly
'De Japanse bezettingspolitiek ten aanzien van de Nederlanders en Indo-Europeanen', in: P.J. Drooglever (ed.), *Indisch intermezzo; Geschiedenis van de Nederlanders in Indonesië*, pp. 61-79. Amsterdam: De Bataafsche Leeuw, 1991. [Second printing 1994.]

1908 *De Tweede Wereldoorlog September 1939-Augustus 1945; De strijd in en rond den Stillen Oceaan*. Melbourne: Nederlandsch Indische Regeerings Publiciteits Dienst, 1945, 36 pp.

1909 Vaillant, R.E.F.
'Van "banzai" naar "bersiap"; Indische Nederlanders in ontreddering, 1942-1946', in: J. Zwaan a.o., *Djojobojo, oorlog en bezetting in Nederlands-Indië, 1940-1946*, pp. 28-35. 1986.

1910 *Van vriend tot vijand; De betrekkingen tusschen Nederlandsch-Indië en Japan.* Amsterdam/Brussel: Elsevier, 1945, 8+382 pp.

1911 Veen, G.H. van der
De krijgsverrichtingen van het Koninklijk Nederlands-Indisch Leger in de Pacific-oorlog. 1977, 79 pp. [MA thesis Erasmus Universiteit, Rotterdam.] (kitlv-smg)

1912 Velde, J.J. van de
'Einde van een tijdperk', in: S.L. van der Wal (ed.), *Besturen overzee; Herinneringen van oud-ambtenaren bij het binnenlands bestuur in Nederlandsch-Indië*, pp. 287-303. Franeker: Wever, 1977.

1913 Velden, D. van
De Japanse interneringskampen voor burgers gedurende de Tweede Wereldoorlog. Groningen: Wolters, 1963, 628 pp. [Second printing, Franeker: Wever, 1977; Also PhD thesis Rijksuniversiteit Utrecht.]

1914 *Verslag van de werkzaamheden in het tijdvak 27 April 1943-27 April 1944.* Melbourne: Netherlands Indies Government Information Service, 1944, 67 pp. (ubl)

1915 Vromans, A.G.
De Indische collectie van het Rijksinstituut voor Oorlogsdocumentatie te Amsterdam. Amsterdam: Rijksinstituut voor Oorlogsdocumentatie, 1954, 35 pp.

1916 Vrijburg, G.S. (ed.)
Een ereschuld ingelost; 25 jaar na de capitulatie van Japan; Het einde van de tweede wereldoorlog. 's-Gravenhage: Comité 15 Augustus 1970, ca. 1972, 16+144 pp.

1917 Ward, O.G.
De militaire luchtvaart van het KNIL in de jaren 1942-1945. Weesp: Romen, 1985, 424 pp.

1918 Weerd, K. de
The Japanese occupation of the Netherlands East Indies. Tokyo: Netherlands Division of the International Prosecution Section, 1946, 129 pp.

1919 Wettelijke regelingen betreffende het staatsbestel van Nederlandsch-Indië, 1942-1944. Londen: n.n., 1945, 83 pp.

1920 Wilhelmina
De Koningin sprak; Proclamaties en radiotoespraken van H.M. Koningin Wilhelmina gedurende de oorlogsjaren 1940-45. Utrecht: Ons Vrije Nederland, 1945, 99 pp.

1921 Wilhelmina
The Netherlands Commonwealth and the future; Important statements of H.M. Queen Wilhelmina on post-war aims. New York: Netherlands Information Bureau, 1945, 59 pp.

1922 Wilhelmina
Rede 7 December 1942. Amsterdam: De Bezige Bij, 1945, 10 pp. (ubl)

1924 Wittert, René
Het vergeten squadron; Het verhaal van de Nederlandse vliegers die tegen Japan hun vergeten strijd vochten. Bussum: Van Holkema en Warendorf, 1976, 512 pp.

1923 Witteveen, Menno
Indië als doel op zich; De Nederlands-Indische regering in ballingschap, 1942-1945. 1981, 74 pp. [MA thesis Rijksuniversiteit Leiden.]

1925 Zonderwijk, P.
Koloniaal beleid in oorlogstijd; Nederlandse bestuurders, Amerikaanse anti-imperialisten en de toekomst van Nederlands-Indië, 1942-1945. 1982, 211 pp. [MA thesis Katholieke Universiteit Nijmegen.]

1926 Zwaan, Jacob
Nederlands-Indië 1940-1946. Vol. I, Gouvernementeel intermezzo 1940-1942. Den Haag: Omniboek, 1980, 269 pp.

1927 Zwaan, Jacob
Nederlands-Indië 1940-1946. Vol. II, Japans intermezzo 9 maart 1942-15 augustus 1945. Den Haag: Omniboek, 1981, 275 pp.

1928 Zwaan, J.
'Het Japanse bestuur in Nederlands-Indië 1942-1945', in: J. Zwaan a.o., *Djojobojo, oorlog en verzet in Nederlands-Indië 1942-1945*, pp. 1-14. 1986.

1929 Zwaan, J.
'Nederlands-Indië onder Japanse bezetting', in: *Oorlog en verzet in Nederlands-Indië 1941-1949 en de voorlichting aan de na-oorlogse generaties*, pp. 7-24. Amsterdam: De Bataafsche Leeuw, 1989.

1930 Zwaan, J.; C. van Dijk; Go Gien Tjwan and R.E.F. Vaillant
Djojobojo, oorlog en verzet in Nederlands-Indië, 1940-1946. N.p.: n.n., 1986, 61 pp.

1931 Zwitzer, H.L.
'Verdediging en val van Nederlands-Indië; Toetsing van een trauma', *Internationale Spectator* 36 (1982):276-283.

1932 Zwitzer, H.L.
'Het Koninklijk Nederlands-Indisch Leger in Australië, 1942-1945', *Mededelingen Sectie Militaire Geschiedenis Landmachtstaf* 8 (1985):67-90. (ubl)

1933 Zwitzer, H.L.
'De oorlog tegen Japan en enkele aspecten van de Japanse bezetting', in: P.J.
Drooglever (ed.), *Indisch intermezzo; De geschiedenis van de Nederlanders in
Indonesië*, pp. 47-60. Amsterdam: De Bataafsche Leeuw, 1991. [Second printing
1994.]

1934 Zyll de Jong, Ellen van
The Netherlands East Indies and Japan. New York: Netherlands Information
Bureau, 1942, 24 pp.

Japanese period
Other authors

1935 Abend, H.E.
Pacific Charter. London: John Lane/The Bodley Head, 1943, 183 pp.

1936 Abend, H.E.
Pacific Charter; Our destiny in Asia. Garden City: Doubleday/Doran, 1943, 302 pp. (vp)

1937 Anderson, Benedict R. O'G.
Some aspects of Indonesian politics under the Japanese occupation, 1944-1945. Ithaca: Cornell University, 1961, 126 pp.

1938 Aziz, M.A.
Japan's colonialism and Indonesia. The Hague: Nijhoff, 1955, 11+271 pp.

1939 Benda, H.J.
'Indonesian Islam under the Japanese occupation, 1942-45', *Pacific Affairs* 28 (1955):350-362.

1940 Benda, Harry
'The beginning of the Japanese occupation of Java', *Far Eastern Quarterly* 15-5 (August 1956):541-560. (ubl)

1941 Benda, Harry J.
The crescent and the rising sun; Indonesian Islam under the Japanese occupation, 1942-1945. The Hague: Van Hoeve, 1958, 15+320 pp. [Second printing, Dordrecht: Foris, 1983; Also PhD thesis Cornell University, Ithaca, 1955.]

1942 Benda, H.J.
Bulan sabit dan Matahari terbit; Islam di Indonesia pada masa pendudukan Jepang. Jakarta: Pustaka Jaya, 1980, 344 pp.

1943 Benda, H.J.; James Irikura and Koichi Kishi (eds)
Japanese military administration in Indonesia; Selected documents. New Haven: Yale University Press, 1965, 279 pp.

1944 Budianta, Melanie
Syahrir and the children of Banda Neira. Jakarta: Gramedia, 1986, 48 pp.

1945 Buisman, Helmut N.
The Eagle and the Lion; The diplomatic relations between the Netherlands government-in-exile and the United States concerning the Dutch Far-Eastern

colonial possessions. 1967, 165 pp. [MA thesis Georgetown University, Washington.]

1946   Chauvel, Richard
       The rising sun in the spice islands; A history of Ambon during the Japanese occupation. Clayton: Monash University, 1985, 38 pp.

1947   Chea Boon Kheng
       'The Japanese occupation of Malaya, 1941-45; Ibrahim Yaacob and the struggle for Indonesia Raya', *Indonesia* no. 28 (1979):84-120.

1948   Cribb, Robert
       The final fruits of war; Japanese interests and the decolonization of Indonesia. Paper JSAA Conference, Griffith University, Nathan (Queensland), 1987, 16 pp.

1949   Daniels, Gordon
       'Japan and Indonesia, 1940-46; Film evidence and propaganda', in: Ian Nish (ed.), *Indonesian experience*, pp. 53-72. London: London School of Economics, 1979.

1950   Demin, L.M.
       The Japanese occupation of Indonesia (1942-1945). Moscow: Izodatelstvo Vostocnoj Literatury, 1963, 235 pp. [In Russian.]

1951   Dubinsky, A.M.
       The Far East in the Second World War; An outline history of international relations and national liberation struggle in East and South East Asia. Moscow: Nauka, 1972, 458 pp. [In Russian.]

1952   Elsbree, Willard H.
       Japan's role in Southeast Asian nationalist movements, 1940 to 1945. Cambridge, Mass.: Harvard University, 1953, 7+182 pp.

1953   Emerson, R.
       The Netherlands Indies and the United States. Boston: World Peace Foundation, 1942, 92 pp.

1954   Franks, H. George
       Oerwoudstrijders onder onze driekleur. Amsterdam: Elsevier, 1946, 276 pp.

1955   Frederick, William H.
       'The Japanese occupation', in: Colin Wild and Peter Carey (eds), *Born in fire; The Indonesian struggle for independence; An anthology*, pp. 75-80. Athens:Ohio University Press, 1986.

1956   Frederick, William H.
       'Pendudukan Jepang', in: Colin Wild and Peter Carey (eds), *Gelora api revolusi*, pp. 83-90. Jakarta: Gramedia, 1986.

1957   Frederick, William H.
       A season of discontent; Understanding mass mobilization efforts and effects in wartime Java, 1942-1945. Paper Symposium on Modern Indonesian History, Jakarta, 1992, 19 pp.

1958   Friend, Theodore
The blue-eyed enemy; Japan against the West in Java and Luzon, 1942-1945.
Princeton, N.J.: Princeton University Press, 1988, 20+325 pp.

1959   Gellhorn, Martha
'The war in Java', in: Martha Gellhorn, *The face of war*, pp. 179-191. Third
revised edition. London: Virago Press, 1986. [First edition 1959; Second edition
1967.]

1960   Goto, Kenichi
'Life and death of "Abdul Rachman" (1906-1949); One aspect of Japanese-
Indonesian relationships', *Indonesia* no. 22 (1976):57-68.

1961   Goto, Kenichi
The life of a Japanese who struggled for Asian liberation. Tokyo: Jiji-Tsushinsha,
1977, 220 pp. [In Japanese.] [59]

1962   Goto, Kenichi
Japanese reactions in 1945 Indonesia. Paper Annual Meeting of the Association
of Asian Studies, Washington, 1984, 46 pp.

1963   Goto, Kenichi
'Kehidupan dan kematian "Abdul Rachman" (1906-1949); Satu aspek dari
hubungan Jepang-Indonesia', in: Akira Nagazumi (ed.), *Pemberontakan Indonesia
pada masa pendudukan Jepang*, pp. 114-131. Jakarta: Yayasan Obor Indonesia,
1988.

1964   Goto, Kenichi
A study of Indonesia under Japanese occupation. Tokyo: Ryukei Shosha, 1989,
357 pp. [In Japanese.] [50]

1965   Goto, Kenichi
' "Bright legacy" or "abortive flower"; Indonesian students in Japan during World
War 2', in: Grant K. Goodman (ed.), *Japanese cultural policies in Southeast Asia
during World War 2*, pp. 7-35. Basingstoke: Macmillan, 1991.

1966   Goto, Kenichi
Education in Indonesia under the Japanese occupation. Paper Symposium on
Modern Indonesian History, Jakarta, 1992, 25 pp.

1967   Habibuddin, S.M.
'Franklin D. Roosevelt's anti-colonial policy towards Asia; Its implications for
India, Indochina and Indonesia (1941-1945)', *Journal of Indian History* 53
(1975):497-522. (ubl)

1968   Haslach, Robert D.
Nishi no kaze, hare; Nederlandsch-Indische Inlichtingendienst contra agressor Japan.
Weesp: Van Kampen, 1985, 224 pp.

1969   Hayakawa, Kiyoshi
Youth in oblivion; A memoir of the struggle for Indonesian independence. Kyoiku
Shuppan Center, 1980, 411 pp. [In Japanese.] [51]

1970   Hayakawa, Kiyoshi
       The Batak and Karo guerillas; A war story of Indonesian independence. Tokyo:
       Bungeisha, 1987, 409 pp. [In Japanese.] [51]

1971   Imamura, Hitoshi
       The war is over. Tokyo: Jiyu-Ajia-Sha, 1960, 298 pp. [In Japanese.] [59]

1972   Iwatake, Teruhiko
       *Economic policy of the Japanese military administration in Southern areas; The record
       of Malaya, Sumatra and Java.* Tokyo, 1981. [In Japanese.] [1986]

1973   Jacobs, G.F.
       Prelude to the monsoon; Assignment in Sumatra. Philadelphia: University of
       Pennsylvania Press, 1982, 34+249 pp.

1974   Jacobs, G.F.
       Wedloop met de moesson; Verslag van een reddingsoperatie op Sumatra. Franeker:
       Wever, 1982, 251 pp.

1975   *Japanese military administration in Indonesia.* Tokyo: Waseda University/
       Washington: US Department of Commerce, 1963, 688 pp.

1976   Jones, F.C.
       Japan's New Order in East Asia; Its rise and fall 1937-45. Oxford: Oxford
       University Press, 1954, 12+498 pp.

1977   Jones, F.C.; Hugh Borton and B.R. Pearn
       The Far East 1942-1946. London: Oxford University Press, 1955, 14+589 pp.
       (ubl)

1978   Jones, Garth N.
       'Soekarno's early views upon the territorial boundaries of Indonesia', *Australian
       Outlook* 18 (1964):30-39.

1979   Kanahele, George Sanford
       The Japanese occupation of Indonesia; Prelude to independence. 1967, 330 pp. [PhD
       thesis Cornell University, Ithaca.]

1980   Kelly, Terence
       Battle for Palembang. London: Hale, 1985, 205 pp.

1981   Kennedy, Raymond
       'Dutch charter for the Indies', *Pacific Affairs* 16 (1943):216-223.

1982   Kirby, S. Woodburn
       The war against Japan; Vol. 5, The surrender of Japan. London: H.M. Stationary
       Office, 1969, 599 pp.

1983   Kurasawa-Shiraishi, Aiko
       Lahirnya tentara Pembela Tanah Air (PETA); Monografi. Jakarta: LEKNAS/LIPI,
       1977, 66 pp.

1984   Kurasawa, Aiko
       'Forced delivery of paddy and peasant uprisings in Indramayu, Indonesia', *The
       Developing Economies* 21-1 (March 1983):52-72. (uba)

1985 Kurasawa, Aiko
'Japanese occupation and leadership changes in Javanese villages', in: J. van Goor (ed.), *The Indonesian revolution*, pp. 57-78. Utrecht: Rijksuniversiteit Utrecht, 1986.

1986 Kurasawa, Aiko
'Propaganda media on Java under the Japanese, 1942-1945', *Indonesia* no. 44 (1987):59-116.

1987 Kurasawa, Aiko
Mobilization and control; A study of social change in rural Java, 1942-1945. 1988, 776 pp. [PhD thesis Cornell University, Ithaca.]

1988 Kurasawa-Shiraishi, Aiko
'Pendudukan Jepang dan perubahan sosial; Penyerahan padi secara paksa dan pemberontakan petani di Indramayu', in: Akira Nagazumi (ed.), *Pemberontakan Indonesia pada masa pendudukan Jepang*, pp. 83-113. Jakarta: Yayasan Obor Indonesia, 1988.

1989 Kurasawa, Aiko
'Marilah kita bersatu! Japanese propaganda in Java, 1942-1945', in: Silva, K.M. de; Sirima Kiribamune and C.R. de Silva (eds), *Asian panorama; Essays in Asian history, past and present*, pp. 486-497. New Delhi: Vikas, 1990.

1990 Kurasawa, Aiko
'Films as propaganda media on Java under the Japanese, 1942-45', in: Grant K. Goodman (ed.), *Japanese cultural policies in Southeast Asia during World War 2*, pp. 36-92. Basingstoke: Macmillan, 1991.

1991 Kurasawa-Inomata, Aiko
Social change in rural Java; A case of a village in Surakarta. Paper Symposium on Modern Indonesian History, Jakarta, 1992, 14 pp.

1992 Larson, George Donald
PETA; The early origins of the Indonesian army. 1970, 392 pp. [MA thesis University of Hawaii, Honolulu.]

1993 Lebra, Joyce C.
Japanese-trained armies in Southeast Asia; Independence and volunteer forces in World War II. Hong Kong/Singapore/Kuala Lumpur: Heinemann, 1977, 10+226 pp.

1994 Leclerc, Jacques
'Afterword; The masked hero', in: Anton Lucas (ed.), *Local opposition and underground resistance to the Japanese in Java 1942-1945*, pp. 323-368. Clayton: Monash University, 1986.

1995 Legge, John D.
'Sukarno the politician', in: C. Wild and P. Carey (eds), *Born in fire; The Indonesian struggle for independence; An anthology*, pp. 98-102. Athens: Ohio University Press, 1986.

1996 Legge, J.D.
Intellectuals and nationalism in Indonesia; A study of the following recruited by Sutan Sjahrir in occupation Jakarta. Ithaca: Cornell University, 1988, 9+159 pp.

1997 Linebarger, Genevieve C.
'The aftermath of Japanese colonialism in Southeast Asia', in: Robert Strausz-Hupé and Harry W. Hazard (eds), *The idea of colonialism*, pp. 187-229. New York: Praeger, 1958.

1998 Long, Gavin
The final campaigns; Australia in the war of 1939-1945. Canberra: Australian War Memorial, 1963, 667 pp.

1999 Long, Gavin
The Six Years War; A concise history of Australia in the 1939-1945 war. Canberra: Australian War Memorial, 1973, 518 pp. (kb)

2000 Lucas, Anton
'The communist anti-fascist movement in Java', in: A. Lucas (ed.), *Local opposition and underground resistance to the Japanese in Java 1942-1945*, pp. 1-119. Clayton: Monash University, 1986.

2001 Lucas, Anton (ed.)
Local opposition and underground resistance to the Japanese in Java 1942-1945. Clayton: Monash University, 1986, 18+368 pp.

2002 Lucas, Anton
Social change during the Japanese occupation; Some reflections on the background to the social revolution in Java. Paper Symposium on Modern Indonesian History, Jakarta, 1992, 22 pp.

2003 Machida, Keiji
Tatakau bunka butai. Tokyo, 1967, 438 pp. [In Japanese.] [71]

2004 McIntyre, Angus
'The "Greater Indonesia" idea of nationalism in Malaya and Indonesia', *Modern Asian Studies* 7-1 (January 1973):75-83.

2005 Makahanap, Nico R.
A hero in the jungle of Kalimantan (Borneo); A true story, as told by W.A. Makahanap. Jakarta: n.n., 1981, 85 pp.

2006 Male, Beverley M.
Australia and the Indonesian nationalist movement 1942-1945. 1965, 96 pp. [MA thesis Australian National University, Canberra.]

2007 Mitsuko, Nanke
Pemerintah daerah di Jawa pada masa pendudukan Jepang; Perubahan dalam kontinuitas. Paper Symposium on Modern Indonesian History, Jakarta, 1992, 13 pp.

2008 Miyamoto, Shizuo
An account of the end of the war in Java. Tokyo: Jawa Shusen Shori-ki Kanko-Kai, 1973, 548 pp. [In Japanese.] [59, 1962, 6272]

2009 Miyamoto, Shizuo
A supplement to the 'Disposal record of the war's end in Java' after reading the 'Independence and revolution of Indonesia' written by M.R. Subardjo. Tokyo, 1974, 68 pp. [25]

2010 Mizugaki, Hirosaburo
      Diary at the time of the Japanese surrender in Sumatra. Tokyo: M.C.C. Shokuhin,
      1984, 247 pp. [In Japanese.] [51]

2011 Mojeiko, I.V.
      Westerly wind – clear weather; Southeast Asia in the Second World War. Moscow:
      Nauka, 1984, 352 pp. [In Russian.]

2012 Mountbatten, Louis (the Earl of)
      *Report to the Combined Chiefs of Staff by the Supreme Allied Commander South East
      Asia 1943-1945.* London: H.M. Stationary Office, 1951, 280 pp. (ubl)

2013 Mrázek, R.
      Pemoeda, bushido and jeunesse dorée; Transfer of values. Paper Conference on
      Youth Movements, Transfer of Values and Ideology/Religion, Royal Institute of
      Linguistics and Anthropology, Leiden, 1990.

2014 Nagazumi, Akira (ed.)
      Pemberontakan Indonesia pada masa pendudukan Jepang. Jakarta: Yayasan Obor
      Indonesia, 1988, 18+140 pp.

2015 Nakamura, Mitsuo
      'General Imamura and the early period of Japanese occupation', *Indonesia* no. 10
      (1970):1-26.

2016 Nakamura, Mitsuo
      'Jenderal Imamura dan periode awal pendudukan Jepang', in: Akira Nagazumi
      (ed.), *Pemberontakan Indonesia pada masa pendudukan Jepang,* pp. 1-37. Jakarta:
      Yayasan Obor Indonesia, 1988.

2017 Nishijima, Shigetada
      'Kisah dari seorang Jepang', in: Colin Wild and Peter Carey (eds), *Gelora api
      revolusi,* pp. 90-95. Jakarta: Gramedia, 1986.

2018 Nishijima, Shigetada
      'The story of a Japanese; An interview with Shigetada Nishijima', in: C. Wild
      and P. Carey (eds), *Born in fire; The Indonesian struggle for independence; An
      anthology,* pp. 81-85. Athens: Ohio University Press, 1986.

2019 Paley, Tony
      The Sparrows. Worcester: The Self Publishing Association, 1992, 256 pp.

2020 Panikkar, K.M.
      The future of South-East Asia; An Indian view. New York: Macmillan, 1943, 126
      pp.

2021 Pelzer, K.J.
      'Postwar plans for Indonesia', *Far Eastern Survey* 12-1 (January 1943):2. (ubl)

2022 Poeppig, Fred
      *Javanisches Abenteuer; Das erwachen Asiens; Erlebtes und Erlittenes in Nieder-
      ländisch-Ost-Indien während der japanischen Besatzungszeit.* Basel: Zbinden, 1951,
      236 pp.

2023 Poppe, Janus
Political development in the Netherlands East Indies during and immediately after the Japanese occupation. 1948, 339 pp. [PhD thesis Georgetown University, Washington.]

2024 Pratt, G.
The Japanese occupation of Indonesia; The role of Putera in the development of Indonesian nationalism. Ca. 1970. [BA thesis Monash University, Clayton.] [58]

2025 Reid, Anthony
'The Japanese occupation and rival Indonesian elites; Northern Sumatra in 1942', *Journal of Asian Studies* 35-1 (November 1975):49-62.

2026 Reid, Anthony
'Indonesia; From briefcase to samurai sword', in: Alfred W. McCoy (ed.), *Southeast Asia under Japanese occupation*, pp. 16-32. New Haven: Yale University, 1980.

2027 Reid, A.J.S.
1942 in Indonesian history. Paper Symposium on Modern Indonesian History, Jakarta, 1992, 18 pp.

2028 Reid, Anthony and Oki Akira (eds)
The Japanese experience in Indonesia; Selected memoirs of 1942-1945. Athens: Ohio University Center for International Studies, Center for Southeast Asian Studies, 1986, 13+411 pp.

2029 Rhys, L.
Jungle Pimpernel; The story of a district officer in central Netherlands New Guinea. London: Hodder and Stoughton, 1947, 239 pp.

2030 Rhys, Lloyd
Aligamè, vriend der Papoea's; Het verhaal over de 'Jungle Pimpernel' Dr. J. Victor de Bruyn onder de Bergpapoea's in Nieuw-Guinea. Amsterdam: Enum, 1952, 240 pp.

2031 Rockwell, Maxine A.
A survey of Japanese propaganda to the Netherlands East Indies during World War II. 1949, 118 pp. [MA thesis University of California at Berkeley.]

2032 Russell, William B.
The Second 14th Batallion; A history of an Australian infantry batallion in the Second World War. Sydney: Angus and Robertson, 1948, 336 pp. (ubl)

2033 Saito, Shizuo
My recollections of military administration on the eve of the Indonesian independence. Tokyo: Nihon-Indonesia Kyokai, 1977, 330 pp. [In Japanese.] [51, 59, 1962]

2034 Sato, Shigeru
War and peasants; The Japanese military administration and its impact on the peasantry of Java, 1942-1945. 1990. [PhD thesis Griffith University, Nathan.] [6193]

2035 Sato, Shigeru
War, nationalism and peasants; Java under the Japanese occupation, 1942-1945.
Armonk, N.Y.: Sharpe, 1994, 20+280 pp.

2036 Shibata, Yaichiro
'Surabaya after the surrender', in: Anthony Reid and Oki Akira (eds), *The
Japanese experience in Indonesia; Selected memoirs of 1942-1945*, pp. 341-374.
Athens: Ohio University Center for International Studies, Center for Southeast
Asian Studies, 1986.

2037 Shimer, Barbara G. and Guy Hobbs (eds)
The Kenpeitai in Java and Sumatra. Ithaca: Cornell University, 1986, 80 pp.

2038 Shiraishi, Saya
'Pemerintahan militer Jepang di Aceh, 1942-1945', in: Akira Nagazumi (ed.),
Pemberontakan Indonesia pada masa pendudukan Jepang, pp. 38-82. Jakarta:
Yayasan Obor Indonesia, 1988.

2039 Silverstein, Josef (ed.)
South-East Asia in World War II; Four essays. New Haven: Yale University, 1966,
86 pp.

2040 *A study of the Japanese occupation in Indonesia.* Tokyo: Kinokuniya Shoten, 1959.
[In Japanese.] [1962]

2041 Sullivan, John A.L.
*The United States, the East Indies and World War II; American efforts to modify the
colonial status quo.* 1968, 275 pp. [PhD thesis University of Massachusetts,
Amherst.]

2042 Sumio, Fukami
'Japanese source materials on the Japanese military administration in Indonesia',
in: J. van Goor (ed.), *The Indonesian revolution*, pp. 33-55. Utrecht, 1986.

2043 Thorne, Chr.
'Engeland, Australië en Nederlands Oost-Indië 1941-1945', *Internationale
Spectator* 29 (1975):493-505.

2044 Thorne, Christopher G.
Allies of a kind; The United States, Britain, and the war against Japan, 1941-1945.
Oxford: Oxford University Press, 1978, 772 pp.

2045 Thorne, Christopher
The issue of war; States, societies, and the Far Eastern conflict of 1941-1945. London:
Hamish Hamilton, 1985, 364 pp.

2046 Tomon, Hiroshi
Merdeka; Indonesian independence movements under Japanese occupation. Tokyo?:
Otori Shuppan, 1975, 459 pp. [In Japanese.] [51, 59]

2047 Ueno, Fukuo
Desa Cimahi; Analysis of a village on Java during the Japanese occupation (1943).
Rotterdam: Erasmus Universiteit, 1988, 291 pp.

2048   Utsumi, Nobuo
       Reminiscences of the occupation of Java. Tokyo: Satsuki-shobo, 1969, 353 pp. [In
       Japanese.] [59]

2049   Van Langenberg, Michael
       'North Sumatra 1942-1945; The onset of a national revolution', in: Alfred W.
       McCoy (ed.), *Southeast Asia under Japanese occupation*, pp. 33-64. New Haven:
       Yale University, 1980.

2050   Webb, Paul
       'Too many to ignore; Flores under the Japanese occupation, 1942-1945',
       Philippine Quarterly of Culture and Society 14-1 (March 1986):54-70. (uba)

2051   Wigmore, Lionel
       The Japanese thrust. Canberra: Australian War Memorial, 1957, 16+715 pp.
       [Second printing 1968.]

2052   Wolthuis, Robert K.
       United States foreign policy towards the Netherlands Indies, 1937-1945. 1968,
       465 pp. [PhD thesis University of Maryland, Baltimore.]

2053   Yamamoto, Moichiro
       My experience of Indonesia; A memoir on the period of my service in the 16th Army.
       Tokyo: Nihon-Indonesia Kyokai, 1979, 226 pp. [In Japanese.] [51, 59, 1962]

2054   Yamazaki, Hajime
       To the North; To the South (a diary). 1977. [In Japanese.] [1962]

2055   Yanagawa, Motoshige
       Captain Yanagawa; An army intelligence officer. Tokyo: Sankei Shimbun-sya, 1967,
       262 pp. [In Japanese.] [59, 1962]

2056   Yano, Narufumi
       Japanese businessmen in Jakarta during the war. Tokyo: Kodansha, 1983, 253 pp.
       [In Japanese.] [59]

Publications from the years 1945-1950
Indonesian authors

2057 *1 tahoen Indonesia merdeka.* Jogjakarta: Kedaulatan Rakjat, 1946, 80 pp.

2058 *1 tahoen Indonesia merdeka, 17-8-1945/17-8-1946.* Boekittinggi: Pedjabat Penerangan Soematera Barat, 1946. [6229]

2059 *1 year East Indonesia, December 24th, 1946-1947.* Makassar: Kem. Penerangan NIT, 1947, 6 pp. (kitlv-m)

2060 *2 tahoen revolusi Indonesia.* Djokja: Madjallah-resmi Pesindo 'Revolusioner', 1947, 80 pp.

2061 *4 tahun sedjarah Indonesia dalam gambaran.* Djakarta: Madjallah Merdeka, 1949, 128 pp.

2062 *17 Agustus 1949; Pidato-pidato.* Djakarta: Kem. Penerangan, 1949. [Various pagings.] (kitlv-m)

2063 Abbas, Loetain
       Repoloesi merah. Medan: Tjerdas, 1946, 37 pp. (kitlv-m)

2064 Abbas, Loetain
       Sedjarah demokrasi. Boekittinggi: Tjerdas, 1946, 37 pp. (kitlv-m)

2065 Abdoelmadjid
       Mentjapai masjarakat sosialistis. Boekittinggi: Dewan Daerah Partai Sosialis Soematera Barat, 1946, 28 pp. (kitlv-m)

2066 Abdoelmadjid
       Sikap Partai Sosialis terhadap warga negara. Boekittinggi: Dewan Daerah Partai Sosialis Soematera Barat, 1946, 22 pp. (kitlv-m)

2067 Adinegoro, Djamaloedin
       Dasar kerakjatan dalam Repoeblik Indonesia. Pematang Siantar: Poestaka Timoer, ca. 1945, 39 pp. (kitlv-m)

2068 Adinegoro, Djamaloedin
       Apa sebab peroendingan Indonesia dan Nederland mesti gagal? Boekittinggi: Kedaulatan Rakjat, 1946, 84 pp. (kitlv-m)

2069 Adinegoro, Djamaloedin
       Perdjoeangan politik loear dan dalam negeri. Boekittinggi: Toko Al-Ma'arif, 1946, 65 pp. (kitlv-m)

2070 *Agitasi dan membangoen; Siaran kilat.* Djakarta: Kem. Penerangan, 1946, 3 pp.

2071   Agung, Ide Anak Agung Gde
       Pidato jang dioetjapkan pada Badan Perwakilan Sementara Indonesia Timoer pada tanggal 28 April 1947. Makassar: n.n., 1947, 29+36 pp.

2072   Agung, Ide Anak Agung Gde
       Mas'alah ketatanegaraan Indonesia. Makassar: Kem. Penerangan Negara Indonesia Timoer, 1948, 8 pp. (kitlv-m)

2073   Agung, Ide Anak Agung Gde
       Ke... Republik Negara Indonesia Serikat; Pidato radio. Makassar: Kementerian Penerangan Indonesia Timur, 1949, 34 pp. (kitlv-m)

2074   Ahmad, Zainal Abidin (ed.)
       Kemerdekaan Indonesia dan Islam. Boekittinggi: Poestaka Negara, 1946, 56 pp. (kitlv-m)

2075   Ahmad, Zainal Abidin
       Konstitoesi negara; Pendjelasan landjoet tentang oendang-oendang dasar negara Repoeblik Indonesia. Boekittinggi: Poestaka Islam, 1946, 54 pp. (kitlv-m)

2076   Ahmad, Zainal Abidin
       Perdjoeangan politik dan sendjata. Pematangsiantar: Poestaka Antara, 1946, 62 pp. (kitlv-m)

2077   Ahmad, Zainal Abidin
       Mentjari negara sempoerna. Jogjakarta, 1947, 48 pp. (kitlv-m)

2078   Ahmad, Zainal Abidin
       Politik dan hukum negara. Third edition. Medan: Saiful, 1951, 80 pp. (kitlv-m) [First edition ca. 1948.]

2079   Ahmad, Zainal Abidin
       Konsepsi tata negara Islam. Djakarta: Sinar Ilmu, 1949, 137 pp.

2080   Ahmad, Zainal Abidin
       Pendidikan bangsa. Tebingtinggi: Alhamba, 1949, 70 pp. [Second edition, Djakarta: Pustaka Antara, 1952, 127 pp. (kitlv-m)]

2081   Ahmad, Zainal Abidin
       Republik Islam demokrasi. Tebing Tinggi: Pustaka Madju, 1949, 95 pp. (ubl)

2082   Aidit, D.N.; Lagiono; Wikana and Mustapha
       Dokumentasi pemuda; Sekitar proklamasi Indonesia merdeka. Jogjakarta: SBPI, 1948, 67 pp.

2083   *Aims in the Pacific.* Jogjakarta: Ministry of Information of the Republic of Indonesia, 1948, 18 pp. (kitlv-m)

2084   Alamsjah, Oemar M.
       Indonesia merdeka koentji perdamaian doenia. Boekittinggi: Penjiaran Ilmoe, 1946, 71 pp. [6]

2085   *Album nasional.* Jogjakarta: Poesat Penerangan GRI Soenda Ketjil, 1947, 32 pp. [49]

2086   *Album nasional; Dokumentasi sedjarah kita.* Djakarta: Mutiara, 194-. [49]

2087 *Album petikan sedjarah; Kenang-kenangan konperensi Kementerian Penerangan Republik Indonesia 30 Nopember-5 Desember 1949.* Jogjakarta: Kem. Penerangan, 1949, 52 pp. (kitlv-m)

2088 I. *Algemene inleiding tot de begroting 1949 van de Staat Oost-Indonesië; II. Comptabiliteitswet.* Makasar: Ministerie van Financiën, 1948, 53 pp.

2089 Alhamid, M.
Sekeliling perdjoeangan warga negara Indonesia toeroenan Arab. Pasoeroean, ca. 1946, 48 pp. (kitlv-m)

2090 Ali, Rifai
Mari menang. Boekittinggi: Tjerdas, ca. 1946, 60 pp. [49]

2091 Alisjahbana, St. Takdir
'The Indonesian language; By-product of nationalism', *Pacific Affairs* 22 (December 1949):388-392.

2092 A.M.
Pedoman oemmat-Islam Indonesia di dalam pertempoeran. Jogjakarta: Al-Djihad, 1946, 32 pp. (kitlv-m)

2093 *Amanat 1 tahoen merdeka.* Padang Pandjang: Penaboer, 1946, 72 pp.

2094 Amin, Soetan Moehammad
Pengetahoean politik oentoek rakjat. Koetaradja: Libreria Indonesiana, 1946, 36 pp. [49]

2095 Aminoellah, H.
Perdjoeangan kita dalam th. 1946; Perdjoeangan kepastian. Boekit Tinggi: Kahamy, 1946, 23 pp. (kitlv-m)

2096 Amir
'De contra-revolutie van Hatta', *Politiek en Cultuur* 3 (1948):375-379. (ubl)

2097 Amir
'De nieuwe situatie in Indonesië', *Politiek en Cultuur* 3 (1948):312-315. (ubl)

2098 Amir
'Wat aan de wapenstilstand vooraf ging', *Politiek en Cultuur* 3 (1948):59-62. (ubl)

2099 Amir
'Indonesië in het Amerikaanse systeem van oorlogsbases', *Politiek en Cultuur* 4 (1949):228-232. (ubl)

2100 Amir
'Koloniale politiek in de praktijk; Drie jaren "onderhandelingen" en "zuiverings-acties" ', *Politiek en Cultuur* 4 (1949):33-39. (ubl)

2101 Amir
'De samenzwering tegen de Republiek Indonesia', *Politiek en Cultuur* 4 (1949):378-384. (ubl)

2102 Amir, Mohammad
Melawat ke Djawa. Medan: Soeloeh Merdeka, 1946, 39 pp.

2103 Anggaran dasar organisasi – Barisan Pemberontakan Rakjat Indonesia. Solo: BPRI, 945, 7 pp.

2104 Anggaran dasar dan program perdjoangan Masjoemi; Partai politik oemmat Islam Indonesia. Jogjakarta: Masjoemi, ca. 1946, 50 pp. (kitlv-m)

2105 Anggaran dasar dan rentjana perdjoeangan Masjoemi; Partai politik Islam Indonesia. Boekit Tinggi: Dewan Pemimpin Daerah Masjoemi Soematera Barat, 1946, 54 pp. (kitlv-m)

2106 Anggaran dasar roemah tangga, program perdjoeangan dan program oesaha-tjepat Masjoemi (partai politik Islam). Bogor: Masjoemi, 1946, 22 pp.

2107 Anggaran dasar Sabil Moeslimaat RI. Padang Pandjang: Barisan Sabil Moeslimaat, 1946, 7 pp.

2108 Anggaran dasar serta pendjelasan dan kesimpulan-kesimpulan Kongres Kebudajaan Nasional Indonesia, Magelang 20-25 Agustus 1949. Djakarta: Lembaga Kebudajaan Indonesia, 1949, 18 pp. (kitlv-m)

2109 Angkasapoetra (ps.)
Ke oedara; Kitab pengetahoean oemoem penerbangan jang pertama dalam bahasa Indonesia. Jogjakarta: Markas Tertinggi Angkatan Oedara Repoeblik Indonesia, 1947, 164 pp. (kitlv-m)

2110 Anshary, M. Isa
'Republik Indonesia Serikat', Aliran Islam 1-2 (December 1948):69-74. (kitlv-m)

2111 Anshary, M. Isa
'Blok anti-imperialis', Aliran Islam 2-4 (1949):194-201. (kitlv-m)

2112 Anshary, Muhammad Isa
Falsafah perdjuangan Islam. Bandung: Pasifik, 1949, 240 pp. (kitlv-m)

2113 Anshary, M. Isa
'Garis perdjuangan kita', Aliran Islam 1-3 (January 1949):122-125. (kitlv-m)

2114 Anwar
Sekeliling oeang kertas. Boekittinggi: Bank Nasional, 1946, 3 pp. [40]

2115 Apa jang dikehendaki Belanda dengan oesoel-oesoelnja? Toentoetan kita berdasarkan kehendak seloeroeh rakjat Indonesia. Djakarta: Merdeka, 1946, 32 pp.

2116 Apa partai kita? Djakarta: PSI-Bagian Penerangan, ca. 1946, 31 pp. (kitlv-m)

2117 Apakah negara itoe? Djakarta: Kem. Penerangan, 1946, 11 pp.

2118 Ardiwilaga, Memed
Masjarakat desa dalam arus revolusi. Djakarta: Pustaka Rakjat, 1949, 27 pp.

2119 Arga, Sakti
Tan Malaka ... datang! Boekit Tinggi: Tjerdas, 1945, 32 pp. (kitlv-m)

2120 Arieffin, Moh. Sjamsoel
Negara Madoera. Soerabaia: Fuhri, 1948, 103 pp.

2121	Arif, Abdullah
	Disekitar peristiwa penchianat Tjoembok. Koetaradja: Semangat Merdeka, 1946,
	26 pp.

2122	Asj'ari, K.H. Hasjim
	Ideologi politik Islam. Jogjakarta: Al-Djihad, 1946, 10 pp. (kitlv-m)

2123	Assaat (gelar Datuk Mudo)
	Hukum tata negara Republik Indonesia dalam masa peralihan. Jogjakarta: Badan
	Penerbit Nasional, 1948, 48 pp. (kitlv-m)

2124	*August 17, 1949; Emergency edition.* Djakarta, 1949, 15 pp. (kitlv-m)

2125	Badaruzzaman (ps. Muh. Dimyati)
	Gema revolusi. Tebing Tinggi: Pustaka Madju, ca. 1949, 72 pp. (kitlv-m)

2126	*Bagaimana? Apa artinja saja djadi warga negara Indonesia? Dan pendoedoek Indo-
	nesia? Oentoek golongan Indo Europa, Tionghoa, Arab dan lain-lain! Siaran kilat.*
	Djakarta: Kem. Penerangan, 1946, 8 pp.

2127	Bahsan, Oemar
	Tjatatan ringkas tentang PETA (Pembela Tahah Air) dan peristiwa Rengasdengklok.
	Bandung: Melati Bandung, 1955, 68 pp.

2128	Bakry, Semaoen
	Setahoen peristiwa Bandoeng. Tasikmalaja, 1946. [1348, 4208]

2129	Balfas, M.
	'Kind van de oorlog', *Oriëntatie* 11 (August 1948):5-15.

2130	Balfas, M.A.
	'A child of the revolution', *Indonesia* no. 17 (1974):43-50.

2131	*Bali; Membuat sedjarah baru, 1938-1948.* Makassar: Kem. Penerangan NIT, 1948,
	56 pp. (kitlv-m)

2132	Banda, Ismail
	Pengakoean Mesir dan politik Arab League. Jogjakarta: Himpoenan Mahasiswa
	Islam, ca. 1947, 31 pp. (kitlv-m)

2133	*Bangoen oentoek membangoen negara! Siaran kilat.* Djakarta: Kem. Penerangan,
	1946, 10 pp.

2134	Barioen, A.S.
	Negara dan ekonomi. Medan: Andalas, 1949, 80 pp.

2135	*Barisan Pemberontakan Rakjat Indonesia; Anggaran dasar organisasi.* Solo: Populair,
	ca. 1945, 7 pp. (kitlv-m)

2136	Basri, Chairoel
	Geo-politik Indonesia; Politik boemi Indonesia. Djakarta: Poestaka Djelita, ca.
	1946, 44 pp. (kitlv-m)

2137	Basri, Chairoel
	Menoedjoe masjarakat baroe (politik, ekonomi, sosial). Medan: Poestaka Nasional,
	ca. 1946, 54 pp. (kitlv-m)

2138 *Bendera dan lagu kebangsaan; Sang Mérah-Putih dan Indonesia Raya.* Makassar: Kem. Penerangan NIT, 1949, 12 pp. (kitlv-m)

2139 *Bertemu kembali.* Jogjakarta: Kem. Penerangan, 1950, 17 pp. (kitlv-m)

2140 *Boekoe peringatan Djawatan Kereta Api Repoeblik Indonesia.* Jogjakarta: Djawatan Kereta Api Repoeblik Indonesia, 1946, 51 pp.

2141 *Boekoe peringatan pelantikan resmi Dewan Koetai, Tenggarong 29 Mei 1947.* Samarinda: Typ Zenit Press, 1947, 37 pp.

2142 *Boekoe peringatan Penghela Rakjat 1 th. Rep. Indonesia.* Malang: Menara Pemoeda Sosialis Indonesia, 1946, 68 pp.

2143 *Boekoe peringatan satoe tahoen NRI di Soematera, 17-8-45 sampai 17-8-46.* Pematang Siantar: Pemerintah Poesat Soematera, 1946. [4854, 6229]

2144 Bongsoe, Datoek Madjo
      Berdjoeang. Boekit Tinggi: Poestaka Bahari, ca. 1945, 56 pp. (kitlv-m)

2145 Brodjonagoro, Sutedjo
      Tatanegara Republik Indonesia. Third edition. Jogjakarta: Kem. P dan K, 1950, 60 pp. [First edition 1947.] (kitlv-m)

2146 *Bubarkan NST.* Medan: Varekamp, 1950, 11 pp. (kitlv-m)

2147 *Bukti.* Medan: Djabatan Penerangan Negara Sumatera Timur, 1949, 47 pp.

2148 *Buku penjongsong Konperensi Ekonomi Antar Indonesia di Jogjakarta, 2-8 Desember 1949.* Semarang: Tanah Air, 1949, 41 pp.

2149 *Constitution of the Indonesian Republic.* Jogjakarta, ca. 1945, 13 pp. (kitlv-m)

2150 *Coup d'etat jang gagal; Soedarsono-Jamin c.s. dihadapan Mahkamah Agung Tentara Djocjakarta.* Sibolga: Gempar, 1948, 44 pp.

2151 *'Daerah Renville' RI.* Djakarta: Kem. Penerangan, 1949, 15 pp. (kitlv-m)

2152 *Daftar kependekan tentang nama-nama gaboengan, persatoean, partai d.l.l. menoeroet abdjad serta dengan artinja jang lengkap.* Djakarta: Kementerian Penerangan (vol. 1)/Indonesisch Translatiebureau Intran, 1947, 1948, 24+38 pp. 2 vols.

2153 Dahlan, A.
      RIS lahir... Medan: Saiful, 1950, 60 pp. (kitlv-m)

2154 Dahler, P.F.
      De Indo in de huidige maatschappij in Indonesia; Siaran kilat. Djakarta: Kem. Penerangan 1946, 16 pp.

2155 Damai, Boroe
      Van goddelijk maaksel. Medan: Phoenix Publishing House, 1947, 94 pp.

2156 Damhoeri, A.
      Sendjata pemoeda; Rangkaian moetiara kemerdekaan. Boekittinggi: Sukses, ca. 1946, 32 pp. (kitlv-m)

2157 *DAMRI dengan pembangunan.* Jogjakarta: Kem. Perhubungan, 1948, 16 pp.

2158 *Dari Digul ke Indonesia merdeka; Uraian ex-Digoelisten.* Bukit Tinggi: Dasmar, 1949, 25 pp. [49]

2159 Darmobroto, Ki
Revolutie pendidikan. Solo: Taman Siswa, ca. 1946, 38 pp. (kitlv-m)

2160 Daroesman, Maroeto
'Aspecten van de Indonesische onafhankelijkheidsstrijd', *Politiek en Cultuur* 2 (1947):101-104. (ubl)

2161 Derita, S.P. (ps.)
Lima minggu sebelum Madiun affair. Medan: Toko Buku Sarkawi, 1949, 48 pp. (kitlv-m)

2162 Dipokusumo
Kearah kemakmoeran dan keadilan sosial di lapangan ekonomi. Jogjakarta, 1945, 12 pp. (kitlv-m)

2163 Diponolo
Bentoek dan isi negara Indonesia. Jogjakarta: Kem. Pertahanan, 1947, 40 pp. (kitlv-m)

2164 *Disekitar oesoel-oesoel pemerintah kita; Siaran kilat.* Jogjakarta: Kem. Penerangan, 1946, 10 pp. (kitlv-m)

2165 *Disekitar pemberontakan Madioen (selajang pandang; Dikarang oentoek teman-teman didaerah pendoedoekan Belanda).* Labroek (Lumadjang), 1948, 18 pp.

2166 Djaja, Asmara
Wanita dimedan pertempuran. Padang Pandjang: Pustaka Merdeka, ca. 1948, 61 pp. (kitlv-m)

2167 Djaja, Tamar
Poesaka Indonesia; Riwajat hidoep orang-orang besar tanah air. Third edition. Djakarta: Penjiaran Ilmoe, 1946, 68 pp. [First edition 1940; Second printing 1941; Fourth edition, Djakarta: Kem. P.P. dan K.; Fifth edition, Bandung: Kolff; Sixth edition, *Pusaka Indonesia; Riwajat hidup orang-orang besar tanah air*, Djakarta: Bulan Bintang, 1965, 830 pp. 2 vols.] (kitlv-m)

2168 Djaja, Tamar
Berontak!!! Menentoekan nasib. Medan: Poestaka Nasional, 1946, 34 pp.

2169 Djaja, Tamar
Panti pengetahuan politik. Second edition. Djakarta: Penjiaran Ilmu, 1950, 1951, 56+41 pp. 2 vols. [First edition 1946-47.]

2170 Djaja, Tamar
Pengertian politik; Tata negara. Boekit Tinggi: Penjiaran Ilmoe, 1946, 36 pp. (kitlv-m)

2171 Djaja, Tamar (gelar St. Rais Alamsjah)
Sedjarah pergerakan politik Indonesia. Boekit Tinggi: Penjiaran Ilmoe, 1946, 74 pp. (kitlv-m)

2172 Djaja, Tamar
Trio komoenis Indonesia; Tan Malaka, Alimin, Semaoen, berikoet Stalin dan Lenin.
Second edition. Boekit Tinggi: Penjiaran Ilmoe, 1946, 53 pp. (kitlv-m)

2173 Djaja, Tamar
Dr. Soekiman Wirjosandjojo; Ketoea oemoem 'Masjoemi'. Boekittinggi: Penjiaran
Ilmoe, 1947, 12 pp.

2174 *Djalan baru untuk Republik Indonesia (Koreksi besar Musso).* Fifth printing,
Djakarta: Bintang Merah, 1951, 30 pp. [First printing 1948.]

2175 Djam'ani
Indonesia Djaja; Ringkasan sedjarah dan kemerdekaan Indonesia. Palembang:
Boedjang Nanang, 1947, 56 pp. [49]

2176 *Djangan menimboen barang! Pelihara oeang Repoeblik! Pelihara masjarakat kita!*
Siaran kilat. Jakarta: Kem. Penerangan, 1946, 4 pp. (kitlv-m)

2177 *Djawa-Tengah didalam setahoen Repoeblik.* Soerakarta: n.n., 1946, 52 pp.

2178 Djawoto
Pers. Jogjakarta: Tjerdas, 1948. (kitlv-m)

2179 Djojodihardjo, Sumarto
Indonesia bangkit. Djakarta: Penerbitan Penerangan Federal, 1949. [unpaged]
(kitlv-m)

2180 Djojohadikoesoemo, Soemitro
Arti oeang didalam soesoenan negara; Sekitar pengeloearan oeang Repoeblik Indonesia.
Siantar: Djabatan Penerangan NRI Soematera Timoer, 1946, 19 pp. (kitlv-m)

2181 Djojohadikoesoemo, Soemitro
Deflasi. Djakarta: Pertjetakan Merdeka, 1946, 7 pp. [49]

2182 Djojohadikoesoemo, Soemitro
Beberapa soal keoeangan. Djakarta: Poestaka Rakjat, 1947, 47 pp. (kitlv-m)

2183 Djojohadikoesoemo, Soemitro
Soal bank di Indonesia. Second edition. Djakarta: Poestaka Rakjat, 1947, 39 pp.
(kitlv-m)

2184 Djojohadikoesoemo, Soemitro
Economic aspects of the Indonesian problem. New York: Republic of Indonesia
Office, 1949, 18 pp. [6194]

2185 Djojohadikoesoemo, Soemitro
'Economic aspects of the Indonesian struggle', *United Asia* 1-5 (1949):428-431.

2186 Djokosoewarno and R. Rooslan Wongsokoesoemo
Verslag pandangan mata upatjara memperingati hari wafatnja almarhum Dr.
Soetomo (bapak pergerakan kebangsaan Indonesia), 30 Mei. Surabaja: Kantjil, 1949,
16 pp.

2187 *Do know more about Indonesia!* Jogjakarta: Kem. Penerangan, ca. 1947, 43 pp.
[49, 6297]

2188 Doeve, W.Chr.A.
Open brief aan het Indo-Comité 'Vrij Indonesië'. Djakarta: Kem. Penerangan, 1946, 4 pp.

2189 *Dutch imperialism exposed; The green hell of Tanah Merah*. Melbourne: Indonesian Independence Committee, 1946, 8 pp.

2190 *Dutch puppet states in Indonesia; East Indonesia, Kartalegawa, West Borneo*. Delhi: Indonesian Information Service, 1947, 21 pp.

2191 *Economy in Indonesia*. Jogjakarta: Kem. Penerangan, ca. 1947, 34 pp. [49, 6297]

2192 Effendi, Roestam
Recht voor Indonesië; Een beroep op democratisch Nederland. Amsterdam: Agentschap Amstel, ca. 1946, 23 pp.

2193 Effendi, Roestam
Demokrasi dan demokrasi. Third printing, Surabaja: Perintis, 1949, 95 pp. [First and second printing 1949.]

2194 Effendi, Rustam
Revolusi nasional. Djakarta: Patriot, 1949, 121 pp. (kitlv-m)

2195 Effendi, Roestam
Perspektip dari finansiel-ekonomi kita. Djakarta: Gapura, 1950, 24 pp.

2196 Effendi, Roestam
Pidato-pidato tentang so'al-so'al 'Negara Demokrasi' dan 'Diktatur Proletariat'. Djakarta: Patriot, 1950, 47 pp.

2197 Effendi, Roestam
Sedikit pendjelasan tentang so'al-so'al Trotskisme. Djakarta: Patriot, 1950, 53 pp.

2198 Effendi, Roestam
So'al-so'al disekitar krisis-kapitalis. Djakarta: Patriot, 1950, 46 pp.

2199 Effendi, Roestam
So'al-so'al mengenai sistem kapitalis. Djakarta: Patriot, 1950, 79 pp.

2200 Effendi, Roestam
Strategie dan taktiek. Djakarta: Patriot, 1950, 87 pp.

2201 *Facts about Indonesia*. Indonesian Information Service in Australia, 1948. [6199]

2202 *Facts about the Republic of Indonesia*. New York: Republic of Indonesia Office, 1948, 15 pp. [6297]

2203 *Fragmenta politica*. Kutaradja: Pedjabat Penerangan Atjeh, 1948, 200 pp. (kitlv-m)

2204 *The freedom of Indonesia*. Jogjakarta: Kem. Penerangan, 1947, 17 pp. [49, 6297]

2205 Gani, A.K.
'Kekoeatan jang menentoekan nasib', in: *Amanat 1 tahoen merdeka*, pp. 36-49. Padang Pandjang: Penaboer, 1946.

2206 Gani, A.K. and Zahari
Ideologi-ideologi politik di Indonesia. Medan: Waktu, ca. 1948, 30 pp.

2207   *Gara-gara.* Jogjakarta: Badan Penerbit Nasional, 1946, 72 pp.

2208   *Gerilja; Djalan mentjapai kemerdekaan.* Malang: BPKKP, 1946, 40 pp. (kitlv-m)

2209   Ghazali, Chaidir
'Perpetjahan; Bahaja perdjuangan nasional', *Aliran Islam* 2-6/7 (1949):309-314.

2210   Gouw Sui Tjiang
Problemen rondom de pranakan-Chinezen als minderheden in een onafhankelijk Indonesië. Djakarta: Federatie van Chinese Studiekringen, 1948, 33 pp.

2211   *Grondwet van de Staat Oost-Indonesië.* Makassar: n.n., 1949, 33 pp.

2212   Habromarkoto
Revoloesi boeroeh dan tani I. Jogjakarta: Barisan Boeroeh Indonesia, 1945, 34 pp. [49]

2213   Hadharyah M.
Perdjoeangan Panglima Batoer Banteng Kalimantan. Kediri: Poestaka Rakjat, 1947, 40 pp. [49]

2214   Hadi, Asmara
Tiang negara jang lima. Fourth edition. Jogjakarta: Kem. Pertahanan, 1946, 31 pp. (kitlv-m)

2215   Hadinoto, Sujono
Riwajat dan dasar-dasar perdjoangan partai; Pidato. Jogjakarta: PNI, 1948. [6234]

2216   Hadinoto, Sujono
Ekonomi Indonesia; Dari ekonomi kolonial ke ekonomi nasional. Djakarta: Jajasan Pembangunan, 1949, 72 pp. (kitlv-m)

2217   Hadiwardojo, Soekendar
Jogja berdjuang selama agresi Belanda ke-2. Djakarta: Quick, ca. 1949, 40 pp. [49, 736]

2218   Halim, Karim
Bataljon X. Boekittinggi: Tjerdas, 1946, 40 pp. (kitlv-m)

2219   Hamid II, Sultan
Speech broadcast by the chairman of the BFO, Sultan Hamid II, kepala daerah of Kalimantan Barat (West Borneo), on Sunday, February 27th, 1949, at 19.40 hours. 1949, 3 pp. [49]

2220   Hamka (ps. H.A.M.K. Amroellah)
Islam dan demokrasi. Boekittinggi: Tjerdas, ca. 1945, 49 pp. (kitlv-m)

2221   Hamka (ps.)
Merdeka. Medan: Tjerdas, 1945, 43 pp. (kitlv-m) [Second printing 1946. (kitlv-m)]

2222   Hamka (ps.)
Adat Minangkabau menghadapi repoloesi. Pandang Pandjang: Anwar Rasjid, 1946, 71 pp. (kitlv-m)

2223 Hamka (ps.)
Djiwa merdeka. Padang Pandjang: Ikatan Peladjar Koellijatoe Moeballighin, ca. 1946, 59 pp. (kitlv-m)

2224 Hamka (ps.)
Moehammadijah melaloei 3 zaman. Padang: Markaz Idarah Moehammadijah Soematera Barat, 1946, 112 pp.

2225 Hamka (ps.)
Revolusi agama. Padang Pandjang: Anwar Rasjid, 1946, 64 pp. (kitlv-m)
[Second edition, Djakarta: Pustaka Antara, 1949, 280 pp. (kitlv-m)]

2226 Hamka (ps.)
Sesudah 'Naskah Renville'. Padang Pandjang: Pemoeda Moehammadijah, 1948, 22 pp. (kitlv-m)

2227 Hanifah, Aboe
Kita berdjoeang; Goebahan koeltoer politis. Djakarta: Merdeka, 1946, 200 pp.

2228 Hanifah, Aboe
Pemoeda. Jogjakarta: GPII, 1946, 18 pp. [49]

2229 Hanifah, Abu
Tjita-tjita perdjoangan; Cultuur-politis-sosiologis. Djakarta: Bulan Bintang, 1948, 229 pp. (kitlv-m)

2230 Harahap, Parada
Sa'at bersedjarah; Ichtisar dan pemandangan jang didapat dari persidangan Komite Nasional Indonesia Poesat, dilangsoengkan di Malang pada tanggal 25 Pebroeari sampai 5 Maart 1947. Djakarta: Kem. Penerangan, 1947, 146 pp. (kitlv-m)

2231 Harahap, Parada
Vietnam merdeka! Djakarta: Tintamas, 1948, 63 pp.

2232 Harahap, Parada
Kemerdekaan pers (persvrijheid). Makassar: Ind.-Ned. Handelsmij, 1949, 79 pp. [49]

2233 Hardjosoediro, Soedjono
Pengakoean internasional atas negara baroe. Djakarta: Tintamas, 1947, 36 pp. (kitlv-m)

2234 *Harian nasional; Kenang-kenangan*. Second edition. Djakarta, 1950, 52 pp. (kitlv-m)

2235 *Haroes awas pada rintangan imperialisme Belanda*. Jogjakarta: A.N. Sebr. Sajap Kiri, 1947, 12 pp. [49]

2236 Hasan, Ghazali (Ar. Muchlis)
Tindjauan Islam Ir. Sukarno, Hamka dan A.M. Pamuntjak. Tebing Tinggi: Pustaka Al Hambra, 1949, 56 pp. (kitlv-m)

2237 Hasjim, K.H.A. Wahid; H.A. Salim and Hamka
The Ministry of Religious Affairs. Djakarta: Kem. Agama, ca. 1947, 19 pp. [49]

2238 Hassan, A.
Kedaulatan... Arti kedaulatan ra'jat pada pandangan Islam. Malang: Toko Timoer, 1946, 36 pp. (kitlv-m)

2239 Hassan, A.
Mereboet kekoeasaan. Malang: Toko Timoer, 1946, 24 pp. [49, 71]

2240 Hassan, A.
Pemerintahan setjara Islam. Malang: Toko Timoer, 1946, 36 pp. [49]

2241 Hassan, Teukoe M.
'Soematera dalam lingkoengan Negara Repoeblik Indonesia', in: *Amanat 1 tahoen merdeka*, pp. 60-71. Padang Pandjang: Penaboer, 1946.

2242 Hatta, Mohammad
Toedjoean dan politik pergerakan nasional di Indonesia; Pidato. Second edition. Jogjakarta: Indonesia Sekarang, 1946, 77 pp. [First printing 1931.] (kitlv-m)

2243 Hatta, M.
Beberapa fasal ekonomi. Third edition. Djakarta: Balai Poestaka, 1946, 160 pp., [First edition 2602 (1942).] (kitlv-m)

2244 Hatta, Moh.
Beberapa toelisan dan pidato beliau pada permoelaan perdjoeangan menegakkan Repoeblik Indonesia. Djakarta: Merdeka Press, 1945, 40 pp.

2245 Hatta, Moh.
Indonesian aims and ideals; A personal message to my old comrades wherever they may be. Djakarta, 1945, 7 pp. (kitlv-m)

2246 Hatta, Mohammad
Pendjadjahan dan kemerdekaan Indonesia; Koetipan karangan Mohammad Hatta. Boekittinggi: Tjerdas, 1945, 24 pp. (kitlv-m)

2247 Hatta, Moh.
'Arti dan hikmah setahoen merdeka', in: *Amanat 1 tahoen merdeka*, pp. 24-32. Padang Pandjang: Penaboer, 1946.

2248 Hatta, M.
Dasar politik loear negeri kita. Jogjakarta: Negara, 1946, 20 pp. (kitlv-m)

2249 Hatta, M.
Ekonomi Indonesia dimasa datang; Pidato. Jogjakarta: Kem. Penerangan, 1946, 38 pp. (kitlv-m)

2250 Hatta, M.
Kedaulatan ra'jat; Pokok pidato jang dioetjapkan pada Permoesjawaratan Pamong Pradja di Solo, tanggal 7 Pebroeari 1946. Jogjakarta: Kem. Penerangan, 1946, 51 pp.

2251 Hatta, M.
Sifat sekolah tinggi Islam. Jogjakarta: Dewan Penerangan Masjoemi, 1946, 15 pp. [49]

2252 Hatta, M.
Ekonomi kita. Siantar: Djabatan Penerangan Soematera Timoer, 1947, 38 pp.

2253 Hatta, M.
Government's statement made by Premier Moh. Hatta before the Working Committee of the Provisional Parliament, Jogjakarta, September 2, 1948. Jogjakarta: Kem. Penerangan, 1948, 17 pp. [49]

2254 Hatta, M.
Mendajung antara dua karang; Keterangan pemerintah diutjapkan oleh Drs. Moh. Hatta dimuka sidang BPKNP di Djokja pada tahun 1948. Djakarta: Kem. Penerangan, 1948, 92 pp. [Second edition, *Mendayung antara dua karang*, Jakarta: Bulan Bintang, 1976, 104 pp.]

2255 Hatta, M.
Politik pemerintah depan Badan Pekerdja KNIP. Jogjakarta: Kem. Penerangan, 1948, 18 pp. (kitlv-m)

2256 Hatta, Moh.
'Politik synthese; Pidato radio pada tanggal 17 November 1948', *Aliran Islam* 1-2 (1948):64-68.

2257 Hatta, Moh.
'Politik pemerintah Republik Indonesia', *Aliran Islam* 2-9/10 (1949):536-541.

2258 Hatta, M.
Tenang dan patuh menghadapi masa datang; Pidato. Djakarta: Kem. Penerangan, 1950, 7 pp.

2259 Hazil
'De Taman Siswa en de revolutie', *Indonesië* 3 (1949-50):541-548.

2260 *Himpoenan pidato pemimpin-pemimpin besar Indonesia.* Pematangsiantar: Perpoestakaan Rakjat, 1946, 20 pp. (kitlv-m)

2261 *Himpunan instruksi pemerintah militer dari Panglima Tentara dan Teritorium Djawa tahun 1948-1949.* N.p.: Staf AD, Sekretariat Markas Besar AD. [1348]

2262 *History of Indonesia's national movement.* New York: Republic of Indonesia Office, 1949, 19 pp. (kitlv-m)

2263 Hurlang, Dja
Dibelakang garis demarkasi atau Bapak Bado. Medan: Boet Singh/Medan Bookstore, ca. 1948, 48 pp.

2264 Idham
'Indonesia and the Netherlands', *Pakistan Horizon* 1-1 (March 1948):5-20. (vp)

2265 Idrus (Idroes)
Soerabaja. Djakarta: Pertjetakan Repoeblik Indonesia/Merdeka Press, 1946, 64 pp. [Many reprints.]

2266 Idrus
'Perempuan dan kebangsaan', *Indonesia* 1 (1949):193-256.

2267 Idrus
'Surabaja', *Oriëntatie* 5 no. 44 (January/June 1952):458-484.

2268 Idrus
'Surabaja', *Indonesia* 5 (1968):1-28.

2269   Idrus
       'Surabaja (fragment)', in: Joop van den Berg (ed.), *Bersiap; Nederlands-Indonesische verhalen*, pp. 9-23. 's-Gravenhage: BZZTôH, 1993.

2270   *The importance of Southeast Asia.* New York: Republic of Indonesia Office, 1948. [3587]

2271   *Impressions of the fights in defense of freedom and democracy in Indonesia.* Jogjakarta: BFI/Negara, 1945. (kitlv-m)

2272   *Indonesia berkibar.* New York: Indonesia League of America, 1947. (kitlv-m)

2273   *Indonesia fights for national independence, democracy and peace.* Issued by the Indonesian delegation to the World Festival of Youth and Students, Budapest, August 1949. Prague: Orbis, 1949, 50 pp.

2274   *Indonesia Raya.* Melbourne: Indonesian Independence Committee, 1945. [6199]

2275   *Indonesia Timur sepintas lalu.* Makasar: Kem. Penerangan NIT, 1948, 15 pp. (kitlv-m)

2276   *Indonesia wants freedom.* Melbourne: Indonesian Independence Committee, 1945, 6 pp.

2277   *Indonesia in world economy.* New York: Republic of Indonesia Office, 1948. [3587]

2278   *Indonesian pamphlet on freedom and self-determination.* Medan: Tjerdas, 1945, 43 pp. (kitlv-m)

2279   *Indonesië bevrijd! Manifest van de Perhimpoenan Indonesia.* Amsterdam: Koersen, 1945, 2 pp.

2280   *Indonesië schrijft.* Amsterdam: Meulenhoff, 1947, 95 pp.

2281   Indra, Soema
       Letoesan torpedo dilautan Padang. Boekittinggi: Djiwa Baroe, ca. 1946, 48 pp. (kitlv-m)

2282   *International recognition of sovereignty.* Djakarta: Ministry of Information of the Republic of the United States of Indonesia (RUSI), 1950, 46 pp.

2283   *Islam dan kebangsaan.* Bangil: Persatuan Islam bag. Poestaka, 1948. [49]

2284   Jacoeb, Jahja
       Disekitar negara Repoeblik Indonesia. Medan: Soeloeh Merdeka, ca. 1946, 87 pp. (kitlv-m)

2285   Jahja, Moechtar
       Islam dan negara. Padang Pandjang: Poestaka Sa'adijah, 1946, 100 pp. (kitlv-m)

2286   *Jajasan Pusat Kebudajaan NIT/Stichting Cultureel Centrum Oost-Indonesië.* Ende: Arnoldus, 1949, 107 pp.

2287   Jassin, H.B. (ed.)
       Gema tanah air; Prosa dan puisi 1942-1948. Djakarta: Balai Pustaka, 1948, 350 pp.

2288 Joenoes, Aminoe'ddin
ABC politik. Padang Pandjang: Penaboer, ca. 1946, 64+64 pp. 2 vols. (kitlv-m)

2289 Joenoes, Aminoe'ddin
Indonesia berdjoeang. Boekittinggi: Penaboer, ca. 1946, 85 pp. (kitlv-m)

2290 Joenoes, Aminoe'ddin
3x5 dari Bung Karno. Bukittinggi: Penabur, 1948, 38 pp. (kitlv-m)

2291 Joenoes, Aminoe'ddin
Memperdjuangkan isi negara. Bukittinggi: TNI-Seksi Penerangan, 1948, 103 pp.
(kitlv-m)

2292 Joenoes, Aminoe'ddin
Naskah Renville sebagai perdjuangan bangsa Indonesia sampai 1949. Bukittinggi:
Penabur, 1948. [49]

2293 Joenoes, Aminoe'ddin
Garis politik Hatta. Bukittinggi: Penabur, 1950, 187 pp.

2294 Joesoef, M.
'De nationale revolutie in Indonesië; Binnen- en buitenlandse factoren', *Politiek
en Cultuur* 1 (1945-46):309-311. (ubl)

2295 Joesoef, M.
'De wapenstilstand in Indonesië', *Politiek en Cultuur* 1 (1945-46):357-360. (ubl)

2296 *Kabinet pertama RIS*. Djakarta: Kem. Penerangan, 1949, 47 pp.

2297 *Kalimantan Barat, 12 Mei 1947*. Pontianak: West-Borneo Raad/RVD Pontianak,
1947, 35 pp. (kitlv-m)

2298 *Kalimantan memperdjoeangkan kemerdekaan*. Jogjakarta: Kantor Goebernoer
Kalimantan, ca. 1946, 42 pp. (kitlv-m)

2299 *Kami berdjoeang dengan poster*. Jogjakarta: PTPI, 1947, 24 pp. [71]

2300 *Kami kaoem Indo Eropah... Siaran kilat*. Djakarta: Kem. Penerangan, 1946, 7 pp.

2301 Karim, A.M.
Tindjauan zaman. Medan: Saiful, 1948, 96 pp. [49]

2302 Kartohadikoesoemo, Soetardjo
Keoeangan daerah. Soerakarta: PRSI, 1946, 60 pp.

2303 Kartohadikoesoemo, Soetardjo
Membangun masjarakat murba. Second, third edition. Djakarta: Bulan-Bintang,
1952, 80 pp. [First edition 1947.]

2304 Kartohadikoesoemo, Soetardjo
*Demokrasi Indonesia asli; Pidato peringatan 4 tahun berdirinja Dewan Pertimbangan
Agung*. Jogjakarta, 1949. [49]

2305 Kartosoewirjo, S.M.
Haloean politik Islam. Garoet: Dewan Penerangan Masjoemi Daerah Priangan,
1946, 42 pp.

2306 Kasimo, I.J.
Dasar perdjuangan PKRI-AMKRI. Jogjakarta: Canisius, 1948, 32 pp. (kitlv-m)

2307 *Kata sepakat; Ichtisar persetudjuan KMB.* Djakarta: Djawatan Penerangan Pemerintah, 1949, 48 pp. (kitlv-m)

2308 Katoppo, E.
'Onderwijsvernieuwing in Oost-Indonesië', *Wending* 4-3 (May 1949):179-192.

2309 *Kearah ketertiban hoekoem baroe di Indonesia; Bahan-bahan oentoek pembangoenan federasi; Disoesoen oentoek Konperensi Federal di Bandoeng.* Djakarta: Pemerintah Federal Sementara, 1948, 44+219 pp. 2 vols.

2310 *Kearah negara Republik Indonesia jang adil dan makmur.* Jogjakarta, 1948, 58 pp. (kitlv-m)

2311 *Kedaulatan.* N.p.: Kementerian Penerangan Negara Indonesia Timur, 1950, 12 pp.

2312 *Kedok Belanda.* Jogjakarta: Kem. Penerangan, ca. 1948, 30 pp. [49]

2313 *Kembali ke pangkuan RI; Menjongsong terbentuknja negara kesatuan pada 17 Agustus 1950.* Semarang: Djawatan Penerangan Propinsi Djawa Tengah, 1950, 92 pp.

2314 *Kementerian Agama.* Jogjakarta: Kem. Agama, 194-. [Various pagings.] (kitlv-m)

2315 *Kenallah sedjarah kebangkitan bangsamu, 20 Mei, 1908-1948.* Surakarta: Kem. Penerangan, 1948. [49]

2316 *Kerapatan permoesjawaratan Belanda-Indonesia; Soesoenan dan kewadjiban; Siaran kilat.* Djakarta: Kem. Penerangan, 1946, 12 pp. (kitlv-m)

2317 Kertapati, Inoe
Risalah 'sahabat peradjoerit'. Malang: n.n., 1946, 71 pp. (kitlv-m)

2318 *Keterangan ringkas dari rentjana persetoedjoean oleh Menteri Penerangan; Pidato radio P.M. St. Sjahrir dan M. Roem.* Djakarta: Kem. Penerangan, 1946, 8 pp. (kitlv-m)

2319 *Kisah perdjalanan Badan Kongres Pemuda Republik Indonesia; Dipersembahkan kepada Kongres Pemuda Indonesia ke-III (di Madiun, 3-4-5 April 1948).* Madiun: Badan-Pekerdja Kongres Pemuda Republik Indonesia, 1948, 29+50 pp.

2320 *Kita memboetoehkan pemimpin jang djoedjoer dan tegoeh pendiriannja oentoek memimpin dan membimbing kita kearah kemerdekaan.* N.p.: A.I.D. Drukkerij, ca. 1948, 52 pp.

2321 *Kita sama kita; Ichtisar dan tindjauan tentang Konperensi Inter-Indonesia I di Jogjakarta dan ke II di Djakarta.* Makasar: Kem. Penerangan NIT, 1949, 79 pp. (kitlv-m)

2322 *Kita tjinta damai, tapi lebih tjinta kemerdekaan.* Jogjakarta: Kem. Penerangan, 1947, 33 pp. (kitlv-m)

2323 *Kitab oendang-oendang hoekoeman Indonesia/ Wetboek van Strafrecht voor Indonesië.* Thirteenth edition. Djakarta: Balai Poestaka, 1948, 356 pp.

2324 *Kitab pembangoenan djiwa merdeka.* Magelang: Pertjetakan Negara, 1947, 19 pp.

2325 *Koempoelan pidato Pres. Soekarno-Hatta-Sjahrir berkenaan dengan satoe tahoen merdeka.* Djakarta: Balai Poestaka, 1946, 38 pp. (kitlv-m)

2326 *Koersoes-koersoes ashrama Repoeblik Indonesia.* Jogjakarta: Kem. Pertahanan, 1947, 39+20+43+29 pp. 4 vols.

2327 Koesnadi
Beberapa oesaha oentoek melenjapkan perang tjatoet. Tegal: Oesaha Penerbit Indonesia, 1946, 18 pp.

2328 Koesnadi
Oeang Repoeblik sebagai koentji kemakmoeran, pembasmi oeang NICA dan harga tjatoet. Tegal: Oesaha Penerbit Indonesia, 1946, 17 pp.

2329 Koesnodiprodjo (ed.)
Himpunan peraturan pegawai negeri, 1945-1949. Djakarta: Seno, 1945-52. 5 vols. [Various pagings.] (kitlv-m)

2330 Koesnodiprodjo (ed.)
Himpunan peraturan-peraturan Komisariat Pemerintah Pusat di Sumatera. Djakarta: S.K. Seno, ca. 1949, 94 pp. (kitlv-m)

2331 Koesnodiprodjo (ed.)
Himpunan undang-undang dan peraturan-peraturan Pemerintah Republik Indonesia. Djakarta: Marataco, 1949, 230 pp. [49]

2332 Koesnodiprodjo (ed.)
Himpunan undang-undang, peraturan-peraturan dan penetapan-penetapan Pemerintah RI 1945. Second edition. Jogjakarta: n.n., 1950, 69 pp.

2333 Koesoemah, Wiranata al'Hadj R.A.A.
Islamietische democratie in theorie en praktijk. Bandung: Pusaka, 1948, 31 pp. (kitlv-m)

2334 *Konggres Muslimin Indonesia, Jogjakarta 20-25 Désember 1949.* Jogjakarta, 1949, 374+80 pp. 2 vols. (kitlv-m)

2335 *Kongres Katholik Indonesia.* Jogjakarta, 1949, 24 pp. (kitlv-m)

2336 *Konperensi Medja Bundar 23 Augustus-2 Nopember.* N.p.: Kementerian Penerangan Republik Indonesia, 1949, 16 pp.

2337 *Kronik ichtisar sekitar peroendingan-peroendingan Indonesia-Inggris/Belanda; Dikoempoelkan dari soerat-soerat kabar.* Jogjakarta: Kem. Penerangan, 1946, 95 pp. (kitlv-m)

2338 Kwee Kek Beng
Doea poeloe lima tahon sebagai wartawan, 1922-1947. Batavia: Kuo, 1948, 114 pp. (kitlv-m)

2339 *Lahirna artos Republik Indonesia; Siaran kilat.* Bandung?: Djawatan Penerangan Propinsi Djawa Barat, ca. 1947, 6 pp. (kitlv-m)

2340 *Lapuran pembukuan tahunan pertama s/d ke-6 (1945 s/d 1950) Bank Dagang Nasional Indonesia NV.* Medan: Bank Dagang Nasional Indonesia, 1951, 55 pp.

2341   Lathief, Abdul Karim
Ichtisar-ichtisar sekitar revolusie di Indonesia. Medan: Gedung Pustaka, 1949, 110 pp. [Second printing 1949.] [49, 71]

2342   Latzim
Sifat-sifat dan bentoek perdjoeangan revoloesi kita. Jogjakarta: Kem. Penerangan, ca. 1946, 32 pp. (kitlv-m)

2343   Leimena, J.
The Dutch-Indonesian conflict. Djakarta: Grafica, 1949, 33 pp.

2344   Leimena, J.
Perselisihan Indonesia-Belanda. Djakarta: Grafica, 1949, 72 pp.

2345   Liem Khiam Soen
Kedoedoekan bangsa Tionghoa di Indonesia/De positie der Chineezen in Indonesië. Soerabaja: Sawahan Chung Hua Hui, 1947, 23 pp. (kitlv-m)

2346   *List of material and personal outrages and injuries against Indonesians by Dutch soldiery in the city of Djakarta (October-December 1945).* Djakarta: Kem. Loearnegeri, 1946, 27 pp.

2347   Loebis, Arif
Imperialisme dan pergerakan di Indonesia. N.p.: 1946, 96 pp. (kitlv-m)

2348   Loebis, Sjamsoeddin
Rahsia pemberontakan di Menado. Boekittinggi: Djiwa Baroe, ca. 1947, 61 pp. [49]

2349   Lubis, Mochtar
'I interview Sjahrir', *United Asia* 1-5 (January-February 1949):391-392.

2350   *Lukisan revolusi rakjat Indonesia, 1945-1949.* Jogjakarta: Kem. Penerangan, 1949, 395 pp.

2351   *Madjallah Mandau; Menudju kesatuan.* Jogjakarta: IPK Pusat Penerangan-Penjiaran, 1948, 90 pp. (kitlv-m)

2352   *Madura kembali ke asalnja.* Jogjakarta: Kem. Penerangan, 1950, 16 pp.

2353   *Makloemat permoesjawaratan Belanda-Indonesia, 21 Oktober 1946; Siaran kilat.* Djakarta: Kem. Penerangan, 1946, 6 pp. (kitlv-m)

2354   *Makloemat politik Pemerintah Repoeblik Indonesia/Political manifesto of the Government of the Republic of Indonesia.* Jogjakarta: Kem. Penerangan, 1945, 24 pp. (kitlv-m)

2355   Malaka, Tan
Massa actie. Second edition. Jakarta: Poestaka Moerba, 1947, 74 pp. [First printing 1926.]

2356   Malaka, Tan
Sitoeasi politik loear dan dalam negeri. Boekit Tinggi: Noesantara, 1946, 48 pp.

2357   Malaka, Tan
Moeslihat. Jogjakarta: Badan Oesaha Penerbitan Nasional Indonesia, 1946, 44 pp. [Various editions and reprints.]

2358   Malaka, Tan
PARI; Partai Repoeblik Indonesia. Boekit Tinggi: Noesantara, 1946, 48 pp.

2359   Malaka, Tan
Politik. Boekittinggi: Jogjakarta: Badan Oesaha Penerbitan Nasional Indonesia, 1946, 32 pp. [Various editions and reprints.]

2360   Malaka, Tan
Rentjana ekonomi. Jogjakarta: Badan Oesaha Penerbitan Indonesia, 1946, 64 pp. (kitlv-m) [Various editions and reprints.]

2361   Malaka, Tan
Thesis. Djakarta: Moerba, 1947, 63 pp. [Various editions and reprints.]

2362   Malaka, Tan
Dari pendjara ke pendjara. Vol. I, Bukit Tinggi: Wakaf Republik, 1948, 183 pp.; Vol. II, Djogjakarta: Pustaka Murba, 1948, 183 pp.; Vol. III, n.p.: n.n., 6+ 119 pp. [Various editions and reprints.]

2363   Malaka, Tan
Islam dalam Madilog. Bukittinggi: Nusantara, 1948, 18 pp. [Various editions and reprints.]

2364   Malaka, Tan
Nasrani-Jahudi dalam Madilog. Second edition. Bukit Tinggi: Nusantara, 1948, 24 pp. (kitlv-m)

2365   Malewa, Nadjamoeddin Daeng
Algemeene beschouwingen voor Malino; Rede. Makassar: n.n., 1946, 21 pp.

2366   Malewa, N.D.
'Some economic aspects of recovery in the Great East', *Asiatic Review* 42 (1946):361-362.

2367   Malewa, Nadjamoeddin Daeng
Algemeene richtlijnen voor de uitbouw van de economische werkzaamheid in Oost-Indonesië. Makassar: n.n., 1947, 59 pp.

2368   Malewa, Nadjamoeddin Daeng
Politik manipes dan pendjawaban Pemerintah dalam bagian pertama/Politiek manifest en Regeeringsantwoord in eerste termijn. Makassar: Celebes-Drukkerij, 1947, 31 pp.

2369   Malik, Adam
Riwajat dan perdjuangan sekitar Proklamasi kemerdekaan Indonesia, 17 Augustus 1945. Bukittinggi: Wakaf Republik, 1948, 80 pp.

2370   Maloekoe, Daeng
Dilarikan gadis Nica. Boekittinggi: Djiwa Baroe, ca. 1946, 65 pp. (kitlv-m)

2371   Manaf, Abdoel
Faham islamisme dan komoenisme. Koetaradja: Partai Komoenis, ca. 1946, 16 pp. (kitlv-m)

2372   Mangkoesasmito, Prawoto and A. Halim
       Apakah maksud dan tudjuan proklamasi kita? Pidato-pidato. Jogjakarta: Kem.
       Penerangan, 1949, 28 pp.

2373   Mangoenkoesoemo, Tjipto
       Pergerakan di India. Jogjakarta: Indonesia Sekarang, 1947, 87 pp. (kitlv-m)

2374   Mangunsarkoro (Mangoensarkoro), Sarmidi
       The sociological and cultural fundamentals for the educational system in Indonesia.
       Djakarta: Pertjetakan Negeri, ca. 1945, 28 pp.

2375   Mangunsarkoro, Sarmidi
       Dasar sosiologi dan kebudajaan untuk pendidikan Indonesia merdeka. Second
       edition. Jogjakarta: Wanita Rakjat, 1948, 32 pp. [49]

2376   Mangunsarkoro, S.
       Pendidikan nasional. Djakarta: Pustaka Timur, 1948, 32 pp. (kitlv-m)

2377   Mangunsarkoro, Sarmidi
       Masjarakat sosialis. Second edition. Medan: Toko Buku Sarkawi, 1949, 48 pp.
       (kitlv-m)

2378   Mangunsarkoro, (Mangoensarkoro) Sri
       Riwajat pergerakan wanita Indonesia. Jogjakarta: Wanita Rakjat, 1946, 38 pp.
       (kitlv-m)

2379   'Manifes politik pemerintah Republik Indonesia', *Aliran Islam* 2-9/10 (1949):
       467-469. (kitlv-m)

2380   *Manifest 20 orang.* Djakarta: Pemandangan, 1947, 45 pp. (kitlv-m)

2381   Mansoer, Tengku
       'Oost-Sumatra in een nieuwe gestalte', *Indonesië* 2 (1948-49):97-101.

2382   Maramis, A.A.
       *No more legal power of the Netherlands in Indonesia/Belanda tidak mempoenjai
       kekoeasaan sjah lagi di Indonesia/Nederland heeft geen wettig gezag meer over
       Indonesia.* Djakarta: Merdeka Press, 1946, 31 pp. (kitlv-m)

2383   *Mari boeng! Bangoen oentoek membangoen; Siaran kilat.* Djakarta: Kem. Pene-
       rangan, 1946, 4 pp.

2384   Matu Mona (ps. Hasbullah Parinduri)
       Pembentoekan negara Repoeblik Indonesia. Djakarta: Loekisan Soeasana, 1946, 56
       pp.

2385   Matu Mona (ps.)
       'Arék Soerobojo', *Loekisan Soeasana* 1-5 (December 1946-January 1947):1-48.

2386   Matu Mona (ps.)
       'Banteng Ketaton', *Loekisan Soeasana* 1-6 (February-March 1947):1-36.

2387   Matu Mona (ps.)
       Menjelidik militer chusus (gedong hantu). Djakarta: Bintang Mas, 1949, 97 pp.

2388 Mbah, Si
Menoedjoe pemerintah jang koeat. Soerakarta: Badan Penerbit Indonesia, 1946, 22 pp. (kitlv-m)

2389 *Membina warga negara.* Makassar: Kem. Penerangan NIT, 1949, 15 pp. (kitlv-m)

2390 *Memorandum outlining acts of violence and inhumanity perpetrated by Indonesian bands on innocent Chinese before and after the Dutch police action was enforced on July 21, 1947.* Batavia: Chung Hua Tsung Hui (Federation of Chinese Associations), 1947, 31 pp. (kitlv-m)

2391 *Menjingkap tirai disekeliling Indonesia-Belanda.* Jogjakarta: Kem. Penerangan, ca. 1946, 29 pp. (kitlv-m)

2392 *Menjingkirkan tentera Djepang; Siaran kilat.* Djakarta: Kem. Penerangan, 1946, 4 pp.

2393 *Menjokong perundingan di Renville; Supplement dari madjallah Mimbar Indonesia.* Djakarta, 1947, 32 pp. (kitlv-m)

2394 *Menoedjoe pembentoekan Negara Indonesia Tengah.* Bandjarmasin: Soeara Kalimantan, ca. 1946, 9 pp. (kitlv-m)

2395 *Menudju ke Kementerian Penerangan Negara Kesatuan.* Jogjakarta: Kem. Penerangan, 1950, 30 pp.

2396 *Menudju kesatuan.* Jogjakarta: IPK Pusat Penerangan-Penjiaran, 1948, 90 pp.

2397 *Menudju negara dari kita, oleh kita dan untuk kita.* Jogjakarta: Kem. Penerangan, ca. 1948, 52 pp.

2398 Meraxa, T.D.
Demokrasi; Toentoenan pemilihan rakjat. Pematang Siantar: Permoeri, ca. 1946, 18 pp. (kitlv-m)

2399 Meraxa, T.D.
Tangga kemerdekaan. Pematang Siantar: Permoeri, ca. 1946, 23 pp. (kitlv-m)

2400 *Merdeka!* Batavia: Kolff, 194-, 8 pp.

2401 *Merdeka; 17 August 1945, Republic Indonesia, 17 August 1946.* Brisbane?: Central Committee of Indonesian Independence, 1946, 36 pp.

2402 *Merdeka; Nomor peringatan 6 boelan Repoeblik Indonesia.* Djakarta: 'Merdeka', 1946, 124 pp.

2403 *Minahassa strijdt voor zelfbeschikkingsrecht en vrijheid; Memorandum betreffende de wenschen van het KKM aangeboden aan de Nederlandsche regeering door de vertegenwoordiging van het KKM.* 's-Gravenhage, 1949, 28 pp.

2404 Moelia, Todoeng gelar Soetan Goenoeng
India; Sedjarah politik dan pergerakan kebangsaan. Djakarta: Balai Pustaka, 1949, 254 pp. (kit) [Third edition, 1959, 372 pp. (kitlv-m)]

2405 Moerba, Hasan (ps. Muhammad Yamin)
Membentoek kabinet jang ketiga. Djakarta: Noesantara, 1945, 32 pp. (kitlv-m)

2406   Moetiara, Dali
        Menoedjoe doenia damai. Bandoeng: Iboenda, ca. 1946, 24 pp. (kitlv-m)

2407   Moetiara, Dali
        Pedoman propaganda. Singapore/Jogjakarta: Moetiara Serikat, ca. 1946, 26 pp.
        (kitlv-m)

2408   Moetiara, Dali
        Manoesia dan propaganda. Jogjakarta: Dali Moetiara, 1947, 26 pp. (kitlv-m)

2409   Moetijar S.
        Soeasana-politika semendjak Indonesia merdeka, 17 Agoestoes-31 Desember 1945.
        Djakarta: Balai Poestaka, 1946, 112 pp.

2410   Mutyara
        Peristiwa Atjeh. Bireuën: Pendekar Rakjat, 1946, 32 pp. (kitlv-m)

2411   Nahar, M.
        'India dan perdjuangan bangsa Indonesia', *Aliran Islam* 2-6/7 (April-May
        1949):315-318.

2412   Nahar, M.
        'Komunisme dalam mas'alah Indonesia', *Aliran Islam* 2-12 (October 1949):664-
        666, 674.

2413   *Naskah persetoedjoean boekan à la Vietnam, boekan reëele unie.* Djakarta: Kem.
        Penerangan, 1946, 13 pp.

2414   *Naskah 'Renville'; Perdjandjian gentjetan sendjata dan pokok dasar politik Indonesia-
        Belanda.* Bukittinggi: Giat, 1948, 27 pp. (kitlv-m)

2415   Nasution, Amir Hamzah
        Sedjarah nasional dan gerakan politik praktis; Pedoman. Medan: Pustaka Ahmad
        Latif, 1949, 47 pp. (kitlv-m)

2416   Nasution, Amir Taät
        Disekitar pertempoeran Tebing Tinggi. Pematang Siantar: n.n., 1946, 48 pp.
        (kitlv-m)

2417   Nasution, M. Yunan
        Riwajat ringkas penghidoepan dan perdjoeangan Ir. Soekarno. Medan: Poestaka
        Timoer, 1945, 64 pp. (kitlv-m) [Third edition, *Riwajat ringkas penghidupan dan
        perdjuangan Ir. Soekarno*, Medan: Pustaka Timur, 1948, 64 pp.]

2418   Nasution, Moechtar
        Ichtisar akar-akar Marxisme dan fascisme. Pematangsiantar: Poestaka Oemika
        Moechtar Nasution, ca. 1946, 37 pp. (kitlv-m)

2419   Nata Permana, R. Hasan
        Peraturan sementara kabupaten autonoom negara Pasundan. Bandung: Parlemen
        Negara Pasundan, 1949, 26 pp. [49]

2420   *Negara Pasundan satu tahun, 24 April 1948-24 April 1949.* Bandung, 1949,
        61 pp.

2421   *Negara Repoeblik Indonesia.* Djakarta: Poesat Komite Nasional Indonesia, 1945,
        52 pp.

2422 *Negara Repoeblik mendjamin golongan Tionghoa; Siaran kilat.* Jogjakarta: Kem. Penerangan, 1947, 31 pp.

2423 *Negara Soematera Timoer sepintas laloe.* Medan: Badan Penerangan Negara Soematera Timoer, ca. 1948, 33 pp.

2424 Negoro, Adi (Adinegoro, Djamaloedin)
'Setahoen merdeka', in: *Amanat 1 tahoen merdeka*, pp. 50-59. Padang Pandjang: Penaboer, 1946.

2425 Negoro, Adi (Adinegoro, Djamaloedin)
Bajangan pergolakan dunia. Djakarta: Pembangunan/Opbouw, 1949, 165 pp.

2426 Negoro, Adi
Revolusi dan kebudajaan. Djakarta: Balai Pustaka, 1950, 44 pp.

2427 *Nehru dan tjita-tjitanja.* Jogjakarta: Badan Penerbit Nasional, 1947. [49]

2428 *New impressions on new neighbor people.* Jogjakarta: Ministry of Information of the Republic of Indonesia, 1946, 23 pp. (kitlv-m)

2429 Ngantoeng, Henk
Impressies dari Linggadjati dan sekitarnja pada boelan Nopember 1946. Djakarta: Pertjetakan Repoeblik Indonesia, 1947, 32 plates.

2430 *Nomor peringatan Repoeblik Indonesia satoe tahoen, 17-8-45/17-8-46.* Bogor: Panitia Besar Oentoek Memperingati Setahoen Berdirinja Repoeblik Indonesia, 1946, 24 pp.

2431 *Nota-balasan pemerintah Repoeblik Indonesia kepada pemerintah Belanda disampaikan pada tanggal 28 Djoeni 1947; Siaran kilat.* Jogjakarta: Kem. Penerangan, 1947, 6 pp. (kitlv-m)

2432 *Notes about Sulawesi.* Bombay: Indonesian Youths' Association India, 1946, 17 pp.

2433 Notosoetarso, R.M.
Het drama van Indië. 's-Gravenhage: Stichting Indië in Nood, Geen Uur te Verliezen!, 1946, 16 pp.

2434 *Notulen moetamar radja-radja jang diadakan di Malino pada tanggal 12 dan 13 boelan Mei, 1948.* Malino, 1948. [Various pagings.] (kitlv-m)

2435 *Oeang Djepang mesti ditjaboet dari peredaran! Simpanlah pada bank! Siaran kilat.* Djakarta: Kem. Penerangan, 1946, 6 pp. (kitlv-m)

2436 *Oeang Repoeblik kita soedah keloear; Siaran kilat.* Djakarta: Kem. Penerangan, 1946, 8 pp. (kitlv-m)

2437 *Oendang-oendang dasar Negara Repoeblik Indonesia dan pendjelasan.* Jogjakarta: Kem. Penerangan, 1945, 30 pp.

2438 *Oendang-oendang no. 3 tahoen 1946 tentang warga negara dan pendoedoek negara Repoeblik Indonesia.* Djakarta, 1946, 17 pp. (kitlv-m)

2439 *Ontwerp der Constitutie van de Republiek der Verenigde Staten van Indonesië.* Djakarta: Kolff, 1949, 48 pp.

2440   *Outline of the Indonesian question.* New York: Kantor Penerangan RI, 1950, 13 pp. (kitlv-m)

2441   Palar, L.N.
'Indonesië na de verkiezingen', *De Brug-Djambatan* 1-3 (June 1946):3-6.

2442   Palar, L.N.
'Gezakt', in: *Indonesië schrijft*, pp. 545-554. Amsterdam: Meulenhoff, 1947.

2443   Palar, L.N.
'Freedom over Indonesia', *United Nations World* 3-12 (December 1949):13-16.
(vp)

2444   *Parlemen Pasundan satu tahun, April 1948-April 1949.* Bandung: Mascotte, 1949, 253 pp.

2445   Parna, Ibnu
Pengantar oposisi rakjat. Malang: Comite Poesat Partai Acoma (Angkatan Communis Indonesia), 1945, 126 pp.

2446   *Partai Buruh; Didirikan di Jogjakarta, 25 Desember 1949.* Djakarta: Menara Pengetahuan, 1949, 33 pp.

2447   *Partai-partai.* Jogjakarta: Kem. Penerangan, 1947-48. [Various pagings.] (kitlv-m)

2448   *Party program.* Mackay: Partai Kebangsaan Indonesia, 1945. [6199]

2449   Pasopati (ps. Hasan Sastraatmadja)
Mengenangkan agressie pertama dari Belanda dalam sedjarah revoloesi Indonesia; Insiden bendera di Soerabaja, tanggal 19 September 1945. Jogjakarta: Pertjetakan Kedaulatan Rakjat, 1947, 16 pp.

2450   *Pedato Wali Negara Soematera Timoer [T. Mansoer] pada ketika pemboekaan sidang pertama Dewan Perwakilan pada hari Senen 15 Maart 1948.* Medan: n.n., 1948, 8 pp.

2451   *Pedoman Kongres Pemoeda Repoeblik Indonesia Sumatera Oetara.* Pematang Siantar: Panitia Kongres, 1946, 80 pp. (kitlv-m)

2452   *Pedoman penghentian permusuhan jang diperintahkan pada tanggal 3 Agustus 1949, djam 20.00 (Jogja) atau djam 20.30 (Djakarta).* Jogjakarta, 1949, 37 pp. (kitlv-m)

2453   *Pedoman untuk Djawatan Penerangan Daerah.* Jogjakarta: Kem. Penerangan Pusat, 1947, 35 pp. (kitlv-m)

2454   *Pelantikan hadat tinggi daerah Selebes Selatan; Pidato-pidato jang dioetjapkan pada tanggal 12 November 1948.* Makassar: Nederlandsche Drukkerij, 1948, 32 pp.

2455   *Pelapoeran Bank Negara Indonesia dalam tahoen boekoe 1 dan 2, 1946-1947.* Batavia: Bank Negara Indonesia, 1948, 38 pp. (kitlv-m)

2456   *Pemandangan-pemandangan umum Konperensi Djawa-Timur, Bondowoso 1948.* Surabaja: Suprapto, 1948, 60 pp. (kitlv-m)

2457   *Pemandangan ringkas ekonomi dan tata Negara Soematera Timoer/Staatkundige en economische schets van Negara Soematera Timoer.* Medan: Varekamp, 1948, 21 pp.

2458 *Pemandangan ringkas tentang moe'tamar di Denpasar.* Batavia: Algemeen Regeerings Commissariaat voor Borneo en de Groote Oost, 1947, 95 pp.

2459 *Pemberantasan boeta hoeroef (koempoelan bahan-bahan).* Djakarta: Dep. P, K dan P, 1947-48, 278 pp.

2460 *Pemuda Puteri Indonesia.* Jogjakarta: PPI, 1950, 43 pp.

2461 Pena Darah (ps.)
Agen provokasi; Tetesan Pena Darah. Boekittinggi: Djiwa Baroe, 1946, 64 pp. (kitlv-m)

2462 *Pendahuluan umum dari anggaran belandja 1949 dari Negara Indonesia-Timur; Undang-undang komptabilitét.* Makassar: Kem. Keuangan NIT, 1948, 56 pp.

2463 *Pendidikan masjarakat 1 tahun, 19 Agustus 1949-17 Agustus 1950.* Jogjakarta?, 1950, 94 pp. (kitlv-m)

2464 *Pendidikan politik rakjat.* Makassar: Kem. Penerangan Negara Indonesia Timur, ca. 1949, 136 pp. (kitlv-m)

2465 *Pendjelasan tentang pembaharoean Komité Nasional Poesat.* Jogjakarta: Badan Pembaharoean KNP, 1946, 8 pp. (kitlv-m)

2466 *Penetapan harga barang; Siaran kilat.* Djakarta: Kem. Penerangan, 1946, 6 pp. (kitlv-m)

2467 *Penjelesaian nasib bangsa kita; Siaran kilat.* Djakarta: Kem. Penerangan, 1946, 4 pp.

2468 *Penoentoen perdjoeangan; Linggardjati nomor; Nomor istimewa.* Boekittinggi: Komandemen Tentara Soematera, 1947, 21 pp.

2469 *Peratoeran pemerintah pengganti oendang-oendang no. 3 tahoen 1946 tentang kewadjiban menjimpan oeang dalam bank; Kearah keoeangan negara jang sehat; Siaran kilat.* Jogjakarta: Kem. Penerangan, 1946, 12 pp. (kitlv-m)

2470 *Peratoeran sementara penjelenggaraan pemerintahan Borneo dan Timoer Besar/Voorlopige voorzieningen bestuursvoering Borneo en de Groote Oost.* Batavia: Algemeen Regeerings Commissariaat voor Borneo en de Groote Oost, 1946, 19 pp. (kitlv-m)

2471 *Peraturan dasar, pendjelasan azas dan garis politik.* Second edition. Jogjakarta: Partai Sosialis Indonesia, 1952, 62 pp. [First edition ca. 1948.] (kitlv-m)

2472 *Peraturan gadji pegawai negeri Republik Indonesia (PGP) 1948.* Jogjakarta: n.n., 1949, 177 pp.

2473 *Peraturan pemilihan anggauta Dewan Flores.* Ende: Kantor Federasi, 1948, 27 pp. [49]

2474 *Peraturan tata-tertib (pada Tentera Nasional Indonesia).* Bukittinggi: Komandemen Sumatera, 1947, 31 pp.

2475 *Perdjandjian gentjetan perang antara tentara serikat dengan tentara Indonesia; Siaran kilat.* Djakarta: Kem. Penerangan, 1946, 8 pp. (kitlv-m)

2476 *Perdjandjian perdamaian antara Repoeblik Indonesia dan Djepang.* Djakarta: Kem. Penerangan, ca. 1946, 38 pp. [22, 40]

2477 *Perdjoangan kemerdekaan dalam kota Bandung.* Second edition. Bandung: Pemerintahan Kota Besar Bandung, 1955. [unpaged] [First edition 1946.] (kitlv-m)

2478 *Perdjoeangan negara dilapangan diplomasi.* Jogjakarta: Kem. Penerangan, ca. 1946, 9 pp. (kitlv-m)

2479 *Perdjoeangan setahoen kemerdekaan di Redjang.* Bengkoeloe, 1946. [4853]

2480 *Perdjuangan di Konperensi Medja Bundar; Penjelesaian pertikaian Indonesia-Belanda, Agustus-November 1949.* Jogjakarta: Kem. Penerangan, 1949, 350 pp.

2481 *Perdjuangan PNI dalam parlemen.* Malang: Pembina Rakjat, 1950, 111 pp. (kitlv-m)

2482 *Perdjuangan rakjat.* Sibolga: Djabatan Penerangan Propinsi Sumatera Timur, 1950, 173 pp. (kitlv-m)

2483 *Peringatan 1 tahoen Kementerian Pertahanan, Biro Perdjoeangan Poesat, 25 Mei 1946-25 Mei 1947.* Jogja: n.n., 1947, 28 pp.

2484 *Peringatan 1 tahoen tentera.* 1946, 26 pp. (lmd)

2485 *Peringatan 40 tahun kebangunan nasional Indonesia.* Djombang?, 1948. (kitlv-m)

2486 *Peringatan satu tahun gerilja.* Lamongan: Panitya Peringatan Lamongan, 1950. [4597]

2487 *Peringatan ulang tahun ke-IV.* Djakarta: Kem. Penerangan, 1949, 43 pp.

2488 *Peringetan Tiong Hoa Siang Hwee Batavia; Berdiri 40 taon, 1908-1948.* Batavia: Perkoempoelan Tiong Hoa Siang Hwee, 1948, 248 pp.

2489 *Permoesjawaratan Indonesia-Belanda; Gentjatan perang; Rentjana persetoedjoean Indonesia-Belanda.* Siantar: Djabatan Penerangan NRI Soematera Timoer, ca. 1946, 32 pp. (kitlv-m)

2490 *Persahabatan Indonesia-Tionghoa; Siaran kilat.* Djakarta: Kem. Penerangan, 1946, 4 pp.

2491 *Persetoedjoean Indonesia-Belanda; Nomor istimewa Nanyang Post.* Batavia: Nanyang Post, 1947, 28 pp.

2492 *Persetoedjoean kita dengan negeri Belanda/Onze overeenstemming met Nederland/Our agreement with the Netherlands.* Djakarta: Balai Poestaka, 1946, 36 pp.

2493 *Pesindo maoe kemana?* Soerakarta: Pesindo, 1946, 16 pp. (kitlv-m)

2494 *PKI dan KNI Poesat.* Jogjakarta: PKI, 1947, 40 pp. (kitlv-m)

2495 *POD: Peratoeran Oeroesan Dalam oentoek sementara.* Poerwokerto: MBO-Bahagian Pendidikan, 1946, 78 pp.

2496 Poedjoboentoro, Soepeni
Kowani. Jogjakarta: Badan Kongres Wanita Indonesia, 1949. [4857]

2497 Poerbaraja
Pantja Sara-sarat Indonesia Djaja. Pematangsiantar: Poestaka Djagoer, 1946. [49]

2498 Poerbopranoto, Koentjoro
Towards the realisation of a real parliament and the position and organisation of the Working Committee. Jogjakarta: Ministry of Information of the Republic of Indonesia, 1949, 12 pp. [49, 1412]

2499 Poerwokoesoemo, Soedarisman
Tafsir Undang-Undang Dasar Republik Indonesia. Jogjakarta: GPII, 1947, 84 pp. (kitlv-m)

2500 Poetera Islam (ps.)
Perdjoeangan pemoeda Islam; Doeloe dan sekarang. Jogjakarta: GPII, 1946, 52 pp. [49]

2501 Poetera Islam (ps.)
Indonesia dalam kantjah pembakaran. Jogjakarta: Persatoean, 1947, 54 pp.

2502 Poetera Negara (ps.)
Sekitar permoesjawaratan Sjahrir-Van Mook. Djakarta: Elita, 1946, 32 pp.

2503 *Political Manifesto of the Republic of Indonesia.* Djakarta: Ministry of Information, 1945. (vp)

2504 *Political parties, armed groups, labour unions and youth organizations in Indonesia.* Djakarta: Republik Indonesia Serikat, Ministry of Information, 1950, 73 pp. (kitlv-m)

2505 *Politiek Manifest der Indonesische Regeering; Siaran kilat.* Djakarta: Kem. Penerangan, 1946, 11 pp.

2506 *Politiek manifest Kabinet Nadjamoeddin.* N.p.: n.n., 1947.

2507 Prawiranegara, Sjafroeddin
Kita peliharalah oeang Repoeblik; Pidato. Siaran kilat. Djakarta: Kem. Penerangan, 1946, 8 pp. (kitlv-m)

2508 Prawiranegara, Sjafruddin
Politik dan revolusi kita. Second edition. Medan: Andalas, 1950, 48 pp. [First edition 1948.] (kitlv-m)

2509 Prawiranegara, Sjafruddin
Tindjauan singkat tentang politik dan revolusi kita. Jogjakarta: Indonesia-Raya, 1948, 18 pp. (kitlv-m)

2510 Prawirodirdjo, Alimin
Analysis. Djokjakarta: Agit-Prop CC Partai Komunis Indonesia, 1947, 43 pp. (kitlv-m) [Other edition, Bukit Tinggi: Partai Komunis Indonesia Sumatera Barat, 1947, 40 pp.]

2511 Prawirodirdjo, Alimin
Perdjoeangan naskah dan mempertegak de facto. Jogjakarta: Bintang Merah, 1947, 12 pp. (kitlv-m)

2512 Prawirodirdjo, Alimin
Sepatah kata dari djaoeh. Jogjakarta: Bintang Merah, 1947, 19 pp. (kitlv-m)

2513   Prawirodirdjo, Alimin
       Tjaranja hidup dua orang besar. Jogjakarta: Bintang Merah, 1948, 19 pp. (kitlv-m)

2514   *Presiden kita P.J.M. Tjokorde Gde Rake Soekawati melawat dari poelau ke poelau di Negara Indonesia Timoer.* Makassar: Kem. Penerangan NIT, ca. 1948, 55 pp.

2515   Prijono
       Ichtisar perdjoeangan oemmat Islam di Indonesia. Jogjakarta: Kem. Agama, ca. 1946, 8 pp. (kitlv-m)

2516   *Program perdjoeangan dan program oesaha-tjepat 'Masjoemi'; Partai politik Islam.* Jogjakarta: Masjoemi, 1945, 16 pp.

2517   Proletar Indonesia (ps.)
       Kesanalah! Kaoem sosialis revoloesioner. Pematang Siantar?: Pesindo, 1946, 25 pp. (kitlv-m)

2518   *PSI-daerah Atjeh.* Koetaradja: PSI, 1946, 35 pp. (kitlv-m)

2519   *Pulau Sumbawa.* Makassar: Kem. Penerangan NIT, 1948, 17 pp. (kitlv-m)

2520   *Putusan Mahkamah Tentara Agung Republik Indonesia di Djogjakarta tanggal 27 Mei 1948 dalam perkaranja terdakwa-dakwa: Djendral-Major Sudarsono, Mr. Muhamad Yamin, Mr. Achmad Subardjo, Mr. Iwa Kusuma Sumantri, c.s.; Peristiwa 3 Djuli 1946.* Djakarta: Van Dorp, 1949, 144 pp.

2521   Radjab, Muhamad
       Tjatatan di Sumatera. Djakarta: Balai Pustaka, 1949, 198 pp. (kitlv-m) [Second edition, 1958, 227 pp.]

2522   *Rakjat berdjoeang.* Jogjakarta: Kem. Penerangan, ca. 1947, 10 pp. (kitlv-m)

2523   Rangkoeti, Bahroem
       Negara tjiptaan rakjat; Sedjarah perdjoeangan dan pembangoenan Repoeblik Indonesia. Djakarta: Tandjoeng, 1946, 68 pp.

2524   *Rantjangan konstitusi RIS/Ontwerp der constitutie van de Republiek der Verenigde Staten van Indonesië.* Bandung: Dua 'R', 1949, 104 pp. [49]

2525   *Rantjangan konstitusi Republik Indonesia Serikat.* Djakarta: Kolff, 1949, 50 pp.

2526   *Rantjangan oendang-oendang tentang anggauta-anggauta dan pemilihan anggauta-anggauta Dewan Perwakilan Rakjat.* Djakarta: Kem. Penerangan, 1946, 24 pp. [49]

2527   Rasid, Gadis
       'Developments in Indonesia; From the Renville Agreement to the resumption of military action', *India Quarterly* 5-3 (1949):253-271.

2528   Rasid, Gadis
       Ditengah-tengah perdjuangan kebudajaan Indonesia; 10 buah intervieu tentang berbagai-berbagai soal kebudajaan dengan St.T. Alisjahbana. Djakarta: Pustaka Rakjat, 1949, 46 pp.

2529   Rasjidi, H.
       Pidato Menteri Agama dalam Konperensi Djawatan Agama seloeroeh Djawa-Madoera
       pada tanggal 17/18-3-1946 di Solo. Jogjakarta: Persatoean, 1946, 16 pp. (kitlv-
       m)

2530   *A record of three years of Republican progress.* London: Republic of Indonesia
       Office, 1948. [6297]

2531   *Repoeblik Indonesia, 17 Augustus 1945-17 Augustus 1946; Herdenkingsnummer ter*
       gelegenheid van het éénjarig bestaan der Repoeblik Indonesia. Amsterdam:
       Weekblad Indonesia, 1946, 32 pp.

2532   *Report on the military situation in Java, Sumatra, and Madura, August 4-September*
       4. Jogjakarta: Kem. Loearnegeri, 1947, 35 pp. (kitlv-m)

2533   *Republic of Indonesia.* Jogjakarta: Kem. Penerangan, 1946, 45 pp.

2534   *Republic of Indonesia.* Brisbane: Central Committee of Indonesian Independence,
       1946, 20 pp. (kitlv-m)

2535   *Republik Indonesia ta' pernah mengakui negara-negaraan.* Jogjakarta: Kem.
       Penerangan, 1950, 15 pp. (kitlv-m)

2536   *Review of the British press.* London: Republic of Indonesia Office, 1949, 16 pp.
       (kitlv-m)

2537   *Revoloesi nasional dan 1 Mei.* Jogjakarta: Sentral Biro SOBSI Bagian Penerangan,
       1947, 32 pp.

2538   *Revolusi Desember '45 di Atjeh atau pembasmian pengchianat tanah air.* Kutaradja:
       Pemerintah RI Daerah Atjeh, 1949, 40 pp.

2539   *Revolusi sosialis (7 November 1917).* Jogjakarta: Bintang Merah, 1947, 33 pp.
       (kitlv-m)

2540   *Revue Indonesia setahoen RI; Merdeka sampai achir zaman.* Djakarta: Badan
       Penerbit Nasional, 1946, 72 pp. (kitlv-m)

2541   *Risalah Kongres Pemuda Peladjar Indonesia I, pada tanggal 25 September 1945*
       sampai dengan tanggal 27 September 1945. Djokja: Pengurus Besar Ikatan
       Pemuda Pelajar Indonesia, 1948, 34 pp.

2542   *Rundingan Badan Perwakilan Sementara Negara Indonesia Timur; Sidang pertama,*
       kedua 1949. Makassar: n.n., 1949, ca. 100 pp. (kitlv-m)

2543   *Rundingan sidang Parlemen Negara Pasundan, 1948-1949.* Bandung, 1949. [49]

2544   Said, Mohamad
       Empat belas boelan pendoedoekan Inggeris di Indonesia. Medan: Kantor Berita
       Antara, 1946, 148 pp.

2545   Said, Mohamad
       Truce atau teroes? Menghentikan atawa meneroeskan penembakan? Medan:
       Poestaka Timoer, 1947, 24 pp. (kitlv-m)

2546   Sajuti, Mohammad Ibnu (= Sajuti Melik)
       Arti Proklamasi dan K.M.B. Jogjakarta: Logika, 1949, 78 pp. (kitlv-m)

2547   Sakirman
       Menindjau perdjuangan PARI. Soeara Lasjkar, ca. 1947, 8 pp. (kitlv-m)

2548   Salim, H.A.
       Artinja gentjatan-perang dalam permoesjawaratan; Siaran kilat. Djakarta: Kem.
       Penerangan, 1946, 4 pp. (kitlv-m)

2549   Salim, H. Agus
       Meningkat ke-kemerdekaan 100%. Jogjakarta: Kem. Penerangan, 1948, 40 pp.

2550   Samawi
       Negara baru di Pasifik. Jogjakarta: Kedaulatan Rakjat, 1948, 65 pp. (kitlv-m)

2551   Sandra
       Siasat massa actie; Dasar dan garis besar Leninisme. Jogjakarta: Pendidikan
       Boeroeh, 1945, 20 pp. (kitlv-m)

2552   Sandra
       Kekoeatan proletar. Jogjakarta: Pendidikan Boeroeh, 1946, 33 pp. (kitlv-m)

2553   Sandra
       Satoe Mei; Hari kemenangan boeroeh sedoenia. Jogjakarta: Pendidikan Boeroeh,
       1946, 50 pp. (kitlv-m)

2554   Sandra
       Upah buruh. Jogjakarta: Pendidikan Buruh, 1947, 58 pp. (kitlv-m)

2555   *Sang Saka; Kenang-kenangan berlangsoengnja Konperensi Daerah jang ke doea.*
       Koetaradja: Badan Penerangan Markas Daerah Pesindo Atjeh, 1946, 35 pp.
       (kitlv-m)

2556   Sardjan, Mohammad
       Manifest politik partai politik Islam Masjumi. Pare: Masjumi, ca. 1948, 25 pp.
       (kitlv-m)

2557   Sardjono
       Indonesia calling! N.p.: Indonesian Political Exiles Association in Australia,
       1945, 6 pp.

2558   Sastroamidjojo, Ali
       Bangsa dan kebangsaan. Tebing Tinggi: Tjerdas, 1947, 27 pp. (kitlv-m)

2559   Sastroamidjojo, Ali
       'Survey of the Indonesian national movement', *Asian Horizon* 2-3 (Autumn-
       Winter 1949-50):29-37. (ubl)

2560   Sastroamidjojo, Ali and Robert Delson
       'The status of the Republic of Indonesia in international law', *Columbia Law
       Review* 49 (1949):344-361.

2561   Sastroamidjojo, Usman
       The Indonesian struggle for freedom. Perth, 1948. [45, 6199]

2562   Sati, A. Manan St. R.
       Peringatan RI; Oendang-Oendang Dasar, tata negara dan berita penting. Padang
       Pandjang, 1945, 41 pp. (kitlv-m)

2563 Sati, A. Manan St. R. and Aboe Bakar S.M.
Perang sabil (perdjoeangan soetji) mempertahankan kemerdekaan Repoeblik Indonesia jang abadi. Padang Pandjang: Poestaka Merdeka, ca. 1946, 45 pp. (kitlv-m)

2564 *Satoe tahoen Indonesia-Timoer, 24 Desember 1946-1947.* Makassar: Kem. Penerangan NIT, 1947, 6 pp. (kitlv-m)

2565 *Satu tahun Badan Pembaharuan Susunan Komite Nasional Pusat, Djuli 1946-Djuli 1947.* Jogjakarta: BPSKNP, 1947, 102 pp. (kitlv-m)

2566 *Sedikit tentang demokrasi dalam Oendang-Oendang Dasar kita.* Djakarta: Kem. Penerangan, 1945, 16 pp. (kitlv-m)

2567 *Sekitar persetudjuan KMB; Kumpulan kupasan dan pemandangan.* Djakarta: Kem. Penerangan, 1950, 45 pp. (kitlv-m)

2568 *Sekitar rentjana persetoedjoean Indonesia-Belanda; No. 2.* Djakarta: Kem. Penerangan, 1946, 24 pp.

2569 *Sekitar statements Rum-Van Royen.* Djakarta: PNI, 1949, 80 pp.

2570 Semaoen
Penoentoen kaoem boeroeh; Dari hal sarekat sekerdja. Solo: Pesindo, 1946, 27 pp. 2 vols. (kitlv-m) [First edition 1920.]

2571 *Setahoen merdeka, 17-8-1945/17-8-1946; Nommer peringatan.* N.p.: Djawatan Kereta Api, 1946, 51 pp.

2572 *Setahoen merdeka; Daerah Bengkoeloe selama setahoen dalam kemerdekaan.* Bengkoeloe: Taman Siswa, 1946. [4853]

2573 *Setahoen Republik Indonesia; Merdeka sampai achir zaman.* Jogja: Revue Indonesia, 1946, 72 pp.

2574 *Setahun Negara Djawa Timur.* Surabaja: Kolff, 1949, 19 pp.

2575 Setiabuddhi, D.
Apakah demokrasi itu? Jogjakarta: Dep. Penerangan, ca. 1947. (kitlv-m)

2576 Setiabuddhi, Danudirdja
Zeventig jaar consequent. Bandung: Nix, 1949, 182 pp.

2577 *Siapa roegi djika kita kirim beras ke India? Siaran kilat.* Djakarta: Kem. Penerangan, 1946, 3 pp.

2578 *Siaran kilat.* Djakarta: Kem. Penerangan, 1946. 18 vols.

2579 *Siaran kilat Badan Penerangan Barisan Boeroeh Indonesia.* Djakarta: Badan Penerangan Barisan Boeroeh Indonesia, 1946. 6 vols.

2580 *Sidang Mahkamah Tentara Agung dalam pemeriksaan proces Sudarsono cs.; Stenografisch verslag.* Jogjakarta: n.n., 1948, 323 pp.

2581 *Sikap Islam terhadap moesoeh jang menjerah.* Bandoeng?: Masjoemi, 1946, 5 pp. (kitlv-m)

2582 Sinaga, Moesa
Harta jang tersemboenji. Pematang Siantar: Pertjetakan Repoeblik Indonesia, 1947, 23 pp. (kitlv-m)

2583   Singodimedjo, R. Kasman (ed.)
       Negara Republik Indonesia. Disusun oleh Pusat Komite Nasional Indonesia.
       Second edition. Jakarta: Mutiara, 1979, 47 pp. [First edition 1945.]

2584   Sipahoetar, A.M.
       Siapa? Loekisan tentang pemimpin-pemimpin. Second edition. Soekaboemi:
       Pertjetakan 'Pemerintah', 1946, 76 pp.

2585   Siregar, Malelo
       Kupasan faham-faham politik. Second printing. Surabaja: Pustaka Baru, n.y.,
       81 pp. [First printing 1948.]

2586   Sitorus, L.M.
       Sedjarah pergerakan kebangsaan Indonesia. Djakarta: Pustaka Rakjat, 1947,
       63 pp.

2587   *The situation in Indonesia.* Melbourne: Indonesian Independence Committee,
       1945, 3 pp.

2588   Sjahrazad (ps. Sutan Sjahrir)
       Indonesische overpeinzingen. Amsterdam: De Bezige Bij, 1945, 182 pp. [Second
       printing 1946; Third printing 1950; Fourth printing 1966; Fifth edition, 1987,
       192 pp.]

2589   Sjahrazad (ps.)
       Renungan Indonesia. Djakarta: Pustaka Rakjat, 1947, 183 pp. (kitlv-m)

2590   Sjahrir, Sutan
       Pergerakan sekerdja. Jogjakarta: Sarekat Boeroeh Pertjetakan Indonesia (S.B.P.I.),
       1947, 34 pp. [First published 1933; Second printing 1948.]

2591   Sjahrir, S.
       Indonesia's fight. London: Perhimpoenan Indonesia, 1945, 13 pp.

2592   Sjahrir
       Perdjoeangan kita. Djakarta: Pertjetakan Repoeblik Indonesia, 1945, 42 pp.

2593   Sjahrir
       Djangan memoeaskan diri kita sendiri sadja; Pidato. Siaran kilat. Djakarta: Kem.
       Penerangan, 1946, 4 pp.

2594   Sjahrir, St.
       'Indonesia berdjoeang mentjapai kesempoernaan kehidoepan manoesia', in:
       Amanat 1 tahoen merdeka, pp. 33-35. Padang Pandjang: Penaboer, 1946.

2595   Sjahrir, Soetan
       *Kebangsaan kita hanja djembatan oentoek mentjapai deradjat kemanoesiaan jang
       sempoerna! Pidato. Siaran kilat.* Djakarta: Kem. Penerangan, 1946. (kitlv-m)

2596   Sjahrir, St.
       *Mendirikan negara kerakjatan dalam revoloesi kerakjatan; Pidato dioetjapkan pada
       pemboekaan konperensi Pamong-Prodjo di Solo pada tanggal 7-2-1946.* Jogjakarta:
       Kem. Penerangan, 1946, 19 pp. (kitlv-m) [Second printing 1950.]

2597   Sjahrir, Soetan
       Onze strijd. Amsterdam: Vrij Nederland, 1946, 35 pp.

2598 Sjahrir
Pidato dimoeka radio Indonesia di Djakarta, tanggal 19 Nopember 1946; Siaran kilat. Djakarta: Kem. Penerangan, 1946, 6 pp. (kitlv-m)

2599 Sjahrir
Rakjat dengan pemerintahnja satoe dan satoe djiwa; Pidato. Siaran kilat. Djakarta: Kem. Penerangan, 1946, 6 pp.

2600 Sjahrir, Soetan
We fight by the code of the ksatryas; Siaran kilat. Djakarta: Kem. Penerangan, 1946, 5 pp.

2601 Sjahrir, St.
Pikiran dan perdjoeangan. Djakarta: Poestaka Rakjat, 1947, 123 pp.

2602 Sjahrir, Soetan
Politik beleid pemerintah; Pedato tanggal 1 Maret 1947 di sidang KNIP. 4 pp. (ubl)

2603 Sjahrir, Soetan
Out of exile. New York: John Day, 1949, 265 pp.

2604 Sjahrir, St.
'Urusan luar negeri', *Aliran Islam* 2-4 (1949):182-189, 217. (kitlv-m)

2605 Sjahrir, St.
Our struggle. Ithaca: Cornell University, 1968, 37 pp.

2606 Sjahrir, St.; H.J. Friedericy and C. Wolf Jr.
'What happened in Indonesia?', *United Nations World* 1-7 (1947):12-15. (ubl)

2607 *Sjair kenang-kenangan kepada Persatoean Latihan Barisan Ra'jat di Padang dan Bedagei.* Tebing Tinggi, 1946, 15 pp. (kitlv-m)

2608 Sjamni, Adnan
Sumatra pulau harapan; Alam dan exploitatie kekajaannja. Djakarta: Grafica, 1949, 144 pp. (kitlv-m)

2609 Slamet, Mas
The afterglow of the Japanese sunset. Batavia, 1946, 15+7 pp. 2 vols.

2610 Slamet, Mas
Dalang Djepang main di Djawa. Betawi, 1946, 23 pp.

2611 Slamet, Mas
Japanese machinations. Batavia, 1946, 8+15+15+19 pp. 4 vols.

2612 Slamet, Mas
Japansche intrigues; De nasleep van de Japansche bezetting. 's-Gravenhage: Stichting Indië in Nood, Geen Uur te Verliezen!, 1946, 16 pp. [Second edition, Amsterdam: Buijten en Schipperheijn, 1946, 16 pp.]

2613 Slamet, Mas
Kommando Tokyo. Betawi, 1946, 8+10 pp. 2 vols.

2614 Slamet, M.
Tipoe moeslihat Djepang. Betawi: n.n., 1946, 14+8+23 +23 pp. 4 vols.

2615   Soal beras dan bahan makan oentoek kota Djakarta; Siaran kilat. Djakarta: Kem. Penerangan, 1946, 5 pp. (kitlv-m)

2616   Soeara pers dari Djawa dan Malaya tentang naskah peroendingan Indonesia-Belanda. Siantar: Djabatan Penerangan Soematera Timoer, ca. 1946, 13 pp. (kitlv-m)

2617   Soeara Proletar (ps.)
        Pembongkaran tiga rahsia penting. Siloengkang: Poestaka Sofjan Pondha, 1946, 34 pp. (kitlv-m)

2618   Soebandrio
        'De facto status at Linggadjati', *Far Eastern Survey* 17 (11 February 1948):29-31. (ubl)

2619   Soedirman
        Order harian Panglima Besar Soedirman pada Hari Angkatan Perang ke-4, 5 Oktober 1949. Jogjakarta, 1949, 4 pp. (kitlv-m)

2620   Soekarno
        Belorong imperialisme. Second edition. Surabaja: Pustaka Nasional, 1949, 16 pp. [First edition 1932.] (kitlv-m)

2621   Soekarno
        Amanah Presiden. Boekittinggi: Pedjabat Penerangan, 1946, 17 pp. (kitlv-m)

2622   Soekarno
        Amanat 1 tahoen merdeka. Padang Pandjang: Penaboer, 1946, 72 pp. (kitlv-m)

2623   Soekarno
        Djangan lengah! Siap-sedia-waspada! Pidato. Siaran kilat. Djakarta: Kem. Penerangan, 1946, 11 pp. (kitlv-m)

2624   Soekarno
        'Proklamasi kemerdekaan Indonesia adalah satoe pekik "berhenti" kepada pendjadjahan 350 tahoen', in: *Amanat 1 tahoen merdeka,* pp. 5-23. Padang Pandjang: Penaboer, 1946.

2625   Soekarno
        Setahoen Repoeblik Indonesia; Pidato Presiden pada oepatjara tanggal 17 Agoestoes tahoen 1946. Soerakarta: Djawatan Penerangan Daerah Soerakarta, 1946, 14 pp.

2626   Soekarno
        Testament politik Ir. Soekarno. Pematang Siantar: Dewan Daerah PNI-Soematera Timoer, 1946, 32 pp. (kitlv-m)

2627   Soekarno
        Ketiga kalinja 17 Agoestoes. Jogjakarta: Kem. Penerangan, 1947, 37 pp.

2628   Soekarno
        Lahirnja Pantjasila; Boeng Karno menggembleng dasar-dasar negara. Jogjakarta: Goentoer, 1947, 41 pp. (kitlv-m)

2629   Soekarno
        Sarinah; Kewadjiban wanita dalam perdjoangan Repoeblik Indonesia. Jogjakarta: Goentoer, 1947, 513 pp.

2630 Soekarno
Tiga kali toedjoehbelas (3 x 17) Agoestoes! Pidato. Jogjakarta: Goentoer, 1947, 17 pp. (kitlv-m)

2631 Soekarno
Kepada bangsaku. Jogjakarta: Goentoer, 1948, 74 pp. (kitlv-m) [Second edition, Jakarta: Haji Masagung, 1988, 7+56 pp.]

2632 Soekarno
Radio speech delivered on 19-9-'48 on the Madiun coup. Jogjakarta: Ministry of Information, 1948, 3 pp. (kitlv-m)

2633 Soekarno
Sarinah; Soal perempuan; Laki dan perempuan; Dari gua ke kota. Tebing Tinggi: Tjerdas, 1948, 94 pp.

2634 Soekarno
Indonesia, kami siap! Pidato. Jogjakarta: Kem. Penerangan, 1949, 33 pp. (kitlv-m)

2635 Soekarno
Melalui tracée baru; Pidato pada waktu memerintahkan penghentian permusuhan pada tanggal 3 Agustus 1949. Jogjakarta: Kem. Penerangan, 1949, 52 pp. (kitlv-m)

2636 Soekarno
Mentjapai Indonesia merdeka. Langsa: Bakti, 1949, 36 pp. (kitlv-m)

2637 Soekarno
'Revolusi Indonesia adalah sebagian dari revolusi dunia', *Aliran Islam* 2-9/10 (1949):458-466. (kitlv-m)

2638 Soekarno
Seluruh Nusantara berdjiwa Republik; 17 Agustus jang ke-4; Pidato. Jogjakarta: Kedaulatan Rakjat, 1949, 35 pp. (kitlv-m)

2639 Soekarno
Tetaplah semangat elang radjawali; Pidato. Djakarta: Kem. Penerangan, 1949, 14 pp. (kitlv-m)

2640 Soekarno
The birth of Pantjasila. Second edition. Djakarta: Ministry of Information, 1952, 32 pp. [First edition 1950.]

2641 Soekarno
Tinggallah tenang dan tenteram; Pidato radio 14 Desember 1949. Jogjakarta: Kem. Penerangan, 1950, 69 pp.

2642 Soekarno (Sukarno)
Sarinah; De taak van de vrouw in de strijd van de Republiek Indonesia. Amsterdam: Van Ditmar, 1960, 262 pp. [First published 1947.]

2643 Soeleiman, M.
Sendjata perdjoeangan. Malang: Soemi, 1946, 51 pp. (kitlv-m)

2644 *Soembangan beras, boeng! Sebagai bingkisan persahabatan kepada saudara kita di India; Siaran kilat.* Djakarta: Kem. Penerangan, 1946, 4 pp.

2645	Soemodilogo, Prawoto (ed.)
	Repoeblik Indonesia contra Tweede Kamer Staten-Generaal. Djakarta: Ma'moer, ca.
	1946. Bagian I, *Laporan Panitia Parlement Hindia-Belanda,* 44 pp.; Bagian II,
	*Pidatonja Luit. G.G. Hindia Belanda, Menteri Oeroesan Daerah Seberang, Mahkota
	Belanda,* 70 pp.; Bagian III, *Pidatonja anggauta dari II Kamer Staten Generaal
	Schouten, Van der Goes van Naters, Van Poll, Bajetto,* 89 pp.; Bagian IV, *Pidato
	anggauta-anggauta Goedhart, Meijerink, Korthals,* 26 pp.; Bagian V, *Pidato
	anggauta-anggauta Palar, Tilanus,* 24 pp. (kitlv-m)

2646	Soemohardjo, Oerip
	Pidato radio J.M. Letnan Djendral Oerip Soemohardjo. Ca. 1946, 11 pp. (lmd)

2647	Soenito
	'De basis-overeenkomst van Linggadjati', *De Nieuwe Stem* 2 (1947):7-12. (ubl)

2648	*Soenting masjarakat.* Pematang Siantar: Badan Penjantoen Perdjoeangan Barisan
	Rakjat, 1946, 52 pp. (kitlv-m)

2649	Soepardi, Imam
	Dibelakang lajar ramalan Djojobojo. Second edition. Surabaja: Pustaka Nasional,
	1949, 24 pp. [First edition 1946.]

2650	Soepardi, Imam
	Bung Karno sebagai Kokrosono; Untuk batjaan rakjat. Second edition. Surabaja:
	Pustaka Nasional, 1950, 24 pp. [First edition 1948.]

2651	*Soerat sebaran oentoek serdadoe-serdadoe TNI (tentara pemerintah) dengan
	petoendjoek-petoendjoek taktik bertempoer.* 1948, 4 pp.

2652	Soeroto, Noto
	Pro swapradja. Solo: Mataram, 1950, 40 pp.

2653	*Soesoenan pemerintah dalam keadaan bahaja; Siaran kilat.* Djakarta: Kem.
	Penerangan, 1946, 3 pp.

2654	Soetardjo, Noerdjana
	Sedjarah pergerakan pemoeda Indonesia. Medan: Poestaka Timoer, 1946, 57 pp.

2655	Soetardjo, Sarwono S. and Mohd. Joesoef Abdoellah
	Perdjoeangan pemoeda revolusioner. Pematang Siantar: Poestaka Revolusioner,
	1946, 74 pp.

2656	Soetomo
	Kepada bangsakoe. Magelang: Pertjetakan Negara, 1946, 63 pp.

2657	Soetomo (Bung Tomo)
	*Manifes politik; Tuntunan bagi mereka jang hendak membentuk persatuan sedjati dan
	menghindarkan negara dan rakjat Indonesia dari bahaja keruntuhannja.* Jogjakarta:
	Balapan, 1948, 43 pp.

2658	*Some graphs concerning Indonesia; Today the youngest republic.* Djakarta: General
	Research Bureau, 1946, 34 pp.

2659	Sosrohadikoesomo
	Oesaha pembangoenan negara. Siantar: Djabatan Penerangan Soematera Timoer,
	ca. 1945, 25 pp. (kitlv-m)

2660 Sosrokoesoemo, R.A.
Keboedajaan Indonesia Raya. Malang: Penerbit Pengetahoean Oemoem, ca. 1946,
36 pp. (kitlv-m)

2661 Sou'yb, Joesoef
Pengetahuan politik. N.p.: TNI-Staf Territorial Sumatra, 1948, 59 pp.

2662 *Staatsregeling van den staat Oost-Indonesië.* Ca. 1949, 34 pp.

2663 *De stem van Makassar over staat en federatie; Keuze uit de vrijdagavondcom-
mentaren.* Makassar: Kem. Penerangan NIT, 1949, 87 pp. (kitlv-m)

2664 Subandrio, Hurustiati
'Ervaringen van mijn zoontje', in: *Indonesië schrijft,* pp. 533-544. Amsterdam:
Meulenhoff, 1947.

2665 Subandrio, H.
'Social reforms in Indonesia', *Asian Horizon* 1-1 (Spring 1948):33-41. (ubl)

2666 Subandrio, H.
'The Muslims in Indonesia', *The Islamic Review* 37 (1949):42-44. (ubl)

2667 Sukma, Ratu
Tan Malaka ..! Bukit Tinggi: Pustaka Rakjat, 1948, 37 pp. (kitlv-m)

2668 Sukonto, Sulianti
'Education and welfare in Indonesia', *Pakistan Horizon* 1 (June 1948):131-136.
(vp)

2669 Sumanang
Beberapa soal tentang pers dan journalistiek. Jogjakarta: Badan Penerbit Nasional,
1948, 96 pp.

2670 Sumarsono
'De hedendaagse staatkundige hervormingen', *Bestuursvraagstukken* 1 (1949):
307-325.

2671 *Sumatera Timur bergolak! Risalah pidato-pidato, resolusi-resolusi, siaran-siaran dan
suara-suara pers jang menudju ke negara kesatuan.* N.p.: Kem. Penerangan R.I.
Sumatera Timur, 1950, 18 pp.

2672 Sunario
Sistem parlementer, sistim partai dan sistem pemilihan. Fourth edition. Djakarta:
Tintamas, 1949, 101 pp. [First edition 1941.]

2673 Sunario, R.M. (Soenario)
Ichtisar ringkas tentang riwajat sosial-ekonomis Indonesia. Djakarta: Badan
Penerbit Nasional, 1945, 44 pp. (kitlv-m)

2674 Sunario, R.M. (Soenario)
The socio-economic history of Indonesia; A brief outline. Djakarta: National
Publishing Co., 1946, 42 pp. (kitlv-m)

2675 Sunario (Soenario)
Parlemen dan parlementarisme; Riwajat dan atoeran-atoerannja. Second edition.
Jogjakarta: Nasional, 1947, 56 pp. [49]

2676   Sunario
       Dasar-dasar kesatuan kebangsaan Indonesia. Second edition. Djakarta: Tintamas,
       1949, 56 pp. [First edition 1946.]

2677   Supena
       Pamong-pradja; Sebelum, waktu dan sesudah Perang Dunia ke-II. Bogor, 1948.
       [1986]

2678   Supomo
       Djiwa angkatan baru. Medan: Saiful, 1949. [49]

2679   Supomo, Iman
       Tata-negara Indonesia; Kitab peladjaran dan batjaan. Jogjakarta: Kedaulatan
       Rakjat, 1949. [49]

2680   Supomo, R.
       Kedudukan hukum adat dikemudian hari; Pidato. Djakarta: Pustaka Rakjat, 1947,
       16 pp.

2681   Supomo, R.
       Soal Negara Indonesia-Serikat dan Uni Belanda-Indonesia. Djakarta: Jajasan
       Dharma, 1948, 64 pp.

2682   Supomo, R.
       *Statut-Uni Indonesia-Belanda; Dengan sekedar pendjelasan di bawah tiap-tiap pasal
       menurut pembitjaraan pada waktu perundingan di Konperensi Medja Bundar di Den
       Haag.* Djakarta/Amsterdam: Djambatan, 1950, 48 pp.

2683   Surapati (ps. M. Saleh Umar)
       100 hari; Sadjak falsafah baru; Tjiptaan ditengah medan perang. Medan: Toko Buku
       Sarkawi, 1947, 16 pp.

2684   Surapati (ps.)
       Indonesia baru. Second edition. Medan: Centraal Courant en Boekhandel, 1949,
       29 pp. (kitlv-m)

2685   *Tafsir urgentie program Masjumi (Masjoemi); Kepoetoesan konferensi kilat tanggal
       19-20 Maart 1947 di Djokjakarta.* Jogjakarta: Masjumi, 1947, 45 pp. (kitlv-m)

2686   Tan Goan Po
       Indonesia dan kerdjasama internasional; Pidato. Djakarta: Perkumpulan
       Memadjukan Ilmu dan Kebudajaan, 1949, 16 pp. [49]

2687   Tan Moh Goan
       Doenia terbalik...?! Djakarta: Tjilik Roman's, 1949, 96 pp.

2688   Tan Toean
       Kearah pembangoenan negara. Boekittinggi: Partai Komunis Indonesia, 1947,
       29 pp.

2689   Tanojo, Raden
       *Djojobojo Indonesia merdeka (djangka Djojobojo sempoerna dengan peristiwa
       Indonesia merdeka).* Solo: Sadoeboedi, ca. 1946, 32 pp. (kitlv-m)

2690   *Tempo dan peristiwa dalam sedjarah RI.* Jogjakarta: Kem. Penerangan, 1948,
       55 pp. (kitlv-m)

2691 *Tentang penjingkiran soldadoe tawanan Djepang serta bekas interniran Serikat;*
Siaran kilat. Djakarta: Kem. Penerangan, 1946, 4 pp. (kitlv-m)

2692 *Tentara dan negara.* Jogjakarta: Al-Djihad, ca. 1946, 23 pp.

2693 Thaib, Aziz
Islam dengan politik. Boekittinggi: Noesantara, 1946, 52 pp.

2694 Thaib, Aziz
'Merdeka'; Menentang NICA. Boekittinggi: Noesantara, ca. 1946, ?+36+76 pp. 3
vols. (kitlv-m)

2695 Thaib, Aziz
Mobilisasi pemoeda Islam. Boekittinggi: Gerakan Keboedajaan Indonesia
Soematera Barat, 1947, 19 pp.

2696 Thaib, Darwis
Toentoetan perdjoeangan. Padang Pandjang: Masjoemi, 1946, 47 pp.

2697 Thaib, Maisir
Sjahrir pegang kemoedi. Boekittinggi: Penjiaran Ilmoe, 1946, 50 pp. (kitlv-m)

2698 Thaib, Maisir and Darwis 'Abbas
Repoloesi Indonesia meletoes. Boekittinggi: Dasmar, ca. 1946, 32 pp. (kitlv-m)

2699 *Tipoe moeslihat Belanda.* Medan: Djabatan Penerangan Soematera Timoer, ca.
1946, 17 pp. (kitlv-m)

2700 Tirtoprodjo, Susanto
Nayaka lelana = Menteri bergerilya; Pengalaman kelana-gerilya waktu aksi militer
Belanda 2; Asli bahasa Jawa-tembang. Second edition. Yogyakarta: UP Indonesia,
1984, 131 pp. [First edition 1949.]

2701 Tirtoprodjo, Susanto
Nejaka lelana (Menteri Gerilja); Dalam bahasa Djawa bersjair disertai terdjemahannja
dalam bahasa Indonesia. Ca. 1949, 64 pp. [22]

2702 Tjan Tjoe Som
'De culturele positie der Chinezen in Indonesië', *Indonesië* 1 (1947-48):53-61.

2703 Tjantrik Mataram (ps. R.W. Dwidjosugondo)
Peranan ramalan Djojobojo dalam revolusi kita. Second edition. Bandung: Masa
Baru, 1950, 189 pp. [First edition 1948.]

2704 *Tjatatan sedjarah dari gerilja ke angkatan perang.* Second edition. Makassar: South
Sulawesi Publication Office, 1950, 51 pp.

2705 Tjoa Sik Ien
Masa'alah warga negara Indonesia. Jogjakarta: Kem. Penerangan, ca. 1947, 26 pp.
(kitlv-m)

2706 Tjoa Sik Ien
Pergerakan kaum buruh; Causerie dalam kongres Serikat Buruh Kehutanan, 16
Oktober 1949. Bukittinggi: Kem. Penerangan, 1949, 24 pp. (kitlv-m)

2707 Tjokroaminoto, Anwar and Soekiman
Tentara dan negara. Jogjakarta: Al-Djihad, 1946, 23 pp.

2708 Tjokrosisworo, Sudarjo
Sedjarah kilat pergerakan kemerdekaan Indonesia, 20 Mei 1908-1948. Solo: Kem. Penerangan, Dinas Propinsi Djawa Tengah, 1948, 22 pp.

2709 Toer, Pramoedya Ananta
Krandji dan Bekasi djatoeh. Djakarta: Pertjetakan Repoeblik Indonesia, 1947, 90 pp.

2710 *Towards the realisation of a real parliament*. Jogjakarta: Kem. Penerangan, ca. 1946, 8 pp. [49]

2711 Trimurti, S.K.
A.B.C. perdjuangan buruh. Jogjakarta: Partai Buruh Indonesia, 1948, 40 pp. (kitlv-m)

2712 *Tudjuan Partai Rakjat Pasundan*. Bandung: Visser, 1949. [4313, 4858]

2713 Tuhuteru, J.M.A.
Riwajat singkat terdirinja negara Pasoendan. Djakarta: Djawatan Penerangan Pemerintah, 1948, 36 pp.

2714 Tumbelaka, J.
Oeraian tentang perdjoangan oemoem di Soelawesi; Sedjak penjerahan Djepang hingga masa pemboebaran PNI. Makassar: Seroean Noesa, 1947, 38 pp. (kitlv-m)

2715 *Tuntutan baru Belanda; Belanda memberi ultimatum lagi! Republik menolak!; Siaran kilat*. N.p.: Djawatan Penerangan Propinsi Djawa Barat, 4 pp. (kitlv-m)

2716 *Two tasks of Allied forces in Indonesia fulfilled*. Jogjakarta: Ministry of Information, 1946, 17 pp. (kitlv-m)

2717 Ubani, B.A.
'The Indonesian question reviewed', *United Asia* 1-4 (December 1948):347-350.

2718 Ubani, B.A.
'Indonesia's fight for freedom', *United Asia* 1-5 (January-February 1949):413-417.

2719 Ubani, B.A.; O.K. Durrani and Mohd. Moein
The Indonesian struggle for independence. Aundh (India): Aundh Publishing Trust, 1946. [45, 75, 6199]

2720 *Undang-undang no. 22, tahun 1948 tentang pemerintah daerah*. Jogjakarta: Kem. Penerangan, 1948, 16 pp. (kitlv-m)

2721 *Undang-undang tentang pemerintahan Sumatera no. 10 tahun 1948; Undang-undang pokok tentang pemerintahan daerah; Pendjelasan; Notulen rapat anggauta DPA dengan PJM Wk Presiden, tanggal 8 April 1948*. Bukittinggi: Kantor Gubernur Propinsi Sumatera, ca. 1948, 37 pp.

2722 *Undang-undang tentang warga negara dan penduduk Negara Republik Indonesia*. Surabaja: Atmantara, ca. 1949, 21 pp. [49]

2723 Usman (Oesman), Sjarif
Sendjata rahsia perdjoeangan kita. Boekittinggi: Markas Komandemen Tentara Soematera, 1947, 53 pp.

2724 Usman, Sjarif
Hendak kemana nasionalisme Asia? Djakarta: Pustaka Mawar, 1949, 58 pp.
(kitlv-m)

2725 *Van onmondige tot burger; Een en ander over groei en achtergrond der
daerahvorming in de staat Oost-Indonesië.* Makassar: Ministerie van Voorlichting
van Oost-Indonesië, 1949, 31 pp.

2726 *Verklaring van de Perhimpoenan Indonesia aan het Nederlandsche volk.* Amsterdam:
Perhimpoenan Indonesia, 1945, 2 pp.

2727 *Verzameling van commentaren en beschouwingen rondom het accoord van de RTC;
Cultureel gedeelte/Kumpulan kupasan dan pemandangan sekitar persetudjuan KMB;
Bagian kebudajaan.* Djakarta, 1950, 30 pp.

2728 *Waarom Chineezen geen vreemde Oosterlingen meer willen zijn in Indonesië; Siaran
kilat.* Djakarta: Kem. Penerangan, 1946, 10 pp.

2729 Warouw, S.J.
Indonesië in Rijksverband. Soestdijk: n.n., 1946, 126 pp.

2730 *Wet op het Staatsburgerschap en het Staatsingezetenschap van de Republikeinse Staat
Indonesië.* Djakarta: Kem. Penerangan, 1946, 12 pp.

2731 *Wie zijn de staatsburgers van de Republiek? Siaran kilat.* Djakarta: Kem.
Penerangan, 1946, 8 pp. (ubl)

2732 Wikana
Organisatie; Pengoempoelan boeah pena. Second edition. Madioen: Oesaha
Penerbitan Tengara, 1947, 30 pp. (kitlv-m)

2733 Wikana
Satu dua pandangan Marxisme. Djokjakarta: Revolusioner, 1948, 23 pp.

2734 Wirjodihardjo, Saroso
Pengiriman beras ke India; Siaran kilat. Jogjakarta: Kem. Penerangan, 1946, 12 pp.
(kitlv-m)

2735 Wirjodihardjo, Wisaksono
Menghendaki negara Djawa Barat; Pidato. Bandung: Vorkink, 1948, 14 pp.

2736 Woerjaningrat, M.M. Daroesman
'De Indonesische nationale beweging', in: M. Ford-van Lennep and W.J. Ford
(eds), *Indonesiërs spreken*, pp. 197-215. 's-Gravenhage: Van Hoeve, 1947.

2737 Wojowasito
Tjongkak (pembangunan politik). Jogjakarta: Nasional, 1947. [49]

2738 Wongsonagoro
Aristocratie dan democratie; Pidato. Boekittinggi: Tjerdas, ca. 1946, 12 pp. (kitlv-
m)

2739 *Wij Indo Europeanen; Siaran kilat.* Djakarta: Kem. Penerangan, 1946, 8 pp.

2740 *Wij waarborgen godsdienstvrijheid! Siaran kilat.* Djakarta: Kem. Penerangan, 1946,
7 pp.

2741 Yamin, Moehammad
      Pembelaan Repoeblik Indonesia; Jaitoe risalah-politik berisi pendjelasan pembelaan
      Republik Indonesia atas kemerdekaan 100% dan penolakan segala bentoek-negara jang
      koerang dari kemerdekaan boelat. Boekittinggi: Noesantara, 1946, 107 pp.

2742 Yamin, M.
      Perdjoangan Tan Malaka. Boekittinggi: Noesantara, ca. 1946, 24 pp. [22, 40]

2743 Yamin, Muhammad
      Tan Malacca; Bapak Repoeblik Indonesia; Riwajat-politik seorang pengandjoer
      revolusioner jang berfikir, berdjoeang dan menderita membentoek negara Repoeblik
      Indonesia. Djakarta: Berita Indonesia, 1946, 48 pp.

2744 Yamin, Muhammad
      Tan Malaka; Bapa Repoeblik Indonesia. Boekit Tinggi: Penjiaran Ilmoe, 1946,
      12 pp.

2745 Yamin, Muhammad
      Tan Malaka; Bapak Republik Indonesia. N.p.: Moerba Berdjoeang, 1946, 18 pp.

2746 Yamin, Muhammad
      Pers merdeka. Jogjakarta: Badan Penerbit Nasional, 1948, 40 pp. (kitlv-m)

2747 Yamin, M.
      Sapta Dharma; Patriotisme Indonesia. Jogjakarta: Panitia Tahanan Politik, 1948,
      202 pp. (kitlv-m) [Second edition, *Sapta Dharma (patriotisme Indonesia)*, Medan:
      Andalas, 1950, 248 pp.; Third edition, *Sapta-Darma; Jaitu apologi-pembelaan*
      tindakan-politik tiga Djuli didepan Mahkamah Tentara Agung di Djokjakarta 1948
      dengan menguraikan nasionalisme-patriotik Indonesia atas dasar tiang tudjuh untuk
      mendjundjung kedaulatan Indonesia meliputi seluruh bangsa dan segenap tanah-air,
      Bukittinggi/Djakarta/Medan: Nusantara, 1957, 410 pp.]

2748 Yamin, Muh.
      'Penglaksanaan kemerdekaan sebagai hak bangsa', *Aliran Islam* 2-3 (January
      1949):190-193. (kitlv-m)

2749 Yatim, Mohammad Dien
      Sekitar politik, negara dan pemerintahan. Boekittinggi: Tjerdas, 1946, 80 pp.
      (kitlv-m)

2750 Zahari
      Kursus ideologie. Pematang Siantar: Poestaka Asmara, 1946, 56 pp. (kitlv-m)

2751 *Zakboek parlemen negara Pasundan; Tahun 1949.* Bandung: Mascotte, 1949,
      414 pp. (kitlv-m)

2752 *Zakboek parlemen Pasoendan 1948-1949.* Bandung: Mascotte, 1948, 286 pp.

2753 Zalecha
      Pulang dari tawanan. Medan: Suasana Baru, 1948, 80 pp.

2754 Zalecha, Maharami
      Pemuda 4 masa. Medan: Pustaka Nasional, 1949, 58 pp. [49]

2755 Zorab, G.
      'De zoogenaamde voorspellingen van Djojobojo, den Javaanschen Nostra-
      damus', *Tijdschrift voor Parapsychologie* 14 (1946):146-153.

Publications from the years 1945-1950
Dutch authors

2756 *2-10 RI, 1945-1949.* 1949. [114, 1216]

2757 *20 Juli 1947; De feiten.* Amsterdam: Vereniging Nederland-Indonesië, 1947, 40 pp.

2758 *20 Juli 1947; Het geweten.* Amsterdam: Vereniging Nederland-Indonesië, 1947, 32 pp.

2759 *37 AAT; Een jaar in de tropen.* 1949, 79 pp. (kitlv-smg)

2760 *100 pages Indonesian economics.* Batavia: Netherlands Indies Government, 1947, 95 pp.

2761 *1948 selajang pandang; Setahun perdjuangan kearah pembangunan, keamanan, ketenteraman dan kesedjahteraan Indonesia.* Djakarta: Regerings Voorlichtings Dienst, 1949, 44 pp.

2762 *De 15.000 gevangenen van de Republiek Djocja; Adhaesiebetuigers aan het woord.* Den Haag: Gemeenschappelijke Actie van Nederlandse Vrouwen, 1949, 51 pp.

2763 Aa, H. and F.R. Böhtlingk
      Undang-undang negara Republik Indonesia. Djakarta: Neijenhuis, 1946. 2 vols.

2764 *Aan onze repatrieerende landgenooten.* N.p.: n.n., 1946, 32 pp.

2765 'Actie Bantam; De geschiedenis van vier maanden bezetting', *Ons Leger* 33-10 (1949):4-8. (ubl)

2766 'De actie van 1-9 RI op 1 October 1946', *De Militaire Spectator* 116 (1947):62-69. (ubl)

2767 *Activities of the Netherlands Red Cross; Indonesian section.* Batavia: Indonesian Section Netherlands Red Cross, 1947, 17+37 pp.

2768 *Activities of the Republican Indonesians in the Netherlands Indies and abroad contrary to the truce agreement and the eighteen Renville principles.* Batavia: Topographical Service, 1948, 141 pp. (kitlv-smg)

2769 *Algemene coördinatie van het onderwijs.* Batavia: Departement van Onderwijs en Eredienst, 1947, 44 pp.

2770 Ansems, H.J. (ed.)
      Eén jaar W-Brigade; Gedenkboek uitgegeven ter gelegenheid van het éénjarig bestaan der W-Brigade. Tjiandjoer, 1947, 72 pp. (kitlv-smg)

2771   Asbeck, F.M. van
       Le statut actuel des pays non autonomes d'outre-mer. Paris: Librairie du Recueil
       Sirey, 1947, 127 pp.

2772   Asbeck, F.M. van
       'Indonesië in Azië', *Indonesië* 1 (1947-48):2-27.

2773   Averink, Annie
       'Vrouwen in de strijd voor een vrij Indonesië', *Politiek en Cultuur* 5 (1950):104-
       107.

2774   Bajetto, M.L.F.
       De katholieken en Indië. 's-Gravenhage: Stichting Libertas, 1946, 7 pp.

2775   Bakker, J.W.M.
       'Godsdienst en nationalisme in Indonesia', *Indisch Missietijdschrift* 32
       (1949):232-243.

2776   *De band Indië-Nederland.* N.p.: n.n., 1945, 20 pp.

2777   Bandy, Lou (ps. Lodewijk Dieben)
       Als ik in m'n klamboe lig te dromen. Utrecht: Buschmann, ca. 1947, 3 pp.

2778   Barents, J.
       'New trends in Dutch foreign policy', *Foreign Affairs* 25 (1947):328-333. (ubl)

2779   Barents, J.
       ' "Dikke" Unie of "dunne" Unie', *Socialisme en Democratie* 5 (1948):152-156. (ubl)

2780   Barents, J.
       'Ondoordacht; Buitenlandse kroniek', *Socialisme en Democratie* 6 (1949):53-61.
       (ubl)

2781   Baruch, F.
       'Indonesië tussen de naties', *Politiek en Cultuur* 2 (1947):201-203.

2782   Baruch, F.
       'Sociaal-democratie en koloniaal-imperialisme', *Politiek en Cultuur* 4 (1949):40-
       45.

2783   Bastiaans, W.Ch.J. (ed.)
       *Personalia van staatkundige eenheden (regering en volksvertegenwoordiging) in
       Indonesië (per 1 Sept. 1949).* N.p.: n.n., 1950, 168 pp.

2784   *Batavia in post-war days.* Batavia: Kappee, 1948, 48 pp.

2785   Baudet, H.
       Aperçu sociologique de la révolution indonésienne. Bruxelles, 1950, 15 pp.

2786   Bavinck, J.H.
       De soldaat in Indië. Den Haag: Bureau Protestants Geestelijke Verzorging der
       Koninklijke Landmacht, ca. 1947, 29 pp.

2787   Beaumont, J.J.A.
       'Kleine oorlog', *De Militaire Spectator* 115 (1946):423-427. (ubl)

2788 Beck, W.J.
Aan den rand van den krater; Nederland en Indonesië; Zooals het was en is en wezen zal. 's-Gravenhage: Van Stockum, 1947, 18 pp.

2789 Beerling, R.F.
'Hamlet zonder Hamlet; Nederland-Indonesië; Van actie I naar actie II', *Wending* 4 (1949):202-216.

2790 *Beknopte mededelingen van den president van de Javasche Bank betreffende de jaren 1941-1946; Uitgebracht in de buitengewone vergadering van aandeelhouders op 18 November 1946.* Amsterdam, 1946, 20 pp.

2791 Bemmelen, J.M. van
Indonesië en oorlogsmisdadigers; Wat moet een officier van het strafrecht weten? Twee inleidende colleges. Leiden: Universitaire Pers, 1947, 24 pp. (ubl)

2792 *Bergcultuurondernemingen op Java; Ondernemingsgegevens.* Batavia, 1947. [Various pagings.] (kitlv-m)

2793 Bess, Jack
Jongen in Indië, hou je maar haaks! Amsterdam: Muziek 'Smith', ca. 1947, 3 pp.

2794 Beuving, Anton and Louis Noiret
'Bataljonslied II-7 R.I.', in: Louis Noiret (ed.), *Voor onze soldaten*, pp. 34-35. Amsterdam: Louis Noiret's Music Publishing Company, ca. 1947.

2795 Beuving, Anton and Louis Noiret
'Bataljonslied II-12 R.I.', in: Louis Noiret (ed.), *Voor onze soldaten*, pp. 36-38. Amsterdam: Louis Noiret's Music Publishing Company, ca. 1947.

2796 Beuving, Anton and Louis Noiret
Jouw thuisfront. Amsterdam: Louis Noiret's Music Company, 1947. [unpaged]

2797 Beuving, Anton and Louis Noiret
'Het lied van de Tijgerbrigade', in: Louis Noiret (ed.), *Voor onze soldaten*, pp. 42-44. Amsterdam: Louis Noiret's Music Publishing Company, ca. 1947.

2798 Beuving, Anton and Louis Noiret
Meisjelief ik zal je schrijven; Opgedragen aan het zingende bataljon 2-7 RI. Amsterdam: Louis Noiret's Music Company, ca. 1947, 3 pp.

2799 *De bevrijders van Tangerang.* N.p.: Legervoorlichtingsdienst, 1946, 14 pp.

2800 'De bevrijders van Tangerang', *Ons Leger* 33-5 (1949):10-15. (ubl)

2801 *Bewaart de eenheid.* 's-Gravenhage: Nationaal Comité Handhaving Rijkseenheid, 1948, 15 pp.

2802 Beyma, U.H. van
'Kerkelijk perspectief in Indonesië', *Wending* 4 (1949):153-163.

2803 *Het 'BIO-besluit'.* Ca. 1948, 122 pp.

2804 *Birth of the so-called 'Republic Indonesia'.* 1945, 15 pp.

2805   Blom, N.S.
'Het rechtskarakter van de besluiten der conferentie van ministers van de Nederlands-Indonesische Unie', *Indonesië* 4 (1950-51):521-535.

2806   Boas, J.H.
Het Indonesische vraagstuk en de Britsche pers. Leiden: Sijthoff, 1946, 43 pp.

2807   Boddeke, B.J.
De strijd om volledige godsdienstvrijheid in de Grondwet van Oost-Indonesië. Batavia: Centraal Missie Bureau, 1949, 62 pp. (kitlv-m)

2808   Boddeke, Ludovicus
De missie in het vicariaat van Pontianak na de Japanse capitulatie. Bussum: n.n., 1950, 49 pp.

2809   Boeke, J.H.
'Economic conditions for Indonesian independence', *Pacific Affairs* 19 (1946):394-402.

2810   Boer, D.W.N. de
Wat iedereen moet weten met betrekking tot 'het Indonesische probleem'. 's-Gravenhage: Stichting Indië in Nood, Geen Uur te Verliezen!, 1946, 8 pp.

2811   Boer, D.W.N. de
Wat iedereen weten moet met betrekking tot het verband tusschen de 'Groot Aziatische gemeenschappelijke welvaartssfeer' en het extremistische standpunt van Soekarno c.s. 's-Gravenhage: Stichting Indië in Nood, Geen Uur te Verliezen!, 1946, 40 pp.

2812   Boer, W. den
Hoe de bevrijding van Nederland en Nederlandsch-Indië door de Nederlandsche regeering in Londen werd voorbereid. N.p.: n.n., 1947, 16 pp.

2813   Boland, B.J.
Zending, wat denkt gij van Indië? 's-Gravenhage: Boekencentrum, 1946, 86 pp.

2814   Boland, B.J.
Bij de geboorte van een staat; Iets over de voor-geschiedenis van de staat Pasoendan. Batavia: n.n., ca. 1948, 33 pp.

2815   Boland, B.J.
Op weg naar oecumenische samenwerking in Indonesië. Batavia, 1949, 54 pp. (kitlv-m)

2816   'De Bondowoso-affaire', *Militair Rechtelijk Tijdschrift* 42 (1949):109-121.

2817   Bongers, H.
Het testament van Sachidananda; Verhaal van een H.B.S.-er. 's-Gravenhage: Van Hoeve, 1949, 306 pp.

2818   Bot, L.J.
Nederland in de mist. Amsterdam: Nederlandse Bond van Vrije Socialisten, 1947, 31 pp.

2819 Both, Pieter
Plan Pieter Both; Conceptvoorstel voor een Rijksplan; Een wereldexperiment in staatkundige vernieuwing, economische ordening en sociale verbetering. Groningen: Niemeijer, 1948, 266 pp.

2820 Brandt, Willem (ps. W.S.B. Klooster)
Demarcatielijn. 's-Gravenhage: Van Hoeve, 1947, 140 pp.

2821 *Bren naar voren partisanen! Het OVW-bataljon 1-12 RI op Java.* Voorwoord van Benjamin Hendrik Erné. Groningen/Batavia: Wolters, 1949, 240 pp.

2822 Brink, E.A.B.J. ten (ed.)
Een bataljon trok voorbij; De belevenissen van een OVW-bataljon, 1944-1948. Eindhoven: Schäfer, 1948, 157 pp. (kitlv-smg)

2823 Brink, H. van den
Een eisch van recht; De koloniale verhouding als vraagstuk getoetst. Amsterdam: Kirchner, 1946, 86 pp.

2824 Brix, W.J.G.
Waarom moeten Nederland en Oost-Indië één zijn? Deventer: Van Hoeve, 1946, 40 pp.

2825 Broek, J.O.M.
'Man and resources in the Netherlands Indies', *Far Eastern Quarterly* 5-2 (February 1946):121-131.

2826 Brouwer, A.M. (ed.)
Tussen sawahs en bergen; Het leven van de soldaat in de Tijger-brigade. Semarang: De Locomotief, 1948, 264 pp.

2827 Brouwer, A.M.
'De houding van de Nederlandse soldaat in de tropen', *Het Gemeenebest* 9 (1948-49):354-368. (ubl)

2828 Brouwer, J.
Ontwaakt het Oosten? Een bijdrage tot het leren kennen van den Javaan. Hilversum: De Atlas, 1945, 33 pp.

2829 Brouwer, J.
Overpeinzingen van een politieken patholoog-anatoom. Hilversum: De Atlas, 1945, 22 pp.

2830 Brouwer, K.J.
Door het geloof alleen; Een rapport en een appèl; Verslag van een reis door Indonesië, Februari-Juli 1948. Oegstgeest: Zendingsbureau, 1948, 50 pp.

2831 Brouwer, K.J.
'Zelfstandigheid van Indonesische kerken', *Indonesië* 2 (1948-49):189-199.

2832 'De brug bij Tjileungsir, West-Java; Of drie keer is scheepsrecht', *De Militaire Spectator* 117 (1948):471-472. (ubl)

2833 'De brug over de Tjitaroem, nabij Batoedjadjar', *De Militaire Spectator* 117 (1948):592-597. (ubl)

2834 Brugmans, I.J.
'Trois siècles et demi de relations hollando-indonésiennes', *Politique Etrangère* 12 (September 1947):409-420. (ubl)

2835 Brunsveld van Hulten, E.
Rapport over de Japansche invloed op de Merdeka-beweging en de gebeurtenissen in de Augustusdagen. 1946. [45]

2836 Bruyn, William F. de (ps. W.K.H. Feuilletau de Bruyn]
The truth about the Indonesian Republic. The Hague: Hofstad, 1946, 38 pp.

2837 *Bijlage Gedenkboek 7 December Divisie 'Wij werden geroepen'.* 's-Gravenhage: Van Hoeve, ca. 1950, 17 pp. (kitlv-smg)

2838 *Bijzonder welvaartsplan 1949.* Buitenzorg: Dep. van Economische Zaken en Landbouw-Visserij, 1949, 116 pp.

2839 *Cease-fire and political discussions with the Security Council's Committee of Good Offices on the Indonesian question.* Batavia: Kolff, 1948, 188 pp.

2840 *Het Christelijk-Historische standpunt inzake de grondwetsherzieningen en het Indië-beleid.* 's-Gravenhage: CHU, 1946, 3 pp. [45]

2841 Christen, P.N.
Indië en wij. Barneveld, 1946, 15 pp.

2842 *Chronologisch overzicht van de ontwikkeling van het Indonesische vraagstuk in de nationale politiek (14 Augustus 1945-1 Januari 1949).* 's-Gravenhage: Regerings Voorlichtings Dienst, 1949, 77 pp.

2843 Cohen Stuart, A.B.
'De Nederlands-Indonesische kwestie en de Veiligheidsraad', *Socialisme en Democratie* 5 (1948):10-23.

2844 Cohen Stuart, A.B.
'Welvaartszorg in Indonesië', *Socialisme en Democratie* 6 (1949):183-189. (ubl)

2845 Cohen Stuart, J.W.Th.
'Wording van de Staat Oost-Indonesië', in: Nooteboom, C.; H.C.J. Gunning and J.W.Th. Cohen Stuart, *Oost-Indonesië*, pp. 19-44. Groningen/Batavia: Wolters, 1948.

2846 Cohen Stuart-Franken, M.
Van Indië tot Indonesië; Voor, in en na het kamp. Amsterdam: Ten Have, 1947, 128 pp.

2847 Colijn, A.W.
Japan en het extremisme. 's-Gravenhage: Van Stockum, 1946, 24 pp.

2848 *Commissarissen-Generaal over de ontwerp-overeenkomst.* Batavia: Regeerings Voorlichtings Dienst, 1946, 17 pp.

2849 *Commissie-Generaal voor Nederlandsch-Indië; Eerste tot en met zevende verslag; September '46-Juli '47.* [45]

2850 *Communism in the Indonesian Republic.* ?Netherlands Information Bureau, ca. 1947, 61 pp. + appendices.

2851 *Communism in the Republic of Indonesia.* New York: Netherlands Information Bureau, 1948, 8 pp. [6297]

2852 *Het communisme in de Indonesische Republiek.* N.p.: n.n., 1948, 29 pp. (kitlv-smg)

2853 *Conclusie van het Coördinatie-College Nederland-Indonesië (September-October 1948-besprekingen).* Batavia: Secretariaat Coördinatie-College Deviezen-instituut, 1948, 63 pp.

2854 *Conclusies en resoluties der conferentie te Malino.* Batavia: Algemeen Regeerings Commissariaat voor Borneo en de Groote Oost, 1946, 23 pp.

2855 *De conferentie te Denpasar, 7-24 December 1946.* Batavia: Algemeen Regeerings Commissariaat voor Borneo en de Groote Oost, 1947, 115+52 pp. 2 vols.

2856 *Conferentie/Permoesjawaratan Malino, 15-24 Juli 1946; Resoluties en/dan moties.* Batavia, 1946, 31 pp. (kitlv-m)

2857 *Constitutionele bepalingen in Indonesië sedert 18 Augustus 1945.* 's-Gravenhage: Ministerie voor Uniezaken en Overzeese Rijksdelen, 1950, 97 pp.

2858 Cort van der Linden, R.A.D.
Bestrijding van de Leidsche professoren die het ontwerp van Cheribon aanbevelen en onze rechten prijsgeven. 's-Gravenhage: Van Stockum, 1946, 5 pp.

2859 Cort van der Linden, R.A.D.
Nederlandsch-Indië; Vijf artikelen over rechtsverzaking en gezagsafstand in Indië. 's-Gravenhage: Van Stockum, 1946, 23 pp.

2860 Cort van der Linden, R.A.D.
De tijger die het Rijk vaneenrijt; Vijf artikelen over Nederlandsch-Indië. 's-Gravenhage: Van Stockum, 1946, 16 pp.

2861 Cort van der Linden, R.A.D.
Linggadjati; Waar het om gaat. 's-Gravenhage: Van Stockum, 1947, 8 pp.

2862 Cort van der Linden, R.A.D.
De rede van Churchill in het Lagerhuis over Britsch-Indië, December 1946; Eene vergelijking met Nederlandsch-Indië en met de tegenkanting in ons land tegen de Regeeringspolitiek. 's-Gravenhage: Van Stockum, 1947, 11 pp.

2863 Court, Alb. de la
Paedagogische richtlijnen voor Indonesië. Deventer: Van Hoeve, 1945, 75 pp.

2864 Court, J.F.H. Alb. de la
Het vraagstuk Indonesië. Deventer: W. van Hoeve, 1945, 68 pp.

2865 Court, Alb. de la
Postwar education in Indonesia. 1946. [...]

2866 Court, J.F.H.A. de la
'Some proposals for postwar education in Indonesia', *Far Eastern Quarterly* 5 (February 1946):152-161.

2867 Court, Alb. de la
'De betekenis van de Ronde Tafel Conferentie', *De Nieuwe Stem* 4 (1949):684-687. (ubl)

2868   Court, J.F.H. Alb. de la
        Soal Indonesia. Bandung: Pusaka, 1949, 80 pp. (kitlv-m)

2869   Cowan, H.K.J.
        'Indische rechtsbedeling na de bevrijding', *Indonesië* 2 (1948-49):64-94.

2870   Cox, P.A.
        'Acties van kleinere eenheden in Nederlandsch-Indië', *De Militaire Spectator* 115
        (1946):414-422. (ubl)

2871   Damsté, Onno and B. Jilderda
        *Nederland en Indonesië in de 20e eeuw; Een beknopte behandeling van de
        ontwikkeling der staatkundige verhoudingen.* Groningen: Noordhoff, Batavia: Kolff,
        1947, 104 pp.

2872   Damsté, Onno and B. Jilderda
        Nederland-Indonesia dalam abad kedua puluh. Djakarta: Kolff, 1949, 108 pp. [40]

2873   *The danger in the Netherlands East Indies.* 's-Gravenhage: Stichting Indië in Nood,
        1946, 8 pp. (riod)

2874   Dassen, J.M.H.
        De staatsrechtelijke verhouding tusschen Nederland en de overzeesche gebiedsdelen.
        Maastricht: Leiter-Nypels, 1946, 37 pp.

2875   *Den Pasar, Pontianak; De geboorte van twee staten.* Batavia: Kolff, 1946, 11 pp.

2876   *Den Pasar, Pontianak; Lahirnja doea negara.* Batavia: Kolff, 1946, 11 pp.

2877   Derksen, J.B.D. and J. Tinbergen
        'Berekeningen over de economische beteekenis van Nederlandsch-Indië voor
        Nederland', *Maandschrift van het CBS* 40 (1945):210-216.

2878   Derksen, J.B.D. and J. Tinbergen
        *Calculations about the economic significance of the Netherlands Indies for the
        Netherlands.* New York: Netherlands Information Bureau, 1947. [3587]

2879   *Desnoods te voet; Een foto-reportage van de zuiverings-acties ondernomen door de
        Mariniersbrigade, 19 December-31 December 1948.* Soerabaja: Kolff, 1949.
        [unpaged]

2880   *Dit vroeg Indië; Indië's wenschen vastgelegd tot op het moment, waarop de Japanners
        kwamen.* 's-Gravenhage: Stichting Indië in Nood, Geen Uur te Verliezen!, 1946,
        12 pp.

2881   *Documents reveal; The government of the Indonesian Republic and the
        implementation of the so-called 'Renville-agreement'.* 1948, 103 pp.

2882   *Documents submitted to the Committee of Good Offices by the Netherlands delegation
        in the period from the beginning of the negotiations up to 17 January 1948.* Batavia:
        Kolff, 1948, 188 pp. (kitlv-m)

2883   Dool, T. van (ed.)
        *In een notedop; De nieuwe demobilisatievoorzieningen voor militairen van de
        Koninklijke Landmacht, die werkelijke dienst in Indië hebben verricht.* Fourth
        printing. 's-Gravenhage: Legervoorlichtingsdienst, 1950, 188 pp. [First edition
        1948.]

2884 Dool, T. van and G. Blokhuis
      De nieuwe demobilisatievoorzieningen in een notedop. Den Haag: Legervoor-
      lichtingsdienst, 1948, 136 pp. (ubl)

2885 Doorn, C.L. van
      Nog is het dag; De toekomst van de zending in Indonesië. 's-Gravenhage: Boeken-
      centrum, 1948, 70 pp.

2886 Doorn, C.L. van
      'De organisatie van het Javaanse dorp in de Republiek', *Indonesië* 2 (1948-
      49):283-284.

2887 Doorn, C.L. van
      'Het eigene als criterium; Sociaal-economische politiek in Indonesië', *Wending* 4
      (1949):125-136.

2888 Doorn, J.A.A. van
      'De Indo-Europeaan in het nieuwe Indonesië', *Het Gemenebest* 9 (1949):290-305.
      (ubl)

2889 Dootjes, F.J.J.
      Kroniek 1941-1946. Amsterdam: Oostkust van Sumatra Instituut, 1948, 192 pp.

2890 Dootjes, F.J.J.
      Kroniek 1947. Amsterdam: Oostkust van Sumatra Instituut, 1949, 182 pp.

2891 Dootjes, F.J.J.
      Kroniek 1948 en 1949. Amsterdam: Oostkust van Sumatra Instituut, 1950,
      292 pp.

2892 *Draft Constitution of the Republic of the United States of Indonesia.* The Hague,
      1949, 48 pp. (kb)

2893 *Drie dagen voor Indië; Lezingen gehouden te Groningen op 24, 25 en 26 Februari
      1947 in het kader van de interacademiale lezingencyclus van het Algemeen Studen-
      tencomité voor Overzeese Gebiedsdelen.* Groningen: Groninger Studentencommissie
      voor Overzeese Gebiedsdelen, 1947, 78 pp.

2894 Dussel, Wim
      Heklichtjes; Humoreskes uit het mariniersleven in Indië. Rotterdam: Wyt, ca. 1948,
      160 pp.

2895 *The Dutch in the Far East; Proud of their achievements, confident in the future.*
      Rotterdam/Amsterdam: Rotterdamsche Bankvereeniging, 1946, 43 pp.

2896 Dijk, R. van (ed.)
      Wetten en verordeningen betreffende het staatsrecht van Nederlandsch-Indië.
      's-Gravenhage: Van Hoeve, 1947, 327 pp.

2897 *Economic and financial survey of Indonesia.* Batavia: ?Department of Economic
      Affairs, 1948, 98 pp.

2898 *The economic situation in Indonesia.* The Hague: Netherlands Government
      Information Service, 1948, 32 pp.

2899 *The economic situation in Indonesia in 1948.* Batavia: n.n., 1949, 43 pp. (ubl)

2900　De economische toekomst van Indonesië. 's-Gravenhage: Centrum voor Staat-kundige Vorming, ca. 1947, 40 pp.

2901　De economische toestand van Indonesië, medio 1948-najaar 1949. Batavia: Departement van Economische Zaken, 1949. [unpaged] (kitlv-m)

2902　Economische voorlichting over Indonesië en het Verre Oosten, 1 September 1947-1 Juli 1948. 's-Gravenhage: Blommendaal, 1948, 290 pp.

2903　Economische voorlichting over het Verre Oosten, 1 Mei-1 September 1947. 's-Gravenhage: Blommendaal, 1947, 183 pp.

2904　Education in Indonesia before, during and after the Pacific War. Batavia: Department of Education, 1948, 20 pp. (ubl)

2905　Het Eerste Eskadron Pantserwagens, Regiment Huzaren van Boreel 10 Januari 1946-22 October 1949. Amsterdam: Becht, 1949, 171 pp.

2906　Eigeman, J.A.
De bouw van het nieuwe Koninkrijk; Staatsrechtelijke en staatkundige studie. 's-Gravenhage: De Kern, 1946, 207 pp.

2907　Ende, E.C. van den
Hoe verder met Indië? Analyse van het Indonesische probleem. 's-Gravenhage/Rijswijk: Blommendaal, 1946, 189 pp.

2908　Engelbrecht, E.M.L.
Algemene verordeningen van Indonesië. N.p.: n.n., ca.1949, 188 pp.

2909　Engers, J.F.
Het Indonesische vraagstuk en de Amerikaansche pers. Leiden: Sijthoff, 1946, 36 pp.

2910　Enthoven, K.L.J.
'Staatkundige hervormingen in en met betrekking tot Indonesië', Indonesië 3 (1949-50):429-446.

2911　Erk, J.P. van
'De berechting van Indië-deserteurs', De Militaire Spectator 117 (1948):356-359.

2912　Evertsen, W.
Vrijwilligers voor. Amsterdam: n.n., 1945, 13 pp. (riod)

2913　Fabricius, Johan
Hoe ik Indië terugvond. 's-Gravenhage: Leopold, 1947, 205 pp.

2914　Fabricius, Johan
Java revisited. London/Toronto: Heinemann, 1947, 156 pp.

2915　Fallentin, M.C.
Onder de klamboe. Den Haag: Voorhoeve, 1948, 28 pp.

2916　Federale Conferentie Bandung 1948-1949; Praeadviezen; Afdelingsverslagen. Many vols.

2917　Feiten en standpunten inzake Nederlandsch-Indië. 's-Gravenhage: Stichting Indië in Nood, Geen Uur te Verliezen!, 1946, 11 pp.

2918 Feuilletau de Bruyn, W.K.H.
Indië's toekomst; Richtlijnen voor het Nederlandsche politieke, economische en sociale beleid over zee na den Tweeden Wereldoorlog. 's-Gravenhage: Stols, 1945, 126 pp.

2919 Feuilletau de Bruyn, W.K.H.
Het politieke en militaire beleid van de Nederlandsche regeering ten aanzien van Nederlandsch-Indië. 's-Gravenhage: Haagsche Drukkerij en Uitgevers Maatschappij, 1945, 27 pp.

2920 Feuilletau de Bruyn, W.K.H.
Herziening van de politieke en staatsrechtelijke structuur van Nederland en zijn gebied over zee na den oorlog. 's-Gravenhage: Stols, 1946, 105 pp.

2921 Feuilletau de Bruyn, W.K.H.
Het oude en het nieuwe leger. 's-Gravenhage: Van Stockum, 1946, 66 pp.

2922 Feuilletau de Bruyn, W.K.H.
Welk aandeel heeft Dr. Van Mook gehad in de gezagsschemering in Nederlandsch-Indië? 's-Gravenhage: Van Stockum, 1946, 31 pp.

2923 Feuilletau de Bruyn, W.K.H.
Naar den financieelen en economischen chaos in Nederland. 's-Gravenhage: Nationaal Comité Handhaving Rijkseenheid, 1947, 39 pp.

2924 Feuilletau de Bruyn, W.K.H.
Naar de Sovjet Republiek Indonesia. 's-Gravenhage: Nationaal Comité Handhaving Rijkseenheid, 1947, 48 pp.

2925 Feuilletau de Bruyn, W.K.H. (W.F. de Bruyn)
The rising Soviet star over Indonesia. 's-Gravenhage: National Committee 'Unity of Kingdom', 1947, 27 pp.

2926 Feuilletau de Bruyn, W.K.H.
Het zelfbeschikkingsrecht in de practijk in Oost-Indonesië. N.p.: n.n., 16 pp.

2927 Fharensbach, Mevr.
Het Roode Kruis verovert Soekaboemi. Buitenzorg: n.n., 1946, 11 pp.

2928 *Financial and economic agreement (between the Kingdom of the Netherlands and the government of the Republik Indonesia Serikat).* 1949, 32 pp. (kitlv-m)

2929 Flink, J.
'De guerilla-oorlog in heuvel- en bergterrein op West-Java', *De Militaire Spectator* 117 (1948):671-679.

2930 Ford-van Lennep, M. and W.J. Ford (eds)
Indonesiërs spreken. 's-Gravenhage: Van Hoeve, 1947, 228 pp.

2931 François, J.H.
37 jaar Indonesische vrijheids-beweging. 's-Graveland: De Driehoek, 1947, 33 pp.

2932 Friedericy, H.J.
'Indonesian problems', *Annals of the American Academy of Political and Social Science* 270 (July 1950):133-139. (ubl)

2933	*From Empire to Union; An introduction to the history of Netherlands-Indonesian relations.* The Hague: Netherlands Ministry for Overseas Territories, Public Relations Department, 1947, 46 pp.

2934	Fruin, Th.A.
	De toekomstige status van Indonesië. Leiden: St Lucas Society, 1945, 22 pp.

2935	Fruin, Th.A.
	De economische politiek van het nieuwe Indonesië. Amsterdam: Vereniging Nederland-Indonesië, ca. 1948, 18 pp.

2936	Fruin, Th.A.
	'De ontwerp-overeenkomst van Linggadjati in het licht der voorafgaande onderhandelingen', *Socialisme en Democratie* 3 (1946):337-348. (ubl)

2937	Fruin, Th.A.
	Het economische aspect van het Indonesische vraagstuk. Amsterdam: Vrij Nederland, 1947, 114 pp.

2938	Fruin, Th.A.
	De worsteling om een nieuwe verhouding tussen Nederland en Indonesië. Amsterdam: Arbeiderspers, 1948, 86 pp.

2939	Fruin, Th.A.
	Dari ekonomi pendjadjahan kearah ekonomi kebangsaan. Djakarta: Djambatan, 1949, 49 pp.

2940	Frijling, J.
	'Slavernij'; Een stukje geschiedenis der Indische buitengewesten, voor wie dat niet overbodig mocht zijn. 's-Gravenhage: Comité Handhaving Rijkseenheid, 1947, 16 pp.

2941	*Gadja Merah op Bali en Lombok.* Batavia: Kolff, ca. 1948, 48 pp.

2942	Gallandat Huet, G.
	'Verrichtingen van het derde Nederlandse mijnenveeg-flottielje', *Marineblad* 58 (1947-48):245-256. (ubl)

2943	'De gebieden overzee', in: *Wat zeggen ze er van? C.H.U. 9 Juli 1908-9 Juli 1948,* pp. 145-229. Den Haag: Christelijk-Historische Unie, 1948.

2944	*Gedenkboek Technische Werkplaatsen van het Koninklijk Nederlands Indonesisch Leger; Artillerie-inrichtingen 1923-1942; Leger-productie-bedrijven 1947-1949.* Bandung: Van Dorp, 1949, 124 pp.

2945	Geemert, J. van and C. Sipkes (eds)
	118 jaar Jagers. Batavia: Het Jagertje, 1947, 48 pp. (kitlv-smg)

2946	Geemert, J. van and C. Sipkes (eds)
	Strijd en opbouw; 119 jaar Jagers. Batavia: Kolff, 1948, 56 pp.

2947	Geest, P. van der and G.M. van Rossum (eds)
	Met 3-3 RI in de tropen; Korpsgeschiedenis 3-3 RI. Medan: Deli Courant, 1949, 135 pp. (kitlv-smg)

2948 Gemmink, Johan
'Churchill en Logemann', in: *Politieke kroniek* 1, pp. 189-195. Utrecht: Den Boer, 1946.

2949 Gerbrandy, P.S.
Het roer moet om! Radiorede. 's-Gravenhage: Voorlichtingsdienst Handhaving Rijkseenheid, 1947, 4 pp.

2950 Gerbrandy, P.S.; J.W. Meyer Ranneft and Ch.J.I.M. Welter
Sinister page in U.S. history. 1949. [45]

2951 Gerretson, C.
'Organisatie van het Koninkrijk of ontbinding van den staat?', *De Gids* 108-9 (October 1945):34-46.

2952 Gerretson, C.
Indië onder dictatuur; De ondergang van het Koninkrijk uit de beginselen verklaard. Amsterdam/Brussel: Elsevier, 1946, 152 pp.

2953 Gerretson, C.
Om Koninkrijk en Constitutie; Rede. 's-Gravenhage: Nationaal Comité Handhaving Rijkseenheid, 1948, 48 pp.

2954 Gerretson, C.
Tilanus contra de Christelijk-Historische Unie; Democratische beginselpartij of autoritaire leiderspartij? Utrecht: Libertas, 1950, 24 pp.

2955 Gideonse, H.D.
American policy in Indonesia. 's-Gravenhage: Sijthoff, 1949, 12 pp.

2956 Gideonse, Harry D.
De Indonesische kwestie; Basis voor correspondentie van Nederlanders met buitenlanders. N.p.: n.n., ca. 1950, 16 pp.

2957 *Gids voor het academiejaar 1949-1950/Pedoman untuk tahun akademia 1949-1950.* Batavia: Universiteit van Indonesië/Universitas Indonesia, 1949, 277 pp. (kitlv-m)

2958 Gobée, E.
'De Masjoemi', *De Nieuwe Stem* 2 (1947):175-184.

2959 Goens, R. van
De schaduwhand; Spook- en kerstverhaal uit Bandoeng anno 1945. 's-Gravenhage/ Batavia: Van Goor, 1946, 188 pp.

2960 Goes van Naters, M. van der
'Tussen einde en begin', *Socialisme en Democratie* 6 (1949):705-709. (ubl)

2961 Goes van Naters, M. van der
'Verklaring', *Socialisme en Democratie* 6 (1949):174. (ubl)

2962 Goossens, L.A.M.
Van man tot man. Radiopraatjes Katholiek Thuisfront. Amsterdam: Diligentia, 1947, 64 pp.

2963 Gooyer, A.C. de
Op wacht in de dessa. Baarn: Bosch en Keuning, 1949, 205 pp.

2964   Gorter, W.S.A.N.
       *Arbitrage en Indonésie? (par un Hollandais). Arbitration in Indonesia? (by a
       Dutchman).* 's-Gravenhage: Van Stockum, 1947, 12 pp.

2965   Gorter, W.S.A.N.
       Open brief aan den Minister-President. 's-Gravenhage, 1947, 2 pp. (uba)

2966   Goudoever, W.A. van
       *Malino maakt historie; Een overzichtelijke bewerking van notulen en tekstueele
       redevoeringen ter conferentie van Malino 15-25 Juli 1946.* Batavia: Regeerings
       Voorlichtings Dienst, 1946, 63 pp.

2967   Goudoever, W.A. van
       *Denpasar bouwt een huis; Een overzichtelijke bewerking van notulen en tekstueele
       redevoeringen ter conferentie van Denpasar, 7-24 December 1946.* Batavia:
       Regeerings Voorlichtings Dienst, 1947, 106 pp.

2968   Goudoever, W.A. van
       Kort overzicht van het behandelde ter conferentie te Den Pasar. Batavia: Kolff, 1947,
       85 pp.

2969   Graaf, Th.M.J. de
       'Beschouwing over het laatste Indonesië-debat', *Katholiek Staatkundig
       Maandschrift* 3 (1949-50):661-664. (kb)

2970   Graaf, Th.M.J. de
       'Korte nabeschouwing op het Indonesië-debat in de Tweede Kamer', *Katholiek
       Staatkundig Maandschrift* 3 (1949-50):429-431. (kb)

2971   Graaf, Th.M.J. de
       'De Nederlands-Indonesische Unie', *Katholiek Staatkundig Maandschrift* 3 (1949-
       50):836-843. (kb)

2972   Graaff, E.A. van de
       'Indonesia's foreign trade, July 1946-June 1947, inclusive', *Economic Review of
       Indonesia* 2-1 (February 1948):23-26. (kitlv-m)

2973   Graaff, E.A. van de
       *Meerjarige overzichten van de in- en uitvoer van Indonesië, 1936/1941, 1946/1948 /
       Ichtisar import dan export Indonesia mengenai beberapa tahun, 1936/1941,
       1946/1948.* Batavia: Departement van Economische Zaken, 1949, 65 pp.

2974   'Grepen uit den huidigen strijd in Indië', *De Militaire Spectator* 114 (1945):78-84.

2975   Groen, C.
       Gedachten over een christelijk Rijksbeleid. Franeker: Wever, 1949, 65 pp.

2976   *Grondslagen van de Nederlands-Indonesische Unie.* Amsterdam: Dr Wiardi
       Beckman Stichting, 1949, 16 pp.

2977   *De Grondwet van de Republiek Indonesia; Officieel afgekondigd op 18 Augustus
       1945.* Vertaald door R.L. Mellema. Amsterdam, 1947, 8 pp. (kit)

2978   Groot, Paul de
       Het militaire avontuur in Indonesië. Amsterdam: Communistische Partij Neder-
       land (De Waarheid), 1947, 20 pp.

2979 Gruyter, P. de
Indonesië in de pers; Het 'Nederlandsche' standpunt. Oegstgeest: n.n., 1946, 16 pp.

2980 *Het 'Haags overleg' (September-October 1948).* 's-Gravenhage: BFO, 1948. 2 vols.
[Various pagings.]

2981 [Haasse, Hella S.]
Oeroeg. Amsterdam: Vereeniging ter Bevordering van de Belangen des Boek-
handels, 1948, 79 pp. [Many reprints; 42th printing, Amsterdam: Uitgeverijen
Singel 262, 1995, 122 pp.]

2982 Haccoû, J.F.
De Indische exportproducten; Hun beteekenis voor Indië en Nederland. Leiden:
Stenfert Kroese, 1947, 12+256 pp.

2983 Haccoû, J.F.
Nederland en Indonesië; Door samenwerking tot welvaart en ontwikkeling. Leiden:
Stenfert Kroese, 1947, 31 pp.

2984 Haccoû, J.F.
The Netherlands and Indonesia; Through cooperation to prosperity and development.
Leyden: Stenfert Kroese, 1949, 32 pp. [34]

2985 Haccoû, J.F.
'De monetaire sanering in Indonesië', *Economisch-Statistische Berichten* 35
(1950):654-657.

2986 Hamel, J.A. van
Nederland, Indonesië en het recht; Rede. N.p.: Nederlandse Vereniging voor
Internationaal Recht, 1949, 4 pp.

2987 Hardeman, J.A.H.
'Leger-pioniers', *De Militaire Spectator* 116 (1947):627-634.

2988 Hartingsveldt, N.W. van
Het Indië-beleid; Van 'koloniaal' tot 'progressief' bewind. 's-Gravenhage: Nationaal
Comité Handhaving Rijkseenheid, 1948, 77 pp.

2989 Has, Jan P. and Louis Noiret
'Wij gaan naar het land van de palmen', in: Louis Noiret (ed.), *Voor onze
soldaten*, pp. 59-61. Amsterdam: Louis Noiret's Music Publishing Company, ca.
1947.

2990 Has, Jan P. and Louis Noiret
'Wij zijn de jongens van "De Zevende December"' , in: Louis Noiret (ed.), *Voor
onze soldaten*, pp. 39-41. Amsterdam: Louis Noiret's Music Publishing
Company, ca. 1947.

2991 *Hasil-hasil Konperensi Medja Bundar sebagaimana diterima pada persidangan umum
jang kedua; Terlangsung tanggal 2 Nopember 1949 di Ridderzaal di kota 's-Gravenhage.* 's-Gravenhage: Sekretariat-Umum Konperensi Medja Bundar, 1949,
127+61 pp.

2992   *Hasil-hasil konperensi menteri Uni Indonesia-Nederland jang kedua; Diadakan di 's-Gravenhage, tanggal 20-29 Nopember 1950.* Djakarta: Sekretariat Uni Indonesia-Nederland, 1950, 200 pp.

2993   Heemstra, J.
       De ambtenaar bij het Binnenlands Bestuur in Indonesië en de souvereiniteitsoverdracht. 's-Gravenhage: Vereniging van Ambtenaren bij het Binnenlands Bestuur in Indonesië, 1949, 38 pp.

2994   Hellings, P.J.
       'De missionaris en de politiek', *Indisch Missietijdschrift* 29 (1946):165-173. (ubl)

2995   Helsdingen, C.C. van
       Cri de coeur; Rede. Batavia: Christelijk Staatkundige Partij, 1946, 30 pp.

2996   Helsdingen, C.C. van
       De openlegging van Borneo; Een fantastiese suggestie? Delft: Delftsche Uitgevers Maatschappij, 1946, 38 pp.

2997   Helsdingen, C.C. van
       'De Indonesische tragedie', *Antirevolutionaire Staatkunde* 19 (1949):361-378.

2998   Helsdingen, W.H. van
       'De nieuwe Rijksgedachte', in: *Democratie; Achtergronden en mogelijkheden,* pp. 171-190. Amsterdam: De Bezige Bij, 1946.

2999   Helsdingen, W.H. van
       De plaats van Nederlandsch Indië in het Koninkrijk; Stemmen van overzee. Leiden: Brill, 1946, 306+128 pp. 2 vols.

3000   Helsdingen, W.H. van
       'The Netherlands-Indonesian agreement', *Pacific Affairs* 20 (1947):184-187.

3001   Helsdingen, W.H. van
       Op weg naar een Nederlandsch-Indonesische Unie; Stemmen van hier en ginds. 's-Gravenhage: Van Hoeve, 1947, 568 pp.

3002   Hendriksen, H.J.M.
       Ik beschuldig de KVP. N.p.: Stichting Voorlopig Katholiek Comité van Actie, 1947, 24 pp.

3003   Hendriksen, H.J.M.
       KVP, rechts omkeert marsch! Delft: Brouwer, 1947, 24 pp.

3004   *Herinneringsalbum 1e Infanterie Brigadegroep C-Divisie '7 December'.* Leiden: Sijthoff, 1948-51, 92+106+96+119 pp. 4 vols.

3005   Hertog, Ary den
       Intermezzo in Batavia; Roman. Leiden: Sijthoff, 1946, 237 pp.

3006   Hertog, A. den
       'De landing van de Nederlandsche troepen op Lombok', *De Militaire Spectator* 115 (1946):80-87.

3007   Hertog, A. den
       'Training der Lichte Infanterie Bataljons op Malakka', *De Militaire Spectator* 115 (1946):279-284.

3008 *De Hervormde Kerk over het Indonesische vraagstuk; Synodale boodschap.* 's-Gravenhage: Boekencentrum, 1946, 8 pp.

3009 Heshusius, C.A.
'Het gebruik van tanks in Nederlands-Indië', *De Militaire Spectator* 116 (1947): 348-353, 515-518, 557-569, 715-728; 117 (1948):109-117.

3010 Hettinga, S.
De 'Repoeblik Indonesia'; Drieërlei houding. Leiden: Sijthoff, 1946, 24 pp.

3011 Heuvel, M. van den
'Het Indisch Instructie-Bataljon', *De Militaire Spectator* 115 (1946):379-386.

3012 Heuvel, M. van den
'De LIB's bestemd voor Nederlandsch-Indië', *De Militaire Spectator* 115 (1946):307-315.

3013 Hidding, K.A.H.
'Mogelijkheden van cultureel contact tussen Nederland en Indonesië', in: *Indonesië*, pp. 15-23. Utrecht: Vrijzinnig Christelijke Jongeren Bond, 1949.

3014 Hoekendijk, J.C. (ed.)
Zending in Indonesië; Verslag en rapporten van de Zendingsconferentie te Batavia gehouden van 10 tot 20 Augustus 1946. 's-Gravenhage: Boekencentrum, 1946, 137 pp.

3015 Hoen, Pieter 't (ps. F.J. Goedhart)
Terug uit Djokja. Amsterdam: Het Parool, 1946, 128 pp.

3016 Hofwijk, J.W. (ps. W. Kint)
De hitte van de dag; Onze soldaten in Indonesië. Heemstede: De Toorts, 1947, 255 pp.

3017 Hofwijk, J.W. (ps.)
Blubber. Heemstede: De Toorts, 1948, 287 pp.

3018 Houtman, Dr.
Een compromis voor het volledig oplossen van het Insulinde-vraagstuk en tevens een aankondiging voor 'De tijd die komt'; Ingeleid door Dr. Plancius. Aalten: De Graafschap, 1946, 14 pp.

3019 Hubenet, L.K. (ed.)
Wetboek van Strafrecht voor Indonesië; Met alphabetisch register; Bijgewerkt tot 1 September 1948. Batavia: Olt, 1948, 213 pp.

3020 Huizinga, Leonhard (Laurens van Sint Laurens)
Zes kaarsen voor Indië. Second edition. Amsterdam: De Bezige Bij, 1945, 46 pp. [Fifth edition, Amsterdam: Van Kampen, 1947, 133 pp.]

3021 *Ik zal handhaven; Extra foto-editie acties Oost-Java, 21 Juli t/m 4 Augustus 1947.* Soerabaia: Voorlichtingsdienst Mariniersbrigade, 1947, 24 pp.

3022 *Ik zal handhaven; Zee-editie a/b m.s. 'Noordam'; Van U.S.A. naar Malakka/Batavia, November 1945-Januari 1946.* Soerabaia: Voorlichtingsdienst Mariniersbrigade/ Kolff, 1947, 104 pp.

3023   Indië en Indonesië; Kranten en knipsels, 1946-1947.

3024   *Indië vrij van Nederlands partijbelang.* Oegstgeest: n.n., 1948, 14 pp.

3025   *Indië; Waar wij naar toe gaan.* 's-Gravenhage: Legervoorlichtingsdienst, 1946, 15 pp.

3026   *Indië; Waarom wij er heen gaan.* 's-Gravenhage: Legervoorlichtingsdienst, 1946, 15 pp.

3027   *Indië wacht.* Den Haag: Nationaal Comité Handhaving Rijkseenheid?, 1948, 15 pp.

3028   *Het Indische beleid van onze regering; Hebt u er óók genoeg van?* 's-Gravenhage: Volkspartij voor Vrijheid en Democratie, ca. 1947, 8 pp.

3029   Het Indische geldwezen in revolutietijd (knipsels 1946-1947). 12 pp.

3030   *Indische Inlichtingendienst.* 's-Gravenhage: Stichting Indië in Nood, Geen Uur te Verliezen!, ca. 1948. [45]

3031   *De Indische pensioenen in gevaar?* Den Haag: Bond van Gepensionneerde Burgerlijke Landsdienaren en Locale Ambtenaren in Nederlandsch-Indië, ca. 1946, 19 pp.

3032   *Indonesia; Annual report 1948 to the Food and Agriculture Organization of the United Nations.* Batavia: n.n., 1948, 72 pp. (kitlv-m)

3033   *Indonesia; Facts and figures.* New York: Netherlands Information Bureau, 1948. [6277]

3034   *Indonesia; History and growth.* New York: Netherlands Information Bureau, 1949, 31 pp.

3035   *The Indonesian problem; Facts and factors; What happened since the end of the Pacific War.* Second edition. Batavia: Netherlands Indies Government Information Service, 1947, 126 pp. [Third edition, 1947, 59 pp. + photographs.]

3036   *Indonesië in de Derde Algemene Vergadering der Verenigde Naties.* 's-Gravenhage: Staatsdrukkerij, 1949, 36 pp.

3037   *Indonesië herleeft! Economisch herstel en wederopbouw in vogelvlucht.* Batavia: Regeerings Voorlichtings Dienst, 1948, 79 pp.

3038   *Indonesië in het parlement; Mei 1946.* Voorwoord van Max van Poll. 's-Gravenhage: Rijks Voorlichtings Dienst, 1946, 82 pp.

3039   *Indonesië in de Veiligheidsraad.* United Nations Security Council, 1947-49. 7 vols. [Various pagings.]

3040   *Indonesië in de Veiligheidsraad van de Verenigde Naties.* 's-Gravenhage: Ministerie van Buitenlandse Zaken, 1947-50, 115+200+160+298+632+470 pp. 6 vols.

3041   *Indonesië's toekomst; Overzicht der plannen van de Nederlandsche regeering/ Indonesia di kemoedian hari; Ichtisar rentjana-rentjana pemerintah Belanda.* Batavia: Regeerings Voorlichtings Dienst, 1946, 40 pp.

3042   *Indonesische documentatie.* 's-Gravenhage: Katholieke Volks Partij, 1948-1950. [Various pagings.]

3043   *The industrial development of Indonesia; Provisional report.* Djakarta: Departement
        van Economische Zaken, 1948. [49]

3044   'Insiders'
        Indische pepertjes; Wist U, dat... 's-Gravenhage: Nationaal Comité Handhaving
        Rijkseenheid, 1947, 19 pp. [Third printing 1947.]

3045   *Een jaar in de tropen, 1948-4 Augustus-1949; Het werk en leven van 6 RS in woord
        en beeld.* 1949, 56 pp.

3046   *Jaarboek III-1 RI, IIe Inf Brigade I Divisie '7 December'.* Batavia: Kolff, 1947,
        79 pp. (lmd)

3047   Jacob, E.H. s'
        *Cheribon? Enkele aanteekeningen bij de concept-overeenkomst van 15 November
        1946.* N.p.: n.n., 1946, 15 pp.

3048   Jacob, E.H. s'
        'De Malino-gebieden', in: *Drie dagen voor Indië; Lezingen gehouden te Groningen op
        24, 25 en 26 Februari 1947 in het kader van de interacademiale lezingencyclus van
        het Algemeen Studentencomité voor Overzeese Gebiedsdelen,* pp. 19-22. Groningen:
        Groninger Studentencommissie voor Overzeese Gebiedsdelen, 1949.

3049   Jaquet, L.G.M.
        'Indonesië op weg naar de democratie', *Bestuursvraagstukken* 1-2 (April
        1949):157-175.

3050   *Java-jaar; Dagboek van het 3e Peloton II-II Regiment Huzaren van Boreel.* Utrecht:
        Smits, 1949, 82 pp.

3051   *Java-jaar II; Dagboek van het 3e Peloton II-II Regiment Huzaren van Boreel.*
        Utrecht: Smits, 1950, 87 pp.

3052   Joekes, A.M.
        'Developments in the administration of Indonesia', in: *Colonial administration by
        European powers,* pp. 20-39. London: Royal Institute of International Affairs,
        1947.

3053   Joekes, A.M.
        'Het Indonesische probleem in een nieuwe phase', *Socialisme en Democratie* 4
        (1947):273-278. (ubl)

3054   Joncheere, J.M.P. de and J.M.J.G. Balendong (eds)
        *Gedenkboek uitgegeven ter gelegenheid van het tweejarig bestaan van het 6e Eskadron
        Pantserwagens Regt. Huzaren van Boreel.* Semarang: De Locomotief, 1948, 63 pp.
        (kitlv-smg)

3055   Jongeneel, D.J.
        Het anti-Nederlandsch beleid in Nederlandsch Indië. Baarn: n.n., 1946, 23 pp.
        [Second printing, 's-Gravenhage: Stichting Indië in Nood, 1946, 22 pp.]

3056   Jongeneel, D.J.
        Het spel dat met Nederlandsch Indië gespeeld wordt. 's-Gravenhage: Van Stockum,
        1946, 46 pp.

3057   Jonkers, A.
        Welvaartszorg in Indonesië; Een geschiedenis en een perspectief. 's-Gravenhage: Van
        Hoeve, 1948, 261 pp.

3058   Jonkman, J.A.
        Het Koninkrijk weer in de branding. 's-Gravenhage: Departement van Overzeese
        Gebiedsdelen, 1946, 11 pp.

3059   Josselin de Jong, J.P.B. de
        Het Indië van Meyer Ranneft. Leiden: Sijthoff, 1945, 20 pp.

3060   Josselin de Jong, J.P.B. de
        'Het Indische nationalisme (1908-1946)', *De Nieuwe Stem* 1 (1946):114-125.

3061   *Jurisprudentie rechtsherstel.* Batavia: Raad voor het Rechtsherstel in Indonesië,
        1949, 204 pp.

3062   Kadt, J. de
        'Open brief aan minister Logemann', in: J. de Kadt, *De deftigheid in het gedrang;
        Een keuze uit de verspreide geschriften*, pp. 274-287. Amsterdam: Van Oorschot,
        1991. [First published in *De Baanbreker*, 12 January 1946.]

3063   Kadt, J. de
        'De leiders der Indonesische nationalisten', *Pembaroean* 1-3 (March 1946):19-30.

3064   Kadt, J. de
        'Rampspoed geboren; Rondom de 20ste Juli 1947', *Socialisme en Democratie* 4
        (1947):278-294. (ubl) [Reprinted in J. de Kadt, *De deftigheid in het gedrang; Een
        keuze uit de verspreide geschriften*, pp. 288-309. Amsterdam: Van Oorschot,
        1991.]

3065   Kadt, J. de
        'Binnenlandse notities', *Socialisme en Democratie* 5 (1948):488-499, 545-557. (ubl)

3066   Kadt, J. de
        'Antwoord aan Mr. M. van der Goes van Naters', *Socialisme en Democratie* 6
        (1949):238-239. (ubl)

3067   Kadt, J. de
        'Begin van een nieuw tijdperk?', *Socialisme en Democratie* 6 (1949):321-326. (ubl)

3068   Kadt, J. de
        'Door het oog van de naald; De Indonesische crisis', *Socialisme en Democratie* 6
        (1949):41-52. (ubl)

3069   Kadt, J. de
        De Indonesische tragedie; Het treurspel der gemiste kansen. Amsterdam: Van
        Oorschot, 1949, 205 pp. [Second edition, 1989, 192 pp.]

3070   Kadt, J. de
        'De R.T.C.-afsluiting; Mogelijkheden en vraagtekens', *Socialisme en Democratie* 6
        (1949):710-718. (ubl)

3071   Kadt, J. de
        'Indonesië, Zuidoost-Azië en Nederland', *Socialisme en Democratie* 7 (1950):86-
        97. (ubl)

3072 *De Katholieke Volks Partij en Indonesië.* 's-Gravenhage: Katholieke Volks Partij, 1947, 4 pp.

3073 *Kearah ketertiban hoekoem baroe di Indonesia; Bahan-bahan oentoek pembangoenan federasi; Disoesoen oentoek Konperensi Federal di Bandoeng. Bagian 1, Pemandangan oemoem.* Batavia: Visser, 1948, 44 pp.

3074 *Keesings historisch archief.* Amsterdam: Systeem Keesing, 1945-1950. Many vols. (ubl)

3075 *Kepada seloeroeh ra'jat Indonesia.* Melbourne: Nederlandsch-Indische Regeerings Publiciteits Dienst, 1945, 13 pp.

3076 *Kesimpoelan-kesimpoelan dan kepoetoesan-kepoetoesan moe'tamar di Malino.* Batavia: Komisariat Pemerintah Oemoem Borneo dan Timoer Besar, 1946, 23 pp.

3077 Keuning, J.
'Amerika's houding in het Indonesische probleem', *Indonesië* 2 (1948-49):474-476.

3078 Kiès, Ch.
Wat de meeste Nederlanders niet weten omtrent Nederlandsch-Indië. Deventer: Van Hoeve, 1946, 63 pp.

3079 Kiès, Ch.
Het Indonesische probleem. Deventer: n.n., 1948, 24 pp.

3080 Kingma, T. (ed.)
Friesland was hier; De lotgevallen van 1-9 RI Bataljon Friesland, 1945-1948. Leeuwarden: Van der Weij, 1948, 240 pp. [Second edition, Franeker: Van Wijnen, 1993, 256 pp.]

3081 *Klare taal; Een bundel radio-redevoeringen van tegenstanders van de overeenkomst van Linggadjati.* N.p.: n.n., 61 pp.

3082 Kleffens, E.N. van
The other side of the medal; Addresses delivered by the Netherlands representative in the Security Council of the UN during the discussions of the Indonesian question (July 31-August 26, 1947). New York: Netherlands Information Bureau, 1947, 32 pp.

3083 Kleimeer, A.G.W.
'Moeilijkheden bij nachtelijke patrouilletochten in het Indisch terrein', *De Militaire Spectator* 118 (1949):45-48. (ubl)

3084 Kluis, A.T.W. de
Ik mis hem zo; Ervaringen en indrukken van een hoofd-legerpredikant in Indonesië. Third edition. 's-Gravenhage: Voorhoeve, 1949, 78 pp.

3085 Knoppers, B.A.
Hoger onderwijs in Indonesië; Rapport uitgebracht naar aanleiding van een oriëntatiereis naar Indonesië in opdracht van het Nederlands Comité voor World Student Relief, van 19 Augustus tot 28 September 1948. Leiden: Nederlands Comité voor World Student Relief, 1948, 43 pp. + appendices.

3086   Knoppers, B.A.
       'Hoger onderwijs in Indonesië', *Indonesië* 3 (1949-50):36-60.

3087   Koekebakker, D.
       'De mariniers bij Soerabaja; Hun verrichtingen in een jaar tijds', *Marineblad* 58 (1947-48):79-81. (ubl)

3088   Koekebakker, D.
       'De Mariniersbrigade', *Ons Leger* 31-2 (1947):5-9. (ubl)

3089   Koene, P.J.
       'De Gevechtsinlichtingendienst (GID)', *De Militaire Spectator* 118 (1949):357-364. (ubl)

3090   *Koers West; In opdracht van de Repatriëringsdienst Indië.* Haarlem: Boom-Ruygrok, 1947, 143 pp.

3091   Kolff, G.H. van der
       'De vooruitzichten van de welvaart voor het nieuwe Indonesië', in: *Drie dagen voor Indië; Lezingen gehouden te Groningen op 24, 25 en 26 Februari 1947 in het kader van de interacademiale lezingencyclus van het Algemeen Studentencomité voor Overzeese Gebiedsdelen*, pp. 23-30. Groningen: Groninger Studentencommissie voor Overzeese Gebiedsdelen, 1947.

3092   Kollewijn, R.D.
       'Nationaliteit en burgerschap in het Koninkrijk der Nederlanden en in de Nederlands-Indonesische Unie', *Indonesië* 1 (1947-48):98-116.

3093   Kollewijn, R.D. and R. van Dijk
       Staatsrecht en rechterlijke organisatie van Indonesië in overgangstijd (met bijlagen); Voor studenten samengesteld. Leiden: n.n., ca.1948, 56+51 pp.

3094   *Konferensi Medja Bundar (KMB) di 's-Gravenhage; Kenjataan-kenjataan dan doku-men-dokumen.* 's-Gravenhage: Sekretariat Umum KMB, 1949, 184 pp. (kitlv-m)

3095   Koningsberger, V.J.
       Achtergronden en oorzaken van het Indische vraagstuk. Utrecht: Utrechtsch Nieuwsblad, 1946, 31 pp.

3096   *Koninklijke woorden over Nederland-Indonesië van Hare Majesteiten Koningin Wilhelmina en Koningin Juliana.* Amsterdam/Antwerpen: Wereldbibliotheek, 1950, 16 pp.

3097   'Korpsgeschiedenis van het 1e Bataljon Infanterie van het KNIL', *De Militaire Spectator* 116 (1947):497-503.

3098   'Korpsgeschiedenis van het 2e Bataljon Infanterie van het KNIL', *De Militaire Spectator* 117 (1948):82-85.

3099   'Korpsgeschiedenis van het 4e Bataljon Infanterie van het KNIL', *De Militaire Spectator* 118 (1949):9-13. (ubl)

3100   *Kort overzicht van het behandelde ter conferentie te Denpasar.* Batavia: Algemeen Regeeringscommissariaat voor Borneo en de Groote Oost, 1947, 85 pp.

3101   *Kort overzicht van feiten en standpunten in Nederlandsch-Indië.* 's-Gravenhage: Stichting Indië in Nood, Geen Uur te Verliezen!, 1946, 11 pp.

3102 *Kort verslag Djawa Timoer Conferentie, Bondowoso, Indonesia, 1948.* Bondowoso, 1949. [49]

3103 Kort, W.L.P.M. de
'De Noodwet-Indonesië', *Katholiek Staatkundig Maandschrift* 2 (1948-49):285-288. (ubl)

3104 Kraemer, H.
'Nederland in de waagschaal', *Wending* 2 (1947):373-386.

3105 Kramer, Diet
Thuisvaart. Amsterdam: Holland, 1948, 236 pp.

3106 Kretschmer de Wilde, C.J.M.
'Koninklijke Marine schrijft geschiedenis in Oost-Java', *Marineblad* 58 (1947-48):100-110.

3107 Kretschmer de Wilde, C.J.M.
'Met de mariniers naar Djember', *Marineblad* 58 (1947-48):111-118.

3108 Kretschmer de Wilde, C.J.M.
Met vlaggen van top; Verrichtingen der Koninklijke Marine in de Nederlandsch-Indische wateren voor herstel van orde en vrede van 1945 tot 1948. Amsterdam: De Boer, 1948, 198 pp.

3109 Kruls, H.J.
Op inspectie. Amsterdam/Brussel: Elsevier, 1947, 112 pp.

3110 Krijgsman, F.H.
Na England-Spiel Indonesien-Spiel? 's-Gravenhage: n.n., 1950, 16 pp.

3111 Kuipers, P.O.
'De neo-zelfbesturen', *Bestuursvraagstukken* 1 (1949):15-28.

3112 *Land- en volkenkunde Indonesië.* 's-Gravenhage: Ministerie van Oorlog, 1947, 72 pp.

3113 Landheer, Bart
'The post-war period in Indonesia', in: B. Landheer, *The Netherlands in a changing world*, pp. 184-200. New York: Roy Publishers, 1947.

3114 *Laporan De Javasche Bank; Tahun buku 1949-1950.* Djakarta: De Javasche Bank, 1950, 169 pp.

3115 Leeuwen, Th. G. van
'De toekomst van de omroep in Indonesië', *Indonesië* 2 (1948-49):455-469.

3116 *Leger? Het vergeten; Neen!* 's-Gravenhage: Legervoorlichtingsdienst, 1946, 32 pp. [28]

3117 Lescens, Roni and Wim Hanraadts
Mooi Priangan-land (krontjong-melodie). Amsterdam: Louis Noiret's Music Company, ca. 1947. [1125]

3118 Levij, J.W.
'Twee jaar Oost-Indonesië', *Indonesië* 2 (1948-49):429-444.

3119   Lezer, A. (ed.)
       Makassar vierde feest. Makassar: Plaatselijk Commando Makassar, 1948, 32 pp.
       (smg)

3120   Ligthart, T.
       'Indische kroniek', *De Economist* 96 (February 1948):135-139. (ubl)

3121   *Linggadjati; De ontwerp-overeenkomst, de toelichting der Commissie-Generaal, de
       Regeeringsverklaring*. 's-Gravenhage: Rijksuitgeverij, 1946, 40 pp.

3122   *The Linggadjati agreement*. 's-Gravenhage: Ministerie van Buitenlandse Zaken,
       1947, 20 pp.

3123   *Linggadjati; Militaire actie; Wat nu?* Amsterdam: Arbeiderspers, 1947, 15 pp.

3124   *Linggardjati*. N.p.: n.n., ca. 1947, 12 pp.

3125   *List of violations by the Republic of Indonesia since the Linggadjati agreement*. New
       York: Netherlands Information Bureau, 1947, 62 pp. [6297]

3126   Locher, G.W.
       'Nederland en Indonesië als deelen van een dynamische wereld', *Wending* 1
       (1946):165-173.

3127   'Locomotieven langs vreemde wegen', *De Militaire Spectator* 117 (1948):131-134.

3128   Löben Sels, T.M.A. van
       Het ontstaan van de Republiek Indonesia. Arnhem: Gouda Quint/Brouwer, 1946,
       51 pp.

3129   Logemann, J.H.A.
       College-aantekeningen over het staatsrecht van Nederlands-Indië. 's-Gravenhage:
       Van Hoeve, Bandung: Vorkink, 1947, 203 pp.

3130   Logemann, J.H.A.
       'The Indonesian problem', *Pacific Affairs* 20 (1947):30-41.

3131   Logemann, J.H.A.
       Indonesië. Amsterdam: Partij van de Arbeid, 1947, 16 pp.

3132   Logemann, J.H.A.
       'Indonesië', *Socialisme en Democratie* 6 (1949):3-11. (ubl)

3133   Logemann, J.H.A.
       Het Indonesische probleem. Antwerpen, 1949, 12 pp. [45]

3134   Luesen, C.J.H.
       De intieme oorlog; Onze jongens in Indië. Batavia: Visser, ca. 1948, 24 pp.

3135   *Lijst van deelnemers aan de Ronde Tafel Conferentie en daarbij betrokkenen*. 1949,
       47 pp. (uba)

3136   Maanen, A. van
       'Het strafrecht in de Republiek', *(Indisch) Tijdschrift van het Recht* 6 (1947):191-
       197.

3137   *Manifest; Aan het Nederlandsche volk... Aan het Indonesische volk*. Amsterdam:
       Vereeniging Nederland-Indonesië, 1946, 6 pp.

3138 *Manifest aan het Nederlandse volk.* 's-Gravenhage: Nationaal Comité Handhaving Rijkseenheid, 1949, 4 pp.

3139 Manschot, H.J.
'Het geld-, bank- en credietwezen in Nederlandsch-Indië in de bezettingsjaren 1942-1945', *Economisch-Statistische Berichten* 31 (1946):196-200, 213-215.

3140 Manschot, H.J.
'De geldzuivering in Indonesië', *Economisch-Statistische Berichten* 35 (1950):268-272.

3141 Margadant, L.
'Ondernemingswachten', *Bestuursvraagstukken* 1 (1949):325-333.

3142 Margadant, L.
'De politie-organisatie in het nieuwe bestel', *Bestuursvraagstukken* 1 (1949):190-197.

3143 Marnix (ps.)
Nieuw Nederland; Gedachten over de vorming van een nieuwe gemeenschap. Amsterdam: Kosmos, 1945, 35 pp.

3144 Maurik, H. van
Djokja achter de horizon. Ingeleid door S.H. Spoor. Nijmegen: De Koepel, 1949, 324 pp.

3145 Mellema, R.L.
'De grondwet van de Republiek Indonesia en de overeenkomst van Linggadjati', in: G.L. Tichelman and H. van Meurs (eds), *Wordend Indonesië*, pp. 65-84. Haarlem: Spaarnestad, 1948.

3146 *Memorandum aangeboden aan de gedelegeerde van het opperbestuur, Zijne Excellentie Minister L. Neher, door de Centrale van Nederlands Personeel in Overheidsdienst.* Batavia: De Centrale, 1948, 67 pp.

3147 *Memorandum aangeboden aan Zijne Excellentie de Minister van Overzeese Gebiedsdelen.* Batavia: Samenwerkende Vakcentrales van Overheidspersoneel, 1948, 12 pp.

3148 *Memorandum Koninklijke Nederlands-Indische Luchtvaart Maatschappij - liquidatie.* 's-Gravenhage: n.n., 1950, 25 pp. + appendices.

3149 Meulen, D. van der
'Muslim problems connected with an independent Indonesia', *The Moslem World* 37 (1947):292-300. (ubl)

3150 Meyer, D.H.
Documenten over Java. Batavia, 1946. 2 vols. [Various pagings.]

3151 Meyer, D.H.
Japan wint den oorlog! Documenten over Java. Maastricht: Leiter-Nypels, 1946, 110 pp.

3152 Meyer, D.H.
'Over het bendewezen op Java', *Indonesië* 3 (1949-50):178-189.

3153   Meyer Ranneft, J.W.
       Rechtvaardigheid voor Indië; Indië in den maalstroom... Maastricht: Leiter-Nypels,
       1945, 34 pp.

3154   Meyer Ranneft, J.W.
       Wat er op het spel staat. Lezing, gehouden op 8 November 1945. N.p.: n.n., 1945,
       16 pp. (uba)

3155   Meyer Ranneft, J.W.
       De weg voor Indië. Amsterdam/Brussel: Elsevier, 1945, 67 pp.

3156   Meyer Ranneft, J.W.
       Indië in nood; Rede. N.p.: n.n., 1946, 21 pp.

3157   Meyer Ranneft, J.W.
       Professor Dr. J.P.B. de Josselin de Jong's 'Indië en de wetenschap'. N.p.: n.n., ca.
       1946, 4 pp. (uba)

3158   Meyer Ranneft, J.W.
       Crisis der waarachtigheid; Dr. J.W. Meyer Ranneft contra Prof. Dr. H. Kraemer. Den
       Haag: Nationaal Comité Handhaving Rijkseenheid, 1947, 24 pp.

3159   Meyer Ranneft, J.W.
       Beschouwing over de gevolgen van het Renville-akkoord. 1948. [45]

3160   Meyer Ranneft, J.W.
       Het land dat verdween; Uitwerking van een rede over Indië in de laatste vijftig jaar.
       Maastricht: Leiter-Nypels, 1949, 88 pp.

3161   Meyer Ranneft, J.W.
       Overdracht van de souvereiniteit over Indonesië. 1949. [45]

3162   Meyer Ranneft, J.W.
       Beschouwing over de actie-Westerling. 1950. [45]

3163   Michels, F.W. and Joh.W.E. Riemens
       Het fiasco van Romme. Amsterdam: Hafkamp, 1949, 108 pp.

3164   Michels, Jan
       Het Lam; Kerstfeest - Indië 1947. Bandung: Visser, 1947, 31 pp.

3165   Middendorp, W.; J.A. Verdoorn and R.J. Ismaël
       Indonesië; Eerst weten, dan oordelen. Amsterdam: Vrij Nederland, 1946, 55 pp.

3166   *Miscellaneous documents covering the period January 1948-June 1948 in connection
       with the truce agreement and the eighteen Renville principles.* Batavia: Topo-
       graphical Service, 1948, 154 pp. (kitlv-smg)

3167   Molenaar, A.N.
       'Stuifzand', *De Gids* 110-1 (1947):36-52.

3168   Mommersteeg, J.A.
       Indonesië; Chronologisch documentair overzicht. Amsterdam: Keesing, 1947,
       40 pp.

3169 Mook, H.J. van
Van Mook spreekt; Drie redevoeringen gehouden te Pangkal Pinang. Amsterdam: Vrij Nederland, 1946, 6 pp.

3170 Mook, H.J. van
'Indonesia', *International Affairs* 25 (July 1949):274-285.

3171 Mook, H.J. van
'Indonesia and the problems of Southeast Asia', *Foreign Affairs* 27 (1949):561-575. (ubl)

3172 Mook, H.J. van
Indonesië, Nederland en de wereld. Amsterdam: De Bezige Bij, 1949, 255 pp.

3173 Mook, H.J. van
The stakes of democracy in South-East Asia. London: Allen and Unwin, 1950, 312 pp.

3174 Morris, Lea (ps. Louise Stolk-Polak)
Vier zonen. Batavia: Kolff, 1948, 213 pp.

3175 Müller, M. and P. van den Roovaart (eds)
Herinneringsboek der 14e Genie Veld Compagnie, Januari 1948 tot Juni 1950. N.p.: n.n., 1950, 55 pp.

3176 *Muktamar Federal Bandung 1948/1949.* Bandung: n.n., 1949. Many vols.

3177 Mulder, J. Henrick
'Van Nederlands-Indië tot Indonesië', in: G.L. Tichelman and H. van Meurs (eds), *Wordend Indonesië*, pp. 13-64. Haarlem: Spaarnestad, 1948.

3178 *Na Linggadjati; Drie voorwaarden voor succes.* Amsterdam: De Brug/Djambatan, 1947, 6 pp.

3179 'Naar de liquidatie van het Koninkrijk?', *Libertas* 12 (September/October 1945):1-32.

3180 *Naar de nieuwe rechtsorde in Indonesië; Bouwstoffen voor de federatie; Samengesteld ten behoeve van de Federale Conferentie te Bandoeng.* Batavia: Visser, 1948, 43+219 pp.

3181 *Naar een nieuwe status; Indonesië gelijkwaardig deelgenoot binnen het Rijksverband.* Batavia: Regeerings Voorlichtings Dienst, 1946, 57 pp.

3182 *Nederland helpt Indië.* 's-Gravenhage: Stichting Nederland Helpt Indië, 1947, 16 pp.

3183 *Nederland en Indië één Rijk!* N.p.: n.n., 1945, 20 pp.

3184 *Nederlanders kent Uw plicht!* Inleiding door Dr. H.J. van Mook. 's-Gravenhage: Militair Gezag, 1945, 15 pp.

3185 'Nederlandsche troepen in Indië', *Ons Leger* 30-9/10 (September/October 1946), 52 pp.

3186 *Het Nederlandse Rode Kruis afdeling Indonesië.* Batavia: Nederlandse Rode Kruis afdeling Indonesië, 1947, 17+37 pp.

3187   *A new system of education for Indonesia*. Batavia: Department of Education, 1948, 7 pp.

3188   *NICA handboek*. NICA Bureau, 1945, 7+147 pp.

3189   *NICA-handboek*. Ca. 1945, 810 pp.

3190   Niet Gz., M. de
       Zending, Indonesië en Nederland. Amsterdam: Nederlands Jongelings Verbond, 1946, 40 pp.

3191   Niet Gz., M. de
       'Gehoorzaamheid-vrijheid-creativiteit (plan-Beel contra Veiligheidsraad-resolutie) 9 Maart 1949', *Wending* 4 (1949):219-237.

3192   Nieuwe Rotterdamsche Courant; Knipsels over de Indonesische kwestie. 2 vols.

3193   *De nieuwe 2-jarige kweekschool*. Batavia: Departement van Onderwijs en Eeredienst, 1947, 79 pp. (kitlv-m)

3194   *De nieuwe vrijheid; De illegaliteit na den oorlog; Het koloniale vraagstuk*. N.p.: n.n., ca. 1945, 45 pp.

3195   Nieuwenhuyze, C.A.O. van
       Er moet wat gebeuren! N.p.: n.n., 15 pp.

3196   Nieuwenhuyze, C.A.O. van
       Mens en vrijheid in Indonesië. 's-Gravenhage/Bandung: Van Hoeve, 1949, 214 pp.

3197   Nieuwenhuijze, C.A.O. van
       'The Dar ul-Islam movement in Western Java', *Pacific Affairs* 23 (1950):169-183.

3198   Nispen tot Sevenaer, O. van
       De Republiek Indonesia, haar leiders en haar soldateska; De eer van het leger is de eer van het volk. 's-Gravenhage: Van Stockum, 1949, 30 pp.

3199   Nispen tot Sevenaer, O. van
       De Ronde Tafel-Conferentie inzake de overdracht der souvereiniteit aan Indonesië; Haar voorgeschiedenis en haar gevolgen. 's-Gravenhage: Van Stockum, 1950, 93 pp.

3200   Noiret, Louis (ed.)
       Voor onze soldaten. Amsterdam: Louis Noiret's Music Publishing Company, ca. 1947, 96 pp.

3201   Nooteboom, C.
       Oost-Indonesië; Een staat in wording. Reprint from: *Zaire* (December 1948), 8 pp. Bruxelles: Editions Universitaires.

3202   Nooteboom, C.; H.C.J. Gunning and J.W.Th. Cohen Stuart
       Oost-Indonesië. Groningen/Batavia: Wolters, 1948, 84 pp.

3203   Norel, K.
       Stille nacht. Nijkerk: Callenbach, 1949, 52 pp.

3204 Nort, Karel (ed.)
Dit is het radio-programma voor de Nederlandse strijdkrachten ter zee, te land en in de lucht; 1945 - 15 Augustus - 1948. 1948, 23 pp.

3205 *Nota inzake het rechtswezen.* Batavia: Departement van Justitie, 1948. [6337]

3206 *Nota omtrent de ontwikkeling van zaken in Indonesië, in zoverre de verhoudingen binnen de Nederlands-Indonesische Unie en de belangen van Nederland daarbij betrokken zijn.* 's-Gravenhage: Staatsuitgeverij, 1950, 52 pp.

3207 *Ons standpunt ten aanzien van: pers en voorlichting, het onderwijs, de verhouding Nederland-Indonesië, het staatsbestel, de economische politiek, in het nieuwe Indonesië is een democratisch standpunt.* Batavia: De Progressieve Groepen, 1946, 40 pp.

3208 *Ontwerp der Constitutie van de Republiek der Verenigde Staten van Indonesië.* 's-Gravenhage: n.n., 1949, 51 pp.

3209 *De ontwikkeling van de federatieve staatsbouw in het jaar 1948.* Batavia: Departement van Binnenlandse Zaken, 1949, 23 pp.

3210 *De ontwikkeling van de ondernemingslandbouw in de federale gebieden van Indonesië gedurende 1947-1948.* Batavia/Djakarta: Departement van Landbouw en Visserij, 1949-50, 47+33+25 pp. 3 vols.

3211 *Onze jongens overzee.* Voorwoord door S.H. Spoor; Inleiding door J.A. Jonkman. Amsterdam: De Geïllustreerde Pers, 1948, 32 pp.

3212 *Onze taak overzee.* 's-Gravenhage: Legervoorlichtingsdienst, 1947, 32 pp.

3213 Ooms, C.M.B.
Wij gingen naar Indië. 's-Gravenhage: Legervoorlichtingsdienst, 1946, 14 pp.

3214 Oorthuys, Cas
Een staat in wording; Foto-reportage over het Indonesië van heden. Met tekst van Alb. de la Court. Amsterdam: Contact, 1947, 126 pp.

3215 *Opening Nood-Universiteit; Redevoeringen uitgesproken door Prof. Dr. P.M. van Wulfften Palthe, president der Nood-Universiteit en P.A. Kerstens, fd. Dir. van Onderwijs en Eeredienst te Batavia op 21 Januari 1946.* Batavia: Wolters, 1946, 15 pp.

3216 Opstal, W. van
We gaan weer naar school; Een woord tot de jongens en meisjes van Indië en tot hun ouders. Melbourne: Nederlandsch-Indische Regeerings Publiciteits Dienst, 1945, 16 pp.

3217 Otten, P.F.S.; E. de Vries a.o.
Aanbevelingen ten behoeve van een snelle en deugdelijke oplossing voor het vraagstuk Nederland-Indonesië. 1947. [45]

3218 'Over groei en achtergrond der daerah-vorming in de staat Oost-Indonesië', *Indonesië* 3 (1949-50):19-35.

3219 Overdijkink, G.W.
Het Indonesische probleem; De feiten. 's-Gravenhage: Nijhoff, 1946, 123 pp.

3220   Overdijkink, G.W.
        Het Indonesische probleem; Nieuwe feiten. Amsterdam: Keizerskroon, 1948,
        208 pp.

3221   'Overzeese gebiedsdelen; Indonesië', in: *Sprekershandboek; Gids voor de Tweede
        Kamerverkiezing van 1946,* pp. 152-163. Amsterdam: Partij van de Arbeid,
        1946.

3222   *Overzicht van de hedendaagse rechtspraak in Indonesië.* Batavia: Departement van
        Justitie, 1948. [6337]

3223   *Overzicht herstelrechtspraak.* 's-Gravenhage: Raad voor het Rechtsherstel in
        Indonesië, 1949, 150 pp. [45]

3224   *Overzicht van het sociaal beleid in Indonesië sinds de instelling van het Departement
        van Sociale Zaken.* Batavia/Djakarta: Departement van Sociale Zaken, ca. 1950,
        94 pp. (kitlv-smg)

3225   *Overzicht van de voornaamste feiten uit de voorgeschiedenis en het gebeuren tijdens de
        conferentie van Malino, 16-24 Juli 1946.* 's-Gravenhage: Staatsuitgeverij, 1946-47.
        (ubl)

3226   *Palang Merah Belanda tjabang Indonesia.* Batavia, 1947, 17 pp. (kitlv-smg)

3227   *Patrouilleboten in actie; De Kleine Vaartuigen Dienst der Koninklijke Marine in
        Indonesië.* Voorwoord van A.S. Pinke. Surabaja: Van Dorp, 1948, 67 pp.

3228   *Peraturan tata-tertib untuk Konperensi Medja Bundar di 's-Gravenhage.* 's-Gra-
        venhage: n.n., 1949, 11 pp.

3229   *Personalia van staatkundige eenheden (regering en volksvertegenwoordiging) in
        Indonesië.* Batavia: Afdeling Documentatie van de Regerings Voorlichtings
        Dienst, 1949, 62 pp.

3230   *Persoverzicht van de Afdeling Documentatie der Regerings Voorlichtings Dienst;
        Overzeese gebiedsdelen.* Batavia, 1945-49. Many vols. (ubl)

3231   *Persstemmen over Indië.* 's-Gravenhage: Militair Gezag, 1945. [Various pagings.]

3232   *Pertemuan untuk Permusjawaratan Federal (PPF) = Bijeenkomst voor Federaal
        Overleg (BFO).* Batavia, 1948-49. Many vols.

3233   Picard, H.W.J.
        En... Japan lacht... tenzij... 1946, 8 pp.

3234   Picard, H.W.J.
        De waarheid over Java; Vijftien AVRO-causerieën in boekvorm. 's-Gravenhage: Van
        Hoeve, 1946, 87 pp.

3235   *Pidato-pidato Radio Batavia, Djuli-Oktober 1947/Lezingen Radio Batavia, Juli-
        October 1947.* Batavia: Departement van Onderwijs en Eredienst, 1948, 79 pp.

3236   Pieters, J.M.
        *Een en ander in verband met een hervatting van de ondernemersactiviteit in Indonesië;
        Rede.* Tilburg: Bergmans, 1947, 18 pp.

3237 Pieters, J.M.
'Grondslagen van de Nederlands-Indonesische Unie', *Katholiek Staatkundig Maandschrift* 3 (1949-50):545-550. (kb)

3238 Pieters, J.M.
'Samenwerking na souvereiniteitsoverdracht', *Katholiek Staatkundig Maandschrift* 3 (1949-50):811-815. (kb)

3239 *De plaats van Indonesië in het herbouwde Koninkrijk.* Leiden: Verbond van Indonesische Burgers, 1945, 31 pp.

3240 Ploeg, J.G. van der
Het Indonesische vraagstuk. Rotterdam: Nederlandse Volksbeweging, 1946, 26 pp.

3241 Poel, H.
'De aan- en afvoertroepen in Indië', *De Militaire Spectator* 116 (1947):151-155, 505.

3242 *The political events in the Republic of Indonesia; A review of the developments in the Indonesian Republic (Java and Sumatra) since the Japanese surrender; Together with statements by the Netherlands and Netherlands Indies Governments, and complete text of the Linggadjati Agreement.* New York: Netherlands Information Bureau, 1947, 64 pp.

3243 *The political events in the Republic of Indonesia.* New York: Netherlands Information Bureau, 1949, 12 pp. [3587, 6297]

3244 *Het politieke gebeuren rondom de Repoeblik Indonesia; Overzicht der ontwikkelingen sedert den oorlog met Japan.* Batavia: Regeerings Voorlichtings Dienst, 1947, 112+78 pp. 2 vols.

3245 *Politieke groeperingen in Indonesië; Een overzicht van de in de laatste tijd op de voorgrond tredende politieke organisaties.* Batavia: Afdeling Documentatie van de Regerings Voorlichtings Dienst, 1948, 106 pp.

3246 Poll, K.J.H.
'Militaire politie in Indonesië', *Ons Leger* 33-6 (1949):5-13. (ubl)

3247 Poll, Max van
'Het Indië-beleid', *Katholiek Cultureel Tijdschrift Streven* 1 (1947-48):607-615, 729-735, 851-859, 952-960, 1065-1072, 1191-1197.

3248 Poll, M.J.M. van (ed.)
Rapport van de Commissie-Van Poll aan de Staten-Generaal; 1 Mei 1946. 's-Gravenhage: Parlementaire Commissie Nederlandsch-Indië, 1946, 14 pp.

3249 Poll, Willem van de
Kerels van de daad; Onze oorlogsvrijwilligers in Malakka en Indië. 's-Gravenhage: Van Hoeve, 1947, 152 pp.

3250 Polman, Jot
De brutale reis; De eerste tocht naar een nieuwe wereld. Meppel: Roelofs van Goor, ca. 1947, 232 pp.

3251   Polman, Jot
        De Stoot; I Bat. Regt. Stoottroepen, 21-7-1947/15-10-1947. Batavia: Kolff, ca.
        1947, 91 pp.

3252   Polman, Jot
        Orde & vrede. Rotterdam: n.n., 1950, 28 pp. (kitlv-smg)

3253   Poortman, C.
        Bestuur en bestel in Indië. 's-Gravenhage: Van Hoeve, 1946, 88 pp.

3254   Pootjes, Joh. Will.
        De ramp in Nederlandsch-Indië. Hilversum: De Vredestichters, 1947, 15 pp.

3255   Portielje, J.N.C. (ed.)
        Wij trokken naar Solo; Gedenkboek 4-9 RI. Semarang: Van Dorp, 1949, 96 pp.

3256   Post, Hans
        Bandjir over Noord-Sumatra. Medan: Pax, 1948, 141 pp.

3257   Post, Hans
        Politionele actie; Boek II van de trilogie Bandjir over Noord-Sumatra. Medan: Pax,
        1948, 172 pp.

3258   Post, Hans
        Bedwongen bandjir. Medan: Pax, 1949, 190 pp.

3259   Post, P.
        'De opbouw van het onderwijs in Indonesië', Indonesië 1 (1947-48):492-506.

3260   Posthuma, S.
        Nederland en Indonesië als economische eenheid. Haarlem: Tjeenk Willink, 1947,
        31 pp.

3261   Preger, W.
        One of many; An Indo-European rebuilds a bit of Java. Batavia: Regerings
        Voorlichtings Dienst, 1948. [24, 45]

3262   Proclamatie aan het Nederlandse volk. Amsterdam: Vereniging Nederland-
        Indonesië, 1947, 3 pp.

3263   De Protestantsche Kerk in Indonesië tijdens bezetting en terreur. Batavia: Bestuur
        van de Protestantsche Kerk in Indonesië, 1946, 64 pp.

3264   Randwijck, S.C. van
        'Geestelijke oordeelvorming in het Indonesische vraagstuk', Wending 3
        (1949):647-654. (ubl)

3265   Rapporten Regeerings Voorlichtings Dienst in Nederlandsch-Indië. Batavia, 1945-
        46. [Various pagings.] (kb)

3266   Rasker, A.J.
        De geestelijke achtergrond van de crisis in Indonesië. Batavia: Protestantsche Kerk
        in Indonesië, 1946, 10 pp.

3267   Rasker, A.J.
        Sebab sebab rohani dibalik krisis di Indonesia. Batavia: Geredja Protestant di
        Indonesia, 1946, 12 pp.

3268 Rasker, A.J.
'Church and state in Indonesia', *International Review of Missions* 37 (July 1948):321-329. (ubl)

3269 Rasker, A.J.
'Higher theological training in Indonesia', *International Review of Missions* 38 (October 1949):412-421. (ubl)

3270 *Recente communistische activiteit in Indonesië.* N.p.: n.n., 1947, 101 pp. + appendices. (kitlv-smg)

3271 *De rechtspositie der burgerlijke overheidsdienaren in Indonesië in verband met de souvereiniteitsoverdracht.* N.p.: n.n., 1949, 36 pp.

3272 *Rechtsreglement voor burgerlijke en strafzaken in Borneo en de Groote Oost.* Makassar: NICA, 1946, 184 pp.

3273 *Redevoeringen gehouden ter gelegenheid van de plechtige opening der Ronde Tafel Conferentie; 's-Gravenhage, 23 Augustus 1949/Pidato-pidato jang diutjapkan pada pembukaan resmi Konperensi Medja Bundar/Speeches delivered at the solemn opening of the Round Table Conference.* 's-Gravenhage: n.n.,1949, 84 pp.

3274 *Redt hen... Zij vergaan.* 's-Gravenhage: Stichting Indië in Nood, Geen Uur te verliezen!, 1946. [unpaged]

3275 *Reglement betreffende de krijgstucht voor Nederlandsch-Indië (R.K.), uitgave 1945.* Melbourne: Netherlands Indies Government Printing Works, 1945, 29 pp.

3276 *Reglement van Orde voor de Ronde Tafel Conferentie te 's-Gravenhage.* 's-Gravenhage: n.n., 1949, 12 pp.

3277 *Report of the president of the Java Bank; Presented on March 10th, 1948.* Batavia: Kolff, 1948, 38+26 pp.

3278 *Report of the president of the Java Bank; Presented on July 9th, 1949.* Batavia: Kolff, 1949, 83+27 pp.

3279 Resink, G.J.
'Contouren van het Uniestatuut', *Oriëntatie* 31 (April 1950):32-53.

3280 *Resultaten van de eerste conferentie van ministers van de Nederlands-Indonesische Unie, gehouden van 25 Maart-1 April 1950 te Djakarta.* 's-Gravenhage: Secretariaat der Nederlands-Indonesische Unie, 1950, 79 pp.

3281 *De resultaten van de Ronde Tafel Conferentie.* Amsterdam: Keesings Historisch Archief, 1949, 15 pp. (ubl)

3282 *Resultaten van de Ronde Tafel Conferentie, zoals aanvaard tijdens de tweede algemene vergadering welke op 2 November 1949 werd gehouden in de Ridderzaal te 's-Gravenhage.* 's-Gravenhage: Secretariaat-Generaal der Ronde Tafel Conferentie, 1950, 130+58 pp.

3283 *Resultaten van de tweede conferentie van ministers van de Nederlands-Indonesische Unie, gehouden van 20-29 November 1950 te 's-Gravenhage.* 's-Gravenhage: Secretariaat der Nederlands-Indonesische Unie, 1950, 168 pp.

3284 Riemens, Joh. W.E. (ed.)
      Wat gebeurt in Indonesië? Amsterdam: Comité voor Vrede in Indonesië, 1949,
      32 pp. [Second printing 1949.]

3285 *Risalah pidato-pidato jang menudju Negara Indonesia Serikat merdeka dan berdaulat.*
      Surabaja: Kolff, 1949, 16 pp.

3286 [Robinson, Tjalie (ps.)]
      *Taaie en Neut in acht en zeventig tekeningen zoals deze in Indonesië verschenen in
      'Wapenbroeders' en bekendheid verwierven bij de troep.* Batavia: Grenzenberg, 1949,
      4+78 pp.

3287 Roelfs, Jan
      Heimwee. Den Haag: Voorhoeve, ca. 1947, 29 pp.

3288 Roetering, G.F.I.
      'Verslag van het transport van het Korps AAT, 1 Divisie "7 December", over de
      periode 1 December 1946 tot 1 December 1947', *De Militaire Spectator* 118-181
      (1949):42-45. (ubl)

3289 Roethof, H.J.
      De toekomstige status van Nederlands-Indië. Port Dickson: n.n., 1946, 23 pp.

3290 Roethof, Hein J.
      Verengde kringen. Batavia: Kolff, 1947, 48 pp. (ubu)

3291 Rombout, M.W. (ed.)
      Ter herinnering aan Uw verblijf op Sumatra; 1-1 RI. Belawan: n.n., 1948, 20 pp.
      (kitlv-smg)

3292 Romein, J.M.
      Revoloesi Roessia. Medan: Partai Boeroeh Indonesia Soematera, 1946, 126 pp.

3293 Romme, C.P.M.
      Rijkseenheid; Het beleid der katholieke 2e Kamerfractie. 's-Gravenhage: Katholieke
      Volks-Partij, 1947, 24 pp.

3294 *Ronde Tafel Conferentie te 's-Gravenhage; Feiten en documenten.* 's-Gravenhage:
      Secretariaat-Generaal der Ronde Tafel Conferentie, 1949, 174 pp.

3295 Roo, J.F. de
      'De Militaire Inlichtingendienst in de gepacificeerde gebieden van Indonesië', *De
      Militaire Spectator* 117 (1948):743-746. (ubl)

3296 Roolvink, E.G.M.
      'Parlementaire kroniek betreffende het Indonesische vraagstuk', *Katholiek
      Staatkundig Maandschrift* 1 (1947-48):49-58, 234-240; 2 (1948-49):32-38. (kb)

3297 Rooy, Peter de
      Herinneringsalbum Verbindingsafd. 1 Div. '7 December'. Bandung: Nix, ca. 1950,
      53 pp.

3298 Rose, H.
      Het Indië dat Nederland vergeet. Varsseveld: Rutgers, 1948, 20 pp.

3299 *Round Table Conference results as accepted in the second plenary meeting, held on 2 November 1949 in the 'Ridderzaal' at The Hague.* The Hague: Secretariat-General of the Round Table Conference, 1950, 126+56 pp.

3300 Routinicus (ps.)
'Economische vooruitzichten van Nederland in Indonesië', *Socialisme en Democratie* 6 (1949):434-439. (ubl)

3301 Rutgers, A.A.L.
'Economische perspectieven in Indonesië', *Antirevolutionaire Staatkunde* 17 (1947):65-74.

3302 Rutgers, A.A.L.
'Indië's zelfstandigheid en Nederlands verantwoordelijkheid', *Antirevolutionaire Staatkunde* 17 (1947):10-26.

3303 Rutgers, S.J.
'Het basis-accoord van Linggadjati', *Politiek en Cultuur* 1 (1945-46):410-411, 422; 2 (1947):7-8. (ubl)

3304 Rutgers, S.J.
'Indonesië in het wereldbeeld', *Politiek en Cultuur* 1 (1945-46):21-22.

3305 Rutgers, S.J.
'De Indonesische nationale beweging vanaf 1927 tot heden', *Politiek en Cultuur* 1 (1945-46):80-84. (ubl)

3306 Rutgers, S.J.
'De verhouding van Nederland tot Indonesië', *Politiek en Cultuur* 1 (1945-46):276-277. (ubl)

3307 Rutgers, S.J.
Indonesië; Het koloniale systeem in de periode tussen de eerste en de tweede wereldoorlog. Amsterdam: Pegasus, 1947, 14+251 pp.

3308 Rutgers, S.J.
'Joris Ivens, de strijder met de camera', *Politiek en Cultuur* 2 (1947):157-161.

3309 Rutgers, S.J.
'Verdeel en heers', *Politiek en Cultuur* 2 (1947):317-320. (ubl)

3310 Ruys de Beerenbrouck, G.A.M.J.
Souvereiniteitsoverdracht aan Indonesië. 's-Gravenhage: Van Stockum, 1950, 55 pp.

3311 Ryckevorsel, L. van
Naar Indië? Beseffen wij, katholieken, onze verantwoordelijkheid voor Indië? Maastricht: Schenk, 1945, 16 pp.

3312 Rijnders, C.B.
Beknopt overzicht van de huidige stand van het zendingswerk der Verenigde Nederlandse Zendingscorporaties. Oegstgeest: Zendingsbureau, 1948, 56 pp.

3313 *Samenvattende overzichten van de invoer in de federale gebieden van Indonesië, 1948.* Batavia: Centraal Kantoor voor de Statistiek, 1949, 20 pp.

3314   *Samenvattende overzichten van de uitvoer in de federale gebieden van Indonesië, 1948.* Batavia: Centraal Kantoor voor de Statistiek, 1949, 25 pp.

3315   *Samenwerking na souvereiniteitsoverdracht.* Amsterdam: Dr Wiardi Beckman Stichting, 1949, 14 pp.

3316   Samkalden, I.
'Het staatkundig uitzicht van Linggadjati', *Internationale Studiën* 1 (January 1948):67-95.

3317   Santen, A. van
Politionele actie 1948; Ve Bataljon Infanterie; W- en T-Brigade. Magelang: n.n., 1949. [Various pagings.]

3318   Schakel, Pieter (ps. D.J. von Balluseck)
Wij, deelgenooten... Amsterdam/Brussel: Elsevier, 1945, 78 pp.

3319   Schalker, J.
'Waarom geen troepen naar Indonesië?', *Politiek en Cultuur* 1 (1945-46):305-308. (ubl)

3320   Scheepens, W.J.
'Eenige factoren, welke het optreden onzer troepen in Ned.-Indië beïnvloeden', *De Militaire Spectator* 116 (1947):207-209.

3321   *Scheepspraet zijnde een reisbeschrijving met tal van wetenswaardigheden en nuttige wenken ten profijte van de Nederlandsche militairen die naar Indië scheep gaan.* Den Haag: Legervoorlichtingsdienst, 1947, 64 pp. [Second printing 1948.]

3322   Schelven, C.M.E. van
'Invloed van het communisme in Indonesië', *Antirevolutionaire Staatkunde* 19 (1949):33-51. (ubl)

3323   Schermerhorn, W.
Rede uitgesproken door den minister-president voor den zender Herrijzend Nederland op Oudejaarsavond 1945. Haarlem: Enschedé, 1946, 15 pp.

3324   Schermerhorn, W.
Indonesië en Neerland's roeping; Radiorede uitgesproken op 12 October 1947. Amsterdam: Arbeiderspers, 1947, 20 pp.

3325   Schermerhorn, W.
'Het Nederlands-Indonesisch conflict', *Socialisme en Democratie* 5 (1948):1-9.

3326   Schmidt, P.J.
Buitenlandse politiek van Nederland. Leiden: Sijthoff, 1945, 156 pp.

3327   Schoonenberg, F.
De troepen terug! Rede. Amsterdam: ANJV, 1947, 18 pp.

3328   Schoonenberg, F.
'Moesoeh of temen - vriend of vijand', *Politiek en Cultuur* 3 (1948):157-161. (ubl)

3329   Schouten, C.
RAPWI; Geschiedkundig overzicht. N.p.: n.n., ca. 1947, 167 pp.

3330 Schouten, J.
'Je Maintiendrai'; Rede over de ontwerp-overeenkomst van Linggadjati in de Tweede Kamer der Staten-Generaal. 's-Gravenhage: Centraal Comité der ARP, 1946, 30 pp.

3331 Schouten, W.A. and H.B. Evers
'Het gebruik van de artillerie, ingedeeld bij de V-Brigade gedurende en na de politionele actie', *De Militaire Spectator* 118 (1949):225-236. (ubl)

3332 Schut, J.
'De territoriale verplegings- en transportdienst in Nederlandsch Oost-Indië', *De Militaire Spectator* 118 (1949):329-334. (ubl)

3333 Schuurmans Stekhoven, W.
Nota inzake de berechting der Indië-deserteurs. Rotterdam, 1948. [5946]

3334 Schuurmans Stekhoven, W.
Tweede nota betreffende de berechting van de (resterende) Indië-deserteurs. Rotterdam: n.n., 1949, 10 pp.

3335 Seijn, W.J.
'Enige werken uitgevoerd door de 16e Cie Legergenietroepen', *De Militaire Spectator* 116 (1947):614-626. (ubl)

3336 Seijn, W.J.
'Technische werkzaamheden uitgevoerd door het Korps Genietroepen van de B-Divisie in West- en Midden-Java voor, tijdens en na de politionele actie 1947', *De Militaire Spectator* 118 (1949):335-349. (ubl)

3337 Sillevis Smitt, J.H.
Met onze mariniers naar Indië. Amsterdam: Ten Have, 1947, 70 pp.

3338 Sipkes, C. (ed.)
120 jaar Jagers; Van Preanger naar Bantam. Batavia: Visser, 1949, 48 pp.

3339 *Situatie en taak in Indonesië; Rapport van de Commissie voor Internationale Zaken van de Oecumenische Raad van Kerken in Nederland.* Amsterdam: Ten Have, 1949, 30 pp.

3340 Sluizer, George
Met de Skymaster naar Indië; Een serie radio-toespraken. Deventer: Van Hoeve, 1946, 48 pp.

3341 Smit, Chr.
'De Communistische Partij van Indonesië 1946-1948 in de strijd voor de bevrijding', *Politiek en Cultuur* 4 (1949):46-48. (ubl)

3342 Snitker, Wim
Om nooit te vergeten. Heemstede: De Toorts, 1949, 64 pp.

3343 Soest, Ems I.H. van
Een wajang in Gods handen. 's-Gravenhage: Van Hoeve, 1946, 126 pp.

3344 *Soldaat in Indië; Dagelijkse belevenissen.* Inleiding door L.A.M. Goossens. Amsterdam: Diligentia, 1948, 79 pp.

3345 *Soldaat overzee.* Hengelo: Smit, 1947, 139 pp. [Second printing 1948.]

3346   *Soldatengids 1949*. Medan: Dienst Welzijnsverzorging, 1949, 56 pp.

3347   *Soldatengids voor Medan*. Medan: Deli Courant, 1947, 24 pp. [49]

3348   *Soldatengids voor Sumatra*. Medan: Leger Voorlichtings Dienst Sumatra, 1946, 44 pp. (kitlv-smg)

3349   Solidarius (ps.)
       Naar een vereeniging Nederland-Indonesië. Amsterdam: De Kameel, 1945, 19 pp.

3350   *Some annotations regarding the Negara Soematera Timoer*. N.p.: n.n., ca. 1948, 6 pp. (kitlv-m)

3351   *Souvereiniteitsoverdracht Indonesië; Penjerahan kedaulatan Indonesia; Transfer of sovereignty Indonesia*. 's-Gravenhage: Staatsdrukkerij, 1949, 52 pp.

3352   Spinosa Cattela, J.E.
       'Monetaire problemen in Indië', *Economisch-Statistische Berichten* 30 (1945):262-264; 31 (1946):5-6.

3353   Sprang, A. van
       En Soekarno lacht...! Journalistieke ervaringen van een Nederlandsch oorlogscorrespondent in Indië. 's-Gravenhage: Van Hoeve, 1946, 109 pp.

3354   Sprang, Alfred van
       Laatste acte; Een cocktail van soldatenleven en politiek in Indonesië. 's-Gravenhage: Van Hoeve, 1949, 80 pp.

3355   Sprang, A. van
       Wij werden geroepen; De geschiedenis van de 7 December Divisie, met zweten en zwoegen geschreven door twintigduizend Nederlandse mannen, in inkt geboekstaafd. 's-Gravenhage: Van Hoeve, 1949, 244 pp.

3356   Star Numan
       Eén minuut voor twaalf. N.p.: n.n., 1947, 6 pp.

3357   Starp, J.E. van der
       Een dolkstoot in de rug van het Nederlandse volk. Dordrecht: Schefferdrukkerij, 1950, 67 pp.

3358   *Statuten en huishoudelijk reglement van de Vereeniging Nederland-Indonesië*. Amsterdam: VNI, ca. 1946, 16 pp.

3359   'Statuut van de Nederlands-Indonesische Unie', *Katholiek Staatkundig Maandschrift* 2 (1948-49):16-26. (ubl)

3360   *Statuut van de Nederlands-Indonesische Unie; Proeve van hoofdlijnen*. 's-Gravenhage: Centrum voor Staatkundige Vorming, 1948, 15 pp.

3361   Stellinga, J.R.
       'De Indonesische kwestie en het parlementaire stelsel', *Antirevolutionaire Staatkunde* 19 (1949):305-309, 401-404. (ubl)

3362   Sterrenwichelaar (ps.)
       Melkweg; Zijnde de kroniek van mijn leven onder de sterren; 100 humoristische schetsen uit het leven te velde der 1e Infanterie Brigade Groep, C Divisie, '7 December'. Buitenzorg: Archipel, ca. 1947, 120 pp.

3363 Stevens, J.A. and Ben Grevedamme
Vrij... Een verzameling foto's uit Indië van den foto-journalist van den Marine Voorlichtings Dienst, Luit. ter zee 3e kl. J.A. Stevens, met brieven van Ben Grevedamme. Deventer: De IJssel, 1946, 96 pp.

3364 Stokvis, J.E.
Men wint een volk door het niet te overwinnen; Rede. Amsterdam: Partijbestuur der SDAP, 1945, 8 pp.

3365 Stokvis, J.E.
Koloniale politiek. Amsterdam: Wiardi Beckman Stichting, 1946, 8 pp.

3366 Stokvis, J.E.
'Een les?', *Socialisme en Democratie* 3 (1946):169-174. (ubl)

3367 Stokvis, J.E.
'Naar de beslissing', *Socialisme en Democratie* 3 (1946):74-77. (ubl)

3368 Stokvis, J.E.
'Rondom de Indonesische crisis', *Socialisme en Democratie* 3 (1946):30-32. (ubl)

3369 Straus, J.
'De luchtmachtpolitie der militaire luchtvaart van het leger in Indonesië', *De Militaire Spectator* 118 (1949):657-659. (ubl)

3370 Straus, J.
'De toekomst der vliegveldverdediging in Nederlands-Indië', *De Militaire Spectator* 118 (1949):148-150. (ubl)

3371 Strien, T. van
'De pioniers in Nederlandsch-Indië', *De Militaire Spectator* 116 (1947):607-613. (ubl)

3372 Suchtelen, B.C.C.M.M. van
De eenheidsgedachte bij 80 millioen Nederlandsche Rijksgenooten. Leiden: Sijthoff, 1945, 61 pp.

3373 Suchtelen, B.C.C.M.M. van
Indië, vrij van Nederlands partijbelang. Oegstgeest: n.n., 1948, 14 pp.

3374 Sunier, A.L.J.
Is Nederland afgeleefd en Indië verloren? N.p.: n.n., 1946, 7 pp.

3375 Sunier, A.L.J.
Nederlandsch-Indië en tientallen millioenen zijner inheemsche bevolking kunnen thans alleen nog maar door krachtig militair optreden gered worden! 's-Gravenhage: Stichting Indië in Nood, Geen Uur te verliezen!, 1946, 11 pp.

3376 Swaay, H. van
Indië in nood; Geen uur te verliezen! 's-Gravenhage: Stichting Indië in Nood, Geen Uur te verliezen!, 1945, 15 pp.

3377 Swaay, H. van
Het Nica-plan voor den economischen wederopbouw van Nederlandsch-Indië; Een opwekkend en tevens een ernstig waarschuwend woord! 's-Gravenhage: Van Stockum, 1945, 32 pp.

3378   Sybesma, F.
       'La fédération indonésienne; Evolution ou révolution?', *Cahiers du Monde Nouveau* 3-6 (1947):143-149. (kb)

3379   Sybesma, F.
       Linggadjati. 's-Gravenhage: Katholieke Volks Partij, 1947, 53 pp.

3380   Tas, S.
       Nederland-Indonesië; Een analyse en een politiek. Amsterdam: Veen, 1945, 40 pp.

3381   *Ter herinnering; 3 jaar U-Brigade; 2 Maart 1946-1949.* Padang: U-Brigade, 1949. [unpaged]

3382   *Ter oriëntatie van de a.s. student aan de Universiteit van Indonesië.* Buitenzorg: Bandoengs Studenten Corps, Bataviaas Studenten Corps en Buitenzorgse Studenten Unie, 1949, 32 pp.

3383   Teunis, Bert; Paul Frische and Mannus Franken
       Vergeefsch vaarwel. Batavia: Geallieerde Militaire Drukkerij, 1946, 16 pp. (ubl)

3384   Thienen, W.A. van
       Er is nog niets verloren; Nederland-Indonesië voor en na de souvereiniteitsoverdracht; De oplossing van het conflict 'Indonesië met de Derde Partij'. Amsterdam: All Ready, 1950, 38 pp.

3385   Thorenaar, A.
       Overvloed in Insulinde; Een landbouw-welvaartsplan. Amsterdam: Arbeiderspers, 1946, 98 pp.

3386   *Three months of truce on Java and Sumatra; Documents submitted to the Committee of Good Offices by the Netherlands delegation, and other related documents in the period 17 January 1948 up to 30 April 1948.* Batavia: Kolff, 1948, 155 pp.

3387   Tibben, W.G.
       Van colbert naar uniform. Met een woord ten geleide van J.C. Koningsberger. 's-Gravenhage: Voorhoeve, 1949, 64 pp.

3388   Tichelman, G.L.
       Indië is toekomst, werk en welvaart. Amsterdam: Van Holkema en Warendorf, 1946. [unpaged]

3389   Tichelman, G.L. and H. van Meurs (eds)
       Indië roept. Amsterdam: Van Holkema en Warendorf, 1947, 205 pp.

3390   Tichelman, G.L. and H. van Meurs (eds)
       Wordend Indonesië. Haarlem: Spaarnestad, 1948, 280 pp.

3391   *De toekomstige positie der ambtenaren; Memorandum van het Verbond van Verenigingen van Overheidsdienaren aan Zijne Excellentie den Minister van Overzeese Gebiedsdelen.* Batavia: Van Dorp, 1949, 11 pp.

3392   Tosseram, B.G.L.M.
       Indonesia; A tropical part of the Netherlands. Amsterdam: Nederland in den Vreemde, 1949, 46 pp.

3393 *Towards a free and sovereign United States of Indonesia; Statements made by the Netherlands representative in the Security Council of the United Nations on December 22 and 24, 1948.* New York: Netherlands Information Bureau, 1949, 42 pp.

3394 *Trade directory of Indonesia, 1949.* Batavia: Departement van Economische Zaken, 1949, 964 pp.

3395 *Translation of the report of the parliamentary commission (States-General) Dutch East Indies.* The Hague: Hofstad, 1946, 48 pp.

3396 *Tropenzakboek voor den soldaat; Ontwerp-voorschrift; No. 1578.* 's-Gravenhage: Chef van den Generalen Staf, 1945, 64 pp.

3397 *Twee jaar 1-1 RI.* Medan: Varekamp, 1947, 17 pp. (kitlv-smg)

3398 Tijmstra, L.F.
Het Indonesische vraagstuk in documenten. Ca. 1948. [1055]

3399 Tijn, B. van
'Politieke verhoudingen binnen de Republiek Indonesië', in: *Drie dagen voor Indië; Lezingen gehouden te Groningen op 24, 25 en 26 Februari 1947 in het kader van de interacademiale lezingencyclus van het Algemeen Studentencomité voor Overzeese Gebiedsdelen*, pp. 69-78. Groningen: Groninger Studentencommissie voor Overzeese Gebiedsdelen, 1947.

3400 Tijn, J. van
'Het wereldvakverbond en Indonesië', *Politiek en Cultuur* 2 (1947):268-270. (ubl)

3401 *The United States of Indonesia; Facts.* New York: Netherlands Information Bureau, 1948. [45]

3402 *Vademecum te gebruiken bij de financieele acquisitie voor de stichtingen 'Indië in Nood' en 'Rijkseenheid'.* Eindhoven: n.n., 1946, 23 pp.

3403 *Vademecum der U-Brigade; Uitgegeven ter gelegenheid van het tweejarig bestaan.* Padang: U-Brigade, 1948, 127 pp.

3404 *Vademecum voor de vormingsofficier.* Bandung: Dienst Vorming HKAG, 1948, 56 pp.

3405 Valk, F.J.E. van der
'Samenwerking in de Nederlands-Indonesische Unie', *Katholiek Staatkundig Maandschrift* 4 (1950-51):49-52. (kb)

3406 Valkhoff, M.
'Le problème indonésien', *Synthèses* 3 (1948):21-35. (uba)

3407 *Van Nederlandsch Oost-Indië tot Indonesië.* Amsterdam: PvdA, 1946, 10 pp.

3408 Veen, H.J. van
'De vermeestering van Tjileungsir door onderdelen van de U-Brigade', *De Militaire Spectator* 117 (1948):473-479.

3409 Veeneklaas, C.
Het rassenconflict in de opvoeding in Indonesië. Groningen: Wolters, 1949, 108 pp.

3410 Veenendaal, C.
'De gevechtsopleiding Indonesië in de practijk', *De Militaire Spectator* 119
(1950):94-107. (ubl)

3411 Veenhoven, W.A.
Dispereert niet! Sta pal! Rede. 's-Gravenhage: Nationaal Reveil, 1949, 7 pp.

3412 Veenstra, J.H.W.
Diogenes in de tropen. Amsterdam: Vrij Nederland, 1947, 155 pp.

3413 Veldhuysen, F.
Hoa-Kiao; Chinezen in Indonesië. Amsterdam: De Keizerskroon, 1948, 77 pp.

3414 Velsen, A. van
'Eenige opmerkingen over de cultureele verhouding Indonesië-Nederland', *De
Gids* 110-2 (1947):164-172.

3415 Velsen, A. van
Feest der cultuur; Vraag en aanbod in de culturele verhouding Oost-West. 's-Gravenhage: Daamen, 1948, 59 pp.

3416 Velsen, A. van
De culturele ontmoeting van Oost en West. Amsterdam: Stichting Grafisch Export-
centrum, 1950, 22 pp.

3417 Ven, C.H.W. van der
*Naar ruimer horizon; Betreffende het contact der schooljeugd Nederland-Overzeese
Gebiedsdelen.* Den Helder: De Boer, 1945, 48 pp.

3418 Vencken, P.A.M.
'Algemene beschouwing over de recente deviezen- en geldsaneringsmaatregelen
in Indonesië', *Maandschrift Economie* 14 (1949-50):527-531.

3419 Venema, R.
'Ontwikkeling van federaal staatsrecht in Indonesië; Verdeling van onderwerpen
van overheidszorg', *Indonesië* 2 (1948-49):163-176.

3420 Venema, R.
'Tendenties in het na-oorlogse staatsrecht der lagere rechtsgemeenschappen in
Indonesië', *Indonesië* 3 (1949-50):289-323.

3421 Verdoorn, J.A.
De zending en het Indonesisch nationalisme. Amsterdam: Vrij Nederland, 1945,
104 pp.

3422 Verdoorn, J.A.
'Indonesia at the crossroads', *Pacific Affairs* 19 (1946):339-350.

3423 Verdoorn, J.A.
'Oostersch nationalisme', *Wending* 1 (1946):147-156.

3424 Verdoorn, J.A.
'De zending in het nieuwe Indonesië', *Wending* 1 (1946):174-180.

3425 Verhoeff, H.G.
'De hoofdstad van de VSI; Een federaal district', *Bestuursvraagstukken* 1
(1949):4-14.

3426 Verhoeven, F.R.J.
'Enige notities over vormen van culturele samenwerking', *Indonesië* 2 (1948-49):364-371.

3427 Verkuyl, J.
De achtergrond van het Indonesische vraagstuk. 's-Gravenhage: Daamen, 1946, 63 pp.

3428 *Het verloren Indië; Vijf opstellen rond de gebeurtenissen van 1945-1946.* N.p.: Stichting Indië in Nood, Geen Uur te verliezen!/Nationaal Reveil, ca. 1946. [Various pagings.]

3429 Vermeulen, J.W.
'De culturele samenwerking tussen Nederland en Indonesië', *Katholiek Staatkundig Maandschrift* 3 (1949-50):844-851. (kb)

3430 *Verslag betreffende Nederlandsch-Indië ingevolge art. 73e van het Handvest der Verenigde Naties, over het jaar 1947.* 's-Gravenhage, 1948, 281 pp.

3431 *Verslag van het buitengewoon congres van de PvdA inzake Indonesië, 15-16 Augustus 1947.* Amsterdam: Partij van de Arbeid, 1947. [1243]

3432 *Verslag van de commissie tot bestudeering van staatsrechtelijke hervormingen.* Batavia: Landsdrukkerij, 1941, 1942, 156+378 pp. 2 vols. [Second edition, New York: Minden Press, 1944.]

3433 *Verslag van de commissie van onderzoek naar de opvattingen in Nederland omtrent de plaats van de overzeesche gebiedsdelen in het Koninkrijk; Ingesteld bij ministerieel besluit van 30 Augustus 1945.* 's-Gravenhage: Rijksuitgeverij, 1946, 90+42+ 215+ 289 pp. 3 vols.

3434 *Verslag van het congres-Indonesië gehouden door de Partij van de Arbeid op 7 September 1946.* Amsterdam: Partij van de Arbeid, 1946, 32 pp.

3435 *Verslag van de lotgevallen van de faculteit der rechtsgeleerdheid en van sociale wetenschap van de Universiteit van Indonesië.* Djakarta: n.n., 1948, 10 pp.

3436 *Verslag van de parlementaire commissie Nederlandsch-Indië.* 's-Gravenhage: Staatsdrukkerij, 1946, 28 pp.

3437 *Verslag van de werkzaamheden van het Departement van Sociale Zaken gedurende de periode 1 December 1946-31 December 1947.* Batavia: Departement van Sociale Zaken, 1948, 158 pp.

3438 *Verslag der werkzaamheden gedurende de periode onmiddellijk volgende op de Japansche capitulatie.* Djakarta: Palang Merah, 1945, 50 pp. [49]

3439 Versloot, H.
'Indonesië na de souvereiniteitsoverdracht', *Socialisme en Democratie* 7 (1950): 337-351. (ubl)

3440 Versluys, J.D.N.
Aspecten van Indonesië's industrialisatie en haar financiering; Rede. Groningen/ Batavia: Wolters, 1949, 40 pp.

3441 Versluys, J.D.N.
'Maatschappelijke vernieuwing op Timor?', *Indonesië* 3 (1949-50):130-150, 201-224.

3442 Versluys, J.D.N.
'Het Uniestatuut; De financiële en economische overeenkomst', *Indonesië* 4 (1950-51):442-465.

3443 *Verzameling bescheiden uitgegeven door de RVD over de Pangkalpinang-conferentie.* Batavia, 1946. [Various pagings.]

3444 Vigilax (ps.)
'De Veiligheidsraad en Indonesië', *Katholiek Staatkundig Maandschrift* 1 (1947-48):245-253. (kb)

3445 Visman, F.H.
The provisional government of the Netherlands East Indies. Paper 9th Conference of the Institute of Pacific Relations, Hot Springs, 1945. [3287]

3446 Visman, Frans H.
The situation in Java; A composite of lectures delivered before the Netherlands Study Group in New York on November 5, 1945, and the Overseas Press Club. New York: Netherlands Information Bureau, 1945, 14 pp.

3447 Vlekke, B.H.M.
'Indonesië en de publieke opinie in de Verenigde Staten', *Indonesië* 1 (1947-48):397-408.

3448 Vlekke, B.H.M.
The Netherlands and its overseas territories. Paper Amsterdam Conference on Overseas Territories, June 9-12, 1948. [24, 3587]

3449 Vlekke, B.H.M.
'The present state of the Dutch empire', *Asiatic Review* 44 (1948):97-100.

3450 Vlekke, B.H.M.
'Indonesia in retrospect', *Pacific Affairs* 22 (1949):290-295.

3451 Vlekke, B.H.M.
'Settlement in Indonesia; The final phase', *The World Today* 6-1 (January 1950):27-37. (ubl)

3452 Vliet, J.L. van der
'De verbindingsdienst in Nederlandsch-Indië', *De Militaire Spectator* 116 (1947):444-448; 117 (1948):46-50. (ubl)

3453 Vogel, Jan and Jaap de Kruyff
Een groet uit Indië. Doetinchem: Muziekuitgeverij De Kruyff, ca. 1948, 2 pp.

3454 Vogel, J.Ph.
The Indonesian question. N.p.: n.n., 1948, 18 pp.

3455 *Voor recht en veiligheid.* Batavia: U-Brigade, 1947, 24 pp.

3456 *Voorbereiding van de Rijksconferentie; Rondschrijven en memorandum.* 's-Gravenhage: n.n., 1945, 16+20 pp.

3457 *Voorbereiding van de Rijksconferentie; Tweede memorandum.* 's-Gravenhage: n.n., 1946, 48 pp. [45]

3458 *Voorlopig leerplan Nieuwe Indonesische Middelbare School; Eerste vier leerjaren.* Batavia: Departement van Onderwijs en Eredienst, 1947, 176 pp.

3459 *Voorlopige en definitieve rehabilitatie-regeling.* Batavia: Ondernemersraad voor Indonesië, 1949, 108 pp. (kitlv-m)

3460 *Voorlopige ranglijsten van de officieren van het Koninklijk Nederlands Indonesisch Leger (afgesloten op 2 November 1948).* Batavia: Topografische Dienst, 1948, 122 pp.

3461 Voortland, Andries and W.G.N. de Keizer
En nu... Indië. Maastricht: Leiter-Nypels, 1944, 199 pp.

3462 Vos, H.
'Geschil om Indonesië', *Socialisme en Democratie* 6 (1949):12-19. (ubl)

3463 Voskuil, Klaas
Waarom? Socialistisch commentaar. Amsterdam: Arbeiderspers, 1947, 7 pp.

3464 Vrande, L.G.W. van de
Ons groot avontuur; Met 2-14 RI Bataljon 'Zeeland' naar Indië. Tilburg: Drukkerij Missiehuis, 1948, 152 pp.

3465 Vreede, F.
Vernieuwing van het hooger onderwijs in Indonesië; Losse aanteekeningen over universeele vorming en vakstudie. Batavia: Van Dorp, 1947, 16 pp.

3466 Vries, C.W. de
'Het aftreden van Mr. Sassen en het aftreden van de minister van Koloniën Mijer (1866)', *Nederlands Juristenblad* 24 (1949):384-387. (ubl)

3467 Vries, D. de
Culturele aspecten in de verhouding Nederland-Indonesië. Amsterdam: Vrij Nederland, 1947, 139 pp.

3468 Vrooland, L.
Ind(ones)ië; Een tropenjournaal. Amsterdam: Scheltens en Giltay, 1949, 304 pp.

3469 Waard, J. de
'Samenwerking na souvereiniteitsoverdracht', *Socialisme en Democratie* 7 (1950):98-99. (ubl)

3470 *Waarom stuurt Beel troepen naar Indonesië?* Amsterdam: De Waarheid, 1946, 31 pp.

3471 *Waarvoor demonstreren wij?* Amsterdam: De Brug/Djambatan, 1947, 8 pp.

3472 Wal, S.L. van der
'Landstaak en staatstaak', *Bestuursvraagstukken* 1 (1949):176-181.

3473 Wanrooij, B.J.
Rapport over de enquête inzake Indonesië. 's-Gravenhage: Mouton, 1945, 31 pp.

3474 *De wapens neer.* Amsterdam: De Waarheid, 1947, 15 pp.

3475   Wasink, P.A.
       Wensdroom of werkelijkheid; Het probleem der keuze voor de Minahassa. Makassar:
       De Unie, 1949, 32 pp.

3476   'Wegherstelling in bergterrein', *De Militaire Spectator* 117 (1948):715-718. (ubl)

3477   *Welkom in Soerabaja.* Soerabaja: Dienst voor Legercontacten, 1947, 16 pp.

3478   Welter, Ch.J.I.M.
       Vrees is een slechte raadgeefster; Radiorede. 's-Gravenhage: Nationaal Comité
       Handhaving Rijkseenheid, 1947, 4 pp.

3479   Werf-Terpstra, G.M. van der
       Hollandsche vrouwen en Indonesië. 's-Gravenhage: Stichting Indië in Nood, Geen
       Uur te verliezen!, 1947, 4 pp. (kb)

3480   Wertheim, W.F.
       Nederland op den tweesprong; Tragedie van den aan traditie gebonden mensch.
       Arnhem: Van Loghum Slaterus, 1946, 36 pp.

3481   Wertheim, W.F.
       'Nederland op den tweesprong; Tragedie van den aan traditie gebonden
       mensch', *De Nieuwe Stem* 1-4 (1946):262-294.

3482   Wertheim, W.F.
       'The Indo-European problem in Indonesia', *Pacific Affairs* 20 (1947):290-298.

3483   Wertheim, W.F.
       'Linggadjati', *De Nieuwe Stem* 2-1 (1947):1-6. (ubl)

3484   Wertheim, W.F.
       Het sociologisch karakter van de Indo-maatschappij; Rede. Amsterdam: Vrij
       Nederland, 1947, 23 pp.

3485   Wertheim, W.F.
       Hintergründe der indonesischen Revolution. Stuttgart: Schmiedel, 1949, 12 pp.

3486   Wertheim, W.F.
       Het rassenprobleem; De ondergang van een mythe. Den Haag: Albani, 1949,
       160 pp.

3487   *Wet Souvereiniteitsoverdracht Indonesië.* 's-Gravenhage: Staatsuitgeverij, 1949, 368
       pp. (ubl)

3488   *Wettelijke regelingen en voorschriften betreffende de overdracht van landstaak aan de
       Staat Oost-Indonesië.* Batavia: De Unie/Tijdschrift Bestuursvraagstukken, 1949,
       205 pp.

3489   Weij, H. van der and G. Bleeker
       De 'illegale' bataljons of LIB's; Hun specifiek karakter en hun verwachting. Batavia:
       Vervoort, 1946, 20 pp. (kitlv-m)

3490   Weijer, G.A.Ph.
       Holland and the Netherlands Indies; Some economic aspects. New York:
       Netherlands Information Bureau, 1945, 9 pp. (uba)

3491 Weijer, G.A.Ph.
Nederland's taak in Indië. Rotterdam: Economisch Statistische Berichten, 1945, 8 pp.

3492 *What about Indonesia?* Leiden: NBBS/ISS, 1948, 16 pp.

3493 *What about Indonesia?* Batavia, 1949, 19 pp.

3494 *What's it about in Indonesia?* Batavia: Netherlands Indies Government Information Service, 1947. [unpaged]

3495 *Why political negotiations between the Netherlands and the Indonesian Republic failed.* 's-Gravenhage: Netherlands Government Information Service, 1948, 18 pp.

3496 Wicherts, A.H.
Het Roode Kruis te Soekaboemi. Buitenzorg: n.n., 1946, 39 pp.

3497 Wielenga, D.K.
De zending op Soemba. Hoenderloo: Nederlandse Zendingsraad/Hoenderloo's Uitgeverij en Drukkerij, 1949, 320 pp.

3498 Wierda, W.
'Grenadiers en Jagers in Indonesië', *Ons Leger* 33-7 (1949):19-21. (ubl)

3499 Willekens, P.J.
'Toespraak tot katholiek Nederland', *Indisch Missietijdschrift* 30 (1947):69-72. (ubl)

3500 Willeumier, J.P. (ed.)
7e Afdeling Veldartillerie 1946-1949. N.p.: n.n., 1949, 75 pp.

3501 Wilmar, H.A. (ed.)
Met de Mariniersbrigade in Oost-Java; Een fotoverhaal over de levensloop der Mariniersbrigade. Haarlem: Spaarnestad, 1948, 158 pp.

3502 Wit, G.H.O. de
'Gebruik de vechtwagens, verbruik ze zo nodig, maar misbruik ze niet', *De Militaire Spectator* 117 (1948):129-148.

3503 Wolde, W.L. ten
Onze jongens overzee. 's-Gravenhage: Van der Linden, ca. 1948, 64 pp.

3504 Wormser, C.
Indië's toekomst. Amsterdam: Stichting voor Volksontwikkeling IVIO, 1945, 16 pp.

3505 Wulfften Palthe, P.M. van
Psychologische aspecten van het Indonesische probleem. Groningen: Wolters, 1946, 20 pp. [71]

3506 Wulfften Palthe, P.M. van
Over het bendewezen op Java. Amsterdam: Van Rossen, 1949, 20 pp.

3507 Wulfften Palthe, P.M. van
Psychological aspects of the Indonesian problem. Leiden: Brill, 1949, 58 pp.

3508 *Wij gingen naar Indië.* Den Haag: Leger Voorlichtings Dienst, 1946, 14 pp.

3509   *Wij van de 'Kompenie'.* Ca. 1945. [unpaged] (lmd)

3510   *Wij waren in... Jogja!* Semarang: Van Dorp, 1949, 30 pp. (kitlv-smg)

3511   Wijnand, J.H.
       Hoe is het in Indië? Een reportage. 's-Gravenhage: Blommendaal, 1948, 59 pp.

3512   Wijnen, D.J. van
       Pangkalpinang; Werkelijkheidszin der minderheden. Batavia: Regeerings Voorlich-
       tings Dienst, 1946, 117 pp.

3513   Zandt, P.
       De Indische kwestie (de ontwerp-overeenkomst van Linggadjati). 's-Gravenhage:
       Staatkundig Gereformeerde Partij, 1947, 30 pp.

3514   Zandt, P.
       Wetsontwerp inzake de overdracht der souvereiniteit over Indonesië. 's-Gravenhage:
       Staatkundig Gereformeerde Partij, 1950, 31 pp.

3515   *Zeven grondslagen voor de ontworpen souvereiniteits-overdracht; Richtlijn voor
       voorlichters/Tudjuh buah pokok-pokok dasar untuk penjerahan kedaulatan jang
       direntjanakan; Pegangan bagi penerangan.* Batavia/Djakarta: Regerings Voorlich-
       tings Dienst/Djawatan Penerangan Pemerintah, 1949, 4+4 pp.

3516   *Zeven lichten over Indië.* 's-Gravenhage: Stichting Indië in Nood, Geen Uur te
       Verliezen!, 1946, 23 pp.

3517   Zeydner, W.A.
       Een waaiende kipas; Brieven uit Batavia, Timor en Medan. 's-Gravenhage: Boeken-
       centrum, 1948, 198 pp.

3518   Zuidema, S.U.
       De Indische kwestie. Franeker: Wever, 1946, 70 pp.

Publications from the years 1945-1950
Other authors

3519 Allen, C.J.
'British trade relations with the new Indonesia', *Great Britain and the East* 63 (February 1947):42-44. (kb)

3520 *American voices that count say that Holland was right.* The Hague: Netherlands Government Information Service, 1949, 48 pp.

3521 Andu, John R.
'The Indonesian struggle for independence', *Crisis* (February 1948):49-50. (uba)

3522 Arondar, E.
'The situation in Indonesia', *Soviet Press Translations* 2 (September 15, 1947):102-104. [6297]

3523 Bidien, Charles
'Indonesia; Asian new democracy', *Political Affairs* 26-9 (September 1947):813-835. [4117]

3524 Bigelow, Jay
'Report from South Celebes', *Asia and the Americas* 46-5 (May 1946):226-228.

3525 Brent, A.R.
'Sidelights on Indonesia', *Common Cause* 3 (September 1949):61-64. [34]

3526 Bridges, F.
'Indonesian dilemma', *Current History* 13 (1947):157-161. (ubl)

3527 Bridges, Flora
'Netherlands' record in Indonesia', *Current History* 13 (1947):217-220. (ubl)

3528 Brockway, J.T.
'The Dutch and Indonesia', *Fortnightly* (July 1949):9-13; (June 1951):364-371. (kb)

3529 Burck, Gilbert
Amerikaans rapport over Indonesië. 's-Gravenhage: Maandblad Succes, 1948, 16 pp.

3530 Burck, Gilbert
'Report from Indonesia', *Fortune* 61 (July 1948):139-143. (ubl)

3531 Chattopadyay, Kamaladevi
'Freedom movements in Indonesia', *United Asia* 1 (May 1948). (kit)

3532   Chaudhry, I.
       The Indonesian struggle. Lahore: Ferozsons, 1950, 273 pp.

3533   Chopra, P.N.
       'Asian conference on Indonesia', *United Asia* 1-5 (January-February 1949):368-373.

3534   Clegg, A.
       Hands off Indonesia. London: Communist Party, 1946, 16 pp. [45]

3535   Colliard, C.A.
       La question d'Indonésie. Paris: Pichon et Durand-Auzias, 1950, 47 pp.

3536   Correspondent, A. (ps.)
       'The Netherlands East Indies after three years of war', *The Asiatic Review* 41 (1945):383-385.

3537   Crockett, Frederick E.
       'How the trouble began in Java', *Harper's Magazine* no. 192 (March 1946):279-284. (ubl)

3538   Dewitz, Jobst von
       Indonesien; Gestern und morgen. Haag/Amper: Linck, 1949, 104 pp.

3539   Dixon, R.
       'The Indonesian conflict', *Communist Review* no. 73 (1947). [6199]

3540   Dunlop, Kathleen E.
       'Indonesia and the Truman Fourth Point', *Current Economic Comment* (August 1949):20-30. [34]

3541   'The Dutch-Indonesian agreement', *Current History* (January 1947):73-76. (ubl)

3542   Dijl, Naboth van
       Constitutional developments in Indonesia. 1949, 129 pp. [MA thesis Stanford University.]

3543   Earle, Frances M.
       'Eurasians - Dutch or Indonesian?', *Far Eastern Survey* 17 (22 December 1948):288-290. (ubl)

3544   Egerton, R.A.D.
       'The Indonesian dispute', *Australian Outlook* 3 (June 1949):117-127.

3545   Elvin, I.
       'International diary; The Indonesian Republic', *Soviet Press Translations* (1 October 1947):138-140. [6297]

3546   Emerson, R.
       'Reflections on the Indonesian case', *World Politics* 1-1 (October 1948):59-81.

3547   Fay, S.B.
       'Revolt in the Netherlands Indies', *Current History* 9 (December 1945):541-546. (ubl)

3548 Fisher, C.
'Crisis in Indonesia', *Political Quarterly* 18 (October-December 1947):295-312. (ubl)

3549 Fisher, Ch.A.
'The Eurasian question in Indonesia', *International Affairs* 23 (October 1947):522-530. (ubl)

3550 Franks, H. George
Oerwoudstrijders onder onze driekleur. Amsterdam: Elsevier, 1946, 276 pp.

3551 Guber, A.A.
The national liberation movement in Indonesia; Lecture. Moscow: Pravda, 1946, 20 pp. [In Russian.]

3552 Guber, A.
'The struggle of Indonesia for independence and the manoeuvers of the Dutch imperialists', *Soviet Press Translations* (31 March 1947):4-8. [6297]

3553 Guber, A.A.
The war in Indonesia; Lecture. Moscow: Pravda, 1947, 32 pp. [5] [In Russian.]

3554 'Hague agreement on Indonesia', *United Nations Bulletin* 7-10 (November 1949):607-610.

3555 Hakim, I.P.
'The problem of Indonesia', *United Asia* 1 (May 1948). (kit)

3556 Hasan, Sarwar
'Indian interests in the Pacific', *Journal of the Indian Institute of International Affairs* 2-4 (October 1946):9-21. (vp)

3557 Hoebel, E. Adamson
The Netherlands East and West Indies. New York: Inter-Allied Publications, 1945, 48 pp.

3558 Hornbeck, Stanley K.
'The United States and the Netherlands East Indies', *Annals of the American Academy of Political and Social Science* vol. 255 (January 1948):124-135.

3559 Hsu, Y.
The Indonesian case. 1949, 141 pp. [MA thesis Columbia University, New York.] [97]

3560 Hyde, Charles Cheney
'The status of the Republic of Indonesia', *Columbia Law Review* 49 (1949):955-966. (vp)

3561 'Indonesia; New and old differences reviewed', *United Nations Bulletin* 5-1 (July 1948):538-540.

3562 'Indonesia; Political and economic realities', *The World Today* (February 1949):52-63. (ubl)

3563 *Indonesia report; The collected dispatches of the American correspondents who died in Bombay, India, July 12, 1949, on their return from a tour of Indonesia.* Tucson: Arizona Daily Star, 1949, 47 pp.

3564   'The Indonesian case in the Security Council', *International Organization* 2 (February 1948):80-85. (ubl)

3565   *The Indonesian question.* Lake Success: United Nations Department of Public Information, 1950, 31 pp.

3566   'The Indonesian settlement', *Round Table* (March 1950):114-120. (ubl)

3567   *Investment in Indonesia; Basic information for U.S. businessmen.* Washington: U.S. Government Printing Office, 1948. [6297]

3568   Isaacs, H.R. (ed.)
       New cycle in Asia; Selected documents on major international developments in the Far East, 1943-1947. New York: Institute of Pacific Relations, 1947, 212 pp. (ubl)

3569   Isaacs, Harold R.
       No peace for Asia. New York: Macmillan, 1947, 295 pp.

3570   Isaacs, Harold R.
       News from Indonesia. New York: Republican Information Centre, 1949. [45, 6362]

3571   J.H.B.
       'Sailor in Sourabaya', *Blackwood's Magazine* no. 1570 (August 1946):73-84. [6186]

3572   Jones, B.W.
       'The Malino conference and after', *Asiatic Review* 42 (1946):370-374. (ubl)

3573   Jones, B.W.
       'Nationalism in Indonesia', *Contemporary Review* 171 (February 1947):80-86. (kb)

3574   Jones, B.W.
       'Nationalism in Indonesia', *The World Today* 4 (February 1948):52-61. (ubl)

3575   Kahin, George McT.
       'The Chinese in Indonesia', *Far Eastern Survey* 15 (23 October 1946):326-329. (ubl)

3576   Kahin, George McTurnan
       The political position of the Chinese in Indonesia. 1946, 123 pp. [MA thesis Stanford University.]

3577   Kahin, George McT.
       'Government in Indonesia', *Far Eastern Survey* 16 (20 February 1947):37-41. (ubl)

3578   Kahin, George McT.
       'The crisis and its aftermath', *Far Eastern Survey* 17 (17 November 1948):261-264. (ubl)

3579   Kahin, George McT.
       'Dispatch from Indonesia', *Far Eastern Survey* 18 (24 January 1949):16-17. (ubl)

3580   Kahin, George McT.
       'Resistance in Indonesia', *Far Eastern Survey* 18 (23 February 1949):45-47. (ubl)

3581 Kahin, George McT.
'Communist leadership in Indonesia', *Far Eastern Survey* 18 (10 August 1949):188-189. (ubl)

3582 Kahin, George McT.
'Indirect rule in East Indonesia', *Pacific Affairs* 22 (1949):227-238.

3583 Kain, Ronald Stuart
'The Netherlands and Indonesia', *Yale Review* 36 (1946):287-302. (ubl)

3584 Kain, Ronald Stuart
'Moscow in Indonesia', *Current History* 17-96 (August 1949):65-70.

3585 Kanetkar, B.D.
Freedom movements in South East Asia; Asian Relations Conference, March-April 1947. Prepared by the Research Staff of the Gokhale Institute of Politics and Economics. Poona-New Delhi: Indian Council of World Affairs, 1947, 56 pp.

3586 Kattenburg, Paul
'Political alignments in Indonesia', *Far Eastern Survey* 15 (25 September 1946):289-294. (ubl)

3587 Kattenburg, Paul M.
The Indonesian question in world politics, August 1945-January 1948. 1949, 447 pp. [PhD thesis Yale University, New Haven.]

3588 Kaushik, B.G.
The Indonesian question. Bombay: Thacker, 1946, 32 pp. [24, 71]

3589 Kelly, Frank
Boycott the Dutch. New South Wales Trades and Labor Council, 1945. [6261]

3590 Kennedy, Raymond
'Dutch plan for the Indies', *Far Eastern Survey* 15 (10 April 1946):97-102. (ubl)

3591 Kennedy, Raymond
'The test in Indonesia', *Asia and the Americas* 46-8 (August 1946):341-345.

3592 Kennedy, Raymond
'Truce in Indonesia', *Far Eastern Survey* 17 (24 March 1948):65-68. (ubl)

3593 Kennedy, Raymond and Paul M. Kattenburg
'Indonesia in crisis', *Foreign Policy Reports* 24-15 (15 December 1948):174-187.

3594 Klinkert, Jan Roelof
The second Netherlands military action against the Republic of Indonesia as reported in the world press; A case study of international reporting. 1949, 169 pp. [MA thesis University of Minnesota, Minneapolis.]

3595 Kobayashi, Yoshimasa
Struggle for Indonesian independence. Tokyo?: Choryu sha, 1949, 45 pp. [51] [In Japanese.]

3596 *Laatste getuigenis; Een Amerikaans document.* Amsterdam: De Vrije Amsterdammer, 1949, 32 pp.

3597　Lasker, Bruno
'The role of the Chinese in the Netherlands Indies', *Far Eastern Quarterly* 5 (February 1946):162-171.

3598　*Last testimony; An American document.* New York: The Knickerbocker, 1949, 31 pp.

3599　Lattimore, E.
Decline of empire in the Pacific. New York: Institute of Pacific Relations, 1947. [24, 3587]

3600　Lattimore, E.H.
Unrest in the colonial world. New York: Institute of Pacific Relations, 1948. [24]

3601　Leyser, J.
'Australia and the post-war settlement in South East Asia', *Australian Outlook* 3 (1949). (kit)

3602　McDonald, A.H.
'Indonesian analysis', *Austral-Asiatic Bulletin* 6 (April 1946):6-12. (kit)

3603　McKay, V.
'Empires in transition; British, French and Dutch colonial plans', *Foreign Policy Reports* 23 (May 1947):34-47. [45, 3587]

3604　*Many American voices that count say that Holland was right when it took action to give Indonesia freedom coupled with order; Here is a representative selection.* New York: Netherlands Information Bureau, 1949, 65 pp.

3605　'Mediation in Indonesia', *United Nations Bulletin* 5-1 (July 1948):540-547.

3606　Mehta, Asoka and Pinakin Patel
The revolt in Indonesia. Bombay: Padma, 1946, 53 pp.

3607　Mohammed, S.
Indonesia's war of independence. Bombay: People's Publishing House, ca. 1949, 40 pp. [45]

3608　Morrell, Charles M.
'The future of the Netherlands East Indies as a world economic unit', *Asiatic Review* 42 (July 1946):262-264.

3609　Morrell, Charles M.
'Indonesian survey', *Asiatic Review* 44 (1948):206-212.

3610　Morrison, Phoebe
'Indonesia; Crossroads in American policy', *American Perspective* 1-6 (November 1947):382-403. (vp)

3611　Mosberg, H.H.B.
'Storm centre: Indonesia', *Fortnightly* (September 1947):200-203. (kb)

3612　Narayanan, T.G.
Freedom movements in Indonesia. New Delhi, 1947, 23 pp. [34]

3613　'Nationalism in Indonesia', *The World Today* 4-2 (February 1948):52-61. (ubl)

3614 Nehru, Jawaharlal
'Crisis in Indonesia', in: Jawaharlal Nehru, *Independence and after; A collection of speeches 1946-1949*, pp. 332-336. New York: The John Day Company, 1950.

3615 *The Netherlands Indies economy in 1946*. Washington: Department of Commerce, 1947. [3587]

3616 'Our neighbour's empire; Constitutional problems of Indonesia', *Round Table* 36 (1945-46):159-164. (kb)

3617 Payne, Robert
The revolt of Asia. New York: Day, 1947, 305 pp.

3618 Peel, Gerald Kingsford
Hands off Indonesia. Sydney: Current Book Distributors, 1945, 15 pp.

3619 Peel, Gerald
Indonesian introduction; What you want to know about the Dutch East Indies. Sydney: Current Book Distributors, 1945, 32 pp.

3620 'The Philippines and Indonesia; A contrast', *Amerasia* 11 (May 1947):147-156.

3621 Pugh, L.H.O.
'Soerabaja (N.E.I.) - 1945', *The Journal of the Royal Artillery* 75-4 (November 1948):320-349.

3622 Purcell, Victor
The Chinese in Southeast Asia. Second edition. London: Oxford University Press, 1965, 625 pp. (First edition, New York: Institute of Pacific Relations, 1949.)

3623 Quelennec, J.F.
Voyages à travers la République de Merdekatie. N.p.: n.n., 1948, 23 pp.

3624 Ray, N.R.
Dutch activities in the East. Calcutta, 1946. [24]

3625 *Red, white and Indonesia; Facts concerning Australia and the Indonesian question*. Melbourne: Australian Constitutional League, 1947, 15 pp.

3626 Renier, G.J.
'Indonesia', *World Affairs* 1 (January 1947):48-54.

3627 Renier, Olive
'Towards the United States of Indonesia', *World Affairs* 3 (October 1949):398-407.

3628 'The rise of the Indonesian republic', *Amerasia* 11-2 (January 1947):16-27.

3629 Roth, Andrew
'Holland's last chance', *The Nation* 163-6 (10 August 1946):153-155. (kb)

3630 Roth, Andrew
'Jokja journal', *The Nation* 166-26 (26 June 1948):715-717. (kb)

3631 Roth, Andrew
'American flipflop in Indonesia', *The Nation* 167-2 (10 July 1948):39-41. (kb)

3632   Roth, Andrew
'The Spice Islands come of age', *The Nation* 167-16 (21 August 1948):203-205.
(kb)

3633   Sanderson, E.B.
The United Nations and the Indonesian problem. 1948, 145 pp. [MA thesis
University of Chicago.]

3634   Sawer, Geoffrey
'Allied policy in Indonesia', *Austral-Asiatic Bulletin* 6 (April 1946):13-16. (kit)

3635   Sawer, G.
'The return of the puppets in Southeast Asia', *Australian Outlook* 1 (June
1947):8-12. (vp)

3636   Schiller, A.A.
Legal and administrative problems of the Netherlands Indies. New York: Institute of
Pacific Relations, 1945, 43 pp. [45, 3587]

3637   Shudnow, B.
U.S. policy in the colonial areas of Southeast Asia, 1920-1946. 1947, 122 pp.
[MA thesis University of Chicago.]

3638   Steiner, H. Arthur
'Postwar government of the Netherlands East Indies', *Journal of Politics* 9
(November 1947):624-651. (uba)

3639   Tantri, K'tut (ps. Sue Manx)
Inside story of Indonesia; Pamphlet by Sourabaya Sue. Sydney, 1947. [6199]

3640   Thompson, John
Hubbub in Java. Sydney: Currawong, 1946, 94 pp.

3641   Thompson, Virginia
'Japan's blueprint for Indonesia', *Far Eastern Quarterly* 5-2 (February 1946):200-
207.

3642   Thompson, Virginia
Labor problems in Southeast Asia. New Haven: Yale University Press, 1947,
18+283 pp.

3643   Thompson-Adloff, Virginia
'Report from Indonesia', *Far Eastern Survey* 16 (23 April 1947):85-88. (ubl)

3644   Thompson, Virginia
'Aspects of planning in Indonesia', *Pacific Affairs* 20 (1947):178-183.

3645   Thompson, Virginia and Richard Adloff
'The communist revolt in Java; The background', *Far Eastern Survey* 17 (17
November 1948):257-260. (ubl)

3646   Thompson, Virginia and Richard Adloff
'Social welfare in Southeast Asia', *Far Eastern Survey* 18 (15 June 1949):136-140.

3647   Thompson, Virginia and Richard Adloff
'Southeast Asia follows the leader', *Far Eastern Survey* 18 (2 November
1949):253-257.

3648 Thompson, Virginia and Richard Adloff
'Empire's end in Southeast Asia', *Far Eastern Survey* 19 (3 May 1950):97-100.
(ubl)

3649 Thompson, Virginia and Richard Adloff
The left wing in Southeast Asia. New York: Sloane, 1950, 14+298 pp.

3650 *Three questions on Indonesia.* London: The Diplomatic Press and Publishing Co.,
1949, 16 pp.

3651 *United Nations Security Council; Official records; Second, third, fourth and fifth year.*
New York (Lake Success): United Nations, 1947-50. [Various pagings.]

3652 'The United States of Indonesia', *Round Table* no. 146 (March 1947):126-132.
(ubl)

3653 Van der Kroef, J.M.
'Social conflict and minority aspirations in Indonesia', *American Journal of
Sociology* 55 (1949-50):450-463. (ubl)

3654 Vandenbosch, Amry
'Indonesia', in: Lennox A. Mills (ed.), *The new world of Southeast Asia*, pp. 79-
125. Minneapolis: University of Minnesota Press, 1949. (kb)

3655 Vandenbosch, Amry
'The Netherlands-Indonesian Union', *Far Eastern Survey* 19 (11 January 1950):1-
7. (ubl)

3656 Vandenbosch, Amry
'Cooperation under the Netherlands-Indonesian Union', *Far Eastern Survey* 19 (8
March 1950):54-55. (ubl)

3657 Vasilyeva, V.
'Events in Indonesia', *Soviet Press Translations* 2 (January 1946):10-19. [6297]

3658 *Views of U.S. voters on the Netherlands and Indonesia; A national survey of public
opinion conducted for Feltus Associates.* New York: Ross Federal Research
Corporation, 1948, 27+31 pp.

3659 Viktorov, Y.
'Foreign troops in friendly territories', *Soviet Press Translations* 3 (14 December
1946):425-428. [3587]

3660 Viktorov, Y.
'The establishment of consular relations between the USSR and the Indonesian
Republic', *Soviet Press Translations* (15 July 1948):425-428. [34, 3587, 6297]

3661 Voina, A.D.
*Defense of the Indonesian Republic by Soviet delegations in the Security Council of the
United Nations.* 1949, 269 pp. [PhD Thesis Shevchenko State University, Kiev.]
[97] [In Russian.]

3662 Wang Jên-shu
On the Indonesian struggle against imperialism. Shanghai: Shêng Huo, 1947,
75 pp. (kitlv-m) [In Chinese.]

3663   Wehl, David
       The birth of Indonesia. London: Allen and Unwin, 1948, 216 pp.

3664   Whittingham-Jones, Barbara
       'The Malino conference and after', *Asiatic Review* 42 (1946):370-374.

3665   Whittingham-Jones, Barbara
       'The Cheribon agreement', *Nineteenth Century* 141 (January-June 1947):16-22.
       (ubl)

3666   Whittingham-Jones, Barbara
       'Nationalism in Indonesia', *Contemporary Review* 171 (February 1947):80-86.
       (ubl)

3667   Wolf Jr., Charles
       'Background of the Indonesian crisis', *United Nations World* 1 (1947):14-15, 61.
       (ubl)

3668   Wolf Jr., Charles
       'Hornet's nest in Indonesia', *The Nation* no. 165 (2 August 1947). (uba)

3669   Wolf Jr., Charles
       'The men who made Merdeka', *Far Eastern Survey* 16 (3 September 1947):181-
       184. (ubl)

3670   Wolf Jr., Charles
       The Indonesian story; The birth, growth and structure of the Indonesian Republic.
       New York: John Day, 1948, 201 pp.

3671   Wolf Jr., Charles
       Indonesian assignment. Washington: U.S. Government Printing Office, 1950.
       [6199, 6297]

3672   Wolf Jr., Charles
       'Problems of Indonesian constitutionalism', *Pacific Affairs* 23 (1950):314-318.

3673   *Work of the United Nations Good Offices Committee in Indonesia.* Washington: U.S.
       Government Printing Office, 1948, 14 pp. [6297]

Revolutionary period
Later Indonesian writings

3674 *10 tahun Genie Angkatan Darat.* Djakarta: Panitya 10 Tahun Genie Angkatan Darat, 1956, 183 pp.

3675 *30 tahun Angkatan Bersenjata Republik Indonesia.* Jakarta: Departemen Pertahanan-Keamanan, Pusat Sejarah ABRI, 1976, 502 pp.

3676 *30 tahun Indonesia merdeka.* Jilid 1. Jakarta: Sekretariat Negara Republik Indonesia, 1978. [42, 4874]

3677 Abdoelmanap, Soerowo and Tanda Huria Manurung
Pelajar berjuang; Roman sejarah. Jakarta: Penerbit Universitas Indonesia (UI-Press), 1983, 372 pp.

3678 Abdoelrachman, K.
Indonesia's Independence Day. Jakarta: Djambatan, 1980, 55 pp. [Third edition, *Hari kemerdekaan Indonesia = Indonesia's Independence Day,* 1985, 77 pp.]

3679 Abduh, Muhammad
'Perjuangan dan pengorbanan rakyat Sulawesi Selatan menegakkan kemerdekaan (suatu pemikiran tentang reinterpretasi nilai sejarah peristiwa korban 40.000 jiwa di Sulawesi Selatan)', in: *Seminar Sejarah Regional Indonesia Timur; Masalah sejarah perjuangan rakyat Sulawesi Selatan,* pp. 10-21. Ujung Pandang: Dep. P dan K, Balai Kajian Sejarah dan Nilai Tradisional, 1993.

3680 Abdulgani, Roeslan
Partij en parlement; Markante punten in de ontwikkeling van de democratie in Indonesië. 's-Gravenhage: Information Service Indonesia, 1953, 16+17 pp. (kitlv-m)

3681 Abdulgani, Roeslan
Hari Pahlawan meletus karena matangnja kondisi-kondisi rakjat Indonesia. Djakarta: Dep. Penerangan, 1962, 20 pp. (kitlv-m)

3682 Abdulgani, Roeslan
Api revolusi tetap berkobar; Himpunan sambutan-sambutan J.M. Wampa bidang chusus Menteri Penerangan mengenai 10 Nopember, Hari Pahlawan. Djakarta: Pradnja Paramita, 1963, 93 pp.

3683 Abdulgani, Roeslan
Asia Tenggara dalam sinar apinja Hari Pahlawan Indonesia. Djakarta: Dep. Penerangan, 1963, 40 pp. (kitlv-m)

3684   Abdulgani, Roeslan
       Api revolusi di Surabaja. Surabaja: Ksatrya, 1964, 88 pp.

3685   Abdulgani, H. Roeslan
       Heroes Day and the Indonesian revolution. Djakarta: Prapantja, 1964, 138 pp.

3686   Abdulgani, Roeslan
       *100 hari di Surabaya yang menggemparkan Indonesia; Kisah singkat tentang
       kejadian-kejadian di kota Surabaya antara tanggal 17 Agustus s/d akhir November
       1945, 28 tahun berselang*. Jakarta: Yayasan Idayu, 1975, 84 pp.

3687   Abdulgani, Roeslan
       *Humanisme dalam heroisme; Tambahan prasaran 'Semangat dan jiwa kepahlawanan
       dalam peristiwa 10 Nopember 1945 untuk kelanjutan pembinaan bangsa'*. Jakarta:
       n.n., 1976, 6 pp.

3688   Abdulgani, Roeslan
       *Semangat dan jiwa kepahlawanan dalam peristiwa 10 Nopember 1945 untuk
       kelanjutan pembinaan bangsa; Prasaran*. Jakarta, 1976, 11 pp.

3689   Abdulgani, Roeslan
       'Mengenangkan Hari Pahlawan demi pembinaan persatuan bangsa', *Gema
       Angkatan 45* no. 34 (1978):3-8. [55]

3690   Abdulgani, Roeslan
       'Melacak jejak revolusi nasional', *Prisma* 10-8 (August 1981):62-72.

3691   Abdulgani, Roeslan
       'Peranan Panglima Besar Soedirman dalam revolusi Indonesia', in: Sides Sud-
       yarto (ed.), *Tingkah laku politik Panglima Besar Soedirman*, pp. 35-60. Jakarta:
       Karya Unipress, 1983.

3692   Abdulgani, Roeslan
       10 Nopember 1945; Saat remaja meledak menjadi dewasa. Jakarta: Sekretariat
       Kelompok Kerja Sejarah 10 November 1945, 1985, 17+339 pp.

3693   Abdulgani, Roeslan
       'Een Indonesische versie van de bersiap-periode', *Indonesia-Holland Line* 5-37
       (January 1987):34-35.

3694   Abdulgani, Roeslan
       'Sejarah asal-mula rumusan haluan politik luar negeri bebas aktif', *Gema
       Angkatan 45* no. 102-103 (1988):46-50.

3695   Abdulgani, Roeslan
       'Partai politik sebagai senjata demokrasi', *Sejarah* 4 (November 1993):51-55.

3696   Abdulgani, H. Roeslan
       'Nilai-nilai kepahlawanan 10 Nopember 1945 sebagai bekal dalam melanjutkan
       perjuangan menatap abad XXI', in: *Museum dan sejarah*, pp. 51-61. Jakarta: Dep.
       P dan K, 1993/1994.

3697   Abdulgani, H. Roeslan
       'Peranan perjuangan pemuda menjelang Proklamasi', in: *Museum dan sejarah*,
       pp. 31-35. Jakarta: Dep. P dan K, 1993/1994.

3698   Abdullah, A.K.
'Semangat pengorbanan seorang wanita', in: *Modal revolusi 45*, pp. 99-100.
Kutaradja: Komite Musjawarah Angkatan 45 DI Atjeh, 1960.

3699   Abdullah, Hamid
Feodalisme dan revolusi 1945 di Sulawesi Selatan; Pidato. Semarang: Universitas
Diponegoro, 1989, 33 pp.

3700   Abdullah, Hamid
Potret tingkah laku pemuda dalam revolusi. Paper Seminar Sejarah Peranan
Generasi Muda dalam Perjuangan Bangsa 1942-1950, Yogyakarta, 1989, 14 pp.

3701   Abdullah, Hamid
Revolusi 1945 dan pembangunan nasional. Paper SSN-V, Semarang, 1990,
17 pp.

3702   Abdullah, Husnial Husin
Sejarah perjuangan kemerdekaan R.I. di Bangka-Belitung. Jakarta: Karya Unipress,
1983, 395 pp.

3703   Abdullah, Ma'moen
Perang lima hari lima malam di Palembang. Paper Lokakarya Sejarah Lisan,
Arsip Nasional, Jakarta, 1982, 11 pp.

3704   Abdullah, R.P.
Susunan pertahanan rakjat di Madura selama Clash ke-1. N.p.: n.n., ca. 1970,
11 pp.

3705   Abdullah, Taufik
'Revolusi pemuda dan dilemma sebuah revolusi', *Prisma* 2-2 (1973):70-75.

3706   Abdullah, Taufik
Revolution and the search for sanctuary; Forgotten aspects of Indonesian
history. Paper Sixth Conference on Asian History, Yogyakarta, 1974, 15 pp.

3707   Abdullah, Taufik
The 1945 generation; The institutionalization of a revolutionary generation and
the ideologization of revolutionary values. Paper Conference on the Indonesian
Revolution, Utrecht, 1986, 28 pp.

3708   Abdullah, Taufik
'PDRI dalam sejarah perang kemerdekaan', in: Abdurrachman Surjomihardjo
and J.R. Chaniago (eds), *Pemerintah Darurat Republik Indonesia dikaji ulang*,
pp. 34-41. Jakarta: Masyarakat Sejarawan Indonesia, 1990.

3709   Abdullah, Taufik
Negotiations for independence; Remembrances and reflections of the past.
Paper Linggarjati Conference, November 1991. [program]

3710   Abdullah, Taufik
'Harga perundingan dalam kancah perjuangan; Kenangan dan refleksi dari
kelampauan', in: A.B. Lapian and P.J. Drooglever (eds), *Menelusuri jalur
Linggarjati; Diplomasi dalam perspektif sejarah*, pp. 21-62. Jakarta: Grafiti, 1992.

3711   Abdullah, Thomas (ed.)
       Prajurit sangkur dan pena; Genderang perjuangan pelajar/TRIP Besuki-Jawa Timur.
       Jakarta: Panitya Penulisan Sejarah Perjuangan Pelajar/TRIP Besuki, 1978,
       77 pp.

3712   Abdulsalam
       Menudju kemerdekaan; A pictorial review of Indonesia's history of independence.
       Djakarta: Aryaguna, 1964, 95 pp. (kitlv-m)

3713   Abdurrachman, H. Omon
       'Brigade-brigade KRU-X menumpas pemberontakan PKI-1948', *Vidya Yudha*
       no. 15 (1972):78-120.

3714   Abdurrachman, Paramita and Mara Karma
       'Menembus blokade', in: Colin Wild and Peter Carey (eds), *Gelora api revolusi*,
       pp. 145-150. Jakarta: Gramedia, 1986.

3715   Abdurrachman, Paramita and Mara Karma
       'Running the blockade; An interview with Paramita Abdurrachman and Mara
       Karma', in: C. Wild and P. Carey (eds), *Born in fire; The Indonesian struggle for
       independence; An anthology*, pp. 132-135. Athens: Ohio University Press, 1986.

3716   Abidin, T.B.M. Zaenal
       Peranan Islam dalam memperjuangkan Proklamasi kemerdekaan Republik
       Indonesia, 1987. [MA thesis IKIP Jakarta.] [Histori]

3717   Abimanyu
       'Penulisan sejarah perjoangan kemerdekaan R.I.', *Gema Angkatan 45* no. 24
       (December 1977):25-27.

3718   Abubakar, H.A.
       'Peristiwa Merah Putih di Sanga-Sanga, Kalimantan Timur', in: *Terbukalah jalan-
       ku; Hasil sayembara mengarang dalam rangka peringatan hari ulang tahun kemer-
       dekaan R.I. yang ke 30*, pp. 167-181. Jakarta: Dewan Harian Nasional Angkatan
       45, Pusat Dokumentasi Sejarah Perjoangan 45/Aries Lima, 1976.

3719   Achmad, R.S.
       Surabaya bergolak. Jakarta: Haji Masagung, 1990, 102 pp.

3720   Adang S.
       Long March Siliwangi. Jakarta: Rosda Jayaputra, 1984, 55 pp.

3721   Adang S.
       Ngungsi; Bandung lautan api. Bandung: Pustaka Buana, 1984, 54 pp.

3722   Adang S.
       Angkatan Perang Ratu Adil (APRA). Bandung: Pustaka Buana, 1985, 71 pp.

3723   Adang S.
       Melacak korban Westerling. Bandung: Pustaka Buana, 1985, 95 pp.

3724   Adiati, Nj.
       Lukisan revolusi; Revolusi di Indonesia gagalkah atau tidak? Medan: Dunia Wanita,
       ca. 1952, 53 pp.

3725 Adihatmodjo, S.; Lukman Ranadipura and Bidin Suriagunawan
'Sejarah perjoangan rakyat kotamadya daerah tingkat II Sukabumi tahun 1945-1950', *Peninjau* 11-1/2 (1984):119-.

3726 Adil, Hilman
'Pers di Kalimantan Selatan sesudah tahun 1945', in: Abdurrachman Surjo-mihardjo (ed.), *Beberapa segi perkembangan sejarah pers di Indonesia*, pp. 125-140. Jakarta: Projek Penelitian Pengembangan Penerangan, Departemen Penerangan, 1977.

3727 Adil, Hilman
'Langkah-langkah diplomatik Australia dan perjanjian Linggarjati', in: A.B. Lapian and P.J. Drooglever (eds), *Menelusuri jalur Linggarjati; Diplomasi dalam perspektif sejarah*, pp. 227-242. Jakarta: Grafiti, 1992.

3728 Adiono, Mohamad
Armada penyelundup Angkatan Laut Republik Indonesia menerobos blokade Belanda tahun 1946-1949. 1986, 74 pp. [MA thesis Universitas Indonesia, Jakarta.] [Histori]

3729 Adiwiratmoko, Soekimin
Perjuangan Magelang dengan putera-puteranya; Pengalaman pribadi. N.p.: n.n., ca. 1980, 37 pp.

3730 Adiwiratmoko, S.
Pertempuran 2 hari di Magelang. N.p.: n.n., ca. 1985, 18 pp.

3731 Adli, Adrial
Perjuangan pemuda dalam revolusi di Sumatera Barat. Paper Musyawarah Kerja Nasional Sejarah, Bandung, 1990, 17 pp.

3732 Adrianatakesuma, Idris
Faktor PBB (Perserikatan Bangsa-Bangsa) dalam repolusi pisik Indonesia. Paper SSN-II, Jogjakarta, 1970, 17 pp.

3733 Adrianatakesuma, Moh. Idris
Suatu studi tentang hubungan Indonesia-Belanda tahun 1945-1950. 1980, 568 pp. [PhD thesis Universitas Gadjah Mada, Yogyakarta.]

3734 Afandi, J. Roestam
Rawe-rawe rantas; Malang-malang putung. Yogyakarta: Mubes & Reuni Ikatan Keluarga ex Tentara Rakyat Mataram di Bedono dan Menyambut Acara Pengukuhan Anggota-anggota Kehormatan TRM di Yogyakarta, 1992, 79 pp.

3735 Agung, Ide Anak Agung Gde
Twenty years Indonesian foreign policy, 1945-1965. The Hague/Paris: Mouton, 1973, 640 pp.

3736 Agung, Ide Anak Agung Gde
'Renville' als keerpunt in de Nederlands-Indonesische onderhandelingen. Alphen aan den Rijn: Sijthoff, 1980, 403 pp.

3737 Agung, Ide Anak Agung Gde
Dari Negara Indonesia Timur ke Republik Indonesia Serikat. Yogyakarta: Gadjah Mada University Press, 1985, 860 pp.

3738 Agung, Ide Anak Agung Gde
'Diplomacy in the service of the revolution', in: Colin Wild and Peter Carey (eds), *Born in fire; The Indonesian struggle for independence; An anthology*, pp. 172-177. Athens: Ohio University Press, 1986.

3739 Agung, Ide Anak Agung Gde
'Diplomasi internasional bagi kepentingan revolusi', in: Colin Wild and Peter Carey (eds), *Gelora api revolusi*, pp. 174-181. Jakarta: Gramedia, 1986.

3740 Agung, Ide Anak Agung Gde
'Federalisme en regionalisme', in: J. van Goor (ed.), *The Indonesian revolution; Conference papers, Utrecht, 17-20 June, 1986*, pp. 201-222. Utrecht: Rijksuniversiteit Utrecht, 1986.

3741 Agung, Ide Anak Agung Gde
'Het dekolonisatieproces in Indonesië tussen 1945 en 1950', *Spiegel Historiael* 22 (1987):399-411.

3742 Agung, Ide Anak Agung Gde
'Een standaardwerk?', in: P. Boomgaard (ed.), *Aangeraakt door Insulinde*, pp. 95-99. Leiden: KITLV Press, 1992.

3743 Agung, Ide Anak Agung Gde
'Negara kesatuan; Negara Indonesia Timur', in: *Seminar Sejarah Regional Indonesia Timur; Masalah penulisan sejarah dan dinamika kesejarahan Indonesia Timur*, pp. 37-59. Ujung Pandang: Departemen P dan K, 1993/1994.

3744 Ahmad, M. Joesoef
Pengalaman semasa revolusi kemerdekaan di Sulit Air. Jakarta: n.n., 1983, 9 pp.

3745 Aidit, D.N.
Aidit accuses; Madiun affair. Djakarta: Pembaruan, 1955, 43 pp.

3746 Aidit, D.N.
Konfrontasi peristiwa Madiun 1948 - peristiwa Sumatera 1956. Djakarta: Pembaruan, 1958, 47 pp. (kitlv-m)

3747 Aidit, D.N.
Aidit menggugat; Peristiwa Madiun. (Pembelaan dimuka Pengadilan Negeri Djakarta, tgl. 24 Februari 1955.) Fourth printing. Djakarta: Pembaruan, 1964, 83 pp.

3748 Aidit, Sobron
Derap revolusi; Kumpulan novelette & tjerpen. Djakarta: Lembaga Kebudajaan Rakjat, 1962, 188 pp. (kitlv-m)

3749 *Aku akan teruskan; Hasil sayembara mengarang dalam rangka peringatan hari ulang tahun kemerdekaan R.I. yang ke 30*. Jakarta: Dewan Harian Nasional Angkatan 45, Pusat Dokumentasi Sejarah Perjoangan 45/Aries Lima, 1976, 239 pp.

3750 *Aku penerus juangmu; Kumpulan karangan hasil sayembara mengarang dalam bahasa Indonesia tingkat SLTP tahun 1975/1976*. Dikumpulkan oleh Pusat Pembinaan dan Pengembangan Bahasa, Dep. P dan K. Jakarta: Balai Pustaka, 1978, 164 pp.

3751 Akustia, Klara
'Sobekan dari lembaran sedjarah', in: Darius Marpaung (ed.), *Bingkisan nasional;*
Kenangan 10 tahun revolusi Indonesia, 17-8-1945/17-8-1955, pp. 112-114.
Djakarta: Usaha Pegawai Nasional Indonesia, 1955.

3752 *Album peristiwa pemberontakan DI-TII di Indonesia.* Bandung: Dinas Sejarah TNI-
AD, 1978, 284 pp.

3753 *Album perjuangan kemerdekaan 1945-1950; Dari negara kesatuan ke negara*
kesatuan. Jakarta: Badan Pimpinan Harian Korps Cacad Veteran R.I./Alda,
1975, 408 pp.

3754 *Album perjuangan TNI Angkatan Darat periode 1945-1950.* Jakarta: Dinas
Sejarah TNI-AD, ca. 1975. [779]

3755 Alfian
Makna politis pemuda dalam revolusi Indonesia. Paper Seminar Lahirnya
Suatu Bangsa, Jakarta, 1990, 38 pp.

3756 Alfian, T. Ibrahim; Zakaria Ahmad; Muhammad Ibrahim; Rusdi Sufi; Nasrud-
din Sulaiman and M. Isa Sulaiman (eds)
Revolusi kemerdekaan Indonesia di Aceh (1945-1949). Banda Aceh: Proyek
Pengembangan Permuseuman Daerah Istimewa Aceh, Dep. P dan K, 1982,
171 pp.

3757 Algadri, Hamid
Suka-duka masa revolusi. Editor Soegiarta Sriwibawa. Jakarta: Penerbit Universitas Indonesia (UI-Press), 1991, 151 pp.

3758 Ali, Sumiarti
Sekitar detik-detik Proklamasi di Sumatera Barat. 1971, 85 pp. [MA thesis
IKIP Djakarta.] [11, Histori]

3759 Alif, M. Nawawi
'Api padam puntung berasap', in: *Bunga rampai perjuangan dan pengorbanan I,*
pp. 304-319. Jakarta: Markas Besar Legiun Veteran RI. 1982.

3760 *Almanak Ex TRIP Jatim.* Jakarta: Sekretariat Darmo 49 Ex Be 17 Det 1 TRIP
Jatim, 1976, 1977, 1979, 129+197+300 pp. 3 vols.

3761 *Almarhum Djendral Sudirman.* Bandung: Umar Mansoor, 1950, 64 pp. [Second
edition, *Almarhum Djenderal Sudirman,* 1950.]

3762 Amar, Djen
Bandung lautan api. Bandung: Dhiwantara, 1963, 151 pp.

3763 Amas, Ateng
Usaha-usaha Tan Malaka untuk menjatuhkan kabinet Sjahrir. 1973, 64 pp.
[MA thesis IKIP Bandung.] [10]

3764 Amidjaja, M. Rosad
Tindjauan sekitar perundingan Linggardjati dalam tahapan revolusi fisik. 1968.
[MA thesis Universitas Padjadjaran, Bandung.] [1, 20, 4858]

3765   Amidjaja, Rosad
       Suatu tindjauan historis tentang adanja gagasan persetudjuan Linggardjati
       sebagai alternatif pemerintah RI dalam usahanja berdjuang dibidang diplomasi.
       Paper SSN-II, Jogjakarta, 1970, 57 pp.

3766   Amidjaja, Rosad and E. Kosim
       Saran-saran dalam rangka pemugaran gedung naskah Linggardjati. Bandung:
       Universitas Padjadjaran, 1973. [99]

3767   Amien, Azinar (ed.)
       *Kenang-kenangan sejarah detik-detik Proklamasi kemerdekaan RI di Bukittinggi dan
       sekitarnya.* Bukittinggi: n.n., n.y., 10 pp.

3768   Amin, S.M.
       'Secuil kenang-kenangan dari perang kemerdekaan', in: *Bunga rampai perjuangan
       dan pengorbanan II*, pp. 167-179. Jakarta: Markas Besar Legiun Veteran RI, 1983.

3769   Amin, Sulaiman
       'Pertempuran lima hari lima malam di kota Palembang', in: *Bunga rampai
       perjuangan dan pengorbanan II*, pp. 371-382. Jakarta: Markas Besar Legiun
       Veteran RI, 1983.

3770   Amiruddin jr. (ed.)
       Sedjarah perdjuangan Harimau Kurandji 1945-1950 di Sumatera Tengah. Padang?:
       Sri Dharma, 1957. [4872, 6229]

3771   Amirudin
       'Serangan Umum 1 Maret 1949', *Intisari* 6-71 (June 1969):73-78.

3772   Amirullah, Andi Magga
       *Sedjarah ringkas PRIW pada pergolakan/perdjoangan kemerdekaan Indonesia di
       daerah Wadjo dan sekitarnja.* Makassar, 1958, 11 pp.

3773   Amura, H.
       Sejarah revolusi kemerdekaan di Minangkabau (1945-1950). Jakarta: Pustaka
       Antara, 1979, 187 pp.

3774   Ananda, M.A. Maya
       Pertempuran di Situjuh Batur, Sumatera Barat. Jakarta: Rosda Jayaputra, 1984,
       76 pp.

3775   Ananda, M.A. Maya
       Detik-detik Proklamasi di Pekanbaru. Jakarta: Serajaya Santra, 1985, 72 pp.

3776   Anas, A. Wahab
       Bahan-bahan untuk Seminar Sejarah Perjuangan Rakyat Sulawesi Selatan Me-
       nentang Penjajahan Asing. Paper Seminar Sejarah Perjuangan Rakyat Sulawesi
       Selatan Melawan Penjajahan Asing, Ujung Pandang, 1982, 8 pp.

3777   *Andil Polri di KODAM III/Sumbar dalam perang kemerdekaan, 1945-1950.* Jakarta:
       Dinas Sejarah Polri, 1981. [4032]

3778   Anhar
       Di bawah Bintang Salib Selatan; Gerakan dan usaha mempertahankan kemer-
       dekaan Indonesia di Australia 1942-1947. 1990, 223 pp. [MA thesis Uni-
       versitas Indonesia, Jakarta.] [Histori]

3779 Anshari, H. Endang Saifuddin
The Jakarta Charter of June 1945; A history of the gentlemen's agreement between the Islamic and the secular nationalists in modern Indonesia. 1976. [MA thesis McGill University, Montreal.] [3780]

3780 Anshari, H. Endang Saifuddin
Piagam Jakarta 22 Juni 1945 dan sejarah konsensus nasional antara nasionalis Islami dan nasionalis 'sekular' tentang dasar negara Republik Indonesia 1945-1959. Bandung: Salman ITB, 1981, 238 pp.

3781 Anshary, M. Isa
'5 tahun revolusi', *Aliran Islam* 3-16 (1950):867-870. (kitlv-m)

3782 Anwar, Ali
'Awal revolusi di daerah; Insiden Kali Bekasi (1945)', *Histori* 1-1 (1991):11-15.

3783 Anwar, Daan
'Moment sejarah yang menentukan rapat raksasa di Lapangan Ikada 19 September 1945', in: *Museum dan sejarah*, pp. 37-49. Jakarta: Dep. P dan K, 1993/1994.

3784 Anwar, Djaruddin
Peranan Padang Pandjang dalam perdjuangan kemerdekaan 1945-1949. 1972. [MA thesis IKIP Padang.] [14]

3785 Anwar, Johnny
Api perjuangan kemerdekaan di kota Padang; Pengalaman pribadi Brigjen Polisi (Purn.) Johnny Anwar. Jakarta: Songo Abadi Inti, 1986, 176 pp.

3786 Anwar, Rosihan
'Tanja djawab saja jang terachir dengan Djenderal Sudirman', in: *Dari penjerangan ke penjerahan*, pp. 37-43. Bukittinggi: Djawatan Penerangan Sumatera Tengah, 1951.

3787 Anwar, Rosihan
Kisah-kisah zaman revolusi; Kenang-kenangan seorang wartawan 1946-1949. Jakarta: Pustaka Jaya, 1975, 111 pp.

3788 Anwar, Rosihan
Kisah-kisah Jakarta setelah Proklamasi. Jakarta: Pustaka Jaya, 1977, 116 pp.

3789 Anwar, Rosihan
'Pengalamanku sebagai reporter dalam perjuangan kemerdekaan Republik Indonesia', *Gema Angkatan 45* no. 14 (1977). [*Gema Angkatan 45* no. 43.]

3790 Anwar, Rosihan
Kisah-kisah Jakarta menjelang clash ke-I. Jakarta: Pustaka Jaya, 1979, 200 pp.

3791 Anwar, Rosihan
Seniman dan wartawan dalam perjuangan 1942-1950. Paper Seminar Sejarah Peranan Generasi Muda dalam Perjuangan Bangsa 1942-1950, Yogyakarta, 1989, 13 pp.

3792 Anwari, Muchtar
'Menjingkap tabir sedjarah pemberontakan di Sanga-Sanga', *Vidya Yudha* no. 4 (1968):107-111.

3793   Any, Andjar
       Siapa penggali Pancasila??? Surakarta: Mayasari, 1981, 96 pp.

3794   Ar, T. Ur-Rakhman
       Semangat perjuangan '45. Jakarta: Pura Jaya, 1984, 80 pp.

3795   Ariathi, Ni Made
       Puputan dalam peristiwa Margarana di kabupaten Tabanan tahun 1945-1946.
       1978. [MA thesis Universitas Gadjah Mada, Yogyakarta.] [Histori]

3796   Arif, Abdullah
       'The affair of the Tjumbok traitors', *Review of Indonesian and Malayan Affairs* 4/5
       (1970-71):29-65.

3797   Arif, M. Syarif
       'Dunia hiburan masa revolusi; Paparan awal terhadap kota Jakarta', *Histori* 1-1
       (1991):16-20.

3798   Arimbi, Diah
       Para pahlawan yang tak dikenal. Jakarta: Pustaka Jaya, 1985, 84 pp.

3799   Ariwiadi
       Perdjuangan rakjat di Bogor selama perang kemerdekaan 2, 1948-1949. 1969.
       [MA thesis Universitas Indonesia, Djakarta.] [18]

3800   Ariwiadi
       Kota dan kabupaten Bogor pada perang kemerdekaan, taraf ke-2. Paper SSN-
       II, Jogjakarta, 1970, 69 pp.

3801   Ariwiadi
       A putsch by the Pasundan People's Party in Bogor on May 23, 1947. Paper
       Sixth International Conference on Asian History, Yogyakarta, 1974, 10 pp. [25,
       4313]

3802   Ariwiadi
       Pengaruh rasionalisasi terhadap badan-badan perjuangan TNI (1947-1950).
       Paper SSN-III, Jakarta, 1982, 22 pp.

3803   Ariwiadi
       'Pengaruh rasionalisasi terhadap badan-badan perjuangan TNI (1947-1950)',
       in: *Seksi Sejarah Mutakhir (1); Seminar Sejarah Nasional III*, pp. 67-82. Jakarta:
       Dep. P dan K, Direktorat Sejarah dan Nilai Tradisional, Proyek Inventarisasi
       dan Dokumentasi Sejarah Nasional, 1982.

3804   Armand, Deddy
       Bandung lautan api. Jakarta: Garuda Metropolitan Press, 1984, 34 pp.

3805   Armand, Deddy
       Proklamasi 17 Agustus 1945. Jakarta: Garuda Metropolitan Press, 1984, 41 pp.

3806   Armansyah, S.
       Kisah pemboman Salatiga; Buku bacaan bergambar. Jakarta: Miswar, 1975, 58 pp.

3807   Armansyah, S.
       Kisah pertempuran Ambarawa. Jakarta: Miswar, 1975, 30 pp.

3808 Armansyah, S.
Perjalanan gerilya Jenderal Sudirman, 19 Desember 1948-10 Juli 1949; Buku bacaan bergambar. Jakarta: Miswar, 1975, 85 pp.

3809 Arnowo, H. Doel
Pengaruh peristiwa 10 Nopember 1945 terhadap sejarah perjuangan kemerdekaan. Surabaya: Dewan Harian Daerah Angkatan 45 Propinsi Jawa Timur, 1974, 29 pp.

3810 Artha, Artum
Proklamasi kemerdekaan dalam jiwa Proklamasi. Second edition. Banjarmasin: Yayasan Pendidikan Seni Budiman, 1973, 27 pp. [First edition 1964.]

3811 'Arti 10 Nopember sebagai Hari Pahlawan bagi bangsa Indonesia', *Vidya Yudha* no. 40 (1980):4-15. [55]

3812 Arto, Soegih
'Pengalaman masa revolusi', in: *Bunga rampai perjuangan dan pengorbanan I*, pp. 545-567. Jakarta: Markas Besar Legiun Veteran RI, 1982.

3813 Ary
Pak Dirman bergerilya; Cerita bergambar perjoangan kemerdekaan. Semarang: Yayasan Telapak, 1982, 47 pp.

3814 Ary
S.O. 1 Maret. Semarang: Yayasan Telapak, ca. 1982, 56 pp.

3815 As, Tamsir
Keluarga gerilya Banteng Blorok. Surabaya: Bina Ilmu, 1984, 72 pp.

3816 Ashari, Mohamad Isa
Kilang minyak Pangkalan Brandan; Usaha-usaha Angkatan Darat dalam menyelamatkan kilang minyak Pangkalan Brandan. 1986, 74 pp. [MA thesis Universitas Indonesia, Jakarta.] [Histori]

3817 Askandar, L.
Perjuangan pasukan 'L'. Jakarta: Dinas Sejarah TNI-AL, 1979. [4895]

3818 Asmadi
Sangkur dan pena. Jakarta: Indira, 1980, 224 pp.

3819 Asmadi
Pelajar pejuang. Jakarta: Sinar Harapan, 1985, 335 pp.

3820 Asmawie, M. Hanafi
'Menegakkan kembali Sang Merah Putih di bumi Sriwijaya; Kisah nyata pada 38 tahun yang lalu', in: *Bunga rampai perjuangan dan pengorbanan II*, pp. 134-139. Jakarta: Markas Besar Legiun Veteran RI, 1983.

3821 Asmudji (ed.)
Pitoyo; Pedjuang muda Belanda - kawan setia pemuda Indonesia dalam perdjuangan untuk menghantjurkan imperialis Belanda. Djakarta: Generasi Baru, 1954, 67 pp.

3822 Asrullah
'Negara Indonesia Timur; Sebuah kreativitas lokal menuju negara kesatuan', in: *Seminar Sejarah Regional Indonesia Timur; Masalah penulisan sejarah dan dinamika*

kesejarahan Indonesia Timur, pp. 60-70. Ujung Pandang: Departemen P dan K, 1993/1994.

3823   Astina, Ida Bagus Ketut
       Sistem kepemimpinan dalam revolusi fisik di Bali, 1945-1950. 1985. [MA thesis Universitas Udayana, Denpasar.] [6333]

3824   Astuti, Sri
       Penarikan tentara Belanda dari Yogyakarta 24-30 Juni 1949. 1981. [MA thesis Universitas Gadjah Mada, Yogyakarta.] [Histori]

3825   Aswad, Hadjrul
       Sekelumit riwajat pentjetusan Proklamasi Indonesia di kota Padang. 1971. [MA thesis IKIP Padang.] [4872]

3826   Atmadinata, Sambas
       'Pengalaman dan anekdote', in: *Bunga rampai perjuangan dan pengorbanan I*, pp. 689-695. Jakarta: Markas Besar Legiun Veteran RI, 1982.

3827   Atmojo, Sulistyo and K. Permadi (eds)
       Tuntunan kepemimpinan (leadership) yang dipancari oleh kepemimpinan alm. Panglima Besar Jenderal Soedirman. Jakarta: Yayasan Panglima Besar Jenderal Soedirman, 1986, 22+138 pp.

3828   Azhari, Eddy
       Sedjarah dan makna Proklamasi kemerdekaan Indonesia 1945. 1963, 74 pp. [MA thesis IKIP Bandung.] [10, 108]

3829   Aziz, H. Aminuddin
       Islam dan tjetusan revolusi Indonesia. Djakarta: Nahdatul Ulama, 1963, 27 pp.

3830   Aziz, T.A.
       'Sekelumit pengabdian pada Republik', in: *Bunga rampai perjuangan dan pengorbanan I*, pp. 31-38. Jakarta: Markas Besar Legiun Veteran RI, 1982.

3831   *Badan-badan perjuangan*. Jakarta: Dep. Pertahanan-Keamanan, Pusat Sejarah ABRI, 1983, 126 pp.

3832   Badaruzzaman (ps. Moh. Dimyati) and Dali Mutiara
       Pengurbanan dan kebaktian. Djakarta: Balai Pustaka, 1950, 67 pp. [Second edition, Jakarta: Kem. P dan K, 1979, 71 pp.]

3833   Badjuri, E. Hassan
       Peristiwa APRA di Tjimahi dan sekitarnja. 1972, 62 pp. [MA thesis IKIP Bandung.] [10]

3834   Badjuri, Johanes Bergman
       'Penyerobotan sebuah pemancar radio milik Kempeitai Jepang', in: *Letusan di balik buku; Hasil sayembara mengarang dalam rangka peringatan hari ulang tahun kemerdekaan RI yang ke 30*, pp. 51-71. Jakarta: Dewan Harian Nasional Angkatan 45/Aries Lima, 1976.

3835   Bagin
       Derap kaki dendam hati. Jakarta: Balai Pustaka, 1980, 159 pp.

3836 Bagin
Mahalnya kemerdekaan. Jakarta: Bunda Karya, 1984, 75 pp.

3837 Bahar, Sjamsul
'Peristiwa Situdjuh, tanggal 15 Januari 1949', in: *Dari penjerangan ke penjerahan*, pp. 128-138. Bukittinggi: Djawatan Penerangan Sumatera Tengah, 1951.

3838 Bahar, Ny. Yusni Y.
Merdeka atau mati. Jakarta: Ikhwan, 1979, 199 pp.

3839 Baharuddin, R.E.
'Tjerita tentang pemerintah darurat Sjafruddin di Sumatera Tengah', in: Darius Marpaung (ed.), *Bingkisan nasional; Kenangan 10 tahun revolusi Indonesia, 17-8-1945/17-8-1955*, pp. 115-119. Djakarta: Usaha Pegawai Nasional Indonesia, 1955.

3840 *Bahaya laten komunisme di Indonesia. Jilid II: Penumpasan pemberontakan PKI (1948).* Jakarta: Markas Besar Angkatan Bersenjata Republik Indonesia, Pusat Sejarah dan Tradisi ABRI, 1992, 208 pp.

3841 Bakri, Ahmad
Rangkaian peristiwa zaman revolusi. Jakarta: Pustaka Jaya, 1986, 116 pp.

3842 Bakry, Zaini
'Sabang diserahkan Belanda kepada Republik Indonesia', in: *Modal revolusi 45*, pp. 105-106. Kutaradja: Komite Musjawarah Angkatan 45 DI Atjeh, 1960.

3843 *Baluwarti; Relief perjuangan bangsa Indonesia sebelum dan sesudah Proklamasi kemerdekaan.* Jakarta: Yayasan Harapan Kita, 1981, 200 pp.

3844 Bangun, Payung
'Perang kemerdekaan di Sumatera Utara; Motivasi untuk berperanserta rakyat', in: *Revolusi nasional di tingkat lokal*, pp. 140-155. Jakarta: Kem. P dan K, 1989.

3845 *Bara api kesusasteraan Indonesia; Chairil Anwar; Memperingati hari 28 April 1949.* Jogjakarta: Kem. P dan K, 1953, 72 pp. (kitlv-m)

3846 Bardosono
Peristiwa Sulawesi Selatan, 1950. Djakarta: Jajasan Pustaka Militer, 1955, 156 pp.

3847 Basjar, Muhammad
Jogjakarta dalam tindjauan sedjarah perdjuangan kemerdekaan. 1970, 88 pp. [MA thesis IKIP Bandung.] [10]

3848 Basra (Bosra), Mustari
Perjuangan lasykar Lipang Bajeng menentang penjajahan Belanda (suatu tinjauan tentang peranan Islam). 1983, 118 pp. [Thesis IAIN 'Alauddin', Ujung Pandang.]

3849 Basri, Chairul
'Pertahanan terakhir Komandemen Sumatera', in: *Bunga rampai perjuangan dan pengorbanan I*, pp. 138-148. Jakarta: Markas Besar Legiun Veteran RI, 1982.

3850   Basri, Hassan
       Catatan seorang pejuang menegakkan Merah Putih di daerah Riau; Menyambut 40
       tahun merdeka. Pekanbaru: n.n., 1985, 300 pp.

3851   Basri, Jusmar
       Gerakan Operasi Militer VI (untuk menumpas 'DI/TII' di Djawa Tengah).
       Djakarta: Mega Bookstore/Pusat Sedjarah ABRI, ca. 1965, 13 pp.

3852   Basry, H. Hassan
       Kisah gerilja Kalimantan (dalam revolusi Indonesia), 1945-1949. Bandjarmasin:
       Jajasan Lektur Lambung Mangkurat, 1961, 115 pp.

3853   Basuki, Djoko
       'Sepi ing pamrih rame ing gawe', in: *Bunga rampai perjuangan dan pengorbanan I,*
       pp. 152-158. Jakarta: Markas Besar Legiun Veteran RI, 1982.

3854   Basuni, Achmad
       'Di Kalimantan: Sebelum dan sesudahnja 17 Agts 1945', in: Darius Marpaung
       (ed.), *Bingkisan nasional; Kenangan 10 tahun revolusi Indonesia, 17-8-1945/17-8-*
       1955, pp. 67-70, 74. Djakarta: Usaha Pegawai Nasional Indonesia, 1955.

3855   Batuah, Djaruddin Amar Dt. Rangkajo
       Peranan Padang Pandjang dalam perdjuangan kemerdekaan tahun 1945-1949.
       1972, 112 pp. [MA thesis IKIP Padang.] [14, 4872]

3856   *Beberapa catatan tentang lahirnya TNI Brigade XVII/Detasemen 1 TRIP Jawa-*
       Timur. Surabaya: Panitya Ziarah dan Monumen MAS TRIP, 1986, 3 pp.

3857   *Beberapa tjatatan tentang lahirnja, tugas dan perdjuangan Pemerintah Darurat*
       Republik Indonesia. Panitia Pusat Peningkatan Lahirnja PDRI, 1969. [3756]

3858   Bedjo
       'Dari Medan-area ke benteng-Huraba', in: *Bunga rampai perjuangan dan*
       pengorbanan II, pp. 51-66. Jakarta: Markas Besar Legiun Veteran RI, 1983.

3859   'Belanda menjerang, pesawat Republik membalas; Gugurnja Komodor Udara
       Prof. Dr. Abdulrachman Saleh', in: *Dari penjerangan ke penjerahan,* pp. 52-56.
       Bukittinggi: Djawatan Penerangan Sumatera Tengah, 1951.

3860   *Berbahagialah perdjuangan bangsa Indonesia.* Djakarta: Kem. Penerangan, 1950,
       32 pp.

3861   *Berita-berita pers dan radio mengenai Panglima Besar Sudirman.* Djakarta: Dep.
       HANKAM, 1969, 34 pp.

3862   Besar, Herry (ed.)
       Peranan POLRI dalam perjuangan kemerdekaan di Jawa Timur tahun 1945-1949.
       Surabaya: KODAK X Jatim, 1982, 154 pp.

3863   *Biografi Djenderal Sudirman.* Bandung: PUSSEMAD, 1959, 130 pp. [22]

3864   Boediardjo, H.
       'Sepercik pengalaman seorang veteran dalam perang kemerdekaan', in: *Bunga*
       rampai perjuangan dan pengorbanan I, pp. 112-120. Jakarta: Markas Besar Legiun
       Veteran RI, 1982.

3865 Boesje, Motinggo
1949; Sebuah novel revolusi. Djakarta: Aryaguna, 1962, 116 pp. (kitlv-m)

3866 Bondan, Mohammad
Genderang Proklamasi di luar negeri. Djakarta: Kawal, 1971, 240 pp.

3867 Brata, A. Sandiwan
Ulama dan perjuangan bangsa. Paper Seminar Sejarah Peranan Generasi Muda dalam Perjuangan Bangsa 1942-1950, Yogyakarta, 1989, 8 pp.

3868 Brata, Suparto
Kadurakan ing kidul Dringu. Surabaja: Arijati, 1964, 82 pp. (kitlv-m) [In Javanese.]

3869 Brata, Suparto
Patriot-patriot kasmaran. Sala: Gema, 1966, 64 pp. [In Javanese.]

3870 Brata, Suparto
Lara lapané kaum Republik. Surabaja: Arijati, 1967, 70 pp. [In Javanese.]

3871 Brata, Suparto
Surabaya tumpah darahku. Surabaya: Surya Raya, 1978, 224 pp.

3872 Brata, Suparto
Mata-mata. Jakarta: Pustaka Jaya, 1979, 180 pp.

3873 Brata, Suparto
Nopember merah; Kisah setetes darah perjuangan bangsa. Surabaya: Bina Ilmu, 1984, 160 pp.

3874 Brata, Suparto
Pahlawan November. Bandung: Citra Aditya Bakti, 1986, 125 pp.

3875 Brodjohudojo, Wisnu
'Nyaris ikut pesawat VT-CLA yang tertembak di atas Yogya', in: Kustiniyati Mochtar (ed.), *Memoar pejuang Republik Indonesia seputar 'zaman Singapura', 1945-1950*, pp. 131-143. Jakarta: Gramedia, 1992.

3876 Buchari, Sjahrul
Tindjauan tentang masalah detik-detik Proklamasi. 1971, 142 pp. [MA thesis IKIP Djakarta.] [11]

3877 Budhiman, Arif
'Analisa bandingan pemberontakan PKI Madiun dan pemberontakan G30S/PKI', *Vidya Yudha* no. 5 (1968):51-56; no. 6 (1969):38-46; no. 7 (1969): 55-61; no. 8 (1969):35-46; no. 10 (1970):20-31.

3878 Budiana, Abud
Tindjauan sedjarah mengenai pembentukan dan pembubaran Uni Indonesia-Belanda. 1972, 41 pp. [MA thesis IKIP Bandung.] [10]

3879 Budiardjo, Ali
Linggar Jati; The first step on the road to the decolonization of Indonesia. Paper Linggarjati Conference, 1991, 17 pp.

3880 Budiardjo, Ali
'Linggarjati; Langkah pertama menuju dekolonisasi Indonesia', in: A.B. Lapian and P.J. Drooglever (eds), *Menelusuri jalur Linggarjati; Diplomasi dalam perspektif Sejarah*, pp. 9-20. Jakarta: Grafiti, 1992.

3881 *Buku kangen-kangenan Mas TRIP Kie 2200 Ex Brigade XVII*. Bojonegoro: Panitya Kerja Pembangunan Monumen Mas TRIP, 1980, 32 pp.

3882 *Buku kenangan pembangunan monumen pahlawan Pekalongan*. Pekalongan, 1964. [5584]

3883 *Buku kenang-kenangan peringatan peristiwa 'Merah Putih' 14 Pebruari 1946*. Jakarta: Panitia Peringatan Peristiwa 'Merah Putih' 14 Pebruari 1946, 1977, 34 pp.

3884 *Buku pantja windhu kebangkitan perdjuangan pemuda Indonesia*. Djakarta: Jajasan Kesedjahteraan Keluarga Pemuda 66, 1970, 128 pp.

3885 *Buku peringatan 5 tahun Chung Hua Tsung Tegal, 1946-1951*. Pekalongan: Tan Poen Hoeiji, 1951, 32 pp.

3886 *Buku peringatan 10 tahun Sin Ming Hui, 1946-1956*. Djakarta: Sin Ming Hui, 1956, 133 pp.

3887 *Buku peringatan pantja warsa Pandu Rakjat Indonesia, 28 Desember 1945-1950*. Djakarta: Pengurus Besar Pandu Rakjat Indonesia, 1951, 155 pp.

3888 *Buku peringatan Persatuan Tionghoa Peranakan (Pertip) Makassar 1945-1953*. Makassar: Pertip, 1953, 174 pp.

3889 *Buku putih tentang peristiwa Madiun*. Djakarta: Sekr. Agitasi-Propaganda C.C.P.K.I., 1953, 32 pp. (kitlv-m)

3890 *Buku riwajat singkat peristiwa perebutan kekuasaan Sulawesi Utara pada tgl. 14 Pebruari 1946*. Djakarta: Panitya 14 Pebruari, 1958, 31 pp.

3891 *Bunga rampai perjuangan dan pengorbanan*. Jakarta: Markas Besar Legiun Veteran RI, 1982-1983, 785+501 pp. 2 vols.

3892 Bunsaman, H.O.
'Pengalaman menerobos blokade Belanda', in: Kustiniyati Mochtar (ed.), *Memoar pejuang Republik Indonesia seputar 'zaman Singapura', 1945-1950*, pp. 144-151. Jakarta: Gramedia, 1992.

3893 Buntaran
Angkatan muda menggugat; Kisah perdjoangan angkatan muda sepandjang tiga djaman; Djaman Bung Karno, djaman Proklamasi RI 17-8-1945 dan djaman sekarang serta hari depannja. Semarang: Musjawarah Kerdja Pemuda Merah Putih Seluruh Indonesia, 1961, 112 pp.

3894 Bustaman
'Perjuangan pemuda pelajar Sumatera selama perang kemerdekaan 1945-1950', *Gema Angkatan 45* no. 14 (1977). [*Gema Angkatan 45* no. 43]

3895 Bustaman
'Beberapa catatan dari medan perang kemerdekaan ke-II, 1948-1949', *Gema Angkatan 45* no. 20 (August 1977):27-31, 46.

3896 Butar-Butar, Djamalam Eduard
Masalah disekitar Konperensi Medja Bundar. 1971, 100 pp. [MA thesis IKIP Djakarta.] [11, Histori]

3897 Butar-Butar, Frans Timbul
Revolusi sosial di Sumatera Timur. 1971, 113 pp. [MA thesis IKIP Djakarta.] [11]

3898 Buyung BA, R.E.S.
Peristiwa 14 Pebruari 1946 di Manado dalam rangka revolusi kemerdekaan bangsa Indonesia. Manado: Djawatan Penerangan RI Propinsi Sulut, 1971. [4871]

3899 *Cahaya dari medan laga; Hasil sayembara mengarang dalam rangka peringatan hari ulang tahun kemerdekaan RI yang ke 30.* Jakarta: Dewan Harian Nasional Angkatan 45/Aries Lima, 1976, 238 pp.

3900 *Case study; Perdjuangan kita, 1945-1949.* Markas Besar Komando Sumatera, 1969. [26]

3901 'Catatan tambahan sekitar beberapa peristiwa; Misi Mayor Ali Djajeng-prawiro', in: Kustiniyati Mochtar (ed.), *Memoar pejuang Republik Indonesia seputar 'zaman Singapura', 1945-1950*, pp. 236-246. Jakarta: Gramedia, 1992.

3902 *Central Museum of the Armed Forces Satriamandala; Guide book.* Djakarta: Dep. HANKAM, 1972, 28 pp.

3903 Chaerudin, Entol
Proklamasi 17 Agustus 1945 dan pemindahan kekuasaan. Jakarta: n.n., 1973, 51 pp.

3904 Chandra, Eva
Peristiwa Situjuh Batur, 15 Januari 1949. 1988, 67+10 pp. [MA thesis Universitas Andalas, Padang.] [58]

3905 Chaniago, Jr.
'Toddo Puli Temmalara; Peristiwa 23 Januari di Palopo', *Gema Angkatan 45* no. 13 (January 1977). [*Gema Angkatan 45* no. 43]

3906 Chaniago, Jr.
'Peranan Komite van Aktie dalam rapat raksasa di Lapangan Ikada', *Gema Angkatan 45* no. 19 (July 1977):24-26.

3907 Chaniago, Jr.
'Badan pekerja KNIP di awal revolusi; Sebuah kerangka', *Gema Angkatan 45* no. 34 (November 1978):19-21.

3908 Chaniago, Jr.
'Kelompok-kelompok pemuda di awal revolusi; Sebuah studi pendahuluan', *Gema Angkatan 45* no. 38 (March 1979):31-34.

3909 Chaniago, Jr.
Wajah dua muka sebuah kekuatan politik; Badan Pekerdja KNIP periode Jakarta (1945-1946). 1979, 8+253 pp. [MA thesis Universitas Indonesia, Jakarta.]

3910   Chaniago, Jr.
       'Wajah dua muka sebuah kekuatan politik; Badan Pekerja KNIP periode
       Jakarta', *Gema Angkatan 45* no. 59-61 (October-December 1981):85-91.

3911   Chaniago, Jr.
       'Wajah dua muka sebuah kekuatan politik; Badan Pekerja KNIP periode
       Jakarta', in: *Seksi Sejarah Mutakhir (1); Seminar Sejarah Nasional III*, pp. 52-66.
       Jakarta: Dep. P dan K, Direktorat Sejarah dan Nilai Tradisional, Proyek
       Inventarisasi dan Dokumentasi Sejarah Nasional, 1982.

3912   Chaniago, Jr.
       'Kaum adat dan revolusi Dewan Perwakilan Negeri di awal Proklamasi', in:
       Revolusi nasional di tingkat lokal, pp. 120-139. Jakarta: Kem. P dan K, 1989.

3913   Chaniago, Jr.
       POPDA dalam perspektif sejarah. Jakarta: Yayasan POPDA, 1990, 20 pp.

3914   Chaniago, Jr.
       'Lintasan sejarah Pemerintah Darurat Republik Indonesia (1948-1949)', in:
       Abdurrachman Surjomihardjo and J.R. Chaniago (eds), *Pemerintah Darurat
       Republik Indonesia dikaji ulang*, pp. 42-54. Jakarta: Masyarakat Sejarawan
       Indonesia, 1990.

3915   Chaniago, Jr.; Tiurma L. Tobing; Sauki Hadiwardoyo a.o.
       PDRI dalam khasanah kearsipan. Jakarta: Arsip Nasional, 1989, 225 pp.

3916   'Chronologie dari Desember 1948 sampai Desember 1949', in: *Dari penjerangan
       ke penjerahan*, pp. 87-105. Bukittinggi: Djawatan Penerangan Sumatera Tengah,
       1951.

3917   Condronagoro, R.T.
       *Riwayat Laskar Putri Indonesia (LPI) di Surakarta, 30 Oktober 1945 - 27 Oktober
       1948.* Solo: Percetakan Wirjowitono, 1976, 27 pp.

3918   *Cuplikan sejarah perjuangan rakyat Propinsi Bengkulu dalam perang merebut dan
       mempertahankan kemerdekaan Republik Indonesia tahun 1945 s/d 1950.* Bengkulu:
       Korps Tenaga Pembangunan Cabang Bengkulu, 1979. [4853]

3919   *Cuplikan sejarah perjuangan TNI-Angkatan Darat.* Bandung: Dinas Sejarah Militer
       TNI-AD, Jakarta: Mahjuma, 1972, 522 pp. [42]

3920   Dahlan, Nursiah
       Tiga putra membela ibu dan tanah air; Cerita di masa perjuangan kemerdekaan.
       Second edition. Jakarta: Kem. P dan K, 1981, 107 pp. [First edition 1963.]

3921   Danukusumo, Sutjipto
       'Catatan perjuangan dalam perang kemerdekaan', in: *Bunga rampai perjuangan
       dan pengorbanan II*, pp. 359-369. Jakarta: Markas Besar Legiun Veteran RI,
       1983.

3922   Darban, A. Adaby
       Sejarah Hisbullah di Yogyakarta; Kelaskaran Islam dalam perjuangan bangsa
       Indonesia. Paper Diskusi Sejarah Lokal IV, Revolusi Kemerdekaan di Tingkat
       Lokal, Bandungan-Ambarawa, 1994, 58 pp.

3923 *Dari penjerangan ke penjerahan.* Bukittinggi: Djawatan Penerangan Sumatera Tengah, 1951, 161 pp.

3924 Dariah, Ny. ('Bu Dar Mortir')
'Wanita komandan tanpa pangkat semasa revolusi kemerdekaan 1945-1949', in: *Bunga rampai perjuangan dan pengorbanan II*, pp. 80-85. Jakarta: Markas Besar Legiun Veteran RI, 1983.

3925 Darmodihardjo, Dardji
'Nostalgia dari masa perjuangan', in: *Bunga rampai perjuangan dan pengorbanan II*, pp. 95-99. Jakarta: Markas Besar Legiun Veteran RI, 1983.

3926 Darmosugondo
'Mengenang peristiwa sekitar 17 Agustus 1945', in: Darius Marpaung (ed.), *Bingkisan nasional; Kenangan 10 tahun revolusi Indonesia, 17-8-1945/17-8-1955*, pp. 42-45, 48. Djakarta: Usaha Pegawai Nasional Indonesia, 1955.

3927 Darusman, Suryono
' "Operation Meriam Bee"; Penyelundupan senjata terbesar', in: Kustiniyati Mochtar (ed.), *Memoar pejuang Republik Indonesia seputar 'zaman Singapura', 1945-1950*, pp. 75-101. Jakarta: Gramedia, 1992.

3928 Darusman, Suryono
'Pendahuluan', in: Kustiniyati Mochtar (ed.), *Memoar pejuang Republik Indonesia seputar 'zaman Singapura', 1945-1950*, pp. 1-16. Jakarta: Gramedia, 1992.

3929 Darusman, Suryono
Singapore and the Indonesian revolution 1945-50. Singapore: Institute of Southeast Asian Studies, 1992, 75 pp.

3930 Daruso, Bambang
Sejarah pembentukan UUD 45. Second edition. Semarang: Aneka Ilmu, 1986, 67 pp. [First edition 1984.]

3931 Daud, Riri Amin
Pahlawan Ranggong Daeng Romo. Makasar: Jajasan Artja Pahlawan, 1971. [4868, 6210]

3932 Daud, Riri Amin
Rakyat Sulawesi Selatan mendobrak dan membubarkan negara Indonesia Timur dan negara-negara bahagian BFO lainnya untuk mempertahankan dan memulihkan kembali kedaulatan negara kesatuan RI 17 Agustus 1945 berdasarkan Pancasila dan berundang-undang dasar dengan UUD 45. Paper Seminar Sejarah Perjuangan Rakyat Sulawesi Selatan Menentang Penjajahan Asing, Ujung Pandang, 1982, 17 pp.

3933 Daya, Syafri
Revolusi fisik di Jambi (1945-1950). 1974, 44 pp. [MA thesis IKIP Bandung.] [10]

3934 Decha
'Penerangan gerilja', in: *Dari penjerangan ke penjerahan*, pp. 106-112. Bukittinggi: Djawatan Penerangan Sumatera Tengah, 1951.

3935   Dekker, I Njoman
       Sedjarah Indonesia baru 1945-1949; Revolusi nasional atau perang kemerdekaan.
       Second edition. Malang: Almamater, 1971, 106 pp.

3936   Dekker, I Njoman
       Sejarah revolusi nasional atau perang kemerdekaan (1945-1949). Malang:
       Almamater, 1975, 107 pp.

3937   Dekker, I Njoman
       Sejarah revolusi nasional. Jakarta: Balai Pustaka, 1980, 94 pp.

3938   *Derap 10 Nopember dalam Orde Baru.* Djakarta: Pusat Pemberitaan ABRI, ca.
       1967, 142 pp. (kitlv-m)

3939   *Detik dan peristiwa 17 Augustus 1945-23 Djanuari 1950.* Jogjakarta: Kem.
       Penerangan, 1950, 82 pp.

3940   Detik-detik peristiwa perjuangan rakyat semesta membela Proklamasi 17-8-
       1945 di wilayah Ex-sub Teritorium 7 Komando Sumatera. Jakarta: Forum
       Komunikasi, 1975, 1010 pp. 2 vols.

3941   *Detik-detik Proklamasi 17 Agustus 1945 di Bukittinggi dan sekitarnja.* Bukittinggi:
       Djawatan Penerangan Kotamadya Bukittinggi, ca. 1970, 12 pp.

3942   Dewi, Witra
       Revolusi di Sumatera Barat; Studi kasus kehidupan pengungsi di Bukittinggi,
       1946-1948. 1989, 76+31 pp. [MA thesis Universitas Andalas, Padang.] [58]

3943   Dharmarata, Imam Mahdi
       Pasukan gerilya Sleman Timur. 1975. [MA thesis Universitas Gadjah Mada,
       Yogyakarta.] [Histori]

3944   Dhofier, Zamaksyari
       Peranan elemen santri dalam proses pencetusan Proklamasi kemerdekaan
       Republik Indonesia 17 Agustus 1945. Paper Seminar Lahirnya Suatu Bangsa,
       Jakarta, 1990, 10 pp.

3945   Diah, B.M.
       *Angkatan baru '45; Lembaga Perjuangan Pemuda menentang Jepang, mendorong
       Proklamasi kemerdekaan Indonesia.* Jakarta: Masa Merdeka, 1983, 39+283 pp.

3946   Diah, Burhanuddin Mohamad
       'Pers dan radio; Suatu pandangan pribadi', in: Colin Wild and Peter Carey
       (eds), *Gelora api revolusi*, pp. 170-174. Jakarta: Gramedia, 1986.

3947   Diah, Burhanuddin Mohamad
       'The press and the radio; An interview with Burhanuddin Mohamad Diah', in:
       Colin Wild and Peter Carey (eds), *Born in fire; The Indonesian struggle for
       independence; An anthology*, pp. 168-171. Athens: Ohio University Press, 1986.

3948   Diasmadi DSG, S.
       Merdeka atau mati; Catatan kisah perjoangan Taruna Patria Sala. Jakarta: Yayasan
       Al-Qalam, 1983, 1984, 226+270 pp. 2 vols.

3949   Diasmadi DSG, S.
       Tentara pelajar Solo mana aksi militer Belanda 2. Jakarta: Pustaka Jaya, 1986,
       54 pp.

3950 Diasmadi DSG, S.
Desa gerilya. Jakarta: Pustaka Jaya, 1992, 45 pp.

3951 *Dimulai dengan senjum; Het begon met een glimlach; It started with a smile.*
Djakarta: Kementerian Penerangan Republik Indonesia Serikat, 1950, 40 pp.

3952 Dimyati, M.
Djokja diduduki. Djakarta: Gapura, 1950, 166 pp.

3953 Dimyati, Muhammad
Manusia dan peristiwa. Second edition. Djakarta: Balai Pustaka, 1964, 221 pp.
[First edition 1951.] (kitlv-m)

3954 Dini, Nh.
Langit dan bumi sahabat kami. Jakarta: Dunia Pustaka Jaya, 1979, 199 pp.
[Second printing, Jakarta: Gramedia, 1988, 139 pp; Third printing 1990; Fourth
printing 1991.]

3955 Dipodilogo, Achmad
'Pengalaman dalam perjuangan', in: *Bunga rampai perjuangan dan pengorbanan I*,
pp. 17-28. Jakarta: Markas Besar Legiun Veteran RI, 1982.

3956 Diro, Pak
'Barisan pelopor', *Gema Angkatan 45* no. 21 (September 1977):21-22.

3957 Djailani, A.K.
'Tjoret-moret sekitar Proklamasi 1945', in: *Modal revolusi 45*, pp. 91-93.
Kutaradja: Komite Musjawarah Angkatan 45 DI Atjeh, 1960.

3958 Djaja, Tamar
Mohd. Natsir dalam revolusi Indonesia. Medan: Menara Islam, ca. 1980, 18 pp.

3959 Djajaatmadja, Wirja
Sekitar peristiwa 10 Nopember 1945. 1968, 93 pp. [MA thesis IKIP Bandung.]
[10, 108]

3960 Djajaatmadja, Wirja
Tindjauan sedjarah mengenai patriotisme pahlawan I Gusti Ngurah Rai. 1970,
61 pp. [MA thesis IKIP Bandung.] [10]

3961 Djajadiningrat, Idrus Nasir
The beginnings of the Indonesian-Dutch negotiations and the Hoge Veluwe talks.
Ithaca: Cornell University, 1958, 128 pp.

3962 Djajadiningrat, R.T.
Herinneringen van een vrijheidsstrijdster. 's-Gravenhage: Nijhoff, 1974, 12+74 pp.
[Second printing 1975.]

3963 Djajadiningrat, Roswita T.
Pengalamanku di daerah pertempuran Malang Selatan. Jakarta: Balai Pustaka,
1974, 111 pp. [Second printing 1975.]

3964 Djajadisastra, Fatah
Tindjauan tentang kedudukan Republik Indonesia dalam hukum internasional
periode 1945-1949. 1970. [MA thesis Universitas Padjadjaran, Bandung.] [20]

3965 Djajakusumah, Warsa
'Api '45 dari masa ke masa', in: *Aku akan teruskan; Hasil sayembara mengarang dalam rangka peringatan hari ulang tahun kemerdekaan R.I. yang ke 30*, pp. 98-127. Jakarta: Dewan Harian Nasional Angkatan 45, Pusat Dokumentasi Sejarah Perjoangan 45/Aries Lima, 1976.

3966 Djajoesman, R.
'Biografi I Gusti Ngurah Rai', *Madjalah Sedjarah Militer Angkatan Darat* no. 7 (1960):61-72.

3967 Djajoesman, R.
'Gerakan tank Belanda di Djawa masa perang kemerdekaan I', *Madjalah Sedjarah Militer Angkatan Darat* no. 15 (1964):21-25.

3968 Djajoesman, R.
'Pendapat Inggeris tentang tjara pemberantasan tentara gerilja Indonesia (1946)', *Madjalah Sedjarah Militer Angkatan Darat* no. 15 (1964):32-37. [55]

3969 Djajoesman, R.
'Perang gerilja didaerah berbukit dan pegunungan Djawa Barat', *Madjalah Sedjarah Militer Angkatan Darat* no. 16 (1964):34-40; no. 17 (1964):36-42. [55]

3970 Djajoesman, R.
'Perebutan Tjileungsir oleh U-Brigade Belanda', *Madjalah Sedjarah Militer Angkatan Darat* no. 16 (1964):17-25. [55]

3971 Djajusman
'Tentara "Tangger Perang" dalam permulaan revolusi fisik', *Vidya Yudha* no. 13 (1971):104-111.

3972 Djajusman
Bandung lautan api; Suatu episode dari perjuangan kemerdekaan. Bandung: Angkasa, 1975, 94 pp. [Third printing 1986.]

3973 Djaka, Baharuddin
'Pengalaman bersama PDRI', in: Abdurrachman Surjomihardjo and J.R. Chaniago (eds), *Pemerintah Darurat Republik Indonesia dikaji ulang*, pp. 160-168. Jakarta: Masyarakat Sejarawan Indonesia, 1990.

3974 *The Djakarta Charter; The spirit of the Constitution of 1945.* Djakarta: Department of Religious Affairs, 1964, 24 pp.

3975 Djakasuria
Lintasan repolusi. Second edition. Djakarta, 1955, 68 pp. [First edition 1953.] (kitlv-m)

3976 Djalil, Halma A.
Peristiwa Rengasdengklok; Hubungannya dengan Proklamasi kemerdekaan Indonesia 17 Agustus 1945. 1987. [MA thesis IKIP Jakarta.] [Histori]

3977 Djamhari, Saleh A.
M.B.K.D.; Markas Besar Komando Djawa (1948-1949). Djakarta: Lembaga Sedjarah HANKAM, 1967, 24 pp.

3978 Djamhari, Saleh A.
The battle of Bojongkokosan, Cibadak, December 9th, 1945. Paper Sixth International Conference on Asian History, Yogyakarta, 1974, 17 pp. [25]

3979 Djamhari, Saleh A.
Kekuatan-kekuatan dalam revolusi di Surabaya. Paper SSN-III, Jakarta, 1981, 17 pp.

3980 Djamhari, Saleh A.
'Pemerintah Darurat RI di Jawa', in: Abdurrachman Surjomihardjo and J.R. Chaniago (eds), *Pemerintah Darurat Republik Indonesia dikaji ulang*, pp. 67-74. Jakarta: Masyarakat Sejarawan Indonesia, 1990.

3981 Djarwadi, Radik
'Hati badja menegak (in memoriam R.W. Mongisidi)', *Madjalah Sedjarah Militer Angkatan Darat* no. 6 (1959):35-46. [55]

3982 Djarwadi, Radik (ed.)
Pradjurit mengabdi; Gumpalan perang kemerdekaan Bataljon Y. Bandung: PUSSEMAD, 1959, 190+62 pp.

3983 Djarwadi, Radik (ed.)
Surat dari sel maut; Kisah pahlawan nasional Robert Wolter Mongisidi. Surabaja: Grip, 1960, 80 pp.

3984 Djarwadi, Radik a.o.
Naskah sedjarah Corps Hasanuddin; Pradjurit tempur dan pembangunan. Udjung Pandang: Corhas, 1972, 126 pp.

3985 Djatikusumo, G.P.H.
'Permulaan terbentuknya suatu tentara', in: Colin Wild and Peter Carey (eds), *Gelora api revolusi*, pp. 79-82. Jakarta: Gramedia, 1986.

3986 *Djendral Soedirman pahlawan sedjati. Jogjakarta: Kem. Penerangan, ca. 1950, 167* pp.

3987 *Djendral Sudirman.* Djakarta: Kem. Pertahanan, ca. 1950, 63 pp.

3988 *Djenderal Sudirman.* Djakarta: Kem. Penerangan, 1960, 61 pp. [22]

3989 Djoehana, A.M.
'Twintig jaar Indonesische dekolonisatie 1942-1962', *Spiegel Historiael* 21 (1986):134-139.

3990 Djohari, Sjamsir
Peristiwa Situdjuh (15 Djanuari 1949). 1971, 106 pp. [MA thesis IKIP Padang.]

3991 (Djojoadisurjo), Achmad Subardjo
'An interpretation of current history in Indonesia', *Penelitian Sedjarah* 2-2 (1961):11-12; 2-4 (1961):10-12.

3992 Djojoadisurjo, Achmad Subardjo
'Annotations on the Indonesian declaration of independence, 17th of August 1945', *Penelitian Sedjarah* 6-9 (1965):4-11.

3993 Djojoadisurjo, Achmad Subardjo
'The Pacific War and Indonesia's independence', *Indonesian Review of International Affairs* 1-2 (July 1971):55-66.

3994   (Djojoadisurjo), Achmad Subardjo
       Lahirnja Republik Indonesia; (Suatu tindjauan dan kisah pengalaman). Djakarta:
       Kinta, 1972, 120 pp.

3995   Djojoadisurjo, Achmad Subardjo
       'Events leading up to the Proclamation of Indonesia's independence', *Indonesian
       Review of International Affairs* 1-5 (April 1975):71-100.

3996   Djojohadikusumo, Margono
       'Haruskah bank asing beroperasi di Indonesia merdeka', *Gema Angkatan 45*
       no. 25 (January 1978):27-29.

3997   Djoko
       'Some notes on the Tiga Daerah Affair; A local event in the Indonesian
       revolution', *Masyarakat Indonesia* 1 (1974):155-163.

3998   Djokolelono
       Hancurnya jembatan Beru. Jakarta: Dunia Pustaka Jaya, 1977, 87 pp.

3999   Djuhari
       Peranan Tentara Nasional Indonesia dalam perang kemerdekaan. 1973, 94 pp.
       [MA thesis IKIP Jakarta.] [11]

4000   Djumarwan
       Aktivitas Laskar Putri Indonesia dalam rangka ikut serta mempertahankan
       kemerdekaan Republik Indonesia. 1984, 138 pp. [MA thesis Universitas
       Gadjah Mada, Yogyakarta.]

4001   Djumarwan; Mudji Hartono and Y.B. Sudjiman
       *Peranan rakyat Segoroyoso dalam perang kemerdekaan 1945-1949; Laporan
       penelitian*. Yogyakarta: IKIP, 1988, 41 pp.

4002   Djunaidi, H. Mahbub
       Dari hari ke hari; Roman. Jakarta: Dunia Pustaka Jaya, 1975, 147 pp.

4003   Djungkung, Murdijo
       Mengenang pertempuran empat hari di kota Solo, Agustus 1949. Solo: n.n., 1988,
       49 pp.

4004   Doelpatah
       Peranan pemuda dalam mempertahankan kemerdekaan 1945-1949. 1970,
       124 pp. [MA thesis IKIP Jogjakarta.] [17]

4005   Doeriatmodjo
       'Pengabdian "Banteng Blorok" dalam perang kemerdekaan', *Gema Angkatan 45*
       nr. 33 (October 1978):36-41.

4006   Doko, I.H. (Tjak)
       *Nusa Tenggara Timur dalam kancah perjuangan kemerdekaan Indonesia; Beberapa
       catatan, ungkapan dan pengalaman pribadi*. Bandung: Masa Baru, 1974, 260 pp.

4007   Doko, I.H.
       Pahlawan-pahlawan suku Timor. Jakarta: Balai Pustaka, 1981, 75 pp.

4008   Doko, I.H.
       Perjuangan kemerdekaan Indonesia di Nusa Tenggara Timur. Jakarta: Balai
       Pustaka, 1981, 280 pp.

4009 *Dokumentasi Republik Indonesia; Djilid 1; 17 Agustus 1945-1 Djanuari 1946.*
Jogjakarta: Kem. Penerangan, 1950, 103 pp.

4010 *Dokumentasi Republik Indonesia; Djilid 2; 1 Djanuari 1946-30 Djuni 1946.*
Jogjakarta: Kem. Penerangan, 1950, 168 pp.

4011 'Dsg'
'11 Desember sepandjang masa; Memperingati 40.000 korban Sulawesi Selatan',
in: Darius Marpaung (ed.), *Bingkisan nasional; Kenangan 10 tahun revolusi
Indonesia, 17-8-1945/17-8-1955*, pp. 80-87. Djakarta: Usaha Pegawai Nasional
Indonesia, 1955.

4012 Dullah
*Teks pidato Seminar Sejarah Peranan Generasi Muda dalam Perjuangan Bangsa
1942-1950.* Yogyakarta: Masyarakat Sejarawan Indonesia, 1989, 32 pp.

4013 Dunia, H. Gazali
Hari Pahlawan 10 Nopember dan kisah-kisah lain. Jakarta: Bulan Bintang, 1976,
56 pp.

4014 Dwidjosoemarto, Sardi
Perjuangan menuju pertemuan. Semarang: Dian Artha, 1985, 100 pp.

4015 Ecip, S. Sinansari
'Korban "40.000" Westerling dari beberapa sudut', *Gema Angkatan 45* no. 20
(August 1977):47-50.

4016 Ecip, S. Sinansari
Jejak kaki Wolter Mongisidi; Sebuah kisah perjuangan. Jakarta: Sinar Harapan,
1981, 139 pp.

4017 Ecip, S. Sinansari
Gerilya pantai. Jakarta: Bunda Karya, 1984, 65 pp.

4018 Edijushanan
Jantan. Jakarta: Gramedia, 1989, 113 pp.

4019 Edisaputra
Bukit Barisan djadi saksi; Suatu epos jang diungkap dari perang kemerdekaan RI.
Medan: Badan Pembina Corps Bukit Barisan, 1967, 100 pp.

4020 Edisaputra
Boetet; Drama perang kemerdekaan. Medan: Badan Pembina Seni Budaja dan
Film Sumatera Utara, 1969, 48 pp.

4021 Edisaputra
Gelora kemerdekaan sepanjang Bukit Barisan. Medan: Patriot, 1972, 64 pp.

4022 Edisaputra
Lintasan dan cukilan perjuangan kemerdekaan se Sumatera dan Kalimantan Barat.
Medan: Bina Satria 45, 1977, 219 pp.

4023 Edisaputra
'Benteng Huraba; Pintu gerbang utara Pemerintahan Darurat Republik
Indonesia', *Gema Angkatan 45* no. 41 (August-September 1979):31-37.

4024   Edisaputra
        'Realisasi Proklamasi kemerdekaan Indonesia terlambat 44 hari di ibukota
        Propinsi Sumatera', *Gema Angkatan 45* no. 42 (October 1979):17-24, 41.

4025   Edisaputra
        Simalungun Jogya-nya Sumatra dalam perang kemerdekaan. Medan: Bina Satria
        45, 1979. [4874]

4026   Edisaputra
        'Indonesia dan Jepang kerja sama menggempur tentara Sekutu di Tanjung
        Morawa', *Gema Angkatan 45* no. 51/53 (February-April 1981):92-94.

4027   Edisaputra
        'Bobolnya "lingkaran maut" Belanda', *Gema Angkatan 45* no. 56/58 (July-
        September 1981):101-107.

4028   Edisaputra
        'Jendral Spoor tertembak mati di Sipirok dalam Perang Kemerdekaan II', *Gema
        Angkatan 45* no. 59/61 (October-December 1981):67-73.

4029   Edisaputra
        'Nopember 1945 diseluruh Indonesia', *Gema Angkatan 45* no. 68/70 (July-
        September 1982):57-61.

4030   Edisaputra
        'Sekitar jalannya rapat Panitya Persiapan Kemerdekaan Indonesia yang
        mensyahkan Undang-Undang Dasar 1945', *Gema Angkatan 45* no. 68/70 (July-
        September 1982):62-64.

4031   Edisaputra
        Bedjo; Harimau Sumatera dalam perang kemerdekaan. Jakarta: Yayasan Bina
        Satria-45, 1985, 248 pp.

4032   Edisaputra
        *Sumatera dalam perang kemerdekaan; Perlawanan rakyat semesta menentang Jepang,
        Inggris dan Belanda*. Jakarta: Yayasan Bina Satria '45, 1987, 560 pp.

4033   Edisaputra; Suwardi Suwardjo and H. Slamet Sudjono
        *Mohamad Rivai; Tanpa pamrih kupertanankan Proklamasi kemerdekaan Indonesia,
        17 Agustus 1945; Ungkapan sejarah perjuangan rakyat Jawa Barat*. Jakarta:
        Intermasa, ca. 1983, 58+720 pp.

4034   Effendi, Achmad
        *Sudirman; Bacaan anak-anak bagi pembinaan generasi Indonesia yang berkepribadian
        nasional*. Jakarta: Tintamas, 1974, 47 pp.

4035   Effendi, M. Amin
        Cukilan riwayat pemberontakan 9 Nopember '45 di Banjermasin; Pidato. Banjer-
        masin, 1975. [4862]

4036   Effendi, Soelaiman
        'Kenang-kenangan pada butiran-butiran pengalaman semasa perang
        kemerdekaan', in: *Bunga rampai perjuangan dan pengorbanan II*, pp. 384-410.
        Jakarta: Markas Besar Legiun Veteran RI, 1983.

4037 Effendie, Danny
Gema perang rakyat di Sumatera Selatan 1945-1949. 1973. [4038]

4038 Effendie, Danny
'Agustus 1945 periode agitasi', in: *Bunga rampai perjuangan dan pengorbanan II*, pp. 87-93. Jakarta: Markas Besar Legiun Veteran RI, 1983.

4039 Effendy, H. Am.
Kapan lahirnya Pancasila? Paper SSN-III, Jakarta, 1981, 19 pp.

4040 Effendy, H. Am.
'Kapan lahirnya Pancasila?', in: *Seksi Sejarah Mutakhir (1); Seminar Sejarah Nasional III*, pp. 1-16. Jakarta: Dep. P dan K, Direktorat Sejarah dan Nilai Tradisional, Proyek Inventarisasi dan Dokumentasi Sejarah Nasional, 1982.

4041 Elias, H.B.
Sejarah pergerakan kebangsaan Indonesia di pulau Siau. Manado: Legiun Veteran RI, 1973, 200 pp.

4042 Enar, Fatimah; Abizar; Nurhadi; Thahar Ramli; Alwir Darwis; Syofyan Naim and Wirda Nur
Sumatera Barat 1945-1950. Padang: Pemerintah Daerah Sumatera Barat, 1976, 40+153 pp.

4043 Enar, Fatimah; Abizar; Nurhadi; Thahar Ramli; Alwir Darwis; Syofyan Naim and Wirda Nur
Sumatera Barat 1945-1949. Padang: Pemerintah Daerah Sumatera Barat, 1978, 68+335 pp.

4044 Erman, Erwiza
Peranan kelompok nasionalis (PNI) dalam KNIP. Paper SSN-IV, Yogyakarta, 1985, 25 pp.

4045 Eryono, A.; R. Soekandar; P. Herukusuma and Moh. Noech (eds)
Memoar perjuangan menegakkan negara Proklamasi 17 Agustus 1945. Yogyakarta: Yayasan Wiratama 45, 1985, 269 pp.

4046 Etek, Syahrul
'Kisahku sebagai ABK kapal PPB 58 LB', in: Kustiniyati Mochtar (ed.), *Memoar pejuang Republik Indonesia seputar 'zaman Singapura', 1945-1950*, pp. 160-174. Jakarta: Gramedia, 1992.

4047 *Ex TRIP Jatim; Mengenang peristiwa-peristiwa perjoangan masa lampau; Dari anggauta oleh anggauta*. Jakarta: Yayasan Darmo 49, 1980, 115 pp.

4048 Fakkih, Markhaban
Golongan santri dan Peristiwa 426 di Klaten; Suatu studi kasus tentang terlibatnya satu kelompok sosial dalam pemberontakan. 1977. [MA thesis Universitas Gadjah Mada, Yogyakarta.]

4049 *Fakta dan dokumen-dokumen untuk menjusun buku 'Indonesia memasuki gelanggang internasional'; Sub-periode kabinet Presiden Soekarno dari tanggal 17.8.45 sampai 14.11.45*. Djakarta: Kem. Luar Negeri, 1958. [6122]

4050 Gade, Usman Nya'
Sekitar pembentukan Angkatan Pemuda Indonesia (API) di Aceh. Kutaraja?:
Kanwil Dep. P dan K Prop. DI Aceh/Masyarakat Sejarawan Indonesia di
Aceh, 1976. [4854]

4051 Gafuri, H. Ahmad
*Sejarah perjuangan gerilya menegakkan Republik Indonesia di Kalimantan Selatan
(1945-1949)*. Banjarmasin: Dep. Penerangan, 1984, 136 pp.

4052 Gaharu, Sjammaun
'Perebutan kekuasaan dari tangan Djepang', in: *Modal revolusi 45*, pp. 27-40.
Kutaradja: Komite Musjawarah Angkatan 45 DI Atjeh, 1960.

4053 Gaharu, Sjammaun
Beberapa catatan tentang perjuangan menegakkan kemerdekaan di Aceh. Medan:
Panitia Seminar Perjuangan Aceh, 1976. [4854, 6286]

4054 Gani, Joyce
Korban 40.000 jiwa; Suatu tinjauan patriotisme dan nasionalisme di Sulawesi
Selatan. Paper Seminar Mahasiswa Sejarah se-Indonesia, Jakarta, 1986, 16 pp.

4055 Gatam, Ny. Nurul Aini S.
' "Sandera" (kenang-kenangan di saat-saat setelah Proklamasi kemerdekaan RI
di Bengkulu)', *Gema Angkatan 45* no. 71/75 (October 1982 - February 1983):65-
70.

4056 Gayatri, Sri Indra
Karesidenan Malang pada masa awal kemerdekaan 1945-1947. 1981, 134 pp.
[MA thesis Universitas Indonesia, Jakarta.] [Histori]

4057 Gayo, M.H.
'Cuplikan Proklamasi pengambil-alihan jawatan kereta api dan trem listrik
Jakarta', *Gema Angkatan 45* no. 29/30 (1978). [*Gema Angkatan 45* no. 43]

4058 *Gelanggang repolusi; Kenangan 10 tahun Proklamasi*. Djakarta: UPMI, 1955, 232
pp.

4059 Ghazali, Zulfikar
Hizbullah salah satu cikal bakal TNI. Paper SSN-V, Semarang 1990, 12 pp.

4060 Gintings, Djamin
Bukit Kadir. Medan: Umum, 1964, 336 pp.

4061 Gintings, Yohannes Pariaman
Suatu tinjauan sejarah tentang perjuangan bangsa Indonesia menentang kolo-
nialisme Belanda di Tanah Karo pada masa mempertahankan kemerdekaan
Republik Indonesia, 1945-1949. 1974, 118 pp. [MA thesis IKIP Medan.] [13]

4062 Gondohutomo, Amino
'Periode revolusi phisik, tahun 1946 sampai dengan akhir tahun 1949', in: M.A.
Hanafiah; Bahder Djohan and Surono (eds), *125 tahun pendidikan dokter di
Indonesia, 1851-1976*, pp. 40-42. Jakarta: Panitya Peringatan 125 tahun
Pendidikan Dokter di Indonesia, 1976.

4063 Gonggong, Anhar
Pemuda berdemokrasi dalam situasi krisis, 1942-1950. Paper Seminar Sejarah Peranan Generasi Muda dalam Perjuangan Bangsa, Yogyakarta, 1989, 15 pp.

4064 Gonggotrisno
Kemerdekaan jang tidak mempunjai arti. Medan: Lathief, 1952, 46 pp. (kitlv-m)

4065 Gumanti, Hamdy El
Selamat jalan Bung Tomo. Jakarta: Aksara Agung, 1981, 127 pp.

4066 Gunawan, Ryadi
'Jagoan dalam revolusi kita', *Prisma* 10-8 (1981):41-50.

4067 Gunawan, Ryadi
'Dinamika wajah antar golongan politik di Indonesia periode revolusi; Sebuah pengantar diskusi', in: *Seminar Sejarah Nasional IV, Sub tema dinamika*, pp. 281-302. Jakarta: Kem. P dan K, 1985.

4068 Gunawan, Ryadi
'Dunia grayak dan revolusi lokal', in: *Revolusi nasional di tingkat lokal*, pp. 29-47. Jakarta: Kem. P dan K, 1989.

4069 Gunawi K.
'Rakjat Luwu Sulawesi menentang pendjadjah', *Vidya Yudha* no. 7 (1969):92-96.

4070 Gurning, Sudarman
Suatu tinjauan tentang pembubaran negara Sumatera Timur. 1974, 87 pp. [MA thesis IKIP Medan.] [13]

4071 Gusti, Aman
Pertumbuhan gerilya RI di Kalimantan. Banjermasin: Utama, 1973. [4862]

4072 Hadi Soewito, Irna H.N.
Lahirnya kelasykaran wanita dan Wirawati Catur Panca. Jakarta: Yayasan Wirawati Catur Panca, 1992, 239 pp.

4073 Hadi Soewito, Irna H.N.
Rakyat Jawa Timur mempertahankan kemerdekaan. Jakarta: Grasindo, 1994, 748 pp. 3 vols.

4074 Hadidjojo, R.M. Sri
Serat gerilja Sala. Djakarta: Balai Pustaka, 1957, 63 pp. [In Javanese.]

4075 Hadimadja, Aoh K.
Manusia dan tanahnja. Second printing. Djakarta: Balai Pustaka, 1972, 107 pp. [First edition 1952.]

4076 Hadiman, H. and Suparmin (eds)
Lintasan perjalanan kepolisian RI sejak Proklamasi-1950. Jakarta: Gadhessa Pura Mas, 1985, 505 pp.

4077 Hadipranoto
Hari Pahlawan 10 November. 1965, 70 pp. [MA thesis IKIP Djakarta.] [11]

4078 Hadisaputro, Imam Basiran
'Sebagai kadet dalam perang kemerdekaan', in: *Bunga rampai perjuangan dan pengorbanan I*, pp. 253-259. Jakarta: Markas Besar Legiun Veteran RI, 1982.

4079   Hadisutjipto, S.Z.
       Bara dan njala revolusi phisik di Djakarta. Djakarta: Pemerintah Daerah Chusus
       Ibukota, Dinas Museum dan Sedjarah, 1971, 104 pp.

4080   Hadjid, Zaran
       'Aku hanya seorang prajurit '45; Cuplikan dari buku harian', in: *Bunga rampai
       perjuangan dan pengorbanan I,* pp. 733-752. Jakarta: Markas Besar Legiun
       Veteran RI, 1982.

4081   Hady, Arto
       Madiun 48. Jakarta: n.n., 1981, 121 pp.

4082   Hadypurnama, K.
       Pertempuran Mendalan Kesamben tahun 1948-1949. 1975, 166 pp. [MA thesis
       IKIP Malang.] [12]

4083   Hakim, Darmiasti Loekman
       Karesidenan Pati 1945-1947. 1981, 113 pp. [MA thesis Universitas Indonesia,
       Jakarta.] [Histori]

4084   Hakim, Masfar R.
       Penembusan blokade Belanda (1946-1949). Paper SSN-III, Jakarta, 1981, 25 pp.

4085   Hakim, Masfar R. and Zamzulis Ismail
       Sejarah pendidikan perwira TNI Angkatan Laut 1945-1950. Jakarta: Dinas Sejarah
       TNI-AL, 1982, 124 pp.

4086   Haliem A.E., A.
       Lintasan perjuangan kemerdekaan RI 1945-1949 di daerah Mandar. Majene: Kantor
       Dep. Penerangan Kabupaten Majene, 1976, 15+61 pp.

4087   Halim, A.
       'Sjahrir yang saya kenal', in: H. Rosihan Anwar (ed.), *Mengenang Sjahrir,*
       pp. 100-115. Jakarta: Gramedia, 1980.

4088   Halim, Abdul
       Di antara hempasan dan benturan; Kenang-kenangan Dr. Abdul Halim 1942-1950.
       Jakarta: Arsip Nasional, 1981, 127 pp.

4089   Halim, Abdul
       'Mengenang perjuangan masa silam selama perjuangan kemerdekaan 1945-
       1950', in: *Bunga rampai perjuangan dan pengorbanan I,* pp. 60-80. Jakarta:
       Markas Besar Legiun Veteran RI, 1982.

4090   Hambali, K.H. Ahmad
       'Peristiwa bersejarah pengibaran bendera Merah Putih pertama di Balikpapan',
       Gema Angkatan 45 no. 71/75 (October 1982 - February 1983):58-64, 154.

4091   Hamengku Buwono IX, Sri Sultan
       'Republik di bawah kepungan', in: Colin Wild and Peter Carey (eds), *Gelora api
       revolusi,* pp. 187-192. Jakarta: Gramedia, 1986.

4092   Hamengku Buwono IX, Sultan
       'Republic under siege; An interview with Sri Sultan Hamengku Buwono IX', in:
       C. Wild and P. Carey (eds), *Born in fire; The Indonesian struggle for independence;
       An anthology,* pp. 184-187. Athens: Ohio University Press, 1986.

4093 Hamid, R.A.
'Cuplikan-cuplikan perjuangan kemerdekaan di sektor barat pulau Madura',
Vidya Yudha no. 18 (1974):47-65.

4094 Hamidiah, R.
Mas TRIP. Jakarta: Balai Pustaka, 1986, 51 pp.

4095 Hamzah, Achmad
Permasalahan P.K.I. dalam perjuangan kemerdekaan Indonesia. 1973, 98 pp.
[MA thesis IKIP Jakarta.]

4096 Handep, Kurnelius
'Pendaratan pasukan-pasukan expedisi di Kalimantan', in: *Letusan di balik buku;
Hasil sayembara mengarang dalam rangka peringatan hari ulang tahun kemerdekaan
RI yang ke 30*, pp. 173-199. Jakarta: Dewan Harian Nasional Angkatan
45/Aries Lima, 1976.

4097 Hanifah, Abu
Tales of a revolution; A leader of the Indonesian revolution looks back. Sydney: Angus
and Robertson, 1972, 377 pp.

4098 Hanifah, Abu
'Revolusi memakan anak sendiri; Tragedi Amir Sjarifudin', in: Abdullah, Taufik;
Aswab Mahasin dan Daniel Dhakidae (eds), *Manusia dalam kemelut sejarah*,
pp. 189-218. Jakarta: Lembaga Penelitian, Pendidikan dan Penerangan
Ekonomi dan Sosial, 1978.

4099 Harahap, A.S.
Rahsia dan akibat Linggardjati. Djakarta: Bintang Mas, 1951, 86 pp.

4100 Harahap, Zainabun
Kolonel anumerta I Gusti Ngurah Rai; Pahlawan dari pulau dewata. Djakarta:
Lembaga Sedjarah HANKAM, 1968, 15 pp.

4101 Hardi, Lasmidjah (ed.)
*Samudera Merah Putih 19 September 1945; Latar belakang peristiwa Ikada dan
dampaknya.* Jakarta: Yayasan 19 September 1945, 1983, 28+238 pp.

4102 Hardjawiganda, Rochmat; Anas Kesdali; J.R. Chaniago and Soeharto
Operasi lintas laut Banyuwangi-Bali. Jakarta: Dep. Pertahanan Keamanan, Pusat
Sejarah ABRI, 1982, 195 pp.

4103 Hardjosoediro, Soejitno
'Sekelumit pengalaman dalam perang kemerdekaan dan pers kebangsaan ikut
berperan', in: *Bunga rampai perjuangan dan pengorbanan I*, pp. 513-542. Jakarta:
Markas Besar Legiun Veteran RI, 1982.

4104 Hardjosoediro, Soejitno
Dari Proklamasi ke perang kemerdekaan. Jakarta: Balai Pustaka, 1987, 231 pp.

4105 *Hari Pahlawan 10 Nopember 1945-10 Nopember 1972.* Djakarta: Dep.
Penerangan, 1972, 12 pp.

4106 *Hari ulang tahun ke-VI Res. Inf. 18; Riwajat singkat Resimen Inf. 18/Terr. V
Brawidjaja.* Malang: n.n., 1954, 18 pp. (kitlv-m)

4107 Hariprasetya, Laserun
Pertemuan Ampelgading tahun 1949. 1975, 165 pp. [MA thesis IKIP Malang.]
[12]

4108 Harjaprayitna, Iskandar Jayusman
Catatan-catatan yang berserakan; Peristiwa-peristiwa nyata selama perjuangan kemerdekaan RI periode tahun 1945-1950. Semarang: Aneka Ilmu, 1984, 104 pp.

4109 Harjono, R.
Pendudukan Jogjakarta oleh tentara kolonial Belanda dan pengaruhnja dalam lapangan pendidikan. 1964, 147 pp. [MA thesis IKIP Djakarta.] [11]

4110 Harnoko, Darto
Gedung bekas tempat kediaman wakil Presiden Republik Indonesia yang pertama di Yogyakarta. Yogyakarta: Dinas Sosial Propinsi DI Yogyakarta/Universitas Gadjah Mada, 1985, 26 pp.

4111 Harnoko, Darto
Magelang pada revolusi phisik periode 1945-1949. Yogyakarta: Kem. P dan K, 1985, 54 pp.

4112 Harnoko, Darto
'Kegiatan pemuda minyak pada awal Proklamasi', in: *Revolusi nasional di tingkat lokal,* pp. 104-119. Jakarta: Kem. P dan K, 1989.

4113 Harnoko, Darto
'Suatu peristiwa bersejarah di Temanggung periode 1948-1949', in: *Peristiwa-peristiwa revolusi di tingkat lokal,* pp. 3-42. Yogyakarta: Dep. P dan K, 1993.

4114 Harnoko, Darto and Poliman
Perang kemerdekaan Kebumen tahun 1942-1950. Yogyakarta: Kem. P dan K, 1986/87, 69 pp.

4115 Hartojo, J. Kadjat
Mentalitas revolusi di Indonesia. Paper Diskusi Sejarah Lokal IV, Revolusi Kemerdekaan di Tingkat Lokal, Bandungan-Ambarawa, 1994, 20 pp.

4116 Hartomo, Ibnu
'Ringkasan pengalaman masa perang gerilya', in: *Bunga rampai perjuangan dan pengorbanan I,* pp. 244-250. Jakarta: Markas Besar Legiun Veteran RI, 1982.

4117 Hartono
The Indonesian communist movement, 1945-1948; Its development and relations with the Soviet Union. 1959, 116 pp. [MA thesis Columbia University, New York.]

4118 Haryono, Ny. Koesnoheni
'Kisah nyata perjuangan keluarga untuk kemerdekaan Republik Indonesia periode 1945-1950', in: *Aku akan teruskan; Hasil sayembara mengarang dalam rangka peringatan hari ulang tahun kemerdekaan R.I. yang ke 30,* pp. 42-66. Jakarta: Dewan Harian Nasional Angkatan 45, Pusat Dokumentasi Sejarah Perjoangan 45/Aries Lima, 1976.

4119 Haryono, Pius Suryo
Kota Yogyakarta pada masa pendudukan Belanda, 19 Desember 1948-30 Juni
1949. 1983, 83 pp. [MA thesis Universitas Indonesia, Jakarta.] [Histori]

4120 Hasan, Said Hamid
Jendral Sudirman. Bandung: Tarate, 1976, 56 pp. [Third printing 1983.]

4121 Hasan, T. Moh.
'PDRI (Pemerintah Darurat Republik Indonesia)', in: Abdurrachman Surjomihardjo and J.R. Chaniago (eds), *Pemerintah Darurat Republik Indonesia dikaji
ulang*, pp. 122-133. Jakarta: Masyarakat Sejarawan Indonesia, 1990.

4122 Hasanah, Siti
Sekitar sedjarah permulaan TNI. 1970. [MA thesis IKIP Bandung.] [10]

4123 Hasibuan, Parlindungan
Rasionalisasi Angkatan Perang 1948. 1986, 75+14 pp. [MA thesis Universitas
Indonesia, Jakarta.] [Histori]

4124 Hasjmy, A.
'Apa sebab Belanda sewaktu agressi pertama dan kedua tidak dapat mema-
suki Atjeh?', in: *Modal revolusi 45*, pp. 53-63. Kutaradja: Komite Musjawarah
Angkatan 45 DI Atjeh, 1960.

4125 Hasjmy, A.
'Pangkalan Lhok Nga yang bersejarah', *Sinar Darussalam* no. 70 (July 1976).
[3756]

4126 Hasjmy, Ali
Bunga rampai revolusi dari Tanah Aceh. Jakarta: Bulan Bintang, 1978, 183 pp.

4127 Hasjmy, A.
'Karena Aceh menentang, gagallah pembentukan Negara Sumatera', *Sinar Darussalam* no. 89 (April 1978). [3756, 4854]

4128 Hasjmy, A.
Kisah Misi Haji RI II; Menjalankan tugas revolusi di negara-negara Arab. Bandung:
Alma'arif, 1984, 180 pp.

4129 Hasjmy, A. and T. Alibasyah Talsya
Hari-hari pertama revolusi 45 di daerah Modal. Banda Aceh: Kanwil Dep. P dan
K Prop. DI Aceh/Masyarakat Sejarawan Indonesia Aceh, 1976. [4854]

4130 Hasmi; Marsoedi and Wid NS
Merebut kota perjuangan. Jakarta: Yayasan Sinar Asih Mataram, 1984, 60 pp.
[Second printing 1985.]

4131 Hassan, H. Chandra
'Kenangan indah dalam perang kemerdekaan ke sidang pengadilan Belanda', in:
Bunga rampai perjuangan dan pengorbanan I, pp. 123-135. Jakarta: Markas Besar
Legiun Veteran RI, 1982.

4132 Hassan, M. Zein
*Diplomasi revolusi Indonesia di luar negeri (perjoangan pemuda/mahasiswa Indonesia
di Timur Tengah)*. Jakarta: Bulan Bintang, 1980, 296 pp.

4133   Hasugian, J.
       Merdeka atau mati. Bandung: Remaja Karya, 1982, 68 pp.

4134   Hasyim, Much.
       Struktur organisasi kelasykaran di Sulawesi Selatan. Paper Seminar Sejarah
       Perjuangan Rakyat Sulawesi Selatan Menentang Penjajahan Asing, Ujung
       Pandang, 1982, 38 pp.

4135   Hasyim, Twk.
       'Detik-detik Proklamasi 1945', *Warta Pendidikan dan Kebudajaan* no. 7 (August
       1971). [4854, 6286]

4136   Hatmanto, Hairkoto
       Rapat raksasa di Lapangan Ikada 19 September 1945; Pemuda dan
       masalahnya. 1983, 79 pp. [MA thesis Universitas Indonesia, Jakarta.] [4101,
       Histori]

4137   Hatta, Mohammad
       'Legende en realiteit omtrent de Proclamatie van 17 Augustus', in: Mohammad
       Hatta, *Verspreide geschriften*, pp. 330-340. Djakarta/Amsterdam/Surabaja:
       Van der Peet, 1952.

4138   Hatta, Moh.
       'Isi Proklamasi', in: Darius Marpaung (ed.), *Bingkisan nasional; Kenangan 10
       tahun revolusi Indonesia, 17-8-1945/17-8-1955*, pp. 8-11. Djakarta: Usaha
       Pegawai Nasional Indonesia, 1955.

4139   Hatta, Mohammad
       Peranan pemuda menudju Indonesia merdeka, adil dan makmur; Pidato. Bandung:
       Angkasa, 1966, 40 pp.

4140   Hatta, Mohammad
       Sekitar Proklamasi 17 Agustus 1945. Djakarta: Tintamas, 1969, 64 pp. [Second
       edition, 1970, 75 pp.]

4141   Hatta, M.
       'Dari hal "testamen politik" kepada Tan Malaka', *Vidya Yudha* no. 18 (1974):6-
       14.

4142   Hatta, Moh.
       'Detik-detik sekitar Proklamasi 1945', *Bulletin Yaperna* 1-2 (1974):3-9.

4143   Hatta, Mohamad
       Kumpulan pidato dari tahun 1942 s/d 1949. Disusun oleh I Wangsa Widjaja dan
       Meutia F. Swasono. Jakarta: Yayasan Idayu, 1981, 332 pp.

4144   Hayati, Chusnul
       Perjuangan di kecamatan Moyudan dalam perlawanan gerilya selama revolusi
       phisik tahun 1948-1949. 1975. [MA thesis Universitas Gadjah Mada,
       Yogyakarta.] [Histori]

4145   Hendraningrat, Abdul Latief
       'Menjelang Proklamasi kemerdekaan penuh ketegangan dan kesibukan; Inilah
       yang paling mengesankan didalam hidup saya', in: *Bunga rampai perjuangan dan
       pengorbanan II*, pp. 14-19. Jakarta: Markas Besar Legiun Veteran RI, 1983.

4146 Hendraningrat, Rukmito
'Yang tak terlupakan dalam perang kemerdekaan; Pasukan elite Marine Brigade musuh kita tawan', in: *Bunga rampai perjuangan dan pengorbanan II*, pp. 286-297. Jakarta: Markas Besar Legiun Veteran RI, 1983.

4147 Henuhili, J.
'Cuplikan pengalaman pribadi', in: *Bunga rampai perjuangan dan pengorbanan I*, pp. 211-217. Jakarta: Markas Besar Legiun Veteran RI, 1982.

4148 Hermanses, Elly Kusumawati
Hubungan kekalahan Jepang dalam Perang Dunia II dengan Proklamasi kemerdekaan Indonesia. 1986. [MA thesis IKIP Jakarta.] [Histori]

4149 Hernawati, Elly
Perjuangan eks tentara PETA bersama rakyat Probolinggo menghadapi Agresi Militer I (periode 1945-1948). 1986. [MA thesis Universitas Gadjah Mada, Yogyakarta.] [Histori]

4150 Hidajat, Wahju
Sedjarah revolusi Indonesia. Djakarta: Dep. Penerangan R.I., 1966, 36+32+41 pp. 3 vols.

4151 *The history of the Armed Forces of the Republic of Indonesia*. Compiled by the Army Headquarters, Military History Division. Djakarta: Dep. Penerangan, ca. 1965, 40 pp. [26, 1412]

4152 Hsu Ching-hsien
Lahirnja Indonesia, 1941-1950. Djakarta: Hsing Chi Jih Pao, 1953, 10+236+16 pp. (kitlv-m)

4153 Husin, Mohd. Firdaus
Kasih di balik kabut. Jakarta: Balai Pustaka, 1974, 47 pp.

4154 Husinsyah, H. Sutan
'Di sepanjang jalan revolusi kemerdekaan 1945-1949', in: *Bunga rampai perjuangan dan pengorbanan I*, pp. 186-207. Jakarta: Markas Besar Legiun Veteran RI, 1982.

4155 Husny, Tengku Haji M. Lah
Revolusi sosial 1946 di Sumatera Timur/Tapanuli disertai pangkal-dan-akibatnya (proloog dan naloog-nya); Sebuah penyegaran ungkapan sejarah. Medan: Usaha Veteran Husny, 1983, 157 pp.

4156 Hussain, Abdullah
Peristiwa. Kuala Lumpur: Pustaka Antara, 1965, 273 pp.

4157 Hussain, Abdullah
Peristiwa kemerdekaan di Aceh. Jakarta: Balai Pustaka, 1990, 259 pp.

4158 Hutagalung, M.S.
Djalan tak ada udjung Mochtar Lubis. Djakarta: Gunung Agung, 1963, 90 pp.

4159 Hutasoit, Marnixius
Percikan revolusi di Sumatera. Jakarta: Gunung Mulia, 1986, 14+90 pp.

4160 Ibrahim, Darlis
Daerah Pariaman dalam perang kemerdekaan 1945-1949. 1971, 175 pp. [MA
thesis IKIP Padang.] [14, 4872]

4161 Ibrahim, H. Gazali
'Pengalaman perjuangan', in: *Bunga rampai perjuangan dan pengorbanan II*,
pp. 109-119. Jakarta: Markas Besar Legiun Veteran RI, 1983.

4162 Ibrahim, H. Gazali
'Membelah Selat Malaka bersama John Lie', in: Kustiniyati Mochtar (ed.),
Memoar pejuang Republik Indonesia seputar 'zaman Singapura', 1945-1950,
pp. 175-190. Jakarta: Gramedia, 1992.

4163 *Ichtisar kemerdekaan Indonesia*. Bandung: Dua-R, ca. 1950, 96 pp.

4164 'Ichtisar-kronologis tentang peristiwa penting dalam negara Indonesia', in:
Darius Marpaung (ed.), *Bingkisan nasional; Kenangan 10 tahun revolusi Indonesia,
17-8-1945/17-8-1955*, pp. 340-373. Djakarta: Usaha Pegawai Nasional Indonesia, 1955.

4165 *Ichtisar sedjarah perdjuangan ABRI*. Djakarta: Pusdjarah ABRI, 1971. [4835]

4166 Idrus
'Surabaja 1945', in: *Indonesian nationalism and revolution*, pp. 18-24. Clayton:
Monash University, 1969.

4167 *Ikhtisar sejarah perjuangan kemerdekaan di Sulawesi Selatan (1945-1949)*. Jakarta:
Markas Besar Angkatan Bersenjata Republik Indonesia, Pusat Sejarah dan
Tradisi ABRI, 1989, 146 pp.

4168 Iljas, Bachtiar
'Sumatra Timur dan sekitarnja', in: Darius Marpaung (ed.), *Bingkisan nasional;
Kenangan 10 tahun revolusi Indonesia, 17-8-1945/17-8-1955*, pp. 59-62.
Djakarta: Usaha Pegawai Nasional Indonesia, 1955.

4169 *Illustrations of the revolution 1945-1950; From a unitary state to a unitary state*.
Djakarta: Ministry of Information, 1954, ca. 500 pp. (ubl)

4170 Ilyas, Muslim
Aziz Chan; Riwayat dan perjuangan. Padang, 1973, 78 pp.

4171 Imran, Amrin
Perebutan-perebutan kekuasaan menegakkan RI (1945). Djakarta: Dep. HANKAM,
1967, 19 pp.

4172 Imran, Amrin
Presidential Decree No.1 of 1948. Paper Sixth International Conference on
Asian History, Yogyakarta, 1974, 8 pp.

4173 Imran, Amrin
Letnan Jenderal Oerip Soemohardjo. Jakarta: Mutiara, 1976, 88 pp.

4174 Imran, Amrin
Pahlawan nasional Jenderal Sudirman; Riwayat hidup dan perjuangannya. Jakarta:
Mutiara, 1976, 91 pp.

4175 Imran, Amrin
Panglima Besar Jenderal Sudirman. Jakarta: Mutiara, 1978, 90 pp.

4176 Imran, Amrin
Jenderal Oerip Soemohardjo. Jakarta: Kem. P dan K, 1980, 91 pp.

4177 Imran, Amrin
Pengiriman perwira-perwira Siliwangi ke Sumatera dalam tahun 1948. Paper SSN-III, Jakarta, 1981, 13 pp.

4178 Imran, Amrin
Pembentukan Tentara Keamanan Rakyat; Antara rasio dan semangat. Paper Musyawarah Kerja Nasional Sejarah, Bandung, 1990, 14 pp.

4179 Imran, Amrin; Hayun Ugaya; Sri Suko and Tanu Suherly
Sedjarah perkembangan Angkatan-Darat. Djakarta: Departemen Pertahanan-Keamanan Pusat Sedjarah ABRI, 1971, 11+184 pp.

4180 Imran, Amrin; Syamsuar Said; T. Sibarani and Zaidir Djalal
Ikhtisar sejarah perang kemerdekaan di Sumatera (1945-1949). Jakarta: Markas Besar Angkatan Bersenjata Republik Indonesia, Pusat Sejarah dan Tradisi ABRI, 1988, 293 pp.

4181 'In memoriam Bung Tomo; Tokoh pejuang 10 Nopember 1945', *Gema Angkatan 45* no. 59/61 (October-December 1981):144.

4182 *Indonesia merdeka sekedar sumbangsih kami.* Jakarta: Badan Kontak Wanita KRIS, 1977, 153 pp.

4183 *Indonesian nationalism and revolution; Six first-hand accounts.* Clayton: Monash University, 1969, 50 pp.

4184 Indra, H.M. Ridhwan
Bung Karno satu-satunya penggali Pancasila. Jakarta: Haji Masagung, 1991, 25+32 pp.

4185 Indra, Muhammad Ridhwan and Sophian Marthabaya
Peristiwa-peristiwa di sekitar Proklamasi 17-8-1945. Second edition. Jakarta: Sinar Grafika, 1989, 184 pp. [First edition 1987.]

4186 Indra, Willem I. Panji
'Peristiwa rapat raksasa 19 September 1945 sebagai hari kebulatan tekat bangsa Indonesia', *Gema Angkatan 45* no. 68/70 (July-September 1982):19-20.

4187 Indradjaja, Erwin
Pelajar pembela kedaulatan Indonesia; Sejarah Tentara Republik Indonesia Pelajar di daerah keresidenan Kediri (1945-1950). 1986, 161 pp. [MA thesis Universitas Indonesia, Jakarta.] [Histori]

4188 Indralaksana, H.B.
Revolusi Indonesia dibanding dengan beberapa revolusi lain. 1968, 118 pp. [MA thesis Universitas 17 Agustus 1945, Djakarta.] [9]

4189 'Insider' (ps.)
Atjeh sepintas lalu. Djakarta: Archapada, 1950, 124 pp.

4190 Irsyam, Mahrus
Nahdlatul Ulama 1945-1952. 1975, 135 pp. [MA thesis Universitas Indonesia, Jakarta.]

4191 Ishak, Buldan Hendra
Sekitar lahirnya Pemerintah Darurat Republik Indonesia (1948-1949). 1974.
[MA thesis Universitas Padjadjaran, Bandung.] [1, 20]

4192 Iskandar, Mohammad
Komité Nasional Indonesia dan pergerakan internal di daerah; Kasus Banten.
Paper Diskusi Sejarah Lokal IV, Revolusi Kemerdekaan di Tingkat Lokal,
Bandungan-Ambarawa, 1994, 20 pp.

4193 Iskandar, N.St.
Udjian masa. Djakarta/Groningen: Wolters, 1952, 499 pp.

4194 Ismail, Muhammad Gade
Ekonomi pada masa revolusi kemerdekaan DI Aceh, 1945-1949. Paper Diskusi
Sejarah Lokal IV, Revolusi Kemerdekaan di Tingkat Lokal, Bandungan-
Ambarawa, 1994, 21 pp.

4195 Ismail, Zamzulis
Angkatan Laut RI daerah Aceh (1945-1950). Jakarta: Dinas Sejarah TNI-AL,
1980, 74 pp.

4196 Ismail, Zamzulis
Ekspedisi-ekspedisi lintas laut ALRI ke Kalimantan. Jakarta: Dinas Sejarah TNI-
AL, 1980, 79 pp.

4197 Isnomo, Suharsono
Perjoangan politik Tan Malaka (suatu tinjauan tentang cita-cita Tan Malaka
dalam usaha pembentukan satu partai persatuan). 1973, 166 pp. [MA thesis
Universitas Indonesia, Jakarta.]

4198 Jacoub, T. Oesman
'Sedjenak kenangan revolusi 1945', in: *Modal revolusi 45*, pp. 94-97. Kutaradja:
Komite Musjawarah Angkatan 45 DI Atjeh, 1960.

4199 Jakobi, Tgk. A.K.
Aceh daerah modal; Long March ke Medan Area. Jakarta: Yayasan 'Seulawah RI-
001', 1992, 350 pp.

4200 Jasin, Aman
Tindjauan sedjarah terhadap peristiwa 3 Djuli 1946. 1970, 91 pp. [MA thesis
IKIP Bandung.] [10]

4201 Jasin, M.
'Surabaya menjelang 10 Nopember 1945 dan sikap patriotik pasukan Polisi
Istimewa', in: *Bunga rampai perjuangan dan pengorbanan II*, pp. 251-257. Jakarta:
Markas Besar Legiun Veteran RI, 1983.

4202 Jatim, Adham
'Episode Bangkok-Singapura masa petualangan penuh risiko', in: Kustiniyati
Mochtar (ed.), *Memoar pejuang Republik Indonesia seputar 'zaman Singapura'*,
1945-1950, pp. 199-206. Jakarta: Gramedia, 1992.

4203 Jayusman, Iskandar
*Catatan-catatan yang berserakan; Peristiwa-peristiwa nyata selama perjuangan
kemerdekaan Republik Indonesia periode tahun 1945-1950*. Semarang: Aneka Ilmu,
1984, 13+104 pp.

4204 Joesoef, Hoesin
'Detik Proklamasi di Atjeh', in: *Modal revolusi 45*, pp. 41-51. Kutaradja: Komite Musjawarah Angkatan 45 DI Atjeh, 1960.

4205 Joesoef, Noerbahrij
Riau dan sahamnja dalam revolusi; Dalam masa-masa revolusi phisik 1945-1950. Pekanbaru: Telagakarya, 1966, 134 pp.

4206 Jogaswara, Jojo
Perdjuangan rakjat kota Bandung dalam awal revolusi fisik (17 Agustus 1945-Maret 1946). 1968. [MA thesis Universitas Padjadjaran, Bandung.] [1, 20]

4207 Jogaswara, Jojo
Perdjoangan rakjat kota Bandung dalam awal revolusi pisik (17 Agustus '45-Maret '46). Paper SSN-II, Jogjakarta, 1970, 19 pp.

4208 Jogaswara, J.
Lahirnya badan-badan perjuangan dan BKR di kota Bandung sampai timbulnya MDPP/MPPP. Paper SSN-III, Jakarta, 1981, 18 pp.

4209 Jogaswara, Jojo
Situasi kota Bandung dalam tahun 1945 ditinjau dari sudut politik dan militer. Bandung: Universitas Padjadjaran, 1981, 70 pp.

4210 Jogaswara, Jojo
Wawancara sejarah lisan sebagai salah satu sumber penulisan kota Bandung, periode revolusi kemerdekaan (1945-1950). Jakarta: Arsip Nasional, 1982, 10 pp.

4211 Johannes, Herman
Peranan generasi muda dalam perjuangan 1942-1950. Paper Seminar Sejarah Peranan Generasi Muda dalam Perjuangan Bangsa 1942-1950, Yogyakarta, 1989, 10 pp.

4212 Juminshon, Eti
Peranan Laskar Rakyat Tirto Nirmolo pada masa Agresi Militer II (1948-1949). 1985. [MA thesis Universitas Gadjah Mada, Yogyakarta.] [Histori]

4213 Junaedi
Runtuhnya negara Pasundan. 1989, 222 pp. [MA thesis Universitas Indonesia, Jakarta.] [Histori]

4214 Junaidi, Mugnie
Peranan Serikat Kerakyatan Indonesia (SKI) dalam perjuangan menegakkan kemerdekaan Indonesia di Kalimantan Selatan. 1975, 223 pp. [MA thesis IKIP Malang.] [12]

4215 Junus, Harun
'Ketawa sedjenak dalam gerilja', in: *Dari penjerangan ke penjerahan*, pp. 141-151. Bukittinggi: Djawatan Penerangan Sumatera Tengah, 1951.

4216 Jusuf, Masjhudi
Udjian bagi Republik Indonesia dalam Peristiwa 3 Djuli 1946. 1969, 61 pp. [MA thesis Universitas Gadjah Mada, Jogjakarta.]

4217 *Kabupaten Bogor selama perdjuangan revolusi phisik (1945-1950).* Bogor: Panitya Penggali-Penjusun Sedjarah, 1971, 198 pp.

4218 Kadarjono, S.
      Swargi Djèndral Sudirman. Surabaja: Panjebar Semangat, 1961, 43 pp. [In
      Javanese.] (kitlv-m)

4219 Kadarjono, Satim
      Timbreng. Surabaya: Yayasan Penerbitan Djojo Bojo, 1994, 82 pp. [First pub-
      lished in 1963.] [In Javanese.]

4220 Kadir, H. Abdul
      'Nilai '45 - setiap insan Indonesia ikhlas berkorban demi negara dan
      bangsanya', in: *Bunga rampai perjuangan dan pengorbanan II,* pp. 21-25. Jakarta:
      Markas Besar Legiun Veteran RI, 1983.

4221 Kadir, Harun a.o.
      *Sejarah perjuangan mempertahankan kemerdekaan Republik Indonesia di Sulawesi
      Selatan.* Ujung Pandang, 1984. [1173]

4222 Kadir, Musa
      'Haji Hasbullah Yasin; Pejuang kemerdekaan RI di Kalimantan Selatan', *Mimbar
      Ulama* 1-10 (1977):62-69.

4223 Kaeng
      *Selajang pandang sedjarah regional perdjuangan kemerdekaan bangsa Indonesia
      Sulawesi Utara-Tengah; Menjongsong peringatan hari ulang tahun ke-XXV
      peristiwa Merah Putih Sulawesi Utara.* Djakarta: Badan Perdjuangan 14 Pebruari
      1946 Merah Putih, 1971, 56 pp.

4224 Kaisiepo, Manuel
      'Murba di tengah persaingan; Tan Malaka dalam revolusi kemerdekaan 1945-
      1949', *Prisma* 11-9 (1982):75-89.

4225 Kalo, Baharuddin
      Peranan Dewan Keamanan dalam penjelesaian sengketa Indonesia-Belanda.
      1965. [MA thesis Universitas Hasanuddin, Makassar.] [111]

4226 Kamajaya
      Revolusi di Surakarta. Yogyakarta: Dep. P dan K, 1993, 29 pp.

4227 Kamaly, Mohammad Husein
      Rakyat Bekasi berjoang; 17 Agustus 1945. Bekasi: n.n., 1973, 29 pp.

4228 Kamil, Mustafa
      Kabupaten Solok dalam perang kemerdekaan, 1945-1949. 1972, 120 pp. [MA
      thesis IKIP Padang.] [14, 4872]

4229 Kamil, Nja' Adam
      'Sekilas-pandang di Medan area', in: *Modal revolusi 45,* pp. 64-71. Kutaradja:
      Komite Musjawarah Angkatan 45 DI Atjeh, 1960.

4230 Kanaana, La Ode
      'Berbagai versi tentang Proklamasi', in: *Letusan di balik buku; Hasil sayembara
      mengarang dalam rangka peringatan hari ulang tahun kemerdekaan RI yang ke 30,*
      pp. 91-115. Jakarta: Dewan Harian Nasional Angkatan 45/Aries Lima, 1976.

4231 Karim, Abdulrahman
      Kalimantan berdjuang (1945-1949). Djakarta: Balai Pustaka, 1956, 68 pp.

4232 Karma, Mara
'Meanwhile in Bukittinggi; An interview with Mara Karma', in: C. Wild and P.
Carey (eds), *Born in fire; The Indonesian struggle for independence; An anthology*,
pp. 127-131. Athens: Ohio University Press, 1986.

4233 Karma, Mara
'Sementara itu, di Bukittinggi', in: Colin Wild and Peter Carey (eds), *Gelora api
revolusi*, pp. 140-145. Jakarta: Gramedia, 1986.

4234 Karneni A.A.
Agus; Pejuang cilik kemerdekaan. Semarang: Bina Pratama, 1985, 70 pp.

4235 Karseno, Ny. Toeti
'Bagimu negeri, jiwa raga kami', in: *Bunga rampai perjuangan dan pengorbanan II*,
pp. 469-479. Jakarta: Markas Besar Legiun Veteran RI, 1983.

4236 Kartasapoetra, G. and S. Darmawan
Peristiwa 3 Juli 1946 ditinjau dari segi hukum dan sejarah. Bandung: Armico,
1982, 58 pp.

4237 Kartasumitra, R. Sulaeman
'Sepintas lalu pengalaman dalam perjuangan', in: *Bunga rampai perjuangan dan
pengorbanan I*, pp. 648-659. Jakarta: Markas Besar Legiun Veteran RI, 1982.

4238 Kartawinata, H.S.Y. Arudji
'Peranan LASWI dalam perjuangan kemerdekaan', *Gema Angkatan 45* no. 13
(1977):28-30. [55]

4239 Kartawiriaputra, Suwarno
Hari pahlawan 10 Nopember. Bandung: Tarate, 1976, 52 pp.

4240 Kartawiriaputra, Suwarno
Bandung lautan api. Bandung: Tarate, 1978, 64 pp.

4241 Kartini, E.
Peristiwa Madiun 1948. 1968, 96 pp. [BA thesis IKIP Bandung.] [10, 108]

4242 Kartodirdjo, Sartono
'The role of struggle organizations as mass movements in the Indonesian
revolution', *Majalah Ilmu-Ilmu Sosial Indonesia* 7-1/2 (1980):1-15.

4243 Kartodirdjo, Sartono
'The role of struggle organizations in the Indonesian revolution', *Review of
Indonesian and Malaysian Affairs* 14-2 (1980):92-110.

4244 Kartodirdjo, Sartono
'Wajah revolusi Indonesia dipandang dari perspektivisme struktural', *Prisma*
10-8 (August 1981):3-13.

4245 Kartodirdjo, Sartono
'Banditry and political change in Java', in: Sartono Kartodirdjo, *Modern
Indonesia; Transformation and tradition; A socio-historical perspective*, pp. 3-29.
Yogyakarta: Gadjah Mada University Press, 1984.

4246 Kartodirdjo, Sartono
'The role of struggle organizations as mass movements in the Indonesian
revolution', in: Sartono Kartodirdjo, *Modern Indonesia; Transformation and*

tradition; A socio-historical perspective, pp. 83-104. Yogyakarta: Gadjah Mada University Press, 1984.

4247 Kartodirdjo, Sartono
'Makna PDRI dalam revolusi Indonesia', in: Abdurrachman Surjomihardjo and J.R. Chaniago (eds), *Pemerintah Darurat Republik Indonesia dikaji ulang*, pp. 27-33. Jakarta: Masyarakat Sejarawan Indonesia, 1990.

4248 Kartodirdjo, Sartono
The bambu runcing behind the conference table. Paper Linggarjati Conference, 1991. [program]

4249 Kartodirdjo, Sartono
'Bambu runcing di belakang meja perundingan', in: A.B. Lapian and P.J. Drooglever (eds), *Menelusuri jalur Linggarjati; Diplomasi dalam perspektif sejarah*, pp. 85-93. Jakarta: Grafiti, 1992.

4250 (Kartodirdjo), Soejatno
'Revolution and social tensions in Surakarta 1945-1950', *Indonesia* no. 17 (1974):99-111.

4251 (Kartodirdjo), Soejatno
'Social and political changes in Surakarta after 1945', *Review of Indonesian and Malayan Affairs* 8-1 (1974):36-44.

4252 (Kartodirdjo), Soejatno
'Feodalisme dan revolusi di Surakarta 1945-1950', *Prisma* 7-7 (August 1978):49-56.

4253 Kartodirdjo, Soejatno
Revolution in Surakarta 1945-50; A case study of city and village in the Indonesian revolution. 1982, 270 pp. [PhD thesis Australian National University, Canberra.] [44, 6326]

4254 *Karya dalam peperangan dan revolusi; Dilukis langsung pada waktu peristiwanya terjadi ketika Yogyakarta sebagai ibu kota Republik Indonesia diserbu dan diduduki oleh tentara Belanda 1948-1949*. Editor: Dullah. Jakarta: Balai Pustaka, 1983, 120 pp.

4255 Kasim, Muh.
Kenanganku. Bandung: Tarate, 1975, 104 pp.

4256 Kaspin, M.D.
'Mengenal pahlawan nasional Brigdjen TNI anumerta Ignatius Slamet Rijadi', *Vidya Yudha* no. 10 (1971):90-97.

4257 Kasturi, Judi
Basis Pesindo di Madiun; Pertumbuhan dan perkembangannya 1945-1948. 1988, 12+113 pp. [MA thesis Universitas Indonesia.] [Histori]

4258 Kawilarang, A.E.
Officier in dienst van de Republiek Indonesië; Ervaringen 1942-1961. Breda: Warung Bambu, 1990, 284 pp. [Second edition, 1992, 238 pp.]

4259 Kawilarang, A.E.
'Pengalaman bulan-bulan akhir 1948 sampai dengan akhir 1949', in: Abdurrachman Surjomihardjo and J.R. Chaniago (eds), *Pemerintah Darurat Republik Indonesia dikaji ulang*, pp. 155-157. Jakarta: Masyarakat Sejarawan Indonesia, 1990.

4260 *Kedaulatan Rakjat lahir 27 September 1945, 40 hari selewat Proklamasi.* Jogjakarta: Kedaulatan Rakjat, ca. 1963, 72 pp.

4261 *Kedjelasan mengenai Pantjasila dan Proklamasi.* Djakarta: Dep. HANKAM, 1968, 82 pp.

4262 Kelabora, Abe L.
'Post-independence life in East Indonesia', in: *Indonesian nationalism and revolution*, pp. 39-45. Clayton: Monash University, 1969.

4263 Kelana, Pandir (ps. R.M. Slamet Danusudirdjo)
Rintihan burung kedasih (sebuah roman revolusi). Jakarta: Sinar Harapan, 1984, 274 pp. [Second edition, Jakarta: Gramedia, 1992, 403 pp.]

4264 Kelana, Pandir (ps.)
Kereta api terakhir. Jakarta: Gramedia, 1991, 210 pp.

4265 *Kenangan 7 tahun revolusi Indonesia.* Djakarta: Kem. Penerangan, 1952, 136 pp. [22, 40]

4266 *Kenang-kenangan kota besar Surakarta, 1945-1953.* Surakarta: Djawatan Penerangan Kota Besar Surakarta, 1953. [6122]

4267 Kertapati, Sidik
Sekitar Proklamasi 17 Agustus 1945. Third edition. Djakarta: Pembaruan, 1964, 182 pp. [First edition 1957; Second edition, 1961, 155 pp.]

4268 Kho Ping Hoo, Asmaraman S.
Merdeka atau mati. Solo: Gema, 1979, 99 pp.

4269 *Kisah-kisah kepahlawanan perang kemerdekaan 1945-1949 dan perang merebut kembali Irian Barat; Kumpulan cerpen.* Jakarta: Balai Pustaka, 1993, 1994, 293+ 288 pp. 2 vols.

4270 Kolit, D.K.
'Di Flores: Merdeka terlebih dahulu terbelakang sendirian', in: Darius Marpaung (ed.), *Bingkisan nasional; Kenangan 10 tahun revolusi Indonesia, 17-8-1945/17-8-1955*, pp. 71-74. Djakarta: Usaha Pegawai Nasional Indonesia, 1955.

4271 *Kongres Persatuan Tionghoa.* Djakarta: Pengurus Pusat Persatuan Tionghoa Djakarta, 1950, 75 pp.

4272 Kosasih, R.A. Yetti Djumiati
'Kisah yang tidak akan dilupakan', in: *Cahaya dari medan laga; Hasil sayembara mengarang dalam rangka peringatan hari ulang tahun kemerdekaan RI yang ke 30*, pp. 49-75. Jakarta: Dewan Harian Nasional Angkatan 45/Aries Lima, 1976.

4273 Kosim, E.; Didi Suryadi; Atja and Rosad Amidjaja
Sejarah sekitar perundingan Linggarjati tahun 1946; Laporan sementara. Bandung: Universitas Padjadjaran, 1973, 118 pp. [62, 4858]

4274 'Kota Palembang dalam lintasan sejarah perjuangan kemerdekaan', *Gema Angkatan 45* no. 59/61 (October-December 1981):61-66, 92.

4275 Kotambonan, W.S.
Kenang-kenangan 5 tahun Trompet Masjarakat, 1947-September-1951. Surabaja: n.n., 1952. [unpaged] (kitlv-m)

4276 Koyohardjo, Kaderi Kandhi
'Merebut kekuasaan dok Surabaya dari Jepang dan perang kemerdekaan', in: *Bunga rampai perjuangan dan pengorbanan II*, pp. 181-187. Jakarta: Markas Besar Legiun Veteran RI, 1983.

4277 Kulit, Joost
'Yang kuingat dari masa Singapore Connection', in: Kustiniyati Mochtar (ed.), *Memoar pejuang Republik Indonesia seputar 'zaman Singapura', 1945-1950*, pp. 191-195. Jakarta: Gramedia, 1992.

4278 *Kumpulan karangan prosa perjoangan; Jiwa pahlawan membara disetiap dada generasi muda; Sembilanbelas prosa perjoangan pada lomba mengarang prosa Hari Pahlawan 1975.* Jakarta: Dep. Sosial, 1977, 414 pp.

4279 *Kumpulan nyanyian 17 lagu perjoangan.* Jakarta: Pradnya Paramita, 1978, 37 pp.

4280 Kuntowidjojo
Angkatan Oemat Islam 1945-1950; Beberapa tjatatan tentang pergerakan sosial. Paper SSN-II, Jogjakarta, 1970, 30 pp.

4281 *Kurir-kurir kemerdekaan; Kisah nyata para pemuda pembawa berita Proklamasi 1945.* Jakarta: Balai Pustaka, 1988, 175 pp.

4282 Kurniadi
Perjanjian Linggarjati sebagai salah satu usaha perjuangan diplomasi untuk mempertahankan pengakuan kedaulatan negara Republik Indonesia. 1988. [MA thesis IKIP Jakarta.] [Histori]

4283 Kurniadi, Deni
Keresidenan Priangan pada masa revolusi; Tinjauan di bidang politik dan militer (dari Proklamasi sampai Hijrah). 1989, 115 pp. [MA thesis Universitas Indonesia, Jakarta.] [Histori]

4284 Kurnianda, Tislinna Savitri
Radio Pemberontakan dalam revolusi di Jawa Timur (1945-1947). 1989, 96 pp. [MA thesis Universitas Indonesia, Jakarta.] [Histori]

4285 Kurniarini, Dina Dwi
Badan Keamanan Rakyat sebagai satu badan yang mengawali pembentukan Tentara Nasional Indonesia. 1981. [MA thesis Universitas Gadjah Mada, Yogyakarta.] [Histori]

4286 Kusnadi, Didi
Pembentukan negara-negara boneka oleh Dr. H.J. van Mook dalam rangka menjepit Republik Indonesia 1946-1950. 1970, 34 pp. [Thesis IKIP Bandung.] [10]

4287 Kusnadi, Endjang
Situasi politik di Indonesia sekitar Agresi Militer Belanda I dan II. 1970, 45 pp.
[Thesis IKIP Bandung.] [10]

4288 Kusnadi, Urip
Kapan berdirinja negara Republik Indonesia? 1964. [MA thesis Universitas
Hasanuddin, Makassar.] [111]

4289 Kuspardani, Rr.
Sedjarah peralihan dari negara Republik Indonesia kenegara kesatuan
Indonesia. 1971, 113 pp. [MA thesis IKIP Djakarta.] [11]

4290 Kutoyo, Sutrisno and Surachman
Riwayat hidup dan perjuangan Mohammad Ramdhan. Jakarta: Kem. P dan K,
1977, 23 pp.

4291 La Hade, M. Saleh
Korban 40.000 jiwa di Sulawesi Selatan dan artinya bagi perjuangan
kemerdekaan RI. Paper Seminar Sejarah Perjuangan Rakyat Sulawesi Selatan
Menentang Penjajahan Asing, Ujung Pandang, 1982, 26 pp.

4292 La Side, R.
Sejarah perjuangan Andi Pangerang. Ujung Pandang: Lembaga Sejarah dan
Antropologi, 1976. [660, 4868]

4293 *Lahirnja Pantjasila dan Undang-Undang Dasar 1945 berikut Piagam Djakarta.*
Djakarta: Tridaja, ca. 1961, 48 pp. (kitlv-m)

4294 'Lahirnya Pancasila', *Gema Angkatan 45* no. 18 (June 1977), 33 pp. [Special
issue.]

4295 Laksmana, Indra
Lembaga Pendidikan Penerbangan Militer pada masa revolusi 1945-1949.
1987, 74 pp. [MA thesis Universitas Indonesia, Jakarta.] [Histori]

4296 Laksmiranti, M. Yuni
Peranan militer dalam menyelesaikan pergolakan di Surakarta dan sekitarnya
tahun 1948-1949. 1987, 75 pp. [MA thesis Universitas Indonesia, Jakarta.]

4297 Lanasir, A.R.
Catatan perjuangan/pergerakan di Luwuk-Banggai. [4869]

4298 Lapian, A.B.
'Partisipasi Kristen dalam revolusi di bidang politik', *Indonesia* (1968):7-35. [99]

4299 Lapian, A.B.
'Linggarjati, Negara Indonesia Timur dan perjuangan Irian Barat', in: *Seminar
Sejarah Regional Indonesia Timur; Masalah penulisan sejarah dan dinamika
kesejarahan Indonesia Timur,* pp. 102-112. Ujung Pandang: Departemen P dan K,
1993/1994.

4300 Lapian, A.B. and P.J. Drooglever (eds)
Menelusuri jalur Linggarjati; Diplomasi dalam perspektif sejarah. Dengan sketsa-
sketsa Henk Ngantung. Jakarta: Grafiti, 1992, 10+318 pp.

4301 *Laporan khusus penyelenggaraan peringatan 4 windu permulaan perang kemerdekaan 2, 19 Desember 1948-19 Desember 1980 di Yogyakarta.* Yogyakarta: Dep. Penerangan, 1981, 162 pp.

4302 *Laporan team sedjarah Pantjasila dan Proklamasi.* Djakarta: Dep. HANKAM, 1968, 82 pp.

4303 Latief, Tadjuddin; Makkateru Sjamsuddin and A. Rasjid Rachman (eds)
Empat puluh ribu pahlawan Sulawesi Selatan. Djakarta: Front Nasional, 1962, 37 pp.

4304 Latonda
Lolos. Jakarta: Pustaka Jaya, 1978, 57 pp.

4305 Legoh, H.M.L.
14 Pebruari 1946 mengisi lembaran sejarah Indonesia. Manado, 1973. [4871]

4306 Leirissa, R.Z.
'Jalur Linggarjati', in: A.B. Lapian and P.J. Drooglever (eds), *Menelusuri jalur Linggarjati; Diplomasi dalam perspektif sejarah*, pp. 1-7. Jakarta: Grafiti, 1992.

4307 *Lembaran sedjarah.* Jogjakarta: Kem. Penerangan, 1950, 75 pp.

4308 *Letusan di balik buku; Hasil sayembara mengarang dalam rangka peringatan hari ulang tahun kemerdekaan RI yang ke 30.* Jakarta: Dewan Harian Nasional Angkatan 45/Aries Lima, 1976, 223 pp.

4309 Lie, John
'Dari pelayaran niaga ke operasi menembus blokade musuh; Sebagaimana pernah diceritakannya kepada wartawan', in: Kustiniyati Mochtar (ed.), *Memoar pejuang Republik Indonesia seputar 'zaman Singapura', 1945-1950*, pp. 152-159. Jakarta: Gramedia, 1992.

4310 Liem Khiem Yang
'Geredja dalam revolusi Indonesia (1942-sekarang)', in: W.B. Sidjabat (ed.), *Partisipasi Kristen dalam nation building di Indonesia*, pp. 93-109. Djakarta: Badan Penerbit Kristen, 1968.

4311 'Lima tahun pertama R.I.', in: Darius Marpaung (ed.), *Bingkisan nasional; Kenangan 10 tahun revolusi Indonesia, 17-8-1945/17-8-1955*, pp. 328-339. Djakarta: Usaha Pegawai Nasional Indonesia, 1955.

4312 *Lima tahun Proklamasi.* Jogjakarta: Kem. Penerangan, 1950, 72 pp.

4313 Lindayanti
Jawa Barat setelah perjanjian Linggajati tahun 1947; Kasus negara Pasundan. 1984, 115 pp. [MA thesis Universitas Gadjah Mada, Yogyakarta.]

4314 Lindayanti
'Negara Pasundan tahun 1947; Uji coba ide politik federal di Jawa Barat', *Sejarah* 4 (November 1993):31-42.

4315 Listianawati
Peranan Jendral Sudirman dalam mempertahankan kemerdekaan Republik Indonesia. 1972, 67 pp. [MA thesis IKIP Yogyakarta.] [17]

4316 Loebis, Aboe Bakar
Pemuda Jakarta sekitar hari-hari Proklamasi. Paper Seminar Lahirnya Suatu Bangsa, Jakarta, 1990, 45 pp.

4317 Loebis, Aboe Bakar
Kilas balik revolusi; Kenangan, pelaku dan saksi. Jakarta: Penerbit Universitas Indonesia, 1992, 13+330 pp.

4318 Loebis, Aboe Bakar
'Tan Malaka's arrest; An eye-witness account', *Indonesia* no. 53 (1992):71-78.

4319 Loebis, Ali Basja
Undang-Undang Dasar RI 1945 (Sedjarah pertumbuhan dan pendjelasan pasal-pasalnja). Djakarta: Loebis, 1963, 68 pp.

4320 Lohanda, Mona a.o.
Sejarah peralihan pemerintah RIS ke RI; Menuju negara kesatuan Republik Indonesia. Jakarta: Kem. P dan K, 1986, 95 pp.

4321 Lubis, Abdul Mukti
Suatu tinjauan historis tentang pengaruh agressi Belanda terhadap Republik Indonesia. 1974. [MA thesis IKIP Medan.] [13]

4322 Lubis, Armen
Suatu tinjauan sejarah tentang kasus pembubaran RIS dan kembalinya negara kesatuan RI tahun 1950. 1974, 154 pp. [MA thesis IKIP Medan.] [13]

4323 Lubis, Mochtar
Tidak ada esok. Second edition. Jakarta: Pustaka Jaya, 1982, 226 pp. [First printing 1950; Fourth printing, Jakarta: Yayasan Obor Indonesia, 1992, 199 pp.]

4324 Lubis, Mochtar
Djalan tak ada udjung. Djakarta: Balai Pustaka, 1952, 127 pp. [Ninth printing, Jakarta: Yayasan Obor Indonesia, 1992, 167 pp.]

4325 Lubis, Mochtar
A road with no end. London: Hutchinson, 1968, 151 pp.

4326 Lubis, Mochtar
Weg zonder eind. Amsterdam/Antwerpen: Wereldbibliotheek, 1969, 112 pp.

4327 Lubis, Mochtar
Maut dan cinta. Jakarta: Pustaka Jaya, 1977, 306 pp. [Fourth printing 1989.]

4328 Lubis, Mochtar
'Kisah wartawan pejuang kemerdekaan', in: Kustiniyati Mochtar (ed.), *Memoar pejuang Republik Indonesia seputar 'zaman Singapura', 1945-1950,* pp. 66-74. Jakarta: Gramedia, 1992.

4329 Lubis, Sjamsudin
Sulawesi Selatan; Dokumentasi penjembelihan 40.000. Djakarta: Analisa, 1954, 127 pp.

4330 Lucas, Bambang Herbramantyo
'Hikmah monumen palagan Ambarawa bagi kita', in: *Cahaya dari medan laga; Hasil sayembara mengarang dalam rangka peringatan hari ulang tahun kemerdekaan*

RI yang ke 30, pp. 193-212. Jakarta: Dewan Harian Nasional Angkatan 45/Aries Lima, 1976.

4331 Luhukay, Hanoch
Peranan KRIM (Kebaktian Rakyat Indonesia Maluku) di Sulawesi Selatan dalam revolusi fisik. Paper Seminar Sejarah Perjuangan Rakyat Sulawesi Selatan Menentang Penjajahan Asing, Ujung Pandang, 1982, 14 pp.

4332 Luhukay, Hanoch
Sejarah lisan dari Sulawesi Selatan dengan kegunaan praktis. Jakarta: Arsip Nasional, 1982, 23 pp.

4333 Luhukay, Hanoch and Ny. S.G. Luhukay
Catatan-catatan pemerintah Belanda dan asing lainnya tentang perjuangan rakyat SUL-SEL selama perang kemerdekaan RI. Paper Seminar Sejarah Perjuangan Rakyat Sulawesi Selatan Menentang Penjajahan Asing, Ujung Pandang, 1982, 19 pp.

4334 Luhukay, Hanoch and M. Shaleh A. Putuhena
Peranan organisasi keagamaan pada awal perjuangan kemerdekaan di Sulawesi Selatan; Suatu studi pendahuluan. Paper Seminar Sejarah Perjuangan Rakyat Sulawesi Selatan Menentang Penjajahan Asing, Ujung Pandang, 1982, 16 pp.

4335 *Lukisan revolusi, 1945-1950; Dari negara kesatuan ke negara kesatuan.* Djakarta: Kem. Penerangan, 1954. [unpaged]

4336 Lumbantobing, Dangol
'Pelajaran sejarah 10 Nopember 1945-10 Nopember 1977', *Gema Angkatan 45* no. 23 (November 1977):31-33.

4337 Lumbantoruan, Mangapul
Suatu tinjauan tentang perjuangan rakyat menegakkan kemerdekaan Indonesia di Sumatera Utara. 1973, 126 pp. [MA thesis IKIP Medan.] [13]

4338 Maas
Piagam Djakarta dan implikasinja dalam Proklamasi kemerdekaan. 1971, 145 pp. [MA thesis IKIP Djakarta.] [11, Histori]

4339 Madjiah, Matia
Kasih di medan perang. Jakarta: Balai Pustaka, 1977, 144 pp.

4340 Madjiah, Matia
Kisah seorang dokter gerilya dalam revolusi kemerdekaan di Banten. Jakarta: Sinar Harapan, 1986, 269 pp.

4341 Madjiah, Matia
Dokter gerilya. Jakarta: Balai Pustaka, 1993, 270 pp.

4342 Madjid, Abubakar
Perserikatan Bangsa-Bangsa dalam menjelesaikan sengketa Indonesia dengan Belanda. 1971, 87 pp. [MA thesis Universitas Djajabaja, Djakarta.] [9]

4343 Madjid, Hamidoen
'Enam anekdote', in: *Bunga rampai perjuangan dan pengorbanan I*, pp. 170-183. Jakarta: Markas Besar Legiun Veteran RI, 1982.

4344 Magenda, B.D.
'The Indonesian and Vietnamese revolutions in comparison; An exploratory analysis', *Prisma* 9 (1978):53-66.

4345 Mahaga
'Di Atjeh: P.T.T. berdjasa', in: Darius Marpaung (ed.), *Bingkisan nasional; Kenangan 10 tahun revolusi Indonesia, 17-8-1945/17-8-1955*, pp. 63-66. Djakarta: Usaha Pegawai Nasional Indonesia, 1955.

4346 Mahdan, Hasjim
'Prapatan 10 di hari-hari pertama Proklamasi adalah pusat perdjuangan pemuda', in: Darius Marpaung (ed.), *Bingkisan nasional; Kenangan 10 tahun revolusi Indonesia, 17-8-1945/17-8-1955*, pp. 18-22. Djakarta: Usaha Pegawai Nasional Indonesia, 1955.

4347 Mahyuni (ed.)
Peristiwa Situjuh, 15-1-49. Situjuh Batur, 1972. [6231]

4348 Majid, M. Saleh
Peranan rakyat Bima terhadap perjuangan kemerdekaan Republik Indonesia tahun 1945-1949. 1981, 99 pp. [MA thesis IKIP Ujung Pandang.] [23]

4349 Makah, Masmimar; Syahbuddin and Mara Karma
Pemuda dan Proklamasi; Gerakan pemuda merealisasi Proklamasi dan mewujudkan pemerintah RI di Bukittinggi-Sumatera. Jakarta: Panitia Penulisan Sejarah Pemuda Pelopor Pejuang Proklamasi 1945 Bukittinggi-Sumatera, 1990, 252 pp.

4350 Makalam, H.M. Sayuti
'Nostalgia perang kemerdekaan, 1945-1950', in: *Bunga rampai perjuangan dan pengorbanan I*, pp. 599-622. Jakarta: Markas Besar Legiun Veteran RI, 1982.

4351 Maksum; Agus Sunyoto and A. Zainuddin
Lubang-lubang pembantaian; Petualangan PKI di Madiun. Disusun oleh Tim Jawa Pos. Jakarta: Grafiti, 1990, 16+190 pp.

4352 Malaka, Tan
Madilog; Materialisme dialektika logika. Djakarta: Widjaya, 1951, 415 pp.

4353 Malaka, Tan
Pandangan hidup; Weltanschauung. Djakarta: Widjaya, 1952, 103 pp. [Reprint of part of 2362, vol. III.]

4354 Malaka, Tan
Uraian mendadak (7 Nop. 1948 [tak ada persiapan] didepan kongres peleburan 3 partai). Djakarta: Komisariat Dewan Partai Partai Murba, 1955, 32 pp. (kitlv-m) [Various editions and reprints.]

4355 Malaka, Tan
Gerpolek (gerilja-politik-ekonomi). Second printing. Djakarta: Jajasan Massa/ Delegasi, 1964, 88 pp. [First printing 1962.] [Various editions and reprints.]

4356 Malaka, Tan
Dari Ir. Soekarno sampai Presiden Soekarno. Djakarta: Jajasan Tjahaja Kita, 1966, 19 pp. [Reprint of part of 2362, vol. III.]

4357   Malako, Sultani St.
       'Sventana; Pemimpin-pemimpin gerilja jang ta' dikenal', in: *Dari penjerangan ke
       penjerahan*, pp. 71-77. Bukittinggi: Djawatan Penerangan Sumatera Tengah,
       1951.

4358   Malau, L. and H. Mansyur
       Perang semesta; Sector II (Sub Terr.) VII Ko. Sumatera. Medan/Jakarta: Yayasan
       Gema Revolusi 45, ca. 1978, 406 pp.

4359   Malik, Adam
       Riwajat dan perdjuangan sekitar Proklamasi kemerdekaan, 17 Agustus 1945. Second
       edition. Djakarta: Widjaya, 1950, 88 pp. [First edition 1948; Sixth edition,
       *Riwayat... Diperlengkap oleh orang-orang yang langsung ikut menyelenggarakan
       Proklamasi 17 Agustus 1945*, Jakarta: Widjaya, 1975, 108 pp.]

4360   Malik, Adam
       'Dari kantor berita Domei Proklamasi 17 Agustus 1975 disiarkan', *Penelitian
       Sedjarah* 1-3 (1962):2-3, 5.

4361   Malik, Adam
       'The first crises', in: C. Wild and P. Carey (eds), *Born in fire; The Indonesian
       struggle for independence; An anthology*, pp. 108-112. Athens: Ohio University
       Press, 1986.

4362   Malik, Adam
       Krisis-krisis pertama', in: Colin Wild and Peter Carey (eds), *Gelora api revolusi*,
       pp. 121-126. Jakarta: Gramedia, 1986.

4363   Malik, Adam; Shigetada Nishijima and Wangsa Wijaya
       'Penulisan Proklamasi; Tiga orang yang menghadirinya', in: Colin Wild and
       Peter Carey (eds), *Gelora api revolusi*, pp. 102-109. Jakarta: Gramedia, 1986.

4364   Malik, M. Raid
       *Riwayat hidup dan perjuangan alm. Chatib Suleiman, gugur dalam peristiwa Situjuh
       Batur, 15 Januari 1949.* Padang Panjang: n.n., 1973, 11 pp.

4365   Maluku, Abd. Wahid
       Memori perjuangan kemerdekaan Indonesia di daerah Donggala, Sulawesi Tengah.
       [4869]

4366   Mamahit, Piet
       Peristiwa Ikada 19 September 1945. Paper Seminar Lahirnya Suatu Bangsa,
       Jakarta, 1990, 9 pp.

4367   Mangandaralam, Sjahbuddin
       Bertempur malam; Sebuah kisah revolusi. Bandung: Pantjasakti, 1965, 20 pp.

4368   Mangitung, Abdul Latief
       Sejarah singkat perjuangan bersenjata di daerah Sulawesi Tengah. [4869]

4369   Mangkualam, H. Asnawi
       Perang kota 120 jam rakyat Palembang. Jakarta: Grafitas Offset, 1985, 179 pp.

4370   Mangkualam, Asnawi
       5 hari 5 malam perang rakyat Palembang 1947. Jakarta: Rineka Cipta, 1990, 65 pp.

4371 Mangkudilaga, Machfudi
'PDRI dalam sumber-sumber Belanda', in: Abdurrachman Surjomihardjo and
J.R. Chaniago (eds), *Pemerintah Darurat Republik Indonesia dikaji ulang*, pp. 171-
174. Jakarta: Masyarakat Sejarawan Indonesia, 1990.

4372 Mangoendiprodjo, H.R. Mohamad
'Kisah pertempuran di Surabaya pada tanggal 30 Oktober dan 10 November
1945', in: *Bunga rampai perjuangan dan pengorbanan I*, pp. 262-273. Jakarta:
Markas Besar Legiun Veteran RI, 1982.

4373 Mangowal, Willy S.P.
'Singapura ajang kegiatan pemuda Indonesia', in: Kustiniyati Mochtar (ed.),
Memoar pejuang Republik Indonesia seputar 'zaman Singapura', 1945-1950,
pp. 196-198. Jakarta: Gramedia, 1992.

4374 Mangunwijaya, Y.B.
'Dilema Sutan Sjahrir; Antara pemikir dan politikus', in: Abdullah, Taufik;
Aswab Mahasin and Daniel Dhakidae (eds), *Manusia dalam kemelut sejarah*,
pp. 63-102. Jakarta: Lembaga Penelitian, Pendidikan dan Penerangan Ekonomi
dan Sosial, 1978.

4375 Mangunwijaya, Y.B.
Burung-burung manyar. Jakarta: Djambatan, 1981, 6+279 pp. [Fifth edition,
1988, 262 pp.]

4376 Mangunwijaya, Y.B.
Het boek van de wevervogel; Roman uit Indonesië. Amsterdam: Meulenhoff, 1987,
309 pp.

4377 Mansyur
Gerilya di Asahan-Labuhan Batu, 1947-1949. Medan: Kaproco, 1977, 467 pp.

4378 Mansyur
*The golden bridge 'Jembatan Emas' 1945; Jilid 1, Kisah-kisah nyata perjuangan
kemerdekaan RI di Sumatera*. Medan: Lembaga Sosial Juang 45 Medan Area
Sumatera Utara, ca. 1980, 580 pp.

4379 Mansyur and Bayo Sutie
Benteng Huraba; Epos perjuangan bersama rakyat Tapanuli Selatan. Medan:
Lembaga Sosial Juang 45 Medan Area Sumatera Utara, 1976, 270 pp.

4380 Manuhutu, E.J.
Peranan TNI pada masa revolusi kemerdekaan. Paper Musyawarah Kerja
Nasional Sejarah, Bandung, 1990, 17 pp.

4381 Marboen, Moela
Gerakan Operasi Militer I untuk menumpas pemberontakan Madiun. Djakarta:
Mega Bookstore/Pusat Sedjarah Angkatan Bersendjata, 1965, 16 pp.

4382 Marboen, Moela
Pembentukan Undang-Undang Dasar 1945 dan penetapannya. Paper SSN-III,
Jakarta, 1981, 25 pp.

4383   Mardawi
'Diplomasi dan senjata', in: *Aku akan teruskan; Hasil sayembara mengarang dalam rangka peringatan hari ulang tahun kemerdekaan RI yang ke-30*, pp. 129-157. Jakarta: Dewan Harian Nasional Angkatan 45/Aries Lima, 1976.

4384   Mardawi
'Diplomasi dan senjata', *Gema Angkatan 45* no. 31 (July-August 1978):17-25.

4385   Marjoto (ed.)
Kenang-kenangan; Sedjarah Republik Indonesia sedjak tanggal 19 Desember 1948 hingga Republik Indonesia Serikat lahir. Jogjakarta: Nasional, 1950, 52 pp. [62]

4386   Marlaut, Rivai
Dokter Haslinda. Djakarta: Gapura, 1950, 126 pp.

4387   Marpaung, Darius (ed.)
Bingkisan nasional; Kenangan 10 tahun revolusi Indonesia, 17-8-1945/17-8-1955. Djakarta: Usaha Pegawai Nasional Indonesia, 1955, 373 pp.

4388   Marpaung, Maruli Tua
Tinjauan sejarah tentang peranan perang gerilya mempertahankan kemerdekaan Republik Indonesia pada masa Agressi ke-II di Tapanuli Tengah. 1975, 116 pp. [MA thesis IKIP Medan.] [13]

4389   Marsoedi a.o.
Merebut kota perjuangan; SU 1 Maret 1949. Jakarta: Yayasan Sinar Asih Mataram, 1985, 59 pp.

4390   Marsudi
Tentara peladjar di Djawa Tengah dalam sedjarah revolusi Indonesia 1945-1951. 1970. [MA thesis Universitas Gadjah Mada, Jogjakarta.] [Histori]

4391   Marsudi, Djamal
Menjingkap-tabir fakta-fakta pemberontakan PKI dalam peristiwa Madiun. Djakarta: Merdeka Press, 1966, 115 pp.

4392   Martoatmodjo, Buntaran
'Tjatatan sekitar Proklamasi kemerdekaan bangsa Indonesia', *Penelitian Sedjarah* 2-2 (1961):36-38; 2-3 (1961):38-40.

4393   Martosewojo, Soejono
'Pengalaman perjuangan', in: *Bunga rampai perjuangan dan pengorbanan I,* pp. 406-446. Jakarta: Markas Besar Legiun Veteran RI, 1982.

4394   Martosewojo, Soejono
Mahasiswa '45 Prapatan-10; Pengabdiannya 1. Bandung: Patma, 1984, 439 pp. [All published.]

4395   Maryoso
Dualisme kepemimpinan Angkatan Perang di Republik Indonesia (1945-1948). 1989, 108 pp. [MA thesis Universitas Indonesia, Jakarta.] [Histori]

4396   Maserin, R.S.S.
Seperseratus sedjarah dan perkembangan Pasukan 'L'. Djakarta: Direktorat Sedjarah dan Perpustakaan ALRI, 1970, 43 pp.

4397 Mashuri
Catatan peristiwa sejarah bangsaku tahun 1945-1950. Jakarta: Intan Pariwara, 1988, 23 pp.

4398 Mattalioe, Bahar
Roman revolusi; Perahu lajar 'Mappasikuwae'. Djakarta: Tekad, 1963, 52 pp. (kitlv-m)

4399 Mattalioe, M. Bahar
Pemberontakan meniti jalur kanan. Jakarta: Grasindo, 1994, 15+328 pp.

4400 Mattata, H.M. Sanusi Daeng
Luwu dalam revolusi. Makasar: n.n., 1967, 340 pp.

4401 Mattulada
The involvement of South Sulawesi in the independence revolution of Indonesia (1945-1950). Kyoto: n.n., 1979, 18 pp.

4402 Matu Mona (ps. Hasbullah Parinduri)
Akibat perang. Djakarta: Gapura, 1950, 72 pp.

4403 Mbeo, Jes Cornelius
Sedjarah perdjuangan rakjat di pulau Timor menudju kemerdekaan Indonesia. 1971, 80 pp. [MA thesis IKIP Djakarta.] [11]

4404 *Medan Area mengisi Proklamasi; Perjuangan kemerdekaan dalam wilayah Sumatera Utara.* Disusun oleh Biro Sejarah PRIMA. Medan: Badan Musyawarah Pejuang Republik Indonesia Medan Area, 1976, 831 pp.

4405 Memed E.R.
'Mengenang kembali Lampung dimasa perjuangan', in: *Bunga rampai perjuangan dan pengorbanan I*, pp. 285-301. Jakarta: Markas Besar Legiun Veteran RI, 1982.

4406 *Mengenang palagan empat hari di Surakarta, tgl. 7 s/d 10 Agt. 1949.* Semarang: Panitia Peringatan 4 Hari Pertempuran Kota Sala, ca. 1965, 83 pp.

4407 *Mengenang puputan Margarana dan pemugaran monumen pahlawan Margarana.* Marga (Bali): Yayasan Kebaktian Proklamasi Daerah Tingkat I Bali, 1978, 88 pp.

4408 *Mengenangkan Hari Proklamasi.* Medan: Deli Drukkerij, ca. 1956, 240 pp. (kitlv-m)

4409 *Mengungkapkan sejarah sebagai kenangan; Riwayat perjuangan kaum perempuan pada saat revolusi kemerdekaan 17-8-1945 di Sumatera Barat (Minangkabau) dalam organisasi Keputerian Republik Indonesia (KRI).* Jakarta: KRI Sumatera Barat, 1990, 40 pp.

4410 *Menyongsong pembangunan 'Museum Perjuangan 45' Jawa Timur.* Surabaya: Dewan Harian Daerah Angkatan 45 Jawa Timur, 1973, 94 pp. [22]

4411 *Merebut kota perjuangan.* Banten: Yayasan Achli Waris Pahlawan, ca. 1989. [Various pagings.]

4412 *Meriam gempur Banteng Blorok; Peranannya dalam perang kemerdekaan R.I.* Disusun oleh TRIP Jawa Timur dan Jarahdam VIII Brawijaya. Jakarta: Dharma Patria, 1987, 85 pp.

4413 Mestoko, Sumarsono
'Sebuah bingkisan bagi remaja pelajar generasi penerus (secercah kisah peninggalan Tentara Pelajar Angkatan 45)', in: *Aku akan teruskan; Hasil sayembara mengarang dalam rangka peringatan hari ulang tahun kemerdekaan R.I. yang ke 30*, pp. 158-188. Jakarta: Dewan Harian Nasional Angkatan 45, Pusat Dokumentasi Sejarah Perjoangan 45/Aries Lima, 1976.

4414 Mihardja, St.
Pemberontakan Madiun (Mr. Amir Syarifuddin). Bandung: Sarana Panca Karya, 1986, 39 pp.

4415 Minawati
Sumbangan organisasi wanita dalam revolusi kemerdekaan Indonesia di Sumatera Barat 1945-1950; Suatu studi tentang Sabil Muslimat. 1989, 73 pp. [MA thesis Universitas Andalas, Padang.] [58]

4416 Mirsha, I Gusti Ngurah Rai
Revolusi fisik 1945 di Bali; Laporan penelitian. Denpasar: Universitas Udayana, 1985, 163 pp.

4417 Mirza, Sidharta
Kenanganku dalam pertempuran 5 hari di Semarang. Semarang: Ramadhani, 1974. [4629]

4418 Mochtar, Kustiniyati (ed.)
Memoar pejuang Republik Indonesia seputar 'zaman Singapura', 1945-1950. Jakarta: Gramedia, 1992, 250 pp.

4419 Mochtar, Sofyan
'Kisah pendirian "Antara Singapore"; Cabang Kantor Berita Indonesia yang pertama di luar negeri', in: Kustiniyati Mochtar (ed.), *Memoar pejuang Republik Indonesia seputar 'zaman Singapura', 1945-1950*, pp. 35-50. Jakarta: Gramedia, 1992.

4420 *Modal revolusi 45*. Kutaradja: Komite Musjawarah Angkatan 45 DI Atjeh, 1960, 108 pp.

4421 Moechtar, H.Z.A. and Slamet Herradi
Merdeka atau mati. Surabaya: Institut Dagang Muchtar, 1984, 80 pp.

4422 Moehadi
Riwayat singkat pembentukan Pemerintah Darurat Republik Indonesia. Semarang: Aneka, 1981, 40 pp.

4423 Moehkardi
'Pertempuran lima hari di Semarang', in: *Terbukalah jalanku; Hasil sayembara mengarang dalam rangka peringatan hari ulang tahun kemerdekaan R.I. yang ke 30*, pp. 19-50. Jakarta: Dewan Harian Nasional Angkatan 45, Pusat Dokumentasi Sejarah Perjoangan 45/Aries Lima, 1976.

4424 Moehkardi
Akademi Militer Yogya dalam perjuangan pisik 1945-1949. Jakarta: Inaltu, 1977, 24+389 pp.

4425 Moehkardi
Pendidikan perwira TNI-AD di masa revolusi I. Jakarta: Inaltu, 1979, 23+331 pp.
[All published.]

4426 Moehkardi
Magelang berjuang. Magelang: Akademi ABRI Bagian Darat, 1983, 112 pp. [42]

4427 Moehkardi
Pelajar pejuang; Tentara Genie Pelajar 1945-1950. Surabaya: Yayasan Ex-Batalyon TGP Brigade XVII, 1983, 22+446 pp.

4428 Moe'in, Anwar A.
'Dari Kantor Berita ke Dinas Luar Negeri', in: Kustiniyati Mochtar (ed.), *Memoar pejuang Republik Indonesia seputar 'zaman Singapura', 1945-1950,* pp. 51-65. Jakarta: Gramedia, 1992.

4429 Moein, Moechtar
'PMT-BPNK dalam total people defense', in: *Dari penjerangan ke penjerahan,* pp. 117-123. Bukittinggi: Djawatan Penerangan Sumatera Tengah, 1951.

4430 Moenir, Abd.
'Mengenang peristiwa perebutan kekuasaan R.I. di kecamatan Donomulyo oleh P.K.I./F.D.R. di Malang Selatan, 20 September 1948', *Gema Angkatan 45* no. 41 (August-September 1979):38-41.

4431 Moerad T.A.
'Indonesia 10 tahun merdeka', in: Darius Marpaung (ed.), *Bingkisan nasional; Kenangan 10 tahun revolusi Indonesia, 17-8-1945/17-8-1955,* pp. 238-242. Djakarta: Usaha Pegawai Nasional Indonesia, 1955.

4432 Moerwanto
Jiwa patriot; Pertempuran lima hari di Semarang. Jakarta: Pustaka Jaya, 1992, 126 pp.

4433 Moerwanto
Jiwa pejuang; Para pelaut remaja membentuk armada. Jakarta: Pustaka Jaya, 1992, 127 pp.

4434 Moestopo
Memori pengalaman May. Jen. Purn. Prof. Dr. Moestopo pada saat-saat setelah Proklamasi kemerdekaan negara Republik Indonesia, tanggal 17 Agustus 1945 sampai dengan tanggal 10 Nopember 1945. Jakarta: Lembaga Pendidikan Tinggi Eksponen 45, 1977, 15 pp.

4435 Moestopo
'Latar belakang perjuangan 10 Nopember 1945 di Surabaya', in: *Bunga rampai perjuangan dan pengorbanan II,* pp. 207-216. Jakarta: Markas Besar Legiun Veteran RI, 1983.

4436 Moestopo
Histori dari Barisan Penggempur Terate. Jakarta, 1984. [4765]

4437 Mohtar, Toha
Pulang; Sebuah novel. Djakarta: Pembangunan, 1958, 117 pp. [Fifth printing, Jakarta: Dunia Pustaka Jaya, 1994, 119 pp.]

4438   Mohtar, Toha
       Gugurnja komandan gerilja. 1962. [902]

4439   Mohtar, Toha
       Daerah tidak bertuan; Sebuah epos revolusi. Djakarta: Pantjaka, 1963, 115 pp.

4440   Mohtar, Toha
       Antara Wilis dan Gunung Kelud. Jakarta: Djambatan, 1989, 110 pp.

4441   *Monumen palagan Ambarawa.* Semarang, 1974, 69 pp.

4442   *Monumen perjuangan.* Jakarta: Kem. P dan K, 1978, 1979, 85+49 pp. 2 vols.

4443   *Monumen perjuangan BKR/TKR Jakarta Raya.* Jakarta: Dinas Sejarah KODAM
       Jaya Jayakarta, 1985, 64 pp.

4444   *Monumen perjuangan Daerah Istimewa Yogyakarta.* Jakarta: Kem. P dan K, 1987,
       89+82 pp.

4445   *Monumen perjuangan Jawa Timur.* Jakarta: Kem. P dan K, 1986, 171 pp.

4446   *Monumen perjuangan di Propinsi Nusa Tenggara Timur.* Jakarta: Kem. P dan K,
       1986, 30+19 pp.

4447   *Monumen perjuangan di Propinsi Sulawesi Utara.* Jakarta: Kem. P dan K, 1986,
       130 pp.

4448   *Monumen Soekarno-Hatta; Proklamator kemerdekaan Indonesia.* Jakarta: Proyek
       Pembangunan Monumen Soekarno-Hatta, 1980, 41 pp.

4449   Muanas, Dasum
       Peranan Komite Nasional Indonesia dalam perjuangan mempertahankan RI
       (1945). 1975. [MA thesis Universitas Padjadjaran, Bandung.] [20]

4450   Muchlis
       Beberapa catatan kecil sejarah perjuangan rakyat di Sulawesi Selatan. Paper
       Seminar Sejarah Perjuangan Rakyat Sulawesi Selatan Menentang Penjajahan
       Asing, Ujung Pandang, 1982, 9 pp.

4451   Muchri and Sugeng Sudarto
       TNI Angkatan Laut dalam gambar 1945-1950. Jakarta: Dinas Sejarah TNI-AL,
       1980, 14+176 pp.

4452   Mufthy, Naga
       Suatu critical study mengenai tatatjara Belanda membentuk negara boneka
       Negara Indonesia Timur. 1964. [MA thesis Universitas Hasanuddin, Makas-
       sar.] [111]

4453   Muginingtyas
       Peranan Hizbullah dalam mempertahankan kemerdekaan Indonesia di Jawa
       Barat 1945-1947. 1987. [MA thesis IKIP Jakarta.] [Histori]

4454   Mukhlis
       Badan perjuangan mobilisasi dan rasionalisasi tentara di Sulawesi Selatan.
       Paper Diskusi Sejarah Lokal IV, Revolusi Kemerdekaan di Tingkat Lokal,
       Bandungan-Ambarawa, 1994, 16 pp.

4455 Mulyadi, Ali
'Sejarah dokumen penyerahan Angkatan Laut Jepang kepada pemerintah RI', in: *Bunga rampai perjuangan dan pengorbanan I*, pp. 41-56. Jakarta: Markas Besar Legiun Veteran RI, 1982.

4456 Mulyadi, Domo
'Route gerilya Gubernur Militer II/DMI II Kol. Gatot Subroto', *Gema Angkatan 45* no. 36 (January 1979):28-33; no. 37 (February 1979):38-41; no. 38 (March 1979):35-38.

4457 Mulyana, Irsda
'Gema kemerdekaan di Sumatra Tengah', in: Darius Marpaung (ed.), *Bingkisan nasional; Kenangan 10 tahun revolusi Indonesia, 17-8-1945/17-8-1955*, pp. 53-58. Djakarta: Usaha Pegawai Nasional Indonesia, 1955.

4458 Mulyo, H.
'Mengenang almarhum bapak Mayjen. Purn. Sungkono; Bapak TNI Jatim', *Gema Angkatan 45* no. 31 (July-August 1978):65-68, 75-76.

4459 Muntholib, Idik
Pemberontakan APRA dan pentrapannja dalam pendidikan untuk memper-tebal semangat nasionalisme. 1970, 113 pp. [MA thesis IKIP Djakarta.] [11]

4460 Murba
'Jogja utara sebagai daerah gerilja semasa agressie Belanda II', *Madjalah Sedjarah Militer Angkatan Darat* no. 17 (1964):43-49. [55]

4461 Murtini, R. Sri
Peristiwa APRA di Bandung dan sekitarnja pada tanggal 23 Djanuari 1950. 1968. [MA thesis Universitas Padjadjaran, Bandung.] [1, 20, 4858]

4462 Muryantoro, Hisbaron
Partisipasi rakyat Bibis selama Clash II pada awal tahun 1949. 1980. [MA thesis Universitas Gadjah Mada, Yogyakarta.] [4463]

4463 Muryantoro, Hisbaron
'Peranan kyai pada masa revolusi di Daerah Istimewa Yogyakarta (1945-1949)', in: *Peristiwa-peristiwa revolusi di tingkat lokal*, pp. 147-172. Yogyakarta: Dep. P dan K, 1993.

4464 *Museum ABRI Satriamandala; Buku panduan*. Second edition. Jakarta: Dep. HANKAM, Pusat Sejarah ABRI, 1980, 112 pp. [First edition 1972; Fourth edition, Jakarta: Markas Besar Angkatan Bersenjata R.I., Pusat Sejarah dan Tradisi ABRI, 1984, 146 pp.]

4465 *Museum Joang 45 - Gedung Joang 45; Jln. Menteng Raya 31*. Jakarta: Dep. P dan K, Proyek Pengembangan Permuseuman DKI Jakarta, 1985, 13+89 pp.

4466 *Museum Mandala Wangsit Siliwangi*. Bandung: Markas Komando Daerah Militer VI Siliwangi, 1982, 12 pp.

4467 *Museum Pusat TNI-AD Dharma Wiratama*. Bandung: Dinas Sejarah TNI Angkatan Darat, 1982, 45 pp.

4468   Musin, Emilia
       Djendral Urip Sumohardjo; Perintis Angkatan Bersendjata R.I. Djakarta: Lembaga
       Sedjarah HANKAM, 1967, 16 pp.

4469   Musin, Emilia Baki
       Persetudjuan Renville; Akibatnja pada bidang pertahanan keamanan. 1969,
       218 pp. [MA thesis Universitas Indonesia, Djakarta.] [18, 99]

4470   Musin, Emilia Baki
       Persetudjuan Renville. Paper SSN-II, Jogjakarta, 1970, 53 pp.

4471   Mustafa, Nurdin
       'Timbul dan tenggelam; Mengenang djawatan "Pe-Ma" dizaman darurat', in:
       Dari penjerangan ke penjerahan, pp. 113-116. Bukittinggi: Djawatan Penerangan
       Sumatera Tengah, 1951.

4472   Musthapa
       Pengantar ke-sejarah perjuangan pers di Kalimantan Selatan, periode 1945-1949.
       Banjarmasin: n.n., 1975, 76 pp.

4473   Mustopo, M. Habib
       *Gerakan hidup baru dan Panca Dharma; Sebuah catatan sejarah menjelang
       Proklamasi kemerdekaan.* Jember: Universitas Jember, 1988, 34 pp.

4474   Muttalib, Jang Aisjah and Sudjarwo
       Gelandangan dalam kancah revolusi. Yogyakarta: Universitas Islam Indonesia,
       1982, 14 pp.

4475   Muttaqien, E.Z.
       Menggali beberapa keping dari sejarah muta-akhir Jawa Barat. Paper Seminar
       Sejarah Jawa Barat, Sumedang, 1974. [4313, 4858]

4476   Mutyara, A.G.
       Banda Aceh pernah berperanan sebagai ibukota RI. Medan: Panitia Seminar
       Perjuangan Aceh, 1976. [3756]

4477   Nalenan, R.
       Proses lahirnya Pancasila. Jakarta: Lembaga Penelitian Sejarah Nasional,
       Universitas 17 Agustus 1945, 1979, 83 pp. [Second edition, 1987, 132 pp.]

4478   Nandang S.
       Medan Area. Bandung: Angkasa, 1984, 34 pp.

4479   Nandang S.
       Pertempuran 5 hari di Palembang. Bandung: Angkasa, 1984, 34 pp.

4480   Nandang S.
       Sulawesi berdarah. Bandung: Angkasa, 1984, 34 pp.

4481   *Napak tilas route gerilya GM II/DMI II Kolonel Gatot Subroto.* Sejarah Militer
       KODAM VII/Diponegoro, 1978. [5111]

4482   Napitupulu, Sontang Pajaman
       Agressi Belanda I dan II merupakan pelanggaran terhadap Proklamasi 17
       Agustus 1945. 1969. [MA thesis IKIP Medan.] [13]

4483   Nas, C.M.
       Kebebasan abadi; Setengkal tragedi kepahlawanan. Djakarta: Pantjaka, 1963, 39 pp.

4484 Nasir S., Muh.
Tinjauan historis terhadap pertempuran tanggal 14 Pebruari 1946 di Selayar.
1979. [Thesis Institut Agama Islam Negeri, Ujung Pandang.] [4334]

4485 Nasution, A.H.
Pokok-pokok gerilya dan pertahanan RI dimasa yang lalu dan yang akan datang.
Fourth edition. Bandung: Angkasa, 1980, 349 pp. [First edition 1953; Second
edition, Djakarta: Pembimbing, 1954, 311 pp.; Third edition, Djakarta: Pembimbing Masa, 1964, 292 pp.]

4486 Nasution, A.H.
'Mengenangkan krisis perang kemerdekaan', in: Darius Marpaung (ed.),
Bingkisan nasional; Kenangan 10 tahun revolusi Indonesia, 17-8-1945/17-8-1955,
pp. 97-111. Djakarta: Usaha Pegawai Nasional Indonesia, 1955.

4487 Nasution, Abdul Haris
*Der Guerillakrieg; Grundlagen der Guerillakriegführung aus der Sicht des indo-
nesischen Verteidigungssystems in Vergangenheit und Zukunft.* Köln: Brückenbauer,
1961, 148 pp.

4488 Nasution, A.H.
Fundamentals of guerrilla warfare. New York: Praeger, 1965, 324 pp. [Second
printing, Djakarta: Seruling Masa, 1970, 324 pp.]

4489 Nasution, A.H.
Sedjarah perdjuangan nasional dibidang bersendjata. Djakarta: Mega Bookstore,
1966, 256 pp.

4490 Nasution, A.H.
Sekitar perang kemerdekaan Indonesia. Second edition. Bandung: Angkasa, 1977-
79. I. *Proklamasi,* 30+515 pp.; II. *Diplomasi atau bertempur,* 30+642 pp.; III.
Diplomasi sambil bertempur, 30+669 pp.; IV. *Periode Linggarjati,* 30+579 pp.; V.
Agresi Militer Belanda I, 30+634 pp.; VI. *Perang Gerilya Semesta I,* 30+562 pp.;
VII. *Periode Renville,* 30+632 pp.; VIII. *Pemberontakan PKI 1948,* 30+575 pp.; IX.
Agresi Militer Belanda II, 30+464 pp.; X. *Perang Gerilya Semesta II,* 30+688 pp.;
XI. *Periode KMB,* 30+503 pp. [First edition 1973.]

4491 Nasution, A.H.
'10 Nopember dan kembali ke UUD '45/November 10th and the return to the
1945 constitution', *Indonesia Magazine* no. 29 (1974):39-51.

4492 Nasution, A.H.
28 tahun Bandung lautan api. Jakarta: n.n., 1974, 7 pp.

4493 Nasution, A.H.
10 Nopember 1945. Bandung: Angkasa, 1976, 59 pp.

4494 Nasution, A.H.
*Proses menyusun naskah Sekitar perang kemerdekaan Indonesia; Ceramah untuk
Masyarakat Sejarawan Indonesia cabang Jakarta, 30 Oktober 1976.* Bandung:
Angkasa, 1976, 24 pp.

4495 Nasution, A.H.
Bandung lautan api. Jakarta: n.n., 1980, 24 pp.

4496   Nasution, A.H.
       'Kepemimpinan Pak Dirman', in: Sides Sudyarto (ed.), *Tingkah laku politik Panglima Besar Soedirman*, pp. 11-32. Jakarta: Karya Unipress, 1983.

4497   Nasution, Abdul Haris
       'Kisah seorang prajurit', in: Colin Wild and Peter Carey (eds), *Gelora api revolusi*, pp. 133-140. Jakarta: Gramedia, 1986.

4498   Nasution, A.H.
       'The story of a soldier; An interview with General Abdul Haris Nasution', in: C. Wild and P. Carey (eds), *Born in fire; The Indonesian struggle for independence; An anthology*, pp. 120-126. Athens: Ohio University Press, 1986.

4499   Nasution, A.H.
       'PDRI dan Komando Jawa', in: Abdurrachman Surjomihardjo and J.R. Chaniago (eds), *Pemerintah Darurat Republik Indonesia dikaji ulang*, pp. 134-141. Jakarta: Masyarakat Sejarawan Indonesia, 1990.

4500   Nasution, Amir Taat
       'Pembentukan BKR-TKR dan pemerintahan RI di Tebingtinggi', *Vidya Yudha* no. 7 (1969):82-84.

4501   Nasution, Harun
       Persetudjuan Linggardjati. 1964, 118 pp. [MA thesis IKIP Djakarta.] [11]

4502   Natasuwarna, H.
       The Indonesian revolution and the paper money issued during that period. Cianjur: n.n., 1979, 43 pp.

4503   Natsir, M.
       'Mengenai sedjarah terdekat', *Aliran Islam* 3-16 (1950):871-875. (kitlv-m)

4504   Natsir, M.
       Revolusi Indonesia. Bandung: Djihad, 1955, 22 pp. [4, 736]

4505   Nawawi, Al Haj (?)
       Sejarah perjuangan revolusi kemerdekaan dalam kabupaten Ogan dan Komering Ulu. Baturaja, 1975. [4873]

4506   Nawawi, Manah
       Perjuangan kemerdekaan di Bengkulu. Bengkulu, 1979. [4853]

4507   Nazar, Bachtul
       Pemberontakan Kapten Andi Abdul Azis di Makasar. 1972. [MA thesis Universitas Padjadjaran, Bandung.] [1]

4508   Nazir, Moh.
       'Butir renungan pada masa revolusi di Sumatera Barat; Bergerilya dari rimba ke rimba', in: Abdurrachman Surjomihardjo and J.R. Chaniago (eds), *Pemerintah Darurat Republik Indonesia dikaji ulang*, pp. 142-146. Jakarta: Masyarakat Sejarawan Indonesia, 1990.

4509   Ngantoeng, Henk
       Menelusuri jalur Linggarjati; Sketsa karya cipta. Jakarta: Agung Offset, 1992, 43 pp.

4510 Ngantung, Piet
'Cukilan pengalaman dalam revolusi kemerdekaan', in: *Bunga rampai perjuangan dan pengorbanan II*, pp. 259-277. Jakarta: Markas Besar Legiun Veteran RI, 1983.

4511 *Nikmat Proklamasi*. Djakarta: Dep. Agama, 1959, 54 pp. (kitlv-m)

4512 Ninnong, H.A.
Otobiografi. Ujung Pandang: n.n., 1975, 39 pp.

4513 Ninnong, H. Andi'
'Pages autobiographiques; Une princesse bugis dans la révolution (traduit et annoté par Chr. Pelras)', *Archipel* 13 (1977):137-156.

4514 Nitimihardjo, Maruto
Sejarah rapat raksasa Ikada tanggal 19 September 1945; Ceramah. Jakarta, 1977. [3908]

4515 Noer, Mohammad
'Kissah suatu perjuangan (kenangan-kenangan tentang liku-likunya perjuangan)', in: *Bunga rampai perjuangan dan pengorbanan II*, pp. 218-225. Jakarta: Markas Besar Legiun Veteran RI, 1983.

4516 Noer, Mohammad
Pengalaman di masa revolusi di medan gerilya Madura. Paper Diskusi Sejarah Lokal IV, Revolusi Kemerdekaan di Tingkat Lokal, Bandungan-Ambarawa, 1994, 17 pp.

4517 Noer'aeni, Nanny
Peranan Ir. Soekarno dalam perang kemerdekaan tahun 1945-tahun 1949. 1972, 67 pp. [MA thesis IKIP Bandung.] [10]

4518 Noor, Anwar D.
Gugurnya pahlawan dirgantara. Bandung: Buana, 1985, 64 pp.

4519 Noor, Djuhar and S. Sigit Wahyudi
Dinamika politik di daerah MMTg Mranggen Semarang (1945-1949). Paper Diskusi Sejarah Lokal IV, Revolusi Kemerdekaan di Tingkat Lokal, Bandungan-Ambarawa, 1994, 24 pp.

4520 Notohamidjojo, Ny. Rr. Soedjariah
'Kehidupanku dan keluarga dalam masa perjuangan 45', in: *Letusan di balik buku; Hasil sayembara mengarang dalam rangka peringatan hari ulang tahun kemerdekaan RI yang ke 30*, pp. 135-154. Jakarta: Dewan Harian Nasional Angkatan 45/Aries Lima, 1976.

4521 Notosoetardjo, H.A.
Dokumen-dokumen Konperensi Medja Bundar; Sebelum, sesudah dan pembubarannja. Djakarta: Endang, 1956, 288 pp.

4522 Notosoetardjo, H.A.
Peristiwa Madiun; Tragedi nasional. Djakarta: Endang/Pemuda/Api Islam, 1966, 227 pp.

4523 Notosusanto, Nugroho
Hudjan kepagian; Kumpulan tjerita pendek. Djakarta: Balai Pustaka, 1958, 83 pp.
[Third printing, 1966, 74 pp.]

4524 Notosusanto, Nugroho
Rasa sajangé; Kumpulan tjerita pendek. Djakarta: Pembangunan, 1961, 135 pp.

4525 Notosusanto, Nugroho
'Hari-hari sesudah Proklamasi', *Intisari* 2-13 (August 1964). [736]

4526 Notosusanto, Nugroho
Pertempuran Surabaja; Monumen jang lajak bagi kepahlawanan Indonesia. Djakarta:
Lembaga Sedjarah HANKAM, 1965, 12 pp. [Second edition, 1968, 15 pp.]

4527 Notosusanto, Nugroho
'Lahirnja UUD 45', *Intisari* 3-37 (August 1966):4-9, 89-90.

4528 Notosusanto, Nugroho
'1 Oktober 1945', *Intisari* 6-63 (October 1968). [736]

4529 Notosusanto, Nugroho
'Awal penerbangan militer di Indonesia', *Intisari* 6-71 (June 1969):13-15, 147-
148.

4530 Notosusanto, Nugroho
'Pasukan-pasukan Belanda dalam perang kemerdekaan Indonesia, 1945-1949',
Intisari 6-65 (1969). [736]

4531 Notosusanto, Nugroho
The battle of Surabaja. Djakarta: Department of Defence and Security, 1970, 15 pp.

4532 Notosusanto, Nugroho
Naskah Proklamasi jang otentik dan rumusan Pancasila jang otentik. Djakarta:
Pusat Sedjarah ABRI, 1971, 38 pp. [Second edition, 1976, 39 pp.]

4533 Notosusanto, Nugroho
Penggunaan sedjarah untuk pewarisan nilai-nilai 1945 dan nilai-nilai TNI 1945.
Djakarta: Dep. HANKAM, 1972, 13 pp.

4534 Notosusanto, Nugroho (ed.)
Markas Besar Komando Djawa. Jakarta: Departemen Pertahanan Keamanan,
Pusat Sejarah ABRI, 1973, 88 pp.

4535 Notosusanto, Nugroho
'The effect of the "gerilya" on the military and society', *Review of Indonesian and
Malaysian Affairs* 8-1 (1974):57-72.

4536 Notosusanto, Nugroho
Some effects of the guerrilla on armed forces and security in Indonesia 1948-1949.
Jakarta: Department of Defence and Security, Centre for Armed Forces History,
1974, 28 pp.

4537 Notosusanto, Nugroho
'The historiography of the Indonesian armed forces; Its first development', *Acta
(of the) International Commission for Military History* no. 2 (1975). [736]

4538 Notosusanto, Nugroho
'Soedirman; Panglima yang menepati janjinya', in: Abdullah, Taufik; Aswab Mahasin dan Daniel Dhakidae (eds), *Manusia dalam kemelut sejarah*, pp. 47-62. Jakarta: Lembaga Penelitian, Pendidikan dan Penerangan Ekonomi dan Sosial, 1978.

4539 Notosusanto, Nugroho
Proses perumusan Pancasila dasar negara. Jakarta: Balai Pustaka, 1981, 68 pp.

4540 Notosusanto, Nugroho
'Riwayat hidup Panglima Besar Soedirman', in: *Mesjid Panglima Besar Soedirman*, pp. 9-16. Jakarta: Pemerintah Daerah K.I. Jakarta, 1981.

4541 Notosusanto, Nugroho
Sumbangan Prof. Supomo kepada perumusan Pancasila dasar negara dan Undang-Undang Dasar 1945. Paper SSN-III, Jakarta, 1981, 13 pp.

4542 Notosusanto, Nugroho
Wawancara simultan; Suatu experimen dalam sejarah lisan. Paper SSN-III, Jakarta, 1981, 6 pp.

4543 Notosusanto, Nugroho (ed.)
Pertempuran Surabaya. Jakarta: Mutiara Sumber Widya, 1985, 276 pp.

4544 *Notulen rapat Panitya Persiapan Kemerdekaan Indonesia, 18 Agustus 1945*. Dikutip oleh W. Bonar Sidjabat. Djakarta: Sinar Kasih, 1969, 32 pp.

4545 Nuh, Muhamad
'Peristiwa Tiga Daerah; Proklamasi kemerdekaan 17 Agustus 1945 di daerah Tegal', *Penelitian Sedjarah* 3-5 (1962):29-32; 3-6 (1962):31-36.

4546 *Nukilan sedjarah Hari Pahlawan 10 Nopember*. Djakarta: Dep. Penerangan, 1969, 12 pp.

4547 Oka, I Gusti Ngurah
Puputan Margarana (20 November 1946). 1967, 130 pp. [MA thesis IKIP Djakarta.] [11]

4548 Onghokham
'Pemberontakan Madiun 1948; Drama manusia dalam revolusi', *Prisma* 7-7 (1978):57-70.

4549 Onghokham
'Revolusi Indonesia; Mitos dan realitas', *Prisma* 14-8 (1985):3-11.

4550 Oudang, M.
Perkembangan kepolisian di Indonesia. Djakarta: Mahabharata, 1952, 218 pp.

4551 Padmawidjaja, Rusjai
Peranan perang gerilja dalam perdjuangan bangsa Indonesia mempertahankan kemerdekaan (1945-1950). 1969, 213 pp. [MA thesis IKIP Bandung.] [10]

4552 Padmosugondo, H. Imam Sudarwo
'Kisah percakapan perjuangan kemerdekaan', in: *Bunga rampai perjuangan dan pengorbanan I*, pp. 232-241. Jakarta: Markas Besar Legiun Veteran RI, 1982.

4553 Paggaru, Andi
Risalah perdjoangan kemerdekaan Republik Indonesia (PKRI) dalam kabupaten Wadjo. Sengkang: n.n., 1968, 15 pp.

4554 Pakpahan, Latif Mula
Suatu analisa tentang sebab-sebab timbulnja peristiwa berdarah 13 Desember 1945 di Tebing Tinggi. 1972, 81 pp. [MA thesis IKIP Medan.] [13]

4555 Pakpahan, Shery
'Pengabdian pedjuang gerilja di Bali; Puputan Margarana, pertempuran 20 Nopember 1946', *Vidya Yudha* no. 5 (1968):90-98.

4556 Pakpahan, Shery
'Peristiwa 13 Desember Tebing Tinggi', *Vidya Yudha* no. 4 (1968):84-90.

4557 Pakpahan, Shery
'Bumi hangus di Pangkalan Berandan, 13 Agustus 1947', *Vidya Yudha* no. 8 (1969):117-123.

4558 Pakpahan, Shery
'Peristiwa gerbong maut (kereta api maut)', *Vidya Yudha* no. 7 (1969):97-101.

4559 Pakpahan, Shery
'Peristiwa Situdjuh Batur', *Vidya Yudha* no. 6 (1969):56-59.

4560 Pakpahan, Shery
'Pertempuran Pajakabung', *Vidya Yudha* no. 10 (1970):110-119.

4561 Pakpahan, Shery
'Pertempuran di Krueng Pandju', *Vidya Yudha* no. 13 (1971):112-116.

4562 Pakpahan, Shery
'Sekelumit kisah sejarah dari Sumut dalam perang kemerdekaan; Pangkalan Berandan lautan api', *Gema Angkatan 45* no. 34 (October 1978):30-32.

4563 'Palagan Ambarawa', *Vidya Yudha* no. 4 (1968):91-100; no. 5 (1968):79-89.

4564 'Palagan Ambarawa', *Vidya Yudha* no. 9 (1970):84-97.

4565 *Palagan Ambarawa.* Semarang: Dinas Sejarah Militer KODAM VII/Diponegoro, 1979, 102 pp.

4566 'Palagan Bali', *Vidya Yudha* no. 9 (1970):116-127.

4567 'Palagan Bandung', *Vidya Yudha* no. 9 (1970):55-75.

4568 'Palagan Makasar', *Vidya Yudha* no. 9 (1970):128-134.

4569 'Palagan Medan', *Vidya Yudha* no. 9 (1970):15-36.

4570 'Palagan Palembang', *Vidya Yudha* no. 9 (1970):37-54.

4571 'Palagan Semarang', *Vidya Yudha* no. 9 (1970):76-83.
4572 'Palagan Surabaja', *Vidya Yudha* no. 9 (1970):98-115.

4573 Palar, L.N.
'A brief for Indonesia's independence', in: Greta O. Wilson (ed.), *Regents, reformers and revolutionaries; Indonesian voices of colonial days; Selected historical readings 1899-1949*, pp. 181-192. Honolulu: University Press of Hawaii, 1978.

4574 *Pameran foto perjuangan di Museum Perjuangan Yogyakarta/Seksi Ilmiah.* Yogyakarta: Kem. P dan K, 1984, 38 pp.

4575 *Pameran foto perjuangan pada masa revolusi fisik di Yogyakarta tahun 1945-1949.* Jakarta: Direktorat Permuseuman, Direktorat Jenderal Kebudayaan, Departemen Pendidikan dan Kebudayaan, 1994, 26 pp.

4576 Pance, H. Maemuna Djud
Ringkasan sejarah kelasykaran GAPRI 5.3.1 di Afdeeling Mandar Sulsel periode tahun 1945-1949. Paper Seminar Sejarah Perjuangan Rakyat Sulawesi Selatan Menentang Penjajahan Asing, Ujung Pandang, 1982, 15 pp.

4577 Pandji, M. Noerdin
'Kotabumi kembali; Kisah perjuangan sepasukan Garuda Hitam di Lampung', in: *Aku akan teruskan; Hasil sayembara mengarang dalam rangka peringatan hari ulang tahun kemerdekaan R.I. yang ke 30*, pp. 68-96. Jakarta: Dewan Harian Nasional Angkatan 45, Pusat Dokumentasi Sejarah Perjoangan 45/Aries Lima, 1976.

4578 Pangaribuan, Bintang
Analisa tentang djalannja perdjuangan Indonesia (1945-1949). 1969. [MA thesis IKIP Medan.] [13]

4579 Panggabean, Maralus
Serangan Umum 1 Maret 1949. 1986, 120 pp. [MA thesis Universitas Indonesia, Jakarta.] [Histori]

4580 *Panglima Besar Djenderal Soedirman.* Djakarta: Kem. Pertahanan RI, 1950. [5065]

4581 Pantouw, G.R.
Perjuangan rakyat Sulawesi Selatan menentang NIT. Paper Seminar Sejarah Perjuangan Rakyat Sulawesi Selatan Menentang Penjajahan Asing, Ujung Pandang, 1982, 11 pp.

4582 Panyarikan, Ktut Sudiri
Kolonel anumerta I Gusti Ngurah Rai. Jakarta: Kem. P dan K, 1976, 91 pp. [Second edition, *I Gusti Ngurah Rai*, 1982, 141 pp.]

4583 Parna, Ibnu
Undang berpikir rakjat berdjoang. Djakarta: Widjaya, 1950, 68 pp.

4584 Patang, Lahadjdji
Sulawesi dan pahlawan-pahlawannja. Djakarta: Jajasan Adil Makmur, 1961, 34 pp.

4585 Patang, Lahadjdji
Sulawesi dan pahlawan-pahlawannya. Jakarta: Yayasan Kesejahteraan Generasi Muda Indonesia, 1976, 347 pp.

4586 Patriawan, Yunus
Profil pejuang wanita di daerah Sulawesi Selatan. Ca. 1986. [MA thesis Universitas Hasanuddin, Ujung Pandang.] [4334]

4587   Paturusi, Saifuddin
        Peranan dan sumbangan pemuda-pemuda Bulukumba dalam revolusi kemerdekaan
        Indonesia. Djakarta: Lembaga Sedjarah Hankam, 1967, 32 pp.

4588   Paturusi, Saifuddin
        'Jatuhnya Kubu Polioi (sumbangan pemuda-pemuda Bulukumba dalam
        perjuangan kemerdekaan Indonesia)', in: *Aku akan teruskan; Hasil sayembara*
        mengarang dalam rangka peringatan hari ulang tahun kemerdekaan R.I. yang ke 30,
        pp. 190-215. Jakarta: Dewan Harian Nasional Angkatan 45, Pusat Dokumen-
        tasi Sejarah Perjoangan 45/Aries Lima, 1976.

4589   Pawiloy, Sarita
        Sejarah revolusi kemerdekaan 1945-1949 daerah Sulawesi Selatan. 1980. [MA
        thesis Universitas Hasanuddin, Ujung Pandang.] [604]

4590   Pawiloy, Sarita
        Arus revolusi di Sulawesi Selatan; Sejarah perjuangan Angkatan 45 di Sulawesi
        Selatan. Ujung Pandang: Dewan Harian Daerah Angkatan 45 Propinsi Sulawesi
        Selatan, 1987, 400 pp.

4591   Pedjuang Nasional (ps.)
        Lintasan peristiwa perdjuangan kemerdekaan Sulawesi Tengah; Gorontalo-
        Donggala/Palu-Posso. Palu: Gerakan Penuntut Propinsi Sulawesi-Tengah, ca.
        1951, 56 pp. [Second edition, *Lintasan peristiwa perdjuangan kemerdekaan Sula-*
        wesi Tengah (Posso-Gorontalo-Donggala), Makasar: Gerakan Penuntut Propinsi
        Sulawesi Tengah, 1958, 117 pp.]

4592   *Pemerintah Darurat Republik Indonesia; Himpunan berita-berita pers dari tg. 10-12-*
        1969 s/d 21-1-1970. Djakarta: n.n., 1970, 82 pp.

4593   Pendit, Njoman S.
        Album Bali berdjuang. Denpasar: Jajasan Kebaktian Pedjuang Daerah Bali,
        1954, 119 pp.

4594   Pendit, Njoman S.
        Bali berjuang. Second edition. Jakarta: Gunung Agung, 1979, 19+397 pp. [First
        edition 1954.]

4595   *Penelitian tentang fungsi DPR dalam teori dan praktek (periode 1945-1950)*.
        Jakarta: LKRN/LIPI, 1985, 185 pp.

4596   'Pengabdian "Banteng Blorok" dalam perang kemerdekaan', *Gema Angkatan 45*
        no. 33 (October 1978):36-41.

4597   *Pengabdian selama perang kemerdekaan bersama Brigade Ronggolawe*. Oleh Panitia
        Penyusunan Sejarah Brigade Ronggolawe. Jakarta: Aries Lima, 1985, 560 pp.

4598   *Pengalaman dalam perang gerilya almarhum Let. Jen. Purn. H. Harun Sohar (10*
        Des. 1919-24 Sep. 1988). Palembang: Badan Pengelola Monumen Perjuangan
        Rakyat Sumatera Bagian Selatan (Sumbagsel), 1993, 5+17 pp.

4599   *Peran sivitas akademika FKUI dalam perjuangan kemerdekaan Indonesia 1945-1949*
        dan operasi pemulangan tentara Jepang dan APWI oleh Republik Indonesia di pulau
        Jawa tahun 1945-1947. Jakarta: Balai Penerbit FKUI, 1988, 26 pp.

4600   *Peranan ABRI dalam revolusi*. Djakarta: Dep. HANKAM, ca. 1965, 9 pp.

4601 *Peranan gemilang Murba Indonesia dalam revolusi kemerdekaan (Sekitar sedjarah Partai Murba).* Djakarta: Biro Agit.-Prop. Dewan Partai Partai Murba, 1959, 71 pp.

4602 *Peranan Kolonel Gatot Subroto dalam menumpas pemberontakan PKI Madiun 1948.* Sejarah Militer KODAM VII/Diponegoro, 1978. [5111]

4603 *Peranan pelajar dalam perang kemerdekaan.* Jakarta: Pusat Sejarah dan Tradisi Angkatan Bersenjata Republik Indonesia, 1985, 19+343 pp.

4604 *Peranan Rengasdengklok sekitar Proklamasi 17 Agustus 1945.* Jakarta: Pemerintah DKI Jakarta, Dinas Museum dan Sejarah, 1979, 40 pp. [42]

4605 *Peranan TNI-Angkatan Darat dalam perang kemerdekaan (revolusi pisik 1945-1950).* Bandung: PUSSEMAD, 1965, 225 pp.

4606 *Peranan wanita Indonesia di masa perang kemerdekaan 1945-1950.* Jakarta: Kem. P dan K, 1985, 146 pp. [Second edition, 1986, 143 pp.]

4607 *Perang rakyat semesta 1948-1949.* Oleh: Yayasan 19 Desember 1948. Jakarta: Balai Pustaka, 1994, 172 pp.

4608 *Peraturan-peraturan dan pengumuman-pengumuman mengenai kedudukan pegawai negeri jang dikeluarkan dalam tahun 1952; Djilid 2, Supplement 1946-1949.* Disusun oleh Mr. Marsoro. Djakarta: Djambatan, 1953, 428 pp.

4609 *Pergelaran fragmen mengenang perjuangan pahlawan 10 November 1945.* Samarinda: Panitya Pergelaran Fragmen Mengenang Perjuangan Pahlawan 10 November 1945, 1984, 111 pp.

4610 *Peringatan Hari Pahlawan 10 Nopember 1977.* Jakarta: Keluarga Besar Bekas Tentara Pelajar, 1979, 128 pp.

4611 'Peristiwa Merah Putih di Galela, tahun 1949', *Vidya Yudha* no. 4 (1968):127-129.

4612 'Peristiwa Merah Putih di Namlea (P. Buru) dan sekitarnja (1946)', *Vidya Yudha* no. 4 (1968):121-126.

4613 *Peristiwa-peristiwa revolusi di tingkat lokal.* Yogyakarta: Dep. P dan K, Balai Kajian Sejarah dan Nilai Tradisional, 1993, 172 pp.

4614 *Perjuangan pelajar bersenjata TRIP Jawa Timur.* Disusun oleh Dinas Sejarah TNI-AD. Jakarta: Dinas Pembinaan Mental TNI-AD, 1986, 396 pp.

4615 'Perjuangan rakyat Jepara periode 45-49 selayang pandang', *Vidya Yudha* no. 38 (1980):31-38. [55]

4616 *Perjuangan rakyat semesta Sumatera Utara.* Jakarta: Forum Komunikasi Ex Sub Teritorium VII Komando Sumatera, 1979, 528 pp.

4617 Permadipura, K.O.
'Mengenang detik Proklamasi kemerdekaan', in: Darius Marpaung (ed.), *Bingkisan nasional; Kenangan 10 tahun revolusi Indonesia, 17-8-1945/17-8-1955,* pp. 13-17. Djakarta: Usaha Pegawai Nasional Indonesia, 1955.

4618 *Pertempuran Empat Hari di Solo dan sekitarnya; Bunga rampai cuplikan-cuplikan sejarah.* Jakarta: Kerukunan Anggota Detasemen II BE 17, 1993, 10+116 pp.

4619 'Pertempuran Palopo', *Vidya Yudha* no. 13 (1971):117-120; no.14 (1971):98-116.

4620 'Pertempuran di Serpong', *Vidya Yudha* no. 4 (1968):88-90.

4621 Perwitorini
Dasar-dasar pemikiran hubungan luar negeri tahun 1945-1949 dalam rangka politik luar negeri (suatu tinjauan sejarah). 1975, 94 pp. [MA thesis Universitas Indonesia, Jakarta.] [19]

4622 Pinardi
Peristiwa coup berdarah P.K.I. September 1948 di Madiun; Sebuah case-study tentang proloog-peristiwa-epiloog dan beberapa analisa tentang sebab dan akibat pemberontakan P.K.I.-Muso jang dilakukan terhadap pemerintah Republik Indonesia jang sah pada bulan September 1948. Djakarta: Inkopak-Hazera, 1966, 176 pp.

4623 Pindha, I Gusti Ngurah
Pertempuran besar Tanah Aron, Karangasem, Bali (periode revolusi fisik 1945-1949); Dikenang kembali. Denpasar: Jajasan Universitas Marhaen, 1964, 21 pp.

4624 Pindha, I Gusti Ngurah
Kirikumi besar-besaran terhadap kota Denpasar. Denpasar, 1973, 82 pp.

4625 Pindha, I Gusti Ngurah
Gempilan perjuangan phisik pasukan induk Ngurah Rai. Denpasar: Upada Sastra, 1990, 14+309 pp.

4626 Poeradisastra, S.I. (ps. Buyung Saleh)
'Oerip Soemohardjo; Kebungkaman yang ampuh', *Prisma* 11-9 (1982):68-74.

4627 Poeradisastra, S.I. (ps.)
'Hubungan Panglima Besar Soedirman dengan Persatuan Perjuangan; Suatu percobaan rekonstruksi latar belakang Peristiwa 3 Juli 1946', in: Sides Sudyarto (ed.), *Tingkah laku politik Panglima Besar Soedirman*, pp. 63-89. Jakarta: Karya Unipress, 1983.

4628 Poerbopranoto, Koentjoro
'Pertempuran 5 hari di Semarang', *Gema Angkatan 45* no. 26 (February 1978):16-20.

4629 Poerwantana, P.K.
'Segi koordinasi pertempuran lima hari Semarang', *Bulletin Yaperna* 3-15 (July 1976):3-20.

4630 Poerwantana, P.K.
Kawasan Samigaluh dalam masa clash II. Paper Musyawarah Kerja Nasional Sejarah, Bandung, 1990, 13 pp.

4631 Polem, T.M.A. Panglima
Memoires van Teuku Muhammed Ali Panglima Polem. Vertaling J.H.J. Brendgen. Kutaradja: n.n., 1972, 51 pp.

4632 Polim (Polem), T.M.A. Panglima
Memoir (tjatatan). Kutaradja: Alhambra, 1972, 60 pp.

4633 Posumah, Jan Piet
Perang kemerdekaan di Minahasa dan Manado sekitar tahun 1950. 1978, 172 pp. [MA thesis Universitas Sam Ratulangi, Manado.]

4634 Prabokusumo, Jailani
'Proklamator tentang Proklamasi', *Gema Angkatan 45* no. 56/58 (July-September 1981):34-39, 116.

4635 Prakoso, E.
Aku jadi tentara pelajar. Jakarta: Pustaka Dian, 1979, 90 pp.

4636 Pranata Ssp
'Perang kemerdekaan di Tegal', *Berita Buana* December 1976-January 1977. [736, 1076]

4637 Pranoto, Naning
Wolter Monginsidi; Pahlawan sejati. Jakarta: Karya Unipress, 1983, 61 pp.

4638 Pranoto, Naning
Panglima Sudirman. Jakarta: Karya Unipress, 1984, 54 pp.

4639 Prawiranegara, Syafruddin
Peranan Islam dalam perjoangan kemerdekaan dan pembangunan RI. Paper Seminar 28 Tahun Kemerdekaan Indonesia, Jakarta, 1973, 11 pp.

4640 Prawiranegara, Sjafruddin
Sejarah sebagai pedoman untuk membangun masa depan (peranan mu'jizat dalam perjoangan kemerdekaan bangsa Indonesia). Second edition. Jakarta: Idayu, 1976, 52 pp. [First edition 1975.]

4641 Prawiranegara, Sjafruddin
'Emergency government; An interview with Syafruddin Prawiranegara', in: C. Wild and P. Carey (eds), *Born in fire; The Indonesian struggle for independence; An anthology*, pp. 193-197. Athens: Ohio University Press, 1986.

4642 Prawiranegara, Syafruddin
'Pemerintah Darurat', in: Colin Wild and Peter Carey (eds), *Gelora api revolusi*, pp. 198-205. Jakarta: Gramedia, 1986.

4643 Prawiranegara, Sjafruddin
'Tugas Pemerintah Darurat RI', in: Abdurrachman Surjomihardjo and J.R. Chaniago (eds), *Pemerintah Darurat Republik Indonesia dikaji ulang*, pp. 119-121. Jakarta: Masyarakat Sejarawan Indonesia, 1990.

4644 Prawirodirdjo, Kadim
Ledakan sumpah pemuda di Surabaja tahun 1945; Kenang-kenangan pertempuran-pertempuran dua hari non-stop, tgl. 28-30 Oktober 1945 diatas bumi kota madya (desa-praja) Surabaja sebagai manifestasi peningkatan aksi sumpah pemuda ke-XVII. Djakarta, 1972, 69 pp.

4645 Prawirodirdjo, Kadim
Dongengan '45; Dari panggung sejarah perang kemerdekaan Indonesia. Djakarta: Mutiara, 1978, 423 pp. 3 vols. [Second edition, Yogyakarta: Kedaulatan Rakyat, 1987, 132 pp.]

4646 Prawirohardjo, Sarwono
'Pendidikan dokter dalam masa pendudukan Jepang dan dalam masa perjuangan kemerdekaan fisik', in: Hanafiah, M.A.; Bahder Djohan and Surono (eds), *125 tahun pendidikan dokter di Indonesia, 1851-1976*, pp. 35-39. Jakarta: Panitya Peringatan 125 tahun Pendidikan Dokter di Indonesia, 1976.

4647 Prawirosudirjo, Garnadi
'Kisah perjuangan kemerdekaan di perioda 1945-1950 sebagai yang kami alami', in: *Letusan di balik buku; Hasil sayembara mengarang dalam rangka peringatan hari ulang tahun kemerdekaan RI yang ke 30*, pp. 19-49. Jakarta: Dewan Harian Nasional Angkatan 45/Aries Lima, 1976.

4648 Prawiroyudo, Sunarto
Sejarah perjoangan; Bom berjiwa Pasukan Berani Mati dalam rangka perjoangan mempertahankan Proklamasi kemerdekaan, tahun 1945-1950. Jakarta: Lembaga Monumen Revolusi 1945, 1982, 108+115 pp.

4649 Prayitno, Mk.
Magelang kembali. Jakarta: Balai Pustaka, 1983, 92 pp.

4650 Prihatin, B.
Kisah-kisah perang gerilja. Djakarta: Jajasan Gadjah Mada, 1957, 191 pp.

4651 Prijadi, Daska
Gerakan Operasi Militer II (operasi penumpasan 'APRA' Westerling Bandung). Djakarta: Mega Bookstore/Pusat Sedjarah Angkatan Bersendjata, 1965, 11 pp.

4652 Princen, J.C.
'Pelarian KNIL berbintang gerilya', *Tempo* 20 no. 19 (7 July 1990):51-65.

4653 Pringgodigdo, A.G.
Sedjarah singkat berdirinja negara Republik Indonesia. Surabaja: Pustaka Nasional, 1958, 40 pp.

4654 Priyanto, Supriya
Amir Fatah Wijayakusumah; Tokoh pencetus revolusi Islam di dataran kali Pemali. Jakarta: LIPI, 1986, 18 pp.

4655 Priyanto, Supriya
Sistem pemerintah militer di daerah gerilya Gunung Sumbing masa kemerdekaan II tahun 1945-1949. Paper Diskusi Sejarah Lokal IV, Revolusi Kemerdekaan di Tingkat Lokal, Bandungan-Ambarawa, 1994, 18 pp.

4656 Priyantono, Yuwono Dwi
Perjuangan pemuda Indonesia di luar negeri 1945-1950; Pengalaman para pelaku di Singapura dan Philipina. Paper Seminar Lahirnya Suatu Bangsa, Jakarta 1990, 26 pp.

4657 Priyantono, Yuwono Dwi
Pembentukan Badan Keamanan Rakyat; Tinjauan di dua daerah. Paper Diskusi Sejarah Lokal IV, Revolusi Kemerdekaan di Tingkat Lokal, Bandungan-Ambarawa, 1994, 16 pp.

4658 *Proces peristiwa Sultan Hamid II*. Disusun oleh Persadja. Djakarta: Express, 1953, 227 pp.

4659 Prodjosoegardo, R.W.
Buku pegangan pamong pradja daerah istimewa Jogjakarta. Jogjakarta: Djawatan Pradja DI Jogjakarta, 1950, 437 pp.

4660 *Proklamasi dan perang kemerdekaan di Kalimantan Barat; Mengenang perjuangan putera-putera daerah Kalimantan Barat.* Pontianak?, 1975. [4861]

4661 Pronohadikusumo, Sukardan
'Pengambil alihan jawatan kereta api di Semarang 1945', in: *Cahaya dari medan laga; Hasil sayembara mengarang dalam rangka peringatan hari ulang tahun kemerdekaan RI yang ke 30*, pp. 77-97. Jakarta: Dewan Harian Nasional Angkatan 45/Aries Lima, 1976.

4662 Puar, Yusuf Abdullah
Jenderal Sudirman patriot teladan. Third printing. Jakarta: Yayasan Panglima Besar Sudirman/Pustaka Antara, 1981, 199 pp. [First printing 1979; Second printing 1981.]

4663 Pulungan, Arifin
Kisah dari pedalaman; Sebuah epos perang kemerdekaan RI di daerah Sumatera Utara dan Aceh. Second edition. Medan: Diancorporation, 1979, 326 pp. [First edition 1974.]

4664 Pulungan, Arifin
Sejarah perjuangan KODAM II (Medan Area sampai perang kemerdekaan I, II). Medan: SEMDAM II/Bukit Barisan, 1976. [4874]

4665 Pulungan, A.; J.A. Siregar; Z. Bustami Lubis; Moestafa Aboe Bakar and A.M. Jamil (eds)
35 tahun kadet Brastagi; Perjuangan bersenjata pemuda/pelajar dalam perang kemerdekaan di wilayah Sumatera Utara/Aceh tahun 1945-1949. Medan: Ikatan Kadet Brastagi, Akademi Militer Perjuangan Brastagi, 1981, 347 pp.

4666 Purwaningsih, Sri Handajani
Pergolakan sosial politik di Serang pada tahun 1945. 1984, 125 pp. [MA thesis Universitas Indonesia, Jakarta.] [Histori]

4667 Purwoko, Dwi
Perjuangan Pemerintah Darurat Republik Indonesia (PDRI); Sebuah renungan bagi generasi muda Muslim. Jakarta: Media Da'wah, 1991, 80 pp.

4668 Purwoko, Dwi
KNI dan pergolakan internal. Paper Diskusi Sejarah Lokal IV, Revolusi Kemerdekaan di Tingkat Lokal, Bandungan-Ambarawa, 1994, 17 pp.

4669 Purwokusumo, Sudarisman
Pemberontakan Madiun ditindjau dari hukum negara kita. Jogja: Sumber Kemadjuan Rakjat, 1951, 37 pp.

4670 *Putera Samudera; Madjallah resmi ALRI; Nomor Angkatan Perang 5 Oktober 1945-5 Oktober 1951.* Djakarta: Pustaka Rakjat, 1951, 84 pp.

4671 Puterajaya, Suripto
Taufan di Sala. Surabaya: Grip, ca. 1975, 135 pp.

4672 Putri, Gusti Ayu
Pemerintahan di Bali tahun 1945-1949. 1985, 151 pp. [MA thesis Universitas Indonesia, Jakarta.] [Histori]

4673 Rachmad, Soendaru
POPDA dalam cakrawala politik luar negeri Indonesia. Jakarta: Yayasan POPDA, 1990, 20 pp.

4674 Rachman, Ambo Tang
'Antara agitasi dan aspirasi NIT menuju NKRI; Implementasinya dalam pengajaran sejarah', in: *Seminar Sejarah Regional Indonesia Timur; Masalah penulisan sejarah dan dinamika kesejarahan Indonesia Timur,* pp. 113-130. Ujung Pandang: Departemen P dan K, 1993/1994.

4675 Rachman, Luthfi
Nostalgia Surabaya '45 dalam puisi perjuangan; Kumpulan puisi perjuangan tahun 1950-1983. Surabaya, 1984, 34 pp.

4676 Radjab, A.
Pelajar dan perang kemerdekaan. Malang: Yayasan Widoro, 1977, 184 pp.

4677 Radjab, A.
TRIP dan perang kemerdekaan. Surabaya: Kasnendra Suminar, 1983, 300 pp.

4678 Radjamin, Ny. Loekitaningsih Irsan
'Partisipasi pemuda puteri Indonesia dalam revolusi 1945 di Surabaya/Jatim', in: *Bunga rampai perjuangan dan pengorbanan II,* pp. 201-205. Jakarta: Markas Besar Legiun Veteran RI, 1983.

4679 Radjamin, S.H.L. Irsan (ed.)
Peristiwa 10 November 1945 dalam lukisan. Surabaya: Enka Parahiyangan, 1988, 92 pp.

4680 Radjasa, Ny. Kartini
'Sekelumit kisah perjuangan pemuda/mahasiswa Jakarta kota Proklamasi 17 Agustus 1945', in: *Bunga rampai perjuangan dan pengorbanan II,* pp. 189-199. Jakarta: Markas Besar Legiun Veteran RI, 1983.

4681 Radjien, M.
Revolusi 17 Agustus 1945. Second edition. Surabaja: Grip, 1967, 32 pp.

4682 Rahardja, Tumi
Sumbangan penduduk Djepang terhadap Proklamasi kemerdekaan Indonesia. 1968, 129 pp. [MA thesis IKIP Jogjakarta.] [17]

4683 Raliby, Osman
Sedjarah Hari Pahlawan. Djakarta: Bulan Bintang, 1952, 80 pp.

4684 Raliby, Osman
Documenta historica; Sedjarah dokumenter dari pertumbuhan dan perdjuangan negara Republik Indonesia I. Djakarta: Bulan Bintang, 1953, 663 pp.

4685 Rama, Ida Bagus
Struktur organisasi perjuangan dalam revolusi fisik di Bali 1945-1950. 1981. [MA thesis Universitas Udayana, Denpasar.] [6333]

4686 Rama, Ida Bagus
'Makna hubungan Bali dan Jawa dalam revolusi fisik di Bali 1945-1950', in: *Seminar Sejarah Nasional IV; Sub tema studi bandingan*, pp. 90-108. Jakarta: Kem. P dan K, 1985.

4687 Ramadhan KH
A.E. Kawilarang; Untuk Sang Merah Putih; (Pengalaman 1942-1961). Jakarta: Sinar Harapan, 1988, 308 pp.

4688 Ramelan
Perdjuangan Republik Indonesia dalam karikatur. Djakarta: Tintamas, 1952, 44 pp.

4689 Ramlan, Ali
Hubungan sistem kabinet parlementer dengan timbulnya Front Demokrasi Rakyat/Partai Komunis Indonesia dalam peristiwa Madiun 1948. 1986. [MA thesis IKIP Jakarta.] [Histori]

4690 *Rangkaian sedjarah kelasjkaran-kelasjkaran, kesatuan-kesatuan dan badan-badan perdjoangan kemerdekaan Republik Indonesia di daerah Sulawesi Selatan/Tenggara 1945-1949*. Makassar: Kantor Urusan Veteran, 1958. [6210]

4691 Rangkuti, Hamsad
Surat dalam tabung. Jakarta: Bunda Karya, 1984, 73 pp.

4692 Rangkuti, Hamsad
Kereta pagi jam 5. Jakarta: Balai Pustaka, 1993, 92 pp.

4693 Ranni, M.Z.
Perlawanan terhadap penjajahan dan perjuangan menegakkan kemerdekaan Indonesia di bumi Bengkulu. Jakarta: Balai Pustaka, 1990, 252 pp.

4694 Ranty, Elly
Dari RIS ke negara kesatuan RI. 1985, 180 pp. [MA thesis Universitas Indonesia, Jakarta.] [Histori]

4695 Ranuwihardjo, A. Dahlan
Pergerakan pemuda setelah Proklamasi (beberapa catatan). Jakarta: Yayasan Idayu, 1979, 40 pp.

4696 Rashi's, P.M.
Djagoan ketjil dari Tembung. Medan: Casso, ca. 1964, 96 pp.

4697 Rasjid, Harun al
Sekitar Proklamasi, Konstitusi dan dekrit Presiden. Djakarta: Pelita Ilmu, 1968, 39 pp.

4698 Rasjid, St. M.
'Memperingati Republik Indonesia empat tahun', in: *Dari penjerangan ke penjerahan*, pp. 57-68. Bukittinggi: Djawatan Penerangan Sumatera Tengah, 1951.

4699 Rasjid, Sutan Mohammad
Di sekitar PDRI (Pemerintah Darurat Republik Indonesia). Jakarta: Bulan Bintang, 1982, 64 pp. [42]

4700 Rasjidi, H.M.
'Pengakuan pertama dari negara-negara Arab', in: *Seratus tahun Haji Agus Salim*, pp. 152-155. Jakarta: Sinar Harapan, 1984.

4701 Rasyid, Abdul Razak
'Episode dramatis penyiaran Proklamasi di studio Radio Bandung', in: *Terbukalah jalanku*, pp. 122-142. Jakarta: Dewan Harian Nasional Angkatan 45/Aries Lima, 1976.

4702 Rasyid, Abdul Razak
'Episode dramatis penyiaran Proklamasi di studio Radio Bandung', *Gema Angkatan 45* no. 31 (July-August 1978):42-47.

4703 Rasyidi, Khalid
'Setelah "19 September" berlalu', *Gema Angkatan 45* nr. 33 (October 1978):30-32.

4704 Ratman, E. Rustam (ed.)
Dari Proklamasi ke Proklamasi 17 Agustus 1945-17 Agustus 1950. Djakarta: Waspada, 1950, 44 pp. (kitlv-m)

4705 Ratna R.
'Perang Cumbok di Aceh tahun 1945', in: *Revolusi nasional di tingkat lokal*, pp. 14-28. Jakarta: Kem. P dan K, 1989.

4706 Ratnawati
Robert Wolter Mongisidi. Jakarta: Kem. P dan K, 1975, 117 pp. [Second edition, 1982, 137 pp.]

4707 Razak, Abdul
Suatu renungan pemikiran tentang arti dan hakekat Proklamasi 17 Agustus 1945. Padang: IKIP Padang, 1977, 17 pp.

4708 Redjeki, Sri
Perang kolonial II di Jogjakarta. 1965, 67 pp. [MA thesis Universitas Gadjah Mada, Jogjakarta.]

4709 Reksopranoto
'Disekitar perebutan kekuasaan Djepang di Jogjakarta', in: Darius Marpaung (ed.), *Bingkisan nasional; Kenangan 10 tahun revolusi Indonesia, 17-8-1945/17-8-1955*, pp. 49-51. Djakarta: Usaha Pegawai Nasional Indonesia, 1955.

4710 Relawati, Sri
Hubungan kesenjangan sosial dengan timbulnya Tiga Daerah sekitar Proklamasi kemerdekaan. 1986. [MA thesis IKIP Jakarta.] [Histori]

4711 *Replika pesawat terbang WEL-1 RI-X; Untuk mewariskan nilai dan semangat 1945*. Bandung: Media Offset, ca. 1981, 24 pp.

4712 Resmana, Min
Mohamad Toha; Pahlawan Bandung Selatan. Jakarta: Pustaka Jaya, 1979, 96 pp.

4713 *Revolusi nasional di tingkat lokal*. Jakarta: Kem. P dan K, 1989, 155 pp.

4714 Rivai, Mohamad
'Memperingati Bandung lautan api', *Gema Angkatan 45* no. 16 (April 1977):26-28; no. 76/80 (March-July 1983):134-137.

4715 *Riwayat-hidup Mas Agustinus Adisutjipto, Laksamana Muda Udara (anumerta)*. Jakarta: Dinas Penerangan Angkatan Udara, 1974, 13 pp.

4716 Riwayat-hidup Prof. Dr. Abdurachman Saleh, Laksamana Muda Udara (anumerta).
Jakarta: Dinas Penerangan Angkatan Udara, 1974, 14 pp.

4717 Rizal, E.
Enam jam di Yogya. Semarang: Ibu Sejati, 1984, 32 pp.

4718 Rizal, E.
Gema mahardika di Semarang. Semarang: Ibu Sejati, 1985, 32 pp.

4719 Rochman, Tuty
Sedjarah pembentukan negara Republik Indonesia Serikat. 1972, 100 pp. [MA
thesis IKIP Bandung.] [10]

4720 Rochwulaningsih, Yeti and Singgih Tri Sulistiyono
Ekologi, ekonomi dan wajah revolusi di pedesaan; Kasus dinamika masyarakat
Desa Gombong tahun 1945-1949. Paper Diskusi Sejarah Lokal IV, Revolusi
Kemerdekaan di Tingkat Lokal, Bandungan-Ambarawa, 1994, 27 pp.

4721 Roekiah S.
Teuku Hassan Djohan Pahlawan. Djakarta: Grafica, ca. 1965, 80 pp.

4722 Roem, Mohamad
Pentjulikan, Proklamasi dan penilaian sedjarah. Djakarta/Semarang: Hudaya,
1970, 74 pp.

4723 Roem, Mohamad
*Tiga peristiwa bersedjarah; Kongres nasional ke-1; Lahirnja Pantjasila; Kembali ke
Djokdja*. Djakarta: Sinar Hudaya, 1971, 62 pp.

4724 Roem, Mohamad
Lahirnya Pancasila. Jakarta: Bulan Bintang, 1977, 20 pp.

4725 Roem, Mohamad
Suka duka berunding dengan Belanda; Ceramah. Jakarta: Idayu Press, 1977, 72 pp.

4726 Roem, Mohamad
'Tragedi Schermerhorn dan Sjahrir', *Budaya Jaya* 10 no. 111 (August 1977):457-
470.

4727 Roem, M.
'Memoirs: the recognition of the Republic Indonesia', *Indonesian Quarterly* 6-3
(1978):103-124.

4728 Roem, Mohamad
'A sad story in spite of its happy ending; Review of Anak Agung's book',
Indonesia no. 31 (April 1981):163-170.

4729 Romankus, Oman
Perdjuangan Divisi Siliwangi dalam masa Hidjrah dan Long March. 1971, 97
pp. [MA thesis IKIP Bandung.] [10]

4730 Romli HM, Usep
Pahlawan tak dikenal. Jakarta: Balai Pustaka, 1982, 60 pp.

4731 Rospina
Peranan diplomasi dalam perang kemerdekaan Indonesia. 1973, 90 pp. [MA
thesis IKIP Jakarta.] [11]

4732 Roza, Octavigeni
Pelaksanaan rekonstruksi dan rasionalisasi dalam bidang militer di Sumatera
Barat (1947-1950). 1989, 68+22 pp. [MA thesis Universitas Andalas, Padang.]
[58]

4733 R.S.W.
'Saat-saat Proklamasi kemerdekaan; Pengalaman di kota Djakarta', *Penelitian
Sedjarah* 3-5 (1962):17-19, 24.

4734 Rudatin, Alex
'Menggali dan mewarisi nilai-nilai luhur yang terkandung di dalam semangat
juang 45', in: *Letusan di balik buku; Hasil sayembara mengarang dalam rangka
peringatan hari ulang tahun kemerdekaan RI yang ke 30*, pp. 157-171. Jakarta:
Dewan Harian Nasional Angkatan 45/Aries Lima, 1976.

4735 Rumahorbo, Sinton
Suatu tindjauan tentang revolusi sosial di Sumatera Timur. 1972. [MA thesis
IKIP Medan.] [13]

4736 Rusad, Djumbang
'Petualangan mengawal tongkang Singapura-Sumatra ulang-alik', in: Kustiniyati
Mochtar (ed.), *Memoar pejuang Republik Indonesia seputar 'zaman Singapura'*,
1945-1950, pp. 102-113. Jakarta: Gramedia, 1992.

4737 Russeng, Rosma Majju
Perjuangan bersenjata di daerah Pare-Pare dan sekitarnya pada tahun 1946-
1947. 1982. [MA thesis Universitas Hasanuddin, Ujung Pandang.] [604]

4738 Ruswendi, Tatang
Peristiwa APRA. 1971, 72 pp. [MA thesis IKIP Bandung.] [10]

4739 Saaman, Hamamy
'Peristiwa rapat raksasa Ikada pada tanggal 19 September 1945 serta
kaitannya dengan Proklamasi kemerdekaan 17 Agustus 1945', *Gema Angkatan
45* no. 68/70 (July-September 1982):100-103.

4740 'Saat-saat jang terachir mendjelang Proklamasi kemerdekaan diutjapkan', in:
Darius Marpaung (ed.), *Bingkisan nasional; Kenangan 10 tahun revolusi Indonesia*,
17-8-1945/17-8-1955, pp. 22-26. Djakarta: Usaha Pegawai Nasional Indonesia,
1955.

4741 Sadulah, R.D.
Zuster Hayati. Surabaya: Karya Pena, 1982, 804 pp.

4742 Saelan, H. Maulwi
'Posisi strategi perjuangan rakyat di Sulawesi Selatan menegakkan negara
kesatuan Republik Indonesia', in: *Seminar Sejarah Regional Indonesia Timur;
Masalah sejarah perjuangan rakyat Sulawesi Selatan*, pp. 49-69. Ujung Pandang:
Dep. P dan K, Balai Kajian Sejarah dan Nilai Tradisional, 1993.

4743 Safwan, Mardanas (ed.)
Peranan Gedung Menteng Raya 31 dalam perjuangan kemerdekaan. Second edition.
Jakarta: Dinas Museum dan Sejarah Pemerintah DKI Jakarta, 1973, 72 pp.
[Second printing 1977.]

4744 Safwan, Mardanas
Arie Frederik Lasut. Jakarta: Kem. P dan K, 1976, 110 pp. [Second edition, 1982, 130 pp.]

4745 Safwan, Mardanas
Pahlawan nasional Mayjen Teuku Nyak Arif. Jakarta: Kem. P dan K, 1976, 203 pp.

4746 Safwan, Mardanas
Riwayat hidup dan perjuangan Abdul Aziz, alias Letnan Kolonel Noto Sunardi. Jakarta: Kem. P dan K, 1977, 27 pp.

4747 Safwan, Mardanas
Iswahyudi. Jakarta: Dep. P dan K, 1979, 121 pp. [Second edition, 1982, 73 pp.]

4748 Sagimun M.D.
Robert Wolter Mongisidi. Jakarta: Bhratara, 1975, 79 pp.

4749 Sagimun M.D.
Calon pahlawan nasional Ranggong Daeng Romo. Jakarta: Kem. P dan K, 1979, 48 pp.

4750 Sagimun M.D.
Calon pahlawan nasional Emmy Saelan. Jakarta: Kem. P dan K, 1981, 57 pp.

4751 Sagimun M.D.
Mas TRIP; Dari brigade pertempuran ke brigade pembangunan. Jakarta: Bina Aksara/Mas TRIP/Kosgoro, 1989, 12+372 pp.

4752 Sagimun M.D. and Sutrisno Kutoyo (eds)
Kebulatan tekad rapat raksasa Ikada; Peristiwa 19 September 1945. Jakarta: Dinas Museum dan Sejarah DKI Jakarta, 1987, 75 pp.

4753 Saharudin
Peristiwa Siantar Hotel dan artinja dalam perdjuangan Sumatera Timur. 1970, 97 pp. [MA thesis IKIP Semarang.] [15]

4754 Sahri
'Kisah nyata perjuangan kemerdekaan RI periode 1945-1950 di daerah kabupaten Indramayu', in: *Terbukalah jalanku; Hasil sayembara mengarang dalam rangka peringatan hari ulang tahun kemerdekaan R.I. yang ke 30*, pp. 201-228. Jakarta: Dewan Harian Nasional Angkatan 45, Pusat Dokumentasi Sejarah Perjoangan 45/Aries Lima, 1976.

4755 Said, Alimuddin
Darah, air mata dan kemarahan rakyat (1945-1947); Awal studi percobaan tentang sejarah gerakan sosial di Sulawesi Selatan. 1982. [MA thesis Universitas Hasanuddin, Ujung Pandang.] [604]

4756 Sa'id, Bermawi
Tindjauan revolusi Indonesia. Djakarta: Pustaka Rakjat, 1950, 46 pp. [Second edition 1950.]

4757 Said, M.
'What was the "social revolution of 1945" in East Sumatra?', *Indonesia* no. 15 (1973):145-186.

4758 Said, Mohammad
'Waspada, harian republiken di daerah NICA', Pers Indonesia 2-8 (October 1976):3-23.

4759 Said, M. Natzir
SOB 11 Desember 1946 sebagai Hari Korban 40.000 Jiwa Sulawesi Selatan. Ujung Pandang: KODAM 14/Hasanuddin, 1974, 147 pp.

4760 Said, M. Natzir
Lahirnya TRI Divisi Hasanuddin di Sulawesi Selatan dan Tenggara. Ujung Pandang: Team Penelitian Sejarah Perjoangan Sulselra, 1981, 353 pp.

4761 Said, M. Natzir (Natsir)
Kegiatan-kegiatan rakyat Sulawesi Selatan menyambut Proklamasi kemerdekaan di Sulawesi Selatan. Paper Seminar Sejarah Perjuangan Rakyat Sulawesi Selatan Menentang Penjajahan Asing, Ujung Pandang, 1982, 11 pp.

4762 Said, M. Natzir
Peristiwa korban 40.000 jiwa rakyat di Sulawesi Selatan. Paper Seminar Sejarah Perjuangan Rakyat Sulawesi Selatan Menentang Penjajahan Asing, Ujung Pandang, 1982. [4764]

4763 Said, M. Natzir
Peristiwa sekitar Proklamasi 17 Agustus 1945 di Sulawesi Selatan. Paper Seminar Sejarah Perjuangan Rakyat Sulawesi Selatan Menentang Penjajahan Asing, Ujung Pandang, 1982. [4764]

4764 Said, M. Natzir
Korban 40.000 jiwa di Sulawesi Selatan; SOB 11 Desember 1946 penyebab banjir darah dan lautan api. Bandung: Alumni, 1985, 300 pp.

4765 Said, Salim
The genesis of power; Civil-military relations in Indonesia during the revolution for independence, 1945-1949. 1985, 302 pp. [PhD thesis Ohio State University, Athens.]

4766 Said, Salim
Genesis of power; General Sudirman and the Indonesian military in politics 1945-49. Singapore: Institute of Southeast Asian Studies, Jakarta: Sinar Harapan, 1992, 20+185 pp.

4767 Said, Sjamsuar
'Sekelumit mengenai keadaan di Sumatra Barat dimasa perang kemerdekaan ke-II', Vidya Yudha no. 8 (1969):124-139.

4768 Said, Syamsuar
Patriot dari pulau Dewata. Semarang: Mandira Jaya Abadi, 1984, 58 pp.

4769 Said, Syamsuar
Perjalanan menuju kemenangan; TNI hijrah dan kembali ke kantong. Semarang: Mandira Jaya Abadi, 1985, 75 pp.

4770 Said, Syamsuar and S. Hadisudaryanto
Palagan Ambarawa. Semarang: Mandira Jaya Abadi, 1984, 83 pp.

4771 Said, Syamsuar and Supriyo Priyanto
Menumpas Tentara Merah; Gerakan Operasi Militer ke-I di Madiun. Second edition. Semarang: Mandira Jaya Abadi, 1985, 68 pp. [First edition 1983.]

4772 Said, Titie
Langit hitam di atas Ambarawa. Jakarta: Media Guna, 1983, 391 pp.

4773 Saili, Imat
'Masuknja rakjat pedjuang Kaltim kedalam slagorde TNI tahun 1949-1950', *Vidya Yudha* no. 8 (1969):108-116.

4774 Sajidiman, Soekamto
'Dai-Ni-Cugakko Surabaya', *Gema Angkatan 45* no. 32 (September 1978):34-36.

4775 Sajudja, Darwas
Peristiwa-peristiwa penting di tanah air sampai 17 Agustus 1950. Djakarta: Tegas, ca. 1952, 78 pp.

4776 Salam, Solichin
Djenderal Soedirman; Pahlawan kemerdekaan. Djakarta: Djajamurni, 1963, 124 pp.

4777 Salam, Solichin
Arti Linggajati dalam sejarah. Jakarta: Gema Salam, 1992, 57 pp.

4778 Saleh, Johana Chairul and Sjamsudin Tjan
Peranan Gedung Menteng 31 dalam perjuangan kemerdekaan; Ceramah. Jakarta, 1977. [3908]

4779 Saleh, R.H.A.
'Cuplikan pengalaman selama masa revolusi kemerdekaan', in: *Bunga rampai perjuangan dan pengorbanan II,* pp. 433-449. Jakarta: Markas Besar Legiun Veteran RI, 1983.

4780 Saleh, R.H.A. (ed.)
Perjuangan bersenjata dari Jakarta & kembali ke Jakarta semasa perang kemerdekaan tahun 1945-1949. Jakarta: Badan Kontak Ex Resimen IV/Tangerang etc., ca. 1990, 72 pp.

4781 Saleh, R.H.A.
Suatu 'mission impossible'; Pemulangan tentara Jepang dan APWI di pulau Jawa pada tahun 1945-1947. Jakarta: Yayasan POPDA, 1990, 12 pp.

4782 Saleh, R.H.A.
Dari Jakarta kembali ke Jakarta; Perjuangan bersenjata 1945-49. Jakarta: Pemerintah DKI Jakarta, Dinas Museum dan Sejarah, 1992, 99 pp.

4783 Salim, Darry
'Riwayat operasi speedboat seputar Singapura', in: Kustiniyati Mochtar (ed.), *Memoar pejuang Republik Indonesia seputar 'zaman Singapura', 1945-1950,* pp. 223-235. Jakarta: Gramedia, 1992.

4784 Salim, Ferdy
'Kisah organisasi operasi speedboat di awal kemerdekaan Republik Indonesia', in: Kustiniyati Mochtar (ed.), *Memoar pejuang Republik Indonesia seputar 'zaman Singapura', 1945-1950,* pp. 207-222. Jakarta: Gramedia, 1992.

4785   Salmun, M.A.
       Masa bergolak. Jakarta: Balai Pustaka, 1987, 190 pp.

4786   Samawi
       Negaraku; Sepuluh tahun revolusi Indonesia dalam lukisan. Jogja: Kedaulatan
       Rakjat, 1955, 100 pp.

4787   Samin, Mansur
       Gerilya Ankola. Bandung: Rosda, 1984, 76 pp.

4788   Samin, Muhammadzen
       Peranan pemuda dalam perjuangan Proklamasi 17 Agustus 1945. 1970,
       175 pp. [MA thesis IKIP Djakarta.] [11]

4789   Sani, Asrul
       Dari suatu masa, dari suatu tempat; Kumpulan tjerita péndék. Djakarta: Pustaka
       Jaya, 1972, 125 pp.

4790   Santoso, Rochmani
       *Bom-waktu kolonialis Belanda meledak di Makasar; Gerakan Operasi Militer III
       menumpas pemberontak Andi Azis serta KNIL/KL.* Djakarta: Mega Bookstore,
       1965, 13 pp.

4791   Santoso, Rochmani
       Pendjelasan mengenai Pantjasila dan Proklamasi. Djakarta: Kem. P dan K, 1968.
       [99]

4792   Santoso, Rokhmani; Yusmar Basri and Djanabung Saragih
       Hari-hari menjelang Proklamasi kemerdekaan 17 Agustus 1945. Jakarta: Markas
       Besar Angkatan Bersenjata Republik Indonesia, Pusat Sejarah dan Tradisi
       ABRI, 1988, 111 pp.

4793   Sanusi, Umar
       Replika sejarah perjuangan rakyat Yogyakarta. Yogyakarta: Dinas Sosial DIY,
       1981.

4794   Sanusie, H.M. Djunaid a.o.
       Secercah perjuangan BPRI Bn. VIII Brig. 'S' Divisi VI (Narotama) di Samarinda.
       Samarinda: Unit Percetakan Pemda Kaltim, 1984, 254 pp.

4795   Sapada, Andi
       Peranan pasukan ekspedisi dalam mempertahankan kemerdekaan RI di
       Sulawesi Selatan. Paper Seminar Sejarah Perjuangan Rakyat Sulawesi Selatan
       Menentang Penjajahan Asing, Ujung Pandang, 1982, 28 pp.

4796   Sapto, Gondo Tatok
       Laskar Wanita (LASWI). 1981, 81 pp. [MA thesis Universitas Indonesia,
       Jakarta.] [Histori]

4797   Sardjono, Imam
       Trajumas. Jakarta: Balai Pustaka, 1986, 66 pp. [In Javanese.]

4798   Sardjono, V. and G.L. Marsadji
       *Pemerintah Darurat Republik Indonesia (PDRI); Penyelamat negara dan bangsa
       Indonesia.* Second edition. Jakarta: Tintamas, 1982, 126 pp. [First edition 1981.]

4799   *Sarimu kupetik kini; Himpunan pikiran pelajar tentang perjoangan 45 untuk pembangunan bangsa; Hasil sayembara mengarang dalam rangka peringatan hari ulang tahun kemerdekaan RI yang ke-30.* Jakarta: Aries Lima, 1976, 224 pp.

4800   Sarumpaet, J.P.
'North Sumatra 1945-1949', in: *Indonesian nationalism and revolution*, pp. 30-38. Clayton: Monash University, 1969.

4801   *Sasmitaloka Panglima Besar Jenderal Sudirman.* Bandung: Dinas Sejarah Tentara Nasional Indonesia Angkatan Darat, 1983, 32 pp.

4802   Sastradiraja, Suparna
'MMC - di lereng Merapi-Merbabu', *Kabar Seberang* 19/20 (1988):133-144.

4803   Sastrapraja, Nurhadi
Sekitar peristiwa Bandung lautan api. 1976, 115 pp. [MA thesis IKIP Jakarta.] [11]

4804   Sastrawijaya, Safiyudin
Sekitar Pancasila, Proklamasi dan Konstitusi. Bandung: Alumni, 1980, 92 pp.

4805   Sastrawiria, Doko
'Pengalaman pribadi pada waktu perang kemerdekaan-I (clash ke-I) di daerah Jawa Barat', in: *Bunga rampai perjuangan dan pengorbanan I*, pp. 161-167. Jakarta: Markas Besar Legiun Veteran RI, 1982.

4806   Sastrosatomo, Soebadio
De Indonesische revolutie; Sjahrir en Schermerhorn. Paper Conference on the Indonesian Revolution, Utrecht, 1986, 18 pp.

4807   Sastrosatomo, Soebadio
Perjuangan revolusi. Jakarta: Sinar Harapan, 1987, 256 pp.

4808   Sastrosatomo, Soebadio
'The Indonesian revolution; Sjahrir and Schermerhorn', *Kabar Seberang* no. 19/20 (1988):107-117.

4809   Sastrosatomo, Soebadio
Pembentukan BKR. Paper Seminar Lahirnya Suatu Bangsa, Jakarta, 1990, 5 pp.

4810   Sastrosatomo, Soebadio
Pembentukan KNIP. Paper Seminar Lahirnya Suatu Bangsa, Jakarta, 1990, 11 pp.

4811   Sastrosatomo, Soebadio
'Perjuangan demokrasi dan demokrasi perjuangan', *Sejarah* 4 (1993):56-60.

4812   Sastrowardojo, Subagio
Kedjantanan di Sumbing; Kumpulan tjerita pendek. Djakarta: Pembangunan, 1965, 91 pp.

4813   Satjadiria, W. Soedarja
Perjuangan rakyat Jabar pada akhir perang kemerdekaan, 1948-1949. Ca. 1975. [MA thesis Universitas Padjadjaran, Bandung.] [1, 20]

4814   Saubari, M.
       'Reflections on economic policy making 1945-51', *Bulletin of Indonesian Economic
       Studies* 23 (1987):118-121.

4815   Saubary, Slamet
       Keluar-masuk perdjoangan. Djakarta: Kompas, 1951, 74 pp. (kitlv-m)

4816   Sawang, Ahmad M.
       Peranan Islam dalam pergerakan KRIS Muda di daerah Mandar. 1980. [Thesis
       Institut Agama Islam Negeri, Ujung Pandang.] [4334]

4817   Sayudi
       Laskar kecil. Jakarta: Dunia Pustaka Jaya, 1975, 92 pp.

4818   Sayudi
       Oratorium Bandung lautan api. Bandung: Pustaka Buana, 1985, 98 pp.

4819   Sebayang, Nas
       Sejarah perjuangan kemerdekaan di Sumatera Utara. 216 pp. [22]

4820   Sebayang, Nas
       '3 orang prajurit gerilya menghancurkan moril 1 kompi pasukan Belanda', *Gema
       Angkatan 45* no. 31 (July-August 1978):77.

4821   Sebayang, Nas
       'Tanah Karo dan perjuangan kemerdekaan', *Gema Angkatan 45* no. 34 (October
       1978):27-29.

4822   Sebul, Istopo
       'Palagan Sidobunder', in: A. Eryono; R. Soekandar; P. Herukusuma and Moh.
       Noech (eds), *Memoar perjoangan*, pp. 187-196. Yogyakarta: Yayasan Wiratama
       45, 1985.

4823   'Sedikit sekitar saat lahirnja R.I. Proklamasi 1945', in: Darius Marpaung (ed.),
       Bingkisan nasional; Kenangan 10 tahun revolusi Indonesia, 17-8-1945/17-8-1955,
       pp. 35-41. Djakarta: Usaha Pegawai Nasional Indonesia, 1955.

4824   *Sedjarah Bataljon 'Y'.* Djakarta: Pussemad, 1959. [4877]

4825   *Sedjarah kelasjkaran di Sulawesi Selatan dan Tenggara.* Makasar: SEMDAM
       XIV/Hasanuddin, 1971. [4868]

4826   *Sedjarah lahirnja Tentara Nasional Indonesia.* Medan: n.n., 1970, 37 pp.

4827   *Sedjarah militer DAM VIII/BRAW; Mengenang pahlawan jang telah gugur di
       medan bhakti pada hari ulang tahun ke-21 KODAM VIII/Brawidjaja.* Malang:
       KODAM VIII/Brawidjaja, 1966, 50 pp.

4828   *Sedjarah singkat proklamasi pemerintahan gubernur tentara ALRI DIV 4 Pertahanan
       Kalimantan Selatan, tanggal 17 Mei 1949.* Bandjermasin: Panitya Pelaksana
       HUT ke-23, 1972, 10 pp.

4829   *Sejarah DKI Jakarta masa revolusi kemerdekaan (revolusi fisik) 1945-1949.* Jakarta:
       Kem. P dan K, 1979, 201 pp.

4830   *Sejarah kota Bandung periode revolusi kemerdekaan (1945-1950).* Bandung:
       Pemerintah Daerah, 1981, 471 pp.

4831 *Sejarah lahirnya Undang-Undang Dasar 1945 dan Pancasila.* Disusun oleh Lembaga Soekarno-Hatta. Jakarta: Inti Idayu Press, 1984, 172 pp.

4832 *Sejarah masa revolusi fisik daerah Riau.* Jakarta: Kem. P dan K, 1982, 161 pp.

4833 *Sejarah masa revolusi fisik daerah Sulawesi Tenggara.* Jakarta: Kem. P dan K, 1982, 97 pp.

4834 *Sejarah Museum Perumusan Naskah Proklamasi.* Jakarta: Kem. P dan K, 1991, 83 pp.

4835 *Sejarah operasi penerbangan Indonesia periode 1945-1950.* Jakarta: Dinas Sejarah Tentara Nasional Indonesia Angkatan Udara, 1980, 95 pp.

4836 *Sejarah pendidikan perwira penerbang periode 1945-1950.* Jakarta: Dinas Sejarah Tentara Nasional Indonesia Angkatan Udara, 1979, 52 pp.

4837 *Sejarah perang kemerdekaan di Sumatera 1945-1950.* Bandung: Dinas Sejarah TNI Angkatan Darat, 1972, 38+387 pp.

4838 *Sejarah perang kemerdekaan di Sumatera 1945-1950.* Second edition. Medan: Dinas Sejarah KODAM II/Bukit Barisan, 1984, 554 pp. [First edition 1973.]

4839 *Sejarah perhubungan/komunikasi dan elektronika TNI Angkatan Udara periode 1945-1949.* Jakarta: Dinas Sejarah TNI Angkatan Udara, 1978, 67 pp.

4840 *Sejarah perjoangan polisi Surabaya 1945-1949.* Surabaya: Panitya Pembuatan Buku Sejarah Perjoangan Polisi Istimewa Surabaya, 1983, 447 pp.

4841 Sejarah perjoangan Tentara Pelajar Kie III Det III Be 17. Jakarta: Yayasan Bhakti TP Kedu, 1987, 92 pp.

4842 *Sejarah perjuangan Indonesian Airways dengan RI-001 'Seulawah'.* Jakarta: Dinas Sejarah Tentara Nasional Indonesia Angkatan Udara, 1979, 79 pp.

4843 *Sejarah perjuangan kemerdekaan Republik Indonesia di Minangkabau 1945-1950.* Jilid 1. Jakarta: Badan Pemurnian Sejarah Indonesia-Minangkabau, 1978, 695 pp. [Second edition, *Sejarah perjuangan kemerdekaan Republik Indonesia di Minangkabau/Riau 1945-1950*, 1991, 37+714 pp.]

4844 *Sejarah perjuangan kemerdekaan Republik Indonesia di Minangkabau 1945-1950.* Jilid 2. Jakarta: Badan Pemurnian Sejarah Indonesia-Minangkabau, 1981, 799 pp.

4845 *Sejarah perjuangan Lasykar Wanita Indonesia.* Jakarta, 1979. [4208]

4846 *Sejarah perjuangan rakyat Jakarta, Tangerang dan Bekasi dalam menegakkan kemerdekaan RI.* Jakarta: Dinas Sejarah Militer Kodam V/Jaya / Virgo Sari, 1975, 191 pp.

4847 *Sejarah perjuangan rakyat kabupaten Klaten; Tahap 1.* Klaten: n.n., 1976, 219 pp.

4848 *Sejarah perjuangan Tentara Pelajar Purwokerto; Ex. Be XVII Tentara Pelajar.* Jakarta: Yayasan Mastepe, 1979, 382 pp.

4849 *Sejarah perjuangan TRIP Bojonegoro.* Bojonegoro: Keluarga Ex-TRIP Bojonegoro, 1980, 233 pp.

4850 *Sejarah perkembangan agama Islam di Jakarta, tahun 1945-1950.* Jakarta: Institut Agama Islam Negeri Syarif Hidayatullah, 1986, 128 pp.

4851 *Sejarah pos dan telekomunikasi di Indonesia; Masa perang kemerdekaan.* Jakarta: Dep. Perhubungan, 1980, 288 pp.

4852 *Sejarah revolusi kemerdekaan (1945-1949) daerah Bali.* Denpasar: Kem. P dan K, 1979, 217 pp.

4853 *Sejarah revolusi kemerdekaan (1945-1949) daerah Bengkulu.* Bengkulu: Kem. P dan K, 1980, 187 pp.

4854 *Sejarah revolusi kemerdekaan (1945-1949) Daerah Istimewa Banda Aceh.* Jakarta: Dep. P dan K; Proyek Inventarisasi Dan Dokumentasi Kebudayaan Daerah, 1980, 5+221 pp. [Second edition, *Sejarah revolusi kemerdekaan (1945-1949) Daerah Istimewa Aceh,* 1983, 198 pp.]

4855 *Sejarah revolusi kemerdekaan (1945-1949) Daerah Istimewa Yogyakarta.* Yogyakarta: Kem. P dan K, 1979, 341 pp. [Second edition, Jakarta: Kem. P dan K, 1991, 300 pp.]

4856 *Sejarah revolusi kemerdekaan (1945-1949) DKI Jakarta.* Second edition. Jakarta: Kem. P dan K, 1991, 160 pp.

4857 *Sejarah revolusi kemerdekaan (1945-1949) daerah Jambi.* Jambi: Kem. P dan K, 1980, 134 pp. [Third edition, Jakarta: Kem. P dan K, 1986, 131 pp.]

4858 *Sejarah revolusi kemerdekaan (1945-1949) daerah Jawa Barat.* Bandung: Kem. P dan K, 1980, 247 pp. [Second edition, Jakarta: Kem. P dan K, 1981, 218 pp.]

4859 *Sejarah revolusi kemerdekaan (1945-1949) daerah Jawa Tengah.* Semarang: Kem. P dan K, 1980, 165 pp. [Second edition, Jakarta: Kem. P dan K, 1983, 172 pp.]

4860 *Sejarah revolusi kemerdekaan (1945-1949) daerah Jawa Timur.* Second edition. Jakarta: Kem. P dan K, 1991, 320 pp. [First edition 1980.]

4861 *Sejarah revolusi kemerdekaan (1945-1949) daerah Kalimantan Barat.* Pontianak: Kem. P dan K, 1980, 6+154 pp.

4862 *Sejarah revolusi kemerdekaan (1945-1949) daerah Kalimantan Selatan.* Banjarmasin: Kem. P dan K, 1979, 5+243 pp.

4863 *Sejarah revolusi kemerdekaan (1945-1949) daerah Kalimantan Tengah.* Jakarta: Kem. P dan K, 1983, 55 pp.

4864 *Sejarah revolusi kemerdekaan (1945-1949) daerah Lampung.* Telukbetung: Kem. P dan K, 1979, 128 pp.

4865 *Sejarah revolusi kemerdekaan (1945-1949) daerah Nusa Tenggara Barat.* Mataram: Kem. P dan K, 1979, 118 pp. [Second edition, Jakarta: Kem. P dan K, 1982, 106 pp.]

4866 *Sejarah revolusi kemerdekaan (1945-1949) daerah Nusa Tenggara Timur.* Jakarta: Kem. P dan K, 1979, 148 pp. [Second edition, Kupang: Kem. P dan K, 1984, 151 pp.]

4867 *Sejarah revolusi kemerdekaan (1945-1949) daerah Riau.* Pekanbaru: Kem. P dan K, 1980, 9+197 pp.

4868 Sejarah revolusi kemerdekaan (1945-1949) daerah Sulawesi Selatan. Ujung Pandang: Kem. P dan K, 1980, 205 pp.

4869 Sejarah revolusi kemerdekaan (1945-1949) daerah Sulawesi Tengah. Palu: Kem. P dan K, 1980, 6+200 pp.

4870 Sejarah revolusi kemerdekaan (1945-1949) daerah Sulawesi Tenggara. Kendari: Kem. P dan K, 1979, 144 pp. [Second edition, Jakarta: Kem. P dan K, 1982, 166 pp.]

4871 Sejarah revolusi kemerdekaan (1945-1949) daerah Sulawesi Utara. Manado: Kem. P dan K, 1979, 6+257 pp. [Second edition, Jakarta: Kem P dan K, 1983, 255 pp.]

4872 Sejarah revolusi kemerdekaan (1945-1949) daerah Sumatera Barat. Padang: Kem. P dan K, 1979, 9+528 pp.

4873 Sejarah revolusi kemerdekaan (1945-1949) daerah Sumatera Selatan. Palembang: Kem. P dan K, 1980, 166 pp.

4874 Sejarah revolusi kemerdekaan (1945-1949) daerah Sumatera Utara. Medan: Kem. P dan K, 1980, 6+168 pp. [Second edition, Jakarta: Kem. P dan K, 1984, 148 pp.]

4875 Sejarah Serangan Umum 1 Maret 1949. Jakarta: Dep. P dan K, Proyek Pembinaan Permuseuman Jakarta, 1993/1994, 31 pp.

4876 Sejarah singkat pertempuran 23 Januari 1946 di Palopo/Luwu. Jakarta: Panitia Peringatan Pertempuran 23 Januari 1946 di Palopo/Luwu, 1976, 57 pp.

4877 Sejarah TNI Angkatan Laut (periode perang kemerdekaan, 1945-1950). Jakarta: Dinas Sejarah Angkatan Laut, 1973, 784 pp.

4878 Sejarah TRIP daerah Kediri. N.p.: n.n., 1980, 88 pp.

4879 Sejarah tugu peringatan Proklamasi kemerdekaan Republik Indonesia. Second edition. Jakarta: Pemerintah DKI JakartaDinas Museum dan Sejarah, 1977, 73 pp. [First edition 1972.]

4880 Sekali di udara, tetap di udara; 40 tahun Radio Republik Indonesia, 11 September 1945-1985. Jakarta: Panitya Peringatan Hari Radio ke-40, 1985, 232 pp.

4881 Sekitar lahirnja TNI. Bandung: Pusat Sedjarah Militer Angkatan Darat, 1965, 43 pp. (kitlv-m)

4882 Sekitar partai-partai kiri di Indonesia. Djakarta: Kem. Penerangan, 1951, 245 pp.

4883 Sekitar perdjuangan peladjar dan penjelesaiannja di KUDP Rayon III Jogjakarta. Jogjakarta: KUDP Rayon III, 1952, 265 pp.

4884 Sekitar perjanjian persahabatan Indonesia-Mesir, tahun 1947. Jakarta: Panitya Peringatan HUT ke-32 Perjanjian Indonesia-Mesir, 1978, 92 pp.

4885 Sekitar TNI hijrah. Jakarta: Dinas Sejarah TNI-AD, 1983, 202 pp.

4886 Selayang pandang sejarah perjuangan rakyat Bima. Bima: Panitya Hari Pahlawan ke-XXXIII Daerah Bima, 1978. [4865]

4887 Selosoemardjan
'Bureaucratic organization in a time of revolution', *Administrative Science Quarterly* 2 (1957):182-199. (ubl)

4888 Seman, M. Sanit
Sejarah politik pendudukan Belanda dan perlawanan rakyat di Kalimantan Selatan 1945-1949. 1972. [MA thesis Universitas Lambung Mangkurat, Banjarmasin.] [4862]

4889 *Semangat '45 dalam rekaman gambar IPPHOS.* Jakarta: Sinar Harapan, 1985, 165 pp.

4890 Sembiring, Sinar
Suatu tindjauan historis tentang peranan gerilja dalam perang menegakkan kemerdekaan Indonesia. 1972, 115 pp. [MA thesis IKIP Medan.] [13]

4891 'Serangan Umum 1 Maret 1949 menjiwai Dwidharma TNI/ABRI dan Dwidharma rakyat dan merupakan test-case doktrin perang wilayah', *Vidya Yudha* no. 18 (1974):42-46.

4892 *Serangan Umum 1 Maret 1949 di Yogyakarta; Latar belakang dan pengaruhnya.* Jakarta: Citra Lamtoro Gung Persada, 1990, 34+425 pp.

4893 *Seri monumen sejarah TNI-AD.* Bandung: Dinas Sejarah TNI-AD. Vol. 2, 1979, 244 pp.; Vol. 3, 1980, 98 pp.

4894 Setiadijaya, Barlan
'Peranan pemuda pelajar dan mahasiswa dalam peristiwa Hari Pahlawan', *Gema Angkatan 45* no. 71/75 (October 1982-February 1983):36-40.

4895 Setiadijaya, Barlan
Merdeka atau mati di Surabaya 1945; Jilid 1: Penyusunan kekuatan. Jakarta: Widyaswara Kewiraan, 1985, 348 pp.

4896 Setiadijaya, Barlan
'Proklamasi kemerdekaan RI dimata orang-orang asing', *Gema Angkatan 45* no. 86/87 (September-October 1985):100-106.

4897 Setiadijaya, Barlan
'Tanggal 19 September 1945 di Jakarta adalah barometer perjuangan mempertahankan kemerdekaan', *Gema Angkatan 45* no. 90/91 (1986):58, 63.

4898 Setiadijaya, Barlan
'Arti pengibaran Sang Merah Putih pertama di Gubernuran Surabaya', *Gema Angkatan 45* no. 102/103 (1988):112-114.

4899 Setiadijaya, Barlan
Arti Hari Pahlawan 10 November 1945. Paper Seminar Lahirnya Suatu Bangsa, Jakarta, 1990, 9 pp.

4900 Setiadijaya, Barlan
10 November '45; Gelora kepahlawanan Indonesia. Jakarta: Yayasan Dwi Warna, 1991, 15+577 pp. [Second edition, Jakarta: Yayasan 10 November 1945, 1992, 32+604 pp.]

4901 Setiawan, A.
Di balik asap dan mesiu. Bandung: Angkasa, 1983, 115 pp.

4902 Setiawan, Dwianto
Pejuang yang terluka. Jakarta: Bunda Karya, 1985, 78 pp.

4903 Setiawati
Peranan pers dalam perjuangan kemerdekaan Indonesia. 1986. [MA thesis IKIP Jakarta.] [Histori]

4904 'Several Indonesian views of the struggle', in: Colin Wild and Peter Carey (eds), *Born in fire; The Indonesian struggle for independence; An anthology*, pp. 206-210. Athens: Ohio University Press, 1986.

4905 Sewang, Ahmad M.
'KRIS Muda; Suatu kajian tentang perjuangan kemerdekaan di Mandar (1945-1950)', in: *Seminar Sejarah Regional Indonesia Timur; Masalah sejarah perjuangan rakyat Sulawesi Selatan*, pp. 39-48. Ujung Pandang: Dep. P dan K, Balai Kajian Sejarah dan Nilai Tradisional, 1993.

4906 *Sewindu Angkatan Udara Republik Indonesia, 9 April 1946-9 April 1954.* Djakarta: Markas Besar Angkatan Udara Republik Indonesia, Biro Penerangan, 1954, 236 pp.

4907 Shahib, M. Roem
Bone kartu mati bagi perkembangan perjuangan Merah-Putih di Sulawesi Selatan pada tahun-tahun 45-50. 1980, 122 pp. [MA thesis Universitas Hasanuddin, Ujung Pandang.]

4908 Shaleh, Mahading
Sumbangsih Islam terhadap perjuangan kemerdekaan di Luwu. 1982. [Thesis Institut Agama Islam Negeri, Ujung Pandang.] [4334]

4909 Siahaan, Ricardo Manik Julius
'Sekelumit perjuangan rakyat Sumatera Timur dalam mempertahankan kemerdekaan R.I.', in: *Bunga rampai perjuangan dan pengorbanan II*, pp. 314-322. Jakarta: Markas Besar Legiun Veteran RI, 1983.

4910 Sianturi, Rudolf
Agresi kolonial Belanda 1948 terhadap Republik Indonesia dan artinja bagi pendidikan bangsa. 1967, 135 pp. [MA thesis IKIP Djakarta.] [11]

4911 Sidhi, Sumaryono
'Ada terjadi sesuatu yang baru di bawah sang surya ini', *Gema Angkatan 45* no. 20 (August 1977):7-11, 52-54.

4912 Sigarlaki, Anton
Rencana persetujuan Linggar Jati; Latar belakang dan akibatnya bagi perjuangan nasional Indonesia. 1972, 127 pp. [MA thesis Universitas Indonesia, Jakarta.] [19, Histori]

4913 Silangit
Sejarah perjuangan KODAM II/Bukit Barisan; Sekitar Proklamasi kemerdekaan 17 Agustus 1945. Medan: SEMDAM II/Bukit Barisan, 1976. [4874]

4914 Simandjuntak, M. Asal
The Australian role in the Indonesian-Dutch dispute between July 21, 1947 and December 27, 1949. 1963, 85 pp. [MA thesis University of Chicago.]

4915   Simangunsong, Mian Pardamean
       Sedjarah Proklamasi kemerdekaan 17 Agustus 1945. 1968, 112 pp. [MA thesis
       IKIP Bandung.] [10, 108]

4916   Simatupang, T.B.
       *Laporan dari Banaran; Kisah pengalaman seorang pradjurit selama perang
       kemerdekaan.* Djakarta: Pembangunan, 1959, 251 pp. [Second edition, Jakarta:
       Sinar Harapan, 1980, 22+277 pp.]

4917   Simatupang, T.B.
       Report from Banaran; Experiences during the people's war. Translated by Benedict
       Anderson and Elizabeth Graves; With an introduction by John R.W. Smail.
       Ithaca: Cornell University, 1972, 186 pp.

4918   Simatupang, T.B.
       'Pentingnya revolusi bagi kita dewasa ini', *Prisma* 5-7 (August 1976):23-32.

4919   Simatupang, T.B.
       'Arti sejarah perjuangan kemerdekaan bagi kita sekarang ini dengan bertolak
       dari buku Laporan dari Banaran', *Majalah Ketahanan Nasional* 9-29 (1980):28-
       42. [55]

4920   Simatupang, T.B.
       Arti sejarah perjuangan kemerdekaan; Ceramah. Jakarta: Yayasan Idayu, 1981,
       39 pp.

4921   Simatupang, T.B.
       *Het laatste jaar van de Indonesische vrijheidsstrijd 1948-1949; Een authentiek
       verslag door Dr. T.B. Simatupang, de voormalig chefstaf van de Indonesische
       strijdkrachten.* Vertaling C.D. Grijns. Kampen: Kok, 1985, 234 pp.

4922   Simatupang, T.B.; Victor Matondang and A.B. Lapian
       'Partisipasi Kristen dalam revolusi dibidang politik', in: W.B. Sidjabat (ed.),
       Partisipasi Kristen dalam nation building di Indonesia, pp. 7-35. Djakarta: Badan
       Penerbit Kristen, 1968.

4923   Sinaga, Khaspar
       Suatu tinjauan sejarah tentang peranan gerilya di Tapanuli Utara untuk
       mempertahankan kemerdekaan Republik Indonesia sejak 1947-1950. 1974,
       136 pp. [MA thesis IKIP Medan.] [13]

4924   Sinar, Tengku Luckman
       'Revolusi sosial pihak kiri 1946 di Serdang', in: *Revolusi nasional di tingkat lokal*,
       pp. 48-103. Jakarta: Kem. P dan K, 1989.

4925   Singo, Darto
       Untuk kemerdekaan. Jakarta: Kurnia Esa, 1978, 56 pp.

4926   Singo, Darto
       Proklamasi kemerdekaan bangsaku. Jakarta: Balai Pustaka, 1979, 63 pp.

4927   Siradz, M.
       'Siliwangi dalam perang kemerdekaan', *Gema Angkatan 45* no. 88/89 (1985):81-
       82, 109, 112.

4928 Siregar, Baginda Panangaran
Dari bukit ke bukit dan gunung ke gunung; Karya menggali sejarah exponen pejuang kemerdekaan Republik Indonesia Propinsi Sumatera Utara 1945-1950. Medan?: n.n., 1974, 593 pp.

4929 Siregar, Becheri
Undang-undang kerdja tahun 1948; Pasal-pasal jang telah berlaku. Jogjakarta: Menara Pengetahuan, 1953, 39 pp. (kitlv-m)

4930 Siregar, M.S.
Pejuang sukarela. Jakarta: Tribuana, 1985, 89 pp.

4931 Siregar, Slamat
Partai Nasional Indonesia, 1945-1950. 1973, 117 pp. [MA thesis Universitas Indonesia, Jakarta.] [19]

4932 Sirie, H.J.
'Menjelang detik-detik "Bandung lautan api"' , in: *Bunga rampai perjuangan dan pengorbanan I,* pp. 697-702. Jakarta: Markas Besar Legiun Veteran RI, 1982.

4933 Siswoyo, S.W.
Kunjungan ke museum ABRI Satriamandala. Jakarta: Ikhwan, 1978, 108 pp.

4934 Sjaaf, Oemar Basri
'Perang kemerdekaan nilai-nilai luhur '45', in: *Bunga rampai perjuangan dan pengorbanan I,* pp. 449-456. Jakarta: Markas Besar Legiun Veteran RI, 1982.

4935 Sjabaroeddin, N.A.
Suatu tindjauan sedjarah tentang persetudjuan Linggardjati. 1967, 188 pp. [MA thesis IKIP Padang.] [14, 4872]

4936 Sjahnan, H.R.
Dari Medan Area ke pedalaman dan kembali ke kota Medan. Medan: Dinas Sejarah KODAM II/Bukit Barisan, 1982, 16+493 pp.

4937 Sjahnan, H.R.
'Kepahlawanan dalam sejarah perjuangan bangsa Indonesia dan Hari Pahlawan 10 Nopember', *Gema Angkatan 45* no. 90/91 (1986):59-63.

4938 Sjam, Noermiah
Peranan perjuangan kaum wanita Indonesia dalam rangka menuju dan mempertahankan Proklamasi kemerdekaan Indonesia 17 Agustus 1945. 1976, 95 pp. [MA thesis IKIP Jakarta.] [11]

4939 Sjamsuddin, Helius; Edi S. Ekadjati; Ietje Marlina and Wiwi Kuswiah
Menuju negara kesatuan; Negara Pasundan. Jakarta: Kem. P dan K, 1992, 108 pp.

4940 Sjamsuddin, Nazaruddin
The course of the national revolution in Aceh, 1945-49. 1974. [MA thesis Monash University, Melbourne.] [6326]

4941 Sjamsuddin, Nazaruddin
'The ulama, the ulebalang and the national revolution in Aceh', in: *Papers of the Dutch-Indonesian Historical Conference,* pp. 359-377. Leiden/Jakarta: Bureau of Indonesian Studies, 1982.

4942   Sjamsuddin, Nazaruddin
       Aceh dalam masa PDRI. Paper Seminar Sejarah PDRI, Jakarta, 1989, 19 pp.

4943   Sjamsuddin, Nazaruddin
       'Aceh pada masa PDRI', in: Abdurrachman Surjomihardjo and J.R. Chaniago
       (eds), *Pemerintah Darurat Republik Indonesia dikaji ulang*, pp. 55-66. Jakarta:
       Masyarakat Sejarawan Indonesia, 1990.

4944   Sjarif, Agus
       'Sekelumit pengabdian masa revolusi', in: *Bunga rampai perjuangan dan
       pengorbanan II*, pp. 28-36. Jakarta: Markas Besar Legiun Veteran RI, 1983.

4945   Slamet, M.
       'West Java 1945-48', in: *Indonesian nationalism and revolution*, pp. 25-29.
       Clayton: Monash University, 1969.

4946   Soe, Herna
       Tangsi Putih. Jakarta: Bunda Karya, 1985, 71 pp.

4947   Soe Hok Gie
       Simpang kiri sebuah djalan (kisah pemberontakan Madiun September 1948).
       1969. [MA thesis Universitas Indonesia, Djakarta.]

4948   Soebagijo I.N.
       'Panglima Besar Jend. Sudirman (1916-1950)', *Gema Angkatan 45* no. 25
       (January 1978):21-22.

4949   Soebagijo I.N.
       Pengalaman masa revolusi. Jakarta: Pustaka Jaya, 1982, 91 pp.

4950   Soebagijo I.N.
       Bagaikan elang rajawali (kisah kepahlawanan Panglima Besar Sudirman). Jakarta:
       Inti Idayu Press, 1984, 96 pp.

4951   Soebagijo I.N.
       Perjuangan pelajar IPI-IPPI. Jakarta: Balai Pustaka, 1987, 258 pp.

4952   Soebekti
       Sketsa revolusi Indonesia 1940-1945. Surabaja: Grip, 1966, 110 pp.

4953   Soebekti
       *Semak-semak berduri; Secuil kenangan perjuangan besar bangsa Indonesia
       pertengahan abad keduapuluh*. Jakarta: n.n., 1986, 270+26 pp.

4954   Soedardjo
       Kenangan dari medan barat. Jakarta: Balai Pustaka, 1985, 112 pp.

4955   Soedarmin
       'Perang gerilya rakyat di ujung timur pulau Jawa dan Wingate action Brigade
       Damarwulan', in: *Bunga rampai perjuangan dan pengorbanan II*, pp. 412-431.
       Jakarta: Markas Besar Legiun Veteran RI, 1983.

4956   Soedarmono
       'Pengalaman masa perjuangan mempertahankan kemerdekaan 1945-1950', in:
       Bunga rampai perjuangan dan pengorbanan I, pp. 459-472. Jakarta: Markas Besar
       Legiun Veteran RI, 1982.

4957 Soedarno
'Pengalaman pada masa revolusi tahun 1945', in: *Bunga rampai perjuangan dan pengorbanan I*, pp. 704-708. Jakarta: Markas Besar Legiun Veteran RI, 1982.

4958 Soedarso Sp.
Karya-karya seni rupa mewarnai sejarah. Paper Diskusi Sejarah Lokal IV, Revolusi Kemerdekaan di Tingkat Lokal, Bandungan-Ambarawa, 1994, 8 pp.

4959 Soedarsono
'Revolusi Djogja dan sekitarnja', *Penelitian Sedjarah* 2-2 (1961):30-35; 2-3 (1961):51-53.

4960 Soedarsono (ed.)
Merdeka, merdeka dan merdeka. Surabaya: Sekretariat Darmo 49 Ex Brig 17 Det 1 TRIP Jawa Timur, 1987, 110 pp.

4961 Soedarsono Pr.
'Anak-anak TRIP terobos pertahanan tentara Sekutu di Surabaya', in: *Terbukalah jalanku; Hasil sayembara mengarang dalam rangka peringatan hari ulang tahun kemerdekaan R.I. yang ke 30* pp. 95-121. Jakarta: Dewan Harian Nasional Angkatan 45, Pusat Dokumentasi Sejarah Perjoangan 45/Aries Lima, 1976.

4962 Soediarto, S.
Album ke-III; Kenangan perjoangan bersenjata; Kegoncangan dalam tubuh TNI Res 24/IV - Be VI/II. Semarang: Yayasan Brigjen S. Soediarto, 1989, 202 pp.

4963 Soedijono, R.
'Pengalaman pribadi dalam perang kemerdekaan', in: *Bunga rampai perjuangan dan pengorbanan I*, pp. 634-645. Jakarta: Markas Besar Legiun Veteran RI, 1982.

4964 Soedirman
Kumpulan amanat Panglima Besar Djenderal Sudirman. Djakarta: Dep. Petahanan-Keamanan, Pusat Sedjarah ABRI, 1970, 46 pp.

4965 Soedirman (Sudirman)
Wawasan kejuangan Panglima Besar Jenderal Sudirman. Jakarta: Yayasan Kejuangan Panglima Besar Sudirman, 1991, 277 pp.

4966 Soedjatmoko
'Choices and circumstances; The Indonesian revolution 45 years on; Some personal reflections', in: C.A. van Minnen (ed.), *Decolonization of Indonesia; International perspectives*, pp. 9-22. Middelburg: Roosevelt Study Center/Stichting V.O.C.-Publicaties Zeeland, 1988.

4967 Soedjatmoko
'Pilihan dan peluang; Revolusi Indonesia 45 tahun; Beberapa refleksi pribadi', *Sejarah* 1 (1991):1-16.

4968 Soedjoko
KODM Sanden pada masa Klas II. 1975. [MA thesis Universitas Gadjah Mada, Yogyakarta.] [Histori]

4969 Soedjono, Lybia
Panglima Besar Sudirman; Pedjuang, pemimpin, pahlawan. Djakarta: Lembaga Sedjarah HANKAM, 1968, 12 pp. [Second edition, 1968, 16 pp.]

4970 Soegijono
Kisah djatuhnja ibu kota Republik Indonesia Jogjakarta. Jogjakarta: Nusantara, 1953, 62 pp. [22, 40]

4971 Soegijono
'Mengenang penjerbuan Belanda atas ibu kota Republik Indonesia Jogjakarta', Penelitian Sedjarah 3-5 (1962):25-28.

4972 Soegito, Ari Tri
Pengaruh Proklamasi terhadap sifat historiografi Indonesia (sebuah studi perbandingan). 1970, 96 pp. [MA thesis IKIP Semarang.] [15]

4973 Soehardjono
Serangan umum di Solo. 1967, 54 pp. [MA thesis Universitas Gadjah Mada, Jogjakarta.] (kitlv-m)

4974 Soeharto
'Pendjelasan tentang Serangan Umum 1 Maret 1949 (Djogjakarta)', Vidya Yudha no. 4 (1968):101-106.

4975 Soehoet, Ali Moechtar Hoeta
'Bung Karno-Hatta ditjulik untuk memproklamirkan kemerdekaan Indonesia atas nama rakjat', in: Darius Marpaung (ed.), Bingkisan nasional; Kenangan 10 tahun revolusi Indonesia, 17-8-1945/17-8-1955, pp. 27-34. Djakarta: Usaha Pegawai Nasional Indonesia, 1955.

4976 Soejatmiko, Basuki (ed.)
Etnis Tionghoa di awal kemerdekaan Indonesia; Sorotan Bok Tok; Pers Melayu-Tionghoa, Desember 1945-September 1946. Surabaya: Liberty, 1982, 326 pp.

4977 Soejatno
Revolusi phisik sebagai thema membentuk warga negara Indonesia sedjati. 1966, 119 pp. [MA thesis IKIP Jogjakarta.] [17]

4978 Soejono, H.
'Kisah perjalanan KSAU PDRI', in: Abdurrachman Surjomihardjo and J.R. Chaniago (eds), Pemerintah Darurat Republik Indonesia dikaji ulang, pp. 147-154. Jakarta: Masyarakat Sejarawan Indonesia, 1990.

4979 Soejono, Nana Nurliana
Pemuda dalam Proklamasi kemerdekaan Indonesia 17 Agustus 1945; Ichtisar tentang peranan jang didjalankan oleh pemuda Indonesia dalam mentjetuskan Proklamasi kemerdekaan tanggal 17-8-45. 1964, 100 pp. [MA thesis Universitas Indonesia, Djakarta.]

4980 Soekadijo
'Perjuangan rakyat diujung timur pulau Jawa', in: Bunga rampai perjuangan dan pengorbanan I, pp. 585-595. Jakarta: Markas Besar Legiun Veteran RI, 1982.

4981 Soekadri K., Heru
'Gerakan pengibaran bendera di kota Surabaya', Gema Angkatan 45 no. 21 (September 1977):17-20.

4982 Soekahar
'Amah pejuang wanita sejati tak dikenal', in: Bunga rampai perjuangan dan pengorbanan II, pp. 341-346. Jakarta: Markas Besar Legiun Veteran RI, 1983.

4983 Soekahar, Ny. Siti Chatimah D.
'Pengabdian', in: *Bunga rampai perjuangan dan pengorbanan I*, pp. 475-485.
Jakarta: Markas Besar Legiun Veteran RI, 1982.

4984 Soekanto S.A.
Tjokli ikut bergerilja. Djakarta: Pustaka Jaya, 1971, 51 pp.

4985 Soekanto S.A.
Perjalanan bersahaja Jenderal Sudirman. Jakarta: Pustaka Jaya, 1981, 212 pp.

4986 Soekardi IS
'Pengalaman dalam perang kemerdekaan', in: *Bunga rampai perjuangan dan pengorbanan I*, pp. 681-687. Jakarta: Markas Besar Legiun Veteran RI, 1982.

• 4987 Soekarno
'Politik Bangka', in: *Dari penjerangan ke penjerahan*, pp. 1-36. Bukittinggi: Djawatan Penerangan Sumatera Tengah, 1951.

➤ 4988 Soekarno
Het ontstaan van de 'Pantjasila'. 's-Gravenhage: Information Service Indonesia, 1952, 26 pp.

◆ 4989 Soekarno
Sepuluh kali tudjuhbelas Agustus. Djakarta: Kem. Penerangan, 1955, 207 pp. (kitlv-m)

▶ 4990 Soekarno
Amanat pada peringatan Hari Pahlawan 10 Nopember 1959 di Jogjakarta. Djakarta: Kem. Penerangan, 1959, 22 pp.

◆ 4991 Soekarno
The rediscovery of our revolution; Political Manifesto Republic of Indonesia. Djakarta: Dep. of Information, 1959, 85 pp. [45]

▶ 4992 Soekarno
Penemuan kembali revolusi kita; Manifesto Politik Republik Indonesia; Pidato. Surabaja: Suara Rakjat, 1959, 34 pp. [Fourth edition, Djakarta: Dep. Penerangan, 1960, 83 pp.]

◆4993 Soekarno
40.000 korban Sulawesi Selatan; Sumbangan kepada perdjoangan revolusi Indonesia. Djakarta: Kem. Penerangan, 1964, 14 pp.

◆4994 Soekarno
Pidato 17 Agustus dalam alam revolusi physik (1945-49). Djakarta: Dep. Penerangan, 1964, 131 pp.

◆ 4995 Soekarno
Koleksi pidato-pidato Bung Karno 45-50; Kenangan lama. Dihimpun kembali oleh Prapti. N.p.: n.n., 1978, 183 pp. (ubl)

4996 Soekarno K.
Himpunan pertanyaan dan jawaban ketatanegaraan dan sistem pemerintahan Indonesia 1945-1949. Jakarta: Miswar, 1982, 215 pp.

4997 Soekito, Wiratmo
'Peranan imaginasi dalam sejarah kemerdekaan kita', _Budaya Jaya_ 10-111 (1977):453-456.

4998 Soelarto, B.
Tanpa nama; Domba-domba revolusi. Bukittinggi/Djakarta: Nusantara, 1964, 99 pp.

4999 Soemantoro
'Sepuluh Nopember '45 di Surabaja', _Penelitian Sedjarah_ 2-4 (1961):2-6, 44.

5000 Soemarmo, A.J.
Perjuangan menegakkan dan mempertahankan kemerdekaan di Magelang tahun 1945. Ca. 1975, 185 pp. [MA thesis IKIP Semarang.] [15]

5001 Soemartini
'Arsip dan sejarah masa revolusi', _Sejarah_ 4 (1993):43-47.

5002 Soemodipoero, Soetandar; Hadipoerwono and Bambang Soejoto (eds)
Sedjarah perdjuangan pegawai kereta api Djawa-Tengah. Semarang: n.n., 1963, 182 pp.

5003 Soenarto
Peranan Divisi Brawidjaja dalam revolusi Indonesia (periode 1945-1956). 1968, 99 pp. [MA thesis IKIP Malang.] [12]

5004 Soenyata, Ny. Christina
'Aceh dimasa revolusi fisik', in: _Terbukalah jalanku; Hasil sayembara mengarang dalam rangka peringatan hari ulang tahun kemerdekaan R.I. yang ke 30_, pp. 77-93. Jakarta: Dewan Harian Nasional Angkatan 45, Pusat Dokumentasi Sejarah Perjoangan 45/Aries Lima, 1976.

5005 Soepanto, H.
Hizbullah Surakarta 1945-1950. Karanganyar: n.n., 1992, 259 pp.

5006 Soepardi
Pemerintah daerah otonom; Ringkesan Undang-Undang No. 22 tahun 1948 tentang pemerintahan daerah dengan pendjelasannja. Second edition. Semarang: Abede, 1952, 32 pp.

5007 Soepono
Jalan masih panjang; Cerita bernafas sejarah perjuangan bangsa Indonesia merebut dan mempertahankan kemerdekaan. Surabaya: Bina Ilmu, 1986, 75 pp.

5008 Soeprapto, Bambang
'Mencari kebenaran sejarah; Indonesia merdeka bukan bikinan Jepang', _Gema Angkatan 45_ no. 90/91 (1986):52-54, 64, 92.

5009 Soeprapto, R.
Rapat raksasa Ikada 19 September 1945; Mengkaji hikmah dan daya getarnya terhadap perjuangan untuk menegakkan, mengisi dan mewujudkan cita-cita kemerdekaan bangsa Indonesia. Jakarta: Pemerintah DKI Jakarta, 1986, 13 pp.

5010 Soeratman, E.
'Penyusupan kembali ke daerah pangkal gerilya', in: *Bunga rampai perjuangan dan pengorbanan I*, pp. 488-494. Jakarta: Markas Besar Legiun Veteran RI, 1982.

5011 Soeripto
Lahirnja Undang-Undang Dasar 1945. Surabaja: Grip, 1962, 147 pp. (kitlv-m)

5012 Soerjono
'Kumpulan humor revolusi', in: Darius Marpaung, *Bingkisan nasional; Kenangan 10 tahun revolusi Indonesia, 17-8-1945/17-8-1955*, pp. 169-171. Djakarta: Usaha Pegawai Nasional Indonesia, 1955.

5013 Soerjono
'On Musso's return', *Indonesia* no. 29 (1980):59-90; no. 30 (1980):163-164.

5014 Soerjono
'Sekelumit pengalaman dalam periode perjuangan phisik melawan Belanda', in: *Bunga rampai perjuangan dan pengorbanan I*, pp. 571-582. Jakarta: Markas Besar Legiun Veteran RI, 1982.

5015 Soerodjo
'Sekelumit perjuangan demi tanah air tercinta', in: *Bunga rampai perjuangan dan pengorbanan II*, pp. 329-339. Jakarta: Markas Besar Legiun Veteran RI, 1983.

5016 Soeroso
Indonesian independence and the United Nations. 1958, 178 pp. [MA thesis Cornell University, Ithaca.]

5017 Soeroto
Sejarah Proklamasi. Bandung: Sanggabuwana, 1976, 44 pp.

5018 Soeroto, A.
Bandung lautan api. Jakarta: Yayasan Cemerlang, 1976, 40 pp. [6]

5019 Soeroto, A.
Pertempuran Ambarawa. Jakarta: Balai Pustaka, 1976, 51 pp. [Third edition, 1987, 64 pp.]

5020 Soeroto, A.
Perlawanan. Second edition. Jakarta: Karya Indah, 1981, 71 pp. [First edition 1979.]

5021 Soeroto, A.
Pasukan payung pertama Republik Indonesia. Jakarta: Alda, 1985, 47 pp.

5022 Soetanto, Himawan
Perintah Presiden Soekarno: 'Rebut kembali Madiun...'. Jakarta: Sinar Harapan, 1994, 323 pp.

5023 Soetanto, Soeranto
Pemberontakan PKI Mr. Mohamad Joesoeph tahun 1946 di Cirebon. 1981, 123 pp. [MA thesis Universitas Indonesia, Jakarta.] [Histori]

5024 Soetanto, Soeranto
Pemberontakan PKI Mr. Mohammad Joesoeph tahun 1946 di Cirebon. Paper SSN-III, Jakarta, 1981, 20 pp.

5025 Soetanto, Soetopo
Djakarta Raya pada masa 'Pemerintahan Nasional Kota', 17 Agustus 1945-21
Djuli 1947. 1971, 243 pp. [MA thesis Universitas Indonesia, Djakarta.] [19,
Histori]

5026 Soetanto, Soetopo
Pemerintahan Nasional Kota Djakarta 1945-1947. Paper SSN-III, Jakarta, 1981,
40 pp.

5027 Soetanto, Soetopo
Jakarta Raya pada awal kemerdekaan; Masalah-masalah ekonomi yang
dihadapi Pemerintahan Nasional Kota dan usaha-usaha menanggulanginya.
Paper Seminar Jakarta pada Perspektif Sejarah, 1987, 23 pp.

5028 Soetanto, Soetopo
'Peranan gedung Jalan Imam Bonjol No. 1 dalam Proklamasi kemerdekaan
Indonesia', in: *Museum dan sejarah*, pp. 129-142. Jakarta: Dep. P dan K,
1993/1994.

5029 Soetojo, R.
'Lintasan sejarah perjuangan di daerah Jember; Sejarah Kompi-I', *Gema
Angkatan 45* no. 76/80 (March-July 1983):123-133.

5030 Soetojo, R.
*Lintasan sejarah perjuangan kemerdekaan di daerah Jember; Sekilas perjuangan rakyat
di daerah Jember dan sejarah Kompi-I Batalyon 25/509*. Jakarta: Mars-26, 1983,
56 pp.

5031 Soetoyo, Harry
'Cukilan pengalaman perjuangan di sarang musuh', in: *Bunga rampai perjuangan
dan pengorbanan I*, pp. 498-509. Jakarta: Markas Besar Legiun Veteran RI, 1982.

5032 Soetoyo, Ny. Mudjinah Harry
'Sekelumit pengabdian seorang wanita dalam revolusi kemerdekaan', in: *Bunga
rampai perjuangan dan pengorbanan I*, pp. 276-281. Jakarta: Markas Besar Legiun
Veteran RI, 1982-83.

5033 Soetrisno
Usaha-usaha Belanda untuk menguasai kembali Indonesia setelah Perang
Dunia II. 1971, 96 pp. [MA thesis IKIP Jogjakarta.] [17]

5034 Soetrisno, Imam
'Mengemban tugas politik membubarkan Negara Jawa Timur dari Besuki', in:
Bunga rampai perjuangan dan pengorbanan II, pp. 141-165. Jakarta: Markas
Besar Legiun Veteran RI, 1983.

5035 Soewandhi
Sekedar tentang Kementerian Pertahanan di Indonesia. Djakarta: Kem. Pertahanan,
1950, 40 pp.

5036 Soewarno (ed.)
Sejarah pertempuran 5 hari di Semarang. Semarang: Suara Merdeka, 1977,
264 pp.

5037 Soewarno, M. Hari
Kehadiran Jenderal Sudirman, senopati perang kemerdekaan, di bumi Pacitan; Dilihat dari gejala adanya perulangan sejarah. Jakarta: Yayasan Kembang Mas, 1986, 145 pp.

5038 Soewarno, Roto
Pak Dirman menuju Sobo. Second edition. Jakarta: Yayasan Kembang Mas, 1986, 514 pp. [First edition 1985.]

5039 Sokowati, S.
Gerilja dalam Pantjasila. Djakarta: n.n., ca. 1954, 83 pp. (kitlv-m)

5040 Sosro, Agus
Peran serta TKR/TRI dalam POPDA. Jakarta: Yayasan POPDA, 1990, 31 pp.

5041 Sriwibawa, Sugiarta
Laskar Putri Indonesia. Jakarta: Pustaka Jaya, 1985, 59 pp.

5042 Sriwibawa, Sugiarta
Laskar Wanita Indonesia (LASWI). Jakarta: Pustaka Jaya, 1985, 64 pp.

5043 Sriwibawa, Sugiarta
Operasi Pasukan Payung 1947. Jakarta: Pustaka Jaya, 1987, 64 pp.

5044 Suarma, I Made
Peranan Djembrana dalam revolusi phisik. 1971. [MA thesis Universitas Udayana, Denpasar.] [6333]

5045 Subakir
Skets parlementer. Djakarta: Pena, 1950, 103 pp.

5046 Subanto, S.
Pertahanan militer di daerah Metro (Lampung Tengah) pada periode Agresi Militer Belanda ke II tahun 1948-1949. 1975. [MA thesis Universitas Gadjah Mada, Yogyakarta.] [Histori]

5047 Subyakto, R.S.
'Membangun generasi pelaut Indonesia', in: *Bunga rampai perjuangan dan pengorbanan II*, pp. 348-357. Jakarta: Markas Besar Legiun Veteran RI, 1983.

5048 Subyanto, Urip
'Cuplikan pengalamanku dalam perang kemerdekaan', in: *Bunga rampai perjuangan dan pengorbanan II*, pp. 493-501. Jakarta: Markas Besar Legiun Veteran RI, 1983.

5049 Sudaldiono, Hamid
Hubungan perlawanan non-militer dengan Agresi Militer Belanda II dalam mempertahankan kedaulatan Indonesia. 1986. [MA thesis IKIP Jakarta.] [Histori]

5050 Sudarini
Komisi Tiga Negara. 1984, 7+173 pp. [MA thesis Universitas Indonesia, Jakarta.] [Histori]

5051 Sudarini
'Komisi Tiga Negara', in: *Seminar Sejarah Nasional IV; Sub tema dinamika*, pp. 179-195. Jakarta: Kem. P dan K, 1985.

5052 Sudarmaji, Kasman
Arti Roem-Royen dan KMB untuk perdjuangan bangsa Indonesia. 1970, 52 pp.
[MA thesis IKIP Bandung.] [10]

5053 Sudarno
Sejarah pemerintahan militer dan peran pamong praja di Jawa Timur selama perjuangan fisik 1945-1950. Jakarta: Balai Pustaka, 1993, 15+390 pp.

5054 Sudarsono, Juwono
'Segi-segi luar negeri PDRI', in: Abdurrachman Surjomihardjo and J.R. Chaniago (eds), *Pemerintah Darurat Republik Indonesia dikaji ulang*, pp. 75-78. Jakarta: Masyarakat Sejarawan Indonesia, 1990.

5055 Sudarto, Sugeng
Monumen TNI-Angkatan Laut; Jilid 1. Jakarta: Dinas Sejarah Angkatan Laut, 1981, 105 pp.

5056 Sudarto, Sugeng
Peranan kekuatan laut dalam perang kemerdekaan Indonesia. 1984. [MA thesis IKIP Jakarta.] [Histori]

5057 Sudarya, Yahya
Oyot pejuang kemerdekaan. Jakarta: Aries Lima, 1978, 138 pp.

5058 Sudarya, Yahya
Negeriku merdeka. Bandung: Angkasa, 1984, 67 pp.

5059 Sudharto, Bondan
Sekitar pertempuran lima hari di Semarang, 14-19 Oktober 1945. 1976, 237 pp. [MA thesis Universitas Sebelas Maret, Surakarta.]

5060 Sudibya, Gde Adnyana
'Puputan tekad patriotisme pejuang Bali', in: *Cahaya dari medan laga; Hasil sayembara mengarang dalam rangka peringatan hari ulang tahun kemerdekaan RI yang ke 30*, pp. 127-151. Jakarta: Dewan Harian Nasional Angkatan 45/Aries Lima, 1976.

5061 Sudibyo
'Retrospeksi dan prospeksi', in: *Cahaya dari medan laga; Hasil sayembara mengarang dalam rangka peringatan hari ulang tahun kemerdekaan RI yang ke 30*, pp. 99-124. Jakarta: Dewan Harian Nasional Angkatan 45/Aries Lima, 1976.

5062 Sudibyo
'Retrospeksi dan prospeksi', *Gema Angkatan 45* no. 33 (October 1978):19-26, 35.

5063 Sudirjo, Radik Utoyo
Album perang kemerdekaan 1945-1950. Sixth edition. Jakarta: Alda, 1983, 381 pp. [First edition 1975.]

5064 Sudirjo, Radik Utoyo
Lima tahun perang kemerdekaan 1945-1949; Album perjuangan kemerdekaan disusun untuk umum dan sekolah-sekolah. Jakarta: Alda, 1976, 48+48+48+48+48 pp. 5 vols.

5065 Sudirjo, Radik Utoyo (ed.)
Panglima Besar Sudirman; Sebuah kenangan perjuangan. Jakarta: Alda, 1985, 264 pp.

5066 Sudirjo, Radik Utoyo
Pelajar Bondowoso menghadapi Agresi Militer 21 Juli 1947. Jakarta: Alda, 1989, 36 pp.

5067 Sudirjo, Radik Utoyo and Tanu Suherly
Lima tahun perang kemerdekaan 1945-1949; Bacaan sejarah untuk angkatan muda dan umum; Dokumentasi revolusi fisik. Third edition. Jakarta: Alda, 1977, 320 pp. [First edition 1976.]

5068 Sudiro
'Saja bahagia ditakdirkan saksikan Proklamasi', in: Darius Marpaung (ed.), *Bingkisan nasional; Kenangan 10 tahun revolusi Indonesia, 17-8-1945/17-8-1955*, pp. 46-48. Djakarta: Usaha Pegawai Nasional Indonesia, 1955.

5069 Sudiro
Pengalaman saya sekitar 17 Agustus 1945; Ceramah. Jakarta: Idayu, 1972, 39 pp. [Second edition, 1975, 44 pp.]

5070 Sudiro
'Mengenang sahabat-sahabat dalam "zaman perjuangan" yang kini telah tiada', in: *Bunga rampai perjuangan dan pengorbanan I*, pp. 392-403. Jakarta: Markas Besar Legiun Veteran RI, 1982.

5071 Sudiro
'Yang telah saya alami antara tanggal 17 Agustus 1945 dan 19 September 1945', *Gema Angkatan 45* no. 88/89 (1985):83-84, 109-110.

5072 Sudjadi GR, Boges
Sekilas-kisah ex pelajar bersenjata TNI-Brigade ke-17 TRIP Jawa Timur Kompi 3400/Nganjuk. Jakarta: n.n., 1981, 238 pp.

5073 Sudjarwo
'Potret diri pemuda dalam revolusi kita', *Prisma* 10-8 (August 1981):21-32.

5074 Sudjarwo
Pasukan Samber Gelap; Potret kemauan merdeka anak kampung. Yogyakarta: Dinas Prop DIY, 1985, 34 pp.

5075 Sudjojono, S.
'Pengalaman saya di zaman Jepang dan di zaman revolusi', *Budaya Jaya* 7-79 (1974):717-731.

5076 Sudrajat, A.
'Revolusi Indonesia; Tekanan internasional dan kelemahan interen', *Tanah Air* (September 1986):44-60. [50]

5077 Sudyarto Ds, Sides
Lilin-lilin empat lima. Jakarta: Aries Lima, 1979, 55 pp.

5078 Sudyarto, Sides
'Tingkah laku politik Panglima Besar Soedirman', in: Sides Sudyarto (ed.), *Tingkah laku politik Panglima Besar Sudirman*, pp. 91-125. Jakarta, 1983.

5079   Sudyarto, Sides a.o. (ed.)
       Tingkah laku politik Panglima Besar Sudirman. Jakarta: Karya Unipress, 1983,
       134 pp.

5080   Sugardo
       'Dari tjomotan dokumentasi; Sekitar 17 Agustus 1945 di Sulawesi Selatan', in:
       Darius Marpaung (ed.), *Bingkisan nasional; Kenangan 10 tahun revolusi Indonesia,*
       17-8-1945/17-8-1955, pp. 75-79. Djakarta: Usaha Pegawai Nasional Indonesia,
       1955.

5081   Sugianto
       TRIP dalam perjuangan mempertahankan kemerdekaan Indonesia (suatu tin-
       jauan perjuangan bersenjata di daerah Malang). 1975, 150 pp. [MA thesis IKIP
       Malang.] [12]

5082   Sugito, Sigit and Suharsana
       Peranan pelajar dan mahasiswa dalam perang kemerdekaan; Sebuah ikhtisar. Jakarta:
       Dep. Pertahanan-Keamanan, Pusat Sejarah ABRI, 1978, 22 pp.

5083   Suhadiyatna, A.
       Sekitar perpindahan pemerintah pusat dari Jakarta ke Yogyakarta. 1976, 103
       pp. [MA thesis IKIP Jakarta.] [11]

5084   Suhardjo
       Serangan Umum 1 Maret 1949 (di Jogjakarta). 1967, 55 pp. [MA thesis
       Universitas Gadjah Mada, Jogjakarta.]

5085   Suhartinah
       Kehidupan persuratkabaran di Yogyakarta pada masa revolusi fisik; Sebuah
       studi awal. Paper Diskusi Sejarah Lokal IV, Revolusi Kemerdekaan di Tingkat
       Lokal, Bandungan-Ambarawa, 1994, 16 pp.

5086   Suhartono
       Surakarta in the early revolution; Trends of social revolution, 1945-1946. Paper
       Sixth International Conference on Asian History, Yogyakarta, 1974, 11 pp.

5087   Suhatno and Poliman
       'Sejarah perjuangan kemerdekaan di Bantul tahun 1942-1949', in: *Peristiwa-*
       peristiwa revolusi di tingkat lokal, pp. 45-97. Yogyakarta: Dep. P dan K, 1993.

5088   Suherly, T.
       'Brigade Tjitarum', *Madjalah Sedjarah Militer Angkatan Darat* no. 19 (1965):26-
       31; no. 20 (1965):31-36.

5089   Suherly, Tanu
       Negara Pasundan dalam tanggapan rakjat Djawa Barat. 1968. [MA thesis
       Universitas Padjadjaran, Bandung.] [1, 20, 4313, 4858]

5090   Suherly, Tanu
       'Ekspedisi ke Kalimantan pada awal revolusi', *Vidya Yudha* no. 7 (1969):74-81.

5091   Suherly, Tanu
       Sekitar Negara Pasundan. Paper SSN-II, Jogjakarta, 1970, 65 pp.

5092 Suherly, Tanu
Kekuatan gerilya di daerah Priangan pada waktu Divisi Siliwangi hijrah tahun 1948. Paper SSN-III, Jakarta, 1981, 13 pp.

5093 Suherly, Tanu a.o.
Pahlawan Ambarawa dan Hari Infanteri. 1968. [99]

5094 Suherly, Tanu; Jusmar Basri; Ariwiadi and Sigit Sugito
Sedjarah perang kemerdekaan Indonesia. Djakarta: Dep. Pertahanan-Keamanan, Pusat Sedjarah ABRI, 1971, 103 pp.

5095 Sujono
'Pertempuran Surabaya adalah pertempuran rakyat', *Gema Angkatan 45* no. 23 (Novermber 1977):20-24.

5096 Sukandar, Kandar
Beberapa peristiwa penting di Jawa Barat pada masa revolusi fisik (1945-1949). 1974, 34 pp. [MA thesis IKIP Bandung.] [10]

5097 Sukardi
Sekitar perdjuangan Sumeru Selatan. Djakarta?, 1950. [1962]

5098 Sukati, Peni Mudji
Negara Indonesia Timur dalam perjuangan menuju persatuan Indonesia. 1985, 215 pp. [MA thesis Universitas Indonesia, Jakarta.] [Histori]

5099 Sukatmo
Latar belakang Peristiwa Tiga Djuli. 1964, 224 pp. [MA thesis Universitas Indonesia, Djakarta.]

5100 Sukinda, Kusnadi Hermawan
Negara Pasundan; Suatu tinjauan sejarah tentang proses pembentukan dan perkembangan tahun 1948-1950. 1986. [MA thesis Universitas Padjadjaran, Bandung.] [4939]

5101 Sukodarsono
'Cepu lautan api; Pelaksanaan tugas pasukan geni pioner', *Gema Angkatan 45* no. 41 (August-September 1979):42-45.

5102 Sukrisno
Belangrijke evenementen in de Indonesische nationale revolutie 1945-1950. 1989, 87 pp. [MA thesis Universiteit van Amsterdam.]

5103 Sulaiman, M. Isa
'Islam et propagande anti-néerlandaise; Abdullah Arief et le Seumangat Atjeh, 1945-1946', *Archipel* 30 (1985):207-217.

5104 Sulaiman, M. Isa
Les ulèebalang, les ulémas, et les enseignants de madrasah; La lutte pour le pouvoir local en Aceh de 1942 à 1951. 1985, 366 pp. [Thesis Ecole des Hautes Etudes et des Sciences Sociales, Paris.]

5105 Sulaiman, Mustafa
Taufan disekitar negara Indonesia. Djakarta: Widjaya, 1950, 136 pp. [Second edition 1951.]

5106 Sularto, B.
Enam jam di Yogya. Jakarta: Bunda Karya, 1985, 80 pp.

5107 Sumadji
'Pengalaman dalam perang kemerdekaan', in: *Bunga rampai perjuangan dan pengorbanan I*, pp. 626-631. Jakarta: Markas Besar Legiun Veteran RI, 1982.

5108 Sumantri, Iwa Kusuma
'Analisa tentang peristiwa-peristiwa disekitar Proklamasi kemerdekaan Indonesia', *Penelitian Sedjarah* 1-1 (1960):3-5; 2-2 (1961):3-4; 2-3 (1961):1-3.

5109 Sumantri, Iwa Kusuma
Sedjarah revolusi Indonesia. Djakarta: Grafica, 1963-69. Vol. 1: *Masa perdjuangan sebagai perintis kemerdekaan*, 162 pp.; Vol. 2, *Masa revolusi bersendjata*, 252 pp.; Vol. 3, *Masa mempertahankan keutuhan negara*, 139 pp.

5110 Sumardjo
Pertahanan gerilya di daerah kabupaten Sragen pada masa 1948-1949. 1976. [MA thesis Universitas Gadjah Mada, Yogyakarta.] [Histori]

5111 Sumarmo, Iwa
Indonesia merdeka atau mati; Sejarah pasukan pelajar I.M.A.M. selama perang kemerdekaan 1945-1949. Jakarta: Keluarga Besar IMAM, 1985, 327 pp.

5112 Sumasto, R.M. Padmo
'Demi rasa cinta tanah air', in: *Bunga rampai perjuangan dan pengorbanan II*, pp. 279-283. Jakarta: Markas Besar Legiun Veteran RI, 1983.

5113 *Sumber sejarah kota Bandung periode revolusi kemerdekaan (1945-1950)*. Bandung: Pemerintah Kotamadya Daerah Tingkat II, 1981, 283 pp. [42]

5114 Sumengkar, Rachmat
'Persembahan sekelumit kisah perjuangan', in: *Bunga rampai perjuangan dan pengorbanan I*, pp. 322-340. Jakarta: Markas Besar Legiun Veteran RI, 1982.

5115 Sumitro, Bambang
'Surabaya membentuk saya', in: *Bunga rampai perjuangan dan pengorbanan II*, pp. 38-50. Jakarta: Markas Besar Legiun Veteran RI, 1983.

5116 Sunaryo
'Kisah sebuah peti mati penuh misteri', in: Kustiniyati Mochtar (ed.), *Memoar pejuang Republik Indonesia seputar 'zaman Singapura', 1945-1950*, pp. 114-130. Jakarta: Gramedia, 1992.

5117 Sundari
Pertempuran lima hari di Semarang. 1975. [MA thesis Universitas Gadjah Mada, Yogyakarta.] [Histori]

5118 Supadmi, Nuning
Pertempuran Rejodani 29 Mei 1949. 1981. [MA thesis Universitas Gadjah Mada, Yogyakarta.] [Histori]

5119 Supardi
Westerling. Jakarta: n.n., 1985, 80 pp.

5120 Suparto D. and Tri Atmono
Surabaya bersembah darah; Pertempuran 10 Nov. 1945. Semarang: Isti, 1984, 33 pp.

5121 Supinah
Hubungan persetujuan Renville dengan kejatuhan kabinet Amir Sjarifuddin. 1986. [MA thesis IKIP Jakarta.] [Histori]

5122 Supono, Wiweko
'Kegiatan AURI selama PDRI di Burma', in: Abdurrachman Surjomihardjo and J.R. Chaniago (eds), *Pemerintah Darurat Republik Indonesia dikaji ulang*, pp. 158-159. Jakarta: Masyarakat Sejarawan Indonesia, 1990.

5123 Supriyanto
Oposisi terhadap Kabinet Sjahrir (1945-1947). 1984, 112 pp. [MA thesis Universitas Gadjah Mada, Yogyakarta.] [Histori]

5124 Supriyanto
Hizbullah Bandung pada awal revolusi tahun 1945-1947. 1986, 128 pp. [MA thesis Universitas Indonesia, Jakarta.] [Histori]

5125 Suraputra, D. Sidik
Republik Indonesia sebagai subyek hukum internasional; Dari Proklamasi sampai dengan perjanjian Linggarjati. 1988, 485 pp. [PhD thesis Universitas Indonesia, Jakarta.]

5126 Suraputra, Dj. Sidik
Revolusi Indonesia dan hukum internasional. Jakarta: Penerbit Universitas Indonesia (UI Press), 1991, 212 pp.

5127 Suratmin
Pers pada masa revolusi fisik di Yogyakarta. Paper Diskusi Sejarah Lokal IV, Revolusi Kemerdekaan di Tingkat Lokal, Bandungan-Ambarawa, 1994, 42 pp.

5128 Suratmin and Moeljono
'Kabupaten Gunung Kidul pada tahun 1942-1949', in: *Peristiwa-peristiwa revolusi di tingkat lokal*, pp. 101-143. Yogyakarta: Dep. P dan K, 1993.

5129 Suratno
Hari Pahlawan ditinjau dari segi sejarah. 1975, 133 pp. [MA thesis IKIP Malang.] [12]

5130 Surbakti, A.R.
Perang kemerdekaan; Jilid 1: Di Karo area. Medan: Yayasan Pro Patria, 1978, 332 pp.

5131 Surbakti, A.R.
Perang kemerdekaan; Jilid 2: Di tanah Karo, Karo Jahe dan Dairi area. Medan: Pro Patria, 1979, 439 pp.

5132 Surbakti, A.R.
Sejarah perjuangan KODAM II/Bukit Barisan (setelah cease-fire - penyerahan kedaulatan). [4874]

5133 Surbakti, Sabar
Hari Pahlawan 10 November. 1964, 96 pp. [MA thesis IKIP Djakarta.] [11]

5134 Surentu, Ari
'Secercah gerakan pemuda-pemuda Langowan dalam revolusi kemerdekaan
Indonesia', in: *Bunga rampai perjuangan dan pengorbanan II*, pp. 451-467.
Jakarta: Markas Besar Legiun Veteran RI, 1983.

5135 Suripto, Ny. Dartiyah
'Sekedar kenangan Lasykar Poetri Indonesia', in: *Bunga rampai perjuangan dan
pengorbanan II*, pp. 68-78. Jakarta: Markas Besar Legiun Veteran RI, 1983.

5136 Surjadi, Didi
Tindjauan sedjarah sekitar lahirnja Divisi Siliwangi pada tanggal 20 Mei 1946.
1967. [MA thesis Universitas Padjadjaran, Bandung.] [1, 20]

5137 Surjadi, Didi
Sebuah setudi sedjarah sekitar lahirnja Divisi Siliwangi pada tanggal 20 Mei
1946. Paper SSN-II, Jogjakarta, 1970, 33 pp.

5138 Surjadi, Didi
Menuju negara kesatuan 1945-1950. Lembang, 1975. [99, 4313]

5139 Surjokartiko, Risa Bambang
Peranan TNI Angkatan Darat dalam merebut kembali kota Jogjakarta dari
pendudukan Belanda (19-12-48/29-6-49). 1969, 144 pp. [MA thesis IKIP
Jogjakarta.] [17]

5140 Surjomihardjo, Abdurrachman
Inventarisasi dan dokumentasi bahan-bahan sedjarah revolusi Indonesia; Tjeramah.
Djakarta: LIPI, 1970. [99]

5141 Surjomihardjo, Abd.
'Rapat samudera di Ikada, Jakarta 19 Sept. 1945', *Budaya Jaya* 10-109
(1977):348-357.

5142 Surjomihardjo, Abdurrachman
'Peristiwa Tiga Daerah; Suatu interpretasi sejarah; Revolusi sosial menyambut
Proklamasi kemerdekaan', *Prisma* 10-8 (August 1981):52-61.

5143 Surjomihardjo, A.
Kisah pelajar pejoang daerah Tegal; Dari bedil kayu, mitralyur ke bangku sekolah.
Jakarta: Takari, 1983, 46 pp.

5144 Surjomihardjo, Abdurrachman
Masa revolusi Indonesia; Suatu tinjauan historiografi. Paper SSN-V, Semarang
1990, 16 pp.

5145 Surjomihardjo, A.
Penulisan sejarah POPDA; Beberapa catatan dan saran untuk perbaikan. Jakarta:
Yayasan POPDA, 1990, 12 pp.

5146 Surjomihardjo, Abdurrachman
'Diambang Proklamasi kemerdekaan bangsa Indonesia dan masa revolusi
Indonesia; Suatu tinjauan historiografi', in: *Museum dan sejarah*, pp. 113-119.
Jakarta: Dep. P dan K, 1993/1994.

5147 Surjomihardjo, Abd. and J.R. Chaniago (eds)
PDRI - Pemerintah Darurat Republik Indonesia dikaji ulang. Jakarta: Masyarakat Sejarawan Indonesia, 1990, 322 pp.

5148 Surono, V.
Pengaruh penyerangan 19 Desember 1948 terhadap masyarakat Yogyakarta. 1975, 79 pp. [MA thesis IKIP Jakarta.] [11]

5149 Suroso, Bambang Edi
Hubungan revolusi Indonesia dengan kolonialisme di Asia-Afrika. 1986. [MA thesis IKIP Jakarta.] [Histori]

5150 Suroyo, A.M. Djuliati
Revolusi dan mentalitas; Cepu sekitar masa revolusi kemerdekaan 1945-1949. Paper Diskusi Sejarah Lokal IV, Revolusi Kemerdekaan di Tingkat Lokal, Bandungan-Ambarawa, 1994, 23 pp.

5151 Suryoatmodjo, F.X.Y.
'Sekitar S.O. 1 Maret di Yogyakarta', in: *Terbukalah jalanku; Hasil sayembara mengarang dalam rangka peringatan hari ulang tahun kemerdekaan R.I. yang ke 30*, pp. 183-198. Jakarta: Dewan Harian Nasional Angkatan 45, Pusat Dokumentasi Sejarah Perjoangan 45/Aries Lima, 1976.

5152 Suryohadiprojo, Sayidiman
'Pemikiran strategi militer Indonesia masa perang kemerdekaan; Antara konsep dan pelaksanaannya', *Histori* 1-2 (1992):41-58.

5153 Susanto, Sewan
Perjuangan Tentara Pelajar dalam perang kemerdekaan Indonesia. Yogyakarta: Gadjah Mada University Press, 1985, 157 pp.

5154 Susatyo, Rachmat
Pemberontakan PKI Muso di Madiun, 18-30 September 1948. 1976. [MA thesis Universitas Padjadjaran, Bandung.] [20]

5155 Sutarna, Tatang
Perdjuangan diplomasi untuk mempertahankan kemerdekaan. 1970, 89 pp. [MA thesis IKIP Bandung.] [10]

5156 Sutarto, Ayu
Sudirman; A simple man; A great general. Jakarta: Gramedia, 1986, 26 pp.

5157 Sutiasumarga, Rusman
Jang terempas dan terkandas. Djakarta: Balai Pustaka, 1951, 129 pp. [Fourth edition, 1965, 127 pp.]

5158 Sutjiatiningsih, Sri
Perekonomian Indonesia dalam masa revolusi kemerdekaan (revolusi fisik) antara tahun 1945-1949. Jakarta: Dep. P dan K, 1979/1980. [4853]

5159 Sutomo (Bung Tomo)
Kenangan bahagia. Jogjakarta: Balapan, ca. 1950, 80 pp. (kitlv-m)

5160 Sutomo
Sepuluh Nopember. Djakarta: Balapan, 1951, 115 pp. [22, 6186]

5161 Sutomo (Bung Tomo)
Kemana bekas pedjuang bersendjata? Second edition. Djakarta: Balapan, 1952, 73 pp. (kitlv-m)

5162 Sutomo (Bung Tomo)
Sesudah 'Madiun' dan 'Gestapu' lantas apa? Djakarta: Balapan, 1965, 52 pp. (kitlv-m)

5163 Sutoto, Sutiko
'Yogyakarta 19 Desember 1948; Sebagaimana saya alami', in: *Bunga rampai perjuangan dan pengorbanan I*, pp. 662-678. Jakarta: Markas Besar Legiun Veteran RI, 1982.

5164 Sutowo, Ibnu
'Peranan Palang Merah Indonesia', in: *Museum dan sejarah*, pp. 73-85. Jakarta: Dep. P dan K, 1993/1994.

5165 Sutoyo, Mudjinah Harry
'Sekelumit pengabdian seorang wanita dalam revolusi kemerdekaan', in: *Bunga rampai perjuangan dan pengorbanan I*, pp. 276-281. Jakarta: Markas Besar Legiun Veteran RI, 1982.

5166 Sutrisno, Try
'Sekilas pengabdian seorang prajurit ditengah negara yang sedang berkembang', in: *Bunga rampai perjuangan dan pengorbanan II*, pp. 481-491. Jakarta: Markas Besar Legiun Veteran RI, 1983.

5167 Su'ud, H. Adhar
'Kenang-kenangan ringkas selama revolusi kemerdekaan', in: *Bunga rampai perjuangan dan pengorbanan I*, pp. 98-109. Jakarta: Markas Besar Legiun Veteran RI, 1982.

5168 Suwagio, Gatot
'Sekelumit pengabdian kepada tanah air', in: *Bunga rampai perjuangan dan pengorbanan II*, pp. 102-107. Jakarta: Markas Besar Legiun Veteran RI, 1983.

5169 Suwanda, H. Aten
Di bawah lindungan Tuhan; Suatu kisah perjalanan penulis sebagai anggota Corps Mahasiswa (CM) dalam perjuangan melawan penjajah Belanda. Jakarta: n.n., 1983, 140 pp.

5170 Suwarno, G.
Peranan pasukan ekspedisi dalam mempertahankan kemerdekaan 17-8-1945 di Sulawesi Selatan. Paper Seminar Sejarah Perjuangan Rakyat Sulawesi Selatan Menentang Penjajahan Asing, Ujung Pandang, 1982, 38 pp.

5171 Suwarno, P.J.
Peranan pemerintah sipil dan rakyat dalam perang kemerdekaan di Yogyakarta 1948-1949. Paper Seminar Sejarah Peranan Generasi Muda dalam Perjuangan Bangsa 1942-1950, Yogyakarta, 1989, 20 pp.

5172 Suwarno, P.J.
Akomodasi gerakan rakyat di Yogyakarta sesudah Proklamasi kemerdekaan. Paper Musyawarah Kerja Nasional Sejarah, Bandung, 1990, 22 pp.

5173 Suwarno, P.J.
Sultan Hamengku Buwono IX memimpin revolusi kemerdekaan di Yogyakarta.
Yogyakarta: Yayasan Ilmu Pengetahuan dan Kebudayaan Panunggalan, 1993,
28 pp.

5174 Suwarno, P.J.
Pemerintah daerah periode 1945-1950 khususnya daerah istimewa Yogyakarta.
Paper Diskusi Sejarah Lokal IV, Revolusi Kemerdekaan di Tingkat Lokal,
Bandungan-Ambarawa, 1994, 25 pp.

5175 Suwiji, Ni Luh Pande
Revolusi physik; Rakyat Klungkung menentang penjajah Belanda 1945-1949.
1972. [MA thesis Universitas Udayana, Denpasar.] [6333]

5176 Suwirta, Andi
Bertempoer atau beroending; Tanggapan pers di Jawa pada awal revolusi
Indonesia. Paper Diskusi Sejarah Lokal IV, Revolusi Kemerdekaan di Tingkat
Lokal, Bandungan-Ambarawa, 1994, 32+3 pp.

5177 Suyatno
'Revolusi Indonesia dan pergolakan sosial di Delanggu', in: *Revolusi nasional di
tingkat lokal,* pp. 1-13. Jakarta: Kem. P dan K, 1989.

5178 Swastika, I Made
Makna hubungan Bali dan Jawa dalam revolusi fisik di Bali (1945-1950). Paper
SSN-IV, Yogyakarta, 1985, 25 pp.

5179 Swetja, I Gusti Ngurah
Latar belakang peristiwa Madiun 18 September 1948. 1968, 193 pp. [MA
thesis IKIP Bandung.] [10]

5180 Syafruddin
Sikap pergerakan rakyat menghadapi pendudukan Belanda di Kalimantan
Selatan, periode 17 Agustus 1945 sampai 1950. 1974. [MA thesis Universitas
Lambung Mangkurat, Banjarmasin.] [4862]

5181 Syahrir, Siti Wahyunah Sutan ('Poppy')
'Peran Singapura pada tahun-tahun pertama kemerdekaan Republik Indonesia;
Sekelumit kenangan', in: Kustiniyati Mochtar (ed.), *Memoar pejuang Republik
Indonesia seputar 'zaman Singapura', 1945-1950,* pp. 17-34. Jakarta: Gramedia,
1992.

5182 Syamsuddin, A. Chumaidi
*Agama dan perubahan sosial di Indonesia; Peranan K.H. Hasyim As'ari dalam masa
revolusi dan perang kemerdekaan.* Jakarta: Dep. Agama, 1982, 54+13 pp.

5183 Syamsuddin, BM.
Harimau kuala. Jakarta: Bunda Karya, 1984, 71 pp.

5184 Syamsuddin, D.N.
Perjuangan Lasykar Lipang Bajeng di daerah Takalar dalam mempertahankan
Proklamasi kemerdekaan Indonesia. 1976. [MA thesis IKIP Ujung Pandang.]
[604]

5185   Tahir, Achmad
'Sekelumit kisah pengalaman seorang veteran pejuang RI', in: *Bunga rampai perjuangan dan pengorbanan I*, pp. 84-95. Jakarta: Markas Besar Legiun Veteran RI, 1982.

5186   Tahir, Ny. Roos Lila
'Sekuntum melati pengikat rasa', in: *Bunga rampai perjuangan dan pengorbanan I*, pp. 343-361. Jakarta: Markas Besar Legiun Veteran RI, 1982.

5187   Taib, M.
Korban nan tak sia-sia; Sekelumit perdjuangan Wolter Robert Mongisidi. Djakarta: Iqbal, ca. 1963, 82 pp. (kitlv-m)

5188   Talsya, Teuku Alibasjah
'Pemantjar radio revolusi di Atjeh', in: *Modal revolusi 45*, pp. 81-90. Kutaradja: Komite Musjawarah Angkatan 45 DI Atjeh, 1960.

5189   Talsya, T. Alibasyah
'Insiden bendera digedung Keimubu titik-mulai dari sedjarah Angkatan Kepolisian Atjeh', *Sinar Darussalam* no. 13 (1969):77-80.

5190   Talsya, T.A.
'Kami tak menerima perintah dari siapapun; Fragmen revolusi '45 di Atjeh', *Sinar Darussalam* no. 24 (1970):49-52.

5191   Talsya, T.A.
'Penegasan Seri Padoeka Toean Besar Goebernoer Soematera NRI Mr. T.M. Hasan kepada General Major Chambers; Fragmen revolusi '45 di Atjeh', *Sinar Darussalam* no. 23 (1970):60-63.

5192   Talsya, Teuku Alibasyah
'Karena tetap setia kepada Republik', *Gema Angkatan 45* no. 59/61 (October-December 1981):75-78.

5193   Talsya, T.A.
'Pasukan Sekutu gagal menyerbu Aceh', *Gema Angkatan 45* no. 59/61 (October-December 1981):28-32.

5194   Talsya, T.A.
'Pesawat terbang "Seulawah" RI 002; Presiden Soekarno mengunjungi Aceh', *Gema Angkatan 45* no. 56/58 (July-September 1981):117-119.

5195   Talsya, T.A.
'Merebut senjata Jepang di Aceh', *Gema Angkatan 45* no. 65/67 (April-June 1982):79-82, 121.

5196   Talsya, T.A.
Banda Aceh pada masa kemerdekaan. Banda Aceh: Panitia Seminar Hari Jadi Kota Banda Aceh, 1988, 22 pp.

5197   Talsya, T.A.
'PKI tidak berhasil menjerat Aceh', *Gema Angkatan 45* no. 102/103 (1988):96-98, 106.

5198 Talsya, T.A.
Batu karang ditengah lautan (Perjuangan kemerdekaan di Aceh) 1945-1946; Buku I.
Medan: Lembaga Sejarah Aceh, 1990, 376 pp.

5199 Talsya, T.A.
Modal perjuangan kemerdekaan (Perjuangan kemerdekaan di Aceh) 1947-1948; Buku II. Medan: Lembaga Sejarah Aceh, 1990, 480 pp.

5200 Talsya, T.A.
Sekali Republikein tetap Republikein (Perjuangan kemerdekaan di Aceh) 1949; Buku III. Medan: Lembaga Sejarah Aceh, 1990, 333 pp.

5201 Tamboto, Johan Hendrik
'Peranan pejuang-pejuang Sulawesi Utara dalam perjuangan kemerdekaan', in:
Letusan di balik buku; Hasil sayembara mengarang dalam rangka peringatan hari ulang tahun kemerdekaan RI yang ke 30, pp. 201-222. Jakarta: Dewan Harian Nasional Angkatan 45/Aries Lima, 1976.

5202 Tamin, M. Arsyad
Sedjarah ringkas Pasukan GAPIS. Watansoppeng: Kantor Urusan Veteran Kabupaten Soppeng, 1957. [4868]

5203 Tamma, H.A. Rachman
'Sulawesi Selatan/Tenggara mempertahankan Negara Proklamasi 17 Agustus 1945', in: *Bunga rampai perjuangan dan pengorbanan II,* pp. 300-312. Jakarta: Markas Besar Legiun Veteran RI, 1983.

5204 Tampenawas, Cris
'Menegakkan kemerdekaan bangsa dilautan; Tjerita kapal ALRI jang menembus blokkade Belanda', in: *Dari penjerangan ke penjerahan,* pp. 44-51. Bukittinggi: Djawatan Penerangan Sumatera Tengah, 1951.

5205 Tandjung, C. Anwar
Anak dalam perang. Jakarta: Balai Pustaka, 1988, 134 pp.

5206 *Tanggal dan tempat lahir Pangsar Jenderal Soedirman; Versi hasil penelitian ABRI.*
Jakarta: Dep. Pertahanan-Keamanan, Pusat Sejarah ABRI, 1978, 79 pp.

5207 Tarjo, N.S.S.
Dari atas tandu; Pak Dirman memimpin perang rakyat semesta (gerilya), 1948-1949. Yogyakarta: Yayasan Wiratama 45, 1984, 144 pp.

5208 Taruna, Joannes Chrysostomus Tukiman
'Fanatis nasionalisme batu penjuru perjuangan kemerdekaan', in: *Letusan di balik buku; Hasil sayembara mengarang dalam rangka peringatan hari ulang tahun kemerdekaan RI yang ke 30,* pp. 73-89. Jakarta: Dewan Harian Nasional Angkatan 45/Aries Lima, 1976.

5209 Taruna, J.Chr. Tukiman
'Fanatis nasionalisme batu penjuru perjuangan kemerdekaan', *Gema Angkatan 45* no. 31 (July-August 1978):26-30, 47.

5210 Tashadi
Hizbullah Sabilillah divisi Sunan Bonang dalam revolusi kemerdekaan; Lahir dan perkembangannya. Paper Diskusi Sejarah Lokal IV, Revolusi Kemerdekaan di Tingkat Lokal, Bandungan-Ambarawa, 1994, 20 pp.

5211 Tashadi; Darto Harnoko; Suratmin and Hisbaron Muryantoro
Peranan desa dalam perjuangan kemerdekaan; Studi kasus keterlibatan beberapa desa di Daerah Istimewa Yogyakarta periode 1945-1949. Jakarta: Kem. P dan K, 1992, 181 pp.

5212 Tatang, Asep
'Doktrin-doktrin perjoangan 45', in: *Terbukalah jalanku; Hasil sayembara mengarang dalam rangka peringatan hari ulang tahun kemerdekaan R.I. yang ke 30,* pp. 145-164. Jakarta: Dewan Harian Nasional Angkatan 45, Pusat Dokumentasi Sejarah Perjoangan 45/Aries Lima, 1976.

5213 Taulu, H.M.
Merah Putih; Novel sejarah. Jakarta: Kem. P dan K, 1983, 224 pp.

5214 Tekang, Nambur Sumbiring
Keradjaan-keradjaan Karo runtuh pada tahun 1946. 1970, 59 pp. [MA thesis IKIP Jogjakarta.] [17]

5215 Tekeja, I Wayan
Revolusi physik di kabupaten Badung, 1945-1949. 1972. [MA thesis Universitas Udayana, Denpasar.] [6333]

5216 *Terbukalah jalanku; Hasil sayembara mengarang dalam rangka peringatan hari ulang tahun kemerdekaan R.I. yang ke 30.* Jakarta: Dewan Harian Nasional Angkatan 45, Pusat Dokumentasi Sejarah Perjoangan 45/Aries Lima, 1976, 229 pp.

5217 Thachir, A. Malik
Pandu cucu seorang pejuang. Jakarta: Balai Pustaka, 1986, 112 pp.

5218 Thaher, Ishaq
Suatu tindjauan sedjarah terhadap masa revolusi physik. 1967, 170 pp. [MA thesis IKIP Padang.] [14, 4872]

5219 Thaher, Ishaq and Alwir Darwis
Bahan kuliah abad Proklamasi sejarah Indonesia. Padang: IKIP, 1978, 32 pp.

5220 Thaib, Alizar
19 September dan angkatan pemuda Indonesia. Jakarta: Yayasan Padepokan Pancuran Mas Jakarta, 1993, 175 pp.

5221 Thaib, Maisir
'Agressi Belanda mempertjepat proses revolusi Indonesia', in: *Dari penjerangan ke penjerahan,* pp. 153-161. Bukittinggi: Djawatan Penerangan Sumatera Tengah, 1951.

5222 Thalib
'Gerilja', in: *Dari penjerangan ke penjerahan,* pp. 80-85. Bukittinggi: Djawatan Penerangan Sumatera Tengah, 1951.

5223 The Siauw Giap
Het Indonesische vraagstuk en de Britse pers (na de conferentie op de Hoge Veluwe). 1955, 105 pp. [MA thesis Universiteit van Amsterdam.]

5224 Tinangon, Rof
'Dari selatan ke utara Sulawesi', in: *Bunga rampai perjuangan dan pengorbanan I*, pp. 365-388. Jakarta: Markas Besar Legiun Veteran RI, 1982.

5225 Tirtayasa, I Gusti Bagus Meraku
Bergerilya bersama Ngurah Rai. Denpasar: Balai Pustaka, 1994, 12+219 pp.

5226 Tirtoprodjo, Susanto
Pelita-gerilja. Paris: n.n., 1958, 21 pp.

5227 Tirtoprodjo, Susanto
Sedjarah revolusi nasional Indonesia; Tahapan revolusi bersendjata, 1945-1950. Djakarta: Pembangunan, 1963, 75 pp. [Third edition 1966.]

5228 Tjokroaminoto, Harsono
Menegakkan benang basah. Djakarta: Bulan Bintang, 1951, 35 pp.

5229 Tjokroaminoto, Harsono
'Tekad menjadi bangsa merdeka', in: *Bunga rampai perjuangan dan pengorbanan II*, pp. 121-133. Jakarta: Markas Besar Legiun Veteran RI, 1983.

5230 Tjokrodiatmodjo, Sukanto
'Kesadaran ber-bangsa dan ber-negara', in: *Bunga rampai perjuangan dan pengorbanan II*, pp. 324-327. Jakarta: Markas Besar Legiun Veteran RI, 1983.

5231 Tjokropranolo
Panglima Besar TNI Jenderal Soedirman; Pemimpin pendobrak terakhir penjajahan di Indonesia; Kisah seorang pengawal. Editor Marzuki Arifin. Jakarta: Surya Persindo, 1992, 29+336 pp.

5232 Tjondronegoro, Purnawan
Merdeka tanahku, merdeka negeriku. Jakarta: Sinar Negara, 1980, 519 pp. [Fourth edition, Jakarta: Nugraha, 1981, 595 pp.]

5233 Tjondronegoro, Purnawan
Enam jam di Yogya. Jakarta: Aries Lima, 1982, 108 pp.

5234 Tjondronegoro, Purnawan
Pertempuran Ambarawa; Gerak siasat Panglima Besar Jenderal Sudirman. Jakarta: Nugraha, 1982, 111 pp.

5235 Tjondronegoro, Purnawan
Berkibarlah Sang Merah Putih. Jakarta: Wiratama, 1984, 92 pp.

5236 *Tjukilan perdjoangan 45*. Djakarta: Lembaga Pembina Djiwa 45, 1972, 60 pp.

5237 Tobing, F. Tagor L.
Partisipasi Tapanuli dalam perjuangan kemerdekaan Republik Indonesia. Jakarta, 1976, 36 pp. [42]

5238 Tobing, K.M.L.
Perjuangan politik bangsa Indonesia; Linggarjati. Jakarta: Gunung Agung, 1986, 230 pp.

5239 Tobing, K.M.L.
Perjuangan politik bangsa Indonesia; Renville. Jakarta: Gunung Agung, 1986, 211 pp.

5240 Tobing, K.M.L.
Perjuangan politik bangsa Indonesia; Persetujuan Roem-Royen dan KMB. Jakarta: Haji Masagung, 1987, 327 pp.

5241 Tobing, Tiurma
Pelaksanaan pemerintahan militer di SWK I/III lewat arsip-arsip yang ada, Juni 1948-Juli 1949. Paper SSN-V, Semarang, 1990, 19 pp.

5242 Toegiman, Noer
'Ibu pertiwi memanggil', in: *Cahaya dari medan laga; Hasil sayembara mengarang dalam rangka peringatan hari ulang tahun kemerdekaan RI yang ke 30,* pp. 173-190. Jakarta: Dewan Harian Nasional Angkatan 45/Aries Lima, 1976.

5243 Toenaro, Loetan Soetan
Pancaran perjuangan radio revolusi. Jakarta: Idayu, 1981, 121 pp.

5244 Toer, Pramoedya Ananta
'Dia jang menjerah', *Pudjangga Baru* 11 (1949-50):245-286.

5245 Toer, Pramoedya Ananta
Keluarga gerilya; Kisah keluarga manusia dalam tiga hari dan tiga malam. Third edition. Kuala Lumpur, 1977, 246 pp. [First edition 1950; Second edition, Bukittinggi: Nusantara, 1962, 244 pp.; Edisi baru, Kuala Lumpur: Antara, 1970, 246 pp.]

5246 Toer, Pramoedya Ananta
Perburuan; Sebuah tjeritera chajali. Djakarta: Balai Pustaka, 1950, 106 pp. [Second edition, Djakarta: Kem. P dan K, 1955, 204 pp.; Third edition, *Perburuan; Sebuah novel,* Jakarta: Hasta Mitra, 1994, 6+173 pp.]

5247 Toer, Pramoedya Ananta
Pertjikan revolusi. Djakarta: Gapura, 1950, 196 pp. [Second edition, Djakarta: Balai Pustaka, 1957, 182 pp.]

5248 Toer, Pramoedya Ananta
Subuh; Tjerita-tjerita pendek revolusi. Third edition. Djakarta: Pembangunan, 1954, 63 pp. [First edition 1950; Fourth edition, Djakarta: Nusantara, 1963, 83 pp.; Also published by Wah Lian, Kuala Lumpur, 1975, 78 pp.]

5249 Toer, Pramoedya Ananta
Ditepi kali Bekasi. Djakarta: Gapura, 1951, 207 pp. (part 1) [Second edition, Djakarta: Balai Pustaka, 1957, 339 pp.]

5250 Toer, Pramoedya Ananta
Mereka jang dilumpuhkan. Djakarta: Balai Pustaka, 1951, 286+295 pp. 2 vols.

5251 Toer, Pramoedya Ananta
'Wier weerstand werd gebroken', *Oriëntatie* no. 40 (1951):3-46.

5252 Toer, Pramoedya Ananta
Tjerita dari Blora. Djakarta: Balai Pustaka, 1952, 368 pp. [Second edition, Djakarta: Balai Pustaka, 1963, 411 pp.; Third edition, *Cerita dari Blora; Kumpulan cerita pendek,* Jakarta: Hasta Mitra, 1994, 13+322 pp.]

5253 Toer, Pramoedya Ananta
The fugitive. Hong Kong: Heinemann, 1975, 142 pp. [Also published by Avon Books, New York, 1991, 171 pp.]

5254 Toer [Tur], Pramoedya Ananta
'Perburuan 1950 and Keluarga gerilya 1950', *Indonesia* no. 36 (1983):24-48.

5255 Toer, Pramoedya Ananta
Spiel mit dem Leben; Roman. Reinbek bei Hamburg: Rowohlt, 1990, 203 pp.

5256 Toer, Pramoedya Ananta
Guerrillafamilie. Breda: De Geus, Amsterdam: Manus Amici, 1991, 311 pp.

5257 Toer, Pramoedya Ananta
De vluchteling. Breda: De Geus, Amsterdam: Manus Amici, 1991, 189 pp.

5258 Toer, Pramoedya Ananta
In de fuik. Breda: De Geus/Manus Amici, 1994, 585 pp.

5259 'Tokoh-tokoh Arab yang turut membantu perjuangan kemerdekaan Indonesia', *Mimbar Ulama* 1-9 (March-April 1977):36-42.

5260 Torar, Jan
Peranan Minahasa dalam perang kemerdekaan. Jakarta: Pelita Buana, 1985, 136 pp.

5261 Triadi B.K., Ganjar
'R.W. Mongisidi; Kesatria belia', in: *Untuk bangsaku II; Kumpulan cerpen perjuangan,* pp. 67-92. Semarang: Yayasan Telapak, 1983.

5262 Trihardjo
'Ilmu perang gerilya tidak diperoleh dibangku sekolah', in: *Bunga rampai perjuangan dan pengorbanan I,* pp. 711-729. Jakarta: Markas Besar Legiun Veteran RI, 1982.

5263 Trimurti, S.K.
'Peranan Ibu Tri sekitar Proklamasi', *Gema Angkatan 45* no. 20 (August 1977):22-24.

5264 Trisaksono, Poedhyarto
Merah Putih jiwaku, Merah Putih semangatku (RAHTIHKU); Derap perjuangan di meja perundingan. Solo: Tiga Serangkai, 1985, 96 pp.

5265 Trisnojuwono
Laki-laki dan mesiu; Kumpulan tjerita pendek. Djakarta: Pembangunan, 1957, 168 pp. [Second edition, 1962, 129 pp.; Third edition, Djakarta: Pustaka Jaya, 1971, 116 pp.]

5266 Trisnojuwono
Pagar kawat berduri; Kisah sebuah revolusi. Second edition. Djakarta: Sulindo, 1961, 175 pp. [First edition 1958; Third edition, Djakarta: Djambatan, 1963, 126 pp.]

5267 Trisnojuwono
Dimedan perang dan tjerita-tjerita lain. Bukittinggi/Djakarta: Nusantara, 1962, 127 pp.

5268   Trisnojuwono
       Sebuah kumpulan kisah-kisah revolusi. Bandung: Sapta, 1965, 97 pp.

5269   Trisnojuwono
       Peristiwa-peristiwa ibukota pendudukan. Djakarta: Balai Pustaka, 1970, 84 pp.

5270   Trisnojuwono
       Petualang. Jakarta: Sinar Harapan, 1981, 314 pp.

5271   Trissaputra, Marjoto
       Peranan Islam bagi berhasilnja Proklamasi 17 Agustus 1945. 1965. [MA thesis
       Universitas Padjadjaran, Bandung.] [1, 20]

5272   Trissaputra, Marjoto
       'Taktik gerilja ular membelit diwilajah MBKS ke-I', *Vidya Yudha* no. 7 (1969):85-
       91; no. 8 (1969):140-149.

5273   Trissaputra, Marjoto
       'Pangsar Sudirman pada hari pertama Agresi Belanda ke II', *Vidya Yudha* no. 10
       (1970):74-84.

5274   Trissaputra, Marjoto
       'Amanat Panglima Besar Sudirman kepada TNI', *Vidya Yudha* no. 13 (1971):93-
       100.

5275   Tryman Ms, Setiadi
       Bintang gerilja. Djakarta: Dasa Warga, ca. 1963, 71 pp. (kitlv-m)

5276   Tugiyono Ks and Eny Sukaeni
       *Sekali merdeka tetap merdeka; Biografi para pejuang bangsa periode revolusi
       bersenjata (1945-1950).* Jakarta: Baru, 1985, 331 pp.

5277   Tugiyono Ks; Sutrisno Kutoyo and Alex Pelatta
       Atlas dan lukisan sejarah nasional Indonesia. Vol. 2. Jakarta: Baru, 1985, 219 pp.

5278   Tujuhbelas Agustus; Kenangan-kenangan sejarah; Detik-detik Proklamasi
       kemerdekaan di Sumatera Barat. Bukittinggi: Dep. Penerangan, 1975, 19 pp.

5279   Twang Peck Yang
       Indonesian Chinese business communities in transformation, 1940-50. 1987, 308 pp.
       [PhD thesis Australian National University, Canberra.]

5280   Ugaja, Hajun
       Sedjarah pembentukan Akademi Militer dalam lingkungan Angkatan Darat.
       1971, 123 pp. [MA thesis IKIP Djakarta.] [11]

5281   *Undang-undang pokok tentang pemerintahan daerah (u.u. no. 22 th. 1948) dan
       undang-undang pemilihan anggauta Dewan Perwakilan Rakjat daerah Propinsi dan
       daerah-daerah dalam lingkungannja (u.u. no. 7 th. 1950).* Djakarta: Noordhoff-
       Kolff, 1951, 112 pp.

5282   *Ungkapan sejarah perjuangan pelajar Surabaya pada tahun 1945; Disampaikan
       dalam rangka peresmian prasasti lahirnya BKR-Pelajar Surabaya di Jalan Raya
       Darmo 49 Surabaya.* Surabaya: Sekretariat Darmo 49 Ex Be 17 Det I TRIP Jatim,
       1986, 27 pp.

5283 *Untuk bangsaku; Kumpulan cerpen perjuangan.* Semarang: Yayasan Telapak, 1983, 96+92 pp. 2 vols.

5284 Usman, Gazali
Pengaruh persetujuan Linggarjati terhadap perjuangan ALRI Divisi IV pertahanan Kalimantan; Periode revolusi fisik 1945-1949. Paper SSN-III, Jakarta, 1981, 31 pp.

5285 Usman, Gazali
'Pengaruh Persetujuan Linggarjati terhadap perjuangan ALRI Divisi IV pertahanan Kalilmantan', in: *Seksi Sejarah Mutakhir (1); Seminar Sejarah Nasional III*, pp. 17-41. Jakarta: Dep. P dan K, Direktorat Sejarah dan Nilai Tradisional, Proyek Inventarisasi dan Dokumentasi Sejarah Nasional, 1982.

5286 Usman, K.
Tabik tuan, eh, merdeka! Jakarta: Bunda Karya, 1984, 68 pp.

5287 Usodo, Poline Pudjiastuti
Tentara Republik Indonesia Pelajar (Jawa Timur). 1984, 105 pp. [MA thesis Universitas Indonesia, Jakarta.] [Histori]

5288 Wahid, Rusli
Pengaruh revolusi fisik terhadap rakyat Aceh. 1978. [Thesis Universitas Syiah Darussalam, Kutaraja.] [4854]

5289 Wahidy, Hasbi
'Mengenang kembali semangat dan tekat 17 Agustus '45', in: *Modal revolusi 45*, pp. 72-78. Kutaradja: Komite Musjawarah Angkatan 45 DI Atjeh, 1960.

5290 Wahyudi, Sigit
Pemogokan kaum buruh di Delanggu pada 1948. 1976, 50 pp. [Thesis Universitas Gadjah Mada, Yogyakarta.]

5291 Wahyudi, Sigit
Peranan SARBUPRI dalam pemogokan kaum buruh di Delanggu pada 1948. 1981, 154 pp. [MA thesis Universitas Gadjah Mada, Yogyakarta.]

5292 Wardhana, F.M.A.
Prahara di Malang Selatan. Semarang: Yayasan Telapak, 1983, 48 pp.

5293 *Wawasan kejuangan Panglima Besar Jenderal Sudirman.* Disiapkan oleh Pusat Pembinaan Mental ABRI. Jakarta: Yayasan Kejuangan Panglima Besar Sudirman, 1992, 10+277 pp.

5294 Wibisono, A. Soni
Serangan akhir tahun; Novel revolusi. Bandung: Rosda, 1985, 95 pp.

5295 Wibisono, Christianto
'Perang kemerdekaan sebagai sumber inspirasi bagi generasi pembangunan Indonesia', in: *Aku akan teruskan; Hasil sayembara mengarang dalam rangka peringatan hari ulang tahun kemerdekaan R.I. yang ke 30*, pp. 18-41. Jakarta: Dewan Harian Nasional Angkatan 45, Pusat Dokumentasi Sejarah Perjoangan 45/Aries Lima, 1976.

5296 Wida, Rani
Untuk Merah-Putih. Jogjakarta: Jaker, 1965, 104 pp.

5297 Widayat, A.
Letikan api perang. Bandung: Rosda, 1985, 155 pp.

5298 Widiatuti, Wiwik
Perkembangan TRIP di Jawa Timur dan masalah yang dihadapinya. 1983. [MA thesis Universitas Gadjah Mada, Yogyakarta.] [Histori]

5299 Widjaya, Roebaie
Merdeka; Tjerita rakjat. Djakarta: Djajamurni, 1962, 84 pp.

5300 Wiharjanto
Latar belakang dan akibat-akibat perjanjian Linggarjati. 1972, 63 pp. [MA thesis IKIP Yogyakarta.] [17]

5301 Wiraatmadja, Soetantya
Palagan empat hari di Sala. Jakarta: Balai Pustaka, 1983, 64 pp.

5302 Wirata, I Ketut
Revolusi phisik daerah kabupaten Buleleng. 1972. [MA thesis Universitas Udayana, Denpasar.] [6333]

5303 Wiwoho, B.
Pasukan meriam Nukum Sanany; Sebuah pasak dari rumah gadang Indonesia merdeka sebagaimana diceritakan kepada penulis B. Wiwoho. Jakarta: Bulan Bintang, 1985, 317+60 pp.

5304 Wongsodirdjo, Moersahid
'17 Agustus dan Kementerian Luar Negeri', in: Darius Marpaung (ed.), *Bingkisan nasional; Kenangan 10 tahun revolusi Indonesia, 17-8-1945/17-8-1955,* pp. 218-234. Djakarta: Usaha Pegawai Nasional Indonesia, 1955.

5305 Wongsonegoro
'Mendjelang saat-saat Proklamasi 17 Agustus di Semarang', *Penelitian Sedjarah* 4-7 (1963):38-39.

5306 Wowor, Ben
Sulawesi Utara bergolak; Peristiwa patriotik 14 Februari 1946 dalam rangka revolusi bangsa Indonesia. Jakarta: Alda, 1977, 96 pp. [Second edition, *Sulawesi Utara bergolak; Peristiwa patriotik Merah-Putih 14 Pebruari 1946 dalam rangka revolusi bangsa Indonesia,* Jakarta: Alda, 1985, 168 pp.]

5307 Wowor, B.
'Peristiwa patriotik 14 Februari 1946 di Sulawesi Utara', *Gema Angkatan 45* no. 26 (February 1978):29-36.

5308 'The writing of the Proclamation; An interview with three participants', in: C. Wild and P. Carey (eds), *Born in fire; The Indonesian struggle for independence; An anthology,* pp. 92-97. Athens: Ohio University Press, 1986.

5309 Wuridal, Bambang
Hubungan Serangan Umum 1 Maret 1949 dengan perjuangan diplomasi. 1974, 96 pp. [MA thesis IKIP Jakarta.] [11]

5310 Wuryani, Emy
Peranan Pasukan Hantu Maut pada Klas II di kota Yogyakarta. 1983. [MA thesis Universitas Gadjah Mada, Yogyakarta.] [Histori]

5311 Xarim, Misbach
'Sekelumit peristiwa permulaan revolusi Agustus 1945 di Bandung', *Penelitian Sedjarah* 1-1 (1960):26-28.

5312 Yadav, Jai Singh
Kobaran semangat pemuda dalam untaian kata (pada masa perjuangan bangsa). Paper Seminar Sejarah Peranan Generasi Muda dalam Perjuangan Bangsa, Yogyakarta, 1989, 14 pp.

5313 Yadav, Jai Singh
Nehru dan Indonesia; Simpati seorang sahabat. Yogyakarta: Universitas Gadjah Mada, 1989, 27 pp.

5314 Yakub, Dt. B. Nurdin
'Dekapan mesra dari ibumu', in: *Cahaya dari medan laga; Hasil sayembara mengarang dalam rangka peringatan hari ulang tahun kemerdekaan RI yang ke 30,* pp. 215-238. Jakarta: Dewan Harian Nasional Angkatan 45/Aries Lima, 1976.

5315 Yamin, Muhammad
Proklamasi dan konstitusi Republik Indonesia. Djakarta/Amsterdam: Djambatan, 1951, 13+242 pp.

5316 Yamin, Muhammad
Pembentukan dan pembubaran Uni; Berisi sedjarah pembentukan dan pembubaran Uni Indonesia-Belanda serta naskah statut-Uni jang telah dihapuskan, bersama protokol pembubaran Uni dan pertukaran-surat dengan pendjelasan. Djakarta: Bulan-Bintang, 1955, 64 pp.

5317 Yamin, Muhammad
Sistema-falsafah Pantja-Sila; Pidato. Djakarta: Kem. Penerangan, 1958, 40 pp.

5318 Yamin, Muhammad
Naskah-persiapan Undang-Undang Dasar 1945; Disiarkan dengan dibubuhi tjatatan. Djakarta: Jajasan Prapantja, 1959-60. 815+848+957 pp. 3 vols. (kitlv-m)

5319 Yamin, Muhammad
Pembahasan Undang-Undang Dasar Republik Indonesia. Djakarta: Jajasan Prapantja, 1960, 593 pp. (kitlv-m)

5320 Yamin, Muhammad
Tan Malaka; Bapak Republik Indonesia. Jakarta: Yayasan Massa, 1981, 42 pp.

5321 Yasin, Mohamad
'Keputusan 9 Nopember 1945 suatu desisi yang menentukan heroisme', *Gema Angkatan 45* nr. 23 (November 1977):25-26.

5322 Yauw, Syamsoeddin
Khususnya untuk pejuang-pejuang 45; Jilid 1. Bengkulu: Dewan Harian Daerah Angkatan 45 Propinsi Bengkulu, 1982, 162 pp.

5323 Yoga (ps. Sajogia Hardjadinata)
Surabaja berdjuang. Second edition. Surabaja: Fadjar, 1958. [6186]

5324 *Yogya benteng Proklamasi; Sejarah perjuangan.* Jakarta: Badan Musyawarah Musea DI Yogyakarta, 1985, 354 pp.

5325 Yudiastuti, Safrida Dewi
Kelaskaran di Surabaya pada awal revolusi tahun 1945-1947. 1981. [MA thesis Universitas Gadjah Mada, Yogyakarta]. [Histori]

5326 Yudiono K.S.
Revolusi kemerdekaan dalam sastra Jawa dan Indonesia. Paper Diskusi Sejarah Lokal IV, Revolusi Kemerdekaan di Tingkat Lokal, Bandungan-Ambarawa, 1994, 22 pp.

5327 Yudosentono, Sudi Suyono
'Lahirnya Hari Pahlawan 10 Nopember 1945 dan kota pahlawan Surabaya; Kegiatan-kegiatan pada hari-hari pertama sesudah Proklamasi', in: *Cahaya dari medan laga; Hasil sayembara mengarang dalam rangka peringatan hari ulang tahun kemerdekaan RI yang ke 30*, pp. 19-47. Jakarta: Dewan Harian Nasional Angkatan 45/Aries Lima, 1976.

5328 Yunus, K.
Indonesian independence; Developments and sequel. 1954. [PhD thesis American University, Washington.] [97, 106]

5329 Yusuf, Musytari
Jatuhnya benteng Batuputih. Jakarta: Pustaka Jaya, 1979, 136 pp.

5330 Yusuf, M. Nurdin
M. Nurdin Yusuf dalam perjuangan menaikkan Merah Putih di Bengkalis; Otobiografi. Bengkalis, 1977. [4867]

5331 Yuwono, Prapto
Ubel-ubel sebagai realitas sejarah dalam novel 'Jalan tak ada ujung' karya Mochtar Lubis. Paper Diskusi Sejarah Lokal IV, Revolusi Kemerdekaan di Tingkat Lokal, Bandungan-Ambarawa, 1994, 16 pp.

5332 Yuwono, Sutopo
'Serangan Umum 1 Maret 1949', in: *Museum dan sejarah*, pp. 63-72. Jakarta: Dep. P dan K, 1993/1994.

5333 Zainuddin
Gerakan Islam di Aceh dan pengaruhnya dalam revolusi kemerdekaan Indonesia 1945-1949. 1986. [MA thesis IKIP Jakarta.] [Histori]

5334 Zainuddin, Emasdia
KGSS atau Kesatuan Gerilya Sulawesi Selatan pada tahun 1945-1950 di Sulawesi Selatan. Ca. 1980. [MA thesis Universitas Hasanuddin, Ujung Pandang.] [4334]

5335 Zakaria, Iskandar
'Kerinci dalam perjuangan pisik 1945-1949', in: *Aku akan teruskan; Hasil sayembara mengarang dalam rangka peringatan hari ulang tahun kemerdekaan R.I. yang ke 30*, pp. 216-239. Jakarta: Dewan Harian Nasional Angkatan 45, Pusat Dokumentasi Sejarah Perjoangan 45/Aries Lima, 1976.

5336 Zed, Mestika
Ekonomi Indonesia zaman revolusi; Kasus Palembang 1945-1950. Paper Diskusi Sejarah Lokal IV, Revolusi Kemerdekaan di Tingkat Lokal, Bandungan-Ambarawa, 1994, 13 pp.

5337 Zein, H.M.
'Lintasan sekelumit turut serta dalam perjuangan mempertahankan Proklamasi', in: *Bunga rampai perjuangan dan pengorbanan I*, pp. 755-765. Jakarta: Markas Besar Legiun Veteran RI, 1982.

5338 Zuhdi
'Pertempuran di kota Tembilahan', *Majalah Canang* no. 6 (June 1978):38-39, etc.

5339 Zuhdi
'Sedjarah perjuangan bersenjata di Riau', *Majalah Canang* no. 10 (Oct.1978):3-4, etc.

5340 Zuhdi, Susanto
The Linggarjati agreement as seen by some local newspapers in Java. Paper Linggarjati Conference, 1991, 14 pp.

5341 Zuhdi, Susanto
'Perjanjian Linggarjati dilihat oleh beberapa surat kabar lokal di Jawa', in: A.B. Lapian and P.J. Drooglever (eds), *Menelusuri jalur Linggarjati; Diplomasi dalam perspektif sejarah*, pp. 135-150. Jakarta: Grafiti, 1992.

5342 Zuhdi, Susanto
Pemerintah gerilya Sewaka dan negara Pasundan Suriakartalegawa; Suatu dinamika politik di daerah pendudukan Belanda di Jawa Barat. Paper Diskusi Sejarah Lokal IV, Revolusi Kemerdekaan di Tingkat Lokal, Bandungan-Ambarawa, 1994, 17 pp.

5343 Zulfadillah
Hubungan Aksi Belanda II dengan timbulnya peristiwa Situjuh di Sumatera Barat 1949. 1987. [MA thesis IKIP Jakarta.] [Histori]

Revolutionary period
Later Dutch writings

5344 *2e Genie Park Cie te Bandoeng-Batavia-Semarang-Purwokerto-Tegal-Djocja-Solo en Magelang, 1947-1950.* N.p.: 2e Genie Park Compagnie, 1950, 72 pp.

5345 *2e Genie Park Cie te Bandoeng-Batavia-Semarang-Purwokerto-Tegal-Djocja-Solo en Magelang, 1950-1990; Speciale editie t.g.v. de reünie.* Utrecht: n.n., 1990. [unpaged]

5346 *4-2 RI; Een bataljon op Noord-Sumatra 1947-1948-1949.* N.p.: n.n., 1992, 28 pp.

5347 *5e Esk. VEW. - 1e Esk. PAW. 1947-1950.* Nijkerk: Callenbach, 1950, 143 pp. (kitlv-smg)

5348 *5-11 RI, 1947-1950.* N.p.: n.n., 1975, 48 pp. (smg)

5349 *42 AAT in Indonesië; De 42e Cie Aan- en Afvoertroepen overzee.* [114, 1216]

5350 *402 Bataljon Infanterie.* Maastricht: Goffin, ca. 1950, 245 pp.

5351 *Vijf jaren beleid met betrekking tot de overzeese gebiedsdelen; De Indonesische kwestie en de staatkundige ontwikkeling in de West (1945-1950).* 's-Gravenhage: Ministerie van Uniezaken en Overzeese Gebiedsdelen, 1951, 121 pp.

5352 *Vijf-zes; Hoe het reilde en zeilde.* Echt. [114, 1216]

5353 Abma, H.
'Doodstraf Nederlands-Indië', *VU Magazine* 20-8(1991):23-28. (ubl)

5354 Acksen, W.H.
De belevenissen van een reserve-officier in vrede en oorlog; Hoe de militaire dienstplicht mijn burgerleven heeft beïnvloed. De Bilt: Acksen, 1988, 126 pp.

5355 *Ada goela, ada semoet; De 3e Geneeskundige Afdeling in Eibergen en 6e Hulp Verbandplaats Afdeling op Sumatra.* Drachten: Commissie Oud-Leden 6e Hulp Verbandplaats Afdeling, 1988, 192 pp.

5356 Alberts, A.
Namen noemen; Zo maar wat ongewone en openhartige herinneringen aan het leven in het verloren paradijs dan Nederlandsch-Indië heette, 1939-1947. Amsterdam: Paris, 1962, 190 pp.

5357 Alberts, A.
Het einde van een verhouding; Indonesië en Nederland tussen 1945 en 1963. Alphen aan den Rijn: Samsom, 1968, 142 pp.

5358 Alberts, A.
In en uit het paradijs getild. Amsterdam: Paris, 1979, 193 pp.

5359 Alers, H.J.H.
Om een rode of groene merdeka; Tien jaren binnenlandse politiek Indonesië 1943-1953. Eindhoven: Vulkaan, 1956, 299 pp.

5360 *Artillerievuur in de tropen; Het boek met zijn herinneringen aan het 8e Regiment Veldartillerie, ingedeeld bij de 3e Infanterie Brigade Groep C Divisie '7 December'.* 's-Gravenhage: Van Hoeve, 1950, 216 pp.

5361 Asbeck, F.M. van
'The birth and decline of the Netherlands-Indonesian Union', *The Yearbook of World Affairs* 7, pp. 204-227. London: Stevens and Sons, 1953. (ubl)

5362 August, David B. and Hans P. van Weeren
Catalogue revolutionary paper money of Indonesia. Leidschendam: n.n., 1983. [unpaged]

5363 Averink, Annie
'De anti-imperialistische strijd van de CPN, II, De geboortedag van de Republiek Indonesië', *Politiek en Cultuur* 24 (1964):1-10. (ubl)

5364 *Awas, Pijp-Pijp datang! Gedenkboek geschreven door en voor de manschappen van 5-5 RI.* N.p.: n.n., 1950, 256 pp.

5365 Baal, J. van
'Uit de nadagen van het Nederlands bestuur over Bali en Lombok', *Bijdragen tot de Taal-, Land- en Volkenkunde* 138 (1982):211-230.

5366 Baardewijk, Frans van
De Indonesische kwestie en de PvdA. 1975, 99+9 pp. [MA thesis Rijksuniversiteit Utrecht.]

5367 Baardewijk, Frans van
'De PvdA van het Koninkrijk 1945-1947', in: *Tweede Jaarboek voor het Democratisch Socialisme*, pp. 164-212. Amsterdam: Arbeiderspers, 1980.

5368 Baardewijk, Frans van; Ria Bargeman; Henk Hendrix and Harrie Verheijen
'Nederland en de Indonesische kwestie onder het kabinet Schermerhorn-Drees', *Kleio* 18 (1977):117-150.

5369 Baljé, Chr.L.
'Dekolonisatie in documenten; Een recensieartikel', *Bijdragen en Mededelingen betreffende de Geschiedenis der Nederlanden* 92 (1977):462-473.

5370 Bals, Kees and Martin Gerritsen
De Indië-weigeraars. Met een voorwoord van Poncke Princen. Amsterdam: Materiaalfonds Vereniging Dienstweigeraars, 1989, 120 pp. [Third edition, Amsterdam: Antimilitaristische Uitgeverij, 1993, 128 pp.]

5371 Bank, J.
'De PvdA en de Indonesische revolutie', *Socialisme en Democratie* 38 (1981):585-593.

5372   Bank, J.Th.M.
'Rubber, religie, rijk; De koloniale trilogie in de Indonesische kwestie 1945-1949',
Bijdragen en Mededelingen betreffende de Geschiedenis der Nederlanden 96
(1981):230-259.

5373   Bank, J.
'Historiography on the revolution; The Western approach', in: *Papers of the
Dutch-Indonesian Historical Conference*, pp. 17-35. Leiden/Jakarta: Bureau of
Indonesian Studies, 1982.

5374   Bank, Jan
Katholieken en de Indonesische revolutie. Baarn: Ambo, 1983, 576 pp. [Also PhD
thesis Universiteit van Amsterdam.]

5375   Bank, Jan
'Indonesië 1948; Na de diplomatie de binnenlandse politiek', *De Gids* 147-1/2
(1984):37-41.

5376   Bank, Jan
'Lijphart malgré lui; The politics of accomodation in the Indonesian question',
Acta Politica 19-1 (1984):73-83. (ubl)

5377   Bank, J.
'Exercities in vergelijkende dekolonisatie; Indonesië in Zuidoost-Azië,
Nederland in West-Europa', *Bijdragen tot de Taal-, Land- en Volkenkunde* 141
(1985):19-36.

5378   Bank, J.Th.M.
'Drees en de Indonesische revolutie', in: H. Daalder en N. Cramer (eds), *Willem
Drees*, pp. 109-136. Houten: De Haan, 1988.

5379   Bargeman, Ria
De Indonesische kwestie en de PvdV/VVD. 1976, 88+14 pp. [MA thesis
Rijksuniversiteit Utrecht.]

5380   Bastiaans, W.Ch.J.
*Indonesia merdeka; Een selectie van mijn reeds eerder verschenen publicaties over het
Indonesië van Soekarno, waaraan zijn toegevoegd reportages van minder bekende
gebeurtenissen en ontmoetingen, die de soevereiniteitsoverdracht zijn voorafgegaan.*
Groningen: Bastiaans, 1969, 164 pp.

5381   Bastiaans, W.Ch.J.
Leven op de brug. Groningen: Van der Kamp, 1970, 183 pp.

5382   Bastings, P.C.; J.G.P. Partouns and L.H.M. Vries
De Nederlandse Militaire Missie in Indonesië, 1950-1954; Organisatie, taak en
functioneren van een randverschijnsel in de Nederlands-Indonesische
betrekkingen. 1988, 142 pp. [MA thesis Rijksuniversiteit Utrecht.]

5383   *Bataljonsgedenkboek 421e Bataljon Garde Regiment Jagers.* Rotterdam: Rouwe, ca.
1950, 242 pp.

5384   Baudet, H.
'Netherland's retreat from Empire', *Internationale Spectator* 21 (1967):1029-1064.

5385 Baudet, H.
'The Dutch retreat from Empire', in: J.S. Bromley and E.H. Kossmann (eds), *Britain and the Netherlands in Europe and Asia*, pp. 207-233. London: Macmillan/St Martin's Press, 1968.

5386 Baudet, H.
'Einde Nederlands wereldrijk', *Spiegel Historiael* 4 (1969):94-102.

5387 Baudet, H.
'The Netherlands after the loss of Empire', *Journal of Contemporary History* 4-1 (January 1969):127-139. (ubl)

5388 Baudet, H.
'Het dagboek van Schermerhorn', *Tijdschrift voor Geschiedenis* 85 (1972):56-63.

5389 Baudet, H.
'Nederland en de rang van Denemarken', *Bijdragen en Mededelingen betreffende de Geschiedenis der Nederlanden* 90 (1975):430-443.

5390 Baudet, H.
'Nederland en Indonesië; Overwegingen bij een recente bronnenpublikatie', *Tijdschrift voor Geschiedenis* 89 (1976):70-75.

5391 Baudet, H.
'Nederland's terugtocht uit Indië; In het perspectief van 1950, in het omzien der jaren '60 en in de terugblik van 1980', in: *Oud-bestuursambtenaren in voormalig Ned. Indië en dekolonisatie*, pp. 30-38. Leiden: Indologenblad, 1980.

5392 Baudet, H.
Some reflections on Art. 14 of the Linggarjati agreement. Paper Linggarjati Conference, 1991, 18 pp.

5393 Baudet, H.
'Aneka renungan terhadap Pasal 14 perjanjian Linggarjati', in: A.B. Lapian and P.J. Drooglever (eds), *Menelusuri jalur Linggarjati; Diplomasi dalam perspektif sejarah*, pp. 121-134. Jakarta: Grafiti, 1992.

5394 Baudet, H. and R.C. Carrière
'Het Nederlandse bedrijfsleven in Nederlands-Indië/Indonesië 1945-1958', *Oost-West* 9 (1970):65-70. (ubl)

5395 Baudet, H. and M. Fennema
Het Nederlands belang bij Indië. Utrecht: Het Spectrum, 1983, 255 pp.

5396 Baudoin, Bruce
De PvdA en de Nederlands-Indonesische betrekkingen (1946-1958); Het beleid van de PvdA, in het bijzonder inzake de Nederlands-Indonesische Unie en de Nieuw-Guinea kwestie, op regerings- en partijniveau doorgelicht. 1988, 152 pp. [MA thesis Universiteit van Amsterdam.] (uba)

5397 Bazen, David; Emiel Schäfer and Henk Wals
'Een onbatig slot; Het belang van de economische factor in de dekolonisatie van Nederlands-Indië', *Skript* 9 (1987):183-192.

5398 Beek, Sjors van
Nederland en India, 1946-1960; Een onderzoek naar de betrekkingen tussen
Nederland en India ten tijde van de Indonesische kwestie en gedurende de
vijftiger jaren. 1988, 105 pp. [MA thesis Katholieke Universiteit Nijmegen.]

5399 *Een beknopt overzicht van de geschiedenis van 4-2 RI.* N.p.: n.n., n.y., 13+6 pp.

5400 *Belevenissen van 5-9 RI in Indië.* Ca. 1950. [114, 1216]

5401 Bentschap Knook, Frans
Het vergeten leger; Onze belevenissen in de jungle van Zuid-Sumatra 1947-1950.
Alphen aan den Rijn 1986, 1990, 183+176 pp. 2 vols.

5402 Berends, P.F.
*Tahoen-tahoen jang soedah loepa; De vergeten jaren; Twentse jongens in Nederlands
Oostindië en Nieuw-Guinea, 1942-1962.* Haaksbergen: Hassink, 1993, 239 pp.

5403 Berg, C.C.
'Nederland en Indonesië; Culturele betrekkingen', *De Gids* 115-2 (1952):83-90.

5404 Berg, J. van den (ed.)
*De keerzijde van de medaille; 1945-1950; Verhalen van Nederlandse en Indonesische
auteurs.* 's-Gravenhage: Leopold, 1982, 255 pp.

5405 Berg, Joop van den
'Kemerdekaan 100%; Honderd procent vrijheid...', *Indische Letteren* 3-1 (March
1988):55-71.

5406 Berg, Joop van den
De wajangfoxtrot. 's-Gravenhage: BZZTôH, 1992, 144 pp.

5407 Berg, Joop van den (ed.)
Bersiap; Nederlands-Indonesische verhalen. 's-Gravenhage: BZZTôH, 1993, 159 pp.

5408 Berg, René van den
'Communistenangst in Batavia; Het Nederlandse beleid, 1945-1949', *Skript* 8-1
(1986):64-75.

5409 Bergh, C.
Logemann en de revolutie in Indië. 1989, 65 pp. [MA thesis Rijksuniversiteit
Leiden.] [Lijst Leiden]

5410 Bessels, G.J.
*Catalogus van de postzegels uitgegeven door het rebellerende regime van de Republiek
Indonesië, 17 augustus 1945/27 december 1949.* Third edition. Ouderkerk aan de
Amstel: Dai Nippon, 1981, 218 pp. [First edition 1963.]

5411 Bessels, G.J.
*Timor en Soemba; Lokale opdrukken aangebracht door de Netherlands Indies Civil
Administration (NICA) 1945.* Hilversum: Dai Nippon, 1983, 36 pp.

5412 Beus, J.G. de
*Morgen, bij het aanbreken van de dag; Nederland driemaal aan de vooravond van
oorlog.* Rotterdam: Donker, 1977, 424 pp.

5413 Beus, J.G. de
Het laatste jaar van Nederlands-Indië; Van de zwaardhouw der Tweede Politionele Actie tot de handtekening onder de soevereiniteitsoverdracht. Rotterdam: Donker, 1987, 175 pp.

5414 Biemans, Ardy W.J. and Regina C.M. Kleingeld
Nederlandse ondernemers in Indonesië, 1945-1957/58. 1985, 131 pp. [MA thesis Rijksuniversiteit Leiden.]

5415 Biemans, A.W.J. and R.C.M. Kleingeld
'Rubber- en tabaksplantages op Sumatra 1945-1957/58', *Leidschrift* no. 6 (1986):24-33.

5416 Binsbergen, J. van
3-41 RVA in de tropen. N.p.: n.n., 1951, 144 pp. (kitlv-smg)

5417 Blauw, Seerp de
'Enige opmerkingen over "Renville" als keerpunt in de Nederlands-Indonesische betrekkingen', *Jambatan* 1-1 (1981):27-30.

5418 Blauw, Seerp de
'De Vereniging Nederland-Indonesië', *Jambatan* 2-1 (1983-84):11-14.

5419 Blauw, Seerp de and Lodewijk Severein
De Vereniging Nederland-Indonesië; Vooruitstrevend Nederland; Dekolonisatie-opvattingen en de houding in het konflikt met Indonesië. 1980, 168 pp. [MA thesis Universiteit van Amsterdam.]

5420 Blokker, J.
'Herinneringen Ketjil', *Moesson* 22 (1977-78) - 30 (1985-86).

5421 Blijleven, C.
'Gepantserde jeeps', *Mars et Historia* no. 21 (1987):108-112. (kb)

5422 Böhm, A.H.
West-Borneo 1940 - Kalimantan Barat 1950. Tilburg: Gianotten, 1986, 150 pp.

5423 Böhtlingk, F.R.
'De nieuwe eenheidsstaat', *Indonesië* 4 (1950-51):106-118.

5424 Böhtlingk, F.R.
Staatsrecht in Indonesië (1942-1951); Samengesteld uit materiaal van het Documen-tatiecentrum voor Overzees Recht te Leiden. Leiden: Dubbeldeman, 1951, 25 pp.

5425 Böhtlingk, F.R.
'De verhouding tussen regering en volksvertegenwoordiging in Indonesië sedert 1945 en in de toekomst', *Indonesië* 7 (1953-54):62-79.

5426 Boer, P.G.J. de
De Indonesische kwestie en de wereld; Een tragedie van verkeerd begrip. Schiedam: Roelants, 1953, 16 pp.

5427 Boer-van Meurs, Louise A. de
De totstandkoming en het functioneren van de Negara Pasoendan, 1947-1950; Collaboratie, coöperatie en verzet. 1984, 122 pp. [MA thesis Rijksuniversiteit Utrecht.]

5428   Boerhout, Richard and Sonja Lindhout
       De Netherlands Eastern Forces Intelligence Service en het Koninklijk Nederlands
       Indisch Leger ten tijde van de dekolonisatie van Indonesië. 1982, 136 pp. [MA
       thesis Universiteit van Amsterdam.]

5429   Bogaarts, A.C.H.
       De Indonesische kwestie. Ca. 1980, 77 pp. [Thesis Koninklijke Militaire Aca-
       demie, Breda.] (kitlv-smg)

5430   Bogaarts, M.D.
       'Lieftinck en de druk op de Indische ketel 1946-1947', in: *Politieke opstellen* 10
       (1990):57-83. Nijmegen: Centrum voor Parlementaire Geschiedenis der Katho-
       lieke Universiteit. (ubl)

5431   Boomsma, Graa
       De idioot van de geschiedenis. Haarlem: In de Knipscheer, 1986, 148 pp.

5432   Boomsma, Graa
       De laatste tyfoon. Amsterdam: Prometheus, 1992, 183 pp.

5433   Boomsma, J.
       Soldaat overzee; Indonesië zoals wij dat zagen; Een fotoboek. Middelharnis:
       Flakkeesche Drukkerij Boomsma, 1950, 194 pp.

5434   Bootsma, N.A.
       De ontdekking van Indonesië; Aspecten van de westerse niet-Nederlandse
       geschiedschrijving over de dekolonisatie. Paper Congres Los van Nederland;
       Dekolonisatie van Indonesië en Suriname, 's-Gravenhage, 1993. [program]

5435   Booy, A. de
       'Herinneringen aan de reis van Hr.Ms. "Karel Doorman" naar Nederlands Oost-
       Indië (1946-47)', *Marineblad* 82 (1972):357-376, 513-528. (ubl)

5436   Bos, Jone
       Tien jaar democratisch-socialisme in de Republiek Indonesië (1945-1955). 1979,
       103 pp. [MA thesis Vrije Universiteit, Amsterdam.]

5437   Bosch, Rob
       'De AR-visie op de Indonesische revolutie', *Antirevolutionaire Staatkunde* 49
       (1979):380-384.

5438   Bosdriesz, Jan and Gerard Soeteman
       Ons Indië voor de Indonesiërs; De oorlog - de chaos - de vrijheid. 's-Gravenhage:
       Moesson, Franeker: Wever, 1985, 138 pp.

5439   Bosscher, D.F.J.
       De Anti-Revolutionaire Partij en de Indonesische revolutie, 1945-1949. 1974.
       [MA thesis Rijksuniversiteit Groningen.] [45]

5440   Bosscher, D.F.J.
       'Niet de chaos maar de rechtsstaat; De Anti-Revolutionaire Partij en de Indo-
       nesische kwestie', *Fibula* 21-23 (1980):12-16. (kb)

5441   Bot, T.H.
       'Les nouvelles relations entre l'Europe et l'Asie; Les Pays-Bas et l'Indonésie',
       Politique Etrangère 15-4 (1950):395-418.

5442 Braak, Berend J. ter
De Indonesische kwestie in de pers. 1985, 110 pp. [MA thesis Rijksuniversiteit Utrecht.] (ubu)

5443 Brendgen, J.H.J.
Belevenissen van een KNIL-officier in de periode 1942-1950; Militaire ervaringen voor en bij politiële akties. Haarlem: Brendgen, ca. 1980, 148 pp.

5444 Brink, H. van den
'De militaire top in Nederlands-Indië na 1945', *Jambatan* 1-1 (1981):20-23; 1-2 (1981-83):53-60.

5445 Broek, Joop van den
Parels voor Nadra. Utrecht: Bruna, 1953, 239 pp. [Second edition, Utrecht/Antwerpen: Bruna, 1967, 189 pp.]

5446 Broeshart, A.C.
Een dagboek over de bersiaptijd in Soerabaja. Rijswijk: n.n., 1987, 49 pp.

5447 Broeshart, A.C.; L.W. Nagtegaal and H.G. Quik
Vrede, maar geen bevrijding; Gebeurtenissen op Midden-Java in de bersiaptijd. Leiden: LIDESCO/Rijksuniversiteit Leiden, Voorburg: Pelita, 1989, 64 pp.

5448 Brouwer, K.J.
Zending in een gistende wereld. Met medewerking van J.H. Bavinck. Amsterdam: Ruys, 1951, 136 pp.

5449 Brouwer, L.
'De marinestaf na 1945; Een organisatie in opbouw', in: Brouwer, L.; K.H.L. Gerretse; J.A.M.M. Janssen; G. Teitler and J.J.A. Wijn (eds), *Tussen vloot en politiek; Een eeuw marinestaf 1886-1986,* pp. 89-125. Amsterdam/Dieren: De Bataafsche Leeuw, 's-Gravenhage: Afdeling Maritieme Historie Marinestaf, 1986.

5450 Brouwers, J.A.
De Indonesiëpolitiek van minister van Buitenlandse Zaken Stikker, augustus-december 1948. 1989, 33 pp. [MA thesis Universiteit van Amsterdam.]

5451 Bruin, C.H.M. de
De proeftuin van Modjokerto. 1981, 128 pp. [MA thesis Rijksuniversiteit Utrecht.]

5452 Bruin, G.C.M. de
De oprichting, het functioneren en de opheffing van de Negara Soematera Timoer. Ca. 1985, 150 pp. [MA thesis Rijksuniversiteit Utrecht.]

5453 Bruin, R. de
'Wankel op vijf zuilen; Indonesië op weg naar een eigen identiteit', in: *Onze jaren 45-70,* pp. 1093-1096. Amsterdam, 1972.

5454 Brusse, Peter
'Net had hij zijn stuk geschreven, of een officier meldde dat 200 republikeinen aan de baleh-baleh waren geprikt; De verslaggever in de Oost en de politionele acties', in: Amerongen, M. van; Jan Blokker and Herman van Run (eds), *Luizen in de pels; 100 jaar journalistiek in Nederland,* pp. 42-47. Amsterdam: Uitgeverij Raamgracht, 1984.

5455   Bulem, Mayra
       Wees niet bang voor je eigen herinneringen; Jaren 1941-1949 Nederlands-Indië. Den
       Helder: Dinky Druk, 1981, 40 pp.

5456   Bunnik, Claartje
       De deelstaat Oost-Indonesië 1946-1949; Invoering van een democratische
       bestuursvorm in de aristocratische samenleving van Oost-Indonesië en van
       Zuid-Celebes in het bijzonder. 1981, 116 pp. [MA thesis Universiteit van
       Amsterdam.]

5457   Bunnik, C.
       'De deelstaat Oost-Indonesië 1946-1949', *Jambatan* 1-3 (1981-83):13-25.

5458   Busselaar, L.F.M.
       *Belevenissen van een Landstormsoldaat gedurende en na afloop van de Tweede
       Wereldoorlog.* Wateringen: n.n., 1955, 36 pp.

5459   Busselaar, Max
       Getuigenis van een wonderrijk leven. Zaandam: Busselaar, 1964, 86 pp.

5460   Bussemaker, H.Th.
       'Montclair; De herovering van Java in 1945', *Marineblad* 76 (1966):535-553. (ubl)

5461   Buurkes, Henk (ed.)
       We hebben het samen beleefd; 40 jaar 9e Afdeling Veldartillerie, 1946-1986.
       Dordrecht: Hijbeek, 1986, 136 pp. (kitlv-smg)

5462   Bijkerk, J.C.
       De laatste landvoogd; Van Mook en het einde van de Nederlandse invloed in Indië.
       Alphen aan den Rijn: Sijthoff, 1982, 295 pp.

5463   Cats, B.C.
       *LIB's in de tropen; Een overzicht van het verblijf van onze oorlogsvrijwilligers bij de
       Lichte Infanterie Bataljons in het voormalige Nederlands-Indië, 1945-49.* Maastricht:
       Departement van Defensie, 1961, 73 pp.

5464   Cats, B.C.
       Overzicht mouwemblemen Nederlands-Indië 1945-1950. Illustraties C. van Ekeris.
       Bussum: n.n., ca. 1965, 31 pp.

5465   Cats, B.C.
       'Beknopt overzicht der OVW-bataljons en hun emblemen', *Mars et Historia* 15-5
       (1981-82):29-36. (smg)

5466   Cats, B.C.
       'Militaire heraldiek in de tropen; De geschiedenis van de mouwemblemen 1945-
       1949 gedragen door KL en KNIL in het voormalige Nederlands-Indië', *Arma-
       mentaria* 16 (1981):182-195, 17 (1982):108-123. (lmd)

5467   Cats, B.C.
       'Parachutisten in voormalig Nederlands-Indië 1946-1950; Uniformen en
       onderscheidingstekens', *Armamentaria* 20 (1985):146-158. (lmd)

5468   Cats, B.C.
       'OVW; Een klasse apart!', *Armamentaria* 21 (1986):130-155. (lmd)

5469 Cats, B.C.
'OVW-bataljons naar de tropen, 1945-1946', *Ons Leger* 70-5 (1986):19-21; 70-6 (1986):15-17. (ubl)

5470 Cats, B.C.
'Dieren in Indië-emblemen 1945-1950', in: Fabri, H.F.; J. van den Berg and C. de Zeeuw (eds), *Mars et Historia 25 jaar*, pp. 47-54. N.p.: Nederlandse Vereniging ter Beoefening van de Militaire Historie, 1991. (kb)

5471 *Compiesboek; Enkele belevenissen uit de Indië-periode opgetekend door de jongens van 2-V-10 RI, 28 Januari 1948-15 Mei 1950*. N.p.: n.n., 1950, 273 pp.

5472 Cortenbach, A. Paul
Mickey achter prikkeldraad. Den Haag: Voorhoeve, 1955, 159 pp.

5473 Cramer, N.
'Stikker en de souvereiniteitsoverdracht', *Liberaal Réveil* 24-23 (1983):44-48. (ubl)

5474 Daalen, K.O.H. van
De terugkeer van het Nederlandse gezag in Batavia in 1945. 1986, 78 pp. [MA thesis Rijksuniversiteit Utrecht.] (kitlv-smg)

5475 Dankbaar, Ben
Dienstweigering en desertie tijdens de oorlog met Indonesië 1945-1950; Achtergrond van het dokument van Wil van Kempen. Amsterdam: Bond voor Dienstplichtigen, ca. 1975, 42 pp.

5476 Dankbaar, Ben
'Dienstweigering en desertie tijdens de oorlog met Indonesië 1945-1950; Achtergrond van het dokument van Wil van Kempen', in: *Jaarboek voor de geschiedenis van socialisme en arbeidersbeweging in Nederland 1977*, pp. 341-366. Nijmegen: SUN, 1977.

5477 Dankbaar, Ben
Soldatenverzet; Politionele akties Indië 48-49. Amsterdam: Bond voor Dienstplichtigen, 1979, 42 pp.

5478 *Dàt was 423; Leven en werken van het 423 Bataljon in Oost-Java*. Heiloo: Kinheim, 1951, 160 pp.

5479 Deelman, A.G.
Ali Bin Joesoep; Roman uit de nadagen van Nederlands-Indië. Franeker: Wever, ca. 1973, 362 pp.

5480 Delden, Mary C. van
'Bersiap in Bandoeng; Een onderzoek naar geweld in de periode van 17 augustus 1945-24 maart 1946', *Jambatan* 7-3 (1989):129-147.

5481 Delden, Mary C. van
Bersiap in Bandoeng; Een onderzoek naar geweld in de periode van 17 augustus 1945 tot 24 maart 1946. Kockengen: Van Delden, 1989, 218 pp.

5482 Derks, H.
'De Indonesische revolutie', in: H. Derks (ed.), *Kroniek van drie eeuwen revoluties*, pp. 296-302. Groningen: Wolters-Noordhoff, 1989.

5483 Derks, J. and J.W. Jennen (eds)
Hun geest heeft overwonnen; Gedenkboek van 5-11 RI met velerlei bijdragen en herinneringen. Tegelen: De Mercuur, 1950. [unpaged] (kitlv-smg)

5484 Deters, G.
Dagboek van een oorlogsvrijwilliger. Ede: Hardeman, 1994, 293 pp.

5485 Dingemans, Frans
Hamid II Alkadrie, sultan van Pontianak; Zijn rol tijdens de Indonesische revolutie 1945-1950. 1989, 94 pp. [MA thesis Rijksuniversiteit Utrecht.]

5486 *Djokjakarta; 1-15 RI.* Ca. 1950, 156 pp.

5487 Doeleman, Frans
De medische geschiedenis van een infanteriebataljon der Koninklijke Landmacht gedurende drie jaar actieve dienst op Java, 1946-1950. Assen: Van Gorcum, 1955, 235 pp. [Also PhD thesis Rijksuniversiteit Utrecht.]

5488 Dolk, Liesbeth
'Wat in De Gids zou kunnen staan, dat moeten wij niet opnemen; Over Rob Nieuwenhuys, Oriëntatie (1947-1954) en Indo-centrisme', *De Gids* 151 (1988): 840-858.

5489 Dommering, E.J.
'De Nederlandse publieke discussie en de politionele acties in Indonesië', *Nederlands Juristenblad* 69(1994):277-290.

5490 Doorn, C.L. van
'Les protestants hollandais', in: Marcel Merle (ed.), *Les églises chrétiennes et la décolonisation*, pp. 325-340. Paris: Armand Colin, 1967.

5491 Doorn, Iens van
Geluk is als een vogel; Roman uit de nadagen van Nederlandsch-Indië. Franeker: Wever, 1981, 271 pp.

5492 Doorn, Iens van
Dreiging onder de tropenzon; Roman uit de nadagen van Nederlandsch-Indië. Franeker: Wever, 1983, 200 pp.

5493 Doorn, J.A.A. van
'Justifying military action; The Dutch return to Indonesia 1945-1949', in: M. Janowitz and J.A.A. van Doorn (eds), *On military ideology*, pp. 75-95. Rotterdam: Rotterdam University Press, 1971.

5494 Doorn, J.A.A. van
'De Indonesische revolutie', in: J.A.A. van Doorn, *Met man en macht; Sociologische studies over maatschappelijke mobilisatie*, pp. 144-161. Meppel: Boom, 1973.

5495 Doorn, J.A.A. van
Orde-opstand-orde; Notities over Indonesië. Meppel: Boom, 1973, 98 pp.

5496 Doorn, J.A.A. van
'De verwerking van het einde van Indië', in: G. Teitler and J. Hoffenaar (eds), *De politionele acties; Afwikkeling en verwerking*, pp. 115-127. Amsterdam: De Bataafsche Leeuw, 1990.

5497 Doorn, J.A.A. van
The past is a strong present; The Dutch-Indonesian conflict and the persistence of the colonial pattern. Paper Linggarjati Conference, 1991, 31 pp.

5498 Doorn, J.A.A. van
'Kelampauan adalah kekinian yang kental; Konflik Belanda-Indonesia dan bertahannya pola kolonial', in: A.B. Lapian and P.J. Drooglever (eds), *Menelusuri jalur Linggarjati; Diplomasi dalam perspektif sejarah*, pp. 243-269. Jakarta: Grafiti, 1992.

5499 Doorn, J.A.A. van
Dekolonisatie in sociologisch perspectief. Paper Congres Los van Nederland; Dekolonisatie van Indonesië en Suriname, 's-Gravenhage, 1993. [program]

5500 Doorn, J.A.A. van and W.J. Hendrix
Ontsporing van geweld; Over het Nederlandsch/Indisch/Indonesisch conflict. Rotterdam: Universitaire Pers Rotterdam, 1970, 309 pp.

5501 Doorn, Jacques van and Willem Hendrix
'Revolution and the struggle for independence in the Sukabumi region of Java, 1945-1949; A preliminary analysis', in: Otto van den Muijzenberg, Pieter Streefland and Willem Wolters (eds), *Focus on the region in Asia*, pp. 231-254. Rotterdam: Erasmus University, 1982.

5502 Doorn, J.A.A. van and W.J. Hendrix
Het Nederlands-Indonesisch conflict; Ontsporing van geweld. Amsterdam/Dieren: De Bataafsche Leeuw, 1983, 363 pp. [Second edition of 5500.]

5503 Doorn, J.A.A. van and W.J. Hendrix
'De planters belegerd; De positie van de Europese planters tussen Nederlandse steun en Indonesisch verzet', in: G. Teitler and P.M.H. Groen (eds), *De politionele acties*, pp. 44-72. Amsterdam: De Bataafsche Leeuw, 1987.

5504 Doorn, Jacques van and Willem J. Hendrix
The process of decolonisation 1945-1975; The military experience in comparative perspective. Rotterdam: Erasmus University, 1987, 46 pp.

5505 Dootjes, F.J.J.
Deli-data 1938-1951. Amsterdam: De Bussy, 1952, 71+14 pp.

5506 Dorren, C.J.O.
Onze Mariniersbrigade (1945-1949); Een veelbewogen episode in de korpsgeschiedenis. 's-Gravenhage: Stok, 1955, 368 pp.

5507 Drees, W.
'Nogmaals de besprekingen op de Hoge Veluwe', *Internationale Spectator* 15 (1961):120-125.

5508 Drees, W.
'De houding van de Nederlandse regering ten aanzien van de Indonesische kwestie', *Groniek* 5 (1971-72):277-292.

5509 Driessen, A.M.A.J.
De gebeurtenissen op Sumatra's Westkust en de houding van het Nederlands bestuur ten aanzien daarvan in de periode oktober 1945-juli 1947. 1979, 126 pp. [MA thesis Katholieke Universiteit Nijmegen.]

5510 Driesum, Robert F. van
Federalisme versus centralisme tijdens het ontstaan van de Indonesische staat.
1982, 105 pp. [MA thesis Universiteit van Amsterdam.] (uba)

5511 Drooglever, P.J.
'The United States and the Dutch applecart during the Indonesian revolution',
in: R. Kroes (ed.), *Image and impact; American influences in the Netherlands since
1945*, pp. 33-47. Amsterdam: Amerika Instituut, 1981.

5512 Drooglever, P.J.
'Dekolonisatie van Oost- en West-Indië', in: *Algemene geschiedenis der Nederlanden*, vol.15, pp. 421-444. Bussum: Fibula-Van Dishoeck, 1982.

5513 Drooglever, P.J.
'Dekolonisatie van Oost- en West-Indië', in: *Overzee; Nederlandse koloniale
geschiedenis 1590-1975*, pp. 229-258. Haarlem: Fibula-Van Dishoeck, 1982.

5514 Drooglever, P.J.
'Nederlands-Indonesische betrekkingen 1945-1950', *Spiegel Historiael* 21
(1986):116-120.

5515 Drooglever, P.J.
'De post-Renvillebesprekingen', in: J. van Goor (ed.), *The Indonesian revolution;
Conference papers*, pp. 223-245. Utrecht: Rijksuniversiteit Utrecht, 1986.

5516 Drooglever, P.J.
'Mars in beweging; Denkbeelden over legerhervorming in het tijdvak van de
dekolonisatie', in: G. Teitler and P.M.H. Groen (eds), *De politionele acties*,
pp. 73-90. Amsterdam: De Bataafsche Leeuw, 1987.

5517 Drooglever, P.J.
'Uneasy encounters; Semarang, Ambarawa and Magelang during the first
months of the revolution', in: Alfian, T. Ibrahim; H.J. Koesoemanto; Dharmono
Hardjowidjono and Djoko Suryo (eds), *Dari babad dan hikayat sampai sejarah
kritis; Kumpulan karangan dipersembahkan kepada Prof. Dr. Sartono Kartodirdjo*,
pp. 34-64. Yogyakarta: Gadjah Mada University Press, 1987.

5518 Drooglever, P.J.
'From coordination to confrontation; The Netherlands and the United States of
America in the period between the two "police actions" in Indonesia', in: C.A.
van Minnen (ed.), *Decolonization of Indonesia; International perspectives*, pp. 39-
54. Middelburg: Roosevelt Study Center/Stichting V.O.C.-Publicaties Zeeland,
1988.

5519 Drooglever, P.J.
'Vreemd volk over de vloer; Interventies in de Indonesische archipel tussen 1941
en 1949', in: A.P. van Goudoever and J. Aalbers (eds), *Interventies in de internationale politiek*, pp. 197-213. Utrecht: Vakgroep Geschiedenis der Universiteit,
1990.

5520 Drooglever, P.J.
'De dekolonisatie en de Indische samenleving', in: P.J. Drooglever (ed.), *Indisch
intermezzo; Geschiedenis van de Nederlanders in Indonesië*, pp. 101-111.
Amsterdam: De Bataafsche Leeuw, 1991. [Second printing 1994.]

5521 Drooglever, P.J.
Diplomacy seen from different angles; Foreign relations as subject and object in Dutch-Indonesian negotiations 1945-1950. Paper Linggarjati Conference, 1991, 18 pp.

5522 Drooglever, P.J.
'Diplomasi dipandang dari berbagai sudut; Hubungan luar negeri sebagai subyek dan obyek dalam perundingan Belanda-Indonesia 1945-1950', in: A.B. Lapian and P.J. Drooglever (eds), *Menelusuri jalur Linggarjati; Diplomasi dalam perspektif sejarah*, pp. 179-205. Jakarta: Grafiti, 1992.

5523 Drooglever, P.J.
Coöperatoren in revolutietijd; De invloed van de met Nederland samenwerkende Indonesiërs op het verloop van het dekolonisatieproces in Indonesië. Paper Congres Los van Nederland; Dekolonisatie van Indonesië en Suriname, 's-Gravenhage, 1993. [program]

5524 Drooglever, P.J.
'De Indonesische kwestie tussen persbericht en egotrip', *Bijdragen en Mededelingen betreffende de Geschiedenis der Nederlanden* 109 (1994):1-16.

5525 Drooglever, P.J.
'Pangkal Pinang en de toekomst van de Nederlandse minderheid in Indonesië', in: Wim Willems and Leo Lucassen (eds), *Het onbekende vaderland; De repatriëring van Indische Nederlanders (1946-1964)*, pp. 45-57. 's-Gravenhage: SDU Uitgeverij Koninginnegracht, 1994.

5526 Dümpel, R.W.
Episode uit mijn leven. N.p.: n.n., ca. 1985, 64 pp.

5527 Dümpel, R.W.
Een blijvende herinnering. N.p.: n.n., ca. 1986, 74 pp.

5528 Duncan Elias, E.R.
'Voyage autour de ma chambre', in: *Bij het scheiden van de markt*, pp. 137-152. Amsterdam: Querido, 1965. [First published in 1950.]

5529 Dunk, H.W. von der
'Bevrijd Nederland en de Indonesische kwestie', *Groniek* no. 40 (1975):2-15, 19.

5530 Dussel, W.
Dat was jij, marinier! De geschiedenis van de Mariniersbrigade. Amsterdam: De Boer, 1950, 320 pp.

5531 Duvekot, M. and P.J.M. Laseroms
Nederlandsch-Indië onvoltooid verleden tijd; In hoeverre is het maatschappelijk klimaat of de directe sociale omgeving bepalend voor de verwerking van ervaringen, opgedaan tijdens de politionele acties in Nederlandsch-Indië? 1986, 135 pp. [Thesis Koninklijke Militaire Academie, Breda.] (kitlv-smg)

5532 Duzee, L.
De schorpioen; Naar de film van Ben Verbong. Amsterdam: Sijthoff, 1984, 138 pp.

5533 *Dwars door Zuid Sumatra; 16e Cie AAT.* Hengelo: Smit, ca. 1950, 88 pp.

5534 Dijk, C. van
'The Muslim contribution to the Indonesian revolution', in: J. van Goor (ed.), *The Indonesian revolution; Conference papers, Utrecht, 17-20 June, 1986*, pp. 147-161. Utrecht: Rijksuniversiteit Utrecht, 1986.

5535 Dijk, C. van
'Strijders op de weg van Allah; De moslims en de Indonesische onafhankelijkheid', in: J. Zwaan; C. van Dijk; Go Gien Tjwan and R.E.F. Vaillant, *Djojobojo, oorlog en bezetting in Nederlands-Indië, 1940-1946*, pp. 15-22. N.p.: n.n., 1986.

5536 Dijk, C. van
Islam, nationalism, and decolonization in Indonesia. Paper Colloque International 'Décolonisations Comparées', Aix-en-Provence, 1993, 19 pp.

5537 Dijk, Friso van and Arie Rijsdijk
Van oude wensen, nieuwe ideeën en de dingen die voorbij gaan; De geschiedenis van het Ministerie van Overzeese Gebiedsdelen na 1945 in historisch perspectief. 1981, 109 pp. [MA thesis Universiteit van Amsterdam.]

5538 Dijk, K. van; A.J. Plas and H. Ulrich
Van Nederlands-Indië tot Indonesië. 's-Hertogenbosch: Malmberg, 1975, 54 pp.

5539 Dijkstra, L.C.
'Een terugblik naar de jaren 1945-1949', *Genie* 27 (1977):186-197. (smg)

5540 Eb, V.L. van der
De overval. Hilversum: De Boer, 1962, 239 pp.

5541 Eb, V.L. van der
Van afgeschreven zaken. Hoorn: West-Friesland, 1967, 248 pp.

5542 Eekman, Alwyna
De politionele acties in Indonesië, of ov · de relatie leger-overheid, 1946-1949. 1993, 69 pp. [MA thesis Erasmus Universiteit, Rotterdam.] (eur)

5543 *Eelder jongens in Indië, 1945-1950.* Tynaarlo: Franken, 1990, 101 pp.

5544 Eggen-Leur, Ingeborg
Op naar Djokja... Neen; Onderzoek naar de werking van het pacificatiemechanisme binnen de Partij van de Arbeid rond de eerste politionele aktie in Indonesië (20 juli 1947). 1981, 83 pp. [MA thesis Universiteit van Amsterdam.]

5545 Eigeman, J.A.
De parlementaire enquêtecommissie en het Indonesische vraagstuk. 's-Gravenhage: Het Vaderland, 1955, 15 pp.

5546 Eigeman, J.A.
Het verlies van Nederlands-Indië. 's-Gravenhage: De Courant/Het Vaderland, 1955, 8 pp.

5547 Eigeman, J.A.
De onjuiste opzet van onze Indonesische staatkunde. 's-Gravenhage: De Courant Het Vaderland, 1957, 28 pp.

5548 Elizen, Jozef G.M.
Genist tot in de kist. Twello: n.n., 1992, 183 pp.

5549   Eng, Pierre van der
'De toegekende zaken kunnen rondlopen; Een katalysator in de dekolonisatie',
in: Pierre van der Eng, *De Marshall-hulp; Een perspectief voor Nederland, 1947-
1953*, pp. 203-227. Houten: De Haan/Unieboek, 1987. (ubl)

5550   Eng, Pierre van der
'Marshall aid as a cataclyst in the decolonization of Indonesia, 1947-49', *Journal
of Southeast Asian History* 19 (1988):335-352.

5551   Eng, Pierre van der
Food supply in Java during war and decolonization, 1940-1950. Hull: Center for
Southeast Asian Studies, University of Hull, 1994, 87 pp.

5552   Engelbrecht, W.A. (ed.)
*Kitab-kitab undang-undang, undang-undang dan peraturan-peraturan, serta
Undang-Undang Dasar Sementara Republik Indonesia/De wetboeken, wetten en
verordeningen benevens de Voorlopige Grondwet van de Republiek Indonesia.* Leiden:
Sijthoff, 1954, 3140 pp.

5553   Engelsman, Herman
Oorlogsmisdadigers op het Binnenhof? Het optreden van Kapitein Westerling
op Zuid-Celebes gerelateerd aan het beleid van het kabinet-Schermerhorn. 1990,
61 pp. [Thesis Nieuwe Leraren Opleiding, Zwolle.] (kitlv-smg)

5554   *Enquêtecommissie Regeringsbeleid 1940-1945; Militair beleid - Terugkeer naar
Nederlandsch-Indië; Deel 8A en B (verslag en bijlagen); Deel 8C (I en II) (verhoren).*
's-Gravenhage: Staatsdrukkerij, 1956.

5555   Esterik, Chris van and Kees van Twist
*Daar werd iets grootsch verricht; Of hoe het Koninkrijk der Nederlanden zijn grootste
kolonie verloor.* Weesp: Heureka, 1980, 112 pp.

5556   Eijkelboom, Jan
'De terugtocht', in: *Bij het scheiden van de markt*, pp. 171-194. Amsterdam:
Querido, 1965. [First published in *Libertinage* 6 (1953):326-346.]

5557   Faber, B.; P.B. Hoff; R.T. Kroon; L.S. Smid; D.A. Swank and G. Vlaar (eds)
Het Derde; Belevenissen van een infanterie-peloton op Zuid-Sumatra, 1947-1950.
Laren: n.n., 1981, 162 pp.

5558   Fasseur, C.
'Het verleden tot last; Nederland, de Tweede Wereldoorlog en de dekolonisatie
van Indonesië', in: Barnouw, David; Madelon de Keizer and Gerrold van der
Stroom (ed.), *1940-1945; Onverwerkt verleden?*, pp. 133-162. Utrecht: HES,
1985. (ubl)

5559   Fasseur, C.
'A not unfriendly big power'; Britain and the decolonization of Indonesia. Paper
Linggarjati Conference, 1991, 14 pp.

5560   Fasseur, C.
'Kekuatan besar yang bukan tidak bersahabat; Inggris dan dekolonisasi Indo-
nesia', in: A.B. Lapian and P.J. Drooglever (eds), *Menelusuri jalur Linggarjati;
Diplomasi dalam perspektif sejarah*, pp. 207-225. Jakarta: Grafiti, 1992.

5561 Feenstra, Fenna
Langs eigen wegen; Roman voor jonge mensen. Amsterdam: Van Holkema en Warendorf, 1953, 328 pp.

5562 Fennema, Meindert
Dutch policy networks in the decolonization of Indonesia. Amsterdam: Universiteit van Amsterdam, 1991, 20 pp.

5563 Feuilletau de Bruyn, W.K.H.
De communistische strijdmethoden in Centraal-, Oost- en Zuidoost-Azië. N.p.: n.n., ca. 1952, 12 pp.

5564 Feuilletau de Bruyn, W.K.H.
De memoires van Kapitein Westerling. 's-Gravenhage: De Vrije Pers, 1952, 16 pp.

5565 Feuilletau de Bruyn, W.K.H.
De ontwaarding van het parlementaire recht van enquête. 's-Gravenhage: De Vrije Pers, 1957, 24 pp.

5566 Fiedeldij Dop, Jan Maarten and Yvonne Simons
Al weer iets groots verricht; Hoe Nederland zijn Indië-deserteurs tot de laatste man berechtte. 1983, 131 pp. [MA thesis Universiteit van Amsterdam.]

5567 Fiedeldij Dop, Jan Maarten and Yvonne Simons
De berechting van de Indië-deserteurs. Amsterdam: Vrij Nederland, 1983, 27 pp.

5568 *Het fiere eendje; Gedenkboek 4-1 RI, Mei 1947-Februari 1950.* 's-Gravenhage: Van Hoeve, 1950, 188 pp.

5569 *Foto-album 2-2 RVA; Ter herinnering aan 3 jaar tropendienst; Aangeboden door de Welzijnsverzorgingsdienst 2-2 RVA.* Ede: Welzijnsverzorgingsdienst 2-2 RVA, 1950, 56 pp.

5570 *Foto-herdenkingsboek van het 3e Eskadron Pantserwagens Regiment Huzaren van Boreel, 10-1-1946/20-10-1949.* Groningen: Steunfonds 3e Eskadron Pantserwagens O.V.W., 1985, 284 pp.

5571 Fris, G. Willem
Van toneelclub tot ere-fronttroep. Maastricht: Leiter-Nypels, 1951, 157 pp.

5572 Gaag, P. van der (ed.)
De geschiedenis van de 1e Infanterie Brigade Werkplaats 87 in Engeland, Nederland en Indië, 1945-1949. Abjat-sur-Bandiat: n.n., 1988, 366 pp.

5573 Gallhofer, I.N.
'Beslissingen betreffende de eerste politionele actie', *Acta Politica* 16 (1981):501-529.

5574 Gallhofer, I.N.
'Beslissingen betreffende de tweede politionele actie', *Acta Politica* 17 (1982):75-110.

5575 Gallhofer, I.N. and W.E. Saris
'A decision-theoretical analysis of decisions of the Dutch government with respect to Indonesia', *Quality and Quantity* 16 (1982):313-344.

5576 Gallhofer, I.N. and W.E. Saris
'A decision-theoretical analysis of decisions of the Dutch government with respect to the intervention of the Security Council in Indonesia in the winter of 1948-1949', *Acta Politica* 18 (1983):63-88.

5577 Gase, Ronald
Beel in Batavia; Van contact tot conflict; Verwikkelingen rond de Indonesische kwestie in 1948. Baarn: Anthos, 1986, 330 pp.

5578 Gastel, P.A. van
'Om de gunst van de marhaen; Leider, politici en leger in de Indonesische staat (1945-1955)', in: *Onze jaren 45-70*, pp. 1097-1100. Amsterdam, 1972.

5579 *Gedenkboek 1e Bataljon, 5e Regiment Infanterie, 1945-1948.* Goes: Oosterbaan en Le Cointre, 1951, 187 pp.

5580 *Gedenkboek 1-4 RI; De belevenissen van 'De Valken' in de jaren 1945-1948; Geschreven door en voor de troep.* Breda: Broese, 1952, 135 pp.

5581 *Gedenkboek 4 LVT; Soldaten langs de strip.* N.p.: n.n., ca. 1950, 90 pp.

5582 *Gedenkboek 43e Zelfstandige Verkenningseskadron.* 1954, 78 pp. [114, 1216]

5583 *Gedenkboek Korps Beroepsofficieren Koninklijk Nederlands Indonesisch Leger 1940-1950.* Amsterdam: Nederlandsch-Indische Officiersvereeniging, 1951, 139 pp.

5584 *Gedenkboek Militaire Luchtvaart Medan.* Medan: n.n., 1950. [unpaged]

5585 *Gedenkboek Tweede Mitrailleur-Bataljon 1947-1950.* Druten, 1951. [114, 1216]

5586 Geelhoed, G.
'De strijd om de vrijheid van Piet van Staveren', *Politiek en Cultuur* 11 (1951):308-312. (ubl)

5587 Gelderblom, Jan Willem
Buitenlandse Zaken en de eerste politionele actie; De gang van zaken die leidde tot de beslissing van minister Van Boetzelaer om zich voor de eerste politionele actie uit te spreken. 1982, 41 pp. [MA thesis Rijksuniversiteit Leiden.]

5588 Gellekink, A.B.
De stem van Wertheim; Een inventarisatie en een analyse van het tijdschrift 'De Nieuwe Stem', jaargang 1-5 (1945/1946-1949/1950). 1991, 31 pp. [Paper Rijksuniversiteit Utrecht.]

5589 Gerbrandy, P.S.
Indonesia. London: Hutchinson, 1950, 224 pp. [Second printing 1975.]

5590 Gerbrandy, P.S.
De scheuring van het Rijk; Het drama van de Indonesische crisis. Kampen: Kok, 1951, 294 pp.

5591 Gerretson, C.
De Rijksgedachte. Utrecht: Oosthoek, 1954, 27 pp.

5592 Gerretson, C.
'Terug naar Colijn! Indonesië's verbrokkeling', in: A.J.M. Goedemans and G. Puchinger (eds), *Gerretson de strijdbare*, pp. 206-211. Amsterdam: De Telegraaf, 1959.

5593 Gerritsen, Hans
De hinderlaag bij Sindoeradja; Militaire acties op Java 1948-1950. Baarn: Hollandia, 1988, 152 pp.

5594 *De geschiedenis van het 4e Bataljon van het 2e Regiment Infanterie.* N.p.: n.n., ca. 1950, 15 pp. (kitlv-smg)

5595 *De geschiedenis van het 425e Bataljon Infanterie 'De Trekvogels'; Indonesië 1949-1950.* N.p.: n.n., 1984, 331 pp. (kitlv-smg)

5596 Giebel, C.
'Nederlandsch-Indië na de Japanse capitulatie', *Ons Leger* 61-10 (1977):59-71.

5597 Giebels, L.J.
'De Indonesiër L.N. Palar; Tussen onafhankelijkheidsverklaring en -overdracht', *Orion* 2-4 (1985-86):22-25; 2-5 (1985-86):38-39; 2-6 (1985-86):18.

5598 Glissenaar, Jan
Terug naar Java; In het spoor van politionele acties. Aalsmeer: DABAR/Luyten, 1992, 78 pp.

5599 Goderbauer, Hans
Herstel van gezag; De Nederlandse bevolkingsgroep op Java en de Indonesische kwestie, 1945-1947. 1982, 173 pp. [MA thesis Katholieke Universiteit Nijmegen.]

5600 Goedhart, J.
Van Nederlands Oost-Indië tot Indonesia. Zutphen: Thieme, 1975, 40 pp.

5601 Goes van Naters, M. van der
'Duynstee en de werkelijkheid', *Socialisme en Democratie* 24 (1967):805-831. (ubl)

5602 Goor, J. van
'Dekolonisatie van Nederlands-Indië', *Spiegel Historiael* 7 (1972):584-589.

5603 Goor, J. van (ed.)
The Indonesian revolution; Conference papers, Utrecht, 17-20 June, 1986. Utrecht: Rijksuniversiteit Utrecht, 1986, 247 pp.

5604 Goossens, P.T.A.
'De troepentransporten per schip naar en van Indonesië', *De Militaire Spectator* 120 (1951):601-610.

5605 Gooyer, A.C. de
Met groot verlof. Baarn: Bosch en Keuning, 1952, 196 pp.

5606 Gorter, Wytze
'Enkele gedachten over de economische betekenis van het verlies van Indonesië', *De Economist* 108 (1960):641-658. (ubl)

5607 Graaf, H.J. de
'Nederlands-Indië na de Japanse overgave', in: H.J. de Graaf (ed.), *Nederlanders over de zeeën; 350 jaar geschiedenis van Nederland buitengaats*, pp. 217-226. Utrecht: De Haan, 1955.

5608 Graaf, H.J. de
'The Indonesian declaration of independence, 17th of August, 1945', *Bijdragen tot de Taal-, Land- en Volkenkunde* 115 (1959):305-327.

5609 Graaf, Th.C. de
Noodwet Indonesië 1948 ongrondwettig en onnodig? Een onderzoek naar de politieke functie van de Noodwet Indonesië 1948 en haar staatsrechtelijk karakter in het licht van art. 210 Grondwet 1948. 1981, 72 pp. [MA thesis Katholieke Universiteit Nijmegen.]

5610 Graaf, Th.C. de
'Een nutteloze Noodwet; Een studie naar de grondwettigheid en de noodzaak van de Noodwet Indonesië 1948', in: *Politieke opstellen*, pp. 20-37. Nijmegen: Centrum voor Parlementaire Geschiedenis der Katholieke Universiteit, 1982.

5611 Graaff, Ant.P. de
De heren worden bedankt; Met het vergeten leger in Indië, 1949-1950. Franeker: Wever, 1986, 174 pp. [Fourth printing, Franeker: Van Wijnen, 1990.]

5612 Graaff, Ant.P. de
De weg terug; Het vergeten leger toen en nu. Franeker: Van Wijnen, 1988, 124 pp. [Second printing 1990.]

5613 Graaff, Ant.P. de
Brieven uit het veld; Het vergeten leger thuis. Franeker: Van Wijnen, 1989, 128 pp.

5614 Graaff, Ant.P. de
Met de TNI op stap; De laatste patrouille van het vergeten leger. Franeker: Van Wijnen, 1991, 201 pp.

5615 Graaff, Ant.P. de
Notities van een soldaat; Het dagboek van soldaat A.A. van der Heiden. Franeker: Van Wijnen, 1994, 91 pp.

5616 Graaff, Bob de
'Pressiegroepen en de Indonesische revolutie', *Jambatan* 2-1 (1983-84):4-5.

5617 Graaff, B.G.J. de
'Intelligence onder de loupe', *Jambatan* 4-2 (1986):30-32.

5618 Graaff, M.G.H.A. de and A.M. Tempelaars
Inventaris van het archief van de Algemene Secretarie van de Nederlands-Indische regering en de daarbij gedeponeerde archieven, 1942-1950. Den Haag: Algemeen Rijksarchief, 1990, 1007 pp. 4 vols.

5619 Groen, Petra
Oprichting, functioneren en opheffing van de deelstaat Oost-Indonesië, 1946-1950. 1979, 179 pp. [MA thesis Rijksuniversiteit Utrecht.]

5620 Groen, P.M.H.
'Koloniale politiek en militaire geschiedschrijving', *Mededelingen Sectie Militaire Geschiedenis Landmachtstaf* 6 (1983):93-119. (kb)

5621 Groen, P.M.H.
'De Stoottroepen in Nederlands-Indië', in: Janssen, J.A.M.M.; P.M.H. Groen and C.M. Schulten, *Stoottroepen 1944-1984*, pp. 59-127. Dieren: De Bataafsche Leeuw, 1984.

5622 Groen, P.M.H.
'Patience and bluff; De bevrijding van de Nederlandse burgergeïnterneerden op Midden-Java (aug.-dec.1945)', *Mededelingen Sectie Militaire Geschiedenis Landmachtstaf* 8 (1985):91-154. (kb)

5623 Groen, Petra M.H.
'Dutch armed forces and the decolonization of Indonesia; The Second Police Action (1948-1949); A Pandora's box', *War and Society* 4-1 (May 1986):79-104.

5624 Groen, P.M.H.
'Ceterum censeo Djogjakartum esse delendum', in: G. Teitler and P.M.H. Groen (ed.), *De politionele acties*, pp. 91-120. Amsterdam: De Bataafsche Leeuw, 1987.

5625 Groen, P.M.H.
'Wapenschouw; De Nederlandse militair-strategische vooruitzichten in de Indische archipel (augustus 1945-maart 1946)', *Mededelingen Sectie Militaire Geschiedenis Landmachtstaf* 10 (1987):90-136.

5626 Groen, P.M.H.
'De aanhouder wint; Spoor en Operatie Kraai', *Mededelingen Sectie Militaire Geschiedenis Landmachtstaf* 11 (1988):97-150.

5627 Groen, P.M.H.
'De eindafrekening; Militaire resultaten van de tweede politionele actie', *Mededelingen Sectie Militaire Geschiedenis Landmachtstaf* 12 (1989):112-195.

5628 Groen, P.M.H.
Marsroutes en dwaalsporen; Het Nederlands militair-strategisch beleid in Indonesië 1945-1950. 's-Gravenhage: SDU Uitgeverij, 1991, 359 pp. [PhD thesis Rijksuniversiteit Leiden.]

5629 Groen, P.M.H.
Treaty under fire; Military power and the Linggarjati agreement. Paper Linggarjati Conference, 1991, 17 pp.

5630 Groen, P.M.H.
'Sebuah perjanjian dalam serangan; Kekuatan militer dan perjanjian Linggarjati', in: A.B. Lapian and P.J. Drooglever (eds), *Menelusuri jalur Linggarjati; Diplomasi dalam perspektif sejarah*, pp. 95-119. Jakarta: Grafiti, 1992.

5631 Groen, P.M.H. and D.W. Staat
Inzet in Nederlands-Indië 1945-1950. Amsterdam: Van Soeren, 1992, 88 pp.

5632 Groenewout, Eric van 't
Indonesia calling; Het verhaal van schepen die niet uitvoeren. 1988, 160 pp. [MA thesis Rijksuniversiteit Leiden.]

5633 Groenhart, R.J. and F.J.M. Smits
Een ander pakje aan... De ideeën van dienstplichtige militairen over het conflict tussen Nederland en de Republiek Indonesië, 1945-1950. 1989, 144 pp. [MA thesis Universiteit van Amsterdam.]

5634 Groot, Corinne
Oog voor het beeld; Persfotografie en de politionele acties. 1989, 136 pp. [MA thesis Universiteit van Amsterdam.]

5635 Groot, Corinne
'Oog voor het beeld; Persfotografie en de politionele acties', *Jambatan* 9-3 (1991):108-121.

5636 Groot, L.F. de
'De rechtspraak inzake oorlogsmisdrijven in Nederlands-Indië (1947-1949)', *Militair Rechtelijk Tijdschrift* 78 (1985):81-90, 161-172.

5637 Groot, L.F. de
'De rechtspraak van de Temporaire Krijgsraad te Batavia (1947-1949)', *Militair Rechtelijk Tijdschrift* 78 (1985):248-257, 361-376.

5638 Groot, L.F. de
Berechting Japanse oorlogsmisdadigers in Nederlands-Indië, 1946-1949; Temporaire Krijgsraad Batavia. 's-Hertogenbosch: Art and Research, 1990, 623 pp.

5639 Groot Heupner, Maureen de
Met het oog op de toekomst; Ideeën van het Indo-Europees Verbond over de toekomst van de Indo-Europeaan in Indonesië, 1946-1949. 1988, 99 pp. [MA thesis Rijksuniversiteit Leiden.] [Lijst Leiden]

5640 Grunsven, G.J. van
Het akkoord van Linggadjati en de KVP in de periode november-december 1946; De houding van de bewindslieden en de Tweede-Kamerfractie ten aanzien van de ontwerp-overeenkomst. Paper Katholieke Universiteit Nijmegen, 1980. [58]

5641 Grunsven, G.J. van
De Nederlandse beleidsvorming met betrekking tot de internationalisering van de Indonesische kwestie, april-augustus 1947. 1987, 152 pp. [MA thesis Katholieke Universiteit Nijmegen.]

5642 Haasen, G. van
Eeuwigheidslicht over het Indonesisch drama; Een verootmoediging en opstanding. 's-Gravenhage: Korthuis, 1950, 31 pp.

5643 Hagens, Jan
Kemajoran; Nederlands-Indisch luchttransport tijdens de roerige jaren 1945-1950. Bergen: Bonneville, 1993, 224 pp.

5644 Ham, M.L. van
De Genie in voormalig Nederlands-Indië; Enkele notities betreffende de geschiedschrijving van het Wapen in het tijdvak 1945-1950. Culemborg: Verschoor, 1971, 16 pp.

5645 Hanswijck de Jonge, H.A.G.J.P. van
Vijf jaar troepen varen. 's-Gravenhage: Ministerie van Defensie, 1979, 328 pp.

5646 Hanswijck de Jonge, H.A.G.J.P. van
Troepentransport naar Nederlandsch-Indië 1946-1950. Bussum: De Boer Maritiem, 1981, 120 pp.

5647 Harlaar, Martin
Achtergronden van de Indië-desertie. 1986, 74 pp. [MA thesis Universiteit van Amsterdam.] [43]

5648   Harmsen, Ger
       'Het politieke en morele gelijk van de Indonesië-weigeraars', *Bulletin van de*
       Nederlandse Arbeidersbeweging no. 17 (1988):3-35.

5649   Harrewijn, J.H.
       Uitdaging en antwoord; De Vierde Afdeling Veldartillerie in de politionele
       acties. 1981, 57 pp. [Thesis Koninklijke Militaire Academie, Breda.] (kitlv-smg)

5650   Harrewijn, (J.)H.
       4e Afdeling Veldartillerie; Van Oldebroek tot Oldebroek. N.p.: n.n., 1989, 144 pp.

5651   Haspel, C.Ch. van den
       De verstandhouding tussen Helfrich en Van Mook van 10 augustus 1945-24
       januari 1946. 1971, 92 pp. [MA thesis Rijksuniversiteit Leiden.]

5652   Hazenkamp, Linda
       De houding van de Gereformeerde zending tegenover het Indonesisch nationa-
       lisme in de periode 1945-1949. 1985, 94 pp. [MA thesis Rijksuniversiteit
       Utrecht.]

5653   Heek, G. van
       Front op Java; Mijn diensttijd in Indonesië 1947-1950. Hengelo: Smit, ca. 1952,
       159 pp. (kitlv-smg)

5654   Heide-Kort, Ans van der
       Tropenvuur; Over een strijd die niet gestreden lijkt. Driebergen-Rijsenburg:
       Zevenster, 1992, 240 pp.

5655   Hekman, Jelle A.
       Nationaal Comité Handhaving Rijkseenheid. 1981, 84 pp. [MA thesis Vrije
       Universiteit, Amsterdam.]

5656   Hekman, J.
       'Het Nationaal Comité Handhaving Rijkseenheid', *Jambatan* 2-1 (1983-84):5-10.

5657   Helder, K. (ed.)
       Tiga doeabelas; Gedenkboek 3-12 RI. Groningen: Van der Kamp, 1951, 327 pp.

5658   Helmer, Hans
       Dit volk is uw vijand niet; Roman. Antwerpen: 't Groeit, 's-Gravenhage: Pax, ca.
       1950, 187 pp.

5659   Helvoort, A. van
       De verzwegen oorlog; Dagboek van een hospik in Indië, 1947-1950. Groningen:
       Xeno, 1988, 184 pp.

5660   Hemkes, Roel
       Herinneringen van een roodborstje; Verhalen uit de periode 1947-1950 doorgebracht
       bij het 4e bataljon 5e Regiment Infanterie op Oost-Java in het voormalige Nederlands
       Oost-Indië. N.p.: Kaveka/J.W.T. Daems, ca. 1993, 48 pp.

5661   Hendriks, Harrie
       De KVP en de Indonesische kwestie tijdens het kabinet Drees-Van Schaik tot en
       met de soevereiniteitsoverdracht. 1980. [BA thesis Katholieke Universiteit
       Nijmegen.] [58]

5662 Hendrikse, Bas
De Nederlands-Indonesische Unie; Het Nederlandse regeringsbeleid inzake de Nederlands-Indonesische Unie gedurende de periode 1949-1954. 1988, 197+40 pp. [MA thesis Katholieke Universiteit Nijmegen.] [43, 58]

5663 Hendrikse, D.
Tropenrit 15 AAT. Voorwoord van J.H. Sijdzes. N.p.: n.n., ca. 1950, 50 pp.

5664 Hendrix, Henk L.
De KVP en de Indonesische kwestie. 1977, 112+40 pp. [MA thesis Rijksuniversiteit Utrecht.]

5665 Hendrix, Willem J.
'Revolusi Indonesia dan generasi 1945', *Prisma* 10-8 (August 1981):14-20.

5666 *Herinneringen aan 43e Z.V.E.* Inleiding door Dick Veenstra. Zwijndrecht: n.n., 1991, 115 pp.

5667 *Herinneringsalbum 5-10 RI; Achter de Sinabun scheen toch de zon... Noord-Sumatra 1948-1950.* Woerden: Zuijderduin, 1950, 208 pp. (kitlv-smg)

5668 Heshusius, C.A.
'Bersiap en het militair gebeuren, gezien vanuit Nederlands perspectief', in: *Oorlog en verzet in Nederlands-Indië 1941-1949 en de voorlichting aan de na-oorlogse generaties*, pp. 29-53. Amsterdam: De Bataafsche Leeuw, 1989.

5669 Heteren, Adrienne van
De Amerikaans-Nederlandse betrekkingen in het dekolonisatieproces van Indonesië, 1945-1949. 1985, 61 pp. [MA thesis Universiteit van Amsterdam.]

5670 Heijboer, Pierre
De politionele acties; De strijd om 'Indië', 1945/1949. Haarlem: Fibula-Van Dishoeck, 1979, 160 pp.

5671 Heijs, J.J.
De bijdrage van Dr. J.W. Meyer Ranneft aan de oplossing van het conflict Nederland-Indië, mei-december 1945. Paper Rijksuniversiteit Utrecht, 1991, 32 pp.

5672 Hisschemöller, Matthijs
Het Nederlands belang; Denken en handelen op de ministeries van Economische Zaken en Financiën met betrekking tot de dekolonisatie van Indonesië tegen de achtergrond van de industrialisatie van Nederland, 1945-1950. 1981, 72 pp. [MA thesis Universiteit van Amsterdam.]

5673 Hoed, Annet den
Het KNIL; Een vergeten leger? Een beleids-historische analyse van de reorganisatie van het KNIL; Het militaire personeelsbeleid van het KNIL in de periode 1945-1951. 1988, 207 pp. [MA thesis Erasmus Universiteit, Rotterdam.]

5674 Hoed, A. den
'Het KNIL in de knel; De ontbinding van het KNIL en het lot van de militairen', in: G. Teitler and J. Hoffenaar (eds), *De politionele acties; Afwikkeling en verwerking*, pp. 21-33. Amsterdam: De Bataafsche Leeuw, 1990.

5675 Hoekstra, H.
Wij waren ingedeeld bij het 4e Bataljon Garde Jagers op Oost-Java en Madoera; Onze belevenissen in de jaren 1946-1950 op Madoera en in Oost-Java; Aan de hand van dagboeken, brieven en gesprekken samengesteld in samenwerking met Kapitein M. Lahm. 's-Gravenhage: n.n., 1988, 124 pp.

5676 Hoffenaar, Jan
'Een doekje voor het bloeden; Onderhandelingen over de status van Indonesië (1945-1949)', *Skript* 6 (1984):47-58.

5677 Hoffenaar, J.
Objectiviteit beoogd, gekleurd betoogd; De berichtgeving over Duitsland, de Republiek Indonesië en de Sowjet-Unie in de militaire kranten 'De Pen Gun' en 'Het Lichtspoor' in de periode juni 1945-april 1949. 1985, 129 pp. [MA thesis Vrije Universiteit, Amsterdam.] (kitlv-smg)

5678 Hoffenaar, J.
'Een "zeer tere kwestie"; Voorlichting aan militairen in de weekbladen De Pen Gun en Het Lichtspoor (1945-1951)', *Mededelingen Sectie Militaire Geschiedenis Landmachtstaf* 9 (1986):75-101.

5679 Hoffenaar, J.
'De Indonesische kwestie (1945-1949); De Nederlandse militaire inbreng nader bekeken', *De Militaire Spectator* 156 (1987):172-179. (ubl)

5680 Hoffenaar, J.
'Geen woorden maar daden; De terugkeer van de Nederlandse militairen uit Indonesië (1947-1951)', in: G. Teitler and J. Hoffenaar (eds), *De politionele acties; Afwikkeling en verwerking*, pp. 79-90. Amsterdam: De Bataafsche Leeuw, 1990.

5681 Hoffenaar, J.
'De militaire aftocht uit Indonesië 1949-1951', *De Militaire Spectator* 159 (1990):412-419. (ubl)

5682 Hoffenaar, J.
'De terugkeer van de militairen van de Koninklijke Landmacht uit Indonesië, 1947-1951', *Mededelingen Sectie Militaire Geschiedenis Landmachtstaf* 13 (1990):99-133.

5683 Hofland, H.J.A.
'Indonesië', in: H.J.A. Hofland, *Tegels lichten; Of ware verhalen over de autoriteiten in het land van de voldongen feiten*, pp. 17-41. Amsterdam: Contact, 1972. [Second printing 1972.]

5684 Hofstad, M. van der (ed.)
Wapenbroeders; Uitgave van en voor de Nederlandse strijdkrachten in Indonesië. Den Dungen: n.n., 1993. [unpaged]

5685 Hofstad, M. van der (ed.)
1e Cie 4e Bataljon 11e Regt. Infanterie; Uit het dagboek van een soldaat van de 1e Cie. Den Dungen: Van der Hofstad, 1994, 143 pp.

5686 Hofstad M. van der (ed.)
3e Cie 4e Bataljon 11e Regt. Infanterie. Den Dungen: Van der Hofstad, 1994, 162 pp.

5687 Hofstad, M. van der (ed.)
5e Cie 4e Bataljon 11e Regt. Infanterie. Den Dungen: Van der Hofstad, 1994, 199 pp.

5688 Hofstad, M. van der (ed.)
Ons Indië. Den Dungen: Van der Hofstad, 1994, 195 pp.

5689 Hogenboom, W.S.R.; J. Lievestro and H.C.J. Lommerse
Het optreden der genietroepen in Indonesië in de periode 1946-1949. 1981, 35 pp. [Thesis Koninklijke Militaire Academie, Breda.] (kitlv-smg)

5690 Holk, G.J. van
'The United States and decolonization', *Leidschrift* 2-6 (1986):70-96.

5691 Holst Pellekaan, R.E. van
Tienduizend vrije vogels; Oorlogsvrijwilligers bij de Koninklijke Marine 1944-1950. Amsterdam: De Bataafsche Leeuw, 1993, 190 pp.

5692 Hooftman, Hugo
Vleugels tegen tropisch blauw; Indonesië en luchtvaart. 's-Gravenhage: Van Hoeve, 1950. [unpaged]

5693 Hooftman, Hugo
'De verkeersluchtvaart in Indonesië', *Indonesië* 6 (1952-53):380-388.

5694 Hooftman, Hugo
Militaire luchtvaart in Nederlandsch-Indië in beeld; Deel 2: 1940-1949. Zaltbommel: Europese Bibliotheek, 1981, 156 pp.

5695 Hoogh, G.J.M. de
Mijn Indische mariniersjaren; Naar herinneringen van B.J. van Gils. Ca. 1975, 380 pp.

5696 Hoogte, Albert van der
Het laatste uur; Kroniek uit het na-oorlogse Indonesië. Amsterdam/Antwerpen: Contact, 1953, 214 pp. [Seventh printing, Amsterdam: Contact, 1975, 214 pp.]

5697 Hoogte, Albert van der
Die Stunde des Gewissens; Roman. Stuttgart: Deutsche Verlags-Anstalt, ca. 1954, 277 pp. (kb)

5698 Hoogte, Albert van der
Huis in de nacht. Amsterdam/Antwerpen: Contact, 1956, 188 pp. [Second printing 1957; Third printing 1961.]

5699 Horninge, J.
'Op patrouille en avontuur; Met de Ceram-killers in de rimboe', *Tong Tong* 12-20 (1967-68):15-17; 12-21 (1967-68):10-20.

5700 Hornman, W.
De hele hap; Jungle-oorlog van de mariniers op Oost-Java. Amsterdam: De Bezige Bij, 1953, 251 pp. [Second edition, Amsterdam: Omega Boek, 1985, 208 pp.

5701 Hornman, W.
De hele hap / Ik wil leven. Baarn: Free Spirit, 1981, 336 pp.

5702 Hornman, Wim
De geschiedenis van de Mariniersbrigade. Amsterdam: Omega Boek, 1985, 450 pp.

5703 Hornman, W.
De laatste man; Mariniers in de gordel van smaragd, 1942-1950. Bergen: Bonneville, 1992, 453 pp.

5704 Horst, Jan van der
Misverstanden en onderschattingen. Paper Rijksuniversiteit Leiden, 1993, 12 pp.

5705 Houben, V.J.H.
'Balans van de dekolonisatie van Indonesië', *Civis Mundi* 29-2 (1989):77-82. (ubl)

5706 Houten, W. van
De commentaren in Het Vrije Volk en De Volkskrant over het Nederlandse Indonesië-beleid, 1945-1949. 1989. [Thesis Hogeschool Interstudie, Nijmegen.] [5322]

5707 Houwer, A.C.M.
Propaganda en politiek; De Regerings Voorlichtings Dienst in Nederlands-Indië 1945-1950. 1986, 79 pp. [MA thesis Rijksuniversiteit Utrecht.] (kitlv-smg)

5708 Huizinga, Leonhard
Gesprek met de Generaal. Voorwoord van L.J.M. Beel. Amsterdam: Van Kampen, 1952, 57 pp.

5709 Hulsbus, Joop
Verborgen dageraad; Nederlands-Indië en Zuidoost-Azië na de Japanse capitulatie, 1945-1947. Baarn: Hollandia, 1988, 195 pp.

5710 Imandt, Florence
De onverbloemde waarheid? Interne legervoorlichting met betrekking tot Indonesië 1945-1950, en de relatie met het moreel. 1988, 128 pp. [MA thesis Erasmus Universiteit, Rotterdam.] (kitlv-smg)

5711 Imandt, F.
'De onverbloemde waarheid; De interne voorlichting aan militairen over Indonesië, 1945-1950', *Mededelingen Sectie Militaire Geschiedenis Landmachtstaf* 12 (1989):79-92.

5712 *Indonesia merdeka; Hoe verloor Nederland de erfenis van Jan Pieterszoon Coen? Een dramatische tv-documentaire van Roelof Kiers over de Indonesische onafhankelijkheidsstrijd.* Hilversum: VPRO, 1977, 23 pp.

5713 'De Indonesische kwestie', in: *Vijfentwintig jaar Vrij Nederland; Een bloemlezing uit het illegale en het na-oorlogse Vrij Nederland,* pp. 56-78. Amsterdam: De Bezige Bij, 1965.

5714 *De Indonesische kwestie; De politionele acties in Indonesië, 1945-1950 en de vermeende Nederlandse excessen begaan door Nederlandse militairen.* Breda: Koninklijke Militaire Academie, 1969, 532 pp. (kma)

5715 Jacob, M. (ps. J. Vredenbregt)
De opstand. 's-Gravenhage: Nijgh en Van Ditmar, 1986, 146 pp.

5716 Jacob, M. (ps.)
Pemberontakan, bukan perang; Sebuah novel. Jakarta: Djambatan, 1986, 172 pp.

5717 Jagt, Bouke
Erven van Indië; Roman. Baarn: De Prom, 1992, 185 pp.

5718 Jalhay, S.M.
Allen zwijgen (Van Merdeka en Andjing-NICA tot APRA). Purmerend: n.n., 1983, 298 pp. [Third edition, Hillegom: Gevana, 314 pp.]

5719 Jansen-Hendriks, Gerda a.o.
Film als historische bron; De kwestie-Indonesië 1945-1950; Een voorlopig verslag. Amsterdam: Historisch Seminarium, 1981, 239 pp. (kitlv-smg)

5720 Jansen-Hendriks, Gerda; Frank Klein and Peter Otten
Een ideaal voor ogen; De kwestie-Indonesië in het bioscoopjournaal; Verantwoording bij de documentaire. 1983, 38 pp. [MA thesis Universiteit van Amsterdam.] (kitlv-smg)

5721 Janssen, Graard
Dorp en dessa; Verhaal van een dorp in Brabant en zijn jongens-soldaten in de vrijheidsstrijd van Indonesië, 1945-1951. Reusel: Heemkunde Werkgroep Reusel, 1989, 351 pp.

5722 Jaquet, L.G.M.
'De Darul-Islam', *Internationale Spectator* 4-3 (1950):6-9.

5723 Jaquet, L.G.M.
'Federalisme en unitarisme in Indonesië', *Internationale Spectator* 4-4 (1950):6-10.

5724 Jaquet, L.G.M.
'The Indonesian federal problem reconsidered', *Pacific Affairs* 25 (1952):170-175.

5725 Jaquet, L.G.M.
Aflossing van de wacht; Bestuurlijke en politieke ervaringen in de nadagen van Nederlandsch-Indië. Rotterdam: Donker, 1978, 320 pp.

5726 Jaquet, L.G.M.
Minister Stikker en de souvereiniteitsoverdracht aan Indonesië; Nederland op de tweesprong tussen Azië en het Westen. 's-Gravenhage: Nijhoff, 1982, 398 pp.

5727 Jaquet, L.G.M.
'Stikker en de souvereiniteitsoverdracht aan Indonesië', *Internationale Spectator* 36 (August 1982):452-459.

5728 Jaquet, L.G.M.
'Inleiding', in: G. Teitler and P.M.H. Groen (eds), *De politionele acties*, pp. 5-10. Amsterdam: De Bataafsche Leeuw, 1987.

5729 Jong, J.J.P. de
'De Indonesië-kwestie 1946-1947; Diplomatie op het breukvlak van Nederlands en Indonesisch krachtenveld', *Internationale Spectator* 37 (1983):48-56.

5730 Jong, J.J.P. de
'Winds of change; Van Mook, Dutch policy and the realities of November 1945', in: J. van Goor (ed.), *The Indonesian revolution; Conference papers, Utrecht, 17-20 June, 1986*, pp. 163-182. Utrecht: Rijksuniversiteit Utrecht, 1986.

5731   Jong, J.J.P. de
'De politieke ontwikkeling van de Indonesische kwestie na de Tweede Wereld-oorlog, 1945-1950', in: *Syllabus Nederland en Nederlands-Indië*, pp. 7-77. Ridderkerk: n.n., 1987.

5732   Jong, J.J.P. de
Diplomatie of strijd; Een analyse van het Nederlands beleid tegenover de Indonesische revolutie 1945-1947. Meppel/Amsterdam: Boom, 1988, 530 pp. [Also PhD thesis Rijksuniversiteit Utrecht.]

5733   Jong, J.J.P. de
'The Indonesian question; International intervention as an option? Aspects of British, Dutch and American policy 1945-1947', in: C.A. van Minnen (ed.), *Decolonization of Indonesia; International perspectives*, pp. 23-37. Middelburg: Roosevelt Study Center/Stichting V.O.C.-Publicaties Zeeland, 1988.

5734   Jong, J.J.P. de
'De Republiek Indonesië tussen strijd en diplomatie (1945-1950)', in: *Oorlog en verzet in Nederlands-Indië 1941-1949 en de voorlichting aan de na-oorlogse generaties*, pp. 59-70. Amsterdam: De Bataafsche Leeuw, 1989.

5735   Jong, J.J.P. de
'De bersiap-periode', in: P.J. Drooglever (ed.), *Indisch intermezzo; Geschiedenis van de Nederlanders in Indonesië*, pp. 81-99. Amsterdam: De Bataafsche Leeuw, 1991. [Second printing 1994.]

5736   Jong, J.J.P. de
Partners in negotiation; Sjahrir and H.J. van Mook. Paper Linggarjati Conference, 1991. [program]

5737   Jong, J.J.P. de
'Mitra dalam perundingan; Sutan Syahrir dan H.J. van Mook', in: A.B. Lapian and P.J. Drooglever (eds), *Menelusuri jalur Linggarjati; Diplomasi dalam perspektif sejarah*, pp. 63-84. Jakarta: Grafiti, 1992.

5738   Jong, L. de
Het Koninkrijk der Nederlanden in de tweede wereldoorlog; Deel 12, Epiloog; Tweede helft: De worsteling met de Republiek Indonesië, pp. 710-1106. Leiden: Nijhoff, 1988. [Popular edition, 's-Gravenhage: SDU Uitgeverij, 1988, pp. 692-1078.]

5739   Jonge, A.B.L. de
De Christelijk-Historische Unie en de Indonesische kwestie. 1980, 159 pp. [MA thesis Rijksuniversiteit Leiden.]

5740   Jonge, A.B.L. de
'De soevereiniteitsoverdracht; Tilanus contra Gerretson', *Christelijk Historisch Tijdschrift* 25 (1980):152-167.

5741   Jonker, Annafiet
Als honden van stro. Amsterdam: Prometheus, 1991, 133 pp.

5742   Jonkman, J.A.
'Nederland en de Indonesische republiek', in: G. Ruygers (ed.), *Socialisme in de branding*, pp. 58-88. Amsterdam: Arbeiderspers, 1951.

5743 Jonkman, J.A.
Nederland en Indonesië beide vrij; Gezien vanuit het Nederlands parlement; Memoires.
Assen/Amsterdam: Van Gorcum, 1977, 298 pp.

5744 Jurg, Wim
'De Waarheid en de Indonesische nationaal-democratische revolutie', in: *Cahiers over de Geschiedenis van de Communistische Partij van Nederland* 5, pp. 108-123.
Amsterdam: Instituut voor Politiek en Sociaal Onderzoek (IPSO), 1980.

5745 Jurg, Wim and Paul van Tongeren
De CPN en de Indonesische onafhankelijkheidsstrijd (mei '45-juli '47); Oftewel: 'Rijksverraad in optima forma' (De Volkskrant); Referaat. N.p.: n.n., n.y., 62 pp.

5746 Kaam, B. van
'Kerstmis dertig jaar geleden; De oorlog die Nederland verloor', *VU-Magazine* 7-11 (1978):34-39. (ubl)

5747 Kaam, B. van
'Foto-verhaal Shahrir-Sjarifudin', *VU-Magazine* 9-3 (1980):17-28. (ubl)

5748 Kaam, B. van
'Een vorstelijke rebel; Nederlands vergissing van 35 jaar geleden', *VU-Magazine* 13-3 (1984):107-115. (ubl)

5749 Kadt, J. de
Jaren die dubbel telden; Politieke herinneringen uit mijn 'Indische' jaren. Amsterdam: Van Oorschot, 1978, 201 pp.

5750 Kakebeen, J.H. a.o. (ed.)
Van Arnhem tot de Poentjak; Herinneringen aan het 412e Bataljon Garderegiment 'Prinses Irene'; Nederland-Indonesië Maart 1948-Augustus 1950. 's-Gravenhage: Zuid-Hollandsche, 1951, 335 pp. (riod)

5751 Kampen, Anthony van
'De verlaten post', in: A. van Kampen, *De laatste leugen*, pp. 47-64. Amsterdam: De Boer, 1953.

5752 Kanters, Antonius
Hij ging, kwam terug en keerde weer. Mierlo: n.n., 1985, 243 pp.

5753 Kappers, Th.
'Nederlandsch-Indië na de Japanse capitulatie (1946-1949)', *Ons Leger* 61-6 (1977):29-47.

5754 Keith, Frank
Liefde en haat in de kampong; Realistische roman. 's-Gravenhage: Lectura, ca. 1954, 217 pp.

5755 Keizer, Madelon de
'Mission impossible; The intermediary role of the Dutch politician and journalist Frans Goedhart in the Dutch-Indonesian conflict, 1945-1947', *Indonesia* no. 55 (1993):113-139.

5756   Kempen, Wil van
        'Na mijn arrestatie; Ervaringen van een Indië-deserteur; Dokument', in: *Jaarboek voor de Geschiedenis van Socialisme en Arbeidersbeweging in Nederland 1977*, pp. 367-380. Nijmegen: SUN, 1977. (ubl)

5757   Kerkhof, Frans
        Duizend dagen. Helmond: Van Stiphout, 1984, 511 pp.

5758   Kersten, Albert E.
        International intervention in the decolonization of Indonesia, 1945-1962. Paper Colloque International 'Décolonisations Comparées', Aix-en-Provence, 1993, 9 pp.

5759   Keyzer-Grooten, S.K.
        Politieke ontwikkelingen op Madoera van 1945 tot 1950. 1984, 80 pp. [MA thesis Rijksuniversiteit Utrecht.]

5760   Kief, Frits
        Vijf jaar Indonesia Merdeka in De Vlam; Een overzicht van de gebeurtenissen in beeld en woord, samengesteld aan de hand van platen, hoofdartikelen en beschouwingen in 'De Vlam' sinds 17 Augustus 1945. Amsterdam: De Vonk, 1950, 47 pp.

5761   Kippers, G.J.
        Het Vrouwenkorps van het Koninklijk Nederlands-Indisch Leger, 1943-1950. 1985, 169 pp. [MA thesis Rijksuniversiteit Utrecht.] (kitlv-smg)

5762   Kippers, Geja
        'Het Vrouwenkorps van het KNIL', *Fibula* 33-1/2 (1992):31-37. (kb)

5763   Klooster, H.A.J.
        'Indonesische publikaties over de revolutiejaren 1945-1949; Een eerste verkenning', *Leidschrift* 2-6 (1986):96-100.

5764   Klijnen, T. and Y. Koopmans (eds)
        5-1 RI in de tropen. Djakarta: n.n., 1950, 100 pp. (lmd)

5765   Koch, D.M.G.
        'H.J. van Mook', *De Nieuwe Stem* 13 (1958):295-299. (ubl)

5766   Kock, W.J.A.M. de
        Commando Luchtvaarttroepen Nederlands-Indië 1947-1950. 's-Gravenhage: Koninklijke Luchtmacht, 1990, 260 pp.

5767   Koenders, W.C.
        'Het binnenlands bestuur en de Indische maatschappij', in: *Wij gedenken... Gedenkboek van de Vereniging van Ambtenaren bij het Binnenlands Bestuur in Nederlandsch-Indië*, pp. 239-362. Utrecht: Oosthoek, 1956.

5768   Koerts, H.J.
        De vrijheid werd duur gekocht; Zuid-Celebes na de Japanse capitulatie. Bunne: Servo, 1991, 323 pp.

5769   Koets, P.J.
        'De voortrekker van de vrijheid; Soekarno (1901-1970), president van Indonesië', in: *Onze jaren 45-70*, p. 351. Amsterdam, 1972. (ubl)

5770 Koets, P.J.
'Beschouwingen naar aanleiding van het proefschrift van Ide Anak Agung Gde Agung: "Renville" als keerpunt in de Nederlands-Indonesische onderhandelingen', *Internationale Spectator* 35 (1981):486-489.

5771 Koets, P.J.
'Nederland op de tweesprong; Van Mook en de dekolonisatie', *Internationale Spectator* 37 (1983):515-521.

5772 Kok, Jean van de
De positie van de Indo-Europese groep tijdens de Indonesische onafhankelijkheidsstrijd 1945-1949. 1979, 45 pp. [MA thesis Rijksuniversiteit Groningen.]

5773 Kolmus-de Vink, Telma
Vlucht naar het vaderland. 's-Gravenhage: Moesson, 1987, 222 pp.

5774 Kool, Nico
De totstandkoming van het naoorlogs staatkundig beleid van Nederland in Indonesië, 1945-maart 1947. 1979, 238 pp. [MA thesis Rijksuniversiteit Utrecht.]

5775 Koops, J.
5-10 RI; Een bataljon in de Karo- en Dairilanden van Noord-Sumatra. 1990, 122 pp. [MA thesis Rijksuniversiteit Utrecht.]

5776 Kooyman, Ad.
Indonesia merdeka; Bagaimana Nederland kehilangan warisan Jan Pieterszoon Coen? Sebuah dokumenter TV tentang perjuangan kemerdekaan Indonesia; Disaksikan oleh Mohammad Hatta, Jenderal Nasution, Johan Fabricius, Dr. Koets dan banyak lain lagi; Suatu acara VPRO oleh Roelof Kiers. Jakarta: Idayu Press, 1977, 85 pp.

5777 Korthof, G.
De Nederlandse arbeidersbeweging en het Indonesische vraagstuk; Politieke standpuntbepaling vanuit de arbeidersbeweging over vraagstukken van internationalisme, revolutie en solidariteit, 1945-1949. 1975, 110 pp. [MA thesis Universiteit van Amsterdam.]

5778 Korthuys, Piet
'Ga uit uw land; Roman in twee delen', in: *De dagen onzer jaren 1 Oct. 1953-30 Sept. 1954*, pp. 105-256. Baarn: Bosch en Keuning, 1954.

5779 Kraamwinkel, Gerard; Wim Roemer; Kees Verhagen and Cor Westerneng (eds)
Met opgeheven hoofd; Herinneringen van LuA-mannen aan hun diensttijd in Nederlands-Indië 1946-1949; 1ste Regiment Lichte Luchtdoel Artillerie. N.p.: n.n., 1987, 88 pp.

5780 Kramer, R.
Inventaris van het archief van de Ronde-Tafelconferentie, Indonesië 1949. 's-Gravenhage: Algemeen Rijksarchief, 1984, 36 pp.

5781 Kramer, R.
Plaatsingslijst van de archieven van de Nederlandse delegatie en van de delegatie van de Voorlopige Federale Regering van Indonesië bij de Ronde-Tafelconferentie (1946) 1949-1950. 's-Gravenhage: Algemeen Rijksarchief, 1985, 28 pp.

5782 Kretschmer de Wilde, C.J.M.
'De laatste Commandant der Zeemacht in Nederlands-Indië', *Marineblad* 76 (1966):983-984. (ubl)

5783 Kreutzer, R.
De PKI/FDR en het voorspel van Madiun. 1979, 31 pp. [Thesis Universiteit van Amsterdam.] (ara)

5784 Kreutzer, R.
'Een stuk geschiedenis; Het voorspel van Madiun', *Tijdschrift voor Diplomatie* 6-10 (1980):685-701.

5785 Kreutzer, R.
The Madiun affair; Hatta's betrayal of Indonesia's first social revolution. Townsville: James Cook University of North Queensland, 1981, 44 pp.

5786 Kreutzer, Ruud
The Madiun affair of 1948; Internal struggle in Indonesia's national movement. Amsterdam: Universiteit van Amsterdam, 1984, 24 pp.

5787 Krimp, R. and J.J. de Ruyter
Operatie Product; De eerste politionele actie in Indonesië. 1980, 62 pp. + appendices. [Thesis Koninklijke Militaire Academie, Breda.] (kitlv-smg)

5788 Kroes, J.
'Genietroepen op Java', *Genie* 7 (1957):143-149, 162-171, 256-267. (smg)

5789 Kroes, J.
'Enige herinneringen aan het optreden der Genietroepen in Indonesië in de periode 1946-1949', *Genie* 28 (1978):236-239. (smg)

5790 Kroes, R.
'Decolonization and the military; The case of the Netherlands', in: M. Janowitz and J.A.A. van Doorn (eds), *On military intervention*, pp. 93-114. Rotterdam: Rotterdam University Press, 1971.

5791 Krosenbrink, Henk (ed.)
Wij de jongens overzee. Doetinchem: Stichting Staring Instituut, 1989, 288 pp.

5792 Kruithof, A.J.
'Het begin van de uitzending der KL-onderdelen naar Indonesië', *Ons Leger* 53-3 (1970):19-22. (ubl)

5793 Kruyt, Laurens
'Over Soekarno zwijgen'; De voorlichting over de dekolonisatie van Nederlands-Indië in de periode 1945-1947. 1988, 95 pp. [MA thesis Universiteit van Amsterdam.] (kitlv-smg)

5794 Kuitenbrouwer, M.
'Dekolonisatie en revolutie in vergelijkend perspectief; Indonesië, India en Indochina', in: J. van Goor (ed.), *The Indonesian revolution; Conference papers, Utrecht, 17-20 June, 1986*, pp. 101-128. Utrecht: Rijksuniversiteit Utrecht, 1986.

5795 Laak, Gerard van der
Belevenissen van een stormpionier van het 4e Eskadron Pantserwagens, 15 juli 1946-19 april 1950. Hengelo: Grafodruk, 1994, 159+22 pp.

5796 Lagendijk, A.
Schakel tussen twee werelden; Repatriërings- en troepenschepen naar en van Indië,
1945-1951. Amsterdam: De Bataafsche Leeuw, 1991, 80 pp.

5797 Lancker, A.F.
'Herinneringen aan Borneo', *Mars et Historia* 14 (1980):15-20. (smg)

5798 Langeraad, Kees van
'De overdracht', in: J. van den Berg (ed.), *Bersiap*, pp. 126-149. 's-Gravenhage:
BZZTôH, 1993. [First published in 1974.]

5799 Lapré, S.A.
Het Andjing NICA Bataljon (KNIL) in Nederlands-Indië (1945-1950). Ermelo:
Lapré, 1987, 334 pp.

5800 Lapré, S.A.
Nederlands-Indië 1940-1950 in kort bestek en enkele gevolgen, o.a. de coup-
Westerling en het Zuidmolukse verzet. Ermelo: Lapré, 1989, 223 pp.

5801 Laurens, Ben
Het peloton; Roman over de Nederlandse soldaat in Nederlands-Indië. Rotterdam:
Donker, 1986, 234 pp.

5802 Laurens, Ben
De vreetpatrouille; Verhalen. Rotterdam: Donker, 1987, 132 pp.

5803 Lee, Jan van der and Erik Peddemors
Een stabiele factor in labiele verhoudingen; Voorlichting en opstelling van de
RVD-Batavia ten aanzien van het Nederlandse beleid in Indonesië, 1946-1949.
1986, 77 pp. [MA thesis Rijksuniversiteit Utrecht.] (kitlv-smg)

5804 Leenders, J.G.M.
Legertop en politiek beleid in het Nederlands-Indonesisch conflict 1945-1947.
1981, 70 pp. [MA thesis Rijksuniversiteit Leiden.] [58]

5805 Leeuwen, Abram van (Prins van Lignac)
Bandjir; Vuurstorm over Java; Een oorlogsroman die echt gebeurd moet zijn tijdens
het drama in Indonesië. Utrecht: Het Spectrum, 1990, 310 pp. [Second printing
1990.]

5806 Lensink, H. (ed.)
Gedenkboek GBI/5e Compagnie INF I-KNIL. Nijmegen: n.n., 1987, 333+299+297
pp. 3 vols.

5807 Liempt, Ad van
Een mooi woord voor oorlog; Ruzie, roddel en achterdocht op weg naar de Indonesië-
oorlog. Den Haag: SDU Uitgeverij Koninginnegracht, 1994, 291 pp.

5808 Limburg, J.H.
Diplomatie in een overgangstijd; De betrekkingen tussen het koninkrijk Egypte
en de Republiek Indonesië in de jaren 1945-1949. 1989, 63 pp. [MA thesis
Rijksuniversiteit Utrecht.]

5809 Limburg, J.H.
'Diplomatie in een overgangstijd; De Republiek Indonesië en Egypte, 1945-
1949', *Jambatan* 9-1 (1991):31-47.

5810 *Limburgs thuisfront 1946-1950; Ontstaan, streven en werken.* Maastricht: Stichting Limburgs Thuisfront, 1951, 95 pp.

5811 Logemann, J.H.A.
'Indonesië's terugkeer tot de Grondwet van 1945', *Bijdragen tot de Taal-, Land- en Volkenkunde* 115 (1959):209-231.

5812 Logemann, J.H.A.
Nieuwe gegevens over het ontstaan van de Indonesische Grondwet van 1945. Amsterdam: Noord-Hollandsche Uitgevers Maatschappij, 1962, 24 pp.

5813 Logemann, J.H.A.
'De Indonesische revolutie', in: I. Schöffer (ed.), *Zeven revoluties*, pp. 127-144. Amsterdam: De Bussy, 1964.

5814 Logemann, J.H.A.
Keterangan-keterangan baru tentang Undang-Undang Dasar Indonesia 1945. Malang: Laboratorium Pancasila IKIP Malang, 1982, 29 pp.

5815 Lukassen, Jo
Een mijlpaal in ons leven; Herinneringen van Nederlandse militairen in de tropen. Zeeland: Lukassen, 1986, 224 pp.

5816 Maaren, Robert van
'Darul Islam; Een vorm van sociaal-banditisme?', *Jambatan* 10 (1992):51-63.

5817 Maas, P.F.
'Dr. H.J. van Mook, onze laatste landvoogd, tot ontslag gedwongen (augustus-oktober 1948)', *Acta Politica* 17 (1982):367-384. Also in: *Politieke opstellen*, pp. 18-32. Nijmegen: Centrum voor Parlementaire Geschiedenis der Katholieke Universiteit, 1982. (ubl)

5818 Maas, P.F.
'Onze minister van Overzeese Gebiedsdelen, Mr. Emmanuel Sassen, abandonneert (februari 1949)', *Acta Politica* 17 (1982):41-71. (ubl)

5819 Maas, P.F.
'Stikker in Kaliurang; Laatste halte op weg naar de tweede politionele actie, nov.-dec. 1948', *Politieke opstellen*, pp. 38-57. Nijmegen: Centrum voor Parlementaire Geschiedenis der Katholieke Universiteit, 1982. (ubl)

5820 Maas, P.F.
Indië verloren, rampspoed geboren; Het moeizame afscheid van Indië van Van Mook, Stikker en Sassen. Dieren: De Bataafsche Leeuw, 1983, 94 pp.

5821 Maas, P.F.
'De Indonesiëpolitiek van minister D.U. Stikker in memoires en geschiedschrijving', *Acta Politica* 19 (1984):359-378. (ubl)

5822 Maas, P.F. and J.E.C.M. van Oerle
'Documents reveal', in: *Politieke opstellen*, pp. 44-66. Nijmegen: Centrum voor Parlementaire Geschiedenis der Katholieke Universiteit, 1983.

5823 Maas, P.F. and J.E.C.M. van Oerle
'Het leger te gelde', in: G. Teitler and P.M.H. Groen (eds), *De politionele acties*, pp. 11-28. Amsterdam: De Bataafsche Leeuw, 1987.

5824 MacGillavry, A.
Je kunt niet altijd huilen; Een Nederlands gezin in de laatste periode van Nederlands-Oostindië. Baarn: De Boekerij, 1975, 208 pp.

5825 Mahieu, Vincent (ps. Jan Boon)
Tjoek. Den Haag: Leopold, 1960, 187 pp. [Second printing, 's-Gravenhage: Moesson, 1975; Fifth printing, *Tjoek.* Met een nawoord van Rudy Kousbroek, Amsterdam: Querido, 1994.]

5826 Mahieu, Vincent (ps.)
'Een bloedbad voor Ferdi', in: Vincent Mahieu, *Schat, schot, schat; Zes vertellingen*, pp. 66-98. Amsterdam: Querido, 1990.

5827 Mahieu, Vincent (ps.)
Tschuk. Berlin: Twenne, 1993, 215 pp.

5828 Mahler, E.
De witte karbouw; Herinneringen aan een oorlog in de tropen. Breda: Warung Bambu, 1992, 187 pp.

5829 Maks, J.
De staatkundig-politieke ontwikkeling van Indonesië. Amsterdam: Koninklijk Instituut voor de Tropen, 1950, 72 pp.

5830 Mays, F.C.
'Ervaringen op watervoorzieningsgebied bij de troepen in Indonesië', *De Militaire Spectator* 119 (1950):237-244. (ubl)

5831 Mei, D.F. van der
Dienstvervulling onder buitengewone en zeer moeilijke omstandigheden; De verantwoordelijkheid van de overheid voor de specifieke problematiek van oud-militairen Indiëgangers. 's-Gravenhage: n.n., 1989, 51 pp.

5832 Meulen, Daniël van der
Ik stond er bij; Het einde van ons koloniale rijk. Baarn: Bosch en Keuning, 1965, 264 pp.

5833 Meulen, Daniël van der
Hoort gij de donder niet? Begin van het einde der Nederlandse gezagvoering in Indië; Een persoonlijke terugblik. Franeker: Wever, 1977, 365 pp.

5834 Meulen, Daniël van der
Don't you hear the thunder? A Dutchman's life story. Leiden: Brill, 1981, 199 pp.

5835 Meulen, Inge van der
'1945-1949; Geleidelijke verwijdering', in: Harry A. Poeze (ed.), *In het land van de overheerser I; Indonesiërs in Nederland 1600-1950*, pp. 331-371, 377. Dordrecht/Cinnaminson: Foris, 1986.

5836 Meulen, J. van der
'Interview met een Indië-veteraan', *Maatschappij en Krijgsmacht* 6 (August 1984):1-13. (ubl)

5837 Minnen, Cornelis A. van (ed.)
The decolonization of Indonesia; International perspectives. Middelburg: Roosevelt Study Center/Stichting V.O.C.-Publicaties Zeeland, 1988, 75 pp.

5838 Mol, Eric
Soldaten willen vrede. Amsterdam: Algemeen Nederlands Jeugd Verbond, 1950, 16 pp.

5839 Mol, Eric
Vrijheid voor Piet van Staveren. Amsterdam: Amnestiecomité voor Dienstweigeraars Indonesië, 1951, 24 pp.

5840 Molen, G.H.J. van der
'Het volkenrechtelijke aspect van de eenzijdige opzegging der Nederlands-Indonesische Unie', *Antirevolutionaire Staatkunde* 26 (1956):33-42. (ubl)

5841 Monster, T.J. and B.H.A. van de Sande
Diplomatie op het scherpst van de snede; De rol van E.N. van Kleffens en H.F.L.K. van Vredenburch tijdens de Indonesische kwestie, mei 1947-juli 1948. Ca. 1985, 181 pp. [MA thesis Rijksuniversiteit Utrecht.] (kitlv-smg)

5842 Montulet, L.F.C. (Loek)
Een ronde tafel met een gat er in; Het einde van een verhouding tussen Nederland en Indonesië. 1984, 107 pp. [MA thesis Rijksuniversiteit Utrecht.]

5843 Moor, J.A. de
'Het Korps Speciale Troepen; Tussen marechaussee-formule en politionele actie', in: G. Teitler and P.M.H. Groen (eds), *De politionele acties*, pp. 121-143. Amsterdam: De Bataafsche Leeuw, 1987.

5844 Moor, J.A. de
'Kapitein Westerling en de APRA-coup; Het einde van een mythe', in: G. Teitler and J. Hoffenaar (eds), *De politionele acties; Afwikkeling en verwerking*, pp. 45-60. Amsterdam: De Bataafsche Leeuw, 1990.

5845 Moor, J.A. de
'Van vrije jongen tot Ratu Adil; De memoires van Kapitein Raymond Westerling', *Indische Letteren* 8 (1993):171-180.

5846 Moraal, Willem
Mariniers in aktie op Oost-Java; Met zware marsbepakking; Memoires uit 1946-1949. Bewerkt door Jaak Venken. Venlo: Van Spijk, 1983, 205 pp.

5847 Morriën, J.
'Schermerhorns dagboek; Démasqué van een koloniale politiek', *Politiek en Cultuur* 31 (1971):53-61. (ubl)

5848 Morriën, J.
Indonesië los van Holland; De CPN en de PKI in hun strijd tegen het Nederlandse kolonialisme. Amsterdam: Pegasus, 1982, 272 pp.

5849 Morris, Lea
En toch haten wij niet. Assen: De Torenlaan, ca. 1961, 227 pp. [Second printing 1977.]

5850 Müller, M.; P. van den Roovaart and H.A. Franssen (eds)
Herinneringsboek der 14e Genie Veld Compagnie, Januari 1948 tot Juni 1950. N.p.: n.n., ca. 1951, 53 pp.

5851 *Mijn diensttijd bij de 3e Compagnie.* 1953, 41 pp. (kitlv-smg)

5852 Nabbe, A.
De Nederlandse liberalen en de kwestie-Indonesië; Een onderzoek naar de houding van de Nederlandse liberalen ten opzichte van de dekolonisatie van Nederlands-Indië, 1945-1949. 1989, 147 pp. [MA thesis Katholieke Universiteit Nijmegen.]

5853 Neden, J.W. van
'De ontwikkeling van een veteranenprobleem', in: G. Teitler and J. Hoffenaar (eds), *De politionele acties; Afwikkeling en verwerking*, pp. 103-113. Amsterdam: De Bataafsche Leeuw, 1990.

5854 *Nederlandsch Indië 1945, Indonesië 1949 en Achter het Nieuws 1969; Teksten van drie Achter het Nieuws uitzendingen over de gebeurtenissen tijdens de twee politionele akties in het voormalig Nederlands Indië.* Hilversum: Omroepvereniging VARA, 1969, 109 pp.

5855 Neuman, H.J.
De W van Willem; Kroniek van een brigade. Semarang: Van Dorp, 1950, 153 pp.

5856 Neut, Ton van der
Daarom zijn we in Indië; Nederlandse militairen schrijven de PvdA. 1982, 122 pp. [MA thesis Universiteit van Amsterdam.]

5857 Neut, Ton van der
'Evert Vermeer en de "jongens overzee", 1947-1950', *Socialisme en Democratie* 40-11 (1983):15-18, 26. (ubl)

5858 Neijssel, Antoinette
Tussen gisteren en vandaag; Twee novellen. Amsterdam: Arbeiderspers, 1957, 66 pp.

5859 Nieskens, Toon
Nacht over de rimboe; Verslag uit het dagboek van Toon Nieskens, bijgehouden tijdens zijn diensttijd in Indonesië, vanaf zijn vertrek op 12 november 1947 tot zijn terugkomst op 1 juni 1950. Montfort: De Ruit, 1993, 96 pp.

5860 *NIWIN, Uw hart was bij hen, 1946-1950; Aangeboden aan allen, die met veel inspanning werkten voor de ontspanning van Neerlands zonen overzee.* 's-Gravenhage: n.n., 1950. [unpaged]

5861 *Noorderlicht op Midden-Java; Gedenkboek 403e Bataljon Infanterie, 1948-1950.* N.p.: n.n., 1992, 160 pp.

5862 Nortier, J.J.
'De Puputan Margarana', *Stabelan* 16-3 (1989/90):33-36. (smg)

5863 *Nota betreffende het archievenonderzoek naar gegevens omtrent excessen in Indonesië begaan door Nederlandse militairen in de periode 1945-1950.* 's-Gravenhage: Ministerie van Algemene Zaken, 1969. [Various pagings; Reprinted 1995.]

5864 Oerle, J.E.C.M. van
'De weg naar Madiun; PKI en CPN tussen twee opstanden, 1927-1948', in: *Politieke opstellen*, pp. 20-37. Nijmegen: Centrum voor Parlementaire Geschiedenis der Katholieke Universiteit, 1982.

5865 *Officiële bescheiden betreffende de Nederlands-Indonesische betrekkingen 1945-1950.* Ed. by S.L. van der Wal; From vol. 9 ed. by P.J. Drooglever and M.J.B. Schouten. 's-Gravenhage: Nijhoff (vols I-XV)/Instituut voor Nederlandse Geschiedenis (vols XVI-XX), 1971-. I. *10 augustus-8 november 1945,* 1971, 24+616 pp.; II. *9 november-31 december 1945,* 1972, 19+628 pp.; III. *1 januari-30 maart 1946,* 1973, 24+739 pp.; IV. *31 maart-16 juli 1946,* 1974, 26+724 pp.; V. *16 juli-28 oktober 1946,* 1975, 24+727 pp.; VI. *29 oktober 1946-5 januari 1947,* 1976, 23+813 pp.; VII. *6 januari-20 maart 1947,* 1978, 23+883 pp.; VIII. *21 maart-20 mei 1947,* 1979, 19+796 pp.; IX. *21 mei-20 juli 1947,* 1981, 24+815 pp.; X. *21 juli-31 augustus 1947,* 1982, 26+770 pp.; XI. *1 september-25 november 1947,* 1983, 27+781 pp.; XII. *26 november 1947-19 februari 1948,* 1985, 30+898 pp.; XIII. *20 februari-4 juni 1948,* 1986, 27+878 pp.; XIV. *5 juni-31 augustus 1948,* 1988, 31+774 pp.; XV. *1 september-30 november 1948,* 1989, 29+873 pp.; XVI. *1 december 1948-12 januari 1949,* 1991, 32+771 pp.; XVII. *13 januari-28 februari 1949,* 1992, 29+759 pp.; XVIII. *1 maart-31 mei 1949,* 1993, 29+839 pp.; XIX. *1 juni-15 september 1949,* 1994, 28+839 pp.; XX. *16 september-31 december 1949,* 1996, 31+929 pp.

5866 Ombroso, Bernardo
Voor de vrijheid. Antwerpen: Zuid-Nederlandse Uitgeverij, Harderwijk: Centrale Uitgeverij, 1974, 124 pp.

5867 *Ons dagboek 1946-1950; 2e Peloton 10e Genie Veldcompagnie.* Roosendaal: n.n., 1989, 228 pp.

5868 *Ons eskadron; Gedenkboek van het derde Eskadron PAW van de tweede afdeling Regiment Huzaren van Boreel, Maart 1947-April 1950.* Haarlem: Tjeenk Willink, 1951, 291 pp. (kitlv-smg)

5869 *Onze kamelenbrug; 3e Peloton 10e Genie Veld Compagnie, 2e Divisie; Reüniebundel.* N.p.: n.n., 1986, 82 pp.

5870 *Oorlog en verzet in Nederlands-Indië 1941-1949 en de voorlichting aan na-oorlogse generaties.* Amsterdam: De Bataafsche Leeuw, 1989, 80 pp.

5871 *Oost-Java; Gedenkboek der 4e Infanterie-brigade.* Tilburg: Bergmans, 1951, 512 pp.

5872 Oppen, L.P. van
'Chris van der Tuin', in: L.P. van Oppen, *Als een goet instrument; 40 jaar strepen, sterren en balken,* pp. 77-100. Utrecht: De Boer Concept, 1993.

5873 *Orde, rust en veiligheid; De operatieve taak van 6 RS.* Heeze: n.n., 1993, 80 pp.

5874 Otte, C. and G.C. Zijlmans
'Wederopbouw en ondergang van de Indische bestuursdienst; Het corps Binnenlands Bestuur op Java 1945-1950', in: *ZWO-jaarboek 1980,* pp. 179-197. 's-Gravenhage: ZWO, 1980.

5875 Otten, Peter H.W.M.
Het Amsterdams belang bij Indië 1945-1950. 1984, 43 pp. [MA thesis Universiteit van Amsterdam.] [58]

5876 *Oud-bestuursambtenaren in voormalig Nederlands-Indië en dekolonisatie.* Leiden: Indologenblad, 1980, 45 pp.

5877 Oijen, L.M.A. van
Soldatenverhalen aan de vergetelheid ontrukt. Breda: Brabantia Nostra, 1988, 144 pp.

5878 Peters, H.C.
Je moet nu gaan. Franeker: Van Wijnen, 1990, 200 pp.

5879 Petri, G.J.
'Met dominee W.L. Steinhart op Sumatra, oktober 1947 tot december 1950', *Documentatieblad Lutherse Kerkgeschiedenis* 7 (1990):2-31. (kb)

5880 Piekaar, A.J.
'A Dutch view of the struggle', in: Colin Wild and Peter Carey (eds), *Born in fire; The Indonesian struggle for independence; An anthology*, pp. 198-205. Athens: Ohio University Press, 1986.

5881 Piekaar, A.J.
'Sebuah pandangan Belanda tentang perjuangan', in: Colin Wild and Peter Carey (eds), *Gelora api revolusi*, pp. 205-212. Jakarta: Gramedia, 1986.

5882 Pinke, A.S.
'De maatregelen in verband met het zeeverkeer in de Indonesische wateren, 1946-1949', *Marineblad* 60 (1950):992-1013.

5883 *Pioniers overzee.* Leiden: n.n., 1950, 339 pp.

5884 Pluvier, Jan M.
'The Dutch press and the Indonesian question (1942-1949)', *Journal of the Historical Society of the University of Malaya* 1-3 (1962-63):58-72.

5885 Pluvier, J.M.
De Indonesische revolutie. Kanttekeningen van G.A.J. Giezeman en N.J. Maarsen. Haarlem: Gottmer, 1970, 48 pp.

5886 Pluvier, Jan
'Dutch war crimes in Indonesia', *Journal of Contemporary Asia* 2-2 (1972):199-202.

5887 Pluvier, J.M.
'Staat in de steigers; De organisatie van de staat Indonesië', in: *Onze jaren 45-70*, pp. 1101-1104. Amsterdam, 1972.

5888 Pluygers, W. and G.A. van Apeldoorn (eds)
3-7 RI op Midden-Java; Gedenkboek van een bataljon van de Koninklijke Landmacht te velde. N.p.: n.n., 1950, 149 pp. (kitlv-smg)

5889 Poeze, Harry
'De Partij van de Arbeid en Indonesië, 1945-1950', in: *Verstrikt in verbondenheid; Nederland, PvdA en Indonesië 1945-1980*, pp. 12-22, 24-26. Amsterdam: Evert Vermeer Stichting, 1980.

5890 Poeze, Harry A.
'De Indonesische kwestie 1945-1950; Sociaal-democratie in de klem', in: Joost Divendal et al. (ed.), *Nederland, links en de koude oorlog; Breuken en bruggen*, pp. 38-57. Amsterdam: De Populier, 1982.

5891 *De politionele acties; Documentatie 27 en 28 november 1986.* Den Haag: Stichting Maatschappij en Krijgsmacht, 1986, 26 pp.

5892 Pollmann, Tessel
'Kolonialgewalt als "Polizeiaktion"; Der niederländische Krieg gegen die indonesischen Nationalisten, 1945-1949', in: M. van der Linden and G. Mergner (eds), *Kriegsbegeisterung und mentale Kriegsvorbereitung; Interdisziplinäre Studien*, pp. 195-218. Berlin: Duncker und Humblot, 1991. (kb)

5893 Pool, R.
Als kwartiermaker naar West-Java voor 1-III Regiment 'Prinses Irene', november 1945-november 1946. Arnhem: n.n., 1986, 47 pp.

5894 Portier, B.F.
'Drie voorbeelden van het gebruik van Baileymateriaal bij de montage', *De Militaire Spectator* 120 (1951):102-106. (kb)

5895 Prince, G.H.A.
'Had Nederland een koloniale ideologie? Na de dekolonisatie; Einde of vervolg', *Kleio* 18 (1977):818-822. (ubl)

5896 *Rapport uit Porrong; Met het 8e Eskadron Vechtwagens naar Oost-Java.* N.p.: n.n., 1950, 184 pp.

5897 Rausch, J.P.C.
'Indië 1946-1950; Jongens-mannen-kerels', *Ons Leger* 70-9 (1986):13-15; 70-10 (1986):7-8. (ubl)

5898 Reenders, Hommo
'De verwerking van de dekolonisatie van Indonesië door de gereformeerden (1945-1963)', in: Alphen, M. van; E. Noort and L. Oranje (eds), *Kerk en vredes- beweging; Bijdragen vanuit de Theologische Hogeschool van de Gereformeerde Kerken in Kampen*, p. 65-82. Kampen: Kok, 1982.

5899 Regenhardt, J.W.
'De affaire Indonesia Calling; Ivens, de CIA en Van Mook', *Skript* 7 (1985):197-207. (ubl)

5900 Remmelink, W.G.J.
'The emergence of the new situation; The Japanese army on Java after the surrender', *De Militaire Spectator* 147 (February 1978):49-66.

5901 Remmelink, W.G.J. and Jang Aisjah Muttalib
'The historiography on the Indonesian revolution; Some remarks on Western approaches', in: *Papers of the Dutch-Indonesian Historical Conference*, pp. 36-46. Leiden/Jakarta: Bureau of Indonesian Studies, 1982.

5902 Rhodius, H.E.R. and E.H. van Eeghen
Op de drempel van een nieuwe tijd of de geschiedenis van een uit Indonesië repatriërend militair. Eindhoven: Eindhovensche Drukkerij, ca. 1955, 22 pp.

5903 Riemersma, Riemer
Hwat west hat. Drachten: Laverman, 1965, 164 pp. [In Frisian.]

5904 Ringoir, H.
'Stoottroepen', *Ons Leger* 59-4 (1975):28-34. (ubl)

5905 Rinzema, Win
Dit was uw Tjideng; Aspecten van de vertraagde afwikkeling van Japanse interne-ringskampen in Batavia met het Tjidengkamp als casus. Utrecht: Stichting ICODO, 1989, 181 pp. [Second edition, 1991, 172 pp.]

5906 Rinzema-Admiraal, W.
'De bersiap tussen Indië en Indonesië', *ICODO-Info* 2-3 (October 1985):14-24.

5907 Robben, Wim
De Indonesië-weigeraars 1945-1950; Een onderzoek naar de omvang, motieven en gevolgen. Zwolle: Stichting Voorlichting Aktieve Geweldloosheid, 1981, 37 pp.

5908 Robinson, Tjalie (ps. Jan Boon)
Taaie en Neut. Heemskerk: Blok, 1980, 89 pp.

5909 *Rond Smeroe en Kawi; Gedenkboek van het 4e Bataljon, 5e Reg. Infanterie, November 1946-April 1950.* Amsterdam: Holdert, 1950, 210 pp.

5910 *De Ronde-Tafelconferentie; Een overzicht van de onderhandelingen met betrekking tot het zelfbeschikkingsrecht der volkeren, het standpunt der Nederlandse regering en de reactie in de Tweede Kamer; Interimrapport. Commissie van Overleg Zuid-Molukkers-Nederlanders; Historisch overzicht eerste deel.* 's-Gravenhage: Staatsuitgeverij, 1978, 59 pp.

5911 Ronner, B.
Van huis en van haard naar het land van de tokkèhs; Indië-dagboek '46-'49-'92. Bedum: Profiel, 1993, 328 pp.

5912 Rooijen, K. van
Tussen goenoeng en guerrilla; Tussen berg en vrijheidsstrijd. Utrecht: n.n., 1986, 146 pp. (kitlv-smg)

5913 Rosheuvel, Ch.A.
Van West naar Oost; De rol van de Curaçaose Rode-Kruiscolonne in het voormalig Nederlands Oost-Indië. Zutphen: De Walburg Pers, 1989, 277 pp.

5914 Rosin, H.
'Geloof en Indonesische revolutie', in: *Geloof en revolutie; Kerkhistorische kanttekeningen bij een actueel vraagstuk,* pp. 210-222. Amsterdam: Bolland, 1977.

5915 Rossum, G.M. van
Groen is de oetan. Leiden: Groen, ca. 1950, 239 pp.

5916 Rossum, G.M. van
Het vreemde leger. N.p.: Vereniging Oud 3-3 RI 1 Divisie '7 December', 1985, 142 pp.

5917 Rottier, R.
'Piet Kerstens; De Tijd vooruit; De hoofdredacteur die struikelde over de Indonesische kwestie', in: *Jaarboek Katholiek Documentatie Centrum* 18 (1988): 156-172. Nijmegen: Katholiek Documentatie Centrum. (ubl)

5918 Rijnbende, R.J.
Gereformeerden en de Indonesische revolutie, 1945-1949. Paper Rijksuniversiteit Utrecht, 1991, 25 pp.

5919 Rijs, J. van; H.J. Reijn and J. Siebenga
Zo was het; Gedenkboek 3-5 RI, 1946-1950. Nijmegen: Leijn, ca. 1950, 176 pp.

5920 Rijsdijk, A.
Repatriëring en opvang van Indische Nederlanders; Departementaal beleid 1945-1958. Paper Universiteit van Amsterdam, 1985, 50 pp.

5921 Sande, Berend van de
De Suripno-affaire; Toedracht en gevolgen. 1984, 29 pp. [Thesis Rijksuniversiteit Utrecht.]

5922 Sande, Kees van de
Een zwarte bladzijde uit het vergeetboek der Nederlandse geschiedenis; De 'Bandung-affaire'; Achtergronden, verloop, nasleep van en reacties op de overval op Bandung op 23 januari 1950. 1985, 100 pp. [MA thesis Rijksuniversiteit Utrecht.]

5923 Sanders, P.
'Sjahrir dan Perjanjian Linggarjati', in: H. Rosihan Anwar (ed.), Mengenang Sjahrir, pp. 272-288. Jakarta: Gramedia, 1980.

5924 Sanders, Pieter
The Linggarjati agreement. Paper Linggarjati Conference, 1991, 13 pp.

5925 Sanders, P.
'Perjanjian Linggarjati', in: A.B. Lapian and P.J. Drooglever (eds), Menelusuri jalur Linggarjati; Diplomasi dalam perspektif sejarah, pp. 151-162. Jakarta: Grafiti, 1992.

5926 Sapu, John (ps.)
De vuile was; Het realistische verhaal van een soldaat tijdens de laatste maanden van het voormalige Nederlands Indië. Rotterdam: SARI, ca. 1970, 240 pp.

5927 Scheffer, C.F.
Het bankwezen in Indonesië sedert het uitbreken van de Tweede Wereldoorlog. Djakarta: Noordhoff/Kolff, 1951, 204 pp. [Also PhD thesis Katholieke Economische Hogeschool, Tilburg.]

5928 Scheltema, H.
'Herinneringen van een vrijheidsstrijdster', in: Peter Boomgaard, Harry A. Poeze and Gerard Termorshuizen (eds), Aangeraakt door Insulinde, pp. 121-124. Leiden: KITLV Uitgeverij, 1992.

5929 Schenkman, Jan
De Indonesiëreizen van Goedhart, alias Pieter 't Hoen; Een land in revolutie; Bevindingen en vertolking. 1990, 69 pp. [MA thesis Katholieke Universiteit Nijmegen.]

5930 Schermerhorn, W.
'Illusie en werkelijkheid over Nederland-Indonesië', in: Bert Bakker, D.H. Couvee and Jan Kassies (eds), Visioen en werkelijkheid; De illegale pers over de toekomst der samenleving, pp. 166-189. 's-Gravenhage: Bakker/Daamen, 1963.

5931 Schie, Laurens van
Kapitaal en politiek; Nederland-Indonesië 1945-1949; Een studie naar de invloed op de dekolonisatie van Indonesië door het georganiseerde Nederlandse

bedrijfsleven dat in Indonesië werkzaam was. 1982, 76 pp. [MA thesis Universiteit van Amsterdam.]

5932 Schie, Laurens van
'De ondernemers en de dekolonisatie van Indonesië 1945-1949', *Jambatan* 2-1 (1983/84):15-21.

5933 Schie, Laurens van
'De verloren strijd van de laatste landvoogd', *De Gids* 151 (1988):831-839.

5934 Schiethart, D.P.
Tussen Washington, Den Haag en Batavia; De Amerikaans-Nederlandse betrekkingen als gevolg van de militaire acties in Indonesië, 1947-1949. 1985, 69 pp. [MA thesis Rijksuniversiteit Groningen.]

5935 Schilling, T.
Spoor, onze generaal door zijn vrienden en soldaten. Amsterdam: Meulenhoff, 1953, 165 pp. [Second edition, 1958, 190 pp.]

5936 Schilt, Jan
Soldaatje spelen onder de smaragden gordel. Amsterdam: Van Gennep, 1969, 196 pp. [Second edition, Amsterdam: Mets, 1989, 192 pp.]

5937 Schneiders, A.L.
'De kanonnen', in: *Bij het scheiden van de markt*, pp. 164-169. Amsterdam: Querido, 1965. [First published in 1950.]

5938 Scholte, Lin
'Surabaya 1945', in: Lin Scholte, *Takdiran en andere verhalen*, pp. 24-64. Amsterdam: Querido, 1977.

5939 Schonagen, Caspar
De PvdA en de Indonesische kwestie; Het dilemma van de koloniale ontvoogding versus de nationale integratie van het socialisme. 1988, 82 pp. [MA thesis Universiteit van Amsterdam.] [43]

5940 Schoonoord, D.C.L.
'Operatie Zeemeeuw', *Marineblad* 79 (1969):27-44. (ubl)

5941 Schoonoord, D.C.L.
'De Mariniersbrigade en de politionele acties', in: G. Teitler and C. Homan (ed.), *Het Korps Mariniers 1942-heden*, pp. 19-28. Amsterdam: De Bataafsche Leeuw, 1985.

5942 Schoonoord, D.C.L.
De Mariniersbrigade 1943-1949; Wording en inzet in Indonesië. 's-Gravenhage: Afdeling Maritieme Historie van de Marinestaf, 1988, 413 pp. [PhD thesis Universiteit van Amsterdam.]

5943 Schoonoord, D.C.L.
'De Nederlandse militaire missie in Indonesië', in: G. Teitler and J. Hoffenaar (eds), *De politionele acties; Afwikkeling en verwerking*, pp. 61-77. Amsterdam: De Bataafsche Leeuw, 1990.

5944 Schotborgh, L.
'De rol, welke Nederland in Indonesië heeft vervuld, meer in het bijzonder voor wat betreft de periode 1940-1949', Antirevolutionaire Staatkunde 23 (1953):229-239. (ubl)

5945 Schulten, C.M.; H.L. Zwitzer and J. Hoffenaar (ed.)
1 Divisie '7 December'. Amsterdam: De Bataafsche Leeuw, 1986, 192 pp.

5946 Schulten, J.W.M.
'Soldaten, legerleiding en thuisfront; Een belangengemeenschap onder een ongelukkig gesternte', in: G. Teitler and P.M.H. Groen (eds), De politionele acties, pp. 29-43. Amsterdam: De Bataafsche Leeuw, 1987.

5947 Schulten, J.W.M.
'Het afgeschreven leger; De Indië-veteranen en hun strijd om erkenning', in: G. Teitler and J. Hoffenaar (eds), De politionele acties; Afwikkeling en verwerking, pp. 91-101. Amsterdam: De Bataafsche Leeuw, 1990.

5948 Schumacher, P.
Indonesië '45-'49; De dilemma's van generaal Spoor, de methodes van kapitein Westerling. Rotterdam: NRC Handelsblad, 1980, 24 pp.

5949 Schumacher, Peter
'Veel paternalisme, weinig racisme?', Wending 39 (1984):431-435. (ubl)

5950 Schutte, G.J.
'De ervaringen van de laatste generatie Indischgasten', Tijdschrift voor Geschiedenis 97 (1984):214-222.

5951 Sigmond, J.P.
'Oorlog en revolutie; Indonesische kindertekeningen uit Djokjakarta 1948-1949 als historische bron', Armamentaria 27(1992):97-106.

5952 Sillevis Smitt, J.H. and A. van Kampen
Het keerpunt. 's-Gravenhage: Verhoeve, 1953, 31 pp.

5953 Simons, Yvonne
Het ANJV en de strijd tegen de Indonesië-politiek van de Nederlandse regering, 1945-1950. Paper Universiteit van Amsterdam, 1985, 33 pp.

5954 Slenter, Marcel
Nederlands Indië/Indonesië in beeld. Roermond: De Vleermuis, ca. 1988, 33 pp.

5955 Sluimers, L.E.L.
'Enige facetten der Indonesische revolutie; Revolutie als dekolonisatieproces', in: B.V.A. Röling (ed.), Opstand en revolutie, pp. 132-175. Assen: Dr. H.J. Prakke & H.M.G. Prakke, 1965.

5956 Sluimers, L.E.L.
Indonesië; Van kolonie tot zelfstandige staat. Amsterdam: Antropologisch-Sociologisch Centrum, 1972, 13 pp. [45]

5957 Smit, C.
De Indonesische quaestie; De wordingsgeschiedenis der souvereiniteitsoverdracht. Leiden: Brill, 1952, 289 pp.

5958 Smit, C.
Het akkoord van Linggadjati; Uit het dagboek van Prof. Dr. Ir. W. Schermerhorn, voorzitter der Commissie-Generaal voor Nederlands-Indië, 14 september 1946-18 september 1947. Amsterdam: Elsevier, 1959, 264 pp.

5959 Smit, C.
'Het begin van de Nederlands-Indonesische onderhandelingen en de besprekingen op de Hoge Veluwe', *Internationale Spectator* 15 (1961):38-48.

5960 Smit, C.
De liquidatie van een imperium; Nederland en Indonesië 1945-1962. Amsterdam: Arbeiderspers, 1962, 232 pp.

5961 Smit, C. (ed.)
Het dagboek van Schermerhorn; Geheim verslag van prof. dr. ir. W. Schermerhorn als voorzitter der Commissie-Generaal voor Nederlands-Indië, 20 september 1946-7 oktober 1947. Groningen: Wolters-Noordhoff, 1970, 956 pp. 2 vols.

5962 Smit, C.
De dekolonisatie van Indonesië; Feiten en beschouwingen. Groningen: Tjeenk Willink, 1976, 154 pp.

5963 Smit, C.
'Twee brieven van Dr. H.J. van Mook over het dekolonisatieproces', *Internationale Spectator* 32 (1978):640-645.

5964 Smits, Frank
'Een ander pakje aan; De ideeën van dienstplichtige militairen over het conflict tussen Nederland en de Republiek Indonesië 1945-1949', *Jambatan* 9-3 (1991): 122-131.

5965 Smulders, R.M.
Een stem uit het veld; Herinneringen van de ritmeester-adjudant van generaal S.H. Spoor. Amsterdam: De Bataafsche Leeuw, 1988, 144 pp.

5966 Sohns, Emile Christiaan
Arbeidsrecht, arbeidsconventies en de samengestelde staatsvorm; De ontwikkeling van Nederlands-Indië tot de Verenigde Staten van Indonesië en de betrekkingen met de internationale arbeidsorganisatie. 's-Gravenhage: Nijhoff, 1950, 177 pp. [PhD thesis Rijksuniversiteit Leiden.]

5967 *Soldatenverzet rond politionele akties in Indonesië, 1948-1949.* Amsterdam: Bond voor Dienstplichtigen, 1982, 48 pp.

5968 Souverijn, Willem
'Pemuda's, jongeren en de Indonesische revolutie', *Fibula* 26-1 (1985):4-12.

5969 Spapens, A.A.M.
De Nederlandse katholieke missie in de Indonesische archipel in de jaren 1940-1950. Paper Rijksuniversiteit Utrecht, 1991, 21 pp.

5970 Spreeuwers, Roelf
De lange weg; Als oorlogsvrijwilliger naar Ned. Indië. Stadskanaal: Roorda, 1980, 207 pp.

5971   Springer, F. (ps. C.J. Schneider)
       'De verovering van Bandoeng', in: F. Springer, Zaken overzee, pp. 7-39. Utrecht:
       E.C.I., 1978.

5972   Spijkerboer, Chris
       P.J. Koets in het naoorlogse Indië. 1982, 67 pp. [MA thesis Universiteit van
       Amsterdam.]

5973   Stallinga, T.
       Soldaten uit de lucht; Oprichting, organisatie en inzet van de eerste Neder-
       landse parachutisteneenheden ten tijde van het Nederlands-Indonesisch con-
       flict, 1945-1949. 1992, 83 pp. [MA thesis Katholieke Universiteit Nijmegen.]

5974   Stallinga, Tamme
       'Aanval van boven; Nederlandse parachutisten en hun rol in het Nederlands-
       Indonesisch conflict, 1945-1949', Kleio 34-5 (June 1993):17-22. (ubl)

5975   Stam, L.
       De Hueting-affaire; Analyse van de reacties op tv-uitzendingen over oorlogsmisdaden
       in het voormalig Nederlands-Indië tijdens de politionele akties. Amsterdam:
       Psychologisch Laboratorium der Universiteit, 1972, 73+12 pp.

5976   Steen, P.A. van der
       De Limmer soldaten in Nederlands Oost-Indië. Limmen: Stichting Oud-Limmen,
       1993, 19 pp.

5977   Stempels, A.
       De parlementaire geschiedenis van het Indonesische vraagstuk. Amsterdam:
       Arbeiderspers, 1950, 317 pp.

5978   Stevens, R.J.J.
       De PvdA en de eerste politionele actie 1945-1947. 1989, 89 pp. [BA thesis
       Katholieke Universiteit Nijmegen.]

5979   Stevens, R.
       Een duister interregnum; De Partij van de Arbeid en de tweede politionele actie.
       1990, 118 pp. [MA thesis Katholieke Universiteit Nijmegen.]

5980   Stevens, Th.
       Een ander geluid, een ander beeld; De Vereniging Nederland-Indonesië, het
       Kamerlid F.J. Goedhart en de groep-Koets over de situatie in de Republik aan
       de vooravond van Linggarjati. Paper Linggarjati Conference, 1991, 11 pp.

5981   Stevens, Th.
       'Lain suara - lain citra; Keadaan Republik menjelang perjanjian Linggarjati
       menurut F.J. Goedhart dan kelompok Koets', in: A.B. Lapian and P.J.
       Drooglever (eds), Menelusuri jalur Linggarjati; Diplomasi dalam perspektif sejarah,
       pp. 163-178. Jakarta: Grafiti, 1992.

5982   Stikker, D.U.
       'The road not taken', Foreign Affairs 52 (1973):184-190. (ubl)

5983   Stolk, Loes
       De Verenigde Staten en de Indonesische kwestie 1945-1949. 1979. [MA thesis
       Katholieke Universiteit Nijmegen.] [45]

5984 Stuldreher, C.J.F.
'De "extremistenkampen" van de Republiek Indonesië', *De Gids* 151 (1988):825-830.

5985 Sytzen, Job
Niet iedere soldaat sneuvelt. Voorwoord van J.C. Koningsberger. Leiden: Sijthoff, 1953, 280 pp. [Many reprints.]

5986 Sytzen, Job
Gods ravijn. Leiden: Sijthoff, 1954, 245 pp. [Many reprints.]

5987 Sytzen, Job
Landgenoten. Leiden: Sijthoff, 1955, 264 pp. [Many reprints.]

5988 Sytzen, Job
Soldaat - Ravijn - Landgenoten. Leiden: Sijthoff, 1960, 656 pp. [Many reprints.]

5989 Talens, Jan
Tussen twee werelden; Peter John Koets - een biografische schets. 1982, 85 pp. [MA thesis Rijksuniversiteit Utrecht.]

5990 Tas, S.
'Indonesië; Een proef op de som', in: S. Tas, *De koude vrede*, pp. 215-243. Amsterdam: Van Oorschot, 1954.

5991 Tas, Sal
'Souvenirs of Shahrir', *Indonesia* no. 8 (1969):135-154.

5992 Tattersall, Sabine
Strijd op Bali in de jaren 1945-1950. Ca. 1990. [MA thesis Rijksuniversiteit Leiden.] [Lijst Leiden]

5993 Teitler, G.
'Liever zag men iets minder goed, doch meer eervol; Marine-reacties op het akkoord van Linggadjati, november-december 1946', *Marineblad* 97 (1987):118-123.

5994 Teitler, G.
'Marine, Generaal Spoor en de eerste politionele actie, juli-augustus 1947', *De Militaire Spectator* 156 (1987):327-333. (ubl)

5995 Teitler, G.
'Een vergeten strijd; Patrouilles, smokkel, infiltratie', in: G. Teitler and P.M.H. Groen (eds), *De politionele acties*, pp. 144-160. Amsterdam: De Bataafsche Leeuw, 1987.

5996 Teitler, G.
'De eerste politionele actie; Aanloop en uitvoering', *KIM-Spiegel* no. 90 (1988): 49-92. (kb)

5997 Teitler, G.
'Onder Britse bevelen, februari-november 1946', *KIM-Spiegel* no. 89 (1988):15-56. (kb)

5998 Teitler, G.
'Smokkel, strategie, unidefensie, augustus 1947-december 1948', *KIM-Spiegel* no. 91 (1988):56-94. (kb)

5999   Teitler, G.
        'Van Helfrich naar Pinke; De Koninklijke Marine en de terugkeer naar Indië,
        augustus 1945-februari 1946', *KIM-Spiegel* no. 88 (1988):2-31. (kb)

6000   Teitler, G.
        '1949; Afsluiting zonder afronding', in: G. Teitler and J. Hoffenaar (eds), *De
        politionele acties; Afwikkeling en verwerking*, pp. 9-19. Amsterdam: De Bataafsche
        Leeuw, 1990.

6001   Teitler, G.
        'Onrust aan de top; De betrekkingen tussen KNIL en KL en het vertrek van
        Generaal-Majoor H.J.J.W. Dürst Britt uit Indië in de zomer van 1948',
        Mededelingen Sectie Militaire Geschiedenis Landmachtstaf 13 (1990):78-98.

6002   Teitler, G.
        *Vlootvoogd in de knel; Vice-Admiraal A.S. Pinke tussen de marinestaf, Indië en de
        Indonesische revolutie.* Assen/Maastricht: Van Gorcum, 1990, 8+258 pp.

6003   Teitler, G.
        'Muiterij in een onverwachte hoek; De Minahassa in opstand, februari-maart
        1946', *Mededelingen Sectie Militaire Geschiedenis* 15 (1993):93-104.

6004   Teitler, G. and P.M.H. Groen (eds)
        De politionele acties. Amsterdam: De Bataafsche Leeuw, 1987, 160 pp.

6005   Teitler, G. and J. Hoffenaar (eds)
        De politionele acties; Afwikkeling en verwerking. Amsterdam: De Bataafsche
        Leeuw, 1990, 128 pp.

6006   Teitler, G. and D. Schoonoord
        'De krijgsmacht in het koloniale avondrood; Het Nederlands-Indonesisch
        conflict in de romanliteratuur', *Maatstaf* 37-8/9 (1989):128-138.

6007   Termorshuizen, Gerard
        '19 december 1948; Lucebert schrijft zijn "Minnebrief aan onze gemartelde bruid
        Indonesia" – Nederlands-Indië in de literatuur na 1940', in: M.A. Schenkeveld-
        van der Dussen (ed.), *Nederlandse literatuur; Een geschiedenis*, pp. 715-721.
        Groningen: Nijhoff, 1993. (ubl)

6008   Thijssen, F.P.A.
        De Partij van de Arbeid en de Indonesische kwestie 1945-49; Verdeeldheid
        binnen de PvdA over de dekolonisatie van Indonesië. 1979. [MA thesis
        Katholieke Universiteit Nijmegen.] [45, 58]

6009   Tichelman, F.
        'Enkele opmerkingen naar aanleiding van "Het dagboek van Schermerhorn" ', *De
        Gids* 135 (1972):327-338.

6010   Touwen-Bouwsma, C. (Elly)
        The Dutch, the Indonesian republicans and the Negara Madura (1945-1950).
        Paper International Conference Madurese Culture and Society, Leiden, 1991, 31
        pp.

6011   Trip, F.H.P.
        Brieven uit Indië 1946-1949. Amsterdam: De Bataafsche Leeuw, 1990, 70 pp.

6012 Tulp, Gerrit
Marsbevel op Java; Aan- en afvoertroepen, april 1946-juli 1949. Bedum: Profiel, 1989, 258 pp.

6013 *Tussen Assen en Lahat, Mei 1947-Februari 1950.* Amsterdam: Holland, 1950. [unpaged]

6014 Uithol, J.C. and J.M. van Wijk
Gods trouw in de tropen; Belevenissen van een aantal oudgedienden in het voormalig Nederlands Oost-Indië gedurende de jaren 1946-1950. Barneveld: Koster, 1993, 399 pp.

6015 *Uniestatuut en RTC-overeenkomsten.* Amsterdam, 1951, 61 pp. (kit)

6016 Vaders, Ger
De verliezers; Indonesië op het tweede gezicht. Amsterdam: Jan Mets, 1993, 143 pp.

6017 Vallen, E.; P. Heurter; J. Reijalt and A. van Oirschot (eds)
402 Bataljon Infanterie; Gedenkboek. Maastricht: Goffin, ca. 1951, 245 pp.

6018 Vanvugt, Ewald
'Maar wat doe jij, Nederlander, op ons veld van eer? De verovering van Bali in 1946', in: Ewald Vanvugt, *Het dubbele gezicht van de koloniaal; Nederlands-Indië herontdekt,* pp. 140-150. Haarlem: In de Knipscheer, 1988.

6019 Varenne, Jan
Eer de haan kraait; Een serdadoe soesoe tussen de peloppers op Java. Amsterdam: Paris, 1969, 118 pp.

6020 Veen, Arie J. van
Tjampoer Marechéplisie; Het Korps Militaire Politie/Koninklijke Marechaussee in Nederlands-Indië, 1945-1951. Amsterdam: De Bataafsche Leeuw, 1991, 112 pp.

6021 Veen, F. van der
'Het optreden van de Nederlandse en de republikeinse strijdkrachten, 17 augustus 1945-15 augustus 1949', in: L. de Jong, *Het Koninkrijk der Nederlanden in de tweede wereldoorlog; Deel 12, Epiloog; De worsteling met de Republiek Indonesië,* pp. 1134-1149. Leiden: Nijhoff, 1988. [Popular edition, 's-Gravenhage: SDU Uitgeverij, 1988, pp. 1108-1123.]

6022 Veenschoten, J.G. van
De 4e Genie Veld Compagnie; Kroniek van een genieveldcompagnie in de tropen. Eindhoven, 1988, 43 pp.

6023 Veer, Paul van 't
'Nederland in Azië', in: Constandse, A.L.; J.L. Heldring and Paul van 't Veer, *Gelijk hebben en krijgen,* pp. 87-157. Amsterdam: De Bezige Bij, 1962.

6024 Veer, Paul van 't
'Geen last van de waarheid', *Hollands Maandblad* no. 277 (1970):3-8. (ubl)

6025 Veer, Paul van 't
'Akkoord van het wantrouwen; De Indië-politiek van Nederland tot en met het akkoord van Linggadjati (25 maart 1947)', in: *Onze Jaren 45-70,* pp. 268-274. Amsterdam, 1972. (ubl)

6026 Veer, Paul van 't
'Indonesia merdeka; De consolidatie van de Republiek Indonesië (1945-1946)',
in: *Onze Jaren 45-70*, pp. 335-342. Amsterdam, 1972. (ubl)

6027 Veer, Paul van 't
'Van aarzeling naar actie en omgekeerd; De Indië-politiek van Nederland van
maart 1947 tot de tweede politionele actie (19 december 1948)', in: *Onze Jaren
45-70*, pp. 776-781. Amsterdam, 1972. (ubl)

6028 Veer, Paul van 't
'Tabéh Insulinde; De Indië-politiek van Nederland tussen 1949 en 1954', in:
Onze Jaren 45-70, pp. 1059-1062. Amsterdam, 1972. (ubl)

6029 Veer, Paul van 't
'De wajangpoppen aan het dansen; De communistische revolte in Madioen
(september 1948)', in: *Onze jaren 45-70*, pp. 1105-1107. Amsterdam, 1972.

6030 Veer, Paul van 't
'Schermerhorn en de hyena's', in: Paul van 't Veer, *De strijdlustige amateur*,
pp. 70-79. Amsterdam: Arbeiderspers, 1973.

6031 Veer, Paul van 't
'Nieuw bericht uit hyenaland', *Hollands Maandblad* no. 339 (1976):13-18. (ubl)

6032 Veer, Paul van 't
'Sjahrir en Schermerhorn', *Hollands Maandblad* no. 347 (1976/77):10-17. (ubl)

6033 Veer, Paul van 't
'De dekolonisatie en de Nederlandse buitenlandse politiek', in: *Nederlands
buitenlandse politiek; Heden en verleden*, pp. 58-70. Baarn: In den Toren, 1978.

6034 Vegt, K. van der
*Toen de tjitjak riep; Belevenissen van een bataljon oorlogsvrijwilligers in Nederlands
Oost-Indië van 1946 tot 1948.* Zeist: Studio Flantua, 1984, 200 pp. (kitlv-smg)

6035 Velde, Jean van de
Oeroeg. Amsterdam: Het Nederlandse Scenario, 1993, 110 pp.

6036 Venema, Rieks and Jan Meeusen
Losse flodders 2-12 RVA; Artillerieherinneringen Midden-Java '47-'50. Assendelft:
n.n., 1994, 164 pp.

6037 Verheijen, Harrie
De houding van CHU en zending in de Indonesische kwestie. 1976, 89+18 pp.
[MA thesis Rijksuniversiteit Utrecht.]

6038 Verheijen, H.
*De houding van de Nederlands Hervormde Kerk en van de zending der Nederlands
Hervormde Kerk ten opzichte van de Indonesische kwestie, 1945-1950.* Schoonhoven:
n.n., 1978, 71 pp.

6039 Verhoeven-van Delden, Mary
'Bersiap in Bandoeng; Een onderzoek gebaseerd op literatuurstudie, interviews
en archieven', in: Wim Willems (ed.), *Bronnen van kennis over Indische Nederlanders.* Bundel artikelen naar aanleiding van de 2e Studiedag Indische Neder-

landers, pp. 201-217. Leiden: Centrum voor Onderzoek van Maatschappelijke Tegenstellingen, Faculteit der Sociale Wetenschappen der Rijksuniversiteit, 1991.

6040 Verhoeven-van Delden, Mary
'Operatie POPDA; De afvoer van het Japanse leger van Java en Madoera en de evacuatie van Nederlandse geïnterneerden uit de Indonesische internerings-kampen 1946-1947', in: *Vierde Jaarboek van het Rijksinstituut voor Oorlogsdo-cumentatie*, pp. 37-64. Zutphen: Walburg Pers, 1993.

6041 Verhoog, A.
Onze laatste oorlog; De voorgeschiedenis van en de strijd om de onafhankelijkheid van Indonesië. Utrecht/Antwerpen: Het Spectrum, 1982, 136 pp.

6042 Verhoog, J.M.
'Overzicht van de opbouw en organisatie van de Nederlandse troepenmacht in Nederlands-Indië in de periode 1945-1950', in: J.M. Verhoog, *Herinnerings-literatuur betreffende het Nederlandse militaire optreden te land in Indonesië 1945-1950*, pp. 3-14. 's-Gravenhage: Sectie Militaire Geschiedenis Landmachtstaf, 1989.

6043 Verkuylen, Charles M.F.
Het verbond verbroken; Het Indo-Europees Verbond in de nadagen van Neder-lands-Indië, 1945-1949; Een studie over Indo-Europeanen en regeringsbeleid. 1985, 268 pp. [MA thesis Katholieke Universiteit Nijmegen.]

6044 Verkuylen, Ch.
'Het belang van de Indo-Europeaan; Het Indo-Europees Verbond in de nadagen van Nederlands-Indië (1945-1949)', *Jambatan* 4-1 (1986):27-46.

6045 Vermeulen, G.J.
Dagboek van een halve mens. Leiden: Sijthoff, 1951, 198 pp.

6046 Verrips, Ger
Zorg dat je een gekkenbriefje krijgt. Fourth edition. Amsterdam/Antwerpen: Manteau, 1984, 144 pp. [First edition, Amsterdam: Elsevier, 1973, 144 pp.]

6047 Verspyck, G.M.
'Hulpverlening aan Indonesië', in: G.M. Verspyck, *Het Nederlandsche Roode Kruis 1867-1967*, pp. 204-214. Nijkerk: Callenbach, 1967.

6048 Verstraaten, Hans
De oorlogsverslaggevers van 1947. Amsterdam: Vrij Nederland, 1980, 26 pp.

6049 Verveer, A.H.
Malino; Revisie en herwaardering. Ca. 1978, 58 pp. [Thesis Katholieke Leergangen, Tilburg.]

6050 Vetten, J.P.M. de
Schermerhorn en de Indonesische kwestie, 1945-1947. 1980, 119 pp. [MA thesis Rijksuniversiteit Leiden.]

6051 Vetten, J.P.M. de
'Schermerhorn en de Indonesische kwestie, 1945-1947', *Spiegel Historiael* 17 (1982):250-256.

6052   *Vier-acht op wacht!* Koog aan de Zaan: Zaanlandsche Stoomdrukkerij, 1950, 96 pp.

6053   Visch Eybergen, H.C. de
       De Nederlandse overheidsvoorlichting inzake de Indonesische kwestie, 1945-1949. 1988, 105 pp. [MA thesis Erasmus Universiteit, Rotterdam.] (eur)

6054   Visser, A.
       'Zuid-Oost Borneo in 1946', in: S.L. van der Wal (ed.), *Besturen overzee; Herinneringen van oud-ambtenaren bij het binnenlands bestuur in Nederlandsch-Indië*, pp. 315-326. Franeker: Wever, 1977.

6055   Visser, M.N. de
       Het ene wee is gegaan, ziet het andere wee is gekomen; Aspecten van de houding van de Staatkundig Gereformeerde Partij en haar achterban tegenover de Indonesische revolutie (1945-1950). 1987, 109 pp. [MA thesis Rijksuniversiteit Utrecht.]

6056   Vlie, Willem van 't
       Het gebruik van de denkmodellen fotografie en holografie als gereedschap voor het ordenen van in feiten zichtbaar te maken informatie ten behoeve van geschiedkundig onderzoek; N.a.v. een gebeurtenis tijdens de eerste politionele actie op Java. 1986, 52 pp. [Thesis Erasmus Universiteit, Rotterdam.] [43]

6057   Vogelpoel, J.F.R. van
       De Koninklijke Landmacht na de Tweede Wereldoorlog; Hoofddeel II: De opbouw ten behoeve van de pacificatie van Nederlands-Indië, 5 Mei 1945-27 December 1949. 's-Gravenhage: Departement van Defensie, 1959, 58 pp.

6058   Voogd, Evert
       De Nederlandse pers over de 'politionele akties' tegen Indonesië, 1947-1948. 1980, 64 pp. [MA thesis Universiteit van Amsterdam.]

6059   *Voor orde en vrede... De geschiedenis van het 3e Bataljon van het Regiment Stoottroepen der 7 December Divisie.* N.p.: n.n., 1986, 144 pp.

6060   Vos, Fred
       'Pantservoertuigen Nederlands Korps Mariniers', *Marineblad* 82 (1972):791-818. (ubl)

6061   Vredenbregt, Jacob
       De opstand; Het relaas van een krijgsgevangene. Amsterdam: Nijgh en Van Ditmar, 1990, 142 pp.

6062   Vreede-de Stuers, Cora
       'Vroedvrouwen van de revolutie; De positie van de vrouw in de Indonesische samenleving', in: *Onze jaren 45-70*, pp. 1115-1117. Amsterdam, 1972.

6063   Vries, Alfred de
       Koloniale politiek van de sociaal-democraten 1945-1946; De houding van de SDAP en PvdA ten aanzien van de Indonesische revolutie. 1985, 136 pp. [MA thesis Rijksuniversiteit Utrecht.]

6064   Vries, J.G. de
       Met 35 AAT op Noord-Sumatra. Enkhuizen: Posthuma, 1950, 55 pp. (kitlv-smg)

6065 Vught, Nell van
De dekolonisatie van Nederlandsch-Indië resp. de Indonesische onafhankelijk-
heidsstrijd in de westerse historiografie. 1982, 143 pp. [MA thesis Katholieke
Universiteit Nijmegen.]

6066 Vusse, M.P. van de
De Partij van de Arbeid, Nederland en de Indonesische revolutie. 1984, 115 pp.
[MA thesis Rijksuniversiteit Utrecht.] (ubu)

6067 Vuyk, Bep
'Verhaal van een toeschouwer', in: Bep Vuyk, *Verzameld werk*, pp. 362-379.
Amsterdam: Querido, 1972. [First published in *Oriëntatie* no. 31 (April
1950):31-.]

6068 Vuyk, Bep
'De jager met zijn schietgeweer', in: Bep Vuyk, *Verzameld werk*, pp. 398-405.
Amsterdam: Querido, 1972. [First published in *De Gids* (December 1958):339-
345.]

6069 Vuyk, Bep
'Full of sound and fury', in: Bep Vuyk, *Verzameld werk*, pp. 406-420. Amsterdam: Querido, 1972. [First published ca. 1960].

6070 *Vijf jaren beleid met betrekking tot de overzeese gebiedsdelen; De Indonesische kwestie.*
's-Gravenhage: Ministerie van Uniezaken en Overzeese Gebiedsdelen, 1951,
121 pp.

6071 Wal, A.L. van der
Djocjakarta, 19 december 1948; De militaire zuiveringsacties van Nederlandse
eenheden in en bij Djocjakarta bij de aanvang van de tweede politiële actie.
1976, 78 pp. [Thesis Koninklijk Instituut voor de Marine, Den Helder.] (kitlv-
smg)

6072 Wal, S.L. van der
'België en het Nederlands-Indonesisch conflict', *Bijdragen en Mededelingen
betreffende de Geschiedenis der Nederlanden* 89 (1974):385-395.

6073 Wal, S.L. van der
Dutch reactions to the Indonesian revolution. Paper Conference on Modern
Indonesian History, Madison (Wis.), 1975, 11 pp.

6074 Ward, O.G.
'Tussen Japanse overgave en geallieerde overname', *Mars et Historia* 20-5
(1986):185-200. (smg)

6075 Ward, O.G.; W.J.A.M. de Kock; M. Onnen and R. van Wijngaarden
De militaire luchtvaart van het KNIL in de na-oorlogse jaren 1945-1950. Houten:
Van Holkema en Warendorf, 1988, 382 pp.

6076 Waterreus, J.C. (ed.)
*Awas 515; Herinneringen aan de zwerftochten der 6e Genie Veldcompagnie verteld
door verschillende leden van dit onderdeel.* N.p.: n.n., 1951, 112 pp. (kitlv-smg)

6077 Weeting, Ben
'Het jaar van het einde', in: Joop van den Berg (ed.), *Bersiap; Nederlands-
Indonesische verhalen*, pp. 73-78. 's-Gravenhage: BZZTôH, 1993.

6078 *Wel en wee der AAT.* N.p.: n.n., ca. 1978, 128+128+256 pp. 3 vols. (kitlv-smg)

6079 Werff, J.L.C. van der
Het akkoord van Linggadjati en de buitenlandse betrekkingen van de Republiek
Indonesië, november 1946-juli 1947. 1981, 59 pp. [MA thesis Rijksuniversiteit
Leiden.]

6080 Westerheijden, D.F.
Vrijheid van handelen; Besluitvorming tussen Linggadjati en de eerste
politionele actie. 1984, 185 pp. [MA thesis Technische Hogeschool Twente,
Enschede.] (kitlv-smg)

6081 Westerling, Raymond
Challenge to terror. London: Kimber, 1952, 222 pp. [71, 6210]

6082 Westerling, R.
Mes aventures en Indonésie. Paris: Hachette, 1952, 254 pp.

6083 Westerling, R.
Ich war kein Rebell; Meine Abenteuer in Indonesien. Wien: Ullstein, 1953, 234 pp.

6084 Westerling, Raymond Paul Pierre
Mijn mémoires... Antwerpen/Amsterdam: Vink, 1952, 308 pp.

6085 Wicherts, A.H.
Herinneringen; De jaren 1941 t/m 1949. Ca. 1974, 36+39 pp.

6086 Wiebes, C. and B. Zeeman
'Stikker, Indonesië en het Noordatlantisch verdrag; Of: hoe Nederland in de
pompe ging', *Bijdragen en Mededelingen betreffende de Geschiedenis der Nederlanden*
100 (1985):225-251.

6087 Wiebes, Cees and Bert Zeeman (eds)
Indonesische dagboeknotities van Dr H.N. Boon, 1946-1949. Houten: De Haan,
1986, 228 pp.

6088 Wiebring, J.C.
De Bandoeng-affaire; Achtergronden en teloorgang van een koloniaal avontuur.
1981, 148 pp. [MA thesis Universiteit van Amsterdam.]

6089 Wieringa, E.P.
'Gara-gara; De julicrisis van 1946 in de Republiek Indonesië besproken door de
clowns Garèng en Pétruk', *Jambatan* 10-1 (1992):3-13.

6090 Wiersma, Erik
'Dienstweigeren rond de Indonesië-kwestie', in: *Dienstplicht/weigerplicht; Feiten
en motieven rond de dienstweigering,* pp. 12-14. Amersfoort: De Horstink, 1981.
(kb)

6091 Wiersma, Gait
Weerzien met Tikoes; De weg van een theeplanter uit de Preanger. Franeker: Wever,
1978, 192 pp.

6092 Wigbold, H. (ed.)
Achter het Nieuws in Zuid-Celebes. Hilversum: Omroepvereniging VARA, 1969,
48 pp.

6093 Wildschut, H.J.
De hervormde zending en de dekolonisatie van Indonesië, 1945-1949; De standpunten van Nico Stufkens en Hendrik Kraemer. 1987, 126 pp. [MA thesis Universiteit van Amsterdam.] [43]

6094 Wind, Jaap
Bericht van je jongen. Voorwoord van J.C. Koningsberger. Baarn: Bosch en Keuning, 1950, 79 pp.

6095 Wit, G.H.O. de and Bas de Jong
Binnen twintig minuten gereed; Het 6e Eskadron Vechtwagens KL/KNIL, 1947-1950; LTD 716/III. 's-Gravenhage: n.n., 1977, 263 pp. (kitlv-smg)

6096 Witteman, N.H.
'Marsroutes en dwaalsporen; De Nederlandse koloniale oorlog 1945-1950', *Spiegel Historiael* 26 (1991):329-331.

6097 Wolff, Joop
'Bij de 9e herdenking van de Proclamatie der Indonesische Republik', *Politiek en Cultuur* 9 (1954):419-425. (ubl)

6098 Wolff, Joop
'Onze anti-koloniale traditie en de strijd in Indonesië', in: *Cahiers over de Geschiedenis van de Communistische Partij van Nederland 1*, pp. 19-34. Amsterdam: Instituut voor Politiek en Sociaal Onderzoek, 1979. (uba)

6099 Wonink, Harry
Speurtocht naar vliegende slangen. Rijssen: Ligtenberg, 1983, 137 pp.

6100 Wuster, H.W.S.
'Tegels lichten; De geschiedenis van een verbazing', *Hollands Maandblad* no. 266 (1969-70):12-20, no.267 (1969-70):10-21. (ubl)

6101 Wijk, A. van
'Bijdragen aan de bevrijding', *Marineblad* 95 (1985):581-590. (ubl)

6102 Wijnmaalen, H.J.
'Aantekeningen betreffende het ontstaan, de ontwikkeling en het optreden van de vakbeweging in Indonesië na de onafhankelijkheidsverklaring van 17 Augustus 1945', *Indonesië* 5 (1951-52):434-461, 539-563.

6103 Wijnmaalen, H.J.
'De Indonesische vakbeweging, haar ontwikkeling en haar problemen', in: W. Lubberink, *Sociaal economische problemen*, pp. 33-47. Second edition, Amsterdam: Koninklijk Instituut voor de Tropen, 1952.

6104 IJzereef, Willem
'De Zuid-Celebesaffaire en de Nederlandse pers 1946-1982', *Groniek* 17-80 (1982-83):49-54. (ubl)

6105 IJzereef, W.
De Zuid-Celebes affaire; Kapitein Westerling en de standrechtelijke executies. Dieren: De Bataafsche Leeuw, 1984, 178 pp.

6106 Zandt, P.
'Souvereiniteitsoverdracht; 27 december 1949', in: _Woord en wet 1918-1988; 70 jaar SGP, Staatkundig Gereformeerde Partij_, pp. 81-112. 's-Gravenhage: Staatkundig Gereformeerde Partij, 1988. (kb)

6107 Zarkel, J.
'Jager op Java; Uit de herinneringen van een dienstplichtige in de tropen', _De Militaire Spectator_ 148 (1979):328-332. (ubl)

6108 Zuring, J.
'De achtergrond van het desertieprobleem', _Militair Rechtelijk Tijdschrift_ 34 (1951):674-683. (ubl)

6109 Zwaan, J.
Soldaat in Indië; De geschiedenis van een peloton. Zwolle: Tijl, 1969, 304 pp. [Second printing, Den Haag: Scheltens en Giltay, 1973.]

6110 Zwaan, Jacob
Nederlands-Indië 1940-1946; III: Geallieerd intermezzo, 15 augustus 1945-30 november 1946. Amsterdam: De Bataafsche Leeuw, 1985, 288 pp.

6111 _Zwart op wit; Liquidatie van een imperium; Een beeld van het na-oorlogse regeringsbeleid in Nederland, ontleend aan De Nieuwsbrief._ Amsterdam: Buijten en Schipperheijn, 1954, 175 pp.

6112 Zweers, L.
De fotoberichtgeving van het dekolonisatieproces van Nederlands-Indië. 1984, 209 pp. [MA thesis Rijksuniversiteit Leiden.] [Lijst Leiden]

6113 Zweers, Louis
' "Een juiste weergave van het leven der troepen in de tropen"; Fotoreportages van de dekolonisatie in drie geïllustreerde weekbladen', in: _Jaarboek Mediageschiedenis 4; Nederlands-Indië_, pp. 115-144. Amsterdam: Stichting Beheer IISG/Stichting Mediageschiedenis, 1992.

6114 Zweers, Louis
Front Indië; Hugo Wilmar, ooggetuige van een koloniale oorlog. Zutphen: Walburg Pers, 1994, 120 pp.

6115 Zwitzer, H.L.
Documenten betreffende de Eerste Politionele Actie (20/21 juli-4 augustus 1947). 's-Gravenhage: Sectie Militaire Geschiedenis van de Landmachtstaf, 1983, 198 pp.

6116 Zijlmans, G.C.
Eindstrijd en ondergang van de Indische bestuursdienst; Het Corps Binnenlands Bestuur op Java 1945-1950. Amsterdam: De Bataafsche Leeuw, 1985, 374 pp. [Also PhD thesis Erasmus Universiteit, Rotterdam.]

Revolutionary period
Other later writings

6117 Albertini, R. von
'The decolonization of the Dutch East Indies', in: Tony Smith (ed.), *The end of European empire; Decolonization after World War II*, pp. 171-177. Lexington, Mass.: Heath, 1975. (ubl)

6118 Alioshin, Yuri
Indonesia dalam Dewan Keamanan PBB tahun 1946-1949; Perdebatan Inggris dan Belanda dan lain-lainnya serta pembelaan Ukraina dan Uni Sovyet. Surabaya: Grip, ca. 1978, 90 pp.

6119 Anderson, Benedict
'The problem of rice', *Indonesia* no. 2 (1966):77-123.

6120 Anderson, Benedict R.O'G.
The pemuda revolution; Indonesian politics 1945-1946. 1967, 660 pp. [PhD thesis Cornell University, Ithaca.]

6121 Anderson, B.R.O'G.
'The cultural factors in the Indonesian revolution', *Asia* 20 (1970-71):48-65.

6122 Anderson, Benedict R.O'G.
Java in a time of revolution; Occupation and resistance, 1944-1946. Ithaca/London: Cornell University Press, 1972, 17+494 pp.

6123 Anderson, Benedict R.O'G.
'The point of no return', in: Colin Wild and Peter Carey (eds), *Born in fire; The Indonesian struggle for independence; An anthology*, pp. 86-91. Athens: Ohio University Press, 1986.

6124 Anderson, Ben
'Saat yang menentukan', in: Colin Wild and Peter Carey (eds), *Gelora api revolusi*, pp. 96-102. Jakarta: Gramedia, 1986.

6125 Anderson, Benedict R.O'G.
Revoloesi pemoeda; Pendudukan Jepang dan perlawanan di Jawa 1944-1946. Jakarta: Sinar Harapan, 1988, 545 pp.

6126 Anderson, David Charles
'The military aspects of the Madiun affair', *Indonesia* no. 21 (1976):1-63.

6127 Anderson, David Charles
Military politics in East Java; A study of the origins and development of the armed forces in East Java between 1945-1948. 1976, 325 pp. [PhD thesis School of Oriental and African Studies, London.]

6128 Aspengren, Evald
Local administration and agricultural development during the upheavals in Java in the 1940's. N.p.: n.n., 1987, 18 pp.

6129 Bajunid, Omar Farouk
The Indonesian Independence League in Bangkok; A profile. Paper 10th IAHA Conference, Singapore, 1986, 14 pp.

6130 Bajunid, Omar Farouk
'The Indonesian Independence League in Bangkok; A profile', *Jebat* 14 (1986):117-125.

6131 Ball, W. MacMahon
Intermittent diplomat; The Japan and Batavia diaries of W. MacMahon Ball. Edited and with an introduction by Alan Rix. Melbourne: Melbourne University Press, 1988, 311 pp.

6132 Beddie, B.D.
'Australian policy towards Indonesia', *Australian Outlook* 22 (August 1968):123-140.

6133 Benda, H.J.
'Indonesia', *Australian Outlook* 4 (1950):41-50, 86-97. (kit)

6134 Benda, H.J.
'Decolonization in Indonesia; The problem of continuity and change', *American Historical Review* 70 (July 1965):1058-1074.

6135 Blazy, Helga
'L'enfant et la révolution dans la littérature indonésienne moderne', *Archipel* 47(1994):146-154.

6136 Bogarde, Dirk
A gentle occupation; A novel. London: Chatto and Windus, 1980, 360 pp. [Second edition, St Albans: Triad/Granada, 1981, 447 pp.]

6137 Bogk, Lari
'Indonesia's struggle for independence on the West Coast USA', *Penelitian Sedjarah* 2-3 (1961):7-10.

6138 Buckley, Ken; Barbara Dale and Wayne Reynolds
'The Indonesian revolution and Australian security', in: Ken Buckley, Barbara Dale and Wayne Reynolds (eds), *Doc Evatt; Patriot, internationalist, fighter and scholar*, pp. 245-263. Melbourne: Longman Cheshire, 1994.

6139 Buckley, Roger
'Responsibility without power; Britain and Indonesia August 1945-February 1946', in: Ian Nish (ed.), *Indonesian experience; The role of Japan and Britain 1943-1948*, pp. 35-52. London: London School of Economics, 1979.

6140 Carew, Tim
All this and a medal too. London: Constable, 1954, 252 pp. (riod)

6141 Carey, Peter
'Introduction', in: Colin Wild and Peter Carey (eds), *Born in fire; The Indonesian struggle for independence; An anthology*, pp. xix-xxvii. Athens: Ohio University Press, 1986.

6142 Carey, Peter
'Mitos, pahlawan dan perang', in: Colin Wild and Peter Carey (eds), *Gelora api revolusi*, pp. 7-14. Jakarta: Gramedia, 1986.

6143 Carey, Peter
'Myths, heroes, and war', in: Colin Wild and Peter Carey (eds), *Born in fire; The Indonesian struggle for independence; An anthology*, pp. 6-11. Athens: Ohio University Press, 1986.

6144 Carey, Peter
'Yogyakarta; From sultanate to revolutionary capital of Indonesia; The politics of cultural survival', *Indonesia Circle* 39 (March 1986):19-29.

6145 Castles, Lance
'Internecine conflict in Tapanuli', *Review of Indonesian and Malaysian Affairs* 8-1 (1974):73-80.

6146 Ciechanowska, Maria
Indonesia and the struggle for independence, 1945-1949. Warsaw: Wydawnictwo Ministerstwa Obrony Narodowej, 1962, 412 pp. [In Polish.]

6147 Coast, John
Recruit to revolution; Adventure and politics in Indonesia. London: Christophers, 1952, 308 pp. [Second edition, New York: AMS Press, 1973, 308 pp.]

6148 Coast, John
'An Englishman joins the struggle; An interview with John Coast', in: Colin Wild and Peter Carey (eds), *Born in fire; The Indonesian struggle for independence; An anthology*, pp. 136-145. Athens: Ohio University Press, 1986.

6149 Colbert, Evelyn
'The road not taken; Decolonization and independence in Indonesia and Indochina', *Foreign Affairs* 51 (1973):608-629. (ubl)

6150 Collins, J. Foster
'The United Nations and Indonesia', *International Conciliation* no. 459 (1950):115-200.

6151 Cribb, Robert
Kota diplomasi? Jakarta in the early revolution. Paper presented to the annual meeting of the Association of Asian Studies, Toronto, 1981, 20 pp.

6152 Cribb, R.
'Political dimensions of the currency question 1945-1947', *Indonesia* no. 31 (1981):113-136.

6153 Cribb, Robert
'Archives, interviews and Indonesian history', *Itinerario* 7-2 (1983):50-58.

6154   Cribb, Robert
       Indonesia in 1945; Looking outwards, looking inwards. Paper presented to the
       annual meeting of the Association of Asian Studies, Washington, 1984. [4765]

6155   Cribb, Robert Bridson
       Jakarta in the Indonesian revolution, 1945-1949. 1984, 341 pp. [PhD thesis School
       of Oriental and African Studies, London.]

6156   Cribb, Robert
       'Jakarta: Cooperation and resistance in an occupied city', in: Audrey R. Kahin
       (ed.), *Regional dynamics of the Indonesian revolution*, pp. 179-205. Honolulu:
       University of Hawaii Press, 1985.

6157   Cribb, Robert
       'The nationalist world of occupied Jakarta, 1946-1949', in: S. Abeyasekere (ed.),
       From Batavia to Jakarta, pp. 91-107. Clayton, 1985.

6158   Cribb, R.B.
       'Administrative competition in the Indonesian revolution; The dual government
       of Jakarta, 1945-1947', in: J. van Goor (ed.), *The Indonesian revolution; Conference
       papers, Utrecht, 17-20 June*, pp. 129-146. Utrecht: Rijksuniversiteit Utrecht,
       1986.

6159   Cribb, Robert
       'The adventures of Captain Mulyono; Indonesian intelligence operations in
       Kalimantan 1946-1948', *Kabar Seberang* 17 (1986):211-221.

6160   Cribb, R.B.
       'A revolution delayed; The Indonesian Republic and the Netherlands Indies,
       August 1945-November 1945', *Australian Journal of Politics and History* 32-1
       (1986):72-85.

6161   Cribb, Robert
       Rice and revolution in Jakarta. Paper presented at the 6th National Conference
       of the Asian Studies Association of Australia, Sydney, 1986, 10 pp.

6162   Cribb, Robert
       Nasution's concept of 'total people's war' in theory and practice. Paper
       presented to the 7th Biennal Conference of the Asian Studies Association of
       Australia, Canberra, 1988, 12 pp.

6163   Cribb, Robert
       'Opium and the Indonesian revolution', *Modern Asian Studies* 22 (1988):701-722.

6164   Cribb, R.B.
       'De HAMOTs van Luitenant Koert Bavinck; Het bendewezen van Djakarta in
       dienst van het Nederlands gezag, 1947-1949', *Mededelingen Sectie Militaire
       Geschiedenis Landmachtstaf* 12 (1989):68-78.

6165   Cribb, Robert
       Heirs to the late colonial state? The Indonesian Republic, the Netherlands
       Indies and the Indonesian revolution, 1945-49. Paper Conference on the Socio-
       Economic Foundations of the Late Colonial State, NIAS, Wassenaar, 1989,
       14 pp.

6166   Cribb, Robert Bridson
       Gejolak revolusi di Jakarta 1945-1949; Pergulatan antara otonomi dan hegemoni.
       Jakarta: Grafiti, 1990, 232 pp.

6167   Cribb, Robert
       Gangsters and revolutionaries; The Jakarta people's militia and the Indonesian revolution, 1945-1949. Sydney: Asian Studies Association of Australia/Allen and Unwin, 1991, 13+222 pp.

6168   Critchley, Susan
       'An Australian Indonesian', *Hemisphere* 26-5 (March-April 1982):282-287.

6169   Crouch, Harold
       'The military and diplomatic notes in the struggle', in: C. Wild and P. Carey (eds), *Born in fire; The Indonesian struggle for independence; An anthology*, pp. 146-151. Athens: Ohio University Press, 1986.

6170   Crouch, Harold
       'Peranan militer dan diplomasi dalam perjuangan', in: Colin Wild and Peter Carey (eds), *Gelora api revolusi*, pp. 150-156. Jakarta: Gramedia, 1986.

6171   Dahm, B.
       'Der Dekolonisationsprozess Indonesiens; Endogene und exogene Faktoren', in: W.J. Mommsen (ed.), *Das Ende der Kolonialreiche; Dekolonisation und die Politik der Grossmächte*, pp. 67-88. Frankfurt am Main: Fischer, 1990.

6172   Dennis, Peter
       Other peoples' empires; Britain and the end of the Second World War in Southeast Asia. Paper 10th IAHA Conference, Singapore, 1986, 16 pp.

6173   Dennis, Peter
       Troubled days of peace; Mountbatten and South East Asia Command, 1945-46. Manchester: Manchester University Press, 1987, 270 pp.

6174   Devillers, Philippe
       Les Pays-Bas devant le régime politique de la République d'Indonésie (1945-1950). Paris: Fondation Nationale des Sciences Politiques, 1963, 34 pp. [45]

6175   Devillers, Philippe
       Indochine, Indonésie; Deux décolonisations manquées. Paper Colloque International 'Décolonisations Comparées', Aix-en-Provence, 1993, 17 pp.

6176   Donnison, F.S.V.
       British military administration in the Far East 1943-1946. London: Her Majesty's Stationary Office, 1956, 483 pp.

6177   Dorling, Philip (ed.)
       Diplomasi; Australia & Indonesia's independence; Documents 1947. Canberra: Australian Government Publishing Service, 1994, 545 pp.

6178   Doulton, A.J.F.
       The fighting cock; Being the history of the Twenty-Third Indian Division, 1942-1947. Aldershot: Gale and Polden, 1951, 318 pp. (kitlv-smg)

6179 Dreyfuss, Jeff
Modes of text-building in the Indonesian story 'Surabaya' by Idrus. 1981, 345 pp.
[PhD thesis University of Michigan, Ann Arbor.]

6180 Drummond, Stuart Hamilton
Britain's involvement in Indonesia 1945-63. 1979, 470 pp. [PhD thesis University
of Southampton.]

6181 Emmerson, D.K.
'Thoughts on "remembered history" as a subject of study, with reference to
Indonesia's revolution', *Review of Indonesian and Malaysian Affairs* 8-1 (1974):3-6.

6182 Faulkner, Norma Mae
The United States and the Indonesian dispute, 1945-1950. 1952, 131 pp. [MA
thesis University of California at Berkeley.]

6183 Finkelstein, Lawrence S.
'The Indonesian federal problem', *Pacific Affairs* 24 (1951):284-295.

6184 Folmer, Henry
'Indonesia 1945-49; An historical survey', *Common Cause* (June-July 1950):577-
583. (vp)

6185 Foulcher, Keith
'The early fiction of Pramoedya Ananta Toer, 1946-1949', in: D.M. Roskies
(ed.), *Text/politics in island Southeast Asia; Essays in interpretation*, pp. 191-220.
Athens: Ohio University, Center for International Studies, 1993.

6186 Frederick, William Hayward
Indonesian urban society in transition; Surabaya 1926-1946. 1978, 840 pp. [PhD
thesis University of Hawaii, Honolulu.]

6187 Frederick, W.H.
'In memoriam: Sutomo (1920-1981)', *Indonesia* no. 33 (1983):127-128.

6188 Frederick, William H.
Reflections on rebellion; Stories from the Indonesian upheavals of 1948 and 1965.
Athens: Ohio University Press, 1983, 168 pp.

6189 Frederick, William H.
Mass mobilization in Java during the Indonesian revolution. Paper Conference
on the Indonesian Revolution, Utrecht, 1986, 29 pp.

6190 Frederick, William H.
Visions and heat; The making of the Indonesian revolution. Athens: Ohio University
Press, 1988, 26+339 pp.

6191 Frederick, William H.
*Pandangan dan gejolak; Masyarakat kota dan lahirnya revolusi Indonesia (Surabaya
1926-1946).* Jakarta: Gramedia, 1989, 33+418 pp.

6192 Frederick, William H.
'Two new studies of the Indonesian revolution; The end of local history?', *Asian
Studies Review* 15 (1992):151-156.

6193   Frederick, William H.
The appearance of revolution; Cloth, uniforms, and the 'pemuda style' in East
Java, 1945-1949. Paper Conference Outward Appearances; Dressing the State
and Society, Leiden, 1993, 28+25 pp.

6194   Freydig, Constance Ann
India and Indonesia's independent foreign policy, 1945-1953. 1954, 149 pp.
[MA thesis University of California at Berkeley.]

6195   Fusayama, Takao
A Japanese memoir of Sumatra 1945-1946; Love and hatred in the liberation war.
Ithaca: Cornell University, 1993, 151 pp.

6196   Geertz, Hildred
'A theatre of cruelty; The contexts of a topéng performance', in: Hildred Geertz
(ed.), *State and society in Bali; Historical, textual and anthropological approaches,*
pp. 165-197. Leiden: KITLV Press, 1991.

6197   George, Margaret
Australia and Indonesian independence, 1942-1949. 1967. [MA thesis
Australian National University, Canberra.] [6132]

6198   George, Margaret Lorraine
*Australian attitudes and policies towards the Netherlands East Indies and Indonesian
independence, 1942-1949.* 1973, 505 pp. [PhD thesis Australian National
University, Canberra.]

6199   George, Margaret
Australia and the Indonesian revolution. Carlton: Melbourne University Press,
1980, 221 pp.

6200   George, Margaret
Australia dan revolusi Indonesia. Jakarta: Pantja Simpati, 1986, 347 pp.

6201   Gidaspov, V.I.
'The British occupation and the international position of the Republik Indonesia
(September 1945-November 1946)', in: *Problems of contemporary Indonesia*, pp. 3-
37. Moscow: Nauka, 1968. [In Russian.]

6202   Gidaspov, Vladimir Ivanovich
The foreign policy of the Republic of Indonesia (1945-1949). Moscow, 1970, 409
pp. [44] [In Russian.]

6203   Gidaspov, V.I.
'Indonesian historiography concerning the foreign policy of the Republic of
Indonesia (1945-1959)', in: V.A. Zharov (ed.), *National historiography in South-
East Asia*, pp. 146-167. Moscow: Nauka, 1974. [In Russian.]

6204   Glover, C.
Reactions of the Indonesian Chinese to two years of Dutch-Indonesian conflict.
Paper Johns Hopkins University, Baltimore 1950. [45, 78]

6205   Göksoy, Ismail Hakki
Dutch policy towards Islam in Indonesia (1945-1949). 1991, 373 pp. [PhD thesis
School of Oriental and African Studies, London.]

6206 Gordenker, Leon
'The role of the United Nations in Indonesian independence', in: C.A. van Minnen (ed.), *Decolonization of Indonesia; International perspectives*, pp. 55-71. Middelburg: Roosevelt Study Center/Stichting V.O.C.-Publicaties Zeeland, 1988.

6207 Gordon, Alec
The Indonesian revolution 1945-1949 as a social revolution. Paper 10th IAHA Conference, Singapore, 1986, 20 pp.

6208 Gupta, Surendra K.
'Indonesian crisis of 1948-1949; A study in great power diplomacy and India's relations with Moscow and Washington', *Asian Profile* 12 (1984):473-484. [25]

6209 Harvey, Barbara S.
Puppets and pejoangs; South Sulawesi in the national revolution, 1945-1949. Paper for the Panel on 'The Regional Dimension of the Indonesian Revolution', Toronto, 13-15 March 1981, 56 pp.

6210 Harvey, Barbara S.
'South Sulawesi: Puppets and patriots', in: Audrey R. Kahin (ed.), *Regional dynamics of the Indonesian revolution*, pp. 207-235. Honolulu: University of Hawaii Press, 1985.

6211 Harvey, Barbara S.
'Review of William H. Frederick: Visions and Heat', *Indonesia* no. 48 (1989):97-100.

6212 Henderson, William
Pacific settlement of disputes; The Indonesian question 1946-1949. New York: Woodrow Wilson Foundation, 1954, 89 pp.

6213 Hogan, Terry
The Labour movement and the Indonesian republicans in Australia, August, 1945-March, 1946. 1972, 104 pp. [BA thesis University of New England, Armidale.]

6214 Homan, G.D.
'The "Martin Behrman" incident', *Bijdragen en Mededelingen betreffende de Geschiedenis der Nederlanden* 94 (1979):253-270.

6215 Homan, G.D.
'The United States and the Indonesian question, December 1941-December 1946', *Tijdschrift voor Geschiedenis* 93 (1980):35-56.

6216 Homan, G.D.
'American business interests in the Indonesian Republic, 1946-1949', *Indonesia* no. 35 (1983):125-132.

6217 Homan, G.D.
'The United States and the Netherlands East Indies; The evolution of American anticolonialism', *Pacific Historical Review* 53 (1984):432-446. (ubl)

6218   Homan, G.D.
        'American military assistance to the Netherlands during the Indonesian struggle for independence, 1945-1949', *Mededelingen Sectie Militaire Geschiedenis Land-machtstaf* 8 (1985):155-161. (ubl)

6219   Homan, Gerlof D.
        'The Indonesian community in the United States, 1941-1950', *Tijdschrift voor Geschiedenis* 103 (1990):43-58.

6220   Homan, G.D.
        'The Netherlands, the United States and the Indonesian question in 1948', *Journal of Contemporary History* 25 (1990):123-141. (ubl)

6221   Hudson, W.J.
        'Australia and Indonesian independence', *Journal of Southeast Asian History* 8 (1967):226-239.

6222   Hurt, William L.
        The establishment of the Republic of Indonesia. 1951. [MA thesis University of Texas, Austin.] [97]

6223   Ibaraki, Seiichi
        Like a flower of melati; The blood of Japanese sacrificed for Indonesian independence. Tokyo: Mainichi Shinbunsha, 1953, 297 pp. [51, 59, 71] [In Japanese.]

6224   Ishihara, Akira
        Hurrah for the Indonesian independence! 1980, 40 pp. [51] [In Japanese.]

6225   Ishii, Masaharu
        From the South; Memoirs of remaining Japanese ex-soldiers. Nishida Shoten, 1984, 246 pp. [51] [In Japanese.]

6226   Jankovec, Miroslav
        Indonésie, 1945-1965. Prague: Svoboda, 1966, 209 pp. (kitlv-m)

6227   Jankovec, Miroslav
        Indonesian foreign policy, 1945-1955. Prague: Ustav Mezinarodnich Vztahu, 1971, 293 pp. [In Czechian.]

6228   Kahin, Audrey
        'Some preliminary observations on West Sumatra during the revolution', *Indonesia* no. 18 (1974):76-117.

6229   Kahin, Audrey Richey
        Struggle for independence; West Sumatra in the Indonesian national revolution 1945-1950. 1979, 402 pp. [PhD thesis Cornell University, Ithaca.]

6230   Kahin, Audrey R. (ed.)
        Regional dynamics of the Indonesian revolution; Unity from diversity. Honolulu: University of Hawaii Press, 1985, 306 pp.

6231   Kahin, Audrey R.
        'West Sumatra: Outpost of the Republic', in: Audrey R. Kahin (ed.), *Regional dynamics of the Indonesian revolution*, pp. 145-176. Honolulu: University of Hawaii Press, 1985.

6232　Kahin, Audrey (ed.)
Pergolakan daerah pada awal kemerdekaan. Jakarta: Grafiti, 1990, 301 pp.

6233　Kahin, George McTurnan
Some aspects of Indonesian politics and nationalism. New York: Institute of Pacific Relations, 1950, 47 pp. (ubl)

6234　Kahin, George McTurnan
Nationalism and revolution in Indonesia. Second edition. Ithaca/London: Cornell University Press, 1970, 12+490 pp. [First edition 1952; Seventh printing 1966.]

6235　Kahin, George McTurnan
'Indonesian politics and nationalism', in: William L. Holland (ed.), *Asian nationalism and the West; A symposium based on documents and reports of the eleventh conference of the Institute of Pacific Relations*, pp. 65-196. New York: Macmillan, 1953.

6236　Kahin, George McT.
'Postwar problems in the Southeast Asia policy of the United States', in: Ph.W. Thayer (ed.), *Southeast Asia in the coming world*, pp. 33-46. Baltimore: Johns Hopkins, 1953.

6237　Kahin, George McT.
'The United States and the anticolonial revolutions in Southeast Asia, 1945-1950', in: Yonosuke Nagai and Akira Iriye (eds), *The origins of the Cold War in Asia*, pp. 338-362. New York: Columbia University Press, Tokyo: University of Tokyo Press, 1977. (ubl)

6238　Kahin, George McTurnan
'A personal view of the war', in: Colin Wild and Peter Carey (eds), *Born in fire; The Indonesian struggle for independence; An anthology*, pp. 188-192. Athens: Ohio University Press, 1986.

6239　Kahin, George
'Sebuah pandangan pribadi tentang perang kemerdekaan', in: Colin Wild and Peter Carey (eds), *Gelora api revolusi*, pp. 192-198. Jakarta: Gramedia, 1986.

6240　Kattenburg, Paul M.
'Indonesia', in: Lawrence K. Rosinger a.o. (ed.), *The state of Asia; A contemporary survey*, pp. 405-442. London: Allen and Unwin, 1951.

6241　Katzenstein, Bertha
The establishment of the Indonesian Republic, 1945-1949. 1960, 69 pp. [MA thesis Columbia University, New York.]

6242　Kennedy, Raymond
Field notes on Indonesia; South Celebes, 1949-1950. New Haven: Human Relations Area Files, 1953, 269 pp.

6243　Kennedy, Raymond
Field notes on Indonesia; Ambon and Ceram, 1949-1950. New Haven: Human Relations Area Files, 1955, 347 pp.

6244　Kenny, E.L.
The United Nations handling of two territorial questions; Palestina and Indonesia. 1959. [MA thesis American University, Washington.] [97]

6245 Kiamilev, E.Kh.
The struggle of the Indonesian people for national independence, 1945-1949.
Moscow: Institute of Asian Peoples of the Academy of Sciences, 1968, 393 pp.
[97] [In Russian.]

6246 Kiamilev, E.Kh.
'The struggle of the Republik Indonesia against imperialist agression in 1945', in:
Countries of the Far East and Southeast Asia; Historical and economic questions,
pp. 42-59. Moscow: Nauka, 1969. [In Russian.]

6247 Kiamilev, E.Kh.
'Civil strife in the Republik Indonesia in 1946', in: *Countries of the Far East and
Southeast Asia; Historical and economic questions,* pp. 74-89. Moscow: Nauka,
1970. [In Russian.]

6248 Kiamilev, E.Kh.
The achievement of Indonesian independence. Moscow: Nauka, 1972, 220 pp. [In
Russian.]

6249 Kinoshita, Hajime
Merdeka... A secret history of Indonesian independence. Tokyo: Naigai Shuppan-
sha, 1958, 321 pp. [51, 1962, 6186] [In Japanese.]

6250 Kitaide, Daita
*The road to Merdeka; Anecdotes of Indonesian independence by an ex-admiral of the
navy.* Tokyo?: Hyodensha, 1986, 242 pp. [50] [In Japanese.]

6251 Koshino, Kikuo
Independence and revolution; Young Indonesia. Tokyo?: Indonesia Keizai
Kenkyujo, 1958, 256 pp. [51] [In Japanese.]

6252 Kratz, Ulrich
'Peranan pers dalam revolusi', in: Colin Wild and Peter Carey (eds), *Gelora api
revolusi,* pp. 49-55. Jakarta: Gramedia, 1986.

6253 Kratz, Ulrich
'The press', in: Colin Wild and Peter Carey (ed.), *Born in fire; The Indonesian
struggle for independence; An anthology,* pp. 46-51. Athens: Ohio University
Press, 1986.

6254 Labrousse-Soemargono, Farida
Cultural life in Yogyakarta during the period of independence (1945-1950).
Paper 6th IAHA Conference, Yogyakarta, 1974, 4 pp.

6255 Leclerc, Jacques
'Aidit dan partai pada tahun 1950', *Prisma* 11-7 (July 1982):61-79.

6256 Leclerc, Jacques
'Aidit and the problem of the party in the year 1950', *Kabar Seberang* no. 17
(1986):102-128.

6257 Lesavre, Pierre
La naissance d'un nouvel état dans le monde; La République des Etats-Unis
d'Indonésie. 1950, 310 pp. [Thesis Université de Paris.]

6258 Leupold, Robert J.
The United States and Indonesian independence 1944-1947; An American response to revolution. 1976, 358 pp. [PhD thesis University of Kentucky, Lexington.]

6259 Lockwood, R.
'The Indonesian exiles in Australia, 1942-1947', *Indonesia* no. 10 (1970):37-56.

6260 Lockwood, Rupert
' "Indonesia Calling" in censored Australian accents', in: *Kabar; Magazine of the Australian-Indonesian Association* 4-2 (1974):3-10. [5632]

6261 Lockwood, Rupert
Black Armada. Sydney: Australasian Book Society, 1975, 352 pp. [Second edition, *Black Armada; Australia and the struggle for Indonesian independence 1942-49*, Sydney: Hale and Iremonger, 1982, 352 pp.]

6262 Lucas, Anton
' "My story" and other sources; An "oral approach" to the Indonesian revolution', *Masyarakat Indonesia* 1 (1974):165-179.

6263 Lucas, Anton
'Social revolution in Pemalang, Central Java, 1945', *Indonesia* no. 24 (1977):87-122.

6264 Lucas, Anthony Edward
The bamboo spear pierces the payung; The revolution against the bureaucratic elite in North Central Java in 1945. 1981, 488 pp. [PhD thesis Australian National University, Canberra.]

6265 Lucas, Anton
'Masalah wawancara dengan informan pelaku sejarah di Jawa', in: Koentjaraningrat and Donald K. Emmerson (eds), *Aspek manusia dalam penelitian masyarakat*, pp. 211-244. Jakarta: Gramedia, 1982.

6266 Lucas, Anton
'Oral sources and the writing of regional history in Java', *Lembaran Berita Sejarah Lisan* 9 (October 1982):53-65.

6267 Lucas, Anton
'Lenggaong, Kyai, Guru; Three revolutionary biographies from North Java', in: R. Hatley and J. Schiller (eds), *Other Javas; Away from the kraton*, pp. 41-48. Clayton: Monash University, 1984.

6268 Lucas, Anton
'The Tiga Daerah affair: Social revolution or rebellion?', in: Audrey R. Kahin (ed.), *Regional dynamics of the Indonesian revolution*, pp. 23-53. Honolulu: University of Hawaii Press, 1985.

6269 Lucas, Anton
Balo and cap doke; Financing the fighting in South Sulawesi. Paper prepared for the Sixth National Conference of the Asian Studies Association of Australia, Sydney, 1986, 10 pp.

6270 Lucas, Anton
'Pemuda revolusi', in: Colin Wild and Peter Carey (eds), *Gelora api revolusi*, pp. 156-163. Jakarta: Gramedia, 1986.

6271 Lucas, Anton
'Revolutionary youth', in: Colin Wild and Peter Carey (eds), *Born in fire; The Indonesian struggle for independence; An anthology*, pp. 152-160. Athens: Ohio University Press, 1986.

6272 Lucas, Anton E.
Peristiwa Tiga Daerah; Revolusi dalam revolusi. Pengantar Sartono Kartodirdjo. Jakarta: Grafitipers, 1989, 16+376 pp.

6273 Lucas, Anton E.
One soul one struggle; Region and revolution in Indonesia. Sydney: Allen and Unwin, 1991, 301 pp.

6274 Ma Shu-li
The history of Indonesia's independence. Hong Kong: Newsdom, 1957, 32+386 pp. [71] [In Chinese.]

6275 Mackie, J.A.C.
'Australia and Indonesia, 1945-1960', in: G. Greenwood and N. Harper (eds), *Australia in world affairs 1956-1960*. Melbourne: Australian Institute of World Affairs, 1960. (kb)

6276 McMahon, Robert James
The United States and decolonization in Southeast Asia; The case of Indonesia, 1945-1949. 1977, 353 pp. [PhD thesis University of Connecticut, Storrs.]

6277 McMahon, Robert J.
Colonialism and Cold War; The United States and the struggle for Indonesian independence, 1945-49. Ithaca/London: Cornell University Press, 1981, 338 pp.

6278 McVey, Ruth T.
The Soviet view of the Indonesian revolution; A study in the Russian attitude towards Asian nationalism. Third edition. Ithaca: Cornell University Press, 1969, 90 pp. [First edition 1957.]

6279 McVey, R.T.
'The Southeast Asian insurrectionary movements', in: C.E. Black and Th.P. Thornton (eds), *Communism and revolution; The strategic use of political violence*, pp. 145-184. Princeton: Princeton University Press, 1964. (ubl)

6280 Mani, P.R.S.
The story of Indonesian revolution, 1945-1950. Madras: Centre for South and Southeast Asian Studies, 1986, 114 pp.

6281 Mani, P.R.S.
Jejak revolusi 1945; Sebuah kesaksian sejarah. Jakarta: Pustaka Utama Grafiti, 1989, 192 pp.

6282 Mariakasih, Frans Kho
'Les catholiques hollandais', in: Marcel Merle (ed.), *Les églises chrétiennes et la décolonisation*, pp. 313-324. Paris: Colin, 1967.

6283 Meek, John P.
The United Nations and Indonesia. 1951, 227 pp. [MA thesis University of Virginia, Charlottesville.]

6284 Michelle, Marion
'Indonesia Calling', in: Georges Sadoul (ed.), _Histoire générale du cinéma VI; L'époque contemporaine (1939-1954)_. Paris: Denoël, 1962. (ubl)

6285 Miyamoto, Shizuo
'Army problems in Java after the surrender', in: Anthony Reid and Oki Akira (eds), _The Japanese experience in Indonesia_, pp. 325-340. Athens: Ohio University Center for International Studies, 1986.

6286 Morris, Eric
'Aceh; Social revolution and the Islamic vision', in: Audrey R. Kahin (ed.), _Regional dynamics of the Indonesian revolution_, pp. 83-110. Honolulu: University of Hawaii Press, 1985.

6287 Mortimer, R.
'Australian support for Indonesian independence', _Indonesia_ no. 22 (1976):171-175.

6288 Mountbatten, Louis
Post surrender tasks; Section E of the Report to the Combined Chiefs of Staff by the Supreme Allied Commander South East Asia 1943-1945. London: His Majesty's Stationary Office, 1951, 42 pp. [Reprinted 1968.] (ubl)

6289 Mountbatten, Louis
Personal diary of Admiral the Lord Louis Mountbatten, Supreme Allied Commander, South-East Asia, 1943-1946. Edited by Philip Ziegler. London: Collins, 1988, 357 pp.

6290 Munro, Dorothy
The first eight months of the British occupation of Indonesia, September, 1945-May, 1946. 1952, 103 pp. [MA thesis Smith College, Northampton, Mass.]

6291 Newsinger, John
'A forgotten war; British intervention in Indonesia 1945-46', _Race and Class_ 30-4 (1989):51-66.

6292 Niimura, Akira
Flames of Jakarta (documents of Japanese who remained in Indonesia). Tokyo: Sairyusha, 1982, 259 pp. [In Japanese.] [51]

6293 Nish, Ian (ed.)
Indonesian experience; The role of Japan and Britain, 1943-1948. London: London School of Economics, 1979, 72 pp.

6294 Nishijima, S.
Riwayat hidup dan perjuangan Nishijima sekitar Proklamasi RI 17-8-1945. Tokyo: Shin-jinbotsu-oraisha, 1975, 246 pp. [In Japanese.] [40]

6295 Nishijima, Shigetada
'The independence proclamation in Jakarta', in: Anthony Reid and Oki Akira (eds), _The Japanese experience in Indonesia_, pp. 299-324. Athens: Ohio University Center for International Studies, 1986.

6296 Nishijima, Shigetada
'Hari-hari di bawah tanah menjelang Proklamasi', _Tempo_ (August 1987):3-16.

6297 Nolton, John S.
The role of the United States in the Indonesian independence movement, 1945-1949.
1972, 311 pp. [PhD thesis American University, Washington.]

6298 Oba, Sadao
'Recollections of Indonesia, 1944-1947', in: Ian Nish (ed.), *Indonesian experience;
The role of Japan and Britain, 1943-1948*, pp. 1-34. London: London School of
Economics, 1979.

6299 Oba, Sadao
'My recollections of Java during the Pacific War and Merdeka', *Indonesia Circle*
no. 21 (March 1980):6-14.

6300 Oey Hong Lee
'The road not taken; Decolonization and independence in Indonesia and
Indochina', *Foreign Affairs* 51 (1972-73):608-628.

6301 Oey Hong Lee
'British-Dutch relations and the Republic of Indonesia', *Asian Affairs* 3 (February
1976):35-53.

6302 Oey Hong Lee
War and diplomacy in Indonesia 1945-50. Townsville: James Cook University of
North Queensland, 1981, 273 pp.

6303 Oey Hong Lee
McArthur, Mountbatten and the beginning of the end of Dutch colonialism in
Indonesia. Paper at the Conference and Annual Meeting of the Association of
Southeast Asian Studies in the United Kingdom, 1982. [38]

6304 Oku, Genzo
Japanese deserters; Behind the Indonesian independence war. Tokyo: Mainichi
Shinbunshya, 1980, 246 pp. [In Japanese.] [51, 1962]

6305 Oku, Genzo
Having survived the independence war of Indonesia. Tokyo?: Sanshin Tosho, 1987,
207 pp. [In Japanese.] [51]

6306 Ong Poh Kee
Trade of Penang with Atjeh, 1945-1955. 1956. [Honor's thesis University of
Malaya, Singapore.] [6286]

6307 Papanek, Hanna
'Note on Soedjatmoko's recollections of a historical moment; Sjahrir's reaction
to Ho Chi Minh's 1945 call for a free peoples federation', *Indonesia* no. 49
(1990):141-144.

6308 Parrott, J.G.A.
'Who killed Brigadier Mallaby?', *Indonesia* no. 20 (1975): 87-111.

6309 Parrott, John George A.
Role of the 49th Indian Infantry Brigade in Surabaya, 25 October-1 November
1945. 1977, 111 pp. [MA thesis Monash University, Clayton.]

6310 Patnaik, Shri Biju
'Menembus blokade udara', *Sejarah* 4 (1993):63-71.

6311 *Peaceful settlement in Indonesia*. New York: United Nations, 1950, 20 pp.

6312 Plychevskii, I.P.
Indonesia, 1945-1949. Moscow: Higher Party School of the Central Committee of the CPSU, 1951, 28 pp. [In Russian.] [5]

6313 Prasad, Birendra
'Indonesian freedom movement and the Indian public opinion (1945-46)', *South East Asian Review* 1-2 (February 1977):167-171.

6314 Prindeville, Susan
The Netherlands' loss of the East Indies; Internal and external pressures on Dutch policy from 1945-1949. 1971, 111 pp. [MA thesis American University, Washington.]

6315 Ray, Jayanta Kumar
Transfer of power in Indonesia 1942-1949. Bombay: Manaktalas, 1967, 224 pp.

6316 Reid, A.
'The birth of the Republic in Sumatra', *Indonesia* no. 12 (1971):21-46.

6317 Reid, A.
Australian military forces and the independence movement in eastern Indonesia, 1945-6. N.p.: n.n., 1973, 13 pp.

6318 Reid, Anthony J.S.
The Indonesian national revolution 1945-1950. Hawthorn: Longman, 1974, 193 pp. [Second edition, Westport (Conn.): Greenwood Press, 1986.]

6319 Reid, A.J.S.
'Marxist attitudes to social revolution, 1946-1948', *Review of Indonesian and Malaysian Affairs* 8-1 (1974):45-56.

6320 Reid, Anthony
The blood of the people; Revolution and the end of traditional rule in northern Sumatra. Kuala Lumpur: Oxford University Press, 1979, 288 pp.

6321 Reid, Anthony
'Indonesia: Revolution without socialism', in: Robin Jeffrey (ed.), *Asia; The winning of independence*, pp. 113-157. London: Macmillan, 1981.

6322 Reid, Anthony
'Social revolution - national revolution', *Prisma* 23 (December 1981):64-72.

6323 Reid, Anthony
'Revolusi sosial - revolusi nasional', *Prisma* 10-8 (August 1981):33-40.

6324 Reid, Anthony
'Australia's hundred days in South Sulawesi', in: David P. Chandler and M.C. Ricklefs (eds), *Nineteenth and twentieth century Indonesia; Essays in honour of Professor J.D. Legge*, pp. 201-224. Clayton: Monash University, 1986.

6325 Reid, Anthony
'Fase kedua; Kemenangan terakhir; Juli 1947 sampai 1950', in: Colin Wild and Peter Carey (eds), *Gelora api revolusi*, pp. 181-187. Jakarta: Gramedia, 1986.

6326 Reid, Anthony
'The revolution in regional perspective', in: J. van Goor (ed.), *The Indonesian revolution; Conference papers*, pp. 183-199. Utrecht: Rijksuniversiteit Utrecht, 1986.

6327 Reid, Anthony J.S.
'The victory of the Republic', in: Colin Wild and Peter Carey (eds), *Born in fire; The Indonesian struggle for independence; An anthology*, pp. 178-183. Athens: Ohio University Press, 1986.

6328 Reid, A.
Perjuangan rakyat; Revolusi dan hancurnya kerajaan di Sumatera. Jakarta: Pustaka Sinar Harapan, 1987, 437 pp.

6329 Reid, Anthony
'The Australian discovery of Indonesia, 1945', *Journal of the Australian War Memorial* no. 17 (October 1990):30-40.

6330 *La République d'Indonésie et la Conférence de la Table Ronde*. Paris: Documentation Française, 1950, 42 pp.

6331 Robinson, Geoffrey
The state and civil war in Bali. 1988, 536 pp. [Thesis Cornell University, Ithaca.]

6332 Robinson, Geoffrey
'State, society and political conflict in Bali, 1945-1946', *Indonesia* no. 45 (April 1988):1-48.

6333 Robinson, Geoffrey Basil
The politics of violence in modern Bali, 1882-1966. 1992, 702 pp. [PhD thesis Cornell University, Ithaca.]

6334 Robles, Eliodoro G.
The role of the United Nations in the Indonesian question. 1954, 267 pp. [MA thesis Cornell University, Ithaca.]

6335 Scharffenorth, Ernst-Albert
Stellungnahmen protestantischer Kirchen zur Dekolonisation von Niederländisch-Indien; Ein zeitgeschichtlich-systematischer Beitrag zur theologischen Ethik des Politischen. 1983, 371 pp. [PhD thesis Ruprecht-Karl-Universität, Heidelberg.]

6336 Scheuner, U.
'Die Entstehung des indonesischen Staates', *Archiv des Völkerrechts* 3 (1951-52):45-67.

6337 Schiller, A. Arthur
The formation of federal Indonesia 1945-1949. Den Haag/Bandung: Van Hoeve, 1955, 472 pp.

6338 Schneider, M.P.
Australia and Indonesian independence; A study in Australian foreign policy. 1955, 153 pp. [BA Honours thesis University of Adelaide.]

6339 *Secret memoirs; Behind the Indonesian independence*. Tokyo?: Indonesia Center, 1974, 36 pp. [In Japanese.] [51]

6340 Sevortyan, R.Z.
'The struggle of the Republik Indonesia against the second Dutch agression (December 1948-May 1949)', in: *Problems of contemporary Indonesia*, pp. 38-53. Moscow: Nauka, 1968. [In Russian.]

6341 Sheedy, F.D.
A study of Australian policies and attitudes to Indonesia before and after independence, in the period 1945-1951, with special reference to the Labour movement. 1970, 130 pp. [BA thesis University of New England, Armidale.]

6342 Shirakawa, Masao
The accomplishment of the original intention; Autobiography of a man who remained there after the war. Tokyo?: Atje Kai, 1981, 76 pp. [In Japanese.] [51]

6343 Simon, W.
De Indonesische kwestie. Ca. 1975, 207 pp. [Thesis Rijkshandelshogeschool, Antwerpen.] [45]

6344 Singh, Rajendra
Post-war occupation forces; Japan and South-East Asia. Kanpur: The Job Press, 1958, 317 pp.

6345 Smail, J.R.W.
Bandung in the early revolution, 1945-6; A study in the social history of the Indonesian revolution. Ithaca: Cornell University, 1964, 169 pp.

6346 Smail, John R.W.
On the style of the Indonesian revolutionaries. Paper at the International Conference on Asian History, Hong Kong, 1964, 7 pp.

6347 Somers-Heidhues, Mary F.
'Citizenship and identity; Ethnic Chinese and the Indonesian revolution', in: Jennifer W. Cushman and Wang Gungwu (eds), *Changing identities of the Southeast Asian Chinese since World War II*, pp. 115-138. Hong Kong: Hong Kong University Press, 1988.

6348 Squire, Clifford William
Britain and the transfer of power in Indonesia 1945-46. 1979, 329 pp. [PhD thesis School of Oriental and African Studies, London.]

6349 Stange, Paul
'Inner dimensions of the Indonesian revolution', in: Laurie J. Sears (ed.), *Autonomous histories, particular truths; Essays in honour of John R.W. Smail*, pp. 219-243. Madison: Center for Southeast Asian Studies, Universit of Wisconsin, 1993.

6350 Stelzer, Hans-Jürgen
Die Indonesienpolitik der Vereinigten Staaten 1940 bis 1949. 1956, 200 pp. [PhD thesis Universität Hamburg.]

6351 Stoler, Ann Laura
'Working the revolution; Plantation laborers and the people's militia in North Sumatra', *Journal of Asian Studies* 47 (1988):227-247.

6352 Sufian, Hiroshi Maeda
Maeda memilih Republik; Kisah perjuangan 1945. Bandung: ITB, 1987, 17+121 pp.

6353   Suryanarayan, V.
'India and the Indonesian revolution', in: *Proceedings 42nd Indian Historical Congress* (1981):549-562. [25]

6354   Sutherland, H.
'The Indonesian revolution; A review', *Indonesia* no. 42 (1986):113-118.

6355   Sutter, J.O.
Indonesianisasi; Politics in a changing economy, 1940-1955. Ithaca: Cornell University, 1959, 1312 pp. 4 vols.

6356   Swift, Elizabeth Ann
Madiun. 1979, 174 pp. [MA thesis Cornell University, Ithaca.]

6357   Swift, Ann
The road to Madiun; The Indonesian communist uprising of 1948. Ithaca: Cornell University, 1989, 12+116 pp.

6358   Tantri, K'tut (ps. Sue Manx)
Revolt in paradise. London: Heinemann, 1960, 305 pp.

6359   Tantri, K'tut (ps.)
Revolusi di nusa damai. Djakarta: Mega Bookstore, 1964, 464 pp. (kitlv-m) [Second edition, Djakarta: Gunung Agung, 1965, 428 pp.; Third edition, Jakarta: Gramedia, 1982, 513 pp.]

6360   Tauber, B.D.
The Soviet attitude towards Indonesia (from August 17, 1945 to the transfer of sovereignty). 1957, 76 pp. [MA thesis Columbia University, New York.] [97]

6361   Taylor, Alastair M.
The United Nations and the Indonesian question; An analysis of the role of international mediation. 1956. [PhD thesis University of Oxford.] [97]

6362   Taylor, Alastair M.
Indonesian independence and the United Nations. London: Stevens, 1960, 503 pp.

6363   Taylor, Jean S.
Some Indonesian perceptions of the revolution; A study in Indonesian historiography. 1969, 246 pp. [MA thesis University of Melbourne.]

6364   Thorne, Christopher
'The British are coming', in: C. Wild and P. Carey (eds), *Born in fire; The Indonesian struggle for independence; An anthology*, pp. 113-119. Athens: Ohio University Press, 1986.

6365   Thorne, Christopher
'Orang-orang Inggris datang', in: Colin Wild and Peter Carey (eds), *Gelora api revolusi*, pp. 126-132. Jakarta: Gramedia, 1986.

6366   Thurston, Donald R.
A study of the Committee of Good Offices on the Indonesian question. 1956, 84 pp. [MA thesis Columbia University, New York.]

6367   Tiat Han Tan
The attitude of Dutch Protestant missions toward Indonesian nationalism, 1945-1949. 1967, 413 pp. [Thesis Princeton Theological Seminary, Princeton.]

6368 Tochikubo, Hiroo
A Japanese Indonesian; The independence war of the ex-Japanese soldier Hassan Tanaka. Tokyo?: Saimaru Shuppan Kai, 1979, 272 pp. [In Japanese.] [51, 59]

6369 Tomon, Hiroshi
Indonesian independence and Japanese soldiers; Merdeka. Tokyo?: Honpo shoseki, 1984, 417 pp. [In Japanese.] [51]

6370 Tran Buu Khanh
L'Indonésie; Introduction à une décolonisation. Bruxelles: Centre pour l'Etude des Problèmes du Monde Musulman Contemporain, 1965, 71 pp.

6371 Trigellis-Smith, S.
'Same war - New country', in: S. Trigellis-Smith, *The Purple Devils; A history of the 2/6 Australian Commando Squadron, Formerly the 2/6 Australian Independent Company, 1942-1946*, pp. 230-261. Melbourne: 2/6 Commando Squadron Association, 1992.

6372 Trullinger, O.O.
Red banners over Asia. Oxford: Pen-in-Hand, 1950, 11+212 pp.

6373 Ushiyama, Mitsuo
'Conflict in Aceh after independence', in; A. Reid and Oki Akira (eds), *The Japanese experience in Indonesia*, pp. 375-395. Athens: Ohio University Center for International Studies, 1986.

6374 Van der Kroef, J.M.
'The Indonesian settlement', *Current History* 18-104 (April 1950):193-196.

6375 Van der Kroef, J.M.
'Indonesia; Federalism and centralism', *Current History* 19-108 (August 1950):88-94. (ubu)

6376 Van der Kroef, J.M.
'The Indonesian revolution in retrospect', *World Politics* 3 (1951):369-398.

6377 Van der Kroef, J.M.
'Dutch policy and the Linggadjati agreement, 1946-1947', *Historian* 15-2 (1953):163-187. (kb)

6378 Van Langenberg, M.
'The establishment of the Republic of Indonesia in North Sumatra; Regional differences and political factionalism', *Review of Indonesian and Malaysian Affairs* 6-1 (1972):1-44.

6379 Van Langenberg, Michael
National revolution in North Sumatra; Sumatera Timur and Tapanuli, 1942-1950. 1976, 22+1030 pp. [PhD thesis University of Sydney.]

6380 Van Langenberg, M.
Minority class and primordial interests in Indonesia's decolonization process; A study of East Sumatra. Paper 8th IAHA Conference, Kuala Lumpur, 1980. [5374, 5452]

6381 Van Langenberg, M.
'Class and ethnic conflict in Indonesia's decolonization process; A study of
East Sumatra', *Indonesia* no. 33 (1983):1-30.

6382 Van Langenberg, Michael
'East Sumatra: Accomodating an Indonesian nation within a Sumatran
residency', in: Audrey R. Kahin (ed.), *Regional dynamics of the Indonesian
revolution*, pp. 113-143. Honolulu: University of Hawaii Press, 1985.

6383 Venner, Dominique
Westerling; Guérrillastory. Paris: Hachette, 1977, 319 pp.

6384 Venner, Dominique
Westerling 'de eenling'. Amsterdam: Spoor, 1982, 399 pp.

6385 Voitenko, A.
Struggle of the Indonesian people for their independence. Kiev: Society for the
Dissemination of Political and Scientific Knowledge of the Ukrainian SSR,
1950, 48 pp. [In Russian?] [5]

6386 Wagner, Hans
Where did the weapons come from? Paper prepared for the Sixth National
Conference of the Asian Studies Association of Australia, Sydney, 1986, 16 pp.

6387 Wagner, H.
'Hoe kwamen de Indonesische strijdkrachten in de jaren '40 aan wapens?', *De
Militaire Spectator* 156 (1987):488-495. (ubl)

6388 *A war journal of the five days of fierce battle in Semarang.* Jakarta?: Hassan
Tanaka, 1986, 206 pp. [In Japanese.] [51]

6389 Weber, Angelika
'Antikolonialer Kampf unter dem Aspekt der Herausbildung bilateraler
Beziehungen zwischen Indien und Indonesien', *Asien, Afrika, Lateinamerika* 16-6
(1988):999-1012.

6390 Wilborn, T.L.
Indonesia and the United Nations, 1945-1961. 1965, 407 pp. [PhD thesis
University of Kentucky, Lexington.]

6391 Wild, Colin
'Pengaruh radio dalam perjuangan', in: Colin Wild and Peter Carey (eds), *Gelora
api revolusi*, pp. 163-170. Jakarta: Gramedia, 1986.

6392 Wild, Colin
'The radio war', in: Colin Wild and Peter Carey (eds), *Born in fire; The Indonesian
struggle for independence; An anthology*, pp. 161-167. Athens: Ohio University
Press, 1986.

6393 Wild, Colin
'De radio als vroedvrouw; De rol van de radio in de Indonesische
onafhankelijkheidsstrijd', in: *Jaarboek Mediageschiedenis 4; Nederlands Indië*,
pp. 71-87. Amsterdam: Stichting Beheer IISG/Stichting Mediageschiedenis,
1992.

6394 Wild, Colin and Peter Carey
BBC Seksi Indonesia mempersembahkan 'Gelora api revolusi'; Sebuah anthologi sejarah. Jakarta: BBC Seksi Indonesia, 1985, 12 pp.

6395 Wild, Colin and Peter Carey (eds)
Born in fire; The Indonesian struggle for independence; An anthology. Athens: Ohio University Press, 1986, 28+215 pp.

6396 Wild, Colin and Peter Carey (eds)
Gelora api revolusi; Sebuah antologi sejarah. Jakarta: Gramedia/BBC Seksi Indonesia, 1986, 236 pp.

6397 Willems, J.
Vergelijkende studie van de ontvoogdingspolitiek van Nederland in Indonesië en België in Kongo. Antwerpen, ca. 1970, 134 pp. [45]

6398 Williams, Michael C.
'Banten: Rice debts will be repaid with rice, blood debts with blood', in: Audrey R. Kahin (ed.), *Regional dynamics of the Indonesian revolution*, pp. 55-81. Honolulu: University of Hawaii Press, 1985.

6399 Wolfsohn, H.A.
'Australia's foreign policy and the Indonesian dispute', in: *Australian papers; Implications for Australia of recent developments in the Far East; 11th Conference of the Institute of Pacific Relations, Lucknow (India) 1950.* [45, 146, 6199]

6400 Yong Mun Cheong
'The Dutch archives as a source for the study of the Indonesian revolution (1945-1949) at the regional level', *Itinerario* 2 (1978):53-55.

6401 Yong Mun Cheong
H.J. van Mook and Indonesian independence; A study of his role in Dutch-Indonesian relations, 1945-48. The Hague: Nijhoff, 1982, 255 pp. [Also PhD thesis University of Singapore, 1981.]

6402 Zaboslaeva, O.I.
On the problem of the declaration of independence by Indonesia, August 17, 1945. Moscow: Eastern Languages Press, 1960, 9 pp. [In Russian.] [5]

6403 Zemba, John Michael
Decolonization and national development; A case study of Indonesia. 1990, 91 pp. [MA thesis California State University, Long Beach.]

West Irian and the South Moluccan question
Indonesian authors

6404 Abdulgani, Roeslan
Perkembangan politik luar negeri Indonesia dalam tahun 1956. Djakarta: Pertjetakan Negara, 1957, 177 pp. (kitlv-m)

6405 Abdulgani, Roeslan
Sumbangan dan peranan tiap-tiap universitas dalam perdjuangan pembebasan Irian Barat. Djakarta: Dewan Pertimbangan Agung, 1962, 22 pp.

6406 Adinegoro
'De Irian-kwestie', *De Gids* (1950, II):45-48.

6407 *Aftermath of colonialism; The 'RMS' question.* Washington: Indonesian Embassy, 1972, 13 pp.

6408 Anantaguna, S.
Dengan TRIKORA membebaskan Irian Barat. Djakarta: Lembaga Kebudajaan Rakjat, 1962, 94 pp. (kitlv-m)

6409 Anwar, Agoes
Soumokil dan hantjurnja RMS; Sebuah tugu bagi kegagalan usaha pemetjah-belah kesatuan bangsa Indonesia. Medan: Pudja Sakti, 1964, 102 pp.

6410 Aroean, L.
Deklarasi ekonomi dengan peraturan-peraturan pelaksanaannja dan peraturan-peraturan ekonomi Irian Barat. Djakarta: Upaja, 1963, 290 pp.

6411 *The autonomous province of West Irian.* Djakarta: Ministry of Information, 1956, 26 pp.

6412 Bachtiar, Harsja W.
'Sedjarah Irian Barat', in: Koentjaraningrat and H.W. Bachtiar, *Penduduk Irian Barat*, pp. 55-94. Djakarta: Penerbitan Universitas Indonesia, 1963.

6413 Brahmanto, Kresno
Sikap Australia terhadap Indonesia dalam masalah Irian Barat 1949-1962. 1990, 18+305 pp. [MA thesis Universitas Indonesia, Jakarta.] [Histori]

6414 *Brief history in chronological order of the dispute about West Irian.* Djakarta: Ministry of Information, 1961, 12 pp.

6415 *Buatlah Irian Barat, satu zamrud jang indah; Kumpulan amanat-amanat dan pidato-pidato penting, 1 Mei '63 - 1 Mei '64.* Djakarta: Dep. Penerangan, 1964, 297 pp.

6416 *Case study mengenai kegiatan-kegiatan Komando Mandala.* Makasar: Komando Mandala Pembebasan Irian Barat, 1963. [6420]

6417 *The case of West Irian (West New Guinea).* Cairo: Indonesian Embassy, 1954, 52 pp. (kitlv-m)

6418 *The case of West Irian (West New Guinea); The dispute between Indonesia and the Netherlands.* Djakarta: Ministry of Foreign Affairs, 1954, 12 pp. (kitlv-m)

6419 Charis, Rizal
Perdjuangan pembebasan Irian Barat dalam rangka revolusi nasional. 1964. [MA thesis Universitas Indonesia, Djakarta.] [18]

6420 Cholil, M.
Sedjarah operasi-operasi pembebasan Irian Barat. Djakarta: Dep. Pertahanan-Keamanan, 1971, 99 pp.

6421 *Colonial purposes in West Irian; An exposé of Dutch intentions.* Djakarta: Department of Foreign Affairs, 1962, 40 pp. (kitlv-m)

6422 Dajoh, M.R.
Patriot, Irian, damai. Djakarta: Grafica, 1958, 410 pp.

6423 Dajoh, M.R.
Irian Barat pukul tifa. Djakarta: Dep. P dan K, 1961, 117 pp.

6424 *Djangan ragu-ragu lagi! Amanat-amanat Soekarno, Moh. Hatta dan pidato pembukaan Soediro pada rapat rakjat, tg. 18 Nopember 1957, di Lapangan Banteng.* Djakarta: Panitya Aksi Pembebasan Irian Barat, 1957, 23 pp. (kitlv-m)

6425 Djojohadikoesoemo, Soemitro
'The West Irian question', *Far Eastern Economic Review* no. 29 (1960). (vp)

6426 Djuanda
Government statement on the struggle for West Irian, delivered by Prime Minister H. Djuanda in the plenary meeting of Parliament held on January 27, 1958. Djakarta: Ministry of Information, 1958, 56 pp.

6427 Djuanda
Keterangan pemerintah tentang perdjoangan Irian Barat, diutjapkan oleh H. Djuanda dalam rapat pleno Dewan Perwakilan Rakjat, tg. 27 Djan.1958. Djakarta: Dep. Penerangan, 1958, 24 pp.

6428 Dongoran, Hiob
Perdjuangan pembebasan Irian Barat di bidang diplomasi. 1972, 73 pp. [MA thesis IKIP Djakarta.] [11]

6429 Effendie, J.
Irian Barat. Djakarta, 1952, 50 pp. (kit)

6430 *The future of West Irian.* London: Embassy of the Republic of Indonesia, 1950, 16 pp.

6431 Hadinoto, Suyatno
Api perjuangan pembebasan Irian Barat. Jakarta: Yayasan Badan Kontak Keluarga Besar Perintis Irian Barat, 1986, 682 pp.

6432 Handojosaputro, Mistesam
Sedjarah perdjuangan merebut kembali Irian Barat. 1971, 145 pp. [MA thesis
IKIP Djakarta.] [11]

6433 Herlina, J.
Pending emas; Pengalaman-pengalaman selama mendarat di Irian Barat. Djakarta:
Second edition. Gunung Agung, 1965, 257 pp. [First edition 1964.] (kitlv-m)

6434 Herlina
'Astaga, kapal perang Belanda berbendera Merah Putih', in: *Bunga rampai
perjuangan dan pengorbanan I*, pp. 220-229. Jakarta: Markas Besar Legiun
Veteran RI, 1982.

6435 Herlina, J.
Pending emas; Bergerilya di belantara Irian; Edisi yang direvisi. Jakarta: Gunung
Agung, 1985, 543 pp.

6436 *Himpunan keputusan tahun 1962-1963 Komando Operasi Tertinggi Pembebasan
Irian Barat.* Djakarta: APRI, 1963, 219 pp.

6437 *Indonesia wants negotiation on the West Irian problem based on transfer of administration from the Netherlands to Indonesia.* Djakarta: Department of Information, 1962. [45]

6438 'Irian; Crisis in Indonesian-Dutch relations', *Indonesian Review* 1-1 (January
1951):41-48.

6439 *Irian Barat adalah wilajah Indonesia.* Djakarta: Djawatan Penerangan Kotapradja
Djakarta Raya, 1956, 42 pp.

6440 *Irian Barat; Bahagian mutlak RI.* Djakarta: Projek Penerbitan Sekretariat
Koordinator Urusan Irian Barat, 1964, 134 pp.

6441 *Irian Barat daerah kita!* Djakarta: Dep. Penerangan, 1962, 51 pp.

6442 *Irian Barat dari masa ke masa.* Djajapura: SEMDAM XVII/Tjenderawasih, 1971,
22+310 pp.

6443 Iskandar, Nur St.
Perdjalinan hidup; Perdjuangan Srikandi Irian Barat untuk kemerdekaan.
Bukittinggi: Nusantara, 1962, 343 pp. (kitlv-m)

6444 Ismaja, Sulaiman Setia Bambang
Peranan Perserikatan Bangsa-Bangsa dalam menjelesaikan masalah Irian Barat.
1970, 136 pp. [MA thesis Universitas Djajabaja, Djakarta.] [9]

6445 Jamlean, V.J.
'Perjuangan 45 untuk pembangunan bangsa strategi perjuangan di Irian Jaya
(1945-1950)', in: *Letusan di balik buku; Hasil sayembara mengarang dalam rangka
peringatan hari ulang tahun kemerdekaan RI yang ke 30*, pp. 117-133. Jakarta:
Dewan Harian Nasional Angkatan 45/Aries Lima, 1976.

6446 Jamlean, V.J.
'Perjuangan 45 untuk pembangunan bangsa strategi perjuangan di Irian Jaya
(1945-1950)', *Gema Angkatan 45* no. 34 (November 1978):22-26.

6447   Kartiningsih, Liena
       Peranan ABRI dalam pembebasan Irian Barat. 1985. [MA thesis IKIP Jakarta.]
       [Histori]

6448   Katoppo, E.
       Perdjoangkan Irian kembali kedalam wilayah Indonesia. Bandung: Kilat Madju,
       1955, 128 pp.

6449   *Komando Mandala pembebasan Irian Barat*. Makasar: Panitya Buku Kenangan,
       1963. [6420]

6450   Kosim, E. Moch.
       'Infiltrasi TRIKORA', *Vidya Yudha* no. 6 (1969):72-81; no. 8 (1969):150-163.

6451   *Laporan-laporan Komando Mandala bidang G-2 (Operasi) dan G-5 (Teritorial dan
       Perlawanan Rakjat)*. Makasar: Komando Mandala Pembebasan Irian Barat,
       1963. [6420]

6452   Latumahina, L. (ed.)
       Irian dan KMB. Jogjakarta: Badan Perdjuangan Irian, 1949, 44 pp. (kitlv-m)

6453   Leimena, J.
       The Ambon question; Facts and appeal. Djakarta: n.n., 1951, 45 pp.

6454   Leimena, J.
       Soal Ambon; Peristiwa dan seruan. Djakarta: n.n., 1951, 48 pp. (kitlv-m)

6455   Leirissa, R.Z.
       Maluku dalam perjuangan nasional Indonesia. Jakarta: Lembaga Sejarah, Fakultas
       Sastra, Universitas Indonesia, 1975, 12+248 pp.

6456   Leirissa, R.Z.
       De Molukken in de nationale strijd van Indonesië; De strijd der onafhankelijkheid. Ja-
       karta?: Organisasi Wanita Indonesia Maluku, 1976, 23 pp.

6457   Leirissa, R.Z.
       'Pemberontakan "Republik Maluku Selatan" ', *Prisma* 7-7 (August 1978):26-39.

6458   Lopa, Baharuddin
       Djalannja revolusi Indonesia membebaskan Irian Barat. Djakarta: Pertjetakan
       Negara, 1962, 300 pp.

6459   Lubis, Nazaruddin
       Irian Barat; Fakta dan angka. Djakarta: Gotong Rojong, 1962, 128 pp.

6460   Luhukay, Hanoch
       Front penentang 'Republik Maluku Selatan' di Makassar (terbentuk pada
       tanggal 26 April 1950). Paper SSN-IV, Yogyakarta, 1985, 18 pp.

6461   Lususina, Teu (ps. Piet de Queljoe)
       Ambon selajang pandang! Djakarta: Pertjetakan Negara, 1950, 139 pp. (kitlv-m)

6462   Manuputty, Joseph
       Peristiwa Republik Maluku Selatan; Suatu projek untuk mempertahankan
       federasi di Indonesia. 1970, 116 pp. [MA thesis IKIP Djakarta.] [11, 58, 99]

6463   Maruapey, M.K.; Trisno Dumadi and Subardjo
        'TNI membebaskan Ambon dari RMS', *Vidya Yudha* no. 10 (1970):120-126.

6464   Matulessy, David
        Patimura-Patimura muda bangkit memenuhi tuntutan sejarah. Jakarta: n.n., 1979,
        150 pp.

6465   *The Moluccas of yesterday and today; History of the Spice Islands; A few facts about
        the self-styled Republic of the South Moluccas.* Bern: Kantor Penerangan Republik
        Indonesia, ca. 1960, 16 pp. [37]

6466   Nainggolan, R.E.
        Pembebasan Irian Barat dengan penjerahan pemerintahan (administrasi) oleh
        Belanda kepada Indonesia. 1962, 63 pp. [MA thesis IKIP Bandung.] [10, 108]

6467   Nainggolan, Zailani Sjah
        Perdjuangan Indonesia dalam Perserikatan Bangsa-Bangsa dari tahun 1950-
        1966. 1971, 113 pp. [MA thesis IKIP Bandung.] [10]

6468   Nanulaitta, I.O.
        Timbulnja militarisme Ambon; Sebagai suatu persoalan politik, social-ekonomis.
        Djakarta: Bhratara, 1966, 145 pp.

6469   Notoadikusumo, Mhd. Hasan
        'Historische afspraken en aanspraken', in: Paul van 't Veer (ed.), *Nieuw-Guinea
        tegen wil en dank; Een historische omschrijving en een waarschuwend toekomst-
        perspectief,* pp. 114-126. Amsterdam: Querido, 1960.

6470   Nurdin, Nurlizar
        Kembalinja Irian Barat kepangkuan negara kesatuan Republik Indonesia. 1971,
        118 pp. [MA thesis IKIP Djakarta.] [11]

6471   *Official documents on the establishment of the province of West Irian.* Djakarta:
        Ministry of Information, 1956, 12 pp. (kitlv-m)

6472   Panggabean, Panagian
        Pertempuran Laut Arafuru menuju pembebasan Irian Barat. 1979. [MA thesis
        Universitas Padjadjaran, Bandung.] [20]

6473   Pello, A.S.
        Irian. Jogjakarta: Sumber Kemadjuan Rakjat, ca. 1955, 88 pp. (kitlv-m)

6474   'Pembebasan Ambon terhadap kekuasaan Republik Maluku Selatan', *Vidya
        Yudha* no. 4 (1968):112-120.

6475   *Penjelesaian persengketaan Irian-Barat; Jaitu rentjana pendirian Komisi Gabungan
        Irian-Barat Bagian Komisi Indonesia; Diangkat oleh kedua negara-peserta Uni Indo-
        nesia-Belanda oleh pemerintah Republik Indonesia Serikat.* Djakarta: Pertjetakan
        Negara, 1950, 272 pp.

6476   *Persetudjuan Indonesia-Nederland mengenai penjerahan Irian Barat kepada Republik
        Indonesia; Ditanda-tangani di markas besar PBB, New York, tg. 15 Agustus 1962.*
        Djakarta: Dep. Penerangan, 1962, 95 pp.

6477   Puar, Jusuf A.
        Peristiwa Republik Maluku Selatan. Djakarta: Bulan Bintang, 1956, 211 pp.

6478   *The question of West Irian.* Djakarta: Ministry of Foreign Affairs, 1955, 38 pp. (kitlv-m)

6479   *The question of West Irian in the United Nations 1954-1957.* Djakarta: Ministry of Foreign Affairs, 1958, 507 pp.

6480   Rapanoi, Supardi; Sjamsuar Said and H. Hutasuhut
       Praja Ghupta Vira/ksatrya pelindung masjarakat; Irian Barat dari masa ke masa. Djajapura: Sedjarah Militer KODAM XVII/Tjenderawasih, 1971, 310 pp.

6481   Reksodiputro, Hertomo
       Act of free choice (PEPERA) sebagai penjelesaian sengketa antara Republik Indonesia dan Keradjaan Negeri Belanda. Djakarta: Universitas Indonesia, 1970, 81 pp.

6482   Said, Syamsuar
       Gagalnya sebuah pemberontakan (GOM IV di Maluku Selatan). Semarang: Mandira Jaya Abadi, 1985, 66 pp.

6483   *Sandjak Irian-Barat tanah pusaka Indonesia.* Bandung: Dua-R, 1962, 43 pp. (kitlv-m)

6484   Sasradipoera, Abdoelkobir
       Dispute between the Kingdom of the Netherlands and the Republic of Indonesia on West Irian (New Guinea) in the United Nations. 1959, 109 pp. [MA thesis Columbia University, New York.]

6485   *Semangat perdjuangan Irian Barat masih tetap menjala-njala.* Djakarta: Dep. Penerangan, 1962, 86 pp. (kitlv-m)

6486   Setiawan, R. Moch. Soemali
       Perjuangan diplomasi Indonesia dalam membebaskan Irian Barat dari kolonialisme Belanda. 1976. [MA thesis Universitas Padjadjaran, Bandung.] [20]

6487   Siagian M.O., A.W.
       Jayapura dulu, sekarang dan esok. Jayapura: Pemerintah Daerah, ca. 1975, 246 pp.

6488   Silaban, M.
       Irian Barat. Medan: Pustaka Sri, 1963, 58 pp.

6489   Siringo-ringo, Djakiras
       Suatu tinjauan sejarah tentang peristiwa Republik Maluku Selatan. 1973, 105 pp. [MA thesis IKIP Medan.] [13, 58]

6490   Sitanggang, Manorsa Togar
       Analisa tentang usaha pengembalian Irian Barat kedalam wilayah Republik Indonesia. 1968, 140 pp. [MA thesis IKIP Medan.] [13]

6491   Soe Hok Gie
       Kisah penumpasan 'RMS' (Gerakan Operasi Militer IV). Djakarta: Mega Bookstore, ca. 1965, 14 pp.

6492   Soebandrio (Subandrio)
       The West Irian issue; Report on Foreign Minister's missions abroad. Djakarta: Ministry of Information, 1959, 12 pp.

6493 Soekarno
Irian Barat adalah tuntunan seluruh rakjat Indonesia; Pidato Presiden Soekarno pada rapat raksasa berkenaan dengan peringatan Hari Pahlawan di Semarang, 10 Nop. 1961. 1961, 23 pp.

6494 Soekarno
Kibarkanlah Sang Merah Putih di Irian Barat! Djakarta: Kem. Penerangan, 1961, 16 pp.

6495 Soekarno
The people's command for the liberation of West Irian. Djakarta: Kementerian Penerangan, 1961, 16 pp.

6496 Soekarno
The door is still open for a peaceful solution of the West Irian problem. Djakarta: Department of Information, 1962, 12 pp.

6497 Soekarno
Membebaskan Irian Barat dengan segala djalan. Djakarta: Kem. Penerangan, 1962, 15 pp. (kitlv-m)

6498 Soekarno
Pembebasan Irian Barat; Kumpulan pidato Presiden Soekarno dan keterangan-keterangan mengenai perdjuangan pembebasan Irian Barat dari 17 Agustus 1961 sampai 17 Agustus 1962. Djakarta: Departemen Penerangan R.I., ca. 1963, 462 pp.

6499 Soenarjo
The West Irian issue. Reprint from *Australian Army Journal* no. 153 (1962), 19 pp.

6500 Soeripto
Dokumen Irian-Barat. Surabaja: Grip, 1962, 63 pp.

6501 *Some facts about West Irian.* New York: Permanent Mission of Indonesia to the United Nations, 1957. [3, 45]

6502 *Some questions and answers concerning the dispute over West Irian.* New York: Permanent Mission of Indonesia to the United Nations, 1957. [3, 45]

6503 Subandrio
Pidato Menteri Luar Negeri pada tg. 20 Nopember 1957 dalam panitya politik PBB tentang Irian Barat. Djakarta: Kem. Penerangan, 1957, 15 pp. (kitlv-m)

6504 Subandrio
Masalah Irian Barat di Perserikatan Bangsa-Bangsa. Djakarta: Dep. Penerangan, ca. 1961, 107 pp.

6505 Subandrio
West Irian; Statement of His Excellency Dr. Subandrio, Minister for Foreign Affairs of the Republic of Indonesia and chairman of the Indonesian delegation to the United Nations, on Monday, 9 October 1961. Karachi: Embassy of Indonesia, 1961, 41 pp.

6506 Sudibjo
West Irian is Indonesian territory. Djakarta: Ministry of Information, 1956, 21 pp. (kitlv-m)

6507   Sujono
Republik Maluku Selatan merupakan gerakan separatisme bagi negara kesatuan
Republik Indonesia. 1968. [MA thesis Universitas Padjadjaran, Bandung.] [1,
20]

6508   Suratmin
Irian Barat dibawah UNTEA (1 Oktober 1962-1 Mei 1963). 1972, 80 pp. [MA
thesis IKIP Yogyakarta.] [17]

6509   Suyasa, Wedastera
Mentjapai Irian merdeka. Bandung: Kontak Biro Umum Mahasiswa, 1955, 41 pp.
(kitlv-m)

6510   Syamsudin
Perjuangan pembebasan Irian Barat. 1975, 169 pp. [MA thesis Universitas
Indonesia, Jakarta.] [19]

6511   Tahija, A.
Irian; Sengketa.... Ca.1955, 19 pp.

6512   The Liang Gie and F. Soegeng Istanto
*Pertumbuhan pemerintahan propinsi Irian Barat dan kemungkinan-kemungkinan
perkembangan otonominja dihari kemudian.* Jogjakarta: Universitas Gadjah Mada,
1968, 135+115 pp. 2 vols.

6513   Tirthayasa, Wajan Kantun
Pembebasan Irian Barat (sebuah studi politik). 1968, 133 pp. [MA thesis
Universitas 17 Agustus 1945, Djakarta.] [9]

6514   Tjondronegoro, M.S.
'Een keerpunt in de Nederlands-Indonesische verstandhouding?', *Wending* 17
(1962-63):471-477. (ubl)

6515   *The truth about West Irian.* Djakarta: Ministry of Information, 1956, 58 pp.

6516   *West Irian; An appalling Dutch injustice.* Djakarta: Indonesian Army Information
Service, 1961, 16 pp.

6517   *West-Irian; An essential part of Indonesia.* Djakarta: Indonesian Army Information
Service, 1961, 35 pp.

6518   *West Irian excerpts from Indonesian National News Agency Antara.* New York:
Antara, 1960, 111 pp. (kitlv-m)

6519   *West Irian is Indonesian territory.* Djakarta: Ministry of Information, 1956, 21 pp.
[6984]

6520   *West Irian liberation campaign.* Djakarta: Ministry of Information, 1957-. Many
vols. (kitlv-m)

6521   *The West Irian problem; Recent comments by prominent Dutch and British people.*
London: Indonesian Embassy, 1961, 30 pp.

6522   *The West Irian question 1950-1957.* Djakarta: Ministry of Information, ca. 1957,
14 pp. [6984]

6523   *West Irian and the world.* Djakarta: Ministry of Foreign Affairs, 1954, 24 pp.
(ubl)

6524 'Wim Reawaru dan kawan-kawannja gugur untuk dasar-dasar Proklamasi 17 Agustus 1945', in: Darius Marpaung (ed.), *Bingkisan nasional; Kenangan 10 tahun revolusi Indonesia, 17-8-1945/17-8-1955*, pp. 88-93. Djakarta: Usaha Pegawai Nasional Indonesia, 1955.

6525 Yamin, Muhammad
Sengkéta Irian Barat; Berisi beberapa naskah mengenai pemetjahan soal Irian Barat, seperti diutjapkan dalam perundingan Indonesia-Belanda dan dalam pembitjaraan di PBB. 's-Gravenhage: Komisariat Agung Republik Indonesia, 1954, 92+125 pp. 2 vols.

6526 Yamin, M.
Kedaulatan Indonesia atas Irian Barat; Jaitu uraian tentang tuntutan rakjat terhadap wilajah Indonesia bagian Irian Barat. Bukittinggi/Djakarta: Nusantara, 1956, 116 pp.

6527 Yamin, Muhammad
Pembebasan Irian Barat atas dasar Proklamasi; Jaitu uraian tentang tuntutan rakjat terhadap wilajah Indonesia bagian Irian Barat atas dasar Proklamasi. Third edition. Bukittinggi/Djakarta: Nusantara, 1961, 139 pp. [First edition 1956.]

6528 Zahari, Said
Irian Barat; Duri dalam daging. Singapore: NTB, 1962, 130 pp.

West Irian and the South Moluccan question
Dutch and RMS authors

6529   *Ambon beroept zich op recht en trouw.* 's-Gravenhage: Bureau Zuid-Molukken, 1950, 24 pp.

6530   *Ambon door de eeuwen; Teksten van een zevendelige documentaire van de IKON-televisie, uitgezonden in januari en februari 1977.* Hilversum: IKON, 1977, 52 pp.

6531   *Ambon; Mena Muria; Om de vrijheid van de Zuid-Molukken.* Eindhoven: Stichting Door de Eeuwen Trouw, 1951, 15 pp.

6532   *Ambonezen in Nederland; Rapport van de Commissie ingesteld bij besluit van de Minister van Maatschappelijk Werk.* 's-Gravenhage: Staatsuitgeverij, 1959, 111 pp.

6533   Andel, H. van
       'Om de toekomst van Nederlands Nieuw-Guinea', *Antirevolutionaire Staatkunde* 26 (1956):211-226.

6534   Antonietti, J.J.M.
       'Ook Papoea's voor de defensie van Nieuw-Guinea!', *De Militaire Spectator* 128 (1959):418-422. (ubl)

6535   Antonietti, J.J.M.
       'Vervoersproblemen bij het optreden in Nieuw-Guinea', *De Militaire Spectator* 129 (1960):94-100. (ubl)

6536   Antonietti, J.J.M.
       'Enige wenken voor het patrouilleren in Nieuw-Guinea', *De Militaire Spectator* 129 (1960):447-455. (ubl)

6537   Ariks, J.; N. Jouwe; M. Kaisiepo and A. Arfan (eds)
       De Papoea's roepen Nederland. 's-Gravenhage: Nationaal Nieuw-Guinea Comité, 1951, 8 pp.

6538   Asbeck, F.M. van
       Aan de politieke partijen in Nederland. Utrecht, 1956, 1 p.

6539   Asbeck, F.M. van
       'Waarheen Nieuw-Guinea?', *Wending* 11 (1956):265-275.

6540   Asbeck, F.M. van
       'Nederland in een Aziatisch stormgebied', *Wending* 13 (1958):100-106.

6541   Baal, J. van
       Het Nieuw-Guinea vraagstuk; Een opgave voor de natie. Kampen: Kok, 1959, 46 pp.

6542 Baal, J. van
'Verzoening in dienst van het onrecht', *Antirevolutionaire Staatkunde* 29 (1959):1-15. (ubl)

6543 Baal, J. van
Ontglipt verleden; Verhaal van mijn jaren in een wereld die voorbijging; Deel I: Tot 1947: Indisch bestuursambtenaar in vrede en oorlog. Franeker: Wever, 1986, 510 pp.

6544 Baal, J. van
Ontglipt verleden; Verhaal van mijn jaren in een wereld die voorbijging; Deel II: Leven in verandering: 1947-1958. Franeker: Van Wijnen, 1989, 619 pp.

6545 Bakker, J.C.M.
Strategie van het economische ontwikkelingswerk in het voormalige Nederlands Nieuw-Guinea. Tilburg: Drukkerij MSC Tilburg, 1965, 189 pp. [PhD thesis Rijksuniversiteit Utrecht.]

6546 Bakker, M.
'Nieuw-Guinea raad en Nieuw-Guinea onraad', *Politiek en Cultuur* 20 (1960): 453-458. (ubl)

6547 Bakker, M.
'Nieuw-Guinea en de democratie', *Politiek en Cultuur* 22 (1962):193-199. (ubl)

6548 Bartels, D.
'Can the train ever be stopped again? Developments in the Moluccan community in the Netherlands before and after the hijackings', *Indonesia* no. 41 (1986):23-45.

6549 Bartels, Dieter
Moluccans in exile; A struggle for ethnic survival; Socialization, identity formation, and emancipation among an East-Indonesian minority in the Netherlands. Leiden: Center for the Study of Social Conflicts, Utrecht: Moluccan Advisory Council, 1989, 544 pp.

6550 Baudet, H. and F.J. Kossmann
'De Zuidmolukken', *Janus* no. 14 (1978):22-27.

6551 Baudet, Henri and Willem A. Veenhoven
Some aspects of the New Guinea problem. Ca. 1955, 13 pp.

6552 Beernink, H.K.J.
De Nieuw-Guinea Raad. Zwolle, 1961. [45]

6553 Berg, C.T.
Rede gehouden op de algemeene ledenvergadering van de Afdeeling Batavia der VKNG op 20 October 1946. Pangkalpinang: n.n., ca. 1946, 9 pp.

6554 Berg, G.W.H. van den
Baalen droefheid; Biak - Nederlands Nieuw-Guinea sche(r)tsenderwijs. 's-Gravenhage: Moesson, 1981, 136 pp.

6555 Berg, Joop van den
'Bellettrie over Nieuw-Guinea van 1945 tot heden', *Indische Letteren* 6 (1991):67-78.

6556   Berg, Joop van den
       Een mors huis; Verhalen over Nieuw-Guinea. Schoorl: Conserve, 1991, 118 pp.

6557   Berge, T. van den
       De Atlantische conceptie op het ministerie van Buitenlandse Zaken tussen twee
       nederlagen. 1981, 44 pp. [MA thesis Erasmus Universiteit, Rotterdam.]

6558   Berghuis, W.P.
       'Nieuw-Guinea; Een terugblik', *Antirevolutionaire Staatkunde* 32 (1962):213-229.

6559   Berghuis, W.P.
       Nieuw-Guinea; Een terugblik. 's-Gravenhage: Antirevolutionaire Partij-Stichting,
       1962, 22 pp.

6560   *De beslissing over Nederlands Nieuw-Guinea... nu!* 's-Gravenhage: Nederlands
       Nieuw-Guinea Blok, 1952, 16 pp.

6561   Betué, Piet de
       *Keesje gooien voor Hare Majesteit; Matroos op Hr. Ms. De Ruyter en in Nieuw-
       Guinea.* Bunnik: Reinders, 1992, 226 pp.

6562   Beuge, J.A. van
       *Het Nederlandse standpunt inzake Nieuw-Guinea; Inleiding, uitgesproken op 20
       januari 1958 voor het Defensie Studie Centrum.* 's-Gravenhage?: n.n., 1958, 19 pp.

6563   Beus, J.G. de
       'De Nieuw-Guinea-kwestie; Een simultaan treurspel op zes tonelen, 1949-1962',
       in: J.G. de Beus, *Morgen, bij het aanbreken van de dag; Nederland drie maal aan de
       vooravond van oorlog,* pp. 245-409. Rotterdam: Donker, 1977.

6564   Blaisse, P.A.
       'Nederlands Nieuw-Guinea', *Katholiek Staatkundig Maandschrift* 15 (1961-
       62):413-422. (ubl)

6565   Blankenstein, M. van
       Indonesië nu; Nieuwe indrukken. 's-Gravenhage/Bandung: Van Hoeve, 1953, 123
       pp.

6566   Blauw, J. and W.P.M. Fleuren
       'Hunters van de Koninklijke Luchtmacht in Nederlands Nieuw-Guinea', *De
       Militaire Spectator* 131 (1962):312-314. (ubl)

6567   *Bloed over Ambon.* Amsterdam: Fix, 1951, 63 pp.

6568   Boer, Anton W. den
       De Republik Maluku Selatan (Republiek der Zuid-Molukken) in Nederland,
       1951-1975. 1976, 95 pp. [MA thesis Universiteit van Amsterdam.] (kitlv-smg)

6569   Boer, A.W. den
       'De Molukkers in Nederland', *Spiegel Historiael* 12 (1977): 526-534.

6570   Boom, Gerton van
       Het Nederlandse ontwikkelingsbeleid in Nederlands Nieuw-Guinea; Nader
       toegespitst op de politieke ontwikkeling van de bevolking van Nieuw-Guinea.
       1987, 108 pp. [MA thesis Rijksuniversiteit Groningen.] (kitlv-smg)

6571 Boom, G. van
'De totstandkoming van de defensiegrondslagen Nieuw-Guinea, 1950-1954',
Mededelingen Sectie Militaire Geschiedenis Landmachtstaf 12 (1989):93-111.

6572 Boomen, Gerard van den and Ruud Metekohy (eds)
Maluku Selatan; Zuid-Molukken; Een vergeten bevrijdingsstrijd. Amsterdam: De
Populier, 1977, 96 pp.

6573 Bos, J.
'De verkiezingen in Nieuw-Guinea', *Socialisme en Democratie* 18 (1961):548-558.
(ubl)

6574 Bosch, Rob; Dik Hoedeman and Wout Oprel
De Zuid-Molukkers en hun aanwezigheid in Nederland. 's-Gravenhage: AR-jon-
gerenorganisatie Arjos, 1978, 21 pp.

6575 Bosscher, D.F.J.
'Enige opmerkingen over de historische aspecten van het Zuidmolukse
vraagstuk', *Groniek* no. 58 (1978):2-7. (ubl)

6576 Bosscher, D.F.J.
'De Partij van de Arbeid en de politieke aspecten van het Zuidmolukse
vraagstuk', *Socialisme en Democratie* 35-4 (1978):164-174.

6577 Bosscher, D.F.J.
'De politieke steun in Nederland aan de Republiek der Zuid-Molukken', *Groniek*
no. 59 (1978):2-3. (ubl)

6578 Bosscher, Doeko and Berteke Waaldijk
Ambon; Eer en schuld; Politiek en pressie rond de Republiek Zuid-Molukken. Weesp:
Van Holkema en Warendorf, 1985, 254 pp.

6579 Bouman, Jan C.
*De sociaal-psychologische en cultureel-anthropologische aspecten van het Zuidmolukse
vraagstuk.* Eindhoven: Stichting Door de Eeuwen Trouw, 1954, 6 pp.

6580 Bouman, Jan C.
'Social-psychological aspects', in: *The South Moluccas; Rebellious province or
occupied state*, pp. 163-171. Leiden: Sythoff, 1960.

6581 Bout, Hendrik
Ambon en het geweten der Kerk; Documentatie inzake het adres van Dr. H. Bout.
Utrecht, 1960, 56 pp. [45]

6582 Brantjes, J.M.J.
Nieuw Guinea; Wat men er wèl en niet van moet verwachten. 's-Gravenhage/
Bandung: Van Hoeve, 1950, 78 pp.

6583 Bruins Slot, J.A.H.J.S.
'Rede op het Partijconvent d.d. 28 april 1962', in: W.P. Berghuis and J.A.H.J.S.
Bruins Slot, *In de stroomversnelling van deze tijd*, pp. 11-21. Groningen: Anti-
Revolutionaire Partij, 1962. (ubt)

6584 Bruyn, J.V. de
Het verdwenen volk. Bussum: Van Holkema en Warendorf, 1978, 372 pp.

6585 Bussemaker, H.Th.
'Nieuw-Guinea; Een historisch-strategische beschouwing', *Marineblad* 72 (1962):27-39. (ubl)

6586 Cannegieter, C.A.
De economische toekomst-mogelijkheden van Nederlands Nieuw-Guinea. Leiden: Stenfert Kroese, 1959, 11+152 pp. [Also PhD thesis Nederlandse Economische Hogeschool, Rotterdam.]

6587 Capelleveen, Jan H. van
De standpunten van de Nederlandse politieke partijen en perscommentaren inzake de likwidatie van het vraagstuk Nieuw-Guinea, 1961-1962. 1980, 60+8 pp. [MA thesis Rijksuniversiteit Utrecht.] [43, 58]

6588 Coerts, H.
De A.R.P. en Nieuw-Guinea; Historische analyse van een partijcrisis. Franeker: Wever, 1983, 104 pp.

6589 *Confrontatie met een kwart eeuw discriminatie van het Zuidmolukse zelfbeschikkingsrecht.* 's-Gravenhage: Voorlichtingsdienst Republiek Zuid-Molukken, 1975, 32 pp.

6590 Coolen, Ingrid
Beter een goede buur dan een verre vriend; Nederland, Australië en de Nieuw-Guineakwestie, 1950-1963. 1992, 184 pp. [MA thesis Rijksuniversiteit Leiden.]

6591 Cort van der Linden, R.A.D.
Nederlandsch Nieuw-Guinea. Amsterdam: Buijten en Schipperheijn, 1962, 35 pp.

6592 *La cuestión de Nueva Guinea Occidental; Memorándum presentado por la delegación holandesa a la novena Asamblea General de las Naciones Unidas.* Nueva York: n.n., 1954, 26 pp.

6593 Derix, Jan
Bapa Papoea; Jan P.K. van Eechoud; Een biografie. Venlo: Van Spijk, 1987, 303 pp.

6594 *Documentatiemap Molukken.* Amsterdam: Tropenmuseum, Educatieve Dienst, 1982, 122 pp.

6595 Droogh, Th.C.
De deurknop in de hand. 's-Gravenhage/Bandung: Van Hoeve, 1956, 32 pp.

6596 Droogh, Th.C.
De koelie wordt toean. Voorhout: Foreholte, 1959, 138 pp.

6597 Drooglever, P.J.
'De vrijheid vanuit Ambons perspectief', in: Knaap, G.J.; W. Manuhutu and H. Smeets (eds), *Sedjarah Maluku; Molukse geschiedenis in Nederlandse bronnen,* pp. 83-108. Amsterdam: Van Soeren, 1992.

6598 Dubois, J.J.W.
Memorie van overgave betreffende Hollandia, periode september 1960-augustus 1961. Hollandia: n.n., 1961, 256 pp.

6599 Duin, K. van
Reader RMS-geschiedenis. Middelburg: RPA, 1981, 66 pp.

6600 *Dutch policy regarding Netherlands New Guinea.* New York: Netherlands Information Service, 1960. [45]

6601 Duynstee, F.J.F.M.
Nieuw-Guinea als schakel tussen Nederland en Indonesië. Amsterdam: De Bezige Bij, 1961, 431 pp.

6602 Eechoud, J.P.K. van
Nota bestuursbeleid Nieuw-Guinea. Hollandia: n.n., 1947, 133 pp.

6603 Eechoud, J.P.K. van
Verslag der residentie Nieuw-Guinea over het jaar 1947. Hollandia: n.n., 1948, 245 pp.

6604 Eechoud, J.P.K. van
Nota inzake kolonisatie van Indo-Europeanen in Nieuw-Guinea. Hollandia: n.n., 1949, 17 pp.

6605 Eechoud, J.P.K. van
Vergeten aarde; Nieuw-Guinea. Amsterdam: De Boer, 1951, 286+30 pp. [Second edition, 1957, 334 pp.]

6606 Eisenga, Ruurd
De mariniers van Klademak. Tjalleberd: Podium, 1982, 251 pp.

6607 *'... En toch draait ze!' En toch: Ambon zàl herrijzen!* Eindhoven: Stichting Door de Eeuwen Trouw, 1956, 36 pp.

6608 Enthoven, K.L.J.
'Om de toekomst van Nieuw-Guinea', *Socialisme en Democratie* 7 (1950):625-636. (ubl)

6609 *Erkenning van Ambon.* 's-Gravenhage: Bureau Zuid-Molukken, 1950, 16 pp.

6610 Esterik, Chris van
Nederlands laatste bastion in de Oost; Ekonomie en politiek in de Nieuw-Guinea-kwestie. Baarn: In den Toren, 1982, 224 pp.

6611 Feuilletau de Bruyn, W.K.H.
Kolonisatie-mogelijkheden op Nieuw-Guinea. 's-Gravenhage: Nieuw-Guinea Studiekring, ca. 1948, 32 pp. [45]

6612 Feuilletau de Bruyn, W.K.H.
Hoe zou in het bestuursbeleid op Nieuw-Guinea verbetering kunnen worden gebracht? Nota van de Groter Nederland Actie aan de Nederlandse regering en de Staten-Generaal. 's-Gravenhage: n.n., 1952, 15 pp.

6613 Feuilletau de Bruyn, W.K.H.
Het Kamerdebat over Nieuw-Guinea. N.p.: n.n., ca. 1953, 12 pp.

6614 Franken, H.M.
Nederland, Nieuw-Guinea en de Papoea's; Schets van het Nederlandse regeringsbeleid inzake Nieuw-Guinea en effectuering van dit beleid door het binnenlands bestuur over de periode 1949-1962. Ca. 1985, 265 pp. [MA thesis Rijksuniversiteit Utrecht.] [58]

6615   Franken, S.
'Nieuw-Guinea - van binnen uit', in: *Terdege ter discussie*, pp. 31-40. Den Haag:
Van Keulen, 1958.

6616   Galis, K.W. and H.J. van Doornik
Een gouden jubileum; 50 jaar Hollandia, 7 maart 1910-7 maart 1960. Hollandia:
Landsdrukkerij, 1960, 84 pp.

6617   Gase, Ronald
*Misleiding of zelfbedrog; Een analyse van het Nederlandse Nieuw Guinea-beleid aan
de hand van gesprekken met betrokken politici en diplomaten*. Baarn: In den Toren,
1984, 224 pp.

6618   *Geen oorlog om Nieuw-Guinea*. Amsterdam: Communistische Partij van
Nederland, 1962, 15 pp.

6619   Gerbrandy, P.S.
Ambon en de A.R. Partij; De vrijheidsstrijd van de Republiek der Zuid-Molukken.
Kampen: Kok, 1956, 35 pp.

6620   Geus, P.B.R. de
'De Nieuw-Guinea-affaire', *Marineblad* 82 (1972):289-301. (ubl)

6621   Geus, P.B.R. de
De Nieuw-Guinea kwestie; Aspecten van buitenlands beleid en militaire macht.
Leiden: Nijhoff, 1984, 11+261 pp. [Also PhD thesis Rijksuniversiteit Leiden.]

6622   Goedhart, L.J.; J.V. de Bruyn and N. Jouwe
*Statements met betrekking tot Nederlands Nieuw-Guinea afgelegd in de VN-
Commissie inzake Rapportage over Niet-Zelfbesturende Gebieden 1960-1962*. Ca.
1962, 73 pp.

6623   Goossens, G.
Nieuw-Guinea, de koude oorlog en de Anti-Revolutionaire Partij. Franeker: Wever,
1962, 79 pp.

6624   Goossens, G.
'Nieuw-Guinea; Recapitulatie en toetsing', *Antirevolutionaire Staatkunde* 32
(1962):347-376.

6625   Goot, S. van der
Nederlands Nieuw-Guinea en de EEG. N.p.: n.n., 1961, 12 pp.

6626   Graaf, H.J. de
De band tussen Ambon en Nederland, historisch-politiek-kultureel. Groningen:
Voorlichtingsdienst Stichting Door de Eeuwen Trouw, 1968, 47 pp.

6627   Graaf, H.J. de
'De band tussen Ambon en Nederland historisch gezien', *Kleio* 10 (1969):278-
288.

6628   Graaf, H.J. de
'De band Ambon-Nederland, meer cultureel gezien', *Kleio* 10 (1969):289-301.

6629   Graaf, H.J. de
De geschiedenis van Ambon en de Zuid-Molukken. Franeker: Wever, 1977, 304 pp.

6630 Graaf, Th.M.J. de
'Te voeren beleid', in: Paul van 't Veer (ed.), *Nieuw-Guinea tegen wil en dank; Een historische omschrijving en een waarschuwend toekomstperspectief*, pp. 100-114. Amsterdam: Querido, 1960.

6631 Grondel, A.H.
Enkele opmerkingen naar aanleiding van de enquête inzake De Stem van Ambon. Bussum: n.n., 1956, 20 pp.

6632 Hahn, K.J.
'Nieuw-Guinea; Nieuwe perspectieven', *Katholiek Staatkundig Maandschrift* 12 (1959):373-378. (ubl)

6633 Hakkert, A.J.
'Nieuw-Guinea', in: G. Teitler and C. Homan (ed.), *Het Korps Mariniers*, pp. 29-38. Amsterdam: De Bataafsche Leeuw, 1985.

6634 Hakkert, A.J.
'De Koninklijke Marine in Nieuw-Guinea (1950-1962)', *Marineblad* 97 (1987):340-355, 388-399.

6635 Halatu, Daan and Elly Pessireron
De pijn van een Molukker. Groningen: Kemper, 1981, 111 pp.

6636 Ham, Ingeborg A. van der
De VS en de Nieuw-Guinea kwestie. 1991, 108 pp. [MA thesis Rijksuniversiteit Utrecht.]

6637 Hanekroot, L.
Nieuw-Guinea; Tijd voor een hernieuwd politiek onderzoek. 's-Gravenhage/ Bandung: Van Hoeve, 1958, 30 pp.

6638 Heeringa, G.
Amboina-Ambon. Rotterdam: Interkerkelijk Contact Comité Ambon-Nederland, 1963, 71 pp.

6639 Helfrich, C.E.L.
Nieuw-Guinea politiek-strategisch. 's-Gravenhage: Stichting Rijksbehoud, 1955, 12 pp.

6640 Helfrich, C.E.L.
De militair-strategische positie van de Republiek Zuid-Molukken. Eindhoven: Stichting Door de Eeuwen Trouw, 1957, 32 pp.

6641 Helfrich, C.E.L.
'The strategic position', in: *The South Moluccas; Rebellious province or occupied state*, pp. 135-147. Leiden: Sythoff, 1960.

6642 Hendrik, H.K.
Ambonezen in Nederland; Vreemden maar geen vreemdelingen. Barneveld, 1975, 50 pp. [38]

6643 Herman, Valentine and Rob van der Laan Bouma
Nationalists without a nation; South Moluccan terrorism in the Netherlands. Rotterdam: Erasmus Universiteit, 1979, 40 pp.

6644   Heuven, W.A. van
       Rapport betreffende de oprichting van een militair corps, bestaande uit Papoea's in
       Nederlands Nieuw-Guinea. Hollandia: n.n., 1960, 50 pp.

6645   Hezik, M.J.M. van
       'Nederlands Nieuw-Guinea in de Verenigde Naties', *Marineblad* 72 (1962):208-
       224, 964-981.

6646   Hintzen, Peter
       Nederland en de Zuidmolukkers. Lelystad: IVIO, 1977, 20 pp.

6647   Hofland, H.J.A.
       'Bijdragen tot de koloniale epiloog', *Podium* 16 (1961-62):163-184. (ubl)

6648   Hofland, H.J.A.
       'Nieuw-Guinea', in: H.J.A. Hofland, *Tegels lichten; Of ware verhalen over de*
       autoriteiten in het land van de voldongen feiten, pp. 42-75. Amsterdam: Contact,
       1972.

6649   Hogendorp, Th.J.
       'Achtergrond van het Indonesische standpunt inzake Nederlands Nieuw-
       Guinea', *Socialisme en Democratie* 15 (1958):129-133. (ubl)

6650   Hokke, C.
       'Nieuw-Guinea en de Gouvernements-marine', *Marineblad* 60 (1950):799-963.

6651   *Holland in Hollandia.* 's-Gravenhage: Van Hoeve, 1948, 79 pp.

6652   Holst Pellekaan, R.E. van; I.C. de Regt and J.F. Bastiaans
       Patrouilleren voor de Papoea's; De Koninklijke Marine in Nederlands Nieuw-Guinea;
       I. 1945-1960. Amsterdam: De Bataafsche Leeuw, 1989, 207 pp.

6653   Holst Pellekaan, R.E. van; I.C. de Regt and J.F. Bastiaans
       Patrouilleren voor de Papoea's; De Koninklijke Marine in Nederlands Nieuw-Guinea;
       II. 1960-1962. Amsterdam: De Bataafsche Leeuw, 1990, 173 pp.

6654   Hoogenband, C. van den
       'De Tweede Wereldoorlog', in: W.C. Klein (ed.), *Nieuw-Guinea III,* pp. 346-374.
       's-Gravenhage: Staatsuitgeverij, 1954.

6655   Huydecoper van Nigtevecht, J.L.R.
       Nieuw-Guinea; Het einde van een koloniaal beleid. 's-Gravenhage: SDU Uitgeverij,
       1990, 193 pp.

6656   Idenburg, P.J.A.
       'De verhouding Nederland-Indonesië', *Socialisme en Democratie* 13 (1956):527-
       552.

6657   Jaarsma, S.R.
       Waarneming en interpretatie; Vergaring en gebruik van etnografische informatie in
       Nederlands Nieuw-Guinea (1950-1962). Hilversum: ISOR, 1990, 247 pp. [PhD
       thesis Katholieke Universiteit Nijmegen.]

6658   *Jaarverslag van de Stichting 'Het Nationaal Nieuw-Guinea Comité'.* 's-Gravenhage,
       1953-61.

6659 Jagt, Bouke B.
De muskietenoorlog en andere verhalen. Amsterdam/Brussel: Elsevier, 1978, 127 pp.

6660 Jansen van Galen, John
Ons laatste oorlogje; Nieuw-Guinea; De pax neerlandica, de diplomatieke kruistocht en de vervlogen droom van een Papoea-natie. Weesp: Van Holkema en Warendorf, 1984, 301 pp.

6661 Jansen Schoonhoven, E.
Nederland en het anti-kolonialisme. 's-Gravenhage: La Rivière & Voorhoeve, 1955, 15 pp.

6662 Jansen Schoonhoven, E.
'Antwoord aan Prof. Van Asbeck', *Wending* 13 (1958):106-112. (ubl)

6663 Jong, J.J.P. de
West Nieuw-Guinea en de Nederlandse belangen in Indonesië. 1969, 123+ 16 pp. [MA thesis Rijksuniversiteit Utrecht.]

6664 Jong, J.J.P. de
'Molukse geschiedenis in nieuw perspectief', *Internationale Spectator* 33 (1979): 120-128.

6665 Jongeling, P.
Ambons rechtvaardige zaak. Groningen: Jongerenorganisatie 'Door de Eeuwen Trouw', 1964, 12 pp.

6666 Jouwe, N.
De stem van de Papoea's. Amsterdam: De Boer, 1952, 14 pp.

6667 Kaam, B. van
Ambon door de eeuwen. Baarn: In den Toren, 1977, 158 pp.

6668 Kaam, Ben van
'Ambon; Geschiedenis in nota en tegennota', *VU-Magazine* 7-3 (March 1978):7-13. (ubl)

6669 Kaam, B. van
The South Moluccans; Background to the train hijackings. London: Hurst, 1979, 151 pp.

6670 Kaam, Ben van and Henk Biersteker (eds)
Van Makassar naar Bovensmilde; Een documentaire in vijf delen over een volksverhuizing die niemand wilde. Hilversum: IKON, 1979, 46 pp.

6671 Kaan, Leonard A.
De ommezwaai van Bruins Slot, 3 oktober 1961. 1983, 76 pp. [MA thesis Rijksuniversiteit Utrecht.] [43]

6672 Kaan, L.A.
'De ommezwaai van Bruins Slot', *Christen-Democratische Verkenningen* 4 (1984):133-144. (ubl)

6673 Kadt, J. de
Kaarten op tafel inzake Nieuw Guinea; Redevoering gehouden op 19 Januari 1951 in de Tweede Kamer der Staten-Generaal. Amsterdam: Partij van de Arbeid, 1951, 16 pp.

6674 Kadt, J. de
'Nuchterheid inzake Nieuw-Guinea', Socialisme en Democratie 12 (1955):81-88.

6675 Kadt, J. de
'Indonesië voor de beslissing; Waar ligt het Nederlands belang?', Socialisme en Democratie 15 (1958):1-12. (ubl)

6676 Kadt, J. de
Huidige stand van het Nieuw-Guinea-vraagstuk. Amsterdam: PvdA, 1960, 22 pp.

6677 Kadt, J. de
'Luns of de ondergang van een politiek handelsreiziger', in: J. de Kadt, De deftigheid in het gedrang; Een keuze uit zijn verspreide geschriften, pp. 428-444. Amsterdam: Van Oorschot, 1991. [First published in Tirade, May 1961.]

6678 Kadt, J. de
'Uit het Nieuw-Guinea slop? Rijkens, Duynstee en verder...', Socialisme en Democratie 18 (1961):505-509. (ubl)

6679 Kampen, Anthony van
Jungle Pimpernel; Controleur B.B. Amsterdam: De Boer, 1949, 342 pp. [Ninth printing 1953.]

6680 Kampen, Anthony van
Het laatste bivak. Amsterdam: De Boer, 1950, 297 pp.

6681 Kampen, Anthony van
De verloren vallei. Amsterdam: De Boer, 1951, 300 pp.

6682 Kampen, Anthony van
Jungle. Bussum: De Boer Jr, 1954, 636 pp.

6683 Kamsteeg, A.
'Nederland en de Republiek der Zuid-Molukken', in: Knot, Gerhard; Henk C. Weltje and Aad Kamsteeg, Wat moeten ze hier? Zuidmolukkers op weg naar vrijheid..., pp. 59-86. Groningen: De Vuurbaak, 1975.

6684 Kappeyne van de Coppello, N.J.C.M.
'Relation to the United Nations', in: The South Moluccas; Rebellious province or occupied state, pp. 85-104. Leiden: Sythoff, 1960.

6685 Kasberg, P.
Nederlands Nieuw-Guinea; Een land in opbouw. Den Haag: Voorhoeve, 1956, 126 pp.

6686 Kenjataan pendirian dari Nieuw-Guinea/Nieuw-Guinea spreekt zich uit. Hollandia: Penerangan Rakjat, 1956, 26 pp.

6687 Kerk en Nieuw-Guinea; Open brief aan de Generale Synode der Nederlandse Hervormde Kerk. Delft: Meinema, 1956, 19 pp.

6688 Kersten, A.E.
'Decolonization of Dutch New Guinea; The Luns plan', in: Philip Everts and Guido Walraven (eds), *The politics of persuasion; Implementation of foreign policy by the Netherlands*, pp. 219-230. Aldershot: Avebury, 1989.

6689 Khleif, B.
Research on Dutch policy towards the Ambonese in Holland. The Hague: Institute of Social Studies, 1958, 26 pp.

6690 Klaassen, M.
'Nieuw-Guinea in de toekomst', *De Gids* (1950, II):31-44.

6691 Klaassen, M.
Pioniers naar Papoealand? Biedt Nieuw-Guinea het Nederlandse volk een toekomst? Amsterdam: De Boer, 1950, 40 pp.

6692 Klaassen, M.
'Zoeklicht op Nieuw-Guinea', *Marineblad* 60 (1950):495-518. (ubl)

6693 Klaassen, M.
'Land en volk van Nieuw-Guinea', *Marineblad* 61 (1951):359-374. (ubl)

6694 Klein, P.W.
Een ondernemer in de politiek; Paul Rijkens (1888-1965) en de kwestie Nieuw-Guinea. 1992. [6754]

6695 Klein, W.C.
'Plannen van resident Van Eechoud inzake de ontwikkeling van Nieuw-Guinea', *Indonesië* 1 (1947-48):178-187.

6696 Klein, W.C.
Nieuw-Guinea problemen. 's-Gravenhage: Van Stockum, 1949, 16 pp.

6697 Klein, W.C. (ed.)
Nieuw-Guinea. 's-Gravenhage: Staatsuitgeverij, 1953-54, 470+491+600 pp. 3 vols.

6698 Kloosterhuis, Henk
Ambon nu! Vier reportages. Wageningen: De Spiegel, 1968. [Various pagings.]

6699 Knaap, G.J.; W. Manuhutu and H. Smeets (eds)
Sedjarah Maluku; Molukse geschiedenis in Nederlandse bronnen. Amsterdam: Van Soeren, 1992, 108 pp.

6700 Knibbe, P.G.
Ambon en onze Anti-Revolutionnaire Partij. Leiden: Knibbe, 1950, 15 pp.

6701 Knot, G.
Het zelfbeschikkingsrecht der Zuidmolukkers; Historisch-juridisch. Groningen: Voorlichtingsdienst Stichting Door de Eeuwen Trouw, ca. 1974, 28 pp.

6702 Knot, G.
De Republik Maluku Selatan. Groningen: Stichting Door de Eeuwen Trouw, 1975, 7 pp.

6703   Knot, G.
        'De Zuidmolukse Republiek', in: Knot, Gerhard; Henk C. Weltje and Aad
        Kamsteeg, *Wat moeten ze hier? Zuidmolukkers op weg naar vrijheid...*, pp. 9-44.
        Groningen: De Vuurbaak, 1975.

6704   Knot, Gerhard; Henk C. Weltje and Aad Kamsteeg
        Wat moeten ze hier? Zuidmolukkers op weg naar vrijheid... Groningen: De Vuur-
        baak, 1975, 96 pp.

6705   Koch, D.M.G. and J.W.E. Riemens (eds)
        *Het geschilpunt West Nieuw Guinea eist een oplossing; Een gecommentarieerde
        bloemlezing.* Monnickendam: Nimo, 1955, 49 pp.

6706   Kock, P.P. de
        De onmisbare schakel. N.p.: Soeara Rajat Maloekoe, 1985, 83 pp.

6707   Koenders, H.J.E.
        Nederland en de Zuid-Pacific Commissie, 1946-1952; De Nederlandse houding
        tegenover de Zuid-Pacific Commissie mede in het licht van de Nieuw-Guinea-
        problematiek. 1982, 241 pp. [MA thesis Katholieke Universiteit Nijmegen.]

6708   Kokkelink, M.Ch.
        *Wij vochten in het bos; De guerillastrijd op Nieuw-Guinea tijdens de Tweede Wereld-
        oorlog.* Amsterdam: Van Kampen, 1956, 256 pp.

6709   Kompagnie, J.H.
        *Inventaris van het persoonlijk archief van Jan P.K. van Eechoud (1904-1958) over de
        periode 1929-1962.* Den Haag: Algemeen Rijksarchief, 1990, 9 pp.

6710   Koole, R.A.
        'De KVP en het kompas Romme-Luns', in: *Jaarboek Documentatiecentrum
        Nederlandse Politieke Partijen*, pp. 103-124. Groningen, 1979. (ubl)

6711   Koole, Ruud
        De KVP en de kwestie Nieuw-Guinea (1950-1962). 1979, 83 pp. [MA thesis
        Rijksuniversiteit Groningen.]

6712   Korn, V.E.
        'Nieuw-Guinea; Een balans en een programma', *Bijdragen tot de Taal-, Land- en
        Volkenkunde* 111 (1955):385-412.

6713   Koster, Ben
        Een verloren land; De regering Kennedy en de Nieuw-Guinea kwestie 1961-1962.
        Baarn: Anthos, 1991, 175 pp.

6714   Kruls, H.J.
        'The strategic importance in the world picture of present and future', in: *The
        South Moluccas; Rebellious province or occupied state*, pp. 123-134. Leiden: Sythoff,
        1960.

6715   Kuijer, Kees de
        De weg van de Zuidmolukkers. 1973, 136 pp. [MA thesis Katholieke Universi-
        teit Nijmegen.]

6716   *De kwestie Nieuw-Guinea; Rapport van de Sociaal-Democratische Studievereniging.*
        Monnickendam, 1961, 24 pp.

6717 Kijne, I.S.
'Met ernst en met spoed', in: Paul van 't Veer (ed.), *Nieuw-Guinea tegen wil en dank; Een historische omschrijving en een waarschuwend toekomstperspectief*, pp. 127-142. Amsterdam: Querido, 1960.

6718 Lafeber, C.V.
Nieuw-Guinea en De Volkskrant. Assen: Van Gorcum, 1968, 135 pp.

6719 Lagerberg, C.S.I.J.
Jaren van reconstructie; Nieuw-Guinea van 1949 tot 1961. 's-Hertogenbosch: South Holland Printery, 1962, 232 pp. [PhD thesis Rijksuniversiteit Utrecht.]

6720 Lagerberg, Kees
'Boekjes hebben hun avonturen; Een Irian-publikatie', *Internationale Spectator* 34 (1980):300-303.

6721 Lagerberg, Kees
West Irian and Jakarta imperialism. London: Hurst, 1979, 10+171 pp. [Second printing, New York: St Martin's Press, 1980.]

6722 Lam, H.J.
Nederlands Nieuw-Guinee op de tweesprong. Schiedam: Centrale Vaderlandse Kring, 1950, 18 pp.

6723 Lapré, S.A.
'Enkele ervaringen opgedaan in Nederlands Nieuw-Guinea', *De Militaire Spectator* 125 (1956):70-74. (ubl)

6724 Lapré, S.A.
'Nederlandse guerillakrijg in Nieuw-Guinea tegen Japan', *De Militaire Spectator* 126 (1957):128-132. (ubl)

6725 Lebelauw, I.A.
Wat gebeurde er op Ambon tot 25 April 1951? 's-Gravenhage: Voorhoeve, 1951, 56 pp.

6726 Leslie-Miller, J.W.H.
Het economisch aspect van het Nieuw-Guinea probleem. 's-Gravenhage: Excelsior, 1952, 79 pp. [Also PhD thesis Rijksuniversiteit Utrecht.]

6727 Leslie-Miller, J.W.H.
'Het politiek aspect van het Nieuw-Guinea vraagstuk', *Socialisme en Democratie* 13 (1956):478-485. (ubl)

6728 Liem Soei Liong and Wim Schroevers
Maluku; Geografie en geschiedenis van de Molukken sinds het kolonialisme. Amsterdam: Koninklijk Instituut voor de Tropen, 1988, 149 pp.

6729 Lieuwen, G.J. and R.J.H. van Maastrigt
De grote confessionele partijen en de rol van de kerk, missie en zending in de Nieuw-Guineakwestie (1949-1962); De marge van christelijke politiek. 1987, 108 pp. [MA thesis Rijksuniversiteit Groningen.] [58]

6730 Lohnstein, M.J.
'De uniformering van het Papoea Vrijwilligerskorps (1961-1963)', *Armamentaria* 26 (1991):19-32. (lmd)

6731   Lohnstein, M.J.
Persevero (ik zet door); Een geschiedenis van het Papoea Vrijwilligerskorps. [6730]

6732   Lokollo, P.W.
Ambon's strijd tegen de leugens van Djocja. 's-Gravenhage: Bureau Zuid-Molukken, 1950, 30 pp.

6733   Lokollo, P.W.
Amboyna's struggle against the lies of Djocja. The Hague: South Molucca Office, 1950, 32 pp.

6734   Lokollo, P.W.
De stem der Ambonnezen. 's-Gravenhage: Bureau Zuid-Molukken, 1950, 11 pp.

6735   Lijphart, Arend
'The Indonesian image of West Irian', *Asian Survey* 1-5 (July 1961):9-16.

6736   Lijphart, A.
'De Nederlandse publieke opinie inzake het Nieuw-Guineavraagstuk medio 1961', *Internationale Spectator* 16 (1962):311-325.

6737   Lijphart, Arend
The West New Guinea problem in Dutch domestic politics. 1963. [PhD thesis Yale University, New Haven.] [97, 106]

6738   Lijphart, Arend
The trauma of decolonization; The Dutch and West New Guinea. New Haven/London: Yale University Press, 1966, 11+303 pp.

6739   Lijphart, A.
'The Dutch and West New Guinea', in: Tony Smith (ed.), *The end of European empire; Decolonization after World War II*, pp. 177-183. Lexington: Heath, 1975. (ubl)

6740   Manuhutu, W.
'Molukkers in Nederland; Migranten tegen wil en dank', *Tijdschrift voor Geschiedenis* 100 (1987):432-445.

6741   Manuhutu, W.
'De Molukse KNIL-militairen; Tussen wal en schip', in: G. Teitler and J. Hoffenaar (eds), *De politionele acties; Afwikkeling en verwerking*, pp. 35-44. Amsterdam: De Bataafsche Leeuw, 1990.

6742   Manuhutu, W. and H. Smeets (eds)
Tijdelijk verblijf; De opvang van Molukkers in Nederland, 1951. Amsterdam: De Bataafsche Leeuw, 1991, 126 pp.

6743   Manusama, J.A.
Om recht en vrijheid; De strijd om de onafhankelijkheid der Zuid-Molukken. Utrecht: Libertas, 1953, 85 pp.

6744   Manusama, J.A.
Political aspects of the struggle for independence. Leiden: Sijthoff/South Moluccan Information Service, 1959, 19 pp.

6745 Manusama, J.A.
'Political aspects of the struggle for independence', in: *The South Moluccas; Rebellious province or occupied state*, pp. 49-63. Leiden: Sythoff, 1960.

6746 Manusama, J.A.
De Zuidmolukse identiteit. N.p.: n.n., 1971, 33 pp.

6747 Mariën, M.H.
De Zuid-Molukkers in Nederland; Migranten tegen wil en dank in de minder-heidssituatie. 1968, 121 pp. [MA thesis Universiteit van Amsterdam.]

6748 Mariën, M.H.
'Het Zuidmolukse radicalisme in Nederland; Nationalistische of emancipatie-beweging?', *Sociologische Gids* 18 (1971):62-76.

6749 Mariën, M.H.
'South Moluccan radicalism in the Netherlands; Nationalist or emancipation movement?', *Sociologia Neerlandica* 9 (1973):77-87. (ubl)

6750 Metzemaekers, L.
'The Western New Guinea problem', *Pacific Affairs* 24 (1951):131-142.

6751 Meulen, E.I. van der
Dossier Ambon 1950; De houding van Nederland ten opzichte van Ambon en de RMS. 's-Gravenhage: Staatsuitgeverij, 1981, 227 pp.

6752 Meijer, Hans
Van Sabang tot Merauke! Indonesië en het Nieuw-Guinea-vraagstuk. 1986, 178 pp. [MA thesis Rijksuniversiteit Groningen.]

6753 Meijer, Hans
'Images of Indonesia in the Dutch press 1950-1962', *Itinerario* 17-2 (1993):53-73.

6754 Meijer, Hans
Den Haag-Djakarta; De Nederlands-Indonesische betrekkingen 1950-1962. Utrecht/ Antwerpen: Het Spectrum, 1994, 712 pp. [Also PhD thesis Universiteit Utrecht.]

6755 Molen, Gesina H.J. van der
'De juridische grondslag van het Nederlands gezag in Nieuw-Guinea', *Anti-revolutionaire Staatkunde* 27 (1957):350-361. (ubl)

6756 Molen, G.H.J. van der
'Indonesia and the Republic of the South Moluccas', *International Relations* 1-9 (April 1958):393-400. (vp)

6757 Molen, Gesina H.J. van der
'The legal position according to international law', in: *The South Moluccas; Rebellious province or occupied state*, pp. 65-83. Leiden: Sythoff, 1960.

6758 Molen, Gesina H.J. van der
The legal position of the Republik Maluku Selatan according to international law. Amsterdam: Vrije Universiteit, ca. 1960, 15 pp.

6759 Molen, Gesina H.J. van der
'Enkele opmerkingen over het zelfbeschikkingsrecht der volken', *Antirevolutio-naire Staatkunde* 32 (1962):73-78. (ubl)

6760   Moll, L.O.A.
       'De Ambonnezenarresten', *Rechtsgeleerd Magazijn Themis* 1977:237-266.

6761   *De Molukken; Terugblik en historisch perspectief.* Lelystad: Stichting IVIO, 1977,
       20 pp.

6762   *Molukker en Nederlander; Perspectieven van een relatie.* 's-Gravenhage:
       Wetenschappelijke Instituten CDA, 1978, 31 pp.

6763   *De Molukkers; Het geweld, de leiders, de toekomst.* Amsterdam: Haagse Post, 1978,
       58 pp.

6764   *De Molukkers; Wat brengt hen tot gijzelingsacties? Achtergronden; Geschiedenis.*
       Rotterdam: Ordeman, 1975, 32 pp.

6765   Muilwijk, A.J.
       Nieuw-Guinea 1919-1949; Continuïteit of discontinuïteit inzake het Neder-
       landse regeringsbeleid? 1986, 97 pp. [MA thesis Erasmus Universiteit, Rotter-
       dam.]

6766   Muralt, R.W.G. de
       'Het volkenrecht en de niet-erkenning van de RMS', *Nederlands Juristenblad* 53
       (1978):176-182. (ubl)

6767   *Naskah dan lampiran dari bagian pokok dari pihak Belanda untuk laporan Komisi
       Gabungan Irian/Nieuw-Guinea.* Djakarta: De Unie, 1950, 108 pp.

6768   Natris, W.G.B.M. de
       Het begin van het einde; Nieuw-Guinea en de buitenlandse politiek, september
       1960-september 1961. 1990, 196 pp. [MA thesis Rijksuniversiteit Leiden.]

6769   *Nederlands Nieuw-Guinea.* 's-Gravenhage: Abraham Kuyper Stichting, ca. 1955,
       19 pp.

6770   *Nederlands Nieuw-Guinea.* 's-Gravenhage: Ministerie van Defensie, ca. 1962, 72
       pp.

6771   *Nederlands Nieuw-Guinea; Algemene oriëntatie.* Amsterdam: Koninklijk Instituut
       voor de Tropen, 1956, 57 pp.

6772   *Nederlands Nieuw-Guinea in de Algemene Vergadering van de Verenigde Naties.*
       's-Gravenhage: Ministerie van Buitenlandse Zaken, 1955-62, 340+58+244+
       234+307 pp. 5 vols.

6773   *Nederlands Nieuw-Guinea en de Verenigde Naties, januari-oktober 1962.* 's-Graven-
       hage: Staatsdrukkerij, 1963, 273 pp.

6774   *De Nederlandse strijdkrachten in Nieuw-Guinea; Studies door de historische secties der
       drie krijgsmachtdelen onder redactie van de Afdeling Maritieme Historie vervaardigd
       in opdracht van de toenmalige Verenigde Chefs van Staven.* 's-Gravenhage: Afdeling
       Maritieme Historie, 1964-89. 6 vols. (amh) [Various pagings; Some sections
       confidential.]

6775   *De Nederlandse strijdkrachten in Nieuw-Guinea; Tweede deel: De politieke ontwikke-
       lingen van 1945 tot 1962.* 's-Gravenhage: Afdeling Maritieme Historie, ca. 1964,
       408 pp.

6776 *Netherlands New Guinea Constitution Act; Basic regulations of the representative bodies.* The Hague: Netherlands Ministry for the Interior, 1961, 47 pp.

6777 *Netherlands New Guinea; A people on the way to self-determination.* Rotterdam: Netherlands New Guinea Institute, 1960, 64 pp.

6778 *The New Guinea Council opened; 5th April 1961.* The Hague: Netherlands Ministry for the Interior, 1961, 12 pp.

6779 *Nieuw-Guinea als probleem van het Nederlandse volk; Rapport van de Commissie voor Internationale Zaken van de Oecumenische Raad van Kerken in Nederland.* Amsterdam: Ten Have, 1956, 24 pp.

6780 'Nieuw-Guinea-manifest', *Podium* 15 (1960-61):312-313. (ubl)

6781 *Nieuw-Guinea torn...* 's-Gravenhage: Ministerie van Marine, ca. 1960, 52 pp.

6782 *Nieuw-Guinea in de Verenigde Naties.* 's-Gravenhage: Ministerie van Binnenlandse Zaken, ca. 1962, 103 pp.

6783 Nikijuluw, J.P.
The forgotten war; An appeal from the RMS. Rotterdam: Department of Public Information of the RMS, 1950, 12 pp.

6784 Nikijuluw, J.P.
La guerra olvidada; Llamamiento... Rotterdam: Ministerio de Información Pública de la República de las Molucas del Sur, ca. 1953, 12 pp.

6785 Nikijuluw, J.P. a.o.
The legal position of the RMS in the international legal order. Rotterdam: Department of Public Information of the RMS, 1950, 48 pp.

6786 Nikijuluw, J.P. and J.A. Kajiadoe
Noodzaak tot beroep op het Uniehof inzake Ambon. 's-Gravenhage: Bureau Zuid-Molukken, 1951, 27 pp.

6787 Nortier, J.
'Een vergeten landmachtonderdeel; Het 6e Infanteriebataljon in Nieuw-Guinea', *Ons Leger* 62-3 (March 1978):50-65. (ubl)

6788 *Nota van de Badan Persatuan.* 's-Gravenhage: Badan Persatuan, 1978, 48+96 pp.

6789 *Nota inzake Nieuw-Guinea.* Batavia: Departement van Sociale Zaken, 1947, 161 pp.

6790 *Un nouveau colonialisme; Document historique publié par le Gouvernement de la République des Moluques du Sud.* La Haye: Département de l'Information Publique de la République des Moluques du Sud, 1958, 15 pp.

6791 Nuis, Aad
De balenkraai; Kroniek uit Oudnederlandsguinea. Amsterdam: Meulenhoff, 1967, 125 pp. [Second edition, *De balenkraai; Kroniek over het einde van Nederlands Nieuw-Guinea*, 1983, 136 pp.]

6792 Oen Kay Liat
Balans van 25 jaar RMS-ideaal Zuid-Molukkers (en onvrede Zuid-Molukkers verklaard met het begrip 'relatieve deprivatie'). 1975, 73 pp. [MA thesis Universiteit van Amsterdam.]

6793   Oerle, J.E.C.M. van
       'Nieuw-Guinea van kwestieus tot kwestie, augustus 1948-augustus 1949', in:
       Politieke opstellen 9 (1989):83-107. (ubl)

6794   *Ontstaan en groei van de kwestie Nieuw-Guinea.* 1962, 28 pp. [45]

6795   'Ontwikkeling van de kwestie Nieuw-Guinea', *Antirevolutionaire Staatkunde* 32
       (1962):60-69. (ubl)

6796   Oosterhoff, J.A.
       'Wat kan Nederland doen tegen Indonesische infiltraties in Nederlands Nieuw-
       Guinea?', *Antirevolutionaire Staatkunde* 27 (1957):259-266. (ubl)

6797   *Open brief aan het Nederlandsche volk.* Bangkok: Nakorn Pathom/Grooter Neder-
       land Actie, 1946, 4 pp. (ubl)

6798   *Oproep van de Generale Synode der Nederlandse Hervormde Kerk tot bezinning op de
       verantwoordelijkheid van het Nederlandse volk inzake de vraagstukken rondom
       Nieuw-Guinea.* 's-Gravenhage: Generale Synode der NHK, 1956, 6 pp. (ubl)

6799   *Overwegingen naar aanleiding van de Oproep tot bezinning inzake Nieuw-Guinea.*
       's-Gravenhage: Generale Synode der NHK, 1956, 6 pp (ubl)

6800   *Papoea's bouwen aan hun toekomst.* 's-Gravenhage: Ministerie van Binnenlandse
       Zaken, 1961, 38 pp.

6801   *Papoea's op de drempel van zelfbeschikking/Papuans on the threshold of self-deter-
       mination.* Hollandia: Gouvernement van Nederlands Nieuw-Guinea, 1961,
       58 pp.

6802   *Partiële herziening bewindsregeling Nieuw-Guinea; Zitting 1959-1960.* 's-Graven-
       hage: Staatsdrukkerij, 1960, 149 pp.

6803   Pels, J.V.M.
       Molukkers in Nederland; Het overheidsbeleid 1951-1978. Amsterdam: Raad voor
       de Jeugdvorming, 1979, 96 pp. (mhm)

6804   Penonton, Bung (ps. G. Knot)
       *Wat gebeurde er na 1950? Schets voor een beschrijving van de nieuwste geschiedenis
       van het Zuidmolukse volk.* Groningen: n.n., 1970, 103 pp.

6805   Penonton, Bung (ps.)
       *De Zuidmolukse republiek; Schets voor een beschrijving van de nieuwste geschiedenis
       van het Zuidmolukse volk.* Fourth edition. Amsterdam: Buijten en Schipperheijn,
       1977, 299 pp. [First edition 1970.]

6806   Persijn, J. (ps. J.J.P. de Jong)
       'Uit de schaduw van het verleden; Legende en realiteit in het Molukse
       vraagstuk', *Internationale Spectator* 30 (1976):103-110.

6807   Persijn, J. (ps.)
       'Out of the shadow of the past', *Review of Indonesian and Malaysian Affairs* 11-2
       (1977):99-111.

6808   Peters, Theo
       Nederlands Nieuw-Guinea 1945-1962; Een na-oorlogse kroniek. 's-Gravenhage:
       Vereniging Belangenbehartiging Militairen VBM/LKV, 1994, 255 pp.

6809   Pluvier, J.M.
       'Nederlands-Indonesische betrekkingen 1950-1963', *Spiegel Historiael* 21
       (1986):121-127.

6810   Pollmann, Tessel and Ingrid Harms
       In Nederland door omstandigheden. Baarn: Ambo, Den Haag: NOVIB, 1987, 158
       pp.

6811   Pollmann, Tessel and Juan Seleky
       Istori-istori Maluku; Het verhaal van de Molukkers. Amsterdam: Arbeiderspers,
       1979, 254 pp.

6812   Pouwer, Jan
       'Kolonisering, dekolonisering en re-kolonisering van West Irian', in: A. Borsboom
       and J. Kommers (eds), *Processen van kolonisatie en dekolonisatie in de Pacific,*
       pp. 108-152. Nijmegen: Centrum voor Studies van Australië en Oceanië, 1987.

6813   Prins, J.
       'De Republiek der Zuid-Molukken een mythe?', *Antirevolutionaire Staatkunde* 29
       (1959):170-182. (ubl)

6814   Prins, J.
       'Location, history, forgotten struggle', in: *The South Moluccas; Rebellious province
       or occupied state,* pp. 9-47. Leiden: Sythoff, 1960.

6815   Prins, J.
       The double problem of the South Moluccan minority. Groningen: Secretariat Dutch-
       Melanesian Aid Foundation, 1977, 47 pp.

6816   *Het probleem Irian zoals Nederlandse democraten het zien.* Amsterdam: Comité
       Vrienden van Indonesië, 1950, 30 pp.

6817   *De problematiek van de Molukse minderheid in Nederland.* 's-Gravenhage: Staats-
       uitgeverij, 1978, 132 pp.

6818   Raalte, E. van
       Onderhandelen met Indonesië; Het Nieuw-Guinea-vraagstuk. 's-Gravenhage: Van
       Hoeve, 1961, 31 pp.

6819   *Rapport van de Commissie van Advies inzake de Agrarische Ontwikkelings-
       mogelijkheden in Nieuw-Guinea.* 's-Gravenhage: Staatsuitgeverij, 1955, 232 pp.

6820   *Rapport van de Commissie Nieuw-Guinea (Irian) 1950.* 's-Gravenhage: Secretariaat
       van de Nederlands-Indonesische Unie, 1950, 7+106+184+159 pp.

6821   *Rapport van de Interdepartementale Commissie voor de Ontwikkeling van Nieuw-
       Guinea.* Ca. 1955, 175 pp.

6822   *Rapport inzake de houding der bevolking en de autochthone leiders in Noord-Nieuw-
       Guinea ten opzichte van de toekomstige status van Nieuw-Guinea.* Hollandia: n.n.,
       1949. [6738]

6823   *Rapport inzake Nederlands Nieuw-Guinea over het jaar... uitgebracht aan de
       Verenigde Naties ingevolge Artikel 73e van het Handvest.* 's-Gravenhage: Ministerie
       van Buitenlandse Zaken/Ministerie van Overzeese Gebiedsdelen, 1950-62.
       1950, 69 pp. + appendices; *1951,* 100 pp. + appendices; *1952,* 79 pp. +

appendices; *1953*, 84 pp. + appendices; *1954*, 120 pp. + appendices; *1955*, 127 pp. + appendices; *1956*, 132 pp. + appendices; *1957*, 151 pp. + appendices; *1958*, 109 pp. + appendices; *1959*, 124 pp. + appendices; *1960*, 157 pp. + appendices; *1961*, 142 pp. + appendices.

6824 *Reacties op de Oproep tot bezinning inzake Nieuw-Guinea.* 's-Gravenhage: Generale Synode der Ned. Hervormde Kerk, 1956, 7 pp. (ubl)

6825 *Recht, onrecht en de Molukken; Tekst van de televisie-uitzending van donderdag 29 januari 1976.* Hilversum: Evangelische Omroep, 1976, 43 pp.

6826 *De rechtsgedingen tussen de Ambonnezen en de K.P.M.; Deel 1: Tekst der voornaamste processtukken in het eerste kort geding.* 's-Gravenhage: Bureau Zuid-Molukken, 1951, 47 pp.

6827 Redeker, A.
De Nieuw-Guineakwestie; Principes tegen alle belangen in; Het Nederlands en Indonesisch Nieuw-Guineabeleid (1956-1962) en de rol van de Amerikaanse regering hierbij. 1992. [MA thesis Universiteit van Amsterdam.] [6754]

6828 *Regeringsuitspraken met betrekking tot het te voeren beleid in en ten aanzien van Nederlands Nieuw-Guinea vanaf september 1952 tot en met 1960.* 's-Gravenhage: n.n., 1961, 403 pp.

6829 Regt, I.C. de
Schema's en overzichten dislocatie schepen, MLD, mariniers, staven en commandanten KM in Nederlands Nieuw-Guinea, periode 1950-1962. [unpaged] (amh)

6830 Renes, P.B.; S.C. van Randwijck and F.M. van Asbeck
'De Republiek der Zuid-Molukken', *Wending* 14 (1959):157-183. (ubl)

6831 Renes, P.B.; S.C. van Randwijck and F.M. van Asbeck
'Nogmaals de Republiek der Zuid-Molukken', *Wending* 15 (1960):228-241. (ubl)

6832 *Report dated 11 October 1950 from the UN Commission for Indonesia to the President of the Security Council concerning the situation in the South Moluccas.* New York, 1950, 3 pp.

6833 *Report on Netherlands New Guinea presented for the year... to the Secretary General of the United Nations pursuant to Article 73 (e) of the Charter.* 's-Gravenhage: Ministry of Foreign Affairs/Ministry of Overseas Territories, 1952-61. *1951*, 171 pp.; *1952*, 9+209 pp.; *1953*, 11+172 pp.; *1955*, 10+190 pp.; *1958*, 11+ 200 pp.; *1960*, 232 pp.; *1961*, 13+232 pp.

6834 Reijs, W.W.
Nieuw-Guinea... Omstreden gebied... Amsterdam: IVIO, 1954, 16 pp.

6835 Riemens, J.W.E.
Naar vriendschap (of oorlog) tussen Nederland en Indonesië? Monnickendam: Nimo, 1961, 11 pp.

6836 Rinsampessy, E.P.
De mogelijke gronden van agressie onder Molukse jongeren (geplaatst in het kader van de integratieproblematiek). Venray: Gerakan Pattimura, 1975, 66 pp.

6837 Rinsampessy, E.P.
Saudara bersaudara; Molukse identiteit in processen van cultuurverandering. Assen: Van Gorcum, Wychen: Pattimura, 1992, 11+284 pp.

6838 Röling, B.V.A.
'Beschouwing over de huidige stand der Nieuw-Guinea kwestie', *Socialisme en Democratie* 15 (1958):13-29. (ubl)

6839 Röling, B.V.A.
Nieuw-Guinea als wereldprobleem. Assen: Van Gorcum, 1958, 104 pp.

6840 *Een roeping, een taak! Bestuursambtenaar in Nederlands Nieuw-Guinea.* N.p.: n.n., ca. 1955, 20 pp.

6841 *Het roer moet om; Geen nieuwe koloniale avonturen! Vlugschrift van de CPN tegen de wijziging van de Dienstplichtwet.* Amsterdam: CPN, ca. 1960, 8 pp. (uba)

6842 Roethof, H.J.
'De internationale positie van Nederlands Nieuw-Guinea', *Rekenschap* 4-1 (March 1957):26-37.

6843 Roethof, H.J.
'The Republic of the South Moluccas; An existing state', in: *Symbolae Verzijl*, pp. 295-313. 's-Gravenhage: Nijhoff, 1958.

6844 Roethof, H.J.
'An existing state', in: *The South Moluccas; Rebellious province or occupied state*, pp. 105-121. Leiden: Sythoff, 1960.

6845 Roethof, H.J.
'Geen last maar dure plicht', in: Paul van 't Veer, *Nieuw-Guinea tegen wil en dank; Een historische omschrijving en een waarschuwend toekomstperspectief*, pp. 143-159. Amsterdam: Querido, 1960.

6846 Roethof, H.J.
'De Nieuw-Guinea Raad', *Marineblad* 72 (1962):225-229. (ubl)

6847 Roolvink, R.
'Nieuw-Guinea; Heroriëntatie noodzakelijk', in: *Terdege ter discussie*, pp. 14-30. Den Haag: Van Keulen, 1958.

6848 Roos, G.K.R. de
De marinierskant van het verhaal, november 1960-november 1962. 's-Gravenhage: Bureau Maritieme Historie, 1979, 285 pp.

6849 Sahalessy, D.O.
Een geïsoleerde oorlog; De dubbele onderdrukking van het Molukse recht op zelfbeschikking; Een memorandum. Groningen: Moluccan Peoples Mission, 1981, 44 pp.

6850 Sahetapy, Abé
Minne strijd voor de RMS. Veenhuizen: n.n., 1980, 129 pp.

6851 Sanders, H.M. and A.M.C. Zegers
De kwestie Nieuw-Guinea opnieuw bekeken. 1981, 319 pp. [MA thesis Rijksuniversiteit Utrecht.]

6852 Schermerhorn, W.
'Nieuw-Guinea', *Wending* 7 (1952-53):165-174. (ubl)

6853 Schmidt, Machteld
'De dekolonisatie van Nieuw-Guinea; Een daad van vrije keuze?', in: *Praesidium Libertatis; Opstellen over het thema vrijheid en recht*, pp. 319-331. Deventer: Kluwer, 1975. (ubl)

6854 Schoe, P.C.
Reis naar Nederlands Nieuw-Guinea van de Commissie Herziening Bewindsregeling, 7 juli-7 augustus 1957. Merauke: n.n., 1957, 170 pp.

6855 Schoonenberg, F.
'De Papoea's onder koloniaal bestuur', *Politiek en Cultuur* 9 (1954):380-388. (ubl)

6856 Schoonenberg, F.
'De Papoea ontwaakt', *Politiek en Cultuur* 9 (1954):407-413. (ubl)

6857 Schrover, H.J. (ed.)
Ambassadeur titulair; Samengesteld door en voor het 434e Bataljon Garde Regiment 'Prinses Irene'. Delft: Brouwer, 1952, 177 pp.

6858 Siahaya, Tete
Mena Muria; Wassenaar '70; Zuid-Molukkers slaan terug; Een persoonlijk verslag van de strijd. Amsterdam: De Bezige Bij, 1972, 182 pp.

6859 Sluysmans, Conny
Habis; Afscheid van Nieuw-Guinea. Amsterdam: Contact, 1963, 160 pp.

6860 Smeets, Henk
Sedjarah kesabaran = De geschiedenis van het geduld; Enkele data uit de geschiedenis van de Molukse bevolkingsgroep in Nederland. Utrecht: Bureau Inspraakorgaan Welzijn Molukkers, 1985, 62 pp.

6861 Smeets, Henk
Moluccans in the Netherlands. Utrecht: Moluks Historisch Museum, 1992, 64 pp.

6862 Smeets, Henk
Molukkers in Nederland. Utrecht: Moluks Historisch Museum, 1992, 64 pp.

6863 Snijtsheuvel, Karel C.
De Indische Nederlanders staan voor een gigantische taak; Stichting van een bakermat op Nieuw-Guinea; Harde feiten. Dordrecht: Schefferdrukkerij, 1950, 88 pp.

6864 Snijtsheuvel, K.C.
Wij en Nieuw-Guinea. Rotterdam: Comité Behoud Nieuw-Guinea, 1952, 16 pp.

6865 Soumokil, Chr.
Rondom de affaire Kapitein Andi Abdul Aziz. 's-Gravenhage: Bureau Zuid-Molukken, 1950, 20 pp.

6866 *The South Moluccan case in the UN machinery*. Rotterdam: Department of Public Information of the RMS, 1955, 30 pp.

6867 *The South Moluccas; Rebellious province or occupied state?* Leiden: Sythoff, 1960, 196 pp.

6868 Spigt, Cees (ed.)
Inspraaknota inzake de problematiek van de Molukkers in Nederland. Samengesteld door de Subgroep Molukkers van de Werkgroep Culturele Minderheden. Den Haag: Stichting Wetenschappelijk Bureau D'66, 1980, 48 pp.

6869 Springer, F. (ps. C.J. Schneider)
Bericht uit Hollandia. 's-Gravenhage: Stols/Barth, 1962, 79 pp.

6870 Springer, F. (ps.)
'Zaken overzee', in: F. Springer, *Zaken overzee,* pp. 41-115. Utrecht: E.C.I., 1978.

6871 Spruit, Ruud
Molukkers onder anderen. Leiden: Spruyt, Van Mantgem en De Does, 1982, 119 pp.

6872 *Staatkundige ontwikkeling in Nederlands Nieuw-Guinea.* 's-Gravenhage: Ministerie van Binnenlandse Zaken, 1960, 7 pp. (ubl)

6873 *Statements met betrekking tot Nederlands Nieuw-Guinea; Afgelegd in de Rapportage Commissie van de Verenigde Naties, 1950-1959.* N.p.: n.n., 1959, 143 pp.

6874 Steijlen, Fridus
'Het ontstaan van een RMS-beweging in Nederland, 1951-1956', in: Carolien Bouw and Bernard Kruithof (eds), *De kern van het verschil; Culturen en identiteiten,* pp. 217-231. Amsterdam: Amsterdam University Press, 1993. (ubl)

6875 Straaten, C. van der
'Is de "hopeloze situatie" werkelijk hopeloos?', in: *Terdege ter discussie,* pp. 7-13. Den Haag: Van Keulen, 1958.

6876 Stratenus, R.J.
Een voorlopig onderzoek naar de economische vooruitzichten in Nederlands Nieuw-Guinea. Amsterdam: Paris, 1952, 170 pp. [Also PhD thesis Rijksuniversiteit Leiden.]

6877 *De strijd van de Molukkers tegen nationale onderdrukking.* Rotterdam: Het Progressieve Boek, 1978, 25 pp.

6878 Teeuw, A.
Het conflict met Indonesië als spiegel voor Nederland. 's-Gravenhage/Bandung: Van Hoeve, 1956, 32 pp.

6879 Telder, P.
'Van Bandoeng begint de nederlaag', in: *Terdege ter discussie,* pp. 41-47. Den Haag: Van Keulen, 1958.

6880 *Terdege ter discussie; Vraagstukken betreffende de verhouding Nederland-Indonesië-Nieuw-Guinea.* Den Haag: Van Keulen, 1958, 72 pp.

6881 Tichelman, G.L.
Nieuw-Guinee; Land der toekomst. Haarlem: Spaarnestad, 1949, 48 pp.

6882 Tichelman, G.L.
Draaiboek van Nieuw-Guinee. 's-Gravenhage: Stichting Nationaal Nieuw-Guinea Comité, Hollandia: Nieuw-Guinea Verbond, 1951, 82 pp.

6883 Tichelman, G.L.
Nieuw-Guinea ... Open kaart ... Amsterdam: IVIO, 1961, 16 pp.

6884 Tichelman, G.L. and W.H. Alting von Geusau
NSB-deportatie naar Oost en West. Amsterdam: DAVID, 1945, 54 pp.

6885 *Toekomstige ontwikkeling van Nieuw-Guinea; Rapport van de interdepartementale commissie, welke tot taak had de huidige ontwikkeling van Nieuw-Guinea te toetsen aan de internationale criteria en daarbij schematisch aan te geven in welke richting verdere ontwikkeling nodig is.* 's-Gravenhage: Staatsdrukkerij, 1953, 315+48 pp. 2 vols.

6886 *Toekomstige status van Nieuw-Guinea.* 's-Gravenhage: Ministerie van Overzeese Gebiedsdelen, 1949, 45 pp.

6887 Tutuarima, W.H.
'Ecclesiastical aspects', in: *The South Moluccas; Rebellious province or occupied state,* pp. 149-161. Leiden: Sythoff, 1960.

6888 Tutupoly, Wiet
Het Nieuw-Guinea verlangen; De invloed van Indo-Europese wensen op en het beleid van de Nederlandse en Indische regering inzake de eis tot migratie naar een Nederlands Nieuw-Guinea, 2 oktober 1945-27 december 1949. 1981, 104+48 pp. [MA thesis Katholieke Universiteit Nijmegen.]

6889 Tutupoly, W.
'Van de regen in de drup komen; Een beschrijving van de positie der Indo-Europeanen in Nederlands-Indië tot 1946 en de rol van Nieuw-Guinea binnen deze positiebepaling', *Jambatan* 2-3 (1983-84):21-32.

6890 Utrecht, Ernst
Ambon; Kolonisatie, dekolonisatie en neo-kolonisatie. Amsterdam: Van Gennep, 1972, 134 pp.

6891 Utrecht, Ernst
Papoea's in opstand (De tweede kwestie Nieuw Guinea); Het verzet van de Papoea's tegen het Indonesiese bewind in West-Irian. Rotterdam: Ordeman, 1978, 96 pp.

6892 Veenman, J. and L.G. Jansma
Molukkers in Nederland; Een probleeminventariserend onderzoek. Deventer: Van Loghum Slaterus, 1981, 292 pp.

6893 Veenstra, J.H.W.
'Ambon; Een blok aan Nederlands been', *Ons Erfdeel* 21 (1978):511-524. (ubl)

6894 Veer, Paul van 't
'Het spektakel Nieuw-Guinea', *Socialisme en Democratie* 12 (1955):1-7. (ubl)

6895 Veer, Paul van 't
Vriend en vijand in de kolonie; Enkele variaties op het thema der menselijke verhoudingen onder koloniale omstandigheden, vooral in Nieuw-Guinea, Suriname, de Nederlandse Antillen, Indonesië en Nederland. Amsterdam: Arbeiderspers, 1956, 156 pp.

6896 Veer, Paul van 't (ed.)
Nieuw-Guinea tegen wil en dank; Een historische omschrijving en een waarschuwend toekomstperspectief. Amsterdam: Querido, 1960, 159 pp.

6897 Veer, Paul van 't
'Dobbelen om een half eiland; De kwestie Nieuw-Guinea tot de bestuursoverdracht aan Indonesië op 1 mei 1963', in: *Onze Jaren 45-70,* pp. 1483-1488. Amsterdam, 1972. (ubl)

6898 Veer, Paul van 't
'Nieuw-Guinea als wraakoefening', *Internationale Spectator* 28 (1974):73-82.

6899 Verhoeff, H.G.
Netherlands New Guinea; A bird's eye view. 's-Gravenhage, 1958, 80 pp.

6900 Verhoeff, H.G.
De Nieuw-Guinea Raad; Geopend: dinsdag 5 april 1961. 's-Gravenhage: Radiorubriek Nederlands Nieuw-Guinea, 1961, 12 pp.

6901 Verhoeven, Bernard
Nieuw-Guinea; Vraagstuk van verantwoordelijkheid. Amsterdam: De Tijd, 1959, 23 pp.

6902 Verkuyl, J.
'Verzoening tussen Nederland en Indonesië', in: *Terdege ter discussie,* pp. 48-69. Den Haag; Van Keulen, 1958.

6903 *Verslag der Nieuw-Guineaconferentie te Den Haag, van 4 tot 27 December 1950.* 's-Gravenhage, 1950. [45]

6904 *Verslag van de parlementaire missie naar Nieuw-Guinea.* 's-Gravenhage: Staatsdrukkerij, 1954, 47+43 pp.

6905 *Verslag van de parlementaire missie naar Nieuw-Guinea.* 's-Gravenhage: Staatsdrukkerij, 1958. (ubl)

6906 *Verslag van de Studiecommissie Nieuw-Guinea.* Batavia: n.n., 1949, 185 pp.

6907 *Verslag over de verkiezingen voor de Nieuw-Guinea Raad 1961.* Hollandia: Dienst van Binnenlandse Zaken, 1961, 28 pp.

6908 Versluis, W.
Hoe wij mogelijk zullen slagen in de nieuwe Nederlandsche volksplanting in Nieuw-Guinea. Soerabaja: n.n., 1948, 12 pp. (kitlv-m)

6909 Vierdag, E.W.
'Enkele volkenrechtelijke kanttekeningen bij het Zuid-Molukken vraagstuk', *Nederlands Juristenblad* 51 (1976):245-255.

6910 Vogel, L.C.
Het beleid van de Dienst van Gezondheidszorg in West Nieuw-Guinea, 1950-1962. Utrecht: Schotanus en Jens, 1965, 383 pp. [PhD thesis Rijksuniversiteit Utrecht.]

6911 *Voice of the negroids in the Pacific to the negroids throughout the world.* Hollandia: Papuan National Committee, 1962, 36 pp. (kitlv-m)

6912   *Voorontwerp voor een handleiding betreffende het patrouilleren in Ned. Nieuw Guinea.* Opgesteld bij het Hoofdkwartier Korps Mariniers. N.p.: n.n., 1957, 131 pp.

6913   *Het vraagstuk Nieuw-Guinea.* Amsterdam: Dr. Wiardi Beckman Stichting, 1958, 32 pp.

6914   *Het vraagstuk van de Republiek der Zuid-Molukken en de Ambonnezen.* 's-Gravenhage: Abraham Kuyper Stichting, 1960, 46 pp.

6915   *Vriendschap met Indonesië.* Amsterdam: CPN, 1962, 14 pp.

6916   Vries, H. de (ps.J. Morriën)
'De strijd rondom Nieuw-Guinea', *Politiek en Cultuur* 13 (1953):503-510. (ubl)

6917   Vries, H. de (ps.J. Morriën)
'Nieuw-Guinea: een koloniaal vraagstuk', *Politiek en Cultuur* 16 (1956):349-355. (ubl)

6918   Vries, H. de (ps.J. Morriën)
'De Wiardi Beckman Stichting en Nieuw-Guinea', *Politiek en Cultuur* 18 (1958):442-450. (ubl)

6919   Vrijburg, B.
Emigratie naar Nieuw-Guinea. N.p.: n.n., 1950, 14 pp.

6920   Waaldijk, Berteke
Mena Muria - ik zal handhaven; De Stichting Door de Eeuwen Trouw en de Zuidmolukse kwestie als probleem in de Nederlandse politiek, 1949-1959. 1982, 64 pp. [MA thesis Rijksuniversiteit Groningen.]

6921   'Waarom wil de Nederlandse regering westelijk Nieuw-Guinea behouden?', *Politiek en Cultuur* 15 (1955):500-503. (ubl)

6922   Weltje, H.C.
Dertigduizend ballingen willen terug naar hun tropisch vaderland. Eindhoven: Stichting Door de Eeuwen Trouw, 1966, 10 pp.

6923   Weltje, H.C.
'Zuidmolukkers in Nederland', in: Knot, Gerhard; Henk C. Weltje and Aad Kamsteeg, *Wat moeten ze hier? Zuidmolukkers op weg naar vrijheid...*, pp. 45-58. Groningen: De Vuurbaak, 1975.

6924   Wentink, J.J.
Nieuw-Guinea, schone slaapster, word wakker! Den Haag: Voorhoeve, ca. 1955, 126 pp.

6925   *Western New Guinea and the Netherlands.* The Hague: Government State Printing Office, 1954, 23 pp.

6926   *Wettelijke regelingen en administratieve voorschriften Nederlands Nieuw-Guinea, 1940-1949.* 's-Gravenhage, 1957. 2 vols. [unpaged]

6927   *Wie is dat en waar is het? Beknopt overzicht van indeling en personalia van het overheidsapparaat, zendings- en missieorganisaties en het particuliere bedrijfsleven in Nederlands Nieuw-Guinea.* Hollandia: Kantoor voor Voorlichting en Radio-omroep, 1958, 79 pp.

6928 Wierikx, Wim
De kwestie-Ambon en de Molukse KNIL-militairen in de Nederlandse publieke opinie. 1985, 74 pp. [MA thesis Rijksuniversiteit Utrecht.]

6929 Willekens, Hanneke
De economische aspecten van de Nieuw-Guineaproblematiek 1949-1962. 1980, 154+23 pp. [MA thesis Universiteit van Amsterdam.] [43, 58]

6930 'Wisselende en blijvende achtergronden van de Nederlands-Indonesische betrekkingen; Door een groep vrienden van Indonesië', *Wending* 11 (1956):361-388. (ubl)

6931 Wolters, R.J.H.
De Nieuw-Guinea Raad; Totstandkomen en functioneren. 1986, 40 pp. [MA thesis Rijksuniversiteit Groningen.]

6932 Wuster, H.W.S.
'Tegels lichten; De geschiedenis van een verbazing', *Hollands Maandblad* no. 268 (1969-70):14-19; no. 270 (1970-71):18-22; no. 271/72 (1970-71):13-22. (ubl)

6933 *Zo zien zij het.* 's-Gravenhage: Nationaal Nieuw-Guinea Comité, ca. 1958, 20 pp. (ubl)

6934 *Zuidmolukse tegennota betreffende de R.M.S. problematiek.* N.p.: R.M.S., 1978, 45 pp.

6935 *Het Zuidmolukse vraagstuk; Enkele realiteiten opnieuw bezien; Discussienota opgesteld door het bestuur van de Stichting Door de Eeuwen Trouw.* Groningen: Stichting Door de Eeuwen Trouw, 1977, 19 pp.

West Irian and the South Moluccan question
Other authors

6936 Albinski, Henry S.
'Australia and the Dutch New Guinea dispute', *International Journal* 16 (1961):358-382. [146, 6960]

6937 Barker, Ralph
Niet hier, maar op een andere plaats; De gijzelingen van Wijster, Amsterdam, De Punt en Bovensmilde. Alphen aan den Rijn: Sijthoff, 1981, 381 pp.

6938 Bone, Robert Clarke
The origin and development of the Irian problem. 1957, 358 pp. [PhD thesis Cornell University, Ithaca.] (ubl)

6939 Bone, Robert C.
The dynamics of the Western New Guinea (Irian Barat) problem. Ithaca: Cornell University, 1958, 170 pp. [Second printing 1962.]

6940 Bramsted, E.K.
'Das Neuguinea Problem und die australisch-indonesischen Beziehungen', *Europa Archiv* 17 (1962):629-644. (ubl)

6941 Brown, Colin P.M.
Indonesia at the United Nations, 1950-1965; A study of Indonesian foreign policy. 1974, 400 pp. [PhD thesis University of Queensland, Brisbane.]

6942 Brown, Colin
'Indonesia's West Irian case in the UN General Assembly, 1954', *Journal of Southeast Asian Studies* 7 (1976):260-274.

6943 Bunnell, Frederick Philip
The Kennedy initiatives in Indonesia, 1962-1963. 1969, 764 pp. [PhD thesis Cornell University, Ithaca.]

6944 Cayrac-Blanchard, F.
'Le règlement du conflit sur l'Irian Occidental; Dernière étape d'une décolonisation', *Revue Française de Science Politique* 24 (1974):328-343. (ubl)

6945 Chauvel, R.
'Their myths and our reality; A review of the debate in the Netherlands on the South Moluccan question', *Review of Indonesian and Malaysian Affairs* 12 (1978):67-94.

6946 Chauvel, R.H.
'Ambon's other half', *Review of Indonesian and Malaysian Affairs* 14-1 (1980):53-67.

6947 Chauvel, Richard H.
Indonesia merdeka! Ambon merdeka? A modern social and political history of the Ambonese islands. 1984, 693 pp. [PhD thesis University of Sydney.]

6948 Chauvel, Richard
'Ambon: Not a revolution but a counterrevolution', in: Audrey R. Kahin (ed.), *Regional dynamics of the Indonesian revolution*, pp. 237-264. Honolulu: University of Hawaii Press, 1985.

6949 Chauvel, Richard
Nationalists, soldiers and separatists; The Ambonese islands from colonialism to revolt, 1880-1950. Leiden: KITLV Press, 1990, 15+432 pp.

6950 Decker, G.
'Die Republik Maluku Selatan; Ein Beitrag zur Diskussion um das Selbstbestimmungsrecht der Nationen und den Antikolonialismus; Mit einem Dokumentenanhang', *Internationales Recht und Diplomatie* (1956):217-235, 333-345. (ubl)

6951 Decker, Günter
Republik Maluku Selatan; Die Republik der Süd-Molukken; Untersuchungen und Dokumente zum Selbstbestimmungsrecht der Ambonesen, zum Föderalismus und Kolonialismus in Indonesien. Göttingen: Schwartz, 1957, 240 pp.

6952 Eppstein, J.
'War in Indonesia; The affair of Ambon', *British Survey* (1950):27-31. (vp)

6953 Finkelstein, L.S.
'Irian in Indonesian politics', *Far Eastern Survey* 20 (1951):76-80.

6954 Fisher, Charles A.
'West New Guinea in its regional setting', in: G.W. Keeton and G. Schwarzenberger (eds), *The year book of world affairs*, pp. 189-210. London: Stevens and Sons, 1952. (ubl)

6955 Goldberg, Harry
Irian; Test of West's sincerity. Djakarta: Ministry of Information, ca. 1955, 7 pp.

6956 Hanna, W.A.
The Irian Barat settlement. New York: American Universities Field Staff, 1962. [44]

6957 Hanna, Willard A.
The Republic of the South Moluccas. Hanover, N.H.: American Universities Field Staff, 1975, 7 pp.

6958 Harper, Norman
'West New Guinea; An Australian view', *International Studies* 3-2 (October 1961):109-132.

6959 Hastings, Peter
New Guinea; Problems and prospects. Melbourne: Cheshire, 1969, 320 pp. [Second edition, 1973, 12+303 pp.]

6960 Haupt, Margaret
Australian policy toward the West New Guinea dispute, 1945-1962. 1970, 466 pp. [PhD thesis Fletcher School of Law and Diplomacy, Tufts University, Medford, Mass.]

6961 Henderson, William
West New Guinea; The dispute and its settlement. South Orange, N.J.: Seton Hall University Press, 1973, 10+281 pp.

6962 Hermanson, J.Th.
The role of good offices and mediation in settling an international conflict; Ellsworth Bunker and the West Irian dispute. Ca. 1970. [PhD thesis Georgetown University, Washington.] [45]

6963 Ito, Hayao
Visit to West Irian; A land of war dead. Tokyo: Shin-jinbutsu-oraisha, 1981, 208 pp. [In Japanese.] [59]

6964 Jawed, Mahmood
West Irian; The problem and its solution. Cairo: Eastern Publications, 1962, 61 pp.

6965 Jeremeyev, M.
Coup d'oeil sur les événements qui sont déroulés dans le Sud-Est Asiatique après la 2ième Guerre Mondiale et dont une des conséquences a été la proclamation de l'indépendence de la République des Moluques du Sud. Genève, 1954. [45]

6966 Kessel'brenner, G.L.
West Irian; An inalienable part of Indonesia. Moscow: State Publishing House for Political Literature, 1958, 80 pp. [In Russian.]

6967 Kessel'brenner, G.L.
West Irian. Moscow: Institute of International Relations Press, 1960, 262 pp. [In Russian.] [5]

6968 Kessel'brenner, G.L.
Irian Barat; Wilayah jang tak terpisahkan dari Indonesia. Djakarta: Lembaga Kebudajaan Rakjat, 1961, 130 pp. (kitlv-m)

6969 Kessel'brenner, G.L.
Out with the colonialists in West Irian. Moscow: State Publishing House for Political Literature, 1962, 48 pp. [In Russian.] [5]

6970 Körner, Ruth
'Der Westneuguinea-Konflikt', *Vierteljahrshefte für Zeitgeschichte* 13 (1965):403-425.

6971 Lasker, B.
'Western New Guinea: past and future', *Far Eastern Survey* 21-6 (1952):53-59. (ubl)

6972 Lewis, Reba
Indonesia; Troubled paradise. London: Hall, 1962, 192 pp.

6973 Leyser, Johannes
'Dispute and agreement on West New Guinea', *Archiv des Völkerrechts* 10 (1963):257-272. (ubl)

6974 Loschagin, V.
A new stage in the struggle of the people of Indonesia for the liberation of Irian. Moscow: Knowledge Publishing House, 1959, 24 pp. [In Russian.] [5]

6975 Mackie, J.A.C.
'The West New Guinea argument', *Australian Outlook* 16 (1962):26-46.

6976 McMullen, Christopher J.
Mediation of the West New Guinea dispute, 1962; A case study. Washington: Georgetown University, 1981, 76 pp.

6977 Müller-Krüger, Th.
Bericht van Ambon. Oegstgeest: Raad voor de Zending van de Ned. Hervormde Kerk, 1957, 134 pp.

6978 Nagarajan, S.
Indonesian society and foreign policy, 1956-1962. 1973, 461 pp. [PhD thesis Jawaharlal Nehru University, Delhi.] [44]

6979 Oey Hong Lee
'Decolonization and racial conflict; The Indonesian-Dutch experience', *Cultures et Développement* 6 (1974):829-850.

6980 Pariury, Izaak Marthen
The forgotten world. East Weymouth: Gemini Book Village, 1974, 37 pp.

6981 Pelras, Christian
'Séquelles d'une décolonisation; Le problème de la République des Moluques du Sud; Déchiffrer un événement', *l'Homme et l'Humanité* 54-1 (1976):17-24.

6982 Poulgrain, Greg
'Sukarno and the international quest for New Guinea', *Kabar Seberang* no. 23 (1992):84-91.

6983 'La question de la Nouvelle Guinée: chronologie et textes', *Notes et Etudes Documentaires* no. 3164 (19 February 1965), 11 pp. (ubl)

6984 Rabe, Bea
De kwestie Nieuw-Guinea. 1959, 102+28 pp. [Thesis Rijkshandelshogeschool, Antwerpen.]

6985 Ritter, C.W.
'Dutch New Guinea', *Contemporary Review* no. 179 (April 1951):222-226. (ubl)

6986 Roscoe, G.T.
Our neighbours in Netherlands New Guinea. Brisbane: Jacaranda Press, 1959, 11+68 pp.

6987 Schreiner, Klaus H.
Die Dekolonisierung Niederländisch-Neuguineas. 1987. [MA thesis Universität Hamburg.] [6171]

6988 Sharp, Nonie
The rule of the sword; The story of West Irian. Malmsbury: Kibble Books, 1977, 76 pp.

6989   Tunnicliff, Kim Hunter
        The United Nations and the mediation of international conflict. 1984, 349 pp. [PhD
        thesis University of Iowa, Iowa City.]

6990   *The United Nations in West New Guinea; An unprecedented story.* New York:
        United Nations, 1963, 32 pp. [3, 45]

6991   Van der Kroef, J.M.
        'The South Moluccan insurrection in Indonesia; A preliminary analysis', *Journal
        of East Asiatic Studies* 1-4 (July 1952):1-20. (ubl)

6992   Van der Kroef, J.M.
        'Around the problem of Western New Guinea', *Pakistan Horizon* 7-4 (December
        1954):210-222; 8-1 (March 1955):278-284. (vp)

6993   Van der Kroef, J.M.
        The West New Guinea dispute. New York: Institute of Pacific Relations, 1958,
        43 pp.

6994   Van der Kroef, J.M.
        'Dutch opinion on the West New Guinea problem', *Australian Outlook* 14
        (1960):269-298.

6995   Van der Kroef, J.M.
        'West New Guinea in the crucible', *Political Science Quarterly* 75 (1960):519-538.
        (ubl)

6996   Van der Kroef, J.M.
        'Nasution, Sukarno and the West New Guinea dispute', *Asian Survey* 1-6
        (August 1961):20-24.

6997   Van der Kroef, J.M.
        'Nationalism and politics in West New Guinea', *Pacific Affairs* 34 (1961):38-53.

6998   Van der Kroef, J.M.
        'The Republic of the South Moluccas after eleven years; A review', *World Justice*
        3-2 (1961):184-198. (kit)

6999   Van der Kroef, J.M.
        'The West New Guinea problem', *The World Today* 17-11 (November 1961):489-
        502. (ubl)

7000   Van der Kroef, J.M.
        'Toward Papua Barat', *Australian Quarterly* 34-1 (1962):17-26.

7001   Van der Kroef, J.M.
        'The West New Guinea settlement; Its origins and implications', *Orbis* 7
        (1963):120-149. (ubl)

7002   Van der Kroef, J.M.
        'Indonesia, the Netherlands and the Republic of the South Moluccas', *Orbis* 16
        (1972):174-210. (ubl)

7003   Van der Kroef, J.M.
        'Separatist movements in Indonesia', *South East Asian Spectrum* 4-4 (July-
        September 1976):9-19.

7004 Van der Veur, P.
      'West Irian; A new era', *Asian Survey* 2-8 (1962):1-8.

7005 Van der Veur, P.
      West New Guinea; Irian Barat or Papua Barat. Canberra: New Guinea Society,
      1962. [45]

7006 Van der Veur, P.W.
      'West Irian in the Indonesian fold', *Asian Survey* 3-7 (1963):332-337.

7007 Vandenbosch, A.
      'Indonesia, the Netherlands and the New Guinea issue', *Journal of Southeast
      Asian Studies* 7 (1976):102-118.

7008 Vandoorne, Fernand
      Het onafhankelijkheidsstreven van de Zuidmolukkers. 1973, 164 pp. [PhD thesis
      Rijksuniversiteit Gent.]

7009 Verrier, June Raye
      Australia, Papua New Guinea and the West New Guinea question, 1949-1969.
      Ca. 1970. [MA thesis Monash University, Clayton.] [80]

7010 Warmenhoven, H.J.
      Prelude to the Irian issue; An evaluation of the exclusion of Dutch New Guinea
      from the transfer of sovereignty to Indonesia in the light of Netherlands colonial
      philosophy. 1965, 352 pp. [MA thesis University of Melbourne.] [97, 6199]

7011 Warmenhoven, H.J.
      Some aspects of Australian concern with the political disposition of New Guinea.
      1971. [PhD thesis University of Melbourne.] [3727]

7012 West, F.J.
      'The New Guinea question; An Australian view', *Foreign Affairs* 39 (1961):504-
      511. (ubl)

7013 Wittermans, Tamme and Noel P. Gist
      'The Ambonese nationalist movement in the Netherlands; A study in status
      deprivation', *Social Forces* 40 (1961-62):309-317. (ubl)

7014 Zavodskii, I.A.
      West Irian. Moscow: Knowledge Publishing House, 1962, 32 pp. [In Russian.]
      [5]

Author index

Index of personal names

Index of geographical names

Subject index

Aan- en Afvoertroepen (AAT) 2759, 3241, 3288, 5349, 5533, 5663, 5878, 6012, 6064, 6078

Adat Law/Kaum Adat 2222, 2680, 3112, 3912

Air Force (Dutch) 1138, 1146, 1215, 1282, 1791, 1792, 1850, 1866, 1917, 1923, 3369, 3370, 5406, 5581, 5584, 5643, 5694, 5766, 6075, 6566, *see also* Aviation

Air Force (Indonesian) 249, 399, 513, 581, 713, 750, 900, 963, 982-984, 2109, 3806, 3859, 3864, 4295, 4529, 4715, 4716, 4747, 4835, 4836, 4839, 4906, 5122, *see also* Aviation

Algemeen Nederlands Jeugd Verbond (ANJV) 3327, 5838, 5953

Andjing NICA Bataljon (KNIL) 5718, 5799

Angkatan Perang Ratu Adil (APRA) 3722, 3833, 4459, 4461, 4651, 4658, 4738, 5718, 5844, 5922, *see also* R.P.P. Westerling

Antara (News Agency) 810, 4419, 5102, 6518

Anti-Revolutionaire Partij (ARP) 1046, 1050, 1051, 1126, 2841, 3330, 3518, 5437, 5439, 5440, 5944, 6533, 6558, 6559, 6578, 6583, 6588, 6619, 6623, 6624, 6671, 6672, 6700, 6729, 6769, 6914

Arab Community 1558, 2089, 2126, 3512, 5259

Archives *see* Sources/Documents/Archives

Armed Forces (Dutch) 33, 96, 114, 1216, 1251, 1267, 1317, 1866, 3109, 3185, 3204, 3211, 3320, 3321, 3344, 3345, 3353, 3354, 3387, 3396, 5444, 5500, 5502, 5504, 5625, 5628, 5631, 5670, 5679, 5790, 6021, 6042, 6096, 6774, 6775, *see also* Air Force, Army, Navy

Armed Forces (Indonesian; ABRI) 8, 116, 119, 120, 122, 126, 130, 161, 186, 197, 223, 274, 414, 494, 496, 515, 518, 520, 538, 541, 543, 589, 764, 766, 771, 780, 781, 844, 921, 1465, 1474, 1486, 1539-1541, 3198, 3675, 3902, 4123, 4151, 4165, 4395, 4464, 4489, 4490, 4537, 4600, 4765, 4766, 4933, 5152, 6021, 6127, 6386, 6387, 6447, *see also* Air Force, Army, Komando Daerah Militer (KODAM), Navy

Army (Dutch; KL) 1119, 1157, 2827, 3016, 3017, 3134, 3468, 4530, 5516, 5682, 5792, 5804, 5823, 6001, 6057, 6787, *see also* Artillery, Cavalry, Engineering, Infantry, Koninklijk Nederlands-Indisch Leger (KNIL)

Army (Indonesian; TNI-AD) 130, 174, 210, 394, 430, 518, 620, 665, 721, 782, 783, 1245, 1329, 1338, 1340, 1447, 1520, 1537, 1538, 2261, 2317, 2474, 2484, 2495, 2651, 3754, 3802, 3803, 3919, 3985, 3999, 4122, 4123, 4172, 4179, 4380, 4467, 4605, 4769, 4826, 4881, 4885, 4893, 4916, 4917, 4921, 6127, *see also* Barisan, Engineering

Artillery (Dutch) 3331, 3500, 5360, 5416, 5461, 5569, 5649, 5650, 5779, 6036

Arts *see* Culture/Cultural Aspects, Fiction (Belles-Lettres), Plastic Arts/Drawing/Painting

658 Subject index

Majlis Syuro Muslimin Indonesia (Masyumi) 200, 245, 362, 524, 530, 533, 551, 788, 798, 1941, 1942, 2104-2106, 2173, 2516, 2556, 2685, 2696, 2958, 4097, 5359
Malino Conference 2365, 2434, 2854, 2856, 2966, 3048, 3076, 3225, 3572, 3664, 6049
Marine Luchtvaart Dienst 1025, 1091, 1122
Markas Besar Komando Jawa 3977, 4534
Marxism 1330, 1337, 1459, 1460, 1526, 2196-2200, 2355-2364, 2418, 2551, 2732, 2733, 4352, 4583, 4882, 6319, see also Socialism
Mass Media 205, 1986, 1989, 1990, 2031, see also Journalism/Press, Newspapers
Masyumi see Majlis Syuro Muslimin Indonesia
Medical Aspects 281, 305, 321, 322, 387, 401, 500, 505, 585, 657, 712, 733, 734, 797, 871, 872, 874, 888, 900, 1176, 1640, 3332, 3955, 4062, 4339-4341, 4386, 4646, 4741, 5355, 5487, 5659, 6910, see also Red Cross
Merdeka (Newspaper) 250, 2402
Militaire Inlichtingen Dienst 3295
Military Police/Marechaussee (Dutch) 3246, 3369, 5859, 6020
Military Police/Marechaussee (Indonesian) 740
Ministerie van Buitenlandse Zaken (Dutch) 5587, 6557
Ministerie van Economische Zaken (Dutch) 5672
Ministerie van Financiën (Dutch) 5430, 5672
Ministerie van (Uniezaken en) Overzeese Gebiedsdelen (Dutch) 5351, 5537, 6070
Mitrailleurbataljon (Dutch Infantry) 5585
Money/Finance 219, 460, 652, 1174, 1268, 1825, 2114, 2176, 2180-2182, 2195, 2302, 2327, 2328, 2339, 2435, 2436, 2462, 2466, 2469, 2507, 2853, 2897, 2923, 2928, 2985, 3029, 3139, 3140, 3352, 3418, 3442, 4502, 5362, 5430, 5823, 6152, 6269, see also Banking, Economy
Monuments 3882, 4330, 4407, 4441-4448, 4879, 4893, 5055
Muhammadiyah 182, 816, 1471, 1472, 2224
Museums 502, 3902, 4410, 4464-4467, 4574, 4575, 4801, 4834, 4933
Music/Songs 208, 280, 349, 375, 409, 603, 792, 793, 823, 866, 896, 897, 996, 1125, 1175, 2138, 2777, 2793-2798, 2989, 2990, 3117, 3200, 3453, 4279, 4818

Nahdatul Ulama 150, 180, 533, 705, 770, 794, 878, 4190
Nationaal Comité Handhaving Rijkseenheid 2801, 2923-2925, 2940, 2949, 2988, 3027, 3044, 3138, 3478, 5655, 5656
Nationaal Nieuw-Guinea Comité 6537, 6658, 6882, 6933
Nationaal Reveil 3411, 3428
Nationalism/Nationalist Movement 134, 136, 194, 209, 221, 252, 257, 266, 327, 332, 333, 360, 404, 458, 472, 477, 568, 693, 694, 717, 795, 806, 937, 958, 971, 1210, 1211, 1213, 1306, 1309, 1355, 1379, 1382, 1519, 1553, 1808, 1952, 2171, 2186, 2242, 2262, 2315, 2347, 2485, 2559, 2586, 2708, 2724, 2736, 2931, 3060, 3305, 3307, 3380, 3421, 3423, 3573, 3574, 3612, 3613, 3666, 3712, 5208, 5209, 6403
Navy (Dutch) 1032, 1111, 1120, 1237, 1796, 1866, 2942, 3106, 3108, 3227, 3363, 5435, 5449, 5691, 5782, 5882, 5993-5999, 6002, 6561, 6650, 6652, 6653, 6774, 6781, 6829, see also Korps Mariniers, Marine Luchtvaart Dienst, Shipping
Navy (Indonesian; TNI-AL) 389, 426, 700, 734, 994, 3728, 3817, 4085, 4102, 4161, 4195, 4196, 4396, 4433, 4451, 4455, 4670, 4828, 4877, 4944, 5047, 5055, 5056, 5114, 5183, 5204, 5284, 5285, 6472
Nederlands-Indonesische Unie 2681, 2682, 2779, 2805, 2971, 2976, 2992, 3001, 3092,

DATE DUE